A FIELD GUIDE TO THE

Nests, Eggs and Nestlings

OF NORTH AMERICAN BIRDS

A FIELD GUIDE TO THE

Nests, Eggs and Nestlings

OF NORTH AMERICAN BIRDS

Colin Harrison

The Stephen Greene Press
Brattleboro, Vermont
Lexington, Massachusetts

First Stephen Greene Press Edition 1984,
published by The Stephen Greene Press,
Fessenden Road, Brattleboro, Vermont 05301
by arrangement with William Collins Sons & Co. Ltd.

Library of Congress Cataloging in Publication Data

Harrison, Colin James Oliver.
A field guide to the nests, eggs, and nestlings of North American birds.

Reprint. Originally published: Cleveland : Collins, 1978.
Includes indexes.
1. Birds—North America—Eggs and nests. 2. Birds—North America—Identification. I. Title.
[QL681.H27 1984] 598.297 83–20708
ISBN 0–8289–0532–0

Made and printed in Hong Kong by South China Printing Co.

CONTENTS

COLOR PLATES

NESTLINGS

All nestlings are painted by Philip Burton

EGGS

PLEASE BEGIN HERE

It is a pity to begin a book with a plea or a warning to the reader, but I feel that I should make these comments at the start. We are studying the nesting of birds, and while this is one of the most interesting aspects of their lives it is also the period at which they are most vulnerable, and it would be deeply regretted if the publication of this work resulted in harm to birds and their young.

During the latter part of the nineteenth century, when collecting of all kinds of natural objects became almost a mania, nesting birds suffered heavily from the attention of egg collectors. The bright and varied colors of egg-shells, their hard form and clean surfaces made them convenient objects to collect. Apart from curiosity there was little reason for such collecting other than a desire, in some instances, to add to our knowledge of birds. This knowledge is now at a stage where little can be added except by careful and controlled scientific study, with any collecting required done under license. *There is no longer any justification for the random, unofficial collecting of birds' eggs by amateurs, and* the casual destruction of nests and nestlings, such as occurred in the past in some rural areas, was not justified at any time.

A more immediate danger to nesting birds at the present time, and one to which even the most well-meaning bird enthusiast may subject them, is unwise disturbance. The bird is a creature which normally evades its enemies by flying or running away. When incubating eggs or brooding young it is tied to one place. If a predator of some kind does attack then it is better that the parent bird should survive and nest again, and so the bird leaves the nest to the attacker. Under natural conditions the predator that finds the nest will destroy it, and probably search there again, and it is therefore safer if the bird does not return. Unfortunately the bird cannot discriminate between a harmful predator and an inquisitive human so a clumsy inspection of a nest when a bird is sitting may cause a bird to desert the nest and its contents completely.

Birds are particularly likely to desert in the early stages of laying and incubation. In addition, when the young of songbirds are growing feathers but still within a few days of being ready to leave the nest, they may leave it prematurely if the nest is touched. This is another device which is designed to save something from a predator, but it may result in most of the brood being lost. If large seabird colonies or such assemblies are disturbed harm may come to eggs or young in the ensuing panic, and once the nests are exposed birds such as gulls will quickly move in to take eggs and young. Disturbance is at its worst in colonies of birds such as pelicans and some terns where disturbance may result in a whole colony deserting and failing to nest for that season.

In addition to all this the slight disturbance of twigs, leaves or grass, necessary in order to see into a nest, may be sufficient to indicate to a sharp-eyed predator the presence of a previously hidden nest; and lingering near a nest may prevent the birds returning and cause eggs and young to become fatally chilled.

The basic rules therefore are – *to disturb as little as possible; preferably examine nests only when the owners are absent; to be as quick as possible; and at all times to exercise the greatest care and caution, remembering that a little carelessness can bring about the accidental destruction of nest and brood.*

There are laws prohibiting the collecting of eggs and protecting nestlings, and anyone hoping to study nesting birds must take care that he knows and complies with them.

*

In most of the field guides to birds that are now available the reader is offered information which assists in the identification of a bird, and some information is given on the habits of the bird and the type of surroundings in which it will be found. The present volume is intended to supplement this by providing additional information on the nesting habits of the species within the area covered. Birds tend to show more variation in their breeding than might be expected, and the information is less easily fitted into a work of this kind than are the data on ordinary species identification. In the present volume the basic information on the nesting cycle has been given, necessarily brief in view of the number of species involved, and covering the habitat and nest-site, the appearance of nest, eggs and young, the season of breeding, and information on the incubation, and the care of the young in the early stages.

I earnestly hope that this work will help in broadening our knowledge and appreciation of birds as living creatures, and not be an incentive to the pointless acquisition of eggs as petty trophies. If there is a need now it is to study the breeding cycle as a whole and to be able to document it to a successful conclusion with the final independence of the fledged young.

It is not possible to prepare a work of this kind without the help of existing sources of reference; and any worker in this field must gain his temporary advantage by building on the labors of earlier workers, adding his own contribution to theirs, and hope that by so doing he will enable those that follow to build still further. Anyone studying the habits of North American birds must pay tribute to the energies of A. C. Bent who compiled the life histories of these birds published by the Smithsonian Institution over a period of 56 years, even though they may have reservations about the way in which the information is presented. I am grateful not only to him but also to the multitude of individuals who over the last half-century have made their contributions, large and small, in various ornithological journals, and steadily increased our knowledge of North American birds.

I am very grateful to Mr John Dupont for his very kind help in obtaining photographs of rarer alcid eggs and those of some other species. I would like to thank my colleague Mr Michael P. Walters for his help; and also to thank the Trustees of the British Museum (Natural History). And last, but by no means least, my very grateful thanks to the artists, Dr Philip Burton who painted the plates of young birds and supplied line drawings for the introduction, Mr Andrew Burton who illustrated most of the nests, and Mr F. Greenaway who took almost all of the egg photographs.

HOW TO USE THIS BOOK

The information given in this book is intended to add to that already available in the ordinary field guides to birds. It covers the North American region from the Arctic to the Southern boundary of the United States. I have omitted Baja California, the Gulf of California, and the Bahamas. I have followed in the main the 1957 A. O. U. Checklist, but I have introduced a few recent taxonomic modifications.

The **Contents List** at the beginning gives a list of bird families and subsidiary groupings arranged in this sequence. The same sequence, with a few modifications, is also used for the color plates of nestlings and of eggs.

The **Introduction** gives the background information needed in using the information that occurs under each heading in the main text on any particular species. The sections deal with habitat and nest-site, nest, breeding season, eggs, incubation, nestlings and the nestling period. Within the introduction each of these is treated in turn, giving the meaning of some of the terms used, and the general background of each section including the scope and limitations of the information on each bird.

The information in the introduction is intended to be read before the book is used, but the first immediately practical part is the section containing three **Identification Keys.** It is not possible, in the case of birds' nests, eggs and young, to give keys which will enable the reader to identify rapidly a particular species unless the bird in question has well-marked peculiarities setting it apart from most others. It has, however, been possible to provide keys to nests, to eggs and to young which may enable the user to narrow rapidly his search to a limited number of species, which he can then limit still further by reference to the plates and text. Since it is usually necessary to take a number of factors into consideration, cross-references to the other two keys are given in each key.

The **Main Text** is in the form of a systematic list. Each section begins with a general note on the family or species group, giving the general information common to the whole group of birds, and then each species is dealt with in turn, the available information being given in slightly abbreviated form. The families and groups may be traced from the index or the contents list at the beginning, while individual species can be traced from the indexes to common and Latin names at the end of the book.

The **Illustrations** consist of color plates and black-and-white drawings in the text. The EGG PLATES are in a section near the end of the book and they show examples of almost every species in the volume. A few are omitted and these may be very rare species or with eggs unknown, or just on the extreme limits of the region covered. Eggs may vary and in most cases it has only been possible to show a single example, although in some instances more than one is included and may indicate the range of variation rather than the typical single example. In the other instances, however, the degree of variation is indicated on the caption pages and can be further checked with the text. The caption pages also give for each group the general information on the eggs and nest-site.

The NESTLING PLATES are distributed at intervals through the text and show young birds at the nestling stage. There is often a close similarity between the nestlings of related species and, apart from some distinctly-patterned downy chicks, in most instances single typical examples representative of a small group of species are shown. Some black-and-white figures of DOWN PATTERNS of chicks as seen from above have been included in the text section. These supplement the color plates, which show a view of young birds from the side, and assist in the identification of downy young which are more often observed from above as they attempt to hide by crouching.

The color plates, used in conjunction with the keys and text, should make it possible to identify most eggs and young.

The NEST ILLUSTRATIONS are also black-and-white drawings in the text. They have been chosen to show the typical nests of the various groups of birds, and also the more striking and more readily identified of the exceptional nests which some birds make. It was not thought necessary to show nests normally concealed in holes.

INTRODUCTION

THE SCOPE OF THE BOOK

This book covers the species found in the North American region, from the Arctic to the southern boundary of the United States, omitting Baja California, the Gulf of California and the Bahamas.

In the main text the basic information of the breeding cycle of each species has been summarised. For species with a wide distribution many of the statements found in literature concerning the nesting refer to particular limited areas, and statements concerning nest-material, nest-site, egg pattern and other aspects of nesting which may be true for a particular region may not hold good for the entire range of the species. As a result some of the information given here is necessarily more generalised and less dogmatic than that found in works referring to more circumscribed areas.

In some instances there is also some uncertainty and doubt about the information now available, and in such instances this has been indicated by a question-mark in the text. The text also gives a clearer picture of the gaps in our knowledge of this part of the lives of many species. It is just possible that in some instances the information was available somewhere, but has been overlooked; but undoubtedly in many cases there is a real lack of information.

The influence of past egg-collecting is apparent in that nest and eggs have usually been described, although some collectors took the eggs without commenting on the appearance of the nest. However, information on the incubation period and the appearance of the nestlings is often lacking; and the period when the young are in the nest, and more especially the period between leaving the nest and final independence, are very poorly documented.

Some of the information common to all the species within a family of species group has been summarised under a general heading at the beginning of that group, and it is therefore advisable, where checking information on a species, to look also at the information under this more general heading. However, in the cases where a family or group is represented by only one or two species, it was not considered necessary to repeat information which would also appear under the species concerned.

For each species information has been arranged in what seemed to be a natural sequence – nest habitat, nest-site, nest, breeding season, eggs, incubation, nestling, and nestling period – to give in the space available an overall picture of this important part in the bird's life cycle.

The introductory notes which follow here give the general background information on each of these stages in the cycle, explain some of the terms used, and indicate where caution is necessary in interpreting the information given. One point that will become apparent from the following notes is that even with a considerable knowledge of nests and eggs the variation in these is such that it is not always possible to identify a species with absolute certainty from its nest and eggs. In many cases the only sure identification lies in recognising the bird itself, and it must be understood that a guide to nests and eggs does not provide an alternative means of recognising the bird species involved.

NEST-SITE

To begin with we indicate the typical habitat in which breeding occurs, and the type of sites in which the nest will be found. Each species of bird is limited to some extent in its distribution by the surroundings, or habitat, which it is prepared to tolerate; and when breeding occurs there are further limitations imposed by the site and nest materials which it is prepared to use. Each species therefore has a typical nest-site and nest structure. Most, however, show some degree of tolerance in adjusting to slightly less suitable sites, the tolerance varying considerably from one species to another. This can create problems in identification of the nests of the more adaptable species. For example, the robin's nest is usually in the branches of a tree or shrub, but it is adaptable and if the necessity arises it may place its nest on a cliff ledge or the ledge of a building, or even on the ground.

The site is not, therefore, a certain clue to the species, although it does indicate the probable occupier. Another problem of identification arises where birds use the old nests of other species. Owls and falcons may use old nests of larger birds such as crows; a cavity in a tree, such as a woodpecker hole, may have a succession of very different tenants; House Sparrows, Rosy Finches, House Finches and wrens will use Cliff Swallow nests; and, perhaps oddest of all, the Solitary Sandpiper, although a shorebird, will utilise old nests in trees, such as those of thrushes, for its nesting. If there is evidence of an old nest being re-used one therefore needs to see the bird to be sure which species is nesting there.

NEST AND NEST-BUILDING

A difficulty that all birds have to overcome is that their future offspring must spend a period as an egg that requires continual protection from predators, and needs warmth. The variety of nests that have been evolved represent partial success in overcoming these difficulties. Nests may form platforms that lift the eggs to a safer site; structures that hide the eggs from view; and insulated cavities that shelter the eggs from cooling winds and allow the body heat of the parent bird to be used to best advantage.

In spite of their considerable diversity we can recognise a limited number of obvious types of nest. Some species make no nest at all other than for the bird to lower itself until the breast rests on the site and then rotate a little to form a shallow hollow if the substrate is soft enough. Such birds usually nest on flat open places, or on rock ledges, or occupy hollow cavities in tree or rocks. Examples of these within our region are the nightjars, owls, falcons, and kingfishers.

Most of the birds nesting in more open places line their shallow scrapes with material of some kind, the quantity varying, even in one species, from almost nothing to a very substantial layer. Most of these birds build by an indirect method called sideways-throwing. From the time that the site is chosen either of the pair when moving away from, or about, the site picks up nest material or small objects and throws these back to either side or beneath them. Such items therefore gradually move towards the nest-site and accumulate there. The sitting bird performs a similar action called sideways-building, pulling in such items and tucking them alongside it. The resultant nest depends almost entirely on the material to hand near the nest, and on the degree of disturbance experienced by the birds. The need to use nearby material results in shorebirds like Piping Plovers lining scrapes with tiny pebbles. The fact that increased disturbance can cause a bird to add more material to the nest is of value in the instance where a bird on a less suitable site, perhaps damp and cold, reacts to increased discomfort by increased building activity which in turn produces a thicker nest and more effective insulation for the eggs and brooding bird. This type of building occurs widely in ducks, gamebirds, cranes, loons, shorebirds and most terns and auks.

Ducks and geese make this type of nest, but add to it an insulating inner layer of down from the breast of the female. Within the above groups some other species build more elaborate nests by this method. Swans pile up their heaps of plant material by sideways-throwing and sideways-building.

Most of the other types of nests are built by birds carrying material directly to a site, and the type of nest is determined to some extent by the size and rigidity of the pieces of nest material used. Birds using lax plant material – for example, grebes with pondweed, cormorants with seaweed, and kittiwakes with mud and grass – build a solid platform or mound with a small hollow in the top for the eggs, the nest being usually consolidated by the trampling of the birds.

Birds using rigid twigs usually build in trees and may produce no more than a thin platform. When the twigs are put in place a small lateral quivering of the bill while it is still holding the twig helps to work the latter into the existing structure. Pigeon nests show this type of construction in its simplest platform stage. Continual additions to nests of this type, such as often occur where nests are re-used in subsequent seasons, produce very bulky structures. Even with the simpler twig nests there is usually some evidence of a tendency for birds, in the later stages of nest-building, to select thinner and finer material which can be used as a lining and may shape an inner cup in which the eggs will lie.

Most of our birds build cup-shaped nests. The material used is usually fairly pliable and the bird sits in the structure as it builds, placing material, pulling in loose ends and tucking them into the existing framework to one side or the other and gradually producing the typical round shape. As the softer lining is added the bird shapes the cup to its own body, sitting in it with bill and tail uplifted, rotating a little, pressing with chin and under-tail coverts, and flexing bill and tail downwards to consolidate the rim. It also pushes backwards with the feet, enlarging the lower cup a little, and the final structure fits snugly around the sitting bird leaving room for the eggs beneath it.

Domed nests with side entrances are much less common, the only larger bird using one being a magpie, with a thin twig roof for its nest; and about a dozen smaller species making more solid structures in trees or bushes, on a ledge or in a crevice, or on the ground.

Another fairly uncommon type of nest in the suspended, pensile nest. This may be a cup slung between twigs to which it is bound at the rim. The Acadian Flycatcher's nest in a horizontal fork tends towards this type and more typical examples are the nests of vireos and some orioles. The nests of kinglets are cups often hanging below a conifer branch and bound on either side to drooping twigs. Some orioles build an elongated pensile bag with an entrance at the top where it is either bound to more than one twig or hangs from a single loop. The Bushtit makes a similar long hanging nest with an entrance at the top but slightly to one side. This nest is peculiar in that it is spiders' webs which bind it together and create an elastic container which the bird stretches downwards as it builds.

Spiders' webs are used as nest material by a number of small birds, especially where the nest is made of small fragmentary material or must be balanced on a large support, as in some of the warblers, the wood pewees and the gnatcatchers. It probably shows its greatest potential however in the delicate cups of the hummingbird nests.

Various birds may incorporate mud or wet woodpulp or leafmold into the nest structure to bind and shape it. This may be found in some crows, blackbirds and thrushes. The phoebes ensure the safety of their nests on the ledges and small supports that they use by building up their cups with mud pellets and plant material, while some swallows use mud extensively, building up nests of mud and plant fiber pellets placed like bricks in a wall, bonded by jabbing the tongue through the wet material, and built up into fine structures that can be stuck to vertical surfaces providing that, like the phoebe nests, they are sheltered from the rain.

The swifts also require adhesives for their nests but create it themselves, using saliva which sticks the material of the nests together. This kind of nest is developed to a high degree in the Chimney Swift which breaks off short dead twigs while in flight and glues them to a vertical surface and to each other to form a strong half-cup.

Although birds show some selection of material when nesting there is a tendency to use whatever is most readily available, and there may be a noticeable variation in the nest structures of a single species, due to this, which may make identification more difficult. Obvious examples of this are the seaweed nests of cormorants on cliffs and the twig nests of pairs in trees, and heron nests may differ if reeds or stems of tall marsh plants are used instead of twigs. More striking differences may be apparent in the nests of species using the sideways-throwing method of building, depending on the amount of material present in the vicinity of the nest.

Provided that they fulfil certain criteria, apparently unlikely man-made materials may be used. Pieces of wire resemble strong flexible twigs and may be used for the nest, while rags and paper form acceptable substitutes for dead leaves. One man-made adjunct to nesting which causes confusion is the niche which is one of a series of identical compartments or divisions in a row, such as occur on some buildings or where a ladder rests against a wall. A bird is not adapted to cope with such situations, which do not occur in the wild. If it selects one such compartment as a nest-site it is likely to become confused and build a series of nests to varying degrees of completion in adjacent identical compartments, and to lay eggs in more than one of these.

BREEDING SEASON

Within the temperate regions birds usually breed in spring and early summer; and the urge to breed appears to be controlled by endocrine gland secretions which in turn are affected by the increasing day-length in the early part of the year. Temperature also appears to have some immediate control on the breeding behavior of birds and can cause variation in the date of commencement of breeding from one year to another. The actual date of commencement of breeding differs from one species to another, and it has been suggested that the hatching of the young is timed to coincide with the period when the necessary food supply is most readily available.

Since commencement of the breeding cycle differs from species to species and year to year only a very general indication of it can be given. It may also differ from one part to another of a species range, usually starting earlier in the south and west. **In the main text references to 'south' or 'north' in the sections on breeding seasons refer to those parts of a species' breeding range within our area.** In the most northerly species, nesting on the arctic tundra, breeding must await the summer thaw, and in cold seasons no breeding may take place.

In the case of some birds, such as seabirds, where there may be a long period of colony-visiting and display before actual breeding starts, I have used the period of egg-laying as the one indicated in the section on the breeding season in order to provide a basis for comparison with more typical groups.

There is a human tendency to note the beginning but not the end of things, and while we know when breeding starts we have little information on when the cycles finish. There are a number of factors that may affect such calculations. Theoretically it is easy to calculate how long the laying, incubation and nesting period of a single brood would take to complete, and we have indicated the number of broods known for the species. Yet a single brood may be destroyed and although in a few species this may finish breeding attempts for the year, in others a replacement clutch will be laid and the whole cycle may occur, but at a later date. Where several broods are involved these may be spaced, or may overlap to a point where the male is feeding the young of one brood while the female is already incubating the eggs of the next one. In addition, where there are several broods, replacements may occur more rapidly if one is lost; and so it is difficult to predict firmly the stage of the breeding cycle at any particular date.

The breeding season usually terminates in late summer or autumn with the moult of feathers of the parents. Some resident species continue producing broods until late in the season. Physiologically birds may be ready to breed again after the autumn moult and it appears to be the decreasing daylength which inhibits them from doing so. Very occasionally, during the periods of abnormally fine weather, individual pairs of some species may attempt to breed.

CLUTCH SIZE

The clutch is the number of eggs laid by a bird and incubated by it at one time. The number of eggs in a clutch may vary with the species. Some species, sometimes referred to as determinate layers, have a fixed clutch size and will produce just that number of eggs and no more. Pigeons with two eggs, usually, are an example of this. Many other species of birds tend to vary the number of eggs a little above or below an average figure, and some appear to continue laying until they have a comfortable number which satisfies the sitting birds, and if eggs are removed they may lay more to make up the number. Birds of the latter type are known as indeterminate layers and if eggs are constantly removed they may lay a very large number. The domestic hen is an example, since under natural conditions it may be satisfied with a clutch of about six eggs but can be induced to lay many more.

A widely distributed species may show variation of clutch size within its range. In the smaller songbirds there is a consistent tendency for the size of the clutch to increase from south to north. It is suggested that this is related to the fact that the northern birds have a longer summer day in which to find food for a larger brood. This is, of course, offset by the shorter breeding season and possibly fewer broods than more southerly birds.

It has been suggested that clutch size is determined by the number of young that a pair of birds can successfully rear. Other factors which have been thought to affect clutch size are the number of eggs that the female is physically capable of producing at one time; the number of eggs that a bird can successfully cover and warm when incubating; and in addition there appears to be some correlation between the size of the clutch and the survival rate and likely length of life of the average individual of the species.

EGG SHAPE

Eggs show a wide range of small individual variations in shape, but only four main shapes are usually recognised. The nomenclature proposed by F. W.

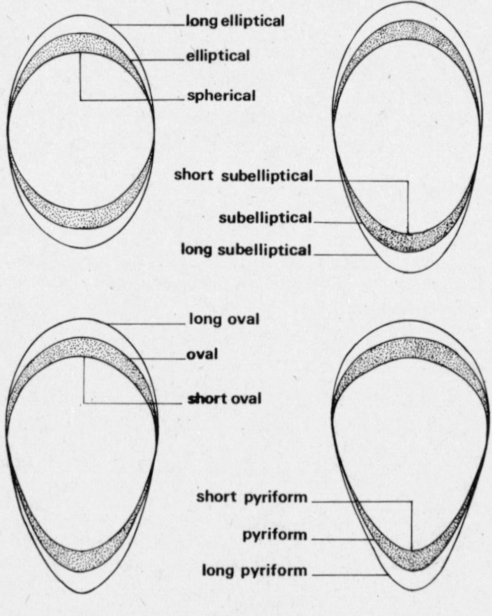

Egg shapes.

Preston is a convenient one for this purpose. At one extreme is the *elliptical* shape, elongated with equally-rounded ends and broadest about the middle. A long, normal, and short form of each shape are recognised, and in the case of the elliptical egg a very short version of the shape would be spherical. The *subelliptical* egg is again rounded at the ends but a little more elongated, tapering more towards the rounded ends, with the broadest part nearer one end than the other. The *oval* egg has the typical egg-shape, rounded and largest at one end, and tapering distinctly towards a narrower end. The term 'ovate' is sometimes used for this. The last shape is the *pyriform,* with the larger end distinctly blunt and rounded, and tapering to a narrower point at the other end. This type of egg is sometimes called 'pear-shaped', but the taper is more even than that of a pear. Two special types that one might like to add to these four are the 'spherical' shape already mentioned, sometimes approached but rarely achieved, and a shape sometimes found in grebe eggs which may have a marked taper towards both ends, producing what is perhaps a special instance of the subelliptical sometimes referred to as 'biconical'.

EGG SIZE

In varying slightly in shape, eggs also vary individually in size, not only between clutches, but also between one egg and another within the clutch itself. The measurements we have given in the text are averages of length and breadth. If one takes a large sample of eggs and measures them there are likely to be variations ranging up to ten to twelve per cent or more on either side of the average measurements. This must be taken into account when attempts are made to use comparative measurements in identifying eggs.

Abnormal-sized eggs occasionally occur, usually single ones in a normal clutch. Exceptionally large ones are unusual in wild birds, but dwarf eggs appear at intervals. These may be tiny yolk-less examples produced when an egg is formed around a small piece of loose tissue, and since they do not hatch they may be found in a nest when a brood has left. They are likely to be more spherical than normal eggs, thick-shelled, and often rough-surfaced.

EGGSHELL COLOR

The shells of most eggs are partly translucent, and when in the nest and complete with their contents they tend to appear darker and deeper in color than the empty shells that appear in collections. Allowance must be made for this when looking at the color plates of the eggs. Apart from this, eggs kept away from the light show little color change save that a fine pinkish flush apparent on some newly-laid eggs such as pigeons' eggs disappears fairly rapidly. This pink tint is due to a fugitive pigment that is rapidly destroyed.

In spite of the considerable range of tints apparent on eggshells only two kinds of pigment, in addition to the fugitive one mentioned above, appear to be present in the eggshells under consideration. One is a blue or greenish-blue pigment. When present this occurs through the whole shell structure, so that the basic shell may be either white or some shade of blue.

The other pigment is a variably-tinted one that may appear as brown, red or black, or intermediate shades of these. When it tints the whole shell it is normally only present in the thin surface covering. For example, small quantities of superficial brown color make the white shell appear yellow or buff and the blue shell green or olive. This pigment also produces the shell markings. In the gamebirds such markings are present only on the surface with the superficial tint, but in most other families these markings are applied at intervals as the shell is formed and occur at varying depths within the shell. The shell being partly translucent, and when in very thin layers partly transparent, markings such as these show through a thin layer of shell, if near the surface. Markings that are black, red or brown may appear gray, pink or buff, in varying degrees of paleness according to their depth, on white shells; and if the shell is blue may appear in shades of purple, lilac and mauve.

If the eggs of a species are patterned they are likely to show considerable minor variation within certain limits. In illustrating the eggs it has usually been possible to show only one of a species and an effort has been made to select a typical 'average' type, although a species may have several distinct types of pattern. Where more than one egg can be shown these have been selected to give some idea of the range of variation rather than the average type. It must therefore be remembered that if only one or a few eggs of two related species have been seen, and appear very different, either may have an unusual variety which may be almost indistinguishable from eggs of the other species; and one must be very cautious of identifying species from their eggs.

Eggs of consistent color and pattern are usually laid by one individual, but some species show fairly consistent variations within clutches. For example, clutches of eggs of some crows and of House Sparrows often have one or two eggs which are much paler and less patterned than others in the same clutch.

For many species the color and pattern of the eggs appears to form a camouflage concealing them from potential enemies. The almost invisible eggs of Piping Plovers and Least Terns on shingle beaches are a good example of this; and it can be assumed that this is true in a number of other instances. Species whose eggs show great individual variation are more difficult to explain, but we know that birds come to recognise the color and pattern of eggs in a particular clutch, and it has been suggested that the very variable pattern and color of Murre eggs allows the parent bird to recognise its own egg among the shuffling crowd on the bare ledge or stack.

The eggs of birds nesting in dark cavities or holes are usually pale blue or white, and this probably helps to ensure that the bird can locate them easily. Where species derived from a group with patterned eggs take to closed nests or holes the eggs tend to be pale but to retain some pattern. Examples of this are the eggs of Rhinoceros Auklets and the Puffins among the auks; and the sparsely speckled or unmarked eggs of titmice, some wrens and sparrows, and the dipper, might be further instances.

ABNORMAL EGGSHELL COLOR

There is always a likelihood that abnormally colored eggs will appear from time to time. This is usually due to some genetic or physiological peculiarity of an individual bird affecting its entire egg production. It usually takes the form of a failure to produce some part of the normal pigmentation. For example, if the superficial pigment is absent an egg normally buff or olive may appear uniform white or blue. An absence of blue can produce a white egg, and may have surprising effects on a patterned egg where spots which normally appear as black or dark brown may appear buff or red when the blue is lost. Other variations occasionally encountered are replacement of black by brown or red, or of brown by red; and there may be increase of pigments to produce very heavily marked or dark eggs, or the other extreme of total loss of color.

These abnormal colors have been recorded more frequently for some species than for others, but might potentially occur in most species; and we have not attempted to deal with them in describing eggs in the text. An excessive attention was paid to them during the heyday of egg-collecting; but they are mainly of interest in providing clues to shell pigmentation and are also of interest in species whose eggs are camouflaged and are assumed to be so colored in order to escape the notice of predators. In these species abnormally colored eggs should be more conspicuous, and it is of interest to see to what extent they survive to hatch in comparison with the normally colored eggs.

INCUBATION

The embryo requires constant warmth if it is to develop inside the egg. This is provided by the body warmth of the parents, usually from the underside where in most species special bare 'brood patches' are present during the breeding season. Exceptions are the waterfowl and the pelicans, cormorants, darters and gannets. The last provides heat from the webs of its feet, covering the egg with these before settling on it.

The incubation period of an egg is the time between the laying and the hatching of a single egg; but unless the eggs are marked as they are laid and closely watched as they hatch this period is difficult to determine. There are other factors that may cause this period to vary and we have therefore given an incubation period which refers not to the individual egg but to the sitting bird, being the period during which a bird incubates and hatches its eggs. Eggs are usually laid at intervals of one to two days. If the parents begin to incubate when the first egg is laid the young may hatch at similar intervals and there will be nestlings of varying age and size in the nest. If the proper incubation is delayed until the last egg is laid the earliest eggs will have been present for some days and may have received some intermittent warmth and undergone some development. The eggs in such a clutch normally hatch in fairly rapid succession, but the precise period of incubation will differ from one egg to another.

In the very early stages of development of the embryo lack of warmth will delay further progress but is not apparently harmful. Later in incubation a period of chilling may prove fatal. A striking exception here are the eggs of petrels which appear to be adapted to possible periods of neglect and can undergo a period of days without incubation during the normal period and still hatch. This is presumably a safeguard in species where the adults change places only at long intervals. There is also some evidence that in ordinary songbirds cold conditions may prolong incubation to some extent, and perhaps add a day or two to the normal period without necessarily harming the young bird.

During incubation the eggs are frequently stirred and turned by the brooding birds. This is said to be necessary for the development of the embryo, although eggs have hatched successfully after being embedded in nest material in such a way that they could not be moved. It also seems that this stirring may be useful in some species for ensuring that the egg, at hatching, is resting in the position in which the chick can most easily emerge.

The part played by the sexes in incubation varies in different species from equal sharing to one sex only incubating. The attentiveness may vary from a constant covering of the eggs by some species to a tendency in others, chiefly those of hotter climates, to leave the eggs uncovered for varying periods.

HATCHING

The chick may be in vocal contact with the outside world a day or two before it emerges from the egg. It will make calls to which the parent responds, and may become silent in response to an alarm call from the parent. Its typical position at hatching is resting on its back or left side, with the head lying on the breast and the bill turned to one side and tucked under the right wing. The bill is usually equipped with a small hard excrescence on the tip of the upper mandible – the egg-tooth. This is often white, and visible on the bill of the newly-hatched young bird, but drops off after a while. A few birds show a similar tooth on the tip of the lower mandible as well.

The chick in the egg is very limited in its movements but is able to raise the bill so that this egg-tooth at the tip comes into contact with the shell and pushes up a small 'pip'; a break in the structure. Some chicks move very little; but as they attempt to bring the head up to a more comfortable position, and continue the bill-raising movement, they make a diagonal break extending from their right to left and up towards the larger end of the egg. At the same time convulsive straightening movements put pressure on the ends of the already weakened shell, and sooner or later it breaks in half and releases the chick.

Chicks of some species are able to move more easily within the shell, and with a series of small movements gradually turn over inside it, pipping it as they go, and making a complete circle, causing the shell to separate into two neat parts.

Breaking out of the egg, *above,* by rupturing shell after chipping rough hole: Curlew. *Below,* by turning in shell and making line of weakness producing two neat pieces: Partridge.

The time taken to escape from the shell may vary from a matter of minutes in the case of small songbirds to one or two days in the case of some larger species. The parent birds may help a little, possibly inadvertently, by pecking at the broken edge of the shell. Once the young bird has emerged, the adult either breaks and eats the shell fragments, or more usually carries them away and drops them some distance from the nest. Were they to remain at the nest they might betray it to passing predators. Birds such as gamebirds whose young leave the nest soon after hatching may not bother to remove the shells.

Young birds may retain the egg tooth for some days, or in some instances a week or two after hatching, the period varying with different species.

THE NESTLING

There are two main types of nestling. One is the down-covered chick which is active soon after hatching and able to leave the nest if necessary. This type of nestling is called *precocial*, or sometimes the term 'nidifugous' is used. The other type is exemplified by the typical songbird nestling, hatched naked, blind and helpless, and wholly dependent on its parents. This type of nestling is called *altricial*, or sometimes 'nidicolous'. These are convenient categories, but are not wholly exclusive since the precocial young have varying degrees of dependence on the adults, and may remain in the nest for some days before leaving it.

The appearance of the young bird at the nestling stage is not always well documented. This may be due in part to a perhaps commendable reluctance of ornithologists to disturb the nesting bird unduly in order to examine the young closely. In the present text we have tried to provide as good a description as possible of this stage in the development of the bird.

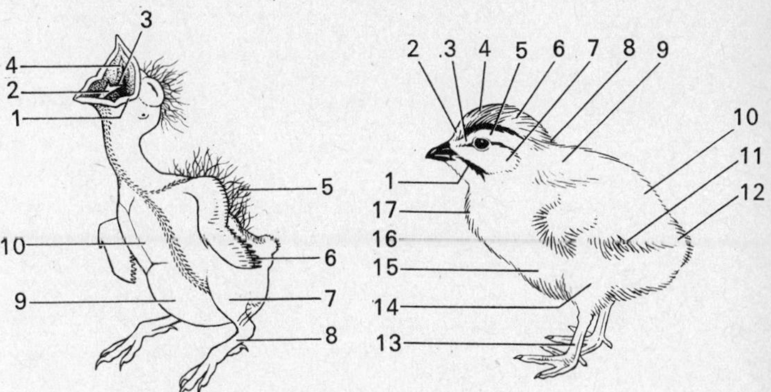

Nestling types, *left,* naked, altricial nestling: 1, gape flanges. 2, tongue. 3, tongue-spurs. 4, palate. 5, down filaments. 6, wing quills. 7, thigh. 8, tarsus. 9, belly. 10, breast. *Right,* downy, precocial chick: 1, moustache streak. 2, forehead. 3, lores. 4, forecrown. 5, eyestripe. 6, hindcrown. 7, ear coverts. 8, nape. 9, mantle. 10, back. 11, flank. 12, rump. 13, tarsus. 14, thigh. 15, belly. 16, wing. 17, upper breast.

Stages in growth of an altricial nestling, a House Sparrow. Stages — 36 hours, 4 days, 6 days, 8 days, 10 days.

The colors of bills, legs, bare skin and irides, which may change to some extent as the nestling grows, are the most poorly documented of all. In illustrating downy young and nestlings the artist has, where direct information was not available, deduced probable colors from preserved material or from juvenile birds. Unless confirmatory information is also given in the text the color shown in the plates should be treated with some caution.

NESTLING PERIOD

This is the period during which the young bird is dependent on its parents for its survival. It is sometimes called the fledging period, but to fledge is to fly, and the points at which the young bird learns to fly and at which it learns to fend for itself usually occur at different times in its development. During the earlier part of this period the young bird is still unable to control its own body temperature and must rely on the adults to brood it and keep it warm. It relies on the parents for food in most species, and also for protection from, or warning against, predators.

For many species with altricial young the pattern is one in which the young are hatched blind, with little or no down, and unable to control their temperature, and spend a period in the nest developing. During this they are brooded by the parents to keep them warm; the one not brooding bringing food. Gradually the young become more active and aware of their surroundings. They grow feathers and become able to keep themselves warm. Finally they leave the nest and follow the parents, still being fed by them for some weeks, but gradually becoming increasingly neglected by them and learning to fend for themselves. Precocial young may be fed for the first few days of their life, and subsequently they still rely on the adults for warmth and warning of danger even though they may feed themselves. Even though they do not feed the young, adults may indicate where the food is to be found.

Stages in growth of a precocial nestling, a Gull-billed Tern. Stages — 30 hours, 9 days 20 days.

Although only two main types of nestling have been referred to, a more precise classification has been proposed by Margaret M. Nice. For the present range of families the grouping under this system would be as follows:

Precocial. (Eyes open, down-covered, leaving nest in a day or two.)

(a) follow parents but find own food. Swans, geese, ducks, grouse, plovers, sandpipers, snipe, avocet, stilt, phalaropes.

(b) follow parents, and are shown food. Grouse, typical gamebirds, oystercatchers, plovers.

(c) follow parents, and are fed by them for varying periods. Loons, grebes, cranes, rails, oystercatchers, snipe.

Semi-precocial. (Eyes open, down-covered, stay at or near nest although able to walk.)

Jaegers, gulls, terns, auks, nightjars.

Semi-altricial. (Down-covered, unable to leave nest.)

(a) eyes open. Petrels, herons, bitterns, ibises, spoonbills, birds of prey.

(b) eyes closed at first. Owls.

Altricial. (Eyes closed, little or no down, unable to leave nest.)

Pelicans, gannets, cormorants, Anhinga, pigeons, cuckoos, swifts, hummingbirds, kingfishers, woodpeckers and songbirds (Passerines.)

The young of some species may remain with the parents after achieving independence, and the family party may not break up until nesting occurs in the following spring. A few are exceptional in that the young may stay and assist with the next nesting. For many young, however, the final break with the parents occurs during the autumn moult.

The roles played by the respective parents vary from one species to another. This may vary from sharing of duties, to independent roles for each, and to complete neglect by one or the other. Intensive observation has revealed that in a variety of species, ranging from grebes to some songbirds, the parents may divide the brood between them as soon as these leave the nest; and one adult will accept full responsibility for feeding some of the young, but will neglect others of the brood or even behave aggressively towards them, these being the responsibility of the other parent.

The severing of contact between adults and young is a gradual process and not a sudden one triggered off at the same instant in all individuals, and so the period of days quoted as the nestling period is necessarily an approximate period rather than a precise one.

Typical methods of feeding young: **a,** pelican, young taking food directly from throat; **b,** hawk, young are fed at first on small morsels taken from larger prey; **c,** dove, young fed on semi-liquid food, placing bill crosswise in that of adult; **d,** gull, young fed on regurgitated food; **e,** warbler, adult places food into bill of young; **f,** finch, adult regurgitates food and places it into bill of young.

NEW INFORMATION

Readers will notice that in a number of instances in the text, I have stated that no information is available on some aspect of the nesting of some species. It is possible, indeed likely, that this information is known to someone who has not realised that it was not more widely available. I would be glad to hear from anybody who feels they possess facts which would help to make this work more complete. Please write c/o Quadrangle, The New York Times Book Co., 10 East 53rd St., New York City, N. Y. 10022.

IDENTIFICATION KEYS

This section has three keys as follows:

It should, in theory, be possible to identify the bird involved from either the nest and its site, or the eggs, or the young one. In actual fact this is more difficult than might be expected. In some instances the same type of nest, eggs or young may be shared by several species; while at the other extreme there is always the possibility of a nest in an unusual site, or of an egg of abnormal color or markings, or with markings absent when they should be present.

It is therefore not possible to offer a key or series of keys which will enable the certain identification of any species in this way; and what has been done here is to group nests, eggs and young in a series of fairly simple subdivisions which should help to narrow down considerably the number of possibilities, and enable the user to refer to likely species, or groups of species, much more rapidly.

With this end in view the various categories have been kept as simple as possible. A capital letter has been assigned to each nest type, a number to each egg type, and a small letter to each type of young with, in some instances, a second letter to indicate whether a nestling is downy or naked. In the lists of species or groups of species in each category, the letters and numbers in brackets following each name indicate the information from the other lists of categories. A question mark indicates lack of information.

For example – the information (8,cn) after the name of the Waxwing in the nests in category 'C. Smaller cup nest in tree or shrub' indicates that the egg is blue or gray-blue marked with brown, black or gray, and that the young have a red or pink mouth and are naked. The entry (A,1) after the name of the Dipper in the section on young, in smaller cup nests, with unpatterned yellow or orange mouths indicates that the nest is domed and the egg unmarked and white.

To trace the birds in the main text the species are indexed under both common and scientific names at the end of the book, and the list of groups of birds and the order in which they are arranged appears on pp. 5-6.

Finally it should be mentioned that a check with data on distribution will sometimes reveal that only one of a group of species is present in a particular region and may also help substantially to reduce the list of possibilities.

Note. The Marbled Murrelet is not included in these keys. See page 162.

Categories used in the Keys

Nests

A. Domed nest.
B. Suspended nest, hanging, or pensile between forked twigs.
C. Smaller nest (up to *c.* 9-10 ins. diameter) in tree or bush.
D. on ground or in herbage layer (including reedbeds).
E. in hole, cavity, crevice or burrow in ground, rocks or buildings.
F. in hole, cavity or crevice in tree.
G. Mud nest, or saliva and debris nest, stuck to buildings, rocks or similar site.
H. Cup nest on ledge of rock or building.
I. Larger nest in tree.
J. on rock ledge or rocky island.
K. by or in water.
L. Little or no nest, on mossy branch, in tree hole or in cavity above ground.
M. in burrow, hole or cavity on or near ground.
N. on rock ledge or rocky island.
O. on the ground, usually near or by water.
P. on open ground.
Q. in growing herbage.
R. on the ground under trees or shrubs.

Eggs

UNMARKED

1. White or cream.
2. Blue or greenish.
3. Buff or olive-buff.

SCRIBBLED, SCRAWLED OR WITH LONG STREAKS

4. Scribbled, scrawled or with long streaks.

SPECKLED, SPOTTED AND BLOTCHED

5. White or creamy, marked with red or reddish-brown.
6. brown, black or gray.
7. Blue or gray-blue, marked with red or reddish-brown.
8. brown, black or gray.
9. Yellowish or pale buff, marked with red or reddish-brown.
10. brown, black or gray.
11. Olive, marked with reddish-brown, brown, olive-brown, black or gray.
12. Greenish, marked with red or reddish-brown.
13. darker green or olive.
14. brown, olive-brown, black or gray.
15. Pinkish or purplish, marked with red or reddish-brown.
16. brown, black or gray.
17. Deep buff, marked with brown, black and gray.

Young Nestlings and Chicks

a. In smaller cup nest, mouth patterned.
b. mouth unpatterned, yellow or orange.
c. pink or red.
d. In unlined cavity in tree, bank or ground, nestling naked.
e. In larger nest on tree or ground, nestling naked.
f. Larger nestling with coarse, hairy down; usually sparse.
g. Larger downy nestling with plain white, gray, buff or light brown down.
h. yellowish or greenish down.
i. down without pattern but with variation in overall dorsal coloration.
j. Larger downy nestling with down boldly striped on head and usually over body, feet lobed.
k. Larger downy nestling with down mainly striped or mottled, short seed-eating bill, bare legs.
l. Larger downy nestling with down mainly striped or mottled, short seed-eating bill, downy legs.
m. Larger downy nestling with down mainly striped or mottled, bill slender and longer.
n. Larger downy nestling with down spotted or mottled, feet webbed.
o. dark brown or blackish, feet unwebbed.
p. three toes webbed.
q. all four toes webbed.

Key 1. Nests

A. DOMED, WITH ENTRANCE HOLE AT SIDE
Rose-throated Becard, suspended from twig (5,6,9,10,15,16,?); Kiskadee and Beardless Flycatchers (5,6,?d); Dipper, ledge or niche by water (1,bd); some wrens (1,5,6,9,10,15,17,bd,cd); Arctic Warbler, on ground (5,bd); Verdin (7,?); Olive Sparrow, on ground (1,cd); Ovenbird, on ground (5,6,?); meadowlarks, on ground (5,?d); House Sparrow (6,cn); magpies (8,10,11,cn).

B. SUSPENDED NEST, HANGING FROM SINGLE SUPPORT, OR SLUNG BETWEEN FORKED TWIGS
Rose-throated Becard, domed suspended nest (5,6,9,10,15,16,?); Acadian Flycatcher (6,?d); kinglets, slung under conifer branch (6,9,bd); Bushtit (1,?d); vireos (1,6,bd); orioles (4,8,16,cd).

C. SMALLER CUP NEST (UP TO C. 9-10 INS. DIAMETER) IN TREE OR SHRUB
Smaller herons and egrets (2,g); Solitary Sandpiper, using other birds' nests (5,9,m); most doves (1,f); cuckoos (1,2,e,k); most hummingbirds (1,g); most flycatchers (1,4,5,6,9,15,16,bd); shrikes (6,10,14,bd,cd); waxwings (8,cn); Phainopepla (6,cd); mockingbirds and thrashers (2,5,7,15,bd): most thrushes (2,7,15,bd); kinglets (6,9,bd); gnatcatchers (7,an); Wrentit (2,?n); sparrows and buntings (1,2,4,5,6,7,8,cd); grosbeaks (1,2,5,6,cd); tanagers (7,8,cd); many warblers (1,5,6,8,9,10,cd); blackbirds and grackles (4,8,16,cd); most finches (1,2,4,5,6,8,cd); cowbirds, parasitic in other birds' nests (2,6,cd); jays (6,8,10,11, 14,16,cn).

D. SMALLER CUP NEST ON GROUND OR IN HERBAGE LAYER, INCLUDING TALL HERBAGE GROWING IN WATER
By or in water. Smaller herons and egrets (2,g); rails (5,9,11,15,17,o); American Coot (10,o); blackbirds and grackles (4,8,16,cd).
Not necessarily near water Ground Dove (1,f); some hummingbirds (1,g); Yellow-bellied and Willow Flycatchers (1,5,6,?d); larks (6,10,14,a); wagtails and pipits (6,10,16,bd,cd); some thrushes (2,7,15,bd); sparrow and buntings (1,2,4,5,6,7,8,cd); longspurs (4,6,8,9,10,11,14,16,cd); Dickcissel (2,?); many warblers (1,5,6,cd); Red-faced Warbler and Painted Redstart (5,6,bd); Bobolink, blackbirds and grackles (4,8,16,cd).

E. SMALLER CUP NEST IN HOLE, CAVITY, CREVICE OR BURROW, IN GROUND, ROCKS OR BUILDING
Rock Dove (1,f); Western Flycatcher (1,5,?); some swallows and martins (1,bd); White Wagtail (6,bd); Water Pipit (6,cd); some wrens (5,6,9,15,?); Wheatear (2,bd); Townsend's Solitaire (5,6,9,10,?); some titmice (1,5,6,bd); Snow Bunting (7,8,cd); Prothronotary and Canada Warblers, and waterthrushes (5,6,9,10,cd); Rosy Finch (1,cd); sparrows (6,cn); starlings (2,bd).

F. SMALLER CUP NEST IN HOLE, CAVITY OR CREVICE IN TREE
Yellow-bellied and Western Flycatchers (1,5,6,?d); Violet-green and Tree Swallows, and Purple Martin (1,?); Bluebirds (2,?); titmice (1,5,6,bd); nut-

hatches (5,6,9,bd); Treecreeper (5,bd): Prothronotary and Lucy's Warblers (5,6,9,?); sparrows (6,cn); starlings (2,bd).

G. MUD NEST, OR SALIVA AND DEBRIS, STUCK TO BUILDING, ROCK OR SIMILAR SITE

Swifts (1,cn,o); Barn, Cliff and Cave Swallows (5,6,bd); phoebes (1,5,6,cd).

H. CUP NEST ON LEDGE OF ROCK OR BUILDING

Rock Dove and Spotted Dove (1,f); phoebes (1,5,6,cd); Canyon Wren (6,?); American Robin (2,bd); Townsend's Solitaire (5,6,9,10,); juncos (5,6,cd).

I. LARGER NEST IN TREE

Pelicans (1,e,g); Cormorants (1,2,e,g,q); Anhinga (1,2,e,g); larger herons and egrets (2,g); Wood Stork (1,g); Roseate Spoonbill (5,6,g); Glossy Ibis (2,o); White Ibis (8,10,14,o); birds of prey (1,5,9,g); Osprey (5,6,9,10,g); Caracara (3,5,9,17,g); some falcons, using old nests of other birds (5,9,15,g); Chachalaca (1,k); Limpkin (10,11,g); Bonaparte's Gull (6,10,11,14,n); Noddy Tern (5,9,15, g); Great Horned, Barred, Spotted, Great Gray, and Long-eared Owls, on old nests of other birds (1,g); ravens and crows (6,8,14,cn); Pinyon Jay (5,7,12,?n); Clarke's Nutcracker (6,14,?n or ?d).

J. LARGER NEST ON ROCK LEDGE OR ROCKY ISLAND

Gannet (1,g); cormorants (1,2,e,g,q); larger herons and egrets (2,g); hawks and eagles (1,5,6,g); Osprey (5,6,9,10,g); Caracara (3,5,9,17,g); many gulls (2,4,6,8, 10,11,14,17,n); Thayer's Gull (6,10,11,p); Kittiwake (6,10,11,14,i); Noddy Tern (5,9,15,g); crows and ravens (8,14,cn).

K. LARGER NEST BY OR IN WATER

Loons (11,17,o); grebes, small nest in Pied-billed (1,3,g,j); pelicans (1,e,g); cormorants, occasionally (1,2,e,g,q); larger herons and egrets (2,g); Bittern (3,h); Roseate Spoonbill (5,6,g); Glossy Ibis (2,o); White Ibis (8,10,14,o); swans (1,2,g); Everglade Kite (5,g); Marsh Hawk (1,6,g); Osprey (5,6,9,10,g); Caracara (3,5,9,17,g); cranes (9,10,11,12,14,i); Limpkin (10,11,g); Forster's and Black Terns (6,10,11,14,17,n); Noddy Tern (5,9,15,g).

L. LITTLE OR NO NEST, IN TREE HOLE, OR CAVITY ABOVE GROUND

Some ducks, usually with down (1,2,3,n,p); California Condor (12,g); vultures (5,6,9,12,g); American Kestrel (5,15,g); Marbled Murrelet, hollow in moss or lichens on a branch (11,14,n); many owls (1,g); Coppery-tailed Trogon (1,d); kingfishers (1,d); woodpeckers (1,d).

M. LITTLE OR NO NEST IN BURROW, HOLE OR CAVITY ON OR NEAR GROUND

Petrels (1,g,p); mergansers (3,p); California Condor (1,2,g); vultures (5,6,9, 12,g); Razorbill (1,4,5,6,9,10,14,15,16,p); guillemots (6,14,p); Xantus's and Ancient Murrelet, Dovekie, auklets and puffins (1,2,3,4,6,8,10,11,14,17,g,i,p); Barn, Great Horned Spotted and Burrowing Owls (1,g); Belted Kingfisher (1,d).

N. LITTLE OR NO NEST, ON ROCK LEDGE OR ROCKY ISLAND

Fulmar (1,g); some geese (1,g,h); California Condor, in cave or recess (1,2,g); vultures, in cave or recess (5,6,9,12,g); falcons (3,5,9,15g); some terns (4, 6,8,10,

11,14,17,n); Razorbill and murres (1,2,4,5,6,7,8,9,10,11,14,15,16,17,p);

O. LITTLE OR NO NEST, ON THE GROUND, USUALLY NEAR OR BY WATER
Loons (11,17,o); pelicans (1,e,g); geese (1,g,h); some ducks (1,2,3,n,p); Jacana, on plants in water (4,m); oystercatchers (6,10,14,m); Avocet and Stilt (10,m); shore plovers (6,10,m); most sandpipers, snipe and phalaropes (5,6,9,10,11,12, 13,14,m); jaegers (10,11,14,17,p); many gulls (2,4,6,8,10,11,14,17,n); terns (4,6,8,10,11,14,17,n); Sooty Tern (5,9,15,n); Skimmer (6,n).

P. LITTLE OR NO NEST, ON OPEN GROUND
Peregrine, rarely (5,9,g); Willow Grouse and ptarmigan (6,10,16,1); Chukar Partridge (9,k); Turkey (6,10,k); Mountain, Golden and Black-bellied Plovers (6,9,10,11,m); some sandpipers (5,6,9,10,11,14,m); jaegers (10,11,14,17,p); Kittlitz's Murrelet (10,11,g,i); Snowy Owl (1,g); Poor-will, Pauraque and nighthawks (6,9,15,i).

Q. LITTLE OR NO NEST, IN GROWING HERBAGE
Some ducks (1,2,3,n,p); some grouse (1,3,6,10,16,17,l); some gamebirds (1,3,9,k); some sandpipers and phalaropes (5,6,9,10,11,12,14,m); Short-eared Owl (1,g).

R. LITTLE OR NO NEST, ON THE GROUND UNDER TREES OR SHRUBS
Some ducks (1,2,3,n,p); vultures (5,6,9,12,g); woodland grouse (1,3,6,9,10,11, 16,l); gamebirds, quail, Turkey (1,3,5,6,9,10,k); Long-eared and Short-eared Owl (1,g); some nightjars (1,6,9,15,16,g,i).

Key 2. Eggs

To assist further with identification, the eggs in the various color categories have been subdivided according to size – **Small,** up to about crow size or to 40 mm., **medium**, from crow to Turkey Vulture size or 40-70 mm., and **large** at 70+mm.

UNMARKED EGGS

1. WHITE OR CREAM
Large. Fulmar (N,g); Gannet (J,g); pelicans (I,K,O,e,g); swans (K,g); geese (N, O,g,h); California Condor (L,M,N,g); Sea and Bald Eagles (I,J,g); Razorbill and murres (M,N,p).
Medium. Grebes (K,g,j); cormorants (I,J,K,e,g,q); Darter (I,e,g); Wood Stork (I,g); some ducks (L,M,O,Q,R,n,p); Mississippi Kite, hawks (I,g); Chachalaca (I,k); Ruffed Grouse (R,l); Lesser Prairie Chicken (Q,l); auklets and puffins (M,p); Roadrunner (C,k); owls (I,L,N,P,Q,R,g); Ringed Kingfisher (M,d).
Small. Petrels (M,g,p); anis (C,e); smaller owls (L. M, g); Poor-will (P,R,g); swifts (G,o,cn); hummingbirds (C,D,g); Coppery-tailed Trogon (L,d); kingfishers (L,M,d); woodpeckers (L,d); *Empidonax* flycatchers (B,C,D,E,F,?d); phoebes (H,cd); some swallows and martins (E,F,bd); Dipper (A,bd); Bushtit (B,?d); Plain and Bridled Titmice (E,F,bd); some sparrows (C,D,cd); Olive

Sparrow (A,cd); Indigo, Lazuli and Varied Buntings (C,cd); Swainson's, Worm-eating and Bachman's Warblers (C,D,?d); some vireos (B,bd); Rosy Finch (E,cd); Lawrence's Goldfinch (C,cd).

2. BLUE OR GREEN

Large. Mute Swan (K,g); California Condor (L,M,N,g); some large gulls (J,O,n); murres (N,p).

Medium. Cormorants, rarely (I,J,K,e,g,q); Anhinga (I,e,g); herons and egrets (C,D,I,J,K,g); Glossy Ibis (I,K,O); some dabbling, diving and sea ducks (L,M,O,Q,R,n,p); some gulls (J,O,n); Dovekie and Parakeet Auklet (M,p).

Small. Green Heron and Least Bittern (C,D,g); *Coccyzus* cuckoos (C,k); anis, rarely (C,e); Short-billed Marsh Wren (A,?); Catbird and Crissal Thrasher (C,bd); some thrushes (C,D,H,bd); Wrentit (C,?n); Lark Bunting (D,?); Black-chinned Sparrow (C,?); Lazuli and Varied Buntings (C,cd); Dickcissel (D,?); Blue Grosbeak (c,cd); Bronzed Cowbird (-,cd); American and Lesser Goldfinches (C,cd); Starling and Crested Mynah (2,bd).

3. BUFF OR OLIVE-BUFF

Medium. Grebes, nest-stained (J,g,j); American Bittern (J,h); some dabbling and sea ducks (L,M,O,Q,R,n,p); Caracara (I,J,K,g); Prairie Falcon (N,g); some grouse (Q,R,l).

SCRIBBLED, SCRAWLED OR WITH LONG STREAKS

4. SCRIBBLED, SCRAWLED OR WITH LONG STREAKS

Large. Razorbills and murres, occasionally (M,N,p).

Medium. Some gulls, occasionally (J,O,n); some terns, occasionally (N,O,n); Xantus's Murrelet, Rhinoceros Auklet and puffins, occasionally (M,p).

Small. Jacana (O,m); *Myiarchus* flycatchers, streaked finely (C,bd); Brown and Abert's Towhees, Vesper and Lark Sparrows, occasionally (C,D,?); Longspurs (D,cd); Bobolink, blackbirds (C,D,cd); orioles (B,cd); Evening Grosbeak, House Finch and Crossbill (C,bd–cd); White-necked Raven, fine longitudinal streaking (I,cd).

SPECKLED, SPOTTED OR BLOTCHED

5. WHITE OR CREAMY, MARKED WITH RED OR REDDISH-BROWN

Large. Vultures (L,M,N,R,g); Golden Eagle (I,J,g); Razorbill and murres (M,N,p).

Medium. Roseate Spoonbill (I,K,g); kites, hawks, Caracara, Osprey (I,J,K,g); falcons (I,N,P,g); rails and gallinules (D,o); Sooty Tern (O,n); Brown Noddy Tern (I,J,K,g).

Small. Merlin and American Kestrel (I,L,N,g); small rails (D,o); Western, Stilt, Upland and Spotted Sandpipers and Woodcock (O,P,Q,m); Solitary Sandpiper (C,m); Rose-throated Becard (B,?); some flycatchers (B,C,D,E,F,H, bd,cd); Barn, Cliff and Cave Swallows (G,bd); some wrens (A,E,bd,cd); Brown, Long-billed and Bendire's Thrashers (C,?); Townsend's Solitaire (E,H,?); Arctic Warbler (A,bd); most titmice (E,F,bd); nuthatches (F,bd); Treecreeper (F,bd); sparrows and buntings (C,D,cd); Painted Bunting (C,cd); most warblers

(A,C,D,E,F,cd); Painted Redstart (D,E,bd); Yellow-headed Blackbird (D,cd); meadowlarks (A,?d); redpolls(C,cd); Pinyon Jay (H,?n).

6. WHITE OR CREAMY, MARKED WITH BROWN, BLACK OR GRAY

Large. Vultures (L,M,N,R,g); Golden Eagle (I,J,g); Razorbill and murres (M,N,p).

Medium. Roseate Spoonbill (I,K,g); hawks and Osprey (I,J,K,g); ptarmigan (P,l); Ruffed Grouse (R,l); oystercatchers (O,m); Golden and Black-bellied Plovers (P,m); some larger sandpipers (O,P,Q,m); some gulls (J,O,i,n,p); Bonaparte's Gull (H,n); most terns (N,O,n); Skimmer (O,n); guillemots, Ancient Murrelet and puffins (M,p).

Small. Most plovers (O,P,m); some sandpipers and phalaropes (O,P,Q,m); Least and Black Terns (K,O,n); nightjars (P,R,g,i); Rose-throated Becard (B,?); some flycatchers (A,B,C,D,bd,cd); larks (D,a); Cliff Swallow (G,?); White Wagtail and pipits (D,E,bd,ce); shrikes (C,bd,cd); Phainopepla (C,cd); Winter, Canyon and Rock Wrens (A,E,H, ?,bd); Townsend's Solitaire (E,H,?); kinglets (B,C,bd); most titmice (E,F,bd); nuthatches (F,bd); sparrows and buntings (C,D,cd); grosbeaks (C,cd); many warblers (A,C,D,E,F,cd); Red-faced Warbler (D,bd); vireos (B,bd); Brown-headed Cowbird (–, cd); European sparrows (A,E,F,cn); crossbills (C,bd-cd); Clark's Nutcracker (H,?n,?d); Green Jay (C,O).

7. BLUE OR GRAYISH-BLUE, MARKED WITH RED OR REDDISH-BROWN

Large. Murres (N,p).

Small. Mockingbirds and most thrashers (C,bd); some thrushes (C,D,bd); gnatcatchers (C,ad); Verdin (A,?); Brown and Abert's Towhees, Savannah and Tree Sparrows, Snow Bunting (C,D,cd); tanagers (C,cd); Pinyon Jay (H,?n).

8. BLUE OR GRAYISH-BLUE, MARKED WITH BROWN, BLACK OR GRAY

Large. Murres (N,p).

Medium. White Ibis (I,K,o); some gulls, rarely (J,O,n); some terns, rarely (N,O,n); Xantus's Murrelet (M,i,p).

Small. Waxwings (C,cn); some sparrows and buntings, Smith's Longspur (C,D,cd); tanagers (C,cd); Olive Warbler (C,cd); Bobolink, Rusty and Brewer's Blackbirds (C,D,cd); orioles (B,cd); some finches (C,cd); jays (C,cn); magpies (A,cn); crows and ravens (H,I,cn).

9. YELLOWISH OR PALE BUFF, MARKED WITH RED OR REDDISH-BROWN

Large. Vultures (L,M,N,R,g); cranes (K,g,i); Razorbill and murres (M,p).

Medium. Kites (I,g); Osprey, Caracara (I,J,K,g); some falcons (I,N,P,g); Blue and Spruce Grouse (Q,l); rails and gallinules (D,o); Golden and Black-bellied Plovers (P,m); some sandpipers (O,P,Q,m); Sooty Tern (O,n); Brown Noddy Tern (I,J,K,g).

Small. Smaller rails (D,o); some sandpipers (O,P,Q,m); Solitary Sandpiper (C,m); Pauraque (P,R,i); Rose-throated Becard (B,?); kingbirds (C,bd); House and Cactus Wrens (A,E,?,cd); Townsend's Solitaire (E,G,?); Brown-headed Nuthatch (F,bd); Lapland Longspur (D,cd); Prothronotary and Blackpoll Warblers and waterthrushes (C,D,E,F,cd).

10. YELLOWISH OR PALE BUFF, MARKED WITH BROWN, BLACK OR GRAY

Large. Cranes (K,g,i); Razorbill and murres (M,N,p).
Medium. White Ibis (I,K,o); Osprey (I,J K,g); grouse (K,i); Limpkin (I,K,g); American Coot (D,o); oystercatchers, Avocet and Stilt (O,m); Golden and Black-bellied Plovers (O,P,m); some sandpipers (O,P,Q,m); jaegers (O,P,p); gulls (J,O,i,n,p); Bonaparte's Gull (I,n); most terns (N,O,n); Forster's Tern (N,n); Kittlitz's Murrelet (P,g,i); Ancient Murrelet (M,g); Puffin (M,p).
Small. Most plovers (O,P,m); some sandpipers and snipe (O,P,Q,m); Least and Black Terns (K,O,n); Rose-throated Becard (B,?); larks (D,a); Yellow Wagtail and pipits (D,cd); shrikes (C,bd,cd); Long-billed Wren (A,?); Townsend's Solitaire (E,H,?); some longspurs (D,cd); Blackpoll Warbler, waterthrushes (C,D,E,cd); Green Jay (C,?); magpies (A,cn).

11. OLIVE, MARKED WITH REDDISH-BROWN, BROWN, OLIVE-BROWN, BLACK AND GRAY

Large. Loons (K,O,o); cranes (K,g,i); murres (N,p).
Medium. Limpkin (I,K,g); some sandpipers (O,P,Q,m); jaegers (O,P,p); gulls (J,O,i,n,p); Bonaparte's Gull (I,n); many terns (K,N,O,n); Marbled Murrelet (L,n); Kittlitz's Murrelet (P,g,i); Xantus's Murrelet (L,i,p).
Small. Sora Rail (D,o); Mountain Plover (P,m); some sandpipers and phalaropes (O,P,Q,m); some longspurs (D,cd); jays (C,cn);); magpies (A,cn).

12. GREENISH, MARKED WITH RED OR REDDISH-BROWN

Large. Black Vulture (L,M,N,R,g); Whooping Crane (K,g,i).
Medium. Common Gallinule (D.p).
Small. Semipalmated Sandpiper (O,Q,m); Pinyon Jay (I,?n).

13. GREENISH, MARKED WITH DARKER GREEN AND OLIVE

Godwits (D,m).

14. GREENISH, MARKED WITH BROWN, OLIVE-BROWN, BLACK OR GRAY

Large. Whooping Crane (K,g,i); Razorbill and murres (M,N,p).
Medium. White Ibis (I,K,o); Oystercatchers, rarely (O,m); some sandpipers (O,P,Q,m); Parasitic and Long-tailed Jaegers (O,P,p); some gulls (J,O,i,n); Bonaparte's Gull (I,n); Arctic and Forster's Tern (K,N,O,n); Marbled Murrelet (L,n); guillemots and Xantus's Murrelet (M,p).
Small. Larks (D,a); Northern Shrike (C,bd,cd); some longspurs (D,cd); jays (C,cn); crows (I,J,cn); Clark's Nutcracker (I,?n,?d).

15. PINKISH OR PURPLISH, MARKED WITH RED OR REDDISH-BROWN

Large. Razorbill and murres (M,N,p).
Medium. Some falcons (L,I,N,g); King, Clapper and Virginia Rails (D,o); Sooty Tern (O,N); Brown Noddy Tern (I,J,K,g).
Small. Pauraque (P,R,i); Rose-throated Becard (B,?); kingbirds (C,bd); House and Cactus Wrens (A,E,?,cd); Mockingbird, occasionally (C,bd); Fieldfare, occasionally (C,D,bd).

16. PINKISH OR PURPLISH, MARKED WITH BROWN, BLACK AND GRAY

Large. Razorbill and murres (M,N,p).
Medium. Some grouse (P,Q,R,l);
Small. Chuck-wills-widow (R,i); Rose-throated Becard (B,?); Olive-sided Flycatcher (C,?); Meadow Pipit (D,cd); McCown's and Smith's Longspurs (D,cd); Bobolink, Rusty and Brewer's Blackbirds (C,D,cd); orioles (B,cd); Blue and Scrub Jays (C,cn).

17. DEEPER BUFF TO PALE BROWN, MARKED WITH BROWN, BLACK AND GRAY

Large. Murres (N,p).
Medium. Caracara (I,J,K,g); Greater Prairie Chicken (Q,1); jaegers (O,P,p); some gulls (J,O,n); a few sea terns (N,O,n); Atlantic Puffin and Xantus's Murrelet (M,p).
Small. Sora Rail (D,o); Black Tern (K,O,n); Long-billed Wren (A,?).

Key 3. Young Nestlings and Chicks

a. IN SMALLER NEST, MOUTH PATTERNED

Larks, mouth yellow with three dark tongue spots (D,6,10,14); gnatcatchers, mouth yellow with two black spots on tongue (C,7); *Coccyzus* cuckoos have ten white spots on palate, Roadrunner has red and white palate with two white spots at throat. *Coccyzus* cuckoos and Catbird have black edge to tongue tip.

b. IN SMALLER NEST, MOUTH UNPATTERNED, YELLOW OR ORANGE

(**All are downy**). Flycatchers (A,B,C,D,E,F,G,1,4,5,6,9,15,16,); swallows (E,F,G,1,5,6); White Wagtail (E,6); Dipper (A,1); Winter Wren (A,1,5,6); Shrikes (C,b,10,14); mockingbirds and thrashers (C,2,5,7,15); thrushes (C,D, E,F,H,2,7,15); Arctic Warbler (A,5); kinglets (B,C,6,9); oystercatchers (C,7); titmice (E,F,1,5,6); nuthatches (f,5,6,9); treecreepers (F,5); Red-faced Warbler and Painted Redstart (D,E,5,6); vireos (B,1,6); Red Crossbill? (C,4,6,8); Starling (E,F,2).

c. IN SMALLER NEST, MOUTH UNMARKED, PINK OR RED

Downy young. Swifts (G,1); Yellow Wagtail and pipits (D,E,6,10,16); shrikes (C,6,10,14); Phainopepla (C,6); Cactus Wren (A,1,5,6,9,10,15); sparrows and buntings (C,D,H,1,2,4,5,6,7,8); Olive Sparrow (A,1); longspurs (D,4,6,8,9,10, 11,14,16); grosbeaks (C,1,2,5,6); tanagers (C,7,8); most warblers (C,D,E,F,1,5, 6,8,9,10); blackbirds (C,D,4,5,6,8,16); orioles (B,4,8,18); cowbirds (-,2,6); finches (C,1,4,5,6,8,); Rosy Finch (E,1).
Naked Young. Swifts, early stage (G,1); waxwings (C,8); European sparrows (A E,F,6); jays (C,6,8,10,11,14,16); magpies (A,8,10,11); crows and ravens (I,J,8,14).

d. IN UNLINED CAVITY IN TREE, BANK OR GROUND, NESTLING NAKED

Coppery-tailed Trogon (L,1); kingfishers (L,M,1); woodpeckers (L,1).

e. IN LARGER NEST ON TREE OR GROUND, NESTLING NAKED
Pelicans (I,K,O,1); cormorants (I,J,K,1,2); Anhinga (I,1,2); anis (C,1,2).

f. LARGER NESTLING WITH COARSE, HAIRY DOWN; USUALLY SPARSE
Coccyzus cuckoos (C,2); Roadrunner (C,1); doves (C,D,E,H,1).

g. LARGER DOWNY NESTLING WITH PLAIN WHITE, GRAY, BUFF OR LIGHT BROWN DOWN
White. Gannet (J,1); pelicans (I,K,O,1); some herons and egrets (C,D,I,J,K,2); Wood Stork (I,1); Roseate Spoonbill (I,K,5,6); California Condor, first down (L,M,N,1,2); Turkey Vulture (L,M,N,R,5,6); White-tailed Kite, pinkish-buff tint on back; hawks, sometimes tinted gray, buff and brown; Golden Eagle, sometimes with gray tips (I,J,1,5,6); falcons (I,L,N,P,3,5,9,15); Brown Noddy Tern, drab white or with greyish-brown on upper parts (I,J,K,5,9,15); many owls (L,M,N,P,R,1).
Gray. Western Grebe (K,1,3); Fulmar (M,1); some petrels (L,1); some cormorants (I,J,K,1, 2); some herons and egrets (C,D,I,J,K,2); swans (K,1,2); Ross's, Emperor and Brent Geese (O,1); California Condor, second down (L,M,N,1,2); White-tailed Kite, second down (I,5,9); some hawks (I,J,1,5,6); Bald Eagle, first down (I,J,1); Peregrine and Merlin, buffish or brownish gray (I,N,P,5,9,15); Ancient Murrelet, blackish (M,6,10); Kittlitz's Murrelet, gray and yellow (P,10, 11); Elf Owl, sooty white (L,1); Burrowing Owl, grayish white (M,I); Great Gray Owl (I,L,1); Some hummingbirds (C,D,1).
Buff. Anhinga, buffish-brown (I,1,2); Least Bittern, white below (C,D,2); Black Vulture (L,M,N,R,5,9,15); some kites, Harris's Hawk, White-tailed Sea Eagle, grayish buff (I,J,K,1,5,6,9); Caracara, pinkish-buff (I,J,K,3,5,9,17); Barn Owl, buffish-cream second down (L,M,1); Hawk and Boreal Owls, buffish-white (L,1); Short-eared Owl (Q,R,1); Poor-will (P,R,1,6); Rubythroat and Costa's Hummingbirds, yellowish (C,D,1).
Light Brown. Anhinga, buffish-brown (I,1,2); Blue Heron with gray, Tricolored Heron with gray and rufous, Black-crowned Night Heron rufous or grayish (I,J,K,2); White-fronted and Barnacle Geese, brown and white (N,O,1); Everglade Kite, grayish-brown second down, Rough-legged Hawk, grayish-brown first down, Harris's Hawk and Bald Eagle, second down (I,J,K,1,5,6); Osprey, brown and white (I,J,K,5,6,9,10); Caracara (I,J,K,3,5,9,17); Limpkin (I,K,10,11); puffins, grayish-brown (M,1,3,4,6,10,17); cranes (K,9,10,11,12, 14).

h. LARGER DOWNY NESTLING WITH YELLOWISH OR GREENISH UNPATTERNED DOWN
American Bittern (K,3); some geese (N,O1).

i. LARGER DOWNY NESTLING WITH DOWN WITHOUT PATTERN BUT WITH VARIATION IN OVERALL DORSAL COLORATION
Cranes (K,9 10,11,12,14); Kittlitz's Murrelet, gray and yellow (P,10,11); nightjars, (P,R,1,6,9,15,16).

j. LARGER DOWNY NESTLING WITH DOWN BOLDLY STRIPED ON HEAD AND USUALLY OVER BODY, FEET LOBED
Grebes (K,1,3).

k. LARGER DOWNY NESTLING WITH DOWN MAINLY STRIPED OR MOTTLED, SHORT SEED-EATING BILL, BARE LEGS
Chachalaca (I,1); typical gamebirds, quails, Turkey (P,Q,R,1,3,5,6,9,10).

l. LARGER DOWNY NESTLING WITH DOWN MAINLY STRIPED OR MOTTLED, SHORT SEED-EATING BILL, DOWNY LEGS
Grouse (P,Q,R,1,3,6,9,10,16,17).

m. LARGER DOWNY NESTLING WITH DOWN MAINLY STRIPED OR MOTTLED, BILL SLENDER AND LONGER
Jacana (O,4); oystercatchers (O,6,10,14); Avocet and Stilt (O,10); plovers (O,P,6,9,10,11); sandpipers, snipe, woodcock and phalaropes (O,P,Q,5,6,9,10, 11,12,13,14); Solitary Sandpiper (C,5,9).

n. LARGER DOWNY NESTLING WITH DOWN SPOTTED OR MOTTLED, FEET WEBBED
Most ducks (L,M,O,Q,R,1,2,3); Avocet, feet half webbed (O,10); most gulls (J,O,2,4,6,8,10,11,14,17); Bonaparte's Gull (I,6,10,11,15); most terns (N,O,4,6, 8,10,11,14,17); Forster's and Black Terns (K,O,6,10,11,14,17); Skimmer (o,6).

o. LARGER DOWNY NESTLING WITH DOWN DARK BROWN OR BLACKISH, FEET UNWEBBED
Loons, toes lobed (K,O,11,17); ibises, with white marks on head (I,K,2,8,10, 14); rails, down black (D,5,9,11,15,17); gallinules, white sheaths on head at first (D,5,9,12); American Coot, orange on head at first (D,10).

p. LARGER DOWNY NESTLING, WITH DOWN DARK BROWN OR BLACKISH, THREE TOES WEBBED
Some petrels (M,1); some diving and sea ducks (L,M,O,Q,1,2,3,); jaegers (O,P,10,11,14,17); Brown Noddy Tern (I,J,K,5,9,15); murres and Razorbill (M,N,1,2,4 – 11,14 – 17); guillemots (M,6,14); Xantus's Murrelet, black and white (M,4,8,10,11,14,17); Dovekie, auklets, puffins (L,1,2,3,4,6,8,10,17); Ancient Murrelet, grayish-black (M,6,10).

q. LARGER DOWNY NESTLING, WITH DOWN DARK BROWN OR BLACKISH, ALL FOUR TOES WEBBED
Cormorants (I,J,K,1,2).

LOONS *Gaviidae*

These breed on waters of the northern regions. They are unable to walk properly on land and nest at the water's edge for easy access, but falling water levels during incubation may leave the nest further from the water's edge. More rarely nests are mounds of material in shallow water near the edge. Nest material is accumulated by sideways-building and the nest may vary from a bare scrape to a mound of vegetation. The nest hollow is often damp. Young are precocial; downy, with a rather short stubby bill. They follow the adults in the water and may be carried on the backs of swimming birds. They are tended by both parents, being fed on fish and Crustacea passed to them by the adults. When small they may hide in waterside vegetation if alarmed.

COMMON LOON *Gavia immer* Pl. 17

Breeds on larger, deeper lakes in bare or wooded country; at varying altitudes. Nest-site is usually on a bare promontory, island or small island mound; usually on raised ground by the water's edge, more rarely on the edge of a reedbed, or on a muskrat house or mass of floating vegetation.

Nest. Usually a slight hollow scrape with little nest material, but in reedbed sites a large heap of vegetation may be assembled. **Breeding season.** Late May or early June to September. Single-brooded. **Eggs.** Normally 2, rarely 1 or ?3. Elliptical oval to long oval. Slightly glossy with a slightly granular or rough texture. Olive-brown, sometimes more greenish; with a few small blackish spots, or larger blotches, or sometimes immaculate. 90 × 57 mm. **Incubation.** By both sexes, beginning with the first egg. 29–30 days. **Nestling.** Precocial, downy. Down thick and short, blackish-brown, paler on throat, foreneck, upper breast and flanks. Belly and lower breast gray-edged, becoming white. First down pushed out by second, paler down with the first attached to its tips. Iris dull reddish-brown. Bill light gray, becoming dark slaty or blackish towards the base. Legs and feet gray, blackish towards the outside. **Nestling period.** Young tended by both adults, but one adult more active and sometimes only one remains until the end of the period. Young may ride on parents' backs for first 2–3 weeks. May feed themselves after 6 weeks; fly at about 12 weeks.

YELLOW-BILLED LOON *Gavia adamsii*

Breeds on bare arctic tundra, north of the tree-line. Nest usually on a raised site at the water's edge, a small mound in the water, or on a small island or peninsula; on a lake, large pool or large rivers.

Nest. Material usually scanty or absent, but the appearance of the mounds suggests an accumulation of muddy material. Hollow usually damp. **Breeding season.** Beginning June to early July, depending on a thaw. Single-brooded. **Eggs.** Normally 2. Variably shaped; usually subelliptical. Like those of Common Loon but at times paler and more buff. 89 × 56 mm. **Incubation.** ? similar to Common Loon. **Nestling.** Like Common Loon. Down dark brownish-gray, but paler than that of Common Loon, with throat to upper breast and flanks paler still. Lower breast and belly white. Bill pale bluish-gray, dark basally and around nostrils. Legs and feet gray. Eyes dark brown. **Nestling period.** Unknown, probably similar to Common Loon.

ARCTIC LOON *Gavia arctica* **Pl. 17**

Breeds on deeper and larger lakes in tundra or wooded country, more rarely on small waters, usually further south than Common Loon. Nest usually on a small island, sometimes on shore, very close to water.

Nest. A shallow scrape on a raised site, or with varying amounts of vegetation and at times a large heap; occasionally a raised heap of vegetation in shallow water. **Breeding season.** Beginning early May in south of range, to mid-June in northern part. Single-brooded; replacement clutches usually have a single egg. **Eggs.** Normally 2, sometimes ?3, replacement clutch 1. Subelliptical to long subelliptical, sometimes oval. Slightly glossy, olive-brown, sometimes greenish or dark brown; with black spots, blotches or streaks. 76 x 47 mm. **Incubation.** By both sexes, beginning with the first egg. 28–29 days. **Nestling.** Precocial, downy. Down thick and short. Back, head and flanks dark brownish-gray, head and neck to upper breast pale gray, underparts grayish-white. Iris brown. Bill dark gray. Legs and feet greenish-gray. **Nestling period.** As for other divers. Tended by both parents, who may fly some distance for food, bringing it back in the bill. Adults may remain with young, which may feed themselves at about 5 weeks. First flight at about 2 months.

Arctic Loon: at a site with plentiful material.

RED-THROATED LOON *Gavia stellata* **Pls. 1, 17**
Breeds on both large and small lakes, and small pools; in open or wooded situations. Nest usually on the shore at water's edge. Usually in solitary pairs but may be sociable with a number of nests near together, at times only a few yards apart.

Nest. A shallow scrape on a mound, with very variable nest material; or a heap of vegetable material, moss, etc., built up in shallow water near the bank. These nests may be built up higher if water rises. **Breeding season.** Late May or early June to September. Single-brooded. **Eggs.** Normally 2, rarely 1 or ?3. Usually long subelliptical but variable. Often glossy, more so than in other species. Olive-buff, sometimes greenish or dark brown; marked with sparse blackish spots or blotches. 74 × 45 mm. **Incubation.** Eggs laid at 2-day intervals. Incubation by both sexes but mainly by female, usually beginning with first egg but some young hatch on same day. 24–29 days. **Nestling.** Precocial, downy. First down thick and short. Variable blackish-brown, blackish-gray, or paler grayish-brown on back; slightly paler on cheeks, throat, foreneck, upper breast and flanks; underparts pale gray. Pushed out by paler second down coat. Iris brown. Bill dark. **Nestling period.** Young tended by both adults, possibly feeding themselves by 4 weeks, first flight at about 6 weeks.

Red-throated Loon: typical bare scrape by water.

GREBES *Podicipedidae*

They breed on freshwater lakes and sometimes rivers. The nests are accumulations of soggy, rotting plant material, in the water, often floating. Both sexes build, the material being carried to the nest by birds swimming from a little distance. It has been suggested that heat generated by rotting nest material assists incubation. The eggs are biconical in shape, thicker at the middle and tapering towards both ends. They are usually quickly covered with a layer of moist nest material by the bird when it leaves the nest, and during incubation become heavily stained brown or buff. The young are precocial, their down patterned in stripes. They follow the adults in the water and may be carried on the backs of swimming adults. They are fed on fish and insects, and given feathers to help form pellets for casting up fishbones. Adults usually divide the brood between them.

RED-NECKED GREBE *Podiceps griseigena* Pl. 18

Breeds on freshwater lakes, lagoons, floodwaters, and calmer rivers; with some vegetation cover.

Nest. A low mound of rotting aquatic and waterside vegetation, floating and anchored by plants or built up in shallows with small hollow on top. Building continues during laying. **Breeding season.** Begins end of April to early June. Single-brooded. **Eggs.** Normally 4–5, more rarely 2–7. Variably shaped, long elliptical to subelliptical with biconical tendency. Smooth and white. 56 × 36 mm. **Incubation.** Eggs laid at 2-day intervals. Incubation by both parents, probably from first egg. 22–25 days. **Nestling.** Precocial, downy. Between white brow stripes crown is black, with small bare spot and narrow median white stripe. Pale neck stripes are dull and buffish, and dark stripes narrow on neck and poorly-defined on upper mantle. Back and sides of body unstriped, black stripes at side of neck broken about halfway, and pair of dark stripes bordering lower throat join to form a V. Center of underside white. Bare scarlet patches on lores and bare patch on crown. Iris olive-brown. Bill buffish with two vertical dark stripes. **Nestling period.** 8–10 weeks. The brood and parents appear to remain together for a long period.

HORNED GREBE *Podiceps auritus* Pl. 18

Breeds on large and small lakes and ponds, floodwaters, sloughs, wet marshes and calmer river and stream backwaters; where vegetation is present. Often solitary, but with a number of nests near each other at times. Nests usually in small bays, with tall vegetation in the water providing cover.

Nest. A low mound of rotting aquatic vegetation built in shallow water, with a shallow nest hollow. **Breeding season.** Begins mid-May to July. Normally single-brooded, possibly occasional second brood. **Eggs.** Usually 4, occasionally 3–5, rarely 8; larger clutches in north of range. Long subelliptical or biconical. Smooth and white. 45 × 31 mm. **Incubation.** Eggs laid at *c.* daily intervals. Incubation by both sexes, with the female taking the major share; normally beginning about the third or fourth egg. Hatching spread over several days. 22–25 days. **Nestling.** Precocial, downy. Bare pinkish spot on crown. Longitudinally striped. Pale stripes on head and throat buff-tinted, on neck and back narrow and gray, and black stripes prominent, making appearance dark. Bill pinkish with two vertical black bands on upper mandible. Iris light gray. Feet dark gray. **Nestling period.** Little information. Young tended by both parents, but only a single adult sometimes apparent with older chicks.

Horned Grebe: *c.* 8-10in. across.

EARED GREBE *Podiceps nigricollis* Pl. 18

A more southerly species than the last, breeding on open freshwater lakes, flood levels, pools, or river backwaters, with reed or vegetation cover. Usually nests colonially, often in close proximity. Nest usually in vegetation cover such as reeds.

Nest. A low mound of aquatic and waterside vegetation. **Breeding season.** Beginning from mid-April in south, late May and June in north. Double-brooded at times. **Eggs.** Normally 3–4, sometimes 5, rarely 2–8. Elliptical to sub-elliptical. Smooth and white at first. 44 × 30 mm. **Incubation.** Eggs laid at intervals of 24–28 hours. Incubated by both parents, beginning with first egg. 20–22 days. **Nestling.** Precocial and downy. With bare pink spots on lores and bare crown spot. The latter can change by flushing. Down darker than on other species, with stripes poorly-defined and broken. Upperparts, including back of head and neck, blackish; with narrow grayish, poorly-defined head and neck stripes and none on the back. Broken, irregular stripes on the sides of head and neck, a narrow inverted black V on sides of chin. Occasional dark central chin streak. Center of underside white, sides blackish with white flecks. Bill flesh-colored or gray with two narrow black vertical bands, tip white. Feet gray, becoming red on lobe edges. Iris dark brown. **Nestling period.** Young first tended by both parents, later the adults divide brood between them. Young feed themselves at 2 weeks, independent at 3 weeks.

LEAST GREBE *Podiceps dominicus* Pl. 18

Resident on lakes and pools of any size, and on quiet rivers and streams. Nest in water often several feet deep, anchored to growing plants, among tall water plants or in the open.

Nest. A mound of rotting aquatic vegetation with shallow nest hollow, anchored to plants. May be used for several successive broods. **Breeding season.** Begins early March. Prolonged. Possibly several broods. **Eggs.** Usually 4–6, sometimes 2–7. Subelliptical to long elliptical or biconical. Smooth and white at first. 33 × 23 mm. **Incubation.** Eggs laid at 1–2-day intervals. Incubation by both sexes, beginning with first egg. 21 days. **Nestling.** Precocial and downy. Head mainly black with large tapering bare red patch on mid-crown, later covered with cinnamon down. Bare orange loral patch. Dark median stripe from chin, down throat to broaden on upper breast and divide to border white underside. Bordered on front of neck by conspicuous white stripes widening over throat to base of bill, with two narrow dark streaks from bill and lores. White stripe on side of neck turns upwards behind ear covert and terminates. Paired narrow white stripes on back of neck join on nape. Short white streak behind eye, and another above it, and tiny white median spot above bill. Pale neck stripes extend along brownish-black back. Bill pale with black tip and culmen, and broken black band near base. Iris dark brown. Feet gray. **Nestling period.** Young tended by both parents. Leave nest after hatching; usually carried on the back of one parent while the other brings food (insects). Nest used for resting and roosting in first two weeks. Young driven from nest but remain near and are visited by adults during incubation of next clutch. Time of full independence and first flight not known.

WESTERN GREBE *Aechmophorus occidentalis* Pl. 18

Breeds on lakes and in sheltered inlets and bays of the coast. Nest built in tall plants, tule and reeds, growing in water on the edge of large stretches of open water. Breeds in colonies that may be large, thousands at times, with nests near each other. Nests on dry land where water has receded after breeding began.

Nest. A solid mound of rotten vegetation, built up from the bottom in shallow water, or floating, anchored to plants, in deep water. Usually well concealed by growing plants. **Breeding season.** Begins mid-May in south to early June in north. **Eggs.** Usually 3–4. Long elliptical to subelliptical. Smooth but not glossy. Greenish or buffish when first laid, becoming white, then nest-stained. 59 × 38 mm. **Incubation.** Eggs laid at daily intervals. Incubation by both sexes beginning with the first egg. 23 days. **Nestling.** Precocial and downy. Triangular bare spot on crown orange, becoming red during excitement; bare loral spot orange. Color of down almost uniform; dull gray above, pale gray to whitish below and on face. Faint indication of pattern visible on close examination. Bill black. Legs and feet grey with greenish lobes. **Nestling period.** Young leave nest at hatching, carried on parents' back and tended by both parents. At nests on dry land young are transported to water under wings of female. No information on later part of nestling period.

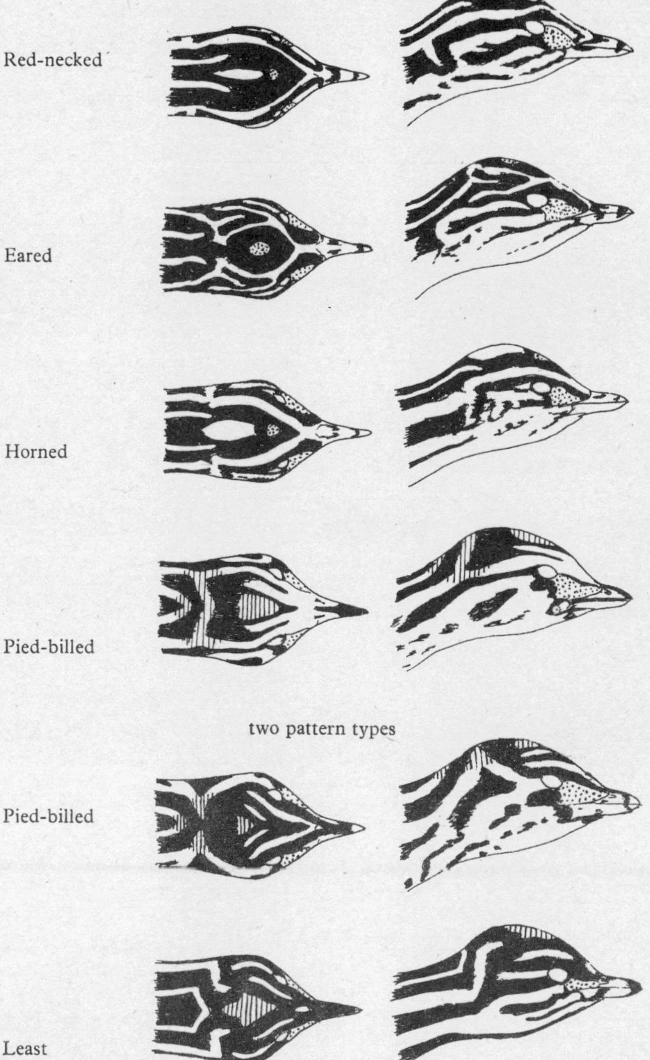

Head patterns of grebe chicks from the side and from above. The pattern of throat and lower face tends to be variable, but the dorsal head pattern is usually diagnostic. Bare areas of colored skin are indicated by stippling.

Plate 1

LOONS. The chicks have two down coats. The second, to the tips of which the first down remains attached, is paler in color.

Red-Throated Loon, *Gavia stellata.* In this species the down may be variably tinted with blackish or gray. The Arctic Loon is dark brownish-gray above with pale gray from throat and neck to upper breast. The Common Loon is blackish-brown, paler on throat, neck and upper breast and the Yellow-billed Loon is similar but paler. **page** 43

GREBES. Young downy, with distinct bold striped patterns (p. 47).

Pied-Billed Grebe, *Podilymbus podiceps.* This species has a more variable head pattern than other species (see p. 47). Stripes are absent on the back of Horned and Eared Grebes, and the Western Grebe has pale gray down with faint patterning. 50

SHEARWATERS. These have two down coats, the second darker in color and longer, and the first clinging to the tips of the second. The young may appear larger than adults before they finally lose their down.

Northern Fulmar, *Fulmarus glacialis.* First down is whitish on head and neck, and blue-gray above; second down is gray on head, neck and back. 50

PETRELS. These are similar to shearwaters, with two successive down coats. There is usually a bare spot on the hind-crown.

Leach's Petrel, *Oceanodroma leucorhoa.* The second down is more blackish than the first. The Fork-tailed Petrel has the first down blackish-brown above and gray below; the second is gray above and paler gray below. In the Ashy Petrel both down coats are brownish-gray. 51

GANNETS.

Gannet, *Morus bassanus.* There is sparser, longer down on a blackish skin at first. The later down is woollier. 52

PELICANS, CORMORANTS and ANHINGAS. These are naked when first hatched but later grow a rather woolly down coat.

Brown Pelican, *Pelecanus occidentalis.* Naked and reddish at first, then turning blackish and growing white down. The White Pelican is flesh-colored on hatching, growing white down. 53

Great Cormorant, *Phalacrocorax carbo.* Naked and dark-skinned, later with dark brown down. The skin is purplish-brown to blackish, followed in the Red-faced Cormorant by dusky-brown down with white mottling below, by black down in Double-crested and Neotropical Cormorants, sooty-gray down in the Pelagic Cormorant, and gray down, mottled white below, in Brandt's Cormorant. 54

Anhinga, *Anhinga anhinga.* The naked buffish skin is later covered with buffish-brown down. 57

Red-throated Loon
Pied-billed Grebe
Northern Fulmar
Leach's Petrel
Gannet
Brown Pelican
Great Cormorant
Anhinga

2

Least
Bittern
Great Blue Heron
Great Egret
Black-crowned
Night Heron
American Bittern
Tricolored Heron
Roseate
Spoonbill
Glossy Ibis
Wood Stork

HERONS. The slender head, narrow bill and upstanding down on the top of the head are typical of nestling herons.

Great Blue Heron, *Ardea herodias.* The Great White Heron is a race with white down in the young. **page** 57

Least Bittern, *Ixobrychus exilis.* 62

Great Egret, *Egretta alba.* Snowy and Cattle Egrets have white down, and the later down of the Little Blue Heron is also white. 60

Black-crowned Night Heron, *Nycticorax nycticorax.* The Yellow-crowned Night Heron has grayish down with a long crest. 61

Tricolored Heron, *Hydranassa tricolor.* The Reddish Egret has gray down tinted cinnamon on the head, the Green Heron has gray down, and the Little Blue Heron pale gray down, tawny on the head, and the later down white. 61

American Bittern, *Botaurus lentiginosus.* 62

SPOONBILL and IBISES. Young hatched with down. Spoonbill has two down coats, the first shorter, the second longer and woollier.

Roseate Spoonbill, *Ajaia ajaja.* 66

Glossy Ibis, *Plegadis falcinellus.* The White Ibis has black down on head with white line in front of eye, smoky-brown on neck, sparse on body and smoky-gray on back and white on underside. 66

STORKS. These usually have two down coats, but in the Wood Stork the first is limited to a little coarse down on the wings, the second thick and woolly.

Wood Stork, *Mycteria americana.* 63

PIED-BILLED GREBE *Podilymbus podiceps* **Pls. 1, 18**

Breeds on lakes and ponds, often very small, floodwaters, marshy borders of large lakes and rivers; exceptionally on quiet parts of estuaries. Nest usually floating in vegetation bordering open water.

Nest. A solid structure of rotting and green vegetation, with distinct nest hollow. Usually floating, anchored to growing plants; sometimes on the bottom in shallow water. Material added during incubation. **Breeding season.** Begins about mid-March in south to mid-May in north. Single or double-brooded. **Eggs.** Usually 4–7, sometimes 2–10. Elliptical to subelliptical. Smooth and non-glossy. Almost white, tinted bluish or buff when first laid; later nest-stained. 44 × 30 mm. **Incubation.** Eggs laid daily, but occasional gap late in brood suggests more than 24-hour interval. Later clutches have longer intervals. Incubation by female at first, then shared, and by female only during period of hatching. 23 days. **Nestling.** Precocial and downy. Head pattern variable. Patches of bare yellowish skin on lores and crown; the latter soon replaced by rufous down. There is rufous color on hind-crown, loral region and eyestripe. Paired white stripes on back of neck meet at nape. Lateral white neck stripes meet on hind-crown, with extension to, or over, eyes. There is a variable double white chevron on forehead and fore-crown. Throat and sides of head are sparsely mottled with black, and thicker black speckling on lower neck and upper breast divides to border white underside. Four whitish stripes from the neck continue down the black back. Bill dark on culmen and tip with small dark marks around base. Iris dark brown. Feet and legs black becoming grayish or greenish. **Nestling period.** Young after hatching follow parents. While small they are carried for periods on parents' backs. Fed on insects at first. Later small fish. No information on fledging and age at independence.

PETRELS AND SHEARWATERS *Hydrobatidae and Procellariidae*

Seabirds with poor powers of movement on land, and reluctant to come to land. Nest in a burrow or natural crevice on island, mainland shore or mountain; coming to site only by night (except for Fulmar). Often colonial nesters. Nest material very variable in quantity; accumulated at mouth of burrow by sideways-throwing and sideways-building and gradually moved down burrow. They produce only a single egg, not replaced if lost; and incubate in long spells, sometimes continuously for several days at a time. There may be long intervals between feeds for the young which are downy, with usually two successive down coats, one attached to the tips of the next, which in turn is attached to tips of first feathers. They become very fat, much larger and heavier than the adults. They take regurgitated food from the bill of the parent, and they are usually finally deserted by the parents and remain in the nest; emerging at night to exercise as the feathers grow and losing weight during this period. They usually leave for sea at night alone.

NORTHERN FULMAR *Fulmarus glacialis* **Pls. 1, 17**

Breeds on cliffs with suitable ledges, or on similar sites on rock outcrops or cliff at times some miles from the sea. More rarely on level tops of cliff stacks, or islands, or level ground on the shore, preferring a slight eminence but needing some shelter at the site.

Nest. A bare rock ledge or slight hollow in a softer substrate. The hollow may contain a few small stems or fragments. **Breeding season.** Mid- to late May, until late September, but adults may be present on the breeding ledges at intervals from November onwards. Single-brooded, with no replacements. **Eggs.** Usually 1, rarely 2 reported. Usually subelliptical. Dull white with a slightly rough texture. 74 × 50 mm. **Incubation.** By both adults in spells of about 4–5 days. 55–57 days. **Nestling.** Altricial and downy. Down long and thick, short and close on crown and chin. In first down, head, neck and underparts white, with a triangular pale blue-gray vent patch. Upperparts pale blue-gray. In second down upperparts are darker gray; and head, chin and throat become a similar gray; and white breast and underside are slightly tinted gray. Bill and legs gray at first, turning black in first week. **Nestling period.** Young one brooded, and fed usually once a day at first but at longer intervals later, both parents taking part. The chick can eject oil, as adults do, from the moment of hatching onwards; and at first even the parents must approach with caution. 46–51 days in nest.

FORK-TAILED PETREL *Oceanodroma furcata*

Breeds on offshore islands, on turf in the open or among trees; rarely among rocks. Nests in colonies.

Nest. A burrow in turf, or rarely a deep natural hole among rocks. Some plant debris may accumulate at nest. **Breeding season.** Begins early to late June. Single-brooded. **Egg.** Single egg. Elliptical to short subelliptical. White, non-glossy, often with wreath of tiny reddish specks around large end. 33 × 25 mm. **Incubation.** By both sexes, changing over at night. Period not recorded. **Nestling.** Altricial and downy. First down blackish-brown above, gray below, with chin and lower face bare. Second down thicker, gray above, pale gray below. **Nestling period.** No information.

LEACH'S PETREL *Oceanodroma leucorhoa* **Pls. 1, 18**

Breeds on offshore islands on turf or rocky slopes, usually bare sites but will use wooded islands. Nests in colonies.

Nest. A burrow excavated in soil, in soft ground, usually 3 ft. long and angled but in some instances up to 6 ft. with several pairs in separate nest-chambers; or natural cavity in fallen rocks, under boulders or buildings, or ruins. Burrow excavated by male in three nights and a day. Some plant debris accumulated in nest. **Breeding season.** Late May to October. Single-brooded. **Egg.** Single egg. Elliptical to subelliptical, blunt ended. White; non-glossy; usually with a zone of fine reddish spots at the larger end. 33 × 24 mm. **Incubation.** By both sexes, each taking an unbroken spell of about 4–6 days. 41–42 days. **Nestling.** Altricial and downy. First down bluish-gray, long and soft, slightly paler on underside. Around eyes, lores, chin and spot on hind-crown nearly bare. Replaced by second down, blackish and as long as first, and a little thicker on more exposed part. Skin around eyes blue-gray. Bill pale with black tip, darkening in first fortnight. Legs and feet gray or flesh-colored. **Nestling period.** Eyes closed when first hatched. Brooded by one parent for first 5 days, then tended at irregular intervals. Eyes open at *c.* 15 days. Deserted when large and fat at *c.* 40 days. Lives on fat reserve and exercises at night, leaving for sea at 63–70 days.

ASHY PETREL *Oceanodroma homochroa*

Breeds on offshore islands in fallen rocks, rock walls, or burrows. Nests in colonies.

Nest. A natural cavity or burrow. Occasionally a lining of plant debris present. **Breeding season.** Apparently prolonged. Eggs found from mid-May to mid-August. Single-brooded. **Eggs.** Single eggs. Elliptical to short subelliptical. White, non-glossy, often with a wreath of tiny reddish-brown specks around large end. 30 × 23 mm. **Incubation period.** Incubation by both sexes, changing over at night. Period not recorded. *c.* 50 days by calculation. **Nestling.** Altricial and downy. Both down coats brownish-gray. **Nestling period.** No information.

MANX SHEARWATER *Puffinus puffinus*

A single recorded breeding on an east coast island. Breeds on offshore islands or mainland cliff slopes, in turf slopes or rocky screes and boulders. In colonies, at times very large.

Nest. A burrow in turf or soil or a natural crevice among rocks. Burrow excavated by both sexes and usually over 3 ft. long, but sometimes only half that length. Usually some material, plants and feathers present. **Breeding season.** In north-western Europe begins early May. Single-brooded. **Eggs.** Only one. Subelliptical to oval. White, non-glossy. 61 × 42 mm. **Incubation.** By both sexes, in spells of 1–4 days, more rarely 5–6. Sitting bird apparently fed by mate, at night, 52–54 days. **Nestling.** Altricial and downy. Down thick, soft and long over most of bird; shorter on lores, chin, and around eyes. First down dull brown to gray-brown. A broad grayish-white band from chin down to center breast then dividing down either side of belly. Mid-belly and other parts gray-brown. Second down darker but similar to first. **Nestling period.** Brooded for first week, then only fed nightly by parents. Parents desert at about 59–62 days; chick remaining in burrow for *c.* 1 fortnight more before leaving.

GANNETS *Sulidæ*

GANNET *Morus bassanus* **Pls. 1, 17**

Breeds mainly on islands, usually with steep cliffs, nesting on the more level top or upper slopes, more rarely on large cliff ledges of islands or coasts. In colonies, often very large, with nests a bill-stab apart.

Nest. A rounded mound of material, mostly seaweed, but plants, feathers and other debris also used. Relieving birds may bring in seaweed during incubation period and this is added to heap by both birds with elaborate ceremony. Shallow nest hollow on top. **Breeding season.** Normally from early April, but May further north in range. Single-brooded. **Eggs.** Usually 1, very rarely 2. Long subelliptical. Dull chalky-white outer layer of irregular thickness, in places showing the bluish shell beneath. Outer layer may become stained buff or brown, and may flake away to reveal the underlying shell. 82 × 49 mm. **Incubation.** By both sexes. There are no brood patches and egg is covered by webs of feet, one over the other, then the bird resting on top. 43–45 days. **Nestling.** Altricial and downy. Skin black. At first sparsely covered with short pale creamy-white down tapering to hair-like tips. This is replaced by longer white down, woolly in appearance which spreads over the whole body but is short on throat, and sparse around base of bill, eyes, and on forehead. Bill grayish. Iris dark brown. Legs and feet dark gray. **Nestling period.** Young fed by both parents, taking regurgitated food from inside the gullet. Tended for 13 weeks, then neglected for about 10 days before leaving for the sea. At sea cannot fly until after *c.* 1 week.

PELICANS *Pelecanidae*

Large fish-eating birds nesting in marshes, islands in lakes, and on coasts. Colonial nesters, with nests placed close together. *Sensitive to disturbance and whole colony likely to desert.* The young are ugly, quick-growing but slow maturing. They tend to leave the nest and huddle together in large groups while still unfeathered. Food, and water, is brought by the adults, and the young put head and neck down into the gullet for it; a method at times accompanied by a struggle and some slight damage to participants. Very small young take regurgitated liquid food from the inside of the tip of the adult's bill.

WHITE PELICAN *Pelecanus erythrorhynchus* Pl 19

Breeds on low, preferably bare, islands, in large waters, fresh or salt, including lakes, sea inlets and shallow coastal bays. Nests in colonies.

Nest. Usually a large mound of earth and debris, 2–3 ft. across and *c.* 1 ft. high, with a central, unlined hollow. Sometimes just a slight depression in the ground. One record of nests on floating tule island. **Breeding season.** Begins early April in south to late May or early June in north. **Eggs.** Usually 2, sometimes 1. Elliptical to long subelliptical. Dull white with thick uneven chalky layer outside, becoming scratched and stained. 87 × 56 mm. **Incubation period.** Incubation by both sexes. 29 days? **Nestling.** Semi-altricial. Naked and flesh-colored at hatching, but covered with thick white down within 10 days. Pouch and bill grayish-white. Iris white. Feet pale yellow. **Nestling period.** Young hatch at intervals and differ in size. Tended by both parents. Brooded at nest for 2–3 weeks and fed mainly on liquid food. Can stand up at 3 weeks. Subsequently they leave and huddle in groups visited by adults for feeding only. Fly at *c* 7–10 weeks.

BROWN PELICAN *Pelecanus occidentalis* Pls. 1, 19

Breeds usually on small coastal islands. Nest on the ground or less frequently on bushes or low trees.

Nest. The structure depends on material available near by. May be a scrape with rim of soil and debris and some feathers for lining, or a similar structure built into a large mound; or a platform of sticks woven into branches and heaped with sticks, reeds, straw and grass. **Breeding season.** Variable in different years and different colonies; but on average may begin mainly March to April with some eggs from February to June. Single-brooded, but lost clutch replaced, possibly by single egg only. **Eggs.** Usually 3, sometimes 2. Long subelliptical. Dull white with thick uneven chalky layer becoming scratched and stained. 75 × 50 mm. **Incubation period.** Eggs laid at intervals of 2 or more days. Incubation by both sexes. Period not certain; 28–30 days? **Nestling.** Semi-altricial. Naked, skin reddish, turning black. Eyes open at 2 days. Coat of white down by 10–12 days.

Pouch and bill pale gray. **Nestling period.** Young tended by both parents. Leave nest at *c.* 5 weeks, huddle together if on ground, or clamber around arboreal nests. Fly at *c.* 9 weeks, but continue to be fed by parents. Age at independence not known.

CORMORANTS *Phalacrocoracidae*

Fish-eating birds of sea-coasts and fresh waters, nesting on ledges, trees, bushes, or on the ground. Coastal nests may be simple seaweed heaps with hollow tops, but at inland sites may be larger twig structures with finer linings. Material may be carried to the nest in flight from a distance. At change-over during incubation the incoming bird may bring nest material. Young birds take food by reaching well into the parent's gullet, or pick up disgorged food. Young regurgitate food if alarmed.

GREAT CORMORANT *Phalacrocorax carbo* Pls. 1, 18

Breeds on cliffs of sea-coasts or by inland waters on cliff ledges; or by lakes and rivers in trees, or bushes; or on the ground on islands. Usually nests colonially. **Nest.** On sea-coasts and offshore islands a heap of seaweed and sticks; but at inland sites a more solid structure of sticks, lined with long leaves, grasses, or water plants. Various other debris may be incorporated. Male brings most of material while female builds. **Breeding season.** Beginning early April in south, to early June in north. Single-brooded. **Eggs.** Usually 3–4, sometimes 5, rarely 6. Subelliptical. Pale blue shell with an uneven chalky-white outer layer, mostly concealing undershell, but becoming scratched and stained. 65 × 40 mm. **Incubation.** Eggs laid at about 2-day intervals. Sitting usually begins with the first egg, but serious incubation not until most are laid. By both sexes. 28–29 days. **Nestling.** Altricial. Eyes closed for first 4–5 days. Naked at first with blackish-brown skin, but down appears within a week. Thick, dark brown down, blacker on head and neck, basally pale. Sparse on throat. Absent around eyes, and on lores and chin. Bill flesh-colored, darkening later. **Nestling period.** Young tended by both adults. In very hot weather they may bring water to the chicks. Young remain in nest for *c.* 5 weeks but can leave and return when younger. They are fledged at 50–60 days, but take 11–12 weeks to become independent. Young regurgitate food if alarmed.

DOUBLE-CRESTED CORMORANT *Phalacrocorax auritus* Pl. 18

Usually breeds on larger water on small islands or islets, isolated rocks or trees standing in water; or in trees in remote swamps, or on cliff ledges overlooking water.

Nest. A large structure of twigs, plant debris and various coarse rubbish, with a finer lining. Nests thin and shallow in first year. Relined and used in subsequent seasons. Foundation built by male, who then brings material while female builds. Male adds material throughout nesting. **Breeding season.** Variable in different years and different seasons. In general begins early March in south to mid-June in north, but eggs recorded in Florida from late December to late October. Single-brooded, but lost clutch may be replaced. **Eggs.** Usually 3–4, sometimes 2–7, exceptionally 9 but possibly from two birds. Long subelliptical. Pale blue shell with uneven chalky outer layer, becoming stained.

Great Cormorant: *left,* stick nest, *c.* 2ft. across; *right,* seaweed nest, *c.* 1½-2ft. across.

51 × 38 mm. **Incubation.** By both sexes, beginning with third egg, or occasionally earlier. 25–29 days. **Nestling.** Altricial. Naked on hatching. Skin brownish turning blackish-purple. Thick, short black woolly down begins to appear at 6 days, complete by 14 days. **Nestling period.** Eggs hatch over 2–7 days. Young tended by both parents. Eyes open at 4–5 days. Young active by 9–10 days. At 14 days not brooded but sometimes shaded. Feathering begins at 16 days, complete at 6–7 weeks. At 3–4 weeks young wander from nest but return to be fed. Fly at 5–6 weeks but can dive before this. After 7 weeks can accompany adults. Independent at 10 weeks.

NEOTROPICAL or OLIVACEOUS CORMORANT *Phalacrocorax olivaceus* **Pl. 18**

Breeds by freshwater lakes and ponds, and on coastal islands. Nests usually in trees or bushes growing in water, or on bare ground or rocks. Nests in colonies. **Nest.** A rough cup or bulkier structure of small sticks, lined with stems and coarse grass. **Breeding season.** May to August. Single-brooded? **Eggs.** Usually 4, sometimes 3–6. Long subelliptical. Pale blue shell with uneven chalky outer layer, becoming stained. 55 × 34 mm. **Incubation.** Period unknown. **Nestling.** Altricial. Naked at hatching. Skin blackish-gray. Later covered with blackish down. **Nestling period.** Young hatch over several days and differ in size. Tended by both parents. Age at independence not known.

BRANDT'S CORMORANT *Phalacrocorax penicillatus* **Pl. 18**

Breeds on offshore, rocky islands. Nest on the ground, usually on a slope towards the top of an island or ridge. Nests colonially, often in company with other cormorant species and seabirds.

Nest. A circular drum, *c.* 1½–2 ft. across and *c.* 6 ins. high. Mostly of seaweed, sometimes with grass or moss, or exceptionally sticks. Built by both sexes, male bringing most material and female building. Material brought throughout incubation period. May be re-used in subsequent season. **Breeding season.** Begins late March in south to early May in north. Single-brooded. **Eggs.** Usually 4, sometimes 3–6. Long subelliptical. Shell pale blue with uneven chalky outer layer, becoming stained. 61 × 38 mm. **Incubation.** By both sexes; beginning with first egg? Period not known. **Nestling.** Altricial. Hatched naked, with black skin. Later covered with down; gray and paler on underside, mottled white on underside and wings. **Nestling period.** No information.

PELAGIC CORMORANT *Phalacrocorax pelagicus* **Pl. 18**

Breeds on ledges and in niches of rocky coastal cliffs and islands. Nests colonially. **Nest.** A heap of seaweed, plant debris and other material if available. Built by both sexes, one (male?) collecting most of material. **Breeding season.** Begins late April in south to early July in north. Single-brooded; but lost clutch replaced, although usually smaller, 2–3 eggs. **Eggs.** Usually 3–5, sometimes 7. Long subelliptical. Shell pale blue with uneven chalky outer layer, becoming nest-stained. 59 × 37 mm. **Incubation.** By both sexes, beginning with first egg. 26 days? **Nestling.** Altricial, hatched naked, skin blackish-gray. Later covered with down; sooty-gray with paler thighs. **Nestling period.** No information.

RED-FACED CORMORANT *Phalacrocorax urile*

Breeds on wider cliff ledges of islands. Nest colonially.

Nest. Large heap of seaweed, plants and shed feathers, and any nearby rubbish; with distinct nest hollow. **Breeding season.** Begins mid-May. Single-brooded but lost clutch replaced. **Eggs.** Usually 3–4. Long elliptical to long subelliptical. Shell pale blue with uneven chalky outer layer, becoming stained. 61 × 37 mm. **Incubation.** By both sexes. Period unknown. **Nestling.** Altricial. Hatched naked with dark purplish-brown skin, white at base of lower mandible. Soon becomes downy. Down dusky-brown with grayish tips, mottled white on underside and with large white spot on outer thighs. **Nestling period.** No information.

ANHINGAS *Anhingidae*

ANHINGA *Anhinga anhinga* **Pls. 1, 18**
Breeds by fresh, brackish or salt water; still or slow-moving. Often in colonies and with colonies of other water birds. Nests in trees or bushes, sometimes low. **Nest.** Built of twigs, or nest of other bird such as a small egret used. Nest lined with leafy twigs. Nests tend to be small. The male brings material which the female incorporates. **Breeding season.** Throughout the year in Florida. Shorter period beginning in April further north. **Eggs.** 3–5, rarely 2. Subelliptical to long subelliptical. Shell bluish with an outer chalky-white layer of irregular thickness. 52 × 35 mm. **Incubation.** Eggs laid at intervals of 1–2 days. Usually both sexes incubate. Rare instances of male incubating and rearing alone. 25–28 days. **Nestling.** Altricial. Naked when hatched. Skin yellowish-buff. Rapid growth of thick, short buff-brown down. Iris dark. Bill dark. Legs and feet yellowish-buff. **Nestling period.** Both sexes tend young. After 2 weeks young will leave nest if disturbed and try to return later. Young regurgitate food if alarmed.

HERONS *Ardeidae*

Long-legged, long-billed wading birds; rather awkward at perching in trees. In spite of this nests are often in trees or bushes. In such sites they are of twigs; while ground nests in reedbeds are of reeds. The twig nests are often thin but are added to annually and may become very large. There is little lining. Nest-building is simple, consisting largely of laying the twig on the existing structure and working it in with lateral quivering bill movements. The male usually brings twigs to the female on the nest, and she builds them in, twig presentation being accompanied by some ritual display. The young are downy, with bristling down on the crown, giving a typical shock-headed appearance. Adults bring food in the crop and are induced to disgorge it by the young seizing the bill of the adult in its bill. The adult regurgitates and the young may take the food directly from the parents' bill or, particularly in the case of larger items, and when the young are larger, will pick up disgorged food from the nest. The young disgorge food when alarmed.

GREAT BLUE HERON *Ardea herodias* (Includes Great White Heron, *A. h. occidentalis*) **Pls. 2, 19**
Breeds by fresh or salt water. Nests built in trees or bushes, on ledges of cliffs or rock outcrops, or on the ground in tule beds or elsewhere. Great White Heron usually in mangrove trees. Nests colonially.

Nest. A large flat platform of twigs. Thin and small when newly-built, but old nests are added to seasonally, becoming very bulky. Nest hollow lined with leaves, grass, fine twigs and other plant material. **Breeding season.** Information is inadequate but breeding appears to begin in November to December in Florida. Very extended in Great White Heron. Elsewhere from early March to April. Single-brooded. **Eggs.** Usually 4, sometimes 3–7. Oval to long oval, long elliptical or subelliptical. Pale greenish-blue. Smooth or slightly rough, and non-glossy. 64 × 45 mm. **Incubation.** By both sexes. 25–29 days. **Nestling.** Semi-altricial and downy. Down on upper parts and flanks long, and on the crown down has long bristle-like tips, and stands up to produce a bristling wig. It is sparser on sides of back and mid-belly; absent around the eyes and on lores, chin, throat and back of neck. Upperparts dark grayish-brown, side pale gray, underside white. Crown is smoky-gray with fine white tips. Bill relatively short and blunt at first. On Great White Heron down is white. **Nestling period.** Young tended by both parents. Always one adult present for first 3–4 weeks. Young fly first at *c.* 60 days, leave nest at 64–90 days.

GREEN HERON *Butorides virescens* Pl. 20

Breeds by water in many habitats; in marshes on tussocks or muskrat house; at varying heights in trees by fresh or salt water, including aerial roots of mangroves; in shrubs and thickets by water and along ditches, and in woods and orchards away from water. Either solitary or in small groups.

Nest. Varies in structure from small flimsy platform when new, to bulky structure re-used in successive seasons. Of twigs, reeds and vines, with lining absent or of similar but finer material. Male builds or relines nest and displays to attract female. Later male brings material and female builds. Some material added until after hatching. **Breeding season.** Begins late April to early May. Often single-brooded, sometimes double-brooded. **Eggs.** Usually 4–5, sometimes 3–6. Elliptical to subelliptical. Pale greenish-blue or more green. Smooth, non-glossy. 38 × 29 mm. **Incubation.** First three eggs laid at 2-day intervals, others at one-day intervals. Incubation by both sexes. 19–21 days. **Nestling.** Semi-altricial and downy. Down thin, thicker on back and bushy on head. Smoky-gray, paler below. **Nestling period.** Young tended by both parents. Eyes open at hatching. Brooding continuous for first week. Young able to move about by third day and show bittern alarm posture at 5 days. Can climb by 1 week, and clamber and jump about in trees by 16–17 days. Fly at 21–23 days, and fly with adults at 25 days. Probably independent at 30–35 days.

LITTLE BLUE HERON *Florida caerulea* Pl. 20

Breeds by fresh, brackish or salt water; in open by lakes, pools, marshes or streams, and by overgrown woodland pools and dense Florida mhumocks. Nest in trees, usually low down, or in shrubs. Nests colonially, often with other species where it tends to be on outskirts of colony.

Nest. Variable in shape and size, usually flat and elliptical with slight central hollow. Usually of sticks, lined with finer twigs, but some reeds and grass may be present. Female builds and male brings material. **Breeding season.** Begins late March to early April in south, to mid-April further north. Probably single-brooded. **Eggs.** Usually 3–5, rarely 2–6. Elliptical to subelliptical. Pale greenish-blue. Smooth and non-glossy. 45 × 33 mm. **Incubation.** Eggs usually laid on alternate days. Incubation by both sexes. 22–24 days. **Nestling.** Semi-altricial

Green Heron: *c.* 1-1½ft. across.

and downy. Down sparse on underside, longer on top of head. On hatching, down very pale gray with tawny tips on head, later down white. Bill pinkish-gray, becoming yellow. Legs and feet gray, becoming greenish-yellow. Iris pale gray to white. **Nestling period.** Hatching takes 3–5 days. Regurgitated food dropped in nest at first; then young take bill of parent. Begins feathering by 1 week, mostly feathered by 12 days. Young can leave nest by 12 days. By 17 days young spend much time on branches near nest. Usually return for food, but parents will visit young on branches. By 1 month young make short flights. Independent probably by 35–40 days.

CATTLE EGRET *Bubulcus ibis* **Pl. 20**

Breeds in a variety of sites, usually near water. Nest often in large trees, not necessarily by waterside; or in small trees or bushes, growing in water or reedbeds; or in dense reedbeds or on small rocky islands. Nests in colonies; often together with other small heron species.

Nest. A shallow structure of varied material; twigs, sticks, dead reeds, or other handy vegetation. Smaller twigs are used for lining. Male usually brings material and female builds. **Breeding season.** Variable, beginning late March to mid-April. Nesting usually synchronised within a colony. Usually single-brooded. **Eggs.** Usually 4–5, rarely 3–6. Elliptical to subelliptical, usually blunt-ended.

Smooth. Non-glossy. Very pale blue or whitish-blue. 46 × 34 mm. **Incubation.** By both sexes. Intermittent incubation from the first egg. 21–25 days. **Nestling.** Semi-altricial and downy. Down white, with fine tips, stiff and upright on the crown. Bill and loral skin greenish-yellow. Legs and feet reddish-buff. Iris yellowish-white. **Nestling period.** Young tended by both parents. Hatching interval produces variation in size of young in nest. Fly at 40 days and possibly not independent until *c.* 60 days.

REDDISH EGRET *Dichromanassa rufescens* Pl. 20

Breeds in coastal areas by salt water, in mangroves or in drier thickets of coastal islands. Nests at heights of up to 15 ft., or on the ground. Nests in colonies where possible.

Nest. A platform of thin sticks, stems and roots, and similar material; with little or no lining. On the ground may be a more solid structure of dry grass with a deep nest hollow. Both sexes appear to collect material and build. **Breeding season.** Usually occurs in late winter in Florida, and spring in Texas; but eggs have been found in both areas in early April. **Eggs.** Usually 3–4, rarely up to 7. Elliptical to short subelliptical. Pale greenish-blue. Smooth, non-glossy. 50–36 mm. **Incubation.** By both sexes. Period not recorded. **Nestling.** Semi-altricial and downy. Down long on top of head, sparse under body. Smoky gray on body, grayish cinnamon on head and neck. Legs feet and bill dark olive. **Nestling period.** No information.

GREAT EGRET *Egretta alba* Pls. 2, 20

Breeds near fresh or salt water, in woodlands and thickets. Nests in trees of woodland and cypress swamps, often high up (60–80 ft. recorded, but 15–40 more usual); in mangroves or nearby trees on saltwater keys; in willow thickets of glades, or waterside thickets of rivers and streams; and in Texas in tule and the scrub of dry islands. Nests singly or in colonies of varying size, large at times; often with other heron species or with Wood Storks.

Nest. A large flat platform or bulkier re-used structure, similar to but thinner and frailer than those of Great Blue Heron. Of sticks, twigs and tule stems; lined with smaller twigs and plant material. Building or repair begun by male, later male brings material and female builds. **Breeding season.** In general may begin in late December in Florida, to mid-April in north of range; but varies in different years, probably with weather. Probably single-brooded. **Eggs.** Usually 4–5, sometimes 3–6. Elliptical to subelliptical. Pale greenish-blue. Smooth and non-glossy. 56 × 41 mm. **Incubation.** Little information. 25–26 days in Europe. **Nestling.** Semi-altricial and downy. Down long and white with fine silky tips. Stiffer on crown producing crest; sparse on neck and underparts, absent from around eyes, on lores, chin, throat, back of neck and central upper breast. Bill pink on hatching, then yellow. Legs and feet, gray-green, becoming gray. Bare facial skin blue-gray, becoming yellow. Iris off-white. **Nestling period.** Both parents tend young. Young begin feathering at one week, mostly complete by 4–5 weeks. At 3 weeks leave nest for branches and return to be fed. By fourth week fed away from nest. Fly short distances by 5 weeks, fly with adults at 6 weeks.

SNOWY EGRET *Egretta thula* **Pl. 20**

Breeds in wide range of sites by fresh or salt water. Nests in trees, including cedar swamp and mangroves, in willows and buttonbush, in prickly pear and huisache on dry Texas islands, and in *Phragmites* reeds, tule and bulrushes in more open marshes. Nests in trees may be up to 30 ft. from ground, but usually at 5–10 ft. Very sociable, nesting in colonies, at times in thousands, and often with other heron species.

Nest. A shallow structure, elliptical and rather flat; of thin twigs, heavier in the foundations and thin in the lining. Building begun by male, continued by female, male bringing material. **Breeding season.** Commencement variable, but usually begin late March in south, to mid-May in north. Probably single-brooded. **Eggs.** Usually 3–4, sometimes up to 6. Elliptical. Greenish-blue. Smooth and non-glossy. 43–32 mm. **Incubation.** Eggs laid on alternate days. Incubation by both sexes, beginning with first egg. Period uncertain. **Nestling.** Semi-altricial and downy. Down long and fine on head. Down white. **Nestling period.** Young tended by both parents. Food dropped on to nest for first few days, later young grasp adult bill. Young leave nest for branches at 3–4 weeks.

TRICOLORED or
LOUISIANA HERON *Hydranassa tricolor* **Pls. 2, 20**

Breeds mainly near salt water. Nest in mangrove or buttonwood, in thickets of tidal marshes, willow thickets or rushes of fresh marshes; on Texas island sites in dry thickets, large cane and prickly pear; and on bare coastal islands in grasses and herbage. Highly sociable, nesting in colonies, sometimes of thousands; often with other heron species.

Nest. A shallow structure, round or oval and *c.* 1–1½ ft. across, with a hollow several inches deep; of slender twigs with a lining of finer twigs, grass and plant stems. Female does most of building, male bringing material. Probably single-brooded. **Breeding season.** Begin mid-March in the south to early May in the north. **Eggs.** Usually 3–4, sometimes up to 7. Usually elliptical. Greenish-blue. Smooth and non-glossy. 45–33 mm. **Incubation.** By both sexes. 21 days? **Nestling.** Semi-altricial and downy. At hatching down dark gray on head, neck, back and wings, with longer tawny down on head, and white on foreneck, underside and thighs. Later head down brownish-red, and neck and back brownish-gray. Bill dark gray. Legs and feet pinkish-gray becoming gray-green. Iris off-white. **Nestling period.** Young tended by both parents. Feathering begins at 4–5 days, complete at *c.* 4 weeks. Young begin to climb from nest at 11–17 days but still fed on nest. By 24 days fed away from nest and tend to form social groups with young of their own species.

BLACK-CROWNED NIGHT HERON *Nycticorax nycticorax* **Pls. 2, 20**

Breeds in a wide variety of sites near fresh, brackish or salt water; in all types of trees, bushes and thickets, from near ground level to *c.* 150 ft up; and in marshes in *Phragmites*, cattails, grass tussocks and *Scirpus*. Nests in colonies, often with herons or other water birds.

Nest. Variable, according to available material. Usually a platform with shallow hollow, of twigs, reeds and similar material. Material often tends to radiate from nest center. Foundation usually heavier, with a finer lining. Male begins building, later bring material for female who builds but may also collect. **Breeding season.** Variable. Beginning in winter in south Florida to early April in the north. **Eggs.** 3–4, sometimes 5. Elliptical to subelliptical. Pale greenish-blue, sometimes more green, or wholly blue. Smooth and non-glossy. 53–37 mm. **Incubation.** Eggs laid at *c.* 2-day intervals. Incubation by both sexes, beginning with first egg. 21 days in Europe, but ? 24–26 days quoted for America. **Nestling.** Semi-altricial and downy. Down sparse with long silky tips, stiff and bristly on crown, producing a crested appearance. Absent about eyes, on lores, chin, throat, lower hind-neck and mid and side belly. Down rufous-brown above, with pale tips forming crest on head, and white on thighs. Later grayish-brown above, darker and more rufous on head and neck. Bill gray. Legs and feet gray-green. Iris grayish or greenish becoming amber. **Nestling period.** Young tended by both parents. Feathering begins at *c.* 12 days, complete in *c.* 4 weeks. Young begin to leave nest at 2–3 weeks, returning to be fed. By 4 weeks fed away from nest. Fly at 6 weeks.

YELLOW-CROWNED NIGHT HERON *Nycticorax violaceus* **Pl. 20**
Breeds by salt and fresh water. Nests in mangroves or adjacent trees, and elsewhere in trees and bushes at varying heights from near ground level to over 50 ft. Nests singly or in colonies, often small, sometimes with other heron species. **Nest.** Usually a stout structure of heavy twigs, lined with finer twigs, rootlets and sometimes leaves. Both adults help build and material is added until young are present. **Breeding season.** Variable. Usually begins about March in south to late April in north of range. Possibly single-brooded. A lost clutch may be replaced. **Eggs.** Usually 2–4, sometimes up to 6. Elliptical. Pale greenish-blue. Smooth and non-glossy. 51 × 37 mm. **Incubation.** By both sexes. Period not known. **Nestling.** Semi-altricial and downy. Down fine and grayish, forming conspicuous long crest on head. Bill brownish and greenish. Leg, feet and loral skin greenish-yellow. Iris deep yellow. **Nestling period.** No information.

LEAST BITTERN *Ixobrychus exilis* **Pls. 2, 20**
Breeds in freshwater marshes. Nest usually in dense stand of *Typha* or *Scirpus*, or similar growth; about a foot above water and near open water. Exceptionally in a bush or tree, or on the old nest of another bird. Usually nests singly, but several adjacent pairs may occur in suitable areas.
Nest. Usually on a base of dried plants bent down, or natural base. Of dead and live stems forming platform with shallow hollow, round to oval, *c.* 6–8 in. across and 2–5 in. thick. Material may radiate from nest center. Both sexes build but the male is more active. **Breeding season.** Variable over the wide range. Begins about mid-March in south, to early June in the north of range. Probably double-brooded. **Eggs.** Usually 4–5, rarely up to 7. Elliptical. Pale bluish to pale greenish. Smooth and non-glossy. 31 × 24 mm. **Incubation.** Eggs usually laid at daily interval. Incubation by both sexes, beginning with second egg. 16–19 days. **Nestling.** Semi-altricial and downy. Down long; buff above and white below. **Nestling period.** Young tended by both parents. They show bittern alarm posture at 3–4 days. Can leave nest for a period at 5 days. May leave nest and remain hidden nearby at 8–10 days, but some remain in nest for 2 weeks. Early moves may be due to disturbance. Age at first flight and full independence unknown.

AMERICAN BITTERN *Botaurus lentiginosus* **Pls. 2, 20**
Breeds in marshy areas of tall vegetation – cattails, bulrushes or reeds; sometimes in wet swales; but has also bred in drier areas of tall grasses. Will use

similar habitats on brackish or tidal marshes. Nest on the ground or raised slightly on platform of thick vegetation. Nests singly, but males may be polygamous, with several females nesting separately within territory.
Nest. A pile of reeds, sedges or similar plant material available near by. Pile 6–13 in. high and 12–16 in. across. Built by female alone. **Breeding season.** Variable. Usually begins late April to May. Apparently single-brooded. **Eggs.** Usually 2–5. Elliptical to short subelliptical. Buffish-brown to deep olive-buff. Smooth or slightly glossy. 49–37 mm. **Incubation.** First four eggs laid at daily intervals, with 2-day interval for the fifth. Incubation by female alone, beginning with first egg. 24–29 days. **Nestling.** Semi-altricial and downy. Down yellowish-olive, darker above. Bill flesh-colored with dark tip. Eyes light olive. **Nestling period.** Young tended by female only. Eggs hatch over several days and young differ in size. Young leave nest after *c.* 2 weeks and are tended nearby. Age at first flight and at independence not known.

STORKS *Ciconiidae*

WOOD STORK *Mycteria americana* — Pls. 2, 19

Breeds in trees by fresh or brackish water, usually in stands of trees growing in water. Prefers large cypress, but will also use smaller trees where necessary, including red mangroves and buttonwoods on creeks. Nests often close together

Wood Stork: *c.* 2-3ft. across.

Plate 3

SWANS. The downy chicks are more uniformly colored and pale.

Trumpeter Swan, *Cygnus buccinator.* The down of the Whistling Swan is similar but extends less far laterally on the sides of the bill. **page** 69

Mute Swan, *Cygnus olor.* 68

GEESE. The downy young lack the more clear-cut patterns of ducklings, and show the stout and narrower goose bill.

White-fronted Goose, *Anser albifrons.* The Pink-footed Goose is brown above, including the crown of the head and around the eyes, and whitish below; sometimes with a greenish-yellow tint on paler parts. 70

Snow Goose, *Anser caerulescens.* The figure on the left shows the downy young of the white form, the right that of the darker, Blue Goose type. The Emperor Goose has pale gray down, darker above and on the head, and Ross's Goose may have down gray, white, yellow, greenish yellow or blackish yellow. 71

Canada Goose, *Branta canadensis.* North-western races tend to be less yellow. 72

Barnacle Goose, *Branta leucopsis.* 72

Brant, *Branta bernicla.* 72

TREE-DUCKS. The downy young are slimly built, boldly patterned and with a typical pale stripe on the nape.

Fulvous Tree-duck, *Dendrocygna bicolor.* 73

Black-bellied Tree-duck, *Dendrocygna autumnalis.* 73

Trumpeter Swan
Mute Swan
White-
fronted
Goose
Snow
Goose
Blue
Goose
Canada
Goose
Barnacle
Goose
Brant
Black-bellied Tree-
duck
Fulvous
Tree-duck

Mallard

Shoveler

Wood Duck

Pintail

American Wigeon

Green-winged Teal

Redhead

Lesser Scaup

DUCKS (see also pl. 5). The young of dabbling ducks in down are mostly brown above and yellow below, with a yellow face and dark eyestripe. Pochards are similar but without bold face markings, and other diving ducks of the genus *Aythya* are dark.

Mallard, *Anas platyrhynchos.* The Black Duck has similar but darker down and the darker mark below the eyestripe may merge with it. The Gadwall resembles the Mallard but with upperparts browner and lighter parts paler, the eyestripe narrow, dorsal patch larger and bill edges flesh-colored. **page** 74

Shoveler, *Anas clypeata.* 76

Wood Duck, *Aix sponsa.* 77

Pintail, *Anas acuta.* 75

American Wigeon, *Anas americana.* 76

Green-winged Teal, *Anas crecca.* The Blue-winged Teal is similar but with the second face streak short and eyestripe broken just before the eye. The Cinnamon Teal is similar to the Blue-winged Teal but with the down greener and yellower. 75

Redhead, *Aythya americana.* The Ring-necked Duck and Canvasback are similar but without the warmer tint on the face, and the back and top of the head dark brown. The Canvasback is larger and with a wedge-shaped bill. 77

Lesser Scaup, *Aythya affinis* 78

and at varying heights from a few feet above water to tree-tops. Nests in colonies. **Nest.** A rather thin platform, about 2–3 ft. across, of sticks with a lining of some finer twigs and leaves. Built by female, male bringing material. **Breeding season.** Variable, usually beginning December to January. **Eggs.** Usually 3–4, rarely 5. Elliptical to subelliptical. Creamy-white, with a finely granular surface. 68 × 47 mm. **Incubation.** Eggs laid at 1–2-day intervals. Incubation by both sexes, beginning with first egg. 28–32 days. **Nestling.** Semi-altricial. On hatching, naked, with coarse, hairy down on wings. By two weeks becomes covered with thick woolly white down. Skin whitish. Bill short and thick, yellow. Legs and feet very pale yellow. Iris and skin around eye pale bluish-white. **Nestling period.** Young tended by both parents. Unless weather is bad young brooded for first week only, but for first 5 weeks one parent always on guard against bands of non-breeding birds which destroy eggs and young. Parents bring and disgorge water over young on hot days. Young leave nest and make short flights at 50–55 days, but return to nest for feeding and roosting until 75 days old. Age of final independence not known.

SPOONBILLS AND IBISES *Threskiornithidae*

Long-legged, long-billed wading birds. Able to perch in trees. Nest on the ground in marshes and reeds, or build nests in trees, the latter quite strongly and competently built although the birds are clumsy on perches. Twigs are fixed by insertion followed by a small lateral shake. The young feed by regurgitation of food into the throat of adults, from which it is taken by the young. When ground nests are used, and possibly elsewhere, young tend to wander from the nest before they can fly.

ROSEATE SPOONBILL *Ajaia ajaja* **Pls. 2, 19**

Breeds in mangroves of Florida, and elsewhere uses trees by or in water if available; in bushy scrub of dry coastal islands in Texas. Sometimes in *Scirpus*, or on the ground in mixed colonies where tree sites are not available. Nests in colonies, often with herons or other water birds.

Nest. A bulky structure, about 16 in. across, of sticks and twigs, with a lining of finer material such as leaves. Male brings material and female usually builds. **Breeding season.** Usually begins November in Florida, April in Texas. Single-brooded. Will replace lost clutch. **Eggs.** Usually 2–3, sometimes 4. Subelliptical. White, with fine speckling and numerous small smudged blotches of reddish-brown or light buffish-brown; larger markings often concentrated in a zone about the larger end. Shell with roughly granular surface. Non-glossy. 65 × 44 mm. **Incubation.** Eggs laid at 2–3-day intervals. Incubation by both sexes. 23–24 days. **Nestling.** Semi-altricial and downy. First down short and white. Bill, legs and feet and bare skin black. After *c.* 1 week second down grows; thicker, longer and woolly. Feet pink. **Nestling period.** Young tended by both parents. When older they begin to leave nest for branches, returning to be fed. They leave finally at 5–6 weeks, being fed nearby until *c.* 8 weeks, when they learn to fly and are progressively neglected by adults.

GLOSSY IBIS *Plegadis falcinellus* **Pls. 2, 19**

Breeds by water, fresh, brackish or salt; or in marshes. Eastern form nests on top of low trees and shrubs growing in water, or on the ground in cordgrass

(*Spartina*). White-faced western form nests mainly in *Scirpus*, tule or *Phragmites*. Nests in colonies, often with herons or other water birds.
Nest. A substantial shallow structure of sticks and twigs, sometimes with leaves and green stems in the lining. On the ground dry stalks of cattails or similar material used. Both sexes build. **Breeding season.** Begins March to late May. Single-brooded. **Eggs.** Usually 3–4. Elliptical to subelliptical. Uniform light blue, much deeper than on heron eggs. Smooth with very slight gloss. 53 × 36 mm. **Incubation.** By both sexes, but mainly by female who sits at night and part of day. 21 days. **Nestling.** Semi-altricial and downy. Down long and sparse; dull black with white patches on crown and white bars on throat; absent on lores. Bill pink with black bands at base, middle and tip. Feet yellowish. **Nestling period.**Young tended by both parents. One parent always present for first 5 days. At 2 weeks young move out to ends of branches but return to nest to be fed. By 6 weeks young fed by parent away from nest, but can fly a little and feed themselves. At 7 weeks they accompany parents. At ground colonies it is likely that adults feed young other than their own once they have left nest.

WHITE IBIS *Eudocimus albus* **Pl. 19**

Breeds near water, fresh, brackish or salt; nesting on low trees or shrubs growing in or by water, and in palmetto. Also nest further west in prickly pear, and in *Scirpus*, or long grasses on the ground. Nests in colonies, often with herons and other water birds. Nest sites tend to be low, and at times on ground of crowded tree colonies.
Nest. A platform of dead sticks, fresh twigs with leaves and other plant material from nearby. Usually some green leaves in the lining. Female does most of building but both sexes collect material. **Breeding season.** Variable, beginning late March to mid-May, but eggs have been found in Florida up to mid-August. **Eggs.** Usually 3–4. Subelliptical to long subelliptical. Pale buffish, bluish or greenish, variably marked with speckling, spots and irregular blotches of light to dark brown, smaller markings fairly evenly distributed, but blotches, where present, sometimes concentrated at larger end. Smooth and non-glossy. 58 × 39 mm. **Incubation.** Begins with completion of clutch. 21–23 days. **Nestling.** Semi-altricial and downy. Down on head, neck, upper breast and wing, but rest of body almost bare. Black down on head; longer smoky-brown down on neck and wings. Narrow white line in front of eye. Skin grayish, and two pink gular patches. Bill pink with broad black bands at base, middle and tip; or only first two. Iris light brown. Later bare parts grow a straggly woolly down; upper parts appear smoky-gray, underside white. **Nestling period.** Young leave nest at *c.* 3 weeks. Fly at *c.* 5 weeks.

WATERFOWL *Anatidae*

SWANS *Cygnus* species

Large waterfowl living and feeding mainly in the water and nesting at its edge. Nest a large heap of plant material accumulated by sideways-throwing and sideways-building; the female usually sitting on the site pulling in and placing material; the male in the water with his back to her, passing material back for the female. Small amounts of down are added to the lining by the female. The precocial, downy young are brooded on nest or shore, but otherwise swim with the parents. Fledged young generally remain with adults until the next season.

MUTE SWAN *Cygnus olor* **Pls. 3, 21**

May breed on any waters, large or small, fresh or brackish, and in swamps and drainage ditches. Usually solitary, aggressive pairs; but semi-domesticated birds may nest colonially, in close proximity to each other. Nest usually at the water's edge on land or small islands, or built in shallow water in reedbeds.

Nest. A large heap of plant material with a raised hollow at the centre. A small amount of down. Usually begun by male, later joined by female. **Breeding season.** Begins mid-April to May. Single-brooded. **Eggs.** 5–7, exceptionally 4–12. Smooth, slightly glossy, slight granular texture. Some almost white, but more often with a pale blue-gray or blue-green tint. Subelliptical to long elliptical. 113 × 74 mm. **Incubation.** Eggs laid on alternate days. Incubation beginning with last egg or a little earlier; by female mainly, with shorter periods by male. 34–38 days. **Nestling.** Precocial and downy. Down pale gray above, underparts white. Bill dark bluish-gray. Feet bluish-gray. **Nestling period.** Young stay on the nest for a day or two; then follow parents. Protected by both adults. Small young are carried on the backs of the adults. Young feed themselves but female pulls up and breaks up plants and roots. Independent by *c.* 4 months.

Mute Swan: *c.* 3-4ft. across.

TRUMPETER SWAN *Cygnus buccinator* **Pls. 3, 21**

Breeds on the edges of large inland waters. Nest on the water's edge, or on a muskrat house. Birds nest in scattered pairs.

Nest. A large heap of nearby plant material, with some white down and small feathers. Building continues during the incubation period. **Breeding season.** Begins late April to early May. Single-brooded. **Eggs.** Usually 5, sometimes 2–9. Clutches smaller in colder seasons. Subelliptical to long subelliptical. Creamy-white to pale yellowish. Smooth, slightly glossy with slightly granular surface texture. 111 × 72 mm. **Incubation.** Eggs laid at 2-day intervals. Incubation by female alone, beginning with completion of clutch, but male may occasionally sit on eggs. Eggs are covered with nest material if left. 33 days. **Nestling.** Precocial and downy. Down pale grayish-white, darker on lower nape, shoulders and wings; underside white. Bill flesh-pink with gray tip and edges. Feet pale orange to flesh colored. A pale phase has down white, bill pinkish, feet yellowish. **Nestling period.** Young may leave nest and feed by first day. Young protected by both parents. They find their own food, aided by parents pulling up and breaking up water plants but much of the food is insects taken from the plants. Young show aggressive behavior at 29 days. They stay with adults until the following spring.

WHISTLING SWAN *Cygnus columbianus* **Pl. 21**

Breeds on tundra near water, beginning while snow is still present. Nests usually built on an islet or at the water's edge, or as a floating mass in water, but land sites may be used before melting snow has surrounded them with water. Pairs nest singly.

Nest. A conspicuous mound of moss, grass, dead leaves and other plant material, with a distinct central hollow. **Breeding season.** Begins late May to June. Single-brooded. **Eggs.** Usually 5, sometimes 3–7. Clutch smaller in colder seasons. Subelliptical. Creamy-white. Smooth and slightly glossy with a finely granular texture. 107 × 68 mm. **Incubation.** Behavior as for Trumpeter Swan. 32 days. **Nestling.** Precocial and downy. Pale grayish-white with some indication of darker patterning; and white on underside. Bill flesh-pink with darker tip and edges. Down extends less far laterally than on Trumpeter Swan. Legs pale orange. **Nestling period.** Similar to that of Trumpeter Swan.

GEESE AND DUCKS *Anserinae* (other than swans) and *Anatinae*

Water-birds. Geese mainly waterside grazers, ducks more aquatic. Nest usually a scrape lined with down and small feathers from the breast of the female, in an open site or cavity; but material is accumulated by sideways-throwing and sideways-building, particularly in some species of geese. Large clutches of cream-colored or pale greenish eggs. Young precocial and downy, brooded by adults but feeding themselves. Young of geese usually remain with adults until the next breeding season, young of duck are normally tended only by female until independent, and separate in the autumn.

PINK-FOOTED GOOSE *Anser fabalis* **Pl. 23**

Breeds in Greenland, preferring ledges of gorges, cliffs and rock outcrops, or river islands; but occasionally on open tundra. Breeds in colonies. Nest-site may be used repeatedly in successive years.

Nest. A shallow scrape lined with plants, mosses, lichens and down. Down tufts brownish-gray with or without paler centers. Feathers gray with pale tips. **Breeding season.** Begins early to mid-June. Single-brooded. **Eggs.** Usually 4–5, sometimes up to 8. Shape variable, elliptical to oval. Creamy-white, smooth with fine granular texture. 80 × 54 mm. **Incubation.** Eggs laid at daily intervals. Incubation by female alone, with male on guard; beginning with completion of clutch. 25–28 days. **Nestling.** Precocial and downy. Color variable but usually brown above, including crown of head and around eye, and whitish below, suffused with greenish-yellow. Pale wing-bar, spot below wing, and area under eye greenish-yellow. Some individuals may lack yellow tint. **Nestling period.** Tended by both parents; leaving nest-site for vicinity of water as soon as down is dry. Begin to feather at 4 weeks, fledged at 8 weeks, but remain with adults until following season.

WHITE-FRONTED GOOSE *Anser albifrons* **Pls. 3, 23**

Breeds on tundra on islands in rivers, or raised places in bogs. Pairs tend to nest in close proximity to others.

Nest. Shallow scrape, with lining of local vegetation, down and some feathers. Built by female only. Down tufts pale gray; and feathers usually larger than those of other geese in region and more variably colored than those of most geese. **Breeding season.** Begins late May to early June. Single-brooded. **Eggs.** 5–6, rarely 4–7. Elliptical to subelliptical. Smooth, slightly glossy. Creamy-white. 79 × 52 mm. **Incubation.** Eggs laid every second day. Incubation by female only, with male on guard; beginning at completion of clutch. 27–28 days. **Nestling.** Precocial and downy. Brown above; grayish-white or yellowish below. Forehead, face, throat and front of neck yellowish-white with dark streak from bill to eye. Pale bar across wing. Bill, legs and feet gray. **Nestling period.** Young tended by both adults and remaining with them until next season.

White-fronted Goose: *c.* 1ft. across.

SNOW GOOSE/BLUE GOOSE *Anser caerulescens* **Pls. 3, 23**

Breeds on tundra, on open grassy areas by freshwater lakes. More rarely, in Greenland, on mountain slopes or ledges.

Nest. A hollow on the ground, often in taller vegetation, lined with plants and dried grasses and built up at the rim; with an inner lining of small white feathers and pale gray down. Built by female alone. **Breeding season.** Begins mid-June. Single-brooded. **Eggs.** Usually 4–7. Elliptical to subelliptical. Smooth with a fine granular texture. White to creamy-white. 79 × 52 mm. **Incubation.** By female only, male remaining near by. 22–25 days. **Nestling.** Precocial and downy. Blue phase nestling has down dusky olive-green, lighter below and blacker on head and back, with a small yellow patch under chin. Legs and feet blackish; bill blackish with whitish nail. White phase has upper parts and hind-neck yellowish-brown, with dark patch over crown and small dark streak through eye. Remainder of head, neck and underparts golden greenish-yellow. Dark patch on thigh and flank, and some yellow on wings. Legs and feet gray. Bill gray with yellowish-brown nail. **Nestling period.** Young led from nest to water's edge soon after hatching. Guarded and brooded by parents. Remain with adults until the following spring.

ROSS'S GOOSE *Anser rossii*

Breeds on small islands and islets in tundra lakes. Nests in colonies on the ground in the open or among dwarf shrubs.

Nest. A hollow lined, thickly at times, with vegetation from near by; often built up with a thick rim several inches high. Lined with white down after eggs are laid. **Breeding season.** Begins early June. Single-brooded, no replacement of lost clutches. **Eggs.** Usually 3–4. Later clutches usually smaller. Elliptical to subelliptical. Smooth with fine granular texture. White. 70 × 47 mm. **Incubation.** Eggs laid at 1½-day intervals. Incubation by female alone, beginning with last egg. Eggs are covered when the nest is left. 21–23 days. **Nestling.** Precocial and downy. Down very thick, with some longer silky tips. Down color varies widely, from almost white to dark gray, to yellow, or greenish or blackish yellow. The color is darker on the back and lower nape, with a small dark patch on the crown and a dark mark through the eye. Legs greenish. Bill black with a pink nail. **Nestling period.** Young hatch almost simultaneously. They leave the nest a few hours after hatching, following the adults and defended by them. They swim well from the first and can dive. They grow rapidly, and feather between three and six weeks old. They remain with the adults until the next spring, not leaving until incubation begins.

EMPEROR GOOSE *Anser canagicus* **Pl. 22**

Breeds on the coastal tundra, by lagoons, on the shore or on low coastal or estuarine islands. Nest on the ground. Pairs nest sociably.

Nest. A hollow thickly lined with grass and plants to form a substantial structure, with inner lining of small feathers and down. **Breeding season.** Begins early to mid-June. Single-brooded. **Eggs.** 3–8, usually 5–6. Elliptical to subelliptical. White to creamy-white. Smooth with a finely granular texture. 78 × 52 mm. **Incubation.** By female only, guarded by male. 24–25 days. **Nestling.** Precocial and downy. Down pale gray, darker above and on head; darkest around eye. Paler below. Legs and bill black. **Nestling period.** The young soon leave the nest and follow the parents. They grow quickly and feather within a few weeks. They remain with the adults until the following spring.

CANADA GOOSE *Branta canadensis* **Pls. 3, 22**

Breeds in a great variety of habitats from forest to open plains and prairie, inland and coastal marshes, muskeg and tundra. The nest is usually by water, and preferably on an islet, or a muskrat or beaver house, but frequently in waterside herbage or among trees. Rarely it may be on a raised site, a rock ledge, tree-stump, broken tree-trunk, or even the large old nest of a large raptor.

Nest. A hollow, lined with a variable amount of plant material, including twigs and plant stems, and at times built up into a substantial structure. It has an inner lining of down and some feathers. Down tufts large, grayish-brown with white centers and pale tips. **Breeding season.** Variable through the range. May begin late April in south or west, early to mid-June in the north. Single-brooded. **Eggs.** Usually 5–6, occasionally 2–11. Elliptical to subelliptical. White to creamy-white. Smooth and non-glossy. Size varies with the different-sized races and may average 87 × 58 mm. in large races, 72 × 48 mm. in small races. **Incubation.** By female alone, with male on guard. 25–30 days. **Nestling.** Precocial and downy. Down greenish-brown above, and on crown and nape; greenish-yellow below, and on forehead, face and neck; with yellow on front and back edges of wings, and on body below wings. In some N.W. races – *fulva, minima, occidentalis* and *taverneri* – the down is less yellow, whitish below and olive above, with a dark mark across the eye. Bill dark blue-gray. Legs and feet blue-gray or greenish. Iris pale blue-gray. **Nestling period.** Young tended by both adults. Flying at *c.* 9 weeks. Young remain with adults until the following spring.

BARNACLE GOOSE *Branta leucopsis* **Pls. 3, 22**

Breeds in arctic valleys on ledges of cliffs and rocky outcrops overlooking rivers or marshes; or occasionally on low estuarine islands. Sociable, nesting in colonies.

Nest. A hollow with little plant material, but quantities of down and some feathers. Down tufts are dark gray with whitish centers; darker than those of Pink-footed Goose, grayer and smaller than Eider's. Nest re-used in subsequent years. **Breeding season.** Begins late May to early June. Single-brooded. **Eggs.** 3–5, sometimes 6. Elliptical to subelliptical. Non-glossy with slight granular texture. Creamy-white. 77 × 51 mm. **Incubation.** By female only, with male on guard. Beginning with completion of clutch. 24–25 days. **Nestling.** Precocial and downy. Back pale brown, and underside white, with a pale brown area on upper breast. Head and neck whitish with a brown crown patch, dark streak from bill to eye, and brownish wash on nape. Small white areas on back and tip of wing and below wing. The whitish down has pale brown bases. **Nestling period.** Young leave nest almost immediately and descend to the vicinity of water. Tended by both adults. Fledged in 7 weeks, but remain with adults.

BRANT *Branta bernicla* **Pls. 3, 22**

Breeds on coastal tundra, usually by lakes, or on islands of coast or deltas. Also along river valleys, uplands with herbage and on stony shores of the north.

Nest. A hollow in the ground, often lined and built up with moss and lichens, particularly on stony sites; with a thick inner lining of down. Down tufts brownish-gray with whitish centers, like Eider down but smaller. **Breeding season.** Begins early to mid-June. Single-brooded. **Eggs.** Usually 3–5, sometimes 2–8. Elliptical to subelliptical, often long. Smooth and slightly glossy.

Creamy-white to yellowish. 71 × 47 mm. **Incubation.** By female alone, the male standing guard. Usually 23–24 days, at times 22–26 days. **Nestling.** Precocial and downy. Down on upperparts drab gray; underside pale gray with darker bases, and with white on chin and upper breast. Head and neck pale with darker gray crown patch, dark patch on lores, and streak through eye. Whitish mark on hind-edge and tip of wings, and on body below wings. In the dark Pacific race the upper parts are a darker gray and a gray cap on the head extends down to the dark eye mark. **Nestling period.** Young are tended by both parents. They leave the nest within a day and are agile and active. They are usually led to the shore by the adults. They swim and dive well when small. They remain with the adults until the next spring.

BLACK-BELLIED TREE-DUCK *Dendrocygna autumnalis* Pls. 3, 23

Breeds in swampy or cultivated areas, and in woodland. Nest in a cavity inside a tree, or in a large fork, or on the ground, concealed in tall herbage such as grasses, reeds or rushes. Not necessarily near water.

Nest. In swampy places a platform of bent-down stems, with some near-by plant material where available. Tree nests are unlined. No down is present. **Breeding season.** Begins early May, but prolonged. Probably single-brooded, some second broods suggested but not proven. **Eggs.** Usually 8–12, sometimes up to 18. Short elliptical. Glossy or glossless, with a finely pitted surface. White to creamy-white. 52 × 39 mm. **Incubation.** By both sexes. 27–28 days. **Nestling.** Precocial and downy. Small, with long neck and legs. Down pattern conspicuous. Blackish-brown above and yellow below and on neck and face. A dark stripe up the hind-neck terminating at a narrow lateral band extending towards the bill. Above this a band of yellow from the base of the bill extending back to, and around the nape; cutting off a dark cap on which is a small pale forehead streak extending back to the eye. There is yellow on the sides of the breast, hind-edge of the wings, a rounded patch on the thigh, and another on each side of the lower back. **Nestling period.** The young are tended by both parents.

FULVOUS TREE-DUCK *Dendrocygna bicolor* Pls. 3, 23

Prefers more open areas but breeds in similar sites to previous species. Usually in tall vegetation such as tule, reeds and grasses, in swampy places or by water; rarely in tree cavities.

Nest. The foundations usually consist of bent-down stems and other plant material from near by may be added. No down lining. **Breeding season.** Begins late April. Period prolonged. Single-brooded. **Eggs.** 8–16. Often several females lay in same nest and large numbers may occur. Short elliptical to short subelliptical. White to creamy-white, and may become nest-stained to shades of buff. Smooth and non-glossy or slightly glossy, the surface finely pitted. 53 × 39 mm. **Incubation.** By both adults, the male possibly playing a major role. 28 days. **Nestling.** Precocial and downy. Small, long-necked and long-legged. Down very pale. Light grayish-brown above and whitish below. Pale gray stripe up hind-neck terminating at short lateral stripe to ear-covert. White stripe from base of bill up to and around nape. Cape darker gray. White on hind edge of wing. Bill and legs dark. **Nestling period.** Young tended by both parents.

MALLARD *Anas platyrhynchos* **Pls. 4, 23**

Breeds near any type of fresh water, in a variety of habitats. Nest usually in cover on the ground, among tall vegetation, grasses, bushes, etc., and on small islands; or in raised sites in tree crotches or holes, in old nests of large birds, on buildings and ruins.

Nest. Built by female. A hollow lined with plant debris, leaves, grass, etc., the lining mixed with down and feathers. Down tufts are brown, with paler centers and tips. Down covers eggs before incubation and when bird is away from the nest. **Breeding season.** Usually March onwards, but feral populations breed at various times through year from February to late autumn. Probably single-brooded normally, but feral birds may have second brood. **Eggs.** Normally 10–12, occasionally 7–16. Elliptical to subelliptical, fairly short. Smooth, waxy rather than glossy. Usually very pale green or blue-green, sometimes creamy with green tinge, buffish-green, or almost blue. 58 × 41 mm. **Incubation.** By female alone; beginning with completion of clutch. 26–29 days. **Nestling.** Precocial and downy. Dark brown above and buffish-yellow below. Dark streak from bill through eye to nape, dark mark at rear of ear-coverts, otherwise sides of head and sides and front of neck yellow. Yellow wing-bar and patches at sides of back and sides of rump. Bill flesh-colored. Legs and feet grayish-black. **Nestling period.** Young take to water soon after hatching; mostly tended by female alone. Fledged at *c.* 7–8 weeks.

BLACK DUCK *Anas rubripes* **Pl. 23**

Breeding habits and nest-sites like those of Mallard.

Nest. Nest like that of Mallard. Down tufts also similar, but the pale centers are less conspicuous. **Breeding season.** Begins late April. Single-brooded. **Eggs.** Usually 8–10, sometimes 6–15. Elliptical to subelliptical. Smooth with rather waxy surface. Green, greenish-buff, yellowish-buff, creamy with a green tinge. 59 × 42 mm. **Incubation.** By female alone. 26–28 days. **Nestling.** Precocial and downy. Down plumage like that of the Mallard but darker above, the dark colour also extending further down on to breast and flanks. Dark marks on the head by the ear-coverts and bill, sometimes forming a dark stripe occasionally coalescing with the dark eyestripe. **Nestling period.** As for the Mallard; the young being tended by the female only, leaving the nest within a few hours of hatching and being led to water.

GADWALL *Anas strepera* **Pl. 23**

Breeds by freshwater lakes, pools or slow streams with waterside vegetation. Nest usually in thicker vegetation and tall plants near water, often using island sites. May breed in close proximity.

Nest. A hollow lined with plant material, down and some feathers. Down tufts dark with small pale center and distinct pale tips. **Breeding season.** Variable, beginning mid-April in south to early June in the north. Single-brooded. **Eggs.** Usually 8–12, rarely 7–16. Elliptical, subelliptical or sometimes oval; usually rather short. Cream-colored or tinted very pale green. Smooth and waxy. 54 × 39 mm. **Incubation.** By female alone; beginning with completion of clutch. 25–27 days. **Nestling.** Precocial and downy. Like Mallard but upper-parts browner, and longer filaments warm buff. Paler stripe over eye and narrower dark eyestreak. Pale dorsal patches and other parts of plumage creamier, less yellow. Bill flesh-colored with gray culmen. Legs and feet greenish-black. **Nestling period.** Young tended by female only; being taken to water almost immediately after hatching. *c.* 7 weeks.

PINTAIL *Anas acuta* **Pls. 4, 24**

Breeds by freshwater lakes, pools, sloughs and lagoons; usually with drier margins. Usually sociable, nesting near each other. Nest in low vegetation, sometimes near water; or on islands; occasionally well away from water.

Nest. A hollow; exposed, or concealed in low vegetation; lined with plant material, down and some feathers. Down tufts longish, light brown with pale centers, like Shoveler's. **Breeding season.** Begins late April in south, to late May or early June in north. Single-brooded. **Eggs.** Usually 7–9, rarely 6–12. Subelliptical to oval, occasionally long. Variable, yellowish-cream to greenish or bluish. 54 × 37 mm. **Incubation.** By female only, beginning with completion of clutch. 25–26 days. **Nestling.** Precocial and downy. Like that of Mallard but light brown above with the longer filaments creamy-buff, light markings paler, underparts grayish-white, and foreneck brownish to grayish-buff. Light patch on side of back sometimes extending towards rump. Cheeks white with light brown patch, eyestripe white and continuing down side of nape to breast. Light brown line through eye, ill-defined towards nape. Bill light gray. Legs and feet greenish-gray. **Nestling period.** Young tended by female, but male usually present. Fledging at *c.* 7 weeks.

GREEN-WINGED TEAL *Anas crecca* **Pls. 4, 24**

Breeds on islands in lakes, the edges of lakes, lagoons and sloughs. Also on higher ground at a little distance from water. The nest is on the ground, well concealed in long grass or under bushes or low trees.

Nest. A hollow lined with dry grass and other plant material; and with a lining of small feathers and down. Down tufts small and very dark with white centers. **Breeding season.** Begins early to mid-May in the south, to early June in the north. Single-brooded. **Eggs.** Usually 10–12, sometimes 6–18. Elliptical to short subelliptical. Smooth. Dull white, cream-colored, creamy-buff or very pale olive-buff. 46 × 32 mm. **Incubation.** By female alone, beginning with completion of clutch. 23–24 days. **Nestling.** Precocial and downy. Down pattern like that of the Mallard, but with a second dark streak from the rear of the ear-coverts to the base of the bill, parallel to the eyestripe; and the longer filaments of down tinted warmer buff-brown. Bill, legs and feet are blackish. **Nestling period.** Young tended by female only. They are led to the nearest water a few hours after hatching. Become independent at *c.* 23 days. Fly at *c.* 44 days.

BLUE-WINGED TEAL *Anas discors* **Pl. 24**

Breeds by small waters – pot-holes, ponds, sloughs and marshes – in prairie and forest regions. Nest on the ground, usually near water and well concealed in herbage.

Nest. A hollow, lined with dry grass and nearby vegetation, with an inner lining of down. Down tufts drab brown, larger and lighter than that of Green-winged Teal, with large whitish centers. **Breeding season.** Begins early May in south, to early June further north. Single-brooded. **Eggs.** Usually 8–12, sometimes 6–16. Elliptical to subelliptical. Smooth and slightly glossy. Dull white, creamy-white, or with pale olive tint. 47 × 33 mm. **Incubation.** Eggs laid at daily intervals. Incubation by female alone, beginning with last egg.

23–24 days. **Nestling.** Precocial and downy. Down brown above and creamy-yellow below, with small yellow patches on either side above the thigh and towards the rump. Rear edge of wing yellow. Sides of face yellow with dark eyestripe from bill to nape, broken just in front of eye, and with short dark streak on ear-coverts. **Nestling period.** Young tended by female alone. They are led to water soon after hatching. They grow and feather rapidly.

CINNAMON TEAL *Anas cyanoptera* **Pl. 24**

Breeds near shallow water, by pools, lake edges or swamps, favoring areas where tule is present. The nest may be in cover by the water's edge, or at some distance. Usually very well concealed, deep in growing herbage, or in marsh or waterside plants on the ground.

Nest. A hollow, usually with a slight lining of grass and plant material, but nests in marsh vegetation may be built up above water level as more substantial structures. The nest is lined with down. Down tufts like those of Blue-winged Teal. **Breeding season.** Begins mid-April in south to early May further north. Single-brooded. **Eggs.** Usually 8–12, sometimes 5–14. Elliptical to subelliptical or oval. Smooth and slightly glossy. White, creamy-white, creamy-buff or warm buff. 48 × 35 mm. **Incubation.** By female alone, but male may maintain contact. 24–25 days. **Nestling.** Precocial and downy. Down pattern like that of Blue-winged Teal, but color a little more olive above and a brighter yellow below and on face. **Nestling period.** Young tended by female or by both parents. Young are led to water soon after hatching. They swim well and escape predators by diving and hiding.

AMERICAN WIGEON *Anas americana* **Pls. 4, 24**

Breeds on lake islands or by lakes or rivers. The nest is on the ground, often at some distance from water, concealed in tall herbage or in more open sites under low bushes or small trees. In northern forests nests may be in leaf-litter by a tree or bush.

Nest. A hollow lined with dry grass or other plant material. Well lined with down and feathers. Down tufts dark with indistinct pale centers and pale tips. **Breeding season.** Begins early May in south to early June in north. Single-brooded. **Eggs.** Usually 9–11, sometimes 6–13. Subelliptical to oval. Cream colored. Smooth and slightly glossy. 54 × 38 mm. **Incubation.** Eggs laid on successive days. Incubation by female alone, beginning with last egg. 24–25 days. **Nestling.** Precocial and downy. Down drab brown above, with some longer buff-tipped filaments, the dark color extending around the foreneck and up over hind-neck and head. Sides of head pale pinkish or cinnamon buff, lighter over eye. Short dark streak behind eye, fainter dark marks on ear-coverts and by bill. Hind-edge of wing, patch at side of lower back, and most of underside cinnamon-buff. **Nestling period.** Young tended by female alone. Independent in *c.* 6–7 weeks.

SHOVELER *Anas clypeata* **Pls. 4, 24**

Breeds by still or sluggish freshwater with vegetation at the edges; by shallow or overgrown pools, marshes, bogs, sloughs or slow creeks. Nest on the ground, in an open site but sheltered by some grass or growing vegetation; usually but not invariably near the water, and on a dry site.

Nest. A hollow lined with plant material, down and some feathers. Down tufts brown with light centers like those of Pintail. **Breeding season.** Begins late March in south to early June in north. Single-brooded. **Eggs.** Usually 8–12, sometimes 7–14. Elliptical to subelliptical. Smooth. Creamy-buff to olive-tinted. 52 × 37 mm. **Incubation.** Eggs laid on successive days. Incubation by female alone, beginning with the last egg. 26 days. **Nestling.** Precocial and downy. Like Mallard but darker above with the longer filaments reddish-buff and light patches paler and less conspicuous. No light wing-bar. Face warm buff and foreneck grayish-buff. Underparts grayish-white tinged with yellow. Bill reddish-brown. Legs and feet greenish-black. **Nestling period.** Young tended by female alone. They are led to water soon after hatching. They are agile divers. Independent in *c.* 6–7 weeks.

WOOD DUCK *Aix sponsa* **Pls. 4, 23**

Breeds near woodland streams and pools. Nest is in a cavity in the trunk or larger limbs of a tree, a natural hole or old hole of a larger woodpecker. More rarely in a similar site in a building such as a barn. Nest boxes are also used. The female can enter a hole as small as 4 in. diameter.

Nest. A bare cavity, unless previously used by another bird or mammal as a nest. No material other than already present, save for a lining of white down. **Breeding season.** Begins early April in south to early May in north. Single-brooded. **Eggs.** Usually 8–10, sometimes 6–15. Subelliptical to oval. Smooth and fairly glossy. White or creamy-white. 52 × 40 mm. **Incubation.** By female alone. 28–32 days. **Nestling.** Precocial and downy. Down dark blackish-brown above and over head. Small whitish rear edge to wing, and whitish spot on either side of lower back. Face and underparts grayish-white. Dark line from eye to nape, sometimes dividing. Bill bluish gray. Feet yellowish and blackish. **Nestling period.** Young tended by female alone. They climb up to nest entrance and drop unaided in response to female's call, following her to water.

REDHEAD *Aythya americana* **Pls. 4, 24**

Breeds by fresh water, usually in the taller vegetation bordering lakes and sloughs, occasionally in more open sites in similar areas. Nest on the ground. **Nest.** In drier sites a hollow sparsely lined with plant material, and in damper sites a substantial cup. There is an inner lining of down. Down tufts very pale, grayish-white. **Breeding season.** Begins late April in south to early June in north. Single-brooded. **Eggs.** Usually 10–15. Difficult to determine since eggs are often laid in nests of other birds including other duck species, and nests may contain a mixture of eggs. Eggs elliptical to sub-elliptical. Smooth and glossy. Greenish to very pale olive or olive-gray. 61 × 43 mm. **Incubation.** By female alone. 24 days. **Nestling.** Precocial and downy. Down very pale, light brownish-olive above and over back of neck and head. Underside and face yellow, with slightly warmer buff tint on face. Bar on hind-wing and two patches at each side of lower back buffish-yellow. Legs, feet and bill dark. Nail at tip of bill broad (narrow on Canvasback). **Nestling period.** Young tended by female alone.

RING-NECKED DUCK *Aythya collaris* **Pl. 24**

Breeds by fresh water, preferring smaller waters of ponds, sloughs and marshes. Nest in herbage on the ground near or by water, or in clumps of tall plants or tussocks in shallow water. Frequently in damp sites.

Nest. A hollow lined with grass and plant material. In wet places the material may be built up into a substantial cup. It is lined with down. Down tufts warm medium brown with whitish centers. **Breeding season.** Begins late May to early June. Single-brooded. **Eggs.** Usually 6–12. Elliptical to subelliptical. Smooth and slightly glossy. Very pale olive, grayish-olive or greenish. 58 × 41 mm. **Incubation.** By female alone. 26 days. **Nestling.** Precocial and downy. Like small Canvasback. Very dark brown above and over back of neck and head. Underparts, face and forehead yellow, brighter on face. Hind-edge of wing and two spots on either side of lower back yellow. Legs and bill dark, bill-tip pale. **Nestling period.** Young tended by female only.

CANVASBACK *Aythya valisineria* **Pl. 25**

Breeds in sloughs and marshes, and other fresh waters with growing vegetation. Nest frequently concealed in a clump of vegetation growing in water. Sometimes in more open sites in sedges, or hidden in tall waterside plants.

Nest. Usually a substantial cup of stems and plant material, well lined with down. Down light grayish-brown with indistinct pale centers. **Breeding season.** Begins mid- to late May. Single-brooded. **Eggs.** Usually 7–9. Eggs of Redhead and Ruddy Duck may also be present. Eggs elliptical to subelliptical or oval. Pale dull green, bluish-green, olive-green or grayish-olive. Smooth and slightly glossy. 63 × 45 mm. **Incubation.** By female alone. 24–27 days. **Nestling.** Precocial and downy. Like larger Ring-necked Duck, but wedge-shaped bill apparent at early stage. Down dark brown above and over back of neck and head. Underside and face yellow. Hind-edge of wings and spots at sides of lower back yellow. Legs and bill dark. Pale tip to bill, and nail at tip narrow (broad on Redhead). **Nestling period.** Young tended by female only. They begin feathering at 5 weeks. Fly at 10–12 weeks.

GREATER SCAUP *Aythya marila* **Pl. 24**

Breeds by fresh water on open ridges and tundra, often using lake islands. Frequently sociable with many pairs together. Nest in fairly open sites, with little or no cover.

Nest. A hollow lined with nearby vegetation, down and feathers. Down tufts dark sooty-brown with indistinct pale centers. **Breeding season.** Beginning from end of May to mid-June. Single-brooded. **Eggs.** 6–15, occasionally 17. Elliptical to subelliptical. Smooth but non-glossy. Pale greenish to olive-gray. 63 × 43 mm. **Incubation.** By female alone, remaining on nest for long periods. 24–28 days. **Nestling.** Precocial and downy. Down dark blackish-brown over much of body. Breast and belly creamy-yellow, upper breast buffish-brown. Sides of head faintly buffish with dark eye-streak and indistinct darker streak bordering yellowish throat. Bill dark blackish-brown with greenish sides and pale tip. Legs and feet olive-gray or blackish. **Nestling period.** Young tended by female, but male present at times. Independent in 5–6 weeks.

LESSER SCAUP *Aythya affinis* **Pls. 4, 25**

Breeds by freshwater ponds, sloughs and creeks, or on lake islands. Nest on the ground, usually near water in grass or waterside plants, exceptionally in vegetation growing in water.

Nest. A hollow, usually sparsely lined with plant material, and with thick inner lining of down and some feathers. Down tufts dark brown with indistinct pale centers. **Breeding season.** Begins early May in south to mid-June in north. Single-brooded. **Eggs.** Usually 8–12, sometimes 6–15. Elliptical to subelliptical. Smooth and slightly glossy. Pale olive or greenish, to olive-buff. 58 × 40 mm. **Incubation.** By female alone. 26–27 days. **Nestling.** Precocial and downy. Like Greater Scaup, but face paler. Down dark blackish-brown above, over much of head and upper breast. Lower breast and belly creamy-buff. Sides of face buffish and throat yellowish; with narrow dark stripe through eye from bill to nape, and indistinct stripe across ear-coverts. Bill blackish-brown with pale tip. Legs and feet blackish. **Nestling period.** Young tended by female alone. Soon after hatching they are led to water. They feed mainly on insects. They dive well from an early age.

COMMON EIDER *Somateria mollissima* Pls. 5, 26

Breeds on coast, or offshore islands, or on lakes or rivers near the sea. Usually on exposed sites. Nest a hollow selected by female reluctantly accompanied by male. Sociable, often nesting in colonies.

Nest. A hollow lined with near-by plant material or seaweed. Lined with copious down and feathers. Down tufts a light grayish-brown with ill-defined pale centers and palish tips. **Breeding season.** Begins late May in south to mid- or late June in north. Single-brooded. **Eggs.** 4–6, sometimes 3–10. Shape variable, elliptical to subelliptical, sometimes oval. Smooth, slightly glossy. Pale green, olive, grayish or bluish, rarely buffish. 77 × 52 mm. **Incubation.** By female alone, sitting closely and leaving only rarely for short periods. 24–27 days. **Nestling.** Precocial and downy. Down mostly blackish-brown, whitish on the lower breast. A broad buffish stripe from the lores, over the eye to the nape and a similar tint on the chin. A darker streak through the eye. Bill and legs dark. **Nestling period.** Young led to water and tended by female, sometimes accompanied by female without young. Young very active and independent. Broods scatter and join up to form larger groups. Independent *c.* 60–75 days.

KING EIDER *Somateria spectabilis* Pl. 26

Breeds on lakes and pools of tundra regions, usually near the sea, in solitary pairs.

Nest. A shallow hollow in grass or heather stems, with little plant lining, but thick down and some feathers. Down tufts sooty-brown, darker than Common Eider's, with indistinct pale centers; and occasional whitish tufts. **Breeding season.** Begins mid-June to mid-July. Single-brooded. **Eggs.** 4–7 occasionally 3–8. Subelliptical. Smooth, slightly glossy. Pale olive. 66 × 44 mm. **Incubation.** By female alone 22–23 days. **Nestling.** Precocial and downy. Sooty-brown above, lighter than Common Eider, whitish-buff below. Sides of head pale buffish with narrow dark streak through eye to nape. Chin, throat and breast whitish-buff. **Nestling period.** Young tended by female alone. Young of several broods tend to group together, attended by only some of the females, or by one only.

SPECTACLED EIDER *Somateria fischeri* Pl. 26

Breeds by pools on coastal marshes of tundra. Nest is set on a drier site, a small islet, or ridge or tussock by the water. The nest is often concealed in herbage.

Nest. A hollow lined with moss and plant debris from nearby, with inner lining of soft down and small feathers. Down tufts medium brown with slightly paler but inconspicuous centers. **Breeding season.** Begins early June. Single-brooded. **Eggs.** Usually 5–7, sometimes 3–9. Elliptical to subelliptical. Smooth, slightly glossy. Green, bluish-green, or olive-buff. 65 × 45 mm. **Incubation.** By female alone. 24 days. **Nestling.** Precocial and downy. Down dark brown, with underside paler and grayer. Narrow dark rim round eye, and around this a large buff spectacle mark with a narrow dark streak across it. Down extends on to the base of the bill. Bill, legs and feet blackish. **Nestling period.** Young tended by female alone.

STELLER'S EIDER *Polysticta stelleri* **Pl. 26**

Breeds on level tundra by freshwater pools.

Nest. A hollow lined with some nearby plant material, down and some feathers. Down tufts very dark brown with occasional white tufts. **Breeding season.** Begins mid-June to mid-July. Single-brooded. **Eggs.** 6–8, occasionally 10. Short subelliptical. Smooth but non-glossy. Pale yellowish-olive, greenish, or olive-buff. 61 × 42 mm. **Incubation.** By female alone. Period not known. **Nestling.** Precocial and downy. Down dark brown above, whitish on underside. Buffish ring round eye and narrow streak from eye to nape, and buffish chin, **Nestling period.** Young tended by female alone.

HARLEQUIN DUCK *Histrionicus histrionicus* **Pls. 5, 26**

Breeds on swift-flowing northern rivers, nesting, sociably at times, on rocky islands in rivers or in sheltered sites on the banks. Nest on the ground, usually concealed in thick shrub cover.

Nest. A hollow lined with a little plant material and with down and feathers. Down tufts light brown with pale centers. **Breeding season.** Begins mid-May to early July, usually in early June. Single-brooded. **Eggs.** Usually 6–8, occasionally 3–9. Elliptical to subelliptical. Smooth, slightly glossy. Pale creamy to pale buff. 58 × 42 mm. **Incubation.** By female alone, beginning before the last egg is laid. 27–33 days. **Nestling.** Precocial and downy. Down blackish-brown above, white below. Sides of head and throat white, crown of head down to below eyes dark brown with small white patch above and before each eye. A whitish patch on wing and either side of back and a whiter one above the thigh. Bill and legs gray. **Nestling period.** Young tended by female only, but the male occasionally present at first. Young can fly in 40 days.

OLDSQUAW *Clangula hyemalis* **Pls. 5, 25**

Breeds in northern forest and tundra; on open tundra, often by pools, and on lake islands. Nest concealed in low vegetation or sheltered by rocks.

Nest. A hollow, lined with a little nearby plant material, down and feathers. Down tufts dark grayish-brown with paler centers. **Breeding season.** Begins late May in south, to June in north. Single-brooded. **Eggs.** Usually 5–9, occasionally 5–11. Subelliptical to elliptical, sometimes oval. Smooth. Yellowish or with faint olive tint, or more greenish. 53 × 38 mm. **Incubation.** By female alone. Male nearby at first. 23–25 days. **Nestling.** Precocial and downy. Brown with golden tips above, grayish-white below with dusky-brown upper breast. Cream spot on lores, whitish streak from rear eye to nape, pale patch above and below eye. Some pale marks may be absent in individuals. Pale down has brownish bases. **Nestling period.** Tended by female alone. Young are led to the sea soon after hatching. They swim and dive well from the first. Some broods may combine. Independent in *c.* 5 weeks.

BLACK SCOTER *Melanitta nigra* **Pls. 5, 25**

Breeds by freshwater lakes and pools on coastal marshes and higher open ground. Nest usually close to water, or on an island, in a slightly sheltered site.

Nest. A hollow lined with a little plant material, down and some feathers. Down tufts medium-sized; dark brown with paler centers. **Breeding season.** Begins early July. Single-brooded. **Eggs.** 6–9, occasionally 5–10. Subelliptical. Smooth and slightly glossy. Pale creamy to creamy-buff. 65 × 45 mm. **Incubation.** By female alone on completion of the clutch. 27–31 days. **Nestling.** Precocial and downy. Down mainly dark brown with whitish lower breast and belly; and white cheeks and throat. Tiny white spot over eye. Bill blackish with reddish-brown nail. Legs and feet dark gray-green. **Nestling period.** Young tended by female alone. Independent at 6–7 weeks.

SURF SCOTER *Melanitta perspicillata* **Pl. 25**

Breeds by ponds, lakes and rivers in wooded, boggy and tundra areas. Nest at times away from water; in wooded areas sheltered by low branches of conifers, in more open areas under bushes or in grasses.

Nest. A hollow lined with grasses and other plants and with an inner lining of down. Down dark brown with whitish centers and tips. **Breeding season.** Begins mid-June. Single-brooded. **Eggs.** 5–7, occasionally up to 9. Subelliptical to oval. Smooth and non-glossy. Creamy-white to pinkish-buff. 62 × 43 mm. **Incubation.** By female only. Period not recorded. **Nestling.** Precocial and downy. Like that of Black Scoter, but tiny white spot over eye is lacking and feathering extends in a wedge on to upper bill (cut off sharply in Black Scoter). Bill appears stout in side view. Down grayish-brown above and silvery-gray below. Cap black and cheeks, throat and chin white. Upper breast brown. **Nestling period.** Young tended by female only.

WHITE-WINGED SCOTER *Melanitta fusca* **Pls. 5, 25**

Breeds on islands or shores of freshwater lakes in wooded, bushy or overgrown sites, or in concealed or bare sites in open tundra.

Nest. A hollow lined with near-by plant material, leaves or twigs, and with down and feathers. Down tufts larger than those of Black Scoter, dark brown with indistinct pale centers. **Breeding season.** Begins mid-June. Single-brooded. **Eggs.** 7–10, sometimes 6–11. Subelliptical. Smooth, non-glossy. Pale creamy to buff. 71 × 48 mm. **Incubation.** By female alone, beginning with the last egg. 27–28 days. **Nestling.** Precocial and downy. Down mainly dark brown above. Cheeks, throat and upper neck, and underside, white, separated by dusky-brown band across upper breast. Small white patches on upper wing and sides of rump. **Nestling period.** Young tended by female alone, who tends to desert them for increasingly long periods. Young independent *c.* 4–5 weeks, fly at *c.* 6–7 weeks.

BUFFLEHEAD *Bucephala albeola* **Pl. 25**

Breeds by freshwater lakes, ponds and rivers in wooded regions, and less frequently in open muskeg with few trees. Nest usually in a flicker hole, occasionally in a natural tree cavity; very exceptionally in a hole in a bank.

Nest. A cavity with the material already present, if any, and down and feathers. Down tufts pale gray tinted purplish or brownish and with indistinct pale centers. **Breeding season.** Begins mid-May in south to early June in north.

Single-brooded. **Eggs.** Usually 8–12, sometimes 7–16. Elliptical to oval. Smooth and slightly glossy. Creamy-white, yellowish-cream and pale olive-buff. 51 × 37 mm. **Incubation.** By female alone. 29 days. **Nestling.** Precocial and downy. Like a small Goldeneye. Down blackish-brown with white patch on cheeks and throat, and white lower breast and belly. Small white patch on hind-wing and three more along each side of back, the foremost two sometimes forming an irregular stripe. **Nestling period.** Young tended by female alone.

COMMON GOLDENEYE *Bucephala clangula* **Pls. 5, 25**

Breeds by lakes and rivers in forest country. Nest in natural cavities in trees or stumps, or in woodpecker holes; will also nest in nest-boxes, or in rabbit burrows.

Nest. No material other than that present, down and some feathers added. Down tufts grayish-white. **Breeding season.** Beginning early May in south, to June in north. Single-brooded. **Eggs.** 6–11, larger clutches probably from two females. Subelliptical. Smooth. Bluish-green; bright at first but fading. 60 × 43 mm. **Incubation.** Eggs laid at intervals of *c.* 1½ days. Incubation by female alone; beginning on completion of clutch; male remaining near by. 27–32 days. **Nestling.** Precocial and downy. Down blackish-brown above, almost white below with upper breast dusky-brown. Dark cap extends just below eyes, but cheeks pale. Grayish-white on wing-bar, patches on either sides of back and rump, and above thigh. Bill gray, legs and feet yellowish-gray. **Nestling period.** Young scramble out of nest and drop unharmed. Tended by female only. Able to fly at 51–60 days.

BARROW'S GOLDENEYE *Bucephala islandica* **Pl. 25**

Breeds by lakes or rivers, including saline lakes in open country. Nest usually in a natural cavity or woodpecker hole in a tree. Has used cavity in roof of barn.

Nest. Only material already present in cavity, with down and some feathers. Down tufts white. **Breeding season.** Begins mid-May. Single-brooded. **Eggs.** 8–14. Elliptical. Smooth. Green or bluish-green. 62 × 45 mm. **Incubation.** By female alone, beginning on completion of clutch. 30 days. **Nestling.** Precocial and downy. Like young of common Goldeneye, but a little larger. Bill grayish with a reddish tip. Legs and feet more greenish-gray than those of common Goldeneye. **Nestling period.** No information.

HOODED MERGANSER *Mergus cucullatus* **Pl. 26**

Breeds by still or slow-moving freshwaters; forest ponds and lakes, flooded forest, riverside swamps and streams. Nest in a cavity in tree or stump, exceptionally between tree-roots, in a fallen hollow log or a hole in a bank. Will use nest boxes and can enter a hole 3½ in. diameter.

Nest. A cavity with any material already present and a lining of down and some feathers. Down tufts very pale gray with centers a little lighter still. **Breeding season.** Begins late April. Single-brooded, but will replace lost clutch. **Eggs.** Usually 5–12. Short elliptical to short subelliptical. Smooth and very glossy. White. 54 × 45 mm. **Incubation.** By female only. 31 days. **Nestling.** Precocial and downy. Down brown on back, over head and on upper breast. Cheeks pale buffish-brown and throat white. Lower breast and belly white, white patch on hind-wing, and two small white patches on each side of back. Bill slender. **Nestling period.** Young tended by female only.

COMMON MERGANSER *Mergus merganser* **Pl. 26**

Breeds by freshwater lakes or rivers, in wooded or, more rarely, open areas. Nest frequently in tree cavity, or in hole in bank or cavity among boulders; will use nest-boxes. Nest-site may be re-used annually.

Nest. Hollow, lined with nearby plants, but no addition in tree cavities other than down. Down tufts large and pale gray. **Breeding season.** Beginning early April in south to late May in north. Single-brooded. **Eggs.** 7–14, rarely 15. Elliptical to subelliptical, slightly long. Smooth and slightly glossy, creamy-white to yellowish. 66 × 46 mm. **Incubation.** Eggs laid on successive days. Incubation by female alone. 28–32 days. **Nestling.** Precocial and downy. Dark brown above and white below. Sides of neck, nape and sides of head rufous-tinted. Narrow whitish streak from bill below eye, and pale loral spot. White patch on wings and either side of rump; and white on fore and hind thigh. **Nestling period.** Tended by female alone. Young said to remain in nest a day or two before leaving with female. Independent in *c.* 5 weeks.

RED-BREASTED MERGANSER *Mergus serrator* **Pls. 5, 26**

Breeds by freshwater ponds, pools and rivers, occasionally on coastal sites or offshore islands. Nest is concealed under thicket or in cavity among rocks or tree-roots, more rarely hollow in bank, or in burrow, or pile of driftwood, or under low tree branches.

Nest. A hollow lined with nearby plant material, down and some feathers. Down tufts darker gray than Merganser's, brown-tinged, with pale centers and palish tips. **Breeding season.** Begins early June. Single-brooded. **Eggs.** Usually 7–12, but up to 21 recorded. Elliptical to subelliptical. Smooth, but non-glossy to slightly glossy. Creamy-stone to greenish-buff. 66 × 45 mm. **Incubation.** By female alone, beginning with completion of clutch. 28–35 days. **Nestling.** Precocial and downy. Like Merganser. Brown above and white below. Crown dark brown, extending to just below eye, cheeks rufous, and throat white. Rufous spot before and above eye and white spot below it. White wing-bar, and white patches either side of back and rump. **Nestling period.** Tended by female alone; broods tending to gather in larger packs with a single female. Flying by 59 days.

RUDDY DUCK *Oxyura jamaicensis* **Pls. 5, 26**

Breeds on freshwater lakes, ponds, sloughs and marshes, where open water is bordered by tall plants growing in water.

Nest. A partly floating structure attached to growing plants, built up above water level, with plants pulled together over it. Of reed stems, weeds or other nearby plants, usually without down. **Breeding season.** Begins late April in south to early June in north. Single-brooded. **Eggs.** 6–10, rarely to 20. Elliptical or short subelliptical. Rough and granular. Dull white. 64 × 42 mm. **Incubation.** By female alone, the male remaining close by. 24 days. **Nestling.** Precocial and downy. Dark gray-brown above, white below. Dark cap; white line from nape to bill, below eye; and slanting dark line below this one separating it from the cheeks and throat which are white freckled with brown. Also a pale spot on either side of the back. **Nestling period.** Exceptional among ducks in that the male remains and accompanies the brood. The young are clumsy on land but swim and dive well.

NEW WORLD VULTURES *Cathartidae*

Medium to large soaring birds, feeding on carrion. No nest built but protected sites such as tree or rock cavities used. May nest sociably. Two eggs laid by smaller species, one by large. Young are downy. Two down coats in California Condor, not certainly recorded for others. Young fed by regurgitation, taking the food directly from inside the adults' throats. Young mature slowly.

TURKEY VULTURE *Cathartes aura* **Pls. 6, 27**

Breeds in a variety of habitats, but tends to select secluded and undisturbed sites. Nest may be in a cave or rock recess, or in unused building, or crevice in rocks, hollow log or stump, or on the ground in thick cover or a swamp. A dark site is preferred. Where conditions are suitable several pairs may nest in proximity, but not contiguously.

Nest. No nest is built; but it is claimed that there may be some preparation of the site. **Breeding season.** Begins late January in south to mid-April in north. Single-brooded. **Eggs.** Usually 2, occasionally 1, rarely 3. Subelliptical to long subelliptical. Smooth and slightly glossy. White or creamy-white, sparsely or heavily marked with spots and small to medium, or rarely large, blotches of reddish-brown, dark brown and faint purple, often concentrated at the larger end. Larger markings often combined with overall fine spotting or speckling of similar colour. 71 × 49 mm. **Incubation.** By both sexes. Sitting birds leave reluctantly. 38–41 days. **Nestling.** Semi-altricial and downy. Down long and white, head mainly bare, with blackish skin, and a little thin white down over crown. **Nestling period.** Young tended by both adults. Fed by regurgitation. Young have eyes open at hatching and are more active than typical hawks. Feather slowly between second and tenth week. Fly at *c.* 11 weeks.

BLACK VULTURE *Coragyps atratus* **Pls. 6, 27**

Breeds in secluded sites in wooded or open country. Nest on ledge in shallow cave or on low cliff or gully side, in hole under rock, in the cavity of a broken tree or tree-stump, or on the ground under a fallen tree or under thick vegetation. Nests singly or with several pairs near each other.

Nest. No nest is made. Birds may move the eggs about within the nesting area. **Breeding season.** Begins late January. Single-brooded but a lost clutch is usually replaced. **Eggs.** Normally 2, rarely 1, exceptionally 3. Subelliptical to blunt oval. Smooth and slightly glossy. Usually very pale gray-green, creamy-white or faintly buff; with sparse small blotches or spots of deep reddish-brown or light brown, faint lilac or purple, and occasionally a few large blotches. The markings sometimes concentrated at the larger end. 76 × 51 mm. **Incubation.** Eggs laid at 2-day intervals. Incubation by both sexes, beginning with first egg. 39–41 days. **Nestling.** Semi-altricial and downy. Down long, thick and creamy-buff, with a more reddish tint on upper parts. Head bare. **Nestling period.** Young tended by both parents. They hatch at intervals and differ in size. They are active at 10 days. Brooded by both parents for first 6 weeks. First feathers at *c.* 17 days, but although full-grown at *c.* 6 weeks are still downy at 8 weeks, not feathered fully until 11 weeks. When younger they hide head and remain motionless when alarmed. At 8 weeks will leave nest cavity if on ground. At 10–11 weeks can fly a little and leave nest. When alarmed food is regurgitated.

CALIFORNIA CONDOR *Gymnogyps californianus* **Pl. 27**

Breeds on mountainsides at 1,500–4,500 ft., once at 6,500 ft. in a limited area of southern California. Nest in a cave on cliff-face, or cavity behind a boulder. Once in a large tree cavity. Nest-site may be re-used, or several sites used alternately.

Nest. No nest is built. A narrow site floored with sand or fine detritus is usually chosen within the nest cavity. **Breeding season.** Begins mid-February. Young mature slowly and successful nesting takes 2 years. **Eggs.** Only one. Long subelliptical. Smooth and glossy surface with very fine elongated pits. White faintly tinted green or blue. 110 × 67 mm. **Incubation.** By both sexes. 42–50 days. **Nestling.** Semi-altricial and downy. Down of first coat white, head and neck bare; skin flesh-pink becoming yellowish. Second down gray and woolly, also extending to head and neck. **Nestling period.** Young one tended by both parents. Brooded continuously for 2–3 weeks, then only at night for next 3–6 weeks. Subsequently visited by parents for feeding once a day. Feathers slowly between seventh and twenty-second week. Young may leave nest at *c.* 5 months, but may not be able to fly for another two months. Flies well at 10–12 months but may rely on feeding by parents until the following summer.

HAWKS AND EAGLES *Accipitridae*

Includes hawks, kites and eagles. Raptors, varying in size from large to small, and hunting live prey or scavenging. Nests are large cups of twigs and various debris; on trees, rock ledges or on the ground. Leafy twigs may be added to the lining during incubation. Eggs are usually rather rounded, often slightly rough-textured, white or with brown blotchings, and frequently stained by leafy nest linings. The young hatch at intervals and vary in size; and the smallest may die of starvation or be killed and eaten by the older ones if food is short. The young are downy, with two down coats, and relatively helpless at first. As they grow they perform bouts of wing-flapping and practise seizing objects. They may leave the nest for nearby branches and return at times before the first real flight. They rely on the parents for food for a period after leaving the nest, while they learn to hunt, but information on this is relatively incomplete.

WHITE-TAILED KITE *Elanus leucurus* **Pl. 28**

Breeds in open country – cultivation, meadows and marshes – with scattered trees. Nest in a tree, usually near water, 12–60 ft. up. Several pairs may nest in near-by trees. Old nests of other birds may be used as nest foundation.

Nest. A loose but well-built twig structure, lined with dry grass, roots, Spanish Moss and other plant material. Nest *c.* 20 in. across by 8 in. deep. For second broods a second nest is built on a different site. Nest built by female, but male may initiate building behavior. **Breeding season.** Begins mid-February. Single-brooded, but will replace a lost clutch. Sometimes double-brooded? **Eggs.** Usually 4–5. Short subelliptical. Smooth and non-glossy or slightly glossy. White or faintly buffish; very heavily mottled and blotched overall with deep reddish-brown, more concentrated towards the larger end, while ground color becomes buff-tinted. 42 × 33 mm. **Incubation.** By female only, the male remaining near by and feeding the female. 28–30 days. **Nestling.** Semi-altricial and downy. First down is short, whitish tinged with pinkish-buff on the back. Second down bluish-gray. **Nestling period.** Young tended by female, but all food brought by male and passed to female away from nest. Female tears up food for first 24 days. Young fly at 35–40 days, but may return to nest to feed or brood. First brood young are tolerated until the second brood has hatched in a different nest.

SWALLOW-TAILED KITE *Elanoides forficatus* **Pl. 28**

Breeds in open or wooded areas, usually by water. Nest in a tree in a clearing or on woodland edge. Usually situated well out on an upper branch, 60–100 ft. up. Several pairs may nest in close proximity.

Nest. A shallow cup of dead twigs broken off in flight; lined with Spanish Moss, more of which may be added during incubation. Nest *c.* 15–20 in. across by 12 in. deep. Cup 6 in. across by 4 in. deep. Built by both sexes. **Breeding season.** Begins early March in south, to early June in north. Single-brooded. **Eggs.** Usually 2, sometimes 3, rarely 4. Shortish elliptical. Smooth, non-glossy or slightly glossy. White, marked, often heavily, with blotches of reddish-brown, usually varied in size and often distributed overall or sometimes concentrated at larger end. Large markings at times combined with profuse minute speckling of similar color. 47 × 37 mm. **Incubation.** By both sexes. **Nestling.** Semi-altricial and downy. First down buffish-white. Second down darker on nape and breast. **Nestling period.** Young tended by female while male brings food.

MISSISSIPPI KITE *Ictinia mississippiensis* **Pl. 28**

Breeds in open pine forest and woodland bordering lakes and rivers of more open regions. In the west in scrub oaks or scattered trees. Nest in a fork or crotch of a tree, high up where possible but low in scrub oaks. A number of pairs may nest in a loose colony.

Nest. Variable twig structures, small flimsy platforms to compact structures; usually irregular or oval. *c.* 14 × 11 in., and 5 in. deep. Cup shallow and lined with green leaves. **Breeding season.** Begins mid-March. Single-brooded; but a lost clutch will be replaced. **Eggs.** Usually 2, sometimes 1–3. Short elliptical to short subelliptical. Bluish-white. Smooth and non-glossy. 41 × 34 mm. **Incubation.** By both sexes. 30–32 days. **Nestling.** Semi-altricial and downy. Down whitish, tinged with buffish-brown on upperparts and nape. Lores grayish. Bill dull blue-gray, cere brownish-orange, gape light orange. Eyes grayish-brown. Legs and feet yellowish-orange. **Nestling period.** Young tended by both parents, bringing food (insects) to the nest. Small young are fed directly, older young have food disgorged on to nest. Young leave nest at *c.* 34 days. Rely on adults for food for several weeks afterwards. Fledged young are fed on the wing.

EVERGLADE KITE *Rostrhamus sociabilis* **Pls. 6, 28**

Breeds in open marsh areas of the Everglades. Nest low in a bush or tree growing in the water, 3–15 ft. up, or on the ground in thick marsh grass or reeds. Pairs usually nest in a colony.

Nest. A loose structure of plant stems or twigs, lined with fine twigs and stems, leaves or sawgrass heads. *c.* 12 in. across. **Breeding season.** Begins mid-February. **Eggs.** Usually 3–4, sometimes 2. Elliptical to shortish elliptical. Smooth and non-glossy. White with usually an overall speckling and spotting of dull or dark brown, or reddish-brown, and with larger irregular blotching of the same color. Often markings concentrated in a zone around or at the larger end.

Sometimes extensive pale blotching. 44 × 36 mm. **Incubation.** By both sexes. **Nestling.** Semi-altricial and downy. First down buff, tinged with cinnamon on crown, wings and rump. Second down thicker; dark grayish-brown. **Nestling period.** Young tended by both parents. Young leave the nest at *c.* 4 weeks.

GOSHAWK *Accipiter gentilis* **Pl. 28**

Breeds in woodland. Nest is in a tree; usually built by the bird, more rarely based on a nest of another species. Old nest may be re-used and a series of alternative sites in the territory utilised.

Nest. A large, shallow, untidy structure of dead twigs, lined with pieces of bark and leafy twigs or bunches of conifer needles which are constantly renewed. Built mainly, or in the case of a new nest entirely, by the male. **Breeding season.** Begins in April in the south to mid-June in the north. Single-brooded. **Eggs.** 2–3, rarely 1–5. Short subelliptical. Non-glossy and rough-textured. Pale bluish-white. 59 × 45 mm. **Incubation.** Eggs laid at 3-day intervals. Incubation mainly or entirely by the female, fed by the male. 36–41 days. **Nestling.** Semi-altricial and downy. First down short, silky and thick above, sparser below; white. Second down longer and woollier; gray-tinged above and white below. Irides gray. Cere and feet light yellow. **Nestling period.** The female closely broods and feeds the young for 8–10 days, and after this remains near by; the male bringing food. The young feather in 18–38 days. They tear up food from *c.* 28 days. The female brings leafy twigs for renewing the nest lining through most of the period. The young leave the nest to perch at *c.* 40 days, and fly at *c.* 45 days, after which the female also hunts. The young begin hunting at *c.* 50 days and are independent at *c.* 70 days.

SHARP-SHINNED HAWK *Accipiter striatus* **Pl. 28**

Breeds in forest, or sometimes in groves of trees in more open country. Prefers thick cover and conifers when available. Nest in a tree, in a crotch or next to the trunk on a horizontal branch, 10–60 ft. up. Occasionally the old nest of a bird or squirrel used as a foundation; rarely nest is in a hollow of tree-trunk or a cliff crevice.

Nest. A large, well-built twig structure; lined with finer twigs and strips of bark, or with chips of bark. Nest usually newly-built annually and not re-used. **Breeding season.** Begins mid-April. Single-brooded. **Eggs.** Usually 4–5, rarely 3–8. Short subelliptical to elliptical. Smooth and non-glossy. Bluish-white; very variably marked with dark or light brown or reddish-brown, and rarely pale grey or lilac. Markings may be sparse large blotches, distinct zones, irregular large and small blotches, speckling, or ill-defined mottling; sometimes concentrated at the larger end. 38 × 30 mm. **Incubation.** By both sexes (beginning with last egg?). 34–35 days. **Nestling.** Semi-altricial and downy. First down short; creamy-white or yellowish. Second down longer and pale purplish-buff to white, sometimes with some grey on the back. **Nestling period.** Young tended by female while male brings food and passes it to female away from nest. Eggs hatch over a short period. Young begin feathering at 14 days, fly at *c.* 23 days.

COOPER'S HAWK *Accipiter cooperii* **Pls. 6, 28**

Breeds in forests, or in groves or trees along rivers, but also in low scrub of treeless areas. Nest in a tree, 20–60 ft. up. Nest usually near to the tree-trunk on a horizontal branch, but may also be built on the foundation of an old nest of bird or squirrel.

Nest. A broad, flat twig platform, lined just before laying with flakes and chips of bark. Bark and, more rarely, leafy twigs are added during incubation and may be several inches deep by hatching. The male does most of the building, although the female may undertake relining if an old nest is used. **Breeding season.** Begins late February in south to late April in north. Single-brooded, but lost clutches will be replaced. **Eggs.** Usually 4, sometimes 5–6. Short subelliptical to elliptical. Smooth and non-glossy. White, tinged pale blue. Rarely with pale brown specks or a few tiny blotches. 49 × 38 mm. **Incubation.** Eggs laid every second day, with extra day interval between fourth and fifth egg. Incubation begins with third egg, by female alone, but male who brings food for female may cover eggs. 36 days (fifth egg takes 35 days). **Nestling.** Semi-altricial and downy. First down short, creamy-white. Second down short, silky and white. Eyes blue-gray, tinged brown at first. **Nestling period.** Young tended by female. Male brings food to female away from nest for first 3 weeks when female is brooding young. Later when female also hunts he takes food to nest. Young grow rapidly for first 17 days; then feather in next 3 weeks. Young become active and feed themselves at 3 weeks. Young male leaves nest at *c.* 30 days, female at *c.* 34 days. For *c.* 10 days young return to nest for food. Young take *c.* 3 weeks to learn to hunt. Become independent at *c.* 8 weeks.

RED-TAILED HAWK *Buteo jamaicensis* (Includes Harlan's Hawk, *B. j. harlani*) **Pl. 28**

Breeds in a wide variety of habitats. Nest normally in a tall tree often bordering open space or in an isolated, commanding position; but low trees may be used if necessary, or large cacti in desert regions, and elsewhere ledges of rock outcrops or cliffs. Nest may be re-used annually.

Nest. A bulky structure of twigs with finer lining of stems and bark, and leafy twigs are added throughout the nesting period. Both sexes build. **Breeding season.** Begins mid-February in south to early April in north. Single-brooded. **Eggs.** Usually 1–3, sometimes 4. Elliptical to short subelliptical. Smooth and non-glossy. White, sometimes with a faint buffish wash; sparsely or heavily marked with blotches of buff, pale reddish-brown, dark brown or purple. Markings often indistinct or combined with fine speckling. 59 × 47 mm. **Incubation.** By both sexes, but mainly by the female, fed by the male. 28–32 days. **Nestling.** Semi-altricial and downy. First down long, soft and silky above, shorter below, grayish or buffish white. Second down shorter and woollier; white. **Nestling period.** Young tended by both parents. They are active from the second day; begin to peck at food at *c.* 1 week, begin feathering at *c.* 16 days. At *c.* 4 weeks may leave the nest for near-by branches. Feed themselves at 4–5 weeks from food brought by parents. Fly at *c.* 6½ weeks. Learn to hunt by *c.* 3 weeks after leaving nest.

RED-SHOULDERED HAWK *Buteo lineatus* **Pl. 28**

Breeds usually in woodland. Nest in a large tree, usually in a large crotch; in Florida may use palmettos. Old nests of birds or squirrels may be used as foundations.

Nest. A bulky twig structure, rather flat on top, lined with stems, leaves, lichens and bark. Leafy twigs are added during nesting. **Breeding season.** Begins late

January in south to mid-April in north. Single-brooded, but more than one clutch may be laid to replace lost clutches. **Eggs.** Usually 2–3, sometimes 4, rarely 5. Short subelliptical to elliptical. Smooth and slightly glossy. Dull white or with faint buff wash. Very variably marked in reddish-brown or dark brown, and rarely pale lilac. Markings bold to indistinct. Large to small blotches, spots or specks. Larger markings often concentrated towards larger end. 55 × 43 mm. (those of southern birds average little smaller). **Incubation.** By both sexes, possibly mainly by female, fed by male. Beginning with first egg. 23–25 days. **Nestling.** Semi-altricial and downy. First down coat long, soft and silky, longest on head, white below and buffish-white above, with purplish-buff tint on back and wings. Second down coat thick and woolly. Pure white below, grayish-white above. **Nestling period.** Young tended by both adults. Young hatch over a period and vary in size. Inactive at first, becoming active at *c.* 10 days. Begin feathering at *c.* 2 weeks. Leave nest at 5–6 weeks.

BROAD-WINGED HAWK *Buteo platypterus* **Pl. 29**

Breeds in forest. Nest in a tree, deciduous or coniferous, usually at a height but has occurred from 3 to 90 ft. up. Nest usually in a main crotch but, especially in conifers, may be next to the trunk on a horizontal branch. Old nests of other birds or of squirrels may be used. Site usually used only once.

Nest. A usually small and loose structure of twigs, sparsely lined with chips of bark and lichens, and with leafy twigs added during nesting. Built by both sexes but lined by female. **Breeding season.** Begins mid-April in south to late May or early June in north. **Eggs.** Usually 2–3, rarely 4. Short subelliptical. Smooth and non-glossy. White usually marked with brown, buff, reddish-brown, purplish-brown, pale lilac or gray; often with profuse tiny speckling and sparser larger irregular blotches. Sometimes almost unmarked. 49 × 39 mm. **Incubation.** By both sexes. 28 days? **Nestling.** Semi-altricial and downy. First down short; buffish-white with gray bases, fading to white. Second down white. **Nestling period.** Young tended by both parents. Brooded by female for 1–2 weeks. Male provides most of food. Begin feathering at *c.* 2 weeks. Leave nest at 29–30 days, begin hunting at 37–46 days, but depend on adults until 50–56 days.

SWAINSON'S HAWK *Buteo swainsoni* **Pl. 29**

Breeds in open country, usually nesting in scattered trees. Nest usually high in a tree, but when necessary in a low tree, on a giant cactus, on a ledge of a rock outcrop or embankment, and exceptionally on the ground. Nests are usually re-used annually.

Nest. An often large and conspicuous structure of twigs and grasses, lined with bark, lichens and plant material, and with leafy twigs added at intervals. Nest may be 3–4 ft. across, with cavity 8–9 in. across, 2–5 in. deep. **Breeding season.** Begins early March in south to mid-May in north. Single-brooded. **Eggs.** Usually 2, rarely 3–4. Short subelliptical to elliptical. Smooth and non-glossy. White, sparsely marked with some dark brown or pale purplish blotches around larger end, or sparse tiny speckling in reddish brown or indistinct buff. 56 × 44 mm. **Incubation.** By both sexes, beginning with first egg. 28 days. **Nestling.** Semi-altricial and downy. First down thick; white with yellowish tint. Second down white. **Nestling period.** Young tended by both parents. Hatch over several days and differ in size. Fly at *c.* 4–5 weeks.

ZONE-TAILED HAWK *Buteo albonotatus*

Breeds in broken or riverside woodland. Nest in a tree. Site and height vary, from 25–100 ft. up and from concealed to exposed. In deciduous or coniferous trees, rarely in mesquite trees.

Nest. A bulky twig structure, lined with plant material and with leafy twigs added. **Breeding season.** Begins late April. Single-brooded. **Eggs.** Usually 2, rarely 1–3. Short subelliptical. Smooth and non-glossy. White or bluish-white, exceptionally with a few fine brown spots. 55 × 43 mm. **Incubation.** No information. **Nestling.** Semi-altricial and downy. Down grayish. **Nestling period.** No information.

WHITE-TAILED HAWK *Buteo albicaudatus* **Pl. 29**

Breeds in open country and low scrub. Nest on a low tree, large shrub, or the crown of a yucca; usually 4–15 ft. up. Usually on a slight eminence and often visible for some distance. Nest re-used annually.

Nest. Large, increasing in size with annual rebuilding. Of twigs, often thorny, and grass tufts, lined with finer plant material, and leafy twigs added. Nests may be 3 ft. across. **Breeding season.** Begins in early March. Single-brooded. **Eggs.** Usually 2, occasionally 1–3. Short subelliptical. White, unmarked or with some faint sparse specklings of pale brown or lavender. 59 × 47 mm. **Incubation.** No information. **Nestling.** Semi-altricial and downy. Down short and yellowish-white with a warm brown tint on head and wings. The down on the head is long and silky. There is a blackish area around the eye. **Nestling period.** No information.

SHORT-TAILED HAWK *Buteo brachyurus*

Breeds in forest, in or near a swamp, or in mangroves. Nest in a tree, 8–90 ft. up. **Nest.** A large stick cup; lined with finer twigs, Spanish Moss and green leaves. About 2 ft. across and 1 ft. deep. Built by both sexes. **Breeding season.** Begins late January. Single-brooded. **Eggs.** Usually 2, occasionally 1–3. Short subelliptical to oval. Smooth and non-glossy. Bluish-white to dull white, or with a buffish wash; unmarked or with sparse speckling or scattered scrawls or spots in pale buff or brown; or heavy irregular spotting and blotching of dark brown, often concentrated at one end. 53 × 43 mm. **Incubation.** No information. **Nestling.** Semi-altricial and downy. Down white. **Nestling period.** No information.

FERRUGINOUS HAWK *Buteo regalis* **Pl. 29**

Breeds in open country, using a tree where available and nesting high in it, but will also use low hillside bushes, a ledge of a rock outcrop or cliff, or among rocks on a hillside. Nests are re-used annually.

Nest. A bulky structure becoming massive and high with constant re-use; of sticks, old bones and similar debris, lined with grass, shredded bark and horse or cow dung. **Breeding season.** Begins mid-April. **Eggs.** Usually 3–4, sometimes 5. Short subelliptical to elliptical. Smooth and non-glossy. White to bluish-white; finely and irregularly speckled and spotted or with additional sparser larger blotching in reddish-brown, medium brown, buffish-brown or light purple. Sometimes almost unmarked. Rarely with sparse faint scribbling. 62 × 49 mm. **Incubation.** *c.* 28 days. **Nestling.** Semi-altricial, and downy. First down white, tinged gray on back and wings. Second down thicker; white. **Nestling period.** Young tended by both parents. Fledge at about 2 months.

ROUGH-LEGGED HAWK *Buteo lagopus* Pl. 29

Breeds in bare, open and mountainous regions; or in open woodland. Nest usually on a ledge or rock outcrop in more open regions, or in a tree in wooded areas. On an outcrop or cliff the nest is usually near the top. Nests may be re-used annually or several sites used alternately.

Nest. A bulky structure of twigs, lined with moss, grass and other green plant material. New nests may be small but with re-use become very large and often very tall if supported at the side. **Breeding season.** Begins early May, possibly later further north. Single-brooded, no replacement clutches laid. Young from late clutches have poor chance of survival. **Eggs.** Usually 2–3. 5–7 in good lemming years. Short subelliptical to short elliptical. Non-glossy. White, very variably marked with blotches or streaks of chestnut-red and brown. 55 × 44 mm. **Incubation.** By both sexes or by female alone, beginning with first egg. 28–31 days. **Nestling.** Semi-altricial and downy. First down pale grayish-brown above, white below. Second down thicker, dark gray. **Nestling period.** Female broods the young closely and feeds them; the male bringing food. Later she remains near by but does not hunt until the young are well-feathered. Young vary in size and small ones may die and be eaten at *c.* 2 weeks old. Second down acquired at *c.* 10 days and feathers by *c.* 35 days. They fly at *c.* 41 days.

GRAY HAWK *Buteo nitidus* Pl. 31

Breeds in or by riverine forest. Nest usually in large tree, up to 90 ft. up; but may be in thorny mesquites at 35–40 ft. up. Nest often hidden in foliage.

Nest. Small and shallow, of twigs often freshly broken off, and lined with leafy stems. **Breeding season.** Begins late March. Single-brooded. **Eggs.** Usually 2, sometimes 1–3. Subelliptical. White or bluish-white. Usually unmarked, or rarely with a few tiny pale brown marks. 51 × 41 mm. **Incubation.** No information. **Nestling.** Semi-altricial and downy. Down dull white below and on head, grayish-brown on back and wings, and a grayish-brown streak behind eye. Cere yellow. Iris brown. Bill black. Feet dull yellow. **Nestling period.** No information.

HARRIS'S HAWK *Parabuteo unicinctus* Pl. 31

Breeds in open areas, dry woodland or scrub. Nest in a small tree, tall shrubby growth, or on a cactus, often low, from 5–30 ft. up.

Nest. A small shallow platform, often compact but sometimes flimsy. Of sticks, twigs, plant stems and roots, lined with leaves, grass, bark, Spanish Moss and roots; and sometimes fur and animal bones. **Breeding season.** Begins early February. **Eggs.** Usually 2–4. Short subelliptical. Smooth and non-glossy. White or bluish-white. Sometimes with small irregular markings of pale brown or lavender gray. 53 × 42 mm. **Incubation.** By both sexes, beginning with first egg. *c.* 28 days. **Nestling.** Semi-altricial and downy. First down light buff. Second down described as rich brown at 5–6 days, and also as buff becoming white. This might be due to fading. **Nestling period.** Young tended by both parents. Well feathered and beginning to feed themselves at 17 days. Leave nest at *c.* 38 days.

BLACK HAWK *Buteogallus anthracinus* **Pl. 31**

Breeds in riverine woodland near water, or on more open coastal lowland. Nest in a tree at very varied heights, from 15–100 ft. up, but often low. Nest may be re-used in successive years.

Nest. Often small at first, becoming very large with re-use. Of large sticks mixed with smaller twigs, stems and debris; lined with finer twigs and green leaves. Twigs are collected in flight. **Breeding season.** Begins April. **Eggs.** One, sometimes 2, rarely 3. Short subelliptical to elliptical. With granular surface. Grayish-white, with small specks and blotches, or indistinct smudging of light brown or purplish-brown and faint purple. 57 × 45 mm. **Incubation.** No information. **Nestling.** Semi-altricial and downy. Down whitish on head and breast but dull gray on back and head, throat and sides of breast. **Nestling period.** No information.

GOLDEN EAGLE *Aquila chrysaetos* **Pls. 6, 30**

Breeds in mountain regions. Nests on rock ledges of outcrops or cliffs, or in trees, individuals using either or both. Several sites within a territory are used alternately.

Nest. New nests on ledges tend to be large but thin, those on trees are thicker; but both become massive with re-use. Building may occur at more than one site during a year. Nests are of thick branches, twigs and stems of any kind, and are lined with leafy twigs or tufts of conifer needles, which may be added continually during the nesting period. **Breeding season.** Begins early February in the south to late May to June in the north. Single-brooded. **Eggs.** Usually 2, sometimes 1, rarely 3. Short subelliptical. Non-glossy, white, usually spotted or blotched with brown, chestnut-red and pale gray; the two in a clutch often varying with one unmarked. 77 × 59 mm. **Incubation.** Eggs laid at 3–4-day intervals. Incubation usually by female alone, sometimes by both, beginning with first egg. 43–45 days. **Nestling.** Semi-altricial and downy. First down white or with pale gray tips. Second down thicker and woollier, white. Irides brown. Cere and legs yellowish-white. **Nestling period.** Young are closely brooded by the female at first, brooding ceasing at *c.* 30 days, the young feathering at 30–50 days. Usually the smaller young one dies. The female feeds young on food brought by the male, continuing until *c.* 40 days when young feed themselves. Later both parents bring food. The young exercise and practise pouncing while on the nest at *c.* 50 days and fly at *c.* 63–70 days, but are weak on the wing for another 3 weeks.

WHITE-TAILED SEA EAGLE *Haliaeetus albicilla* **Pl. 30**

Breeds by coasts, large rivers or lakes. Nests on the ground or a rock outcrop. In solitary pairs, using several alternative nest sites within a territory.

Nest. A massive structure, built slowly and added to continually. Of branches and twigs, the cup lined with green plants and leafy twigs. Both sexes build, the male tending to bring most material and the female incorporating it. **Breeding season.** Begins late March. Single-brooded. **Eggs.** Usually 2, sometimes 1–3, rarely 4. Short subelliptical to elliptical. Slightly glossy. Dull white. 76 × 59 mm. **Incubation.** Eggs laid at 2–4-day intervals. Incubation by both sexes or by female alone, beginning with the first egg. Green branches for lining brought during incubation. 35–45 days. **Nestling.** Semi-altricial and downy. First down thin and long, creamy to grayish-buff, darker on wings and rump, paler on throat. Replaced at *c.* 3 weeks by second down; longer, coarse and woolly. Pale grayish-buff above, darker on sides and underside. Feathering begins at *c.* 30 days. **Nestling period.** Young brooded and tended closely by female for 2 weeks, female in attendance near by for further 2 weeks; male bringing all food during this period. Young become active at *c.* 10 days, pick up food at *c.* 35–40 days, move from nest at *c.* 56 days. No loss of smallest. They fly at *c.* 70 days, remaining near nest and relying on parents for food for a further 35–40 days.

BALD EAGLE *Haliaeetus leucocephalus* **Pls. 6, 30**

Breeds usually by lakes, large rivers and on coasts. Nest a large, conspicuous structure on a site with a wide view; in a large tree, or on a rocky outcrop, or may be on the ground on islands. Usually close to water. Site usually re-used annually.

Nest. A massive structure of sticks and branches; the deep cup lined with grass and plant stems. Leafy twigs are added throughout the nesting period. With constant annual additions nests may become huge, sometimes ultimately *c.* 12 ft. high and 8½ ft. across. **Breeding season.** Begins late autumn, early November, in Florida, to May in north. Single-brooded. **Eggs.** Usually 2, rarely 1–3, short subelliptical to short oval. Rough-shelled. White and non-glossy. 71 × 54 mm. **Incubation.** Eggs laid at several day intervals. Incubation by both sexes. 35–46 days. **Nestling.** Semi-altricial and downy. First down gray, slightly paler on head and underparts, almost white on chin and throat. Second down drab dark brown. **Nestling period.** Young tended by both parents. First hatched young frequently kills or starves the second. Feathers at at *c.* 5 weeks. Leaves nest at 10–11 weeks, but may return to nest to feed and rest.

MARSH HAWK *Circus cyaneus* **Pl. 31**

Breeds on meadows and open marshland. Nest on the ground; usually in the shelter of taller vegetation, shrubs or grasses. Built mainly by the female. The same area but not the same site may be re-used. Pairs associate in a loose colony at times.

Nest. On dry sites a thin layer of small sticks and reeds, lined with grass. On wet ground it is a larger and substantially thicker structure. **Breeding season.** Begins mid-March in the south to mid-May in the north. Single-brooded. Replacement clutches may be laid. **Eggs.** 4–6, rarely up to 12. Short subelliptical. Bluish-white, rarely blotched with light brown; inside of shell green. 47 × 36 mm. **Incubation.** Eggs laid at intervals of 2 days or more. Incubation by female alone, beginning with second to fourth egg. 29–39 days, **Nestling.** Altricial and downy. First down mainly white with buffish on back and wings, and sides of head and neck; and a dark patch surrounding the eye. Second down buffish-brown above, becoming paler on the sides and whitish below. Irides blue-gray. Cere and feet pinkish, turning yellow. **Nestling period.** Young closely brooded and fed by female for *c.* 2 weeks, the male bringing food and passing it to the female in mid-air. The young begin to feather at *c.* 14 days and this is complete in *c.* 35 days. During this period they leave the nest and hide in near-by vegetation, returning when the parent brings food. Very small young often die. Young fly at *c.* 37 days, at first remaining near by while the adults bring food, later accompanying them. The point of independence is not known but maturation may be slow. Males occasionally have 2 or 3 females but this forces the females to hunt too, with a greater likelihood of nest loss.

OSPREYS *Pandionidae*

OSPREY *Pandion haliaetus* **Pls. 6, 31**

Large, fish-eating raptor. Breeds near water on lakes, rivers, estuaries and coasts. The nest-site usually on a tree-top or rocky outcrop overlooking a stretch of water. Sometimes on ruins, low bushes or the ground on undisturbed sites; and artificial sites, e.g., cartwheels, on poles, may be used. Solitary at times, but in colonies in suitable areas.

Nest. A massive accumulation of sticks and various debris, re-used and added to in successive years. The cup lined with finer material, stems and grasses. Both sexes build, the male tending to bring material and the female to incorporate it. **Breeding season.** Begins late April in south, to early June in north. Single-brooded. **Eggs.** Usually 3, rarely 2–4. Shortish subelliptical. Slightly glossy. Creamy to yellowish, spotted and blotched variably with chestnut-red to dark brown, some pale grayish markings. 61 × 46 mm. **Incubation.** By both sexes, beginning with the first egg; female taking the greater part and being fed by the male. 32–33 days. **Nestling.** Altricial and downy. First down short and thick. Mottled smoky-brown above and creamy-white below. A sandy-buff streak down the central back and on the head. Second down similar above but dorsal streak whitish; and speckled with brown tips on pale underside. Feathering

Osprey: *c.* 3-5ft. across.

begins at *c.* 4 weeks. **Nestling period.** Young varying in size and the smallest may die if food is scarce. They become active at *c.* 2 weeks. For *c.* 30 days female remains at nest brooding, feeding and tending young; male bringing food. Young feather towards end of this period; pick up food after *c.* 42 days; fly first at 51–59 days. Family remain about nest for up to 8 weeks. Young said to become independent *c.* 1 week after flying.

FALCONS *Falconidae*

Small to medium-sized raptors, usually capable of swift flight and capturing prey on the wing. They breed in solitary pairs or colonies. They make no nest, using a natural cavity or ledge, or the nest of another large bird. The Caracara is an exception, feeding on carrion and building a large nest. The eggs are rather rounded and usually mostly, or entirely, chestnut-red in color. The young are downy, having two successive down coats before feathering. Within a brood young usually hatch at intervals, varying in size; and the smallest may die if food is scarce, but not through the aggression of other young.

CARACARA *Polyborus plancus* **Pls. 6, 32**

Breeds in various habitats. Nests may be in trees, usually concealed among branches, or palm fronds, or on cacti; from 8–80 ft. up. In treeless areas nests may be on rock ledges or under overhanging rocks, or on the ground in a secluded site such as a marsh island. Nests often re-used annually.

Nest. A large untidy structure, of sticks, plant stems and weeds, unlined or lined with debris including dung and animal remains. Nest often bulky with re-use, and with a deep cup. **Breeding season.** Begins January. Lost clutches are replaced. Possibly double-brooded at times. **Eggs.** Usually 2–3, rarely 4. Short subelliptical to elliptical. Smooth and non-glossy or slightly glossy. White to pinkish-white, buff, orange-buff or purplish; marked with chestnut-red, reddish-brown or brown. Often so heavily speckled, mottled, blotched or smeared as to obscure ground color which in most instances is tinted with profuse fine speckling. 59 × 46 mm. **Incubation.** By both sexes. *c.* 28 days. **Nestling.** Semi-altricial and downy. First down pinkish-buff? Second down similar but with dark rich brown on upper head, and patches on shoulders, thighs and rump. **Nestling period.** Young tended by both parents. 2–3 months in nest. Fed on fragments torn from carcases in typical falcon fashion.

GYRFALCON *Falco rusticolus* **Pl. 32**

Breeds in open tundra regions and within the northern forest limits. Nest usually on a ledge of a cliff or outcrop, often of a river gorge; at times nests of other large birds are utilised on ledges, and more rarely in trees. Breeding frequency varies with weather conditions, and pairs appear not to breed every year.

Nest. A hollow scrape with no additional material, or an old nest of another bird such as raven or buzzard. Ledge nests are usually under overhangs. The site is usually heavily stained with droppings. **Breeding season.** Begins May. Single-brooded. **Eggs.** 3–4, sometimes 2–8. Short subelliptical to short elliptical. Smooth, non-glossy. Pale buffish or yellowish-white, rarely white; finely spotted with red or reddish-brown. 59 × 46 mm. **Incubation.** Eggs laid at *c.* 3-day intervals. Incubation usually by female alone, beginning with the first egg, and disturbance of the sitting bird may cause fatal chilling. The male rarely assists, but normally brings food. 28–29 days. **Nestling.** Semi-altricial and downy. Down thicker and short on the upperparts, thinner below, absent at the base of neck. White with a creamy tint. Irides dark. Cere and feet pale yellow. **Nestling period.** The female closely broods the young at first, feeding them; the male bringing food. Later both adults hunt and feed young. Young feather at 31–35 days, and fly at 46–49 days. The young remain near by for another 4 weeks, relying on the adults for food, before becoming independent.

PEREGRINE FALCON *Falco peregrinus* **Pl. 32**

Breeds in a wide range of habitats. Nest normally on a ledge of a cliff or rocky outcrop; more rarely on a raised mound on the ground in bare open regions; or in the top of a hollow stump. Sometimes on ledges of large city buildings.

Nest. A hollow scrape with no material added to it. **Breeding season.** Begins in early March in the south to mid-May in the north. Single-brooded. **Eggs.** 3–4, sometimes 2–6. Short subelliptical to short elliptical. Smooth, non-glossy. Creamy or buff, very heavily marked and usually obscured by dense fine red or chestnut-red specklings, irregularly marked at times with pale patches and gray or purple blotches. 53 × 41 mm. **Incubation.** Eggs laid at 2–3-day intervals. Incubation by both sexes, but mainly by the female, beginning with the second to third egg, the male bringing food. 28–29 days for a single egg. **Nestling.** Semi-altricial and downy. First down sparse, short and creamy-white. Second down long and woolly, buffish-gray above and creamy below. Irides dark. Cere and legs pale gray. **Nestling period.** The female closely broods and feeds young for the first 14 days, but later leaves them more. For most of the period she feeds the young and the male brings food for all; but after the first period of intensive care he will feed the young if she is absent. Young begin to feather at *c.* 18 days, and exercise at 21 days. During the later period they tear up prey themselves. They fly at 35–42 days, but appear to be dependent on the adults for a further 2 months.

PRAIRIE FALCON *Falco mexicanus* **Pl. 32**

Breeds in open regions, with rock outcrops or cliffs. Nest on a ledge under an overhang, or in a pothole or shallow cave in cliff face. Sometimes old nests of other birds in such sites are used. Often several sites used alternately.

Nest. A scrape in any soft substrate, or any old nest material already present. **Breeding season.** Begins mid-April. Single-brooded. **Eggs.** Usually 4–5, occasionally 3–6. Subelliptical to short subelliptical. Smooth and non-glossy. White or pinkish-white, with very fine overall speckling and spotting of reddish-brown or brown, tinting ground color, and usually extensive but indistinct blotches or smears in buff, purplish-pink or light reddish-brown. Sometimes more heavily marked with small blotches of brown or reddish-brown and lilac; or almost uniform buff or pinkish-buff. Paler generally than most other falcon eggs. 52 × 41 mm. **Incubation.** Usually by female; male rarely assists, but feeds female. Incubation begins with first egg. 29–31 days. **Nestling.** Semi-altricial and downy. Both down coats white. **Nestling period.** Young tended by both parents. They hatch over a period of days and differ in size. Quill feathers grow at *c.* 2 weeks. Young move about nest ledge at *c.* 30 days, leave nest at *c.* 40 days.

APLOMADO FALCON *Falco femoralis*

Breeds in open or lightly wooded or scrub country. Uses the old nests of large birds such as ravens, which are usually in yuccas, mesquites or other low trees, at 7–25 ft. up.

Nest. No nest other than the material already present. **Breeding season.** Begins mid-March. Single-brooded. **Eggs.** Usually 2–3, rarely 4. Subelliptical to short subelliptical. Smooth and non-glossy. White to pinkish-white; profusely marked with speckling, spots and blotches of light brown or chestnut-red. 45 × 35 mm. **Incubation.** By both sexes. Period not known. **Nestling.** No information. **Nestling period.** No information.

MERLIN (PIGEON HAWK) *Falco columbarius* **Pls. 6, 32**

Breeds in forest, in sparse woodland bordering open areas, in mountain areas, and open plain or prairie with scattered trees. Nest in large old nests of other birds in trees, in open tree cavities, on cliff-ledges or rocky hillsides, or on the ground.

Nest. Normally a bare hollow; but nests on the ground may have a plant lining apparently pulled in by the sitting bird; while old nests have their original material. **Breeding season.** Begins from mid- to late May. Single-brooded. **Eggs.** Usually 5–6, occasionally 2–7. Short subelliptical to short elliptical. Smooth, non-glossy. Pale buff, usually obscured by a heavy sprinkling of red, purplish-red or brown and often appearing wholly of the latter colors. 40 × 31 mm. **Incubation.** Eggs laid at about 2-day intervals. Incubation mainly by the female, beginning before completion of the clutch, the male bringing all food. 28–32 days. **Nestling.** Altricial and downy. First down, thinner and shorter, creamy-white. Second down longer and coarser, brownish-gray above, pale gray below, and white with gray bases on chin, throat and belly. **Nestling period.** Young closely brooded by female in the early stages, the male bringing food but rarely feeding the young. Later both adults hunt. The young are mainly feathered by 18 days, and fly at 25–30 days. They remain near by and take *c.* 6 weeks to become independent.

AMERICAN KESTREL (SPARROWHAWK) *Falco sparverius* **Pl. 32**

Breeds in open country, areas with scattered trees, or woodland edge. Nest in a hole, a natural cavity or crevice in a tree, a woodpecker hole, or a similar cavity in a building or a rocky or earth bank. Rarely in the old nest of another bird. Will use nest-boxes.

Nest. A shallow scrape. No material added other than what is already present. **Breeding season.** Begins early March in the south to late May in the north. Single-brooded. **Eggs.** Usually 4–5, sometimes 3–7. Short subelliptical to subelliptical. Smooth and non-glossy. White, creamy or pale pink, with minute speckling tinting the ground color pale buff or pink, with indistinct mottling or fine spotting and occasionally small blotches in reddish-brown or medium brown. Darker tint often concentrated towards one end. 35 × 29 mm. **Incubation.** Eggs laid at 2–3-day intervals. Incubation mostly by female, the male bringing food and occasionally assisting. 29–30 days. **Nestling.** Semi-altricial and downy. First down rather scanty, white. Second down thicker and creamy or yellowish-white. **Nestling period.** Young tended by both parents, being brooded and fed by female at first, the male bringing all food. Later both hunt. Young feed themselves at 20 days, leave nest at 30 days.

GUANS *Cracidae*

CHACHALACA *Ortalis vetula* **Pls. 7, 33**

Breeds in chapparal thickets. Nest in a small tree, often in a clump near water. Nest well out on a branch, hidden in thick foliage, 5–25 ft. up. The nest is built from material plucked from branches within reach of the nest.

Nest. A small, frail platform, of twigs, lined with a few leaves. **Breeding season.** Begins in April. **Eggs.** Usually 3. Subelliptical to oval. Smooth but surface very finely granular. Non-glossy or slightly glossy. White, but often nest-stained. 66 × 53 mm. **Incubation.** By female alone, the male remaining nearby. 22–26 days. **Nestling.** Precocial and downy. Down cinnamon-buff with a black spot on forehead, a black reddish-tinted stripe over centre of crown and nape; warmer cinnamon-buff with fine blackish mottling on sides of neck; cinnamon-buff and dark brown mottling on back; chin, throat and belly white. Bill black. Legs and feet pinkish. **Nestling period.** Young, tended by both parents, leave nest for ground on day of hatching. Food is passed to them by adults and feeding continues for a long period, at least until young are half-grown. Adults roost on perches above ground, and young clamber and flutter up to roost with them, one under each adult wing. Wing feathers are well-grown within the first few days, and young fly well at 3 weeks. The throat begins to become bare at *c.* 1 month. Young stay with adults and join flocks.

GROUSE *Tetraonidae*

Gamebirds of tundra, mountains, scrub, and floors of northern woodland. Nests are usually open hollows, rather exposed, relying on the camouflaged plumage of the female birds for concealment. Very rarely an old nest in a tree is used by some species. In ground nests sideways-throwing and sideways-building by sitting birds may produce a substantial nest-lining of nearby grasses or other vegetation, especially in damper sites. Eggs are strikingly patterned for concealment against backgrounds of moorland-type vegetation. The coloring is on the surface of the eggs and may be smudged on newly-laid eggs. The eggs may be partly covered with vegetation when the bird leaves the nest. The chicks can follow the female as soon as the down is dry. In some species the male assists in care and protection of young. Young birds are led to places where food is available, the position of food being indicated by the pecking female, but the young are not fed directly. The wing feathers grow very rapidly and the young may be able to flutter some distance at a few days.

SAGE GROUSE *Centrocercus urophasianus* **Pls. 7, 34**

Breeds in sagebrush areas. Nest on the ground, sheltered by shrubby growth. Males have communal display leks and are promiscuous. Females nest alone.

Nest. A shallow scrape; bare or with a slight lining of near-by plants. **Breeding season.** Begins mid-March to early May. Probably few lost clutches are replaced. **Eggs.** Usually 7–8, sometimes up to 13. Subelliptical to oval. Smooth and moderately glossy. Pale drab olive to olive-buff; with profuse spots, specks and tiny blotches of dark brown. 55 × 38 mm. **Incubation.** By female alone. 25–27 days. **Nestling.** Precocial and downy. Down has general spotted pattern, mottled in black, brown, buff and white. Head whiter with bolder spots and short stripes in black and brown over most of it. Two brownish, black-edged spots on foreneck. Upper breast buff mottled with black. Bill black. **Nestling period.** Young tended by female alone. Young leave nest as soon as down is dry, feeding themselves and brooded and guarded by female. Brood move to a moister site where feeding is better.

BLUE GROUSE *Dendragapus obscurus* **Pls. 7, 33**

Breeds in montane forest. Nest on the ground, well-concealed, near or under fallen logs, low tree branches or tree-roots; usually in a dry site, often near forest edge. Occasionally by solitary trees or bushes in the open.

Nest. A shallow scrape lined with a little vegetation pulled in from around the site. **Breeding season.** Begins mid-April in south to late May in north. Single-brooded. **Eggs.** Usually 6–8, sometimes 7–12. Short subelliptical to oval. Smooth and slightly glossy or non-glossy. Very pale pinkish-buff or buff, with very fine speckling of reddish-brown or light brown, and with sparse irregular spotting. 50 × 35 mm. **Incubation.** Eggs laid at 1½-day intervals. Incubation by female alone. 26 days. **Nestling.** Precocial and downy. Down pattern varies in color. Pale whitish-buff below, darker and grayer on upper breast. Upperparts heavily mottled in black, brown and buff; the blackish markings tending to form two broken stripes on the lower back. Crown has a zone of warmer buff with broken transverse black markings. Neck of similar color with fine black mottling. Dark longitudinal mark and some mottling behind eye. **Nestling period.** Young tended by female alone. Young feed themselves from hatching, brooded and guarded by female. Can fly some way at 6–7 days, well at 2 weeks. Brooding ceases at *c.* 8–10 days. Brood moves from nest area to thicker cover. Disperse by late summer.

SPRUCE GROUSE *Dendragapus canadensis* **Pls. 7, 33**

Breeds in forest areas. Nest on the ground, well-concealed, often under low branches, or in brush, or in deep moss by or in spruce thickets.

Nest. A slight scrape lined with a few twigs, stems or leaves from near by. **Breeding season.** Begins in May. Single-brooded. **Eggs.** Usually 7–8, sometimes 4–10. Subelliptical. Smooth and slightly glossy. Buff or pinkish-buff, finely speckled, spotted and with small irregular blotches; of dull reddish-brown or brown. Smaller markings often profuse and overall. 44 × 32 mm. **Incubation.** By female alone. *c.* 24 days. **Nestling.** Precocial and downy. Down pattern rather similar to that of ptarmigans but lacks distinctive dorsal pattern and feathered toes of latter. Young are pale whitish-buff below, yellowish-buff on head with chestnut-red patch bordered with black on crown tapering to nape, two black spots on forehead and irregular black line through eye. Back indistinctly mottled in buff and blackish-brown. **Nestling period.** Young tended by female alone. Young begin growing wing feathers in few days, and can fly a little at 10–12 days. Feathered when half-grown.

WILLOW PTARMIGAN *Lagopus lagopus* **Pls. 7, 33**

Breeds in zones of willow, birch, or juniper scrub, often in partially open and rather boggy places on tundra, or on more open areas in low, close, shrubby growth on rocks, or in grassy heathland. Nests are often partly in the shelter of a small shrub or taller tuft of vegetation.

Nest. A shallow hollow made by the female, lined at times with a sparse layer of grasses, moss and heather stems. **Breeding season.** Begins mid-May in south to early June in north. Single-brooded. **Eggs.** Usually 6–11, sometimes 4–17. Sub-elliptical. Smooth and glossy. Yellowish, or sometimes slightly reddish; heavily and irregularly blotched and mottled all over with dark chocolate-brown to reddish-brown. Markings very variable. 44 × 32 mm. **Incubation.** Eggs laid at intervals of 36–48 hours. Incubation by the female only, beginning with the next-to-last egg or complete clutch. The male remains near by. 20–26 days. **Nestling.** Precocial and downy; the down extending to legs and feet but toe-nails bare. Down is pale sandy-buff below and on sides and extending to cheeks; throat a little paler, upper breast warmer. Crown of head chestnut-red with a blackish border, and patches of similar color on the ear-coverts. Pale sandy-buff streak from lores back over eye. Another pale streak breaks the ear-coverts to join broad pale patches on either side of a dark nape streak. The body pattern is irregular. A central dorsal stripe of warm or rufous-buff is bordered with irregular blackish bands, and broadens into a saddle on mid-back, with darker bands extending to the shoulders. There are irregular dark patches either side of the rump. The wings are rufous with black edges. The bill dark. **Nestling period.** Young hatch in a short period, and are led away by female soon afterwards. The male helps to guard the young, which are brooded by the female but find their own food. Wing feathers grow quickly while the young are still small. They fly at 12–13 days. The family remain together until late autumn and may group with others to form winter flocks.

ROCK PTARMIGAN *Lagopus mutus* **Pls. 7, 33**

Breeds on rocky arctic tundra and on high latitude zones of similar vegetation further south. Nest a scrape in an open site, sometimes slightly sheltered by a plant tuft or rock.

Nest. A rather bare hollow scrape, scantily lined with pieces of grass, plants and a few feathers. **Breeding season.** Begins late May to early June. Single-brooded. **Eggs.** 5–10, sometimes 3–12. Subelliptical. Smooth and glossy. Tends to have paler ground color and darker markings than Willow Ptarmigan. Whitish to pale creamy-yellow with irregular blotching and mottling of dark chocolate brown. 43 × 31 mm. **Incubation.** Eggs laid at intervals of 1–2 days. Incubation by female alone, beginning with the next-to-last egg, the male remaining near by. 24–26 days. **Nestling.** Precocial and downy; down extending over legs and feet to toe-nails. The pattern similar to that of Willow Ptarmigan but tending to be bolder, with conspicuous black zones edging the rufous and rufous-buff areas, and across the sides of the head. The pale parts lacking most of the yellow, and a more pale grayish-buff. Bill blackish. **Nestling period.** Young are tended by both parents at first; brooded by the female, guarded by the male, but finding their own food. Wing-feathers grow first and they can fly weakly at *c.* 10 days. In the latter part of the period the males tend to leave the family and flock together, joining unmated males. Females and young remain together, joining with others later to form winter flocks.

WHITE-TAILED PTARMIGAN *Lagopus leucurus* **Pls. 7, 33**

Breeds in alpine tundra areas of mountains, where dwarf willows are present. **Nest.** A shallow scrape, usually lined with slight vegetation such as grasses which are pulled in to line the hollow. **Breeding season.** Begins mid-June.

Single-brooded. **Eggs.** Usually 4–7, sometimes 3–9. Subelliptical to long elliptical. Smooth and slightly glossy. Very pale warm buff to pinkish-buff with sparse but regular small spotting in dark brown; and very fine overall speckling. More sparsely marked than other ptarmigan eggs and resembling those of the Spruce Grouse. 43 × 29 mm. **Incubation.** Eggs laid at 1½-day intervals. Incubation by female alone, the male remaining near by. 22–23 days. **Nestling.** Precocial and downy. Down colors paler than on other ptarmigans. Chestnut-red cap poorly defined with narrow margins. Forehead pale buff with broken dark markings, black streak behind eye, and throat whitish. Dorsal stripe tends to be indistinct, but this area is warmer buff, bordered and mottled with black, the rest of the back being mottled with buff, gray, brown and black. Underparts grayish-white. Toes feathered. **Nestling period.** Young tended by both parents, finding their own food. Can fly at *c.* 10 days. Broods remain together until the following spring.

RUFFED GROUSE *Bonasa umbellus* **Pls. 7, 33**

Breeds in forest areas with some deciduous trees. Nest on the ground at the base of a tree or stump, under logs, bushes or brush piles.

Nest. A shallow scrape, lined with any near-by plant material that can be pulled in, including dead leaves and pine needles. **Breeding season.** Begins early April in south to early May in north. Will replace lost clutches but with fewer eggs. **Eggs.** Usually 9–12, replacement clutches often *c.* 7. Subelliptical to oval. Smooth and moderately glossy. Creamy or ivory to very pale buff or pinkish-buff; often unmarked, sometimes with very fine speckling of brown. 40–30 mm. **Incubation.** Eggs laid at rate of 2 every 3 days. Incubation by female alone, beginning with last egg. 23–24 days, or longer in cold seasons. **Nestling.** Precocial and downy. Down pattern dark. From crown of head to rump reddish-brown, paler on the crown. Pale yellowish-buff on sides of head, breast and flanks, and underparts yellow to yellowish-white. There may be slightly darker markings on crown, and a black stripe extends from eye to nape. **Nestling period.** Young tended by female alone. Young leave nest soon after hatching. Feed themselves, brooded and guarded by female. Wings grow rapidly and young can flutter up to tree-branches while small. Fly at 10–12 days. Broods begin to break up at *c.* 12 weeks.

GREATER PRAIRIE CHICKEN *Tympanuchus cupido* **Pls. 7, 34**

Breeds on open grassland and prairies. Nest on the ground in growing herbage, in the open or on the edge of marshes, bushes or scrub woodland. Males have a communal lek display and are promiscuous. Females nest alone.

Nest. A shallow scrape with a little of the surrounding vegetation pulled in as lining, and may be concealed by overhanging plants possibly pulled over by birds. **Breeding season.** Begins early April in south to late May in north. Single-brooded, but will replace lost clutches. **Eggs.** Usually 12–14. Short subelliptical to short oval. Smooth and moderately glossy. Ground color in shades of buff, light ivory-buff to deep buff, very finely and minutely speckled and spotted in dark brown, sometimes almost or completely unmarked. 45 × 34 mm. **Incubation.** Eggs laid at a little more than 1-day intervals. Incubation by female alone, beginning a little before or after laying of last egg. 23–26 days. **Nestling.** Precocial and downy. Down pattern like that of Lesser Prairie Chicken and Sharp-tailed Grouse, but with deeper color above. Mainly yellowish with a rufous-brown tinge above. Head with several black spots on crown and nape and some indication of a median brown stripe. Tiny black patch immediately behind eye, and row of three dark spots across ear-coverts. Upper parts marked with irregular black patches. Bill light brown with black along the upper edge. Feet yellowish. **Nestling period.** Young leave the nest after the first day, tended by female alone. Young brooded frequently during first week, less often after this. Become independent at *c.* 6–8 weeks.

LESSER PRAIRIE CHICKEN *Tympanuchus pallidicinctus*
(possibly a race of the previous species) **Pl. 34**

Breeds on more arid grasslands. Nest on the ground in grassy places. Males have a communal lek display and are promiscuous. Females nest alone.

Nest. A shallow scrape lined with grasses and with other plant material from near by. **Breeding season.** Begins early May. Single-brooded. **Eggs.** Usually 11–14. Short subelliptical to short oval. Pale ivory-buff to ivory-yellow, with or without minute speckling. 42 × 32 mm. **Incubation.** Eggs laid at a little over 1-day intervals. Incubation by female alone, beginning a little before or after last egg. 23–26 days. **Nestling.** Precocial and downy. Down pattern like that of Greater Prairie Chicken, but paler and less brownish above, without a median streak. **Nestling period.** As for Greater Prairie Chicken.

SHARP-TAILED GROUSE *Tympanuchas phasianellus* **Pls. 7, 34**

Breeds in areas of mixed open grassland with woodland or scrub. Nest on the ground, usually near to or within tree or shrub cover, exceptionally in open sites, typically on the borders of open areas, usually partly or wholly concealed by tall herbage or bushes.

Nest. A shallow scrape scantily lined with plant material pulled in from near by. **Breeding season.** Begins early April in south and west, to early May in north. Single-brooded. **Eggs.** Usually 10–13. Subelliptical to oval. Smooth and slightly to moderately glossy. Usually buff or slightly olive-buff, pinkish or warm buff; unmarked or with fine speckling and a few larger spots of dark brown. 43 × 32 mm. **Incubation.** Eggs laid at daily intervals. Incubation by female alone, beginning with last egg. 23–24 days. **Nestling.** Precocial and downy. Down pattern like that of prairie chickens, but lacks the warmer tints above and is a yellowish color overall. There are small black marks along mid-crown and some spots on nape, and only one or two black spots on ear-coverts. Upper parts have irregular black patches or streaks. **Nestling period.** Young tended by female only. Young soon leave nest and are led by females to moister areas. Can fly a little at 10 days. Become increasingly independent in period from 10 days to 6–8 weeks, when broods disperse.

TYPICAL GAMEBIRDS *Phasianidae*

Birds of open spaces, scrub and woodland. Nest usually a hollow scrape on the ground, made by the female. As with the grouse, the scanty nest lining is added by sideways-throwing and sideways-building. The part played by the male varies from full participation to relative indifference. Eggs are usually uniformly colored or finely marked. In some groups shells are very thick and hard. The chicks are precocial and very active, leaving the nest within a day of hatching.

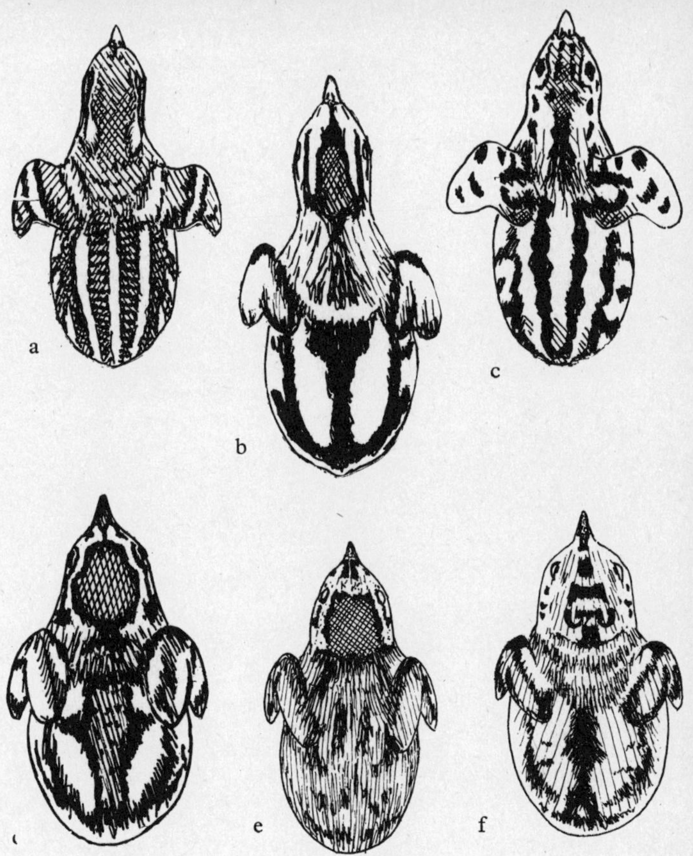

Dorsal patterns of downy chicks: a, Chukar; b, Ring-necked Pheasant; c, Partridge; d, Willow Ptarmigan; e, Spruce Grouse; f. Prairie Chicken.

They are led to places where food is available, and its position may be indicated by the pecking female, but the young pick it up for themselves. They are brooded by the adults. The down is long and fluffy on the body, shorter and closer on the head, and boldly patterned. Wing-feathers grow first and grow quickly while the young are still small. They can flutter some distance at a few days old. Parental care is not always effective and small young seem to be easily lost from larger broods. Broods tend to remain together until the following breeding season.

MOUNTAIN QUAIL *Oreortyx pictus* **Pls. 8, 34**

Breeds on the edge of mountain woodland and scrub. Nest on the ground, usually well-concealed; in herbage or shrubs at the base of large tree, under fallen pine branch, and under or in shrubby growth. It is usually near a pathway and at no great distance from water.

Nest. A shallow scrape, lined with plant material pulled in from near by. **Breeding season.** Begins mid-March. Single-brooded, but lost clutches replaced. **Eggs.** Usually 7–10, large clutches of 19–22 eggs usually attributed to two females, but see comments below. Oval. Slightly glossy and smooth. Deep pinkish-buff to pale creamy; unmarked. 35 × 27 mm. **Incubation.** By female alone? with male near by. But male has brood patch and has been seen tending young and might possibly incubate one of two separate clutches laid by female, as in some other species. 24–25 days. **Nestling.** Precocial and downy. Down pattern rather like that of Bobwhite, but body color generally paler and markings blacker with larger mark on ear-coverts. Upperparts and head buffish-white, and underside grayish or yellowish-white. There is a broad chestnut-red stripe bordered, and in places marked, with black. It extends up the middle of the back, is narrow and blacker at shoulders, broad again on nape and hind-crown, and tapers to point on mid-crown. There is a black streak from the eye across the ear-coverts, broadening posteriorly. There is a chestnut and black patch on the inner wing, and a blackish band on the upper flanks. **Nestling period.** Young tended by both parents, or by either alone. Wings and other feathers begin rapid growth in first few days. Young are very active, feeding themselves, brooded and guarded by parents.

SCALED QUAIL *Callipepla squamata* **Pls. 8, 34**

Breeds in arid grassland, brush or desert, where some water is available. Nest on the ground usually under or sheltered by a shrub or herbage, but not usually in even herbage such as grass or grain.

Nest. A shallow scrape with a lining, often sparse, of nearby grasses or other plants. **Breeding season.** Season prolonged, may begin early March in south, although early May is more typical as in north. Possibly double-brooded. Breeding may be completely inhibited in dry seasons. **Eggs.** Usually 12–14, sometimes 9–16. Female may sometimes lay two clutches. In some instances two females lay in one nest. Subelliptical to oval. Glossy and smooth. Very pale creamy to pale ivory with very fine speckling in pale buffish- or reddish-brown. 33 × 25 mm. **Incubation.** Usually by female with male sometimes near by. 22–23 days. **Nestling.** Precocial and downy. Down pattern like those of Gambel's and California Quails; but grayer on body, with almost white paired lines on back. Small grayish tuft where adult has crest. Forehead to crown, and sides of head, cinnamon-buff or pinkish-buff. Throat whitish. Elongated dark chestnut-red streak on rear edge of ear-coverts. Broad chestnut-red stripe from mid-crown to nape, with blackish edges, and bordered with narrow whitish stripe. On back paired blackish lines, joining on upper back, area between stripes mottled buff and chestnut. Dark stripe bordered by a pair of whitish stripes, and a blackish broken band along the flank. Flanks and breast grayish-buff becoming paler on underside. **Nestling period.** Young tended by both or either parents. Plumage grows rapidly and young can fly when half-grown. Male possibly takes over brood while female raises second brood. Young remain with adults and later join to form large coveys.

GAMBEL'S QUAIL *Callipepla gambeli* Pls. 8, 34

Breeds in arid desert scrub. Nest on the ground at the base of the trunk of small tree or shrub, or under a low shrub, or fallen branches, or sheltered and shaded by a tall tuft of herbage.

Nest. A shallow scrape, variably lined with grasses or other plant material. **Breeding season.** Begins late April. Single-brooded, or double-brooded in good seasons. **Eggs.** Usually 12–14, sometimes 10–19. Oval to subelliptical or short pyriform. Smooth and slightly to moderately glossy. Pale creamy-buff with fine over-all speckling, occasionally lacking, and sparser irregular spotting and blotching in light reddish-brown, buffish-brown or dark brown. 32 × 24 mm. **Incubation.** Eggs laid at 25–28-hour intervals. Incubation by female alone, with male near by. 21–23 days. **Nestling.** Precocial and downy. Like pale California Quail. Forehead and sides of head pinkish-buff or paler; dark chestnut streak on hind ear-covert. Tiny topknot tuft. From mid-crown to nape broad band of chestnut-red bordered with black and with a pale cream band along the side. Upper parts pale pinkish-buff with four longitudinal dark brown bands on lower back, a single band and some dark blotches on upper back. Underparts pale grayish-buff. **Nestling period.** Young tended by both parents; but if conditions are good male may take care of young and female nest again; or after *c.* 4 weeks chicks may be left with other adults and the pair re-nest. Young leave the nest soon after hatching. Normally female broods young while male guards. Young feed themselves, mostly on insects, and grow rapidly. *C.* 3 months to rear brood.

CALIFORNIA QUAIL *Callipepla californica* Pls. 8, 34

Breeds in a wide range of habitats, from moister forest edges through chaparral regions to scrub desert; where bushy cover is combined with open areas of herbage. Nest usually on the ground; rarely in the nest of another bird in tree or shrub, or on suitable raised site formed by branches and creepers, or on tree stump.

Nest. A shallow hollow, usually lined with vegetation from near by. **Breeding season.** Begins January in south to mid-May in north. Sometimes, possibly often, double-brooded, and lost clutches are replaced. **Eggs.** Usually 12–17, sometimes 6–28. Short subelliptical to short oval, or short pyriform. Smooth and glossy. Creamy-white to creamy-buff or yellowish; often with fine overall speckling, and with irregular spotting and blotching, often heavy, of golden-brown, buffish, or dull brown. 31 × 24 mm. **Incubation.** Eggs laid at a little more than 24-hour interval, averaging five per week. Incubation normally by female with male near by, but male may incubate if female dies. 21–23 days. **Nestling.** Precocial and downy. Down pattern like young Gambel's or Scaled Quail, but with yellower tint. Underside buffish-white. Sides of head and forehead, warm yellowish-buff; crown and nape rufous-brown with blackish edges, tapering to point on forecrown, and bordered by pale creamy-buff stripe. Short black mark on hind-edge of ear-covert. Back dark brown with three broad longitudinal yellowish-buff stripes. Flanks and wings with broken pattern of dark brown and buff. **Nestling period.** Young very active soon after hatching. Tended by both parents, but often, perhaps regularly, female appears to leave male to tend young and re-nests to produce second brood. Young drop from raised nests without harm. Wing feathers grow rapidly, and young can flutter some way at 10 days. Broods may gather into flocks while young are still small.

Dorsal patterns of downy chicks (*left to right*): Bobwhite Quail, California Quail, Mountain Quail.

BOBWHITE QUAIL *Colinus virginianus* **Pls. 8, 34**

Breeds in a wide variety of habitats, but basically a species of scrub, scattered cover in grassland or cultivated areas, and on woodland edge. Nest on the ground, usually in low cover bordering an open space.

Nest. A shallow hollow, lined with plant material pulled in from near by, and with growing plants pulled over to hide it. Both sexes build. **Breeding season.** Begins mid-March in south to late May in north. Single-brooded, possibly double-brooded in south. Lost clutches replaced. **Eggs.** Usually 12–16, sometimes 7–28. Short subelliptical to short oval or short pyriform. Smooth and slightly glossy. Dull white to creamy-white. 30 × 24 mm. **Incubation.** Eggs laid at a little over one-day intervals (14 eggs in 18–20 days). **Nestling.** Precocial and downy. Grayish-buff on underside. Sides of head yellowish-buff with blackish streak from eye to nape. Forehead rufous-buff, and crown and nape chestnut-red, deeper at edges, tapering on to forehead. Blackish streak from eye to nape. Broad chestnut-red band continues down middle of back, bordered with narrow creamy-buff stripes; and flanks mottled chestnut, blackish and buff. Some individuals show more rufous over all of back. **Nestling period.** Young tended by both parents. In captivity male is known to take over brood while female re-nests. Feathers grow rapidly and young can fly at 2 weeks. Feather in 4–8 weeks, and are full-grown in 2 months. Brood remains together until spring.

MONTEZUMA QUAIL *Cyrtonyx montezumae* **Pls. 8, 34**

Breeds in montane pine-oak and oak scrub. Nest on the ground, sometimes under a bush, and usually built into the side of a tuft of grass or herbage.

Nest. A scrape several inches deep, *c.* 5–6 in. across, among grasses, lined with grass and leaves, and with grass-stems worked together at the sides and pulled over at the top to form a closed cavity. Male may help to build? **Breeding season.** Begins late April, but actual nesting probably not until June. **Eggs.** Usually 6–14. Oval to subelliptical or short pyriform. Smooth and moderately glossy. White to creamy-white. 32 × 25 mm. **Incubation.** By female, with male on guard, but some records of males sitting. 25–26 days. **Nestling.** Precocial and downy. Down lacks a distinct dorsal pattern. Head pale cinamon-buff with narrow black line from eye to nape. Light chestnut patch on crown and nape, tapering into forehead. Back and wings mottled brown and chestnut with some cinnamon-buff forming two indistinct pale streaks on upper back. Rear edge of wing yellowish. Grayish-white on underside. Whiter on throat. **Nestling period.** Young tended by both parents. Fed on insects and seeds, but gradually feeding themselves. Broods remain together and coalesce into larger groups in autumn.

RING-NECKED PHEASANT *Phasianus colchicus* **Pls. 8, 34**

Breeds in reedbeds, on waste ground among cultivation, hedgerows, scrub and woodland. Introduced in cultivated regions. Males are polygamous and females nest alone. Nest normally on the ground in cover of tall plants, briers or shrubs; rarely on raised sites on stacks or overgrown ruins, or flattish old bird nests or squirrel dreys in trees.

Nest. A shallow hollow, unlined, or sparsely lined with near-by plants, grass or dead leaves. **Breeding season.** Begins mid-April to early May. Single-brooded. **Eggs.** 7–15. Subelliptical. Smooth and glossy. Uniform olive-brown, sometimes more definite brown, or olive, or blue-gray. 46 × 36 mm. **Incubation.** Eggs laid on consecutive days. Incubation by female alone, beginning with completion of the clutch. 23–27 days. **Nestling.** Precocial and downy. Down varies in color, dark parts dark brown to rufous, pale parts creamy to rufous-buff. Rufous forms have less distinct pattern. Creamy-buff below, extending to sides of neck and forehead. Dark mark behind eye and narrow dark streak over it. Broad stripe over nape, rufous-centered and dark-edged. Back dark brown, with a pair of longitudinal broad pale cream stripes tending to terminate just before the tail-end. Wing rufous with pale edge. **Nestling period.** Young all hatch within a short period, and are tended by the female alone, led to food, and brooded. They can fly at 12–14 days. When the young are half-grown they tend to roost in trees at night.

PARTRIDGE *Perdix perdix* **Pls. 8, 32**

Breeds on grassland, the borders of scrub and cultivation. Nest on the ground in tall grasses or growing crops or in the base of hedgerows or shrubs, or young trees; very rarely above ground in stacks.

Nest. A shallow hollow, usually sheltered by taller plants, and lined with dead grasses and leaves. **Breeding season.** Begins late May to early June. Single-brooded. **Eggs.** 9–20, sometimes 8–23, larger broods probably from two females. Subelliptical to short oval or short pyriform. Smooth and glossy. Uniform shades of buff, brown or olive. 36 × 27 mm. **Incubation.** Eggs laid at 1–2-day intervals and covered with nest material until incubation. Incubation by female alone, with the male in close attendance, beginning on completion of clutch. 23–25 days. **Nestling.** Precocial and downy. Creamy-yellowish on underside; yellower on throat and sides of head. Crown light orange-buff with four longitudinal blackish lines usually broken into short streaks or spots and more rufous between middle pair. Black spots on broken lines around eyes and ear-coverts, nape and neck. Mantle mottled. Back dark brown, rufous towards rump, with three pale cream longitudinal streaks breaking up flanks. Wings dark, rufous-edged, with two pale bars. **Nestling period.** Young hatch within a short period, and may leave the nest on the first day. They are tended and brooded by both parents. They grow quickly. Wing-feathers appear at 5–6 days; the young can flutter at 10–11 days, fly at 16 days, and feather by 28 days. They remain together until the following spring.

CHUKAR *Alectoris chukar* **Pls. 8, 32**
Breeds mainly in sagebrush-grassland on hill slopes. Nest on the ground, usually under the shelter of a rock or shrub, or against a grass-tuft in more open sites. **Nest.** A shallow hollow, with a variable, usually sparse, lining of near-by vegetation, leaves and stems. **Breeding season.** Begins March to early June. Single-brooded. **Eggs.** Usually 8–15, up to 20 at times. On some occasions at least the female produces two clutches at one period. Subelliptical. Smooth and glossy. Pale yellowish, buff or brown, with fine light red speckling; often heavily marked. 43 × 31 mm. **Incubation.** By the female only, on completion of the clutch. A separate additional clutch may be incubated independently by the male. 22–23 days. **Nestling.** Precocial and downy. Creamy-white below, more grayish on breast. Sides of head and thin streak over eye cream-colored, and blackish streak from eye to nape. Top of head light brown, dark-speckled; browner on nape. Back mottled blackish-brown with three dark-edged cream stripes down the back, the central one narrow, two shorter lateral ones, and one across each wing. **Nestling period.** Young cared for by the adult that incubates them. The brood remain together and join with others into larger groups in autumn.

TURKEYS *Meleagridae*

TURKEY *Meleagris gallopavo* **Pls. 8, 33**
Breeds in more open deciduous forest, along forest edges and in clearings; and in more open and scattered woodland of drier regions. Nest on the ground. Usually by or under shrubby cover or against a fallen log or foot of a tree; occasionally among rocks or in an open site. Apparent sharing of nest by several females recorded. Males are polygamous and take no part in nesting.
Nest. A shallow hollow, sparsely lined with near-by vegetation or dead leaves. **Breeding season.** Begins mid-March. Single-brooded. **Eggs.** Usually 8–12, sometimes up to 20 .Elliptical to oval. Smooth and glossy. Pale buff or yellowish,

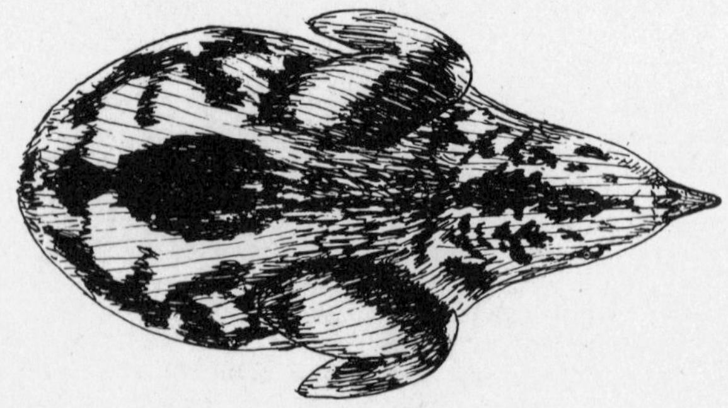

Turkey: dorsal pattern of downy chick.

rarely white, heavily spotted and speckled overall with light to dark brown or purplish-brown, and rarely buff. 63 × 45 mm. **Incubation.** By female alone. 28 days. **Nestling.** Precocial and downy. Down pinkish-cinnamon on head and back, slightly lighter on upper breast and flanks. Crown and upper parts heavily spotted with dark brown. Sides of head and underparts pale pinkish-buff to yellowish. Throat white. **Nestling period.** Young tended by female alone. Feed themselves and are brooded and guarded by adult. Wings grow rapidly and young can fly into trees at *c.* 2 weeks, and roost on branch with female. Broods remain together until winter.

CRANES *Gruidae*

Large, long-legged birds of marsh and grassland, preferring extensive areas of marshland for breeding. Nests are built by both members of the pair by sideways-throwing and sideways-building to produce large, low heaps of loose plant material. As is usual with this type of building the amount of material may vary considerably and on dry sites may be almost absent. Downy young appear very feeble at first and are carefully tended and fed directly by both adults, but soon become able to follow the adults from the nest. They grow very quickly but remain in down until well-grown. They tend to remain with the parents after fledging.

WHOOPING CRANE *Grus americana* **Pls. 9, 35**

Breeds in large marshes, open or with rank herbage. Nest on the ground, often surrounded by shallow water where material has been gathered to form nest.

Nest. A heap of plant material thrown in from around site, *c.* 4–5 ft. across, and 8–18 in. high. Central nest depression slight. **Breeding season.** Begins early May. Single-brooded. **Eggs.** Usually 2, sometimes 1, rarely 3. Subelliptical. Creamy-buff to olive-buff or greenish; spotted and blotched and finely speckled with light brown or darker reddish-brown and paler purple and lilac. 100 × 63 mm. **Incubation.** By both sexes. 33–35 days. **Nestling.** Precocial and downy. Down cinnamon to light brown, darker brown or rufous-brown along middle of back and on rump. Paler and grayer on neck. Drab buffish-gray or brownish-white on underside. Bill brown at tip, flesh-colored at base. Legs and feet brownish. **Nestling period.** Young tended by both parents. Leave nest within *c.* 1 day of hatching. Fly at *c.* 3½ months. Remain with adults until following year.

SANDHILL CRANE *Grus canadensis* **Pls. 9, 35**

Breeds in north on open tundra near water, or on grassy flats with drier ridges; further south in large marshes with some open water and areas of tall grasses or rushy vegetation. Nest on the ground. In north tends to be on low ridges and may be a dry hollow; but in water nests are large. More southerly nests usually in shallow water with vegetation, or on small islands, and screened by tall herbage or some shrubs.

Nest. A large heap of plant material thrown in from around site; with a slight central hollow; in dry sites may be only a hollow with a thin grass lining. **Breeding season.** Begins in January in Florida, April in mid-USA to mid-May in north. Single-brooded. **Eggs.** Usually 2, sometimes 1, rarely 3. Subelliptical to long subelliptical. Smooth and moderately glossy. Pale to medium buff to olive-buff; spotted and blotched with light to medium brown or reddish-brown, and with paler purple and lilac. The markings often concentrated towards the larger end. 94 × 60 mm. **Incubation.** Eggs laid at intervals of two days. Incubation by both sexes. 30–32 days. **Nestling.** Precocial and downy. Dark brown on top of head, tapering to forehead; forehead and sides of face light buff, with a darker line under eye becoming a dark mark in front of eye. Diamond-shaped dark brown area on upper back, tapering on mid-back and expanding to diamond-shaped area on rump. Hind neck gray, throat whitish, underside grayish-white. Bill dull flesh-color with dark tip. Irides gray. Legs and feet flesh-colored, becoming gray. **Nestling period.** Young tended by both parents. Hatch *c.* 1 day apart. Leave nest soon after both hatched. Fed directly by adults at first, on small items; begin to feed themselves in second week. Wing feathers begin to grow at *c.* 16 days. Young fly at *c.* 70 days. Remain with adults to following year.

Sandhill Crane: *c.* 3-4ft. across.

LIMPKINS *Aramidae*

LIMPKIN *Aramus guarauna* **Pls. 9, 35**

Breeds in marshes and swamp forests. Nest in sawgrass clumps, or on low trees, or bushes, overgrown with climbing plants; occasionally on a stump.

Nest. A loosely constructed saucer of plant stems, dead leaves, dead vines and various plant material, including Spanish Moss. In sawgrass the blades of growing plants are incorporated. The fragile nest is usually resting on a substantial base of growing plant material. **Breeding season.** Begins in January. Single-brooded. **Eggs.** Usually 4–8. Subelliptical. Smooth and slightly glossy. Pale creamy-buff or olive-buff, with spots and blotches of medium brown, dark brown, and pale gray or lilac. Markings mostly concentrated at the larger end. 59 × 44 mm. **Incubation.** No information. **Nestling.** Precocial and downy. Down long, soft and thick. Upper parts warm brown, paler on sides of head and on underparts. Almost white on chin. **Nestling period.** No information.

RAILS *Rallidae*

Birds of swamp and waterside, usually long-legged and preferring to swim rather than fly. They nest in low vegetation, by or just in water. The nests are bulky cups; and material is carried to the site. Clutches are relatively large. There is evidence that occasionally eggs or young may be carried to another site near by after disturbance of the nest. Downy young have a claw at the carpal joint of the wing.

KING RAIL *Rallus elegans* Pl. 35

Breeds in large freshwater marshes with rank vegetation. Nest on the ground in a grass tussock or waterside vegetation, or raised on plants growing in shallow water.

Nest. On dry sites a cup of grasses with growing stems pulled over to form a canopy. In wet site stems of plants are bent down to form a base and a substantial cup several inches thick is built up from plant material, and may be 6–18 in. up. Leaves are pulled over and interwoven to form a canopy. Nest *c.* 8–9 in. across, *c.* 1–4 in. thick. Nest built by both sexes. **Breeding season.** Begins early to mid-May. **Eggs.** Usually 8–11, sometimes 6–15. Subelliptical. Smooth and glossy. Creamy white or tinted very pale buff or pinkish-buff; with sparse spotting in dark reddish-brown and purple, and sometimes small blotches concentrated at the larger end. 41 × 30 mm. **Incubation.** By both sexes. 21–24 days. **Nestling.** Precocial and downy. Down short, thick and black. **Nestling period.** Young tended by both parents. Leave nest soon after hatching.

CLAPPER RAIL *Rallus longirostris* Pl. 35

Breeds on salt marshes. Nest on the ground, hidden in growing or dead herbage, or under a small bush; or raised above ground in a grass tuft or clump of rushes.

Nest. A bulky cup built up well above the ground in a concealed hollow. Of grasses and plant stems, lined with finer material. Growing plants are pulled over to form a canopy. Nest *c.* 7–10 in. diameter, 3–6 in. thick; with cavity 5–6 in. across and 1–1½ in. deep. **Breeding season.** Begins mid-March to mid-April. Single-brooded but lost clutches replaced. **Eggs.** Usually 8–11, sometimes 4–14. Replacement clutches may be only 4–6. Subelliptical to long subelliptical. Smooth and glossy. Very pale buff, pinkish-buff or creamy-white. Sparsely spotted or blotched with dark reddish-brown or purplish-red, and paler purple or gray. The larger markings sometimes concentrated towards the larger end. 42 × 30 mm. **Incubation.** By both sexes. 20–24 days. **Nestling.** Precocial and downy. Down black, with a slight greenish gloss on upper part, dull black on underside, and usually a little white down just below and behind the wings. **Nestling period.** Young tended by both parents. Leave nest soon after hatching. Can swim at 1 day.

VIRGINIA RAIL *Rallus limicola* **Pl. 9, 35**

Breeds on freshwater marshes or in rank vegetation bordering fresh water. Nest on the ground concealed in a grass tussock or waterside vegetation, or built up among plants on mud, or raised in tall vegetation in water.

Nest. A substantial cup, in a hollow, or built up well above water in a wet site, or suspended in bases of tall vegetation; of coarse grass, rushes, cat-tails and similar material. *c.* 8 in. diameter, with cup 4–5 in. across and rather shallow. Leaves or stems are pulled over to hide the nest. **Breeding season.** Begins early April in south and west to mid-May in north. **Eggs.** Usually 7–12. Subelliptical. Smooth and glossy. Creamy-white or faintly tinted buff or pinkish-buff; with sparse speckling, spotting and a few small blotches of light to dark reddish-brown and pale gray or purple. 32 × 24 mm. **Incubation.** By both sexes, beginning before completion of clutch. 20 days. **Nestling.** Precocial and downy. Down long, thick and rather coarse. Black with greenish gloss on back and bluish gloss on head. Sometimes a little white down under the wings. Bill longer than on Sora Rail, pinkish at first, then orange-red, with a broad black band across the middle. **Nestling period.** Young tended by both parents. Young leave nest soon after completion of hatching. Active, swimming and diving at an early age. Food is given to young by adults.

SORA RAIL *Porzana carolina* **Pls. 9, 35**

Breeds in swamps, sloughs, bogs and wet meadows. Nest raised in grass tussock or in bases of tall plants such as reed-mace or bulrushes, by water's edge or in water; sometimes in a more exposed site.

Nest. A substantial cup of dead reed-mace, sedges and grasses, with finer lining of grass and sedges. *c.* 6 in. across, 3 in. cavity *c.* 2 in. deep. Plants are pulled over to form a cavity and there may be a runway of nesting material leading up to it from the water. **Breeding season.** Begins late April in south to late May in north. Single-brooded. **Eggs.** Usually 8–12, sometimes 5–18. Subelliptical to oval. Smooth and glossy. Buff or olive-buff; with some minute dark speckling, and with sparse spots and small blotches of chestnut-red or light purple. 31 × 22 mm. **Incubation.** Eggs laid on consecutive days. Incubation by both sexes beginning with first to third egg. 16–20 days. **Nestling.** Precocial and downy. Down long with fine silky tips. Black, with tip of upper parts glossed greenish. Tuft at apex of chin, of long and coarse, hair-like yellowish down. **Nestling period.** Young tended by both parents. Eggs hatch over several days. Young leave nest within 1–2 days of hatching, but may return for brooding at night. Can fly at *c.* 36 days.

YELLOW RAIL *Coturnicops novaboracensis*

Probably breeds over a wide area but nest rarely found. Where found nests are in bogs or wet meadows, on the ground in grassy vegetation, or among grasses or plant tufts in several inches of water.

Nest. A thick cup of plant material, concealed in a natural hollow with an overhanging tuft of vegetation or with grasses bent over to form a concealing canopy. 4–5 in. diameter, 1–1½ in. thick, with rather deep cup. **Breeding season.** Begins in May? **Eggs.** Usually 8–10. Subelliptical to oval. Slightly glossy and smooth. Warm buff; with sparse marking of fine spots and specks of light reddish-brown and lilac, usually mostly concentrated in a small cap or wreath at the larger end. 28 × 21 mm. **Incubation.** No information. **Nestling.**

Sora Rail: *c.* 7-9ins. across.

Precocial and downy. Down long and glossy black. No bare patch on forehead. Bill pinkish-flesh. Feet grayish-brown. **Nestling period.** Young leave the nest soon after hatching.

BLACK RAIL *Laterallus jamaicensis* **Pls. 9, 35**

Breeds on salt or brackish marshes. Nest on the ground concealed in a tuft of grasses or *Salicornia*.

Nest. A neat, small and deep cup of grasses and sedges, overhanging adjacent grasses or plant stems being pulled and woven together to form a concealing canopy. 4–5 in. across, cup about 3½ in., and 2¼ deep. **Breeding season.** Begins mid-March. **Eggs.** Usually 6–10, sometimes up to 13. Subelliptical to elliptical. Smooth and moderately glossy. White, or faintly tinted buffish or pinkish, with very fine speckling in reddish-brown and purple; mainly concentrated towards the larger end. 26 × 20 mm. **Incubation.** No information. **Nestling.** Precocial and downy. Down black. **Nestling period.** No information.

PURPLE GALLINULE *Porphyrula martinica* **Pls. 9, 35**

Breeds in marshes and by ponds, lakes and rivers where tall dense waterside vegetation occurs. Nest on the ground in tall marsh herbage, or among plants

growing in water, on branches of shrubs at water level, and exceptionally in more open sites.
Nest. A bulky cup of dead or green plant material, built up well above the water. May be up to 8 in. thick and 8–10 in. across, with cup *c.* 3 in. deep. **Breeding season.** Begins early to mid-April. **Eggs.** Usually 6–8, sometimes 5–10. Subelliptical to oval. Smooth and slightly glossy. Pale creamy-buff to cream-colored, with speckling and fine spotting in dark reddish-brown and light purple. 39 × 29 mm. **Incubation.** No information. **Nestling.** Precocial and downy. Down, thick and long, but scanty around bill and eyes. Black, glossy on the back, dull on the underside, and on crown cheeks and throat retains sheaths, appearing whitish and hair-like. Bill yellowish at base, black towards end with white tip. **Nestling period.** No information.

COMMON GALLINULE *Gallinula chloropus* **Pls. 9, 35**
Breeds at the edge of waters of all kinds, from lakes and rivers to tiny marshes and ditches. Nest usually on the ground by water, or among plants in water, but sometimes above ground in thick shrubs or in large old nests of other birds in trees. Additional nests may be built in territory, especially in marshy sites, and are used for brooding young.
Nest. Usually a bulky platform of dead plant material and debris. Tall growing plants near by are pulled over to conceal it. Built by both sexes, the male bringing most of the material. **Breeding season.** Begins early to mid-May. **Eggs.** Usually 5–11, sometimes 2–21, but larger clutches may be from two females. Subelliptical. Smooth and glossy. Grayish-white to pale buff or greenish, with spots or small blotches of reddish-brown and blue-gray. 44 × 31 mm. **Incubation.** Eggs laid on consecutive days. Incubation by both sexes, and may begin at various times in the laying period. 19–22 days. **Nestling.** Precocial and downy. Down long and black with long fine tips except on head. Sparse round eye and bill. Black, glossed green above, browner below; and on chin, throat and sides of head coarse, with whitish sheaths. Down thin on top of head, skin shows light blue on crown, pinkish on nape. Bill red and orange with yellow tip, fading after *c.* 3 weeks to dull yellowish-green. Legs and feet blackish-olive. **Nestling period.** Young may hatch together or over a period, and stay in the nest for several days, tended by both parents. Young of earlier broods of same year may help to feed later ones. Young able to feed alone in 3 weeks, independent in 5 weeks, and can fly in 6–7 weeks. Tend to remain with adults for some period after.

AMERICAN COOT *Fulica americana* **Pls. 9, 36**
Breeds on lakes, larger pools and slower rivers, usually with waterside vegetation. Also in swamps with some open water and tall reeds or similar cover. Nest usually on the ground among reeds or growing vegetation in or by water, or at water level in branches lying in or hanging into water. Extra nest platforms may be built and used by young for resting.
Nest. A bulky cup of dead leaves and stems of waterside plants. Often well raised. Both sexes build, the male bringing most material, the female building it in. **Breeding season.** Begins mid-April in south to mid-May in north. **Eggs.** Usually 6–9, sometimes 5–15. Subelliptical, smooth and slightly glossy. Pale buffish-stone, fairly uniformly marked overall with specks and fine spots of dark brown and black. 49 × 34 mm. **Incubation.** Eggs laid on consecutive days.

Incubation by both sexes, beginning early in the laying of the clutch, or with the first egg. 21–24 days. **Nestling.** Precocial and downy. Down thick and soft, with long, fine hair-like tips except on the underside. Grayish on underside, black on back and head. Reddish to orange waxy tips on down of neck, throat and front of head, yellow sheaths on down of mantle and wings. On larger young reddish tips and sheaths are lost and the bird is black above, and white on the throat, front of neck and belly. Bare crown reddish, blue skin over eyes. Bill reddish, white-tipped. Legs and feet blackish-gray. **Nestling period.** Young may hatch over several days. Tended by both parents. Usually brooded by the female and fed by male for first 3–4 days. Later young follow adults, and are brooded on nest or platforms. Adults tend to divide brood and feed certain young only. Young feed themselves by 1 month; independent at 8 weeks.

JACANAS *Jacanidae*

JACANA *Jacana spinosa* **Pls. 11, 35**

Breeds on marshes, lakes and other areas of open water which are in part covered with floating plants which will support the birds. The nest is laid on a mass of floating plants, or on water hyacinths or lily pads, and is at water level, sometimes sinking slightly into the water when the bird is sitting. The male is smaller and duller in color than the female and the sex roles are reversed, the male incubating the eggs and caring for the young alone.

Nest. An often thin, damp layer of water plant material, or a few loosely-arranged stems, lying on plants floating on the surface. **Breeding season.** Begins late April. **Eggs.** Usually 3–4. Subelliptical to oval or sometimes elliptical. Smooth and highly glossy. Golden-buff to buff or golden-brown, heavily scrawled and scribbled overall with irregular patterns of thin black lines. 30 × 22 mm. **Incubation.** By male alone. **Nestling.** Precocial and downy. Down white below and on sides of face. Crown of head orange-buff with a dark band extending on to crown from nape, and narrow black line from nape to eye on each side. There is a chestnut band down mid-back, with blackish edges, bordered by a pair of whitish-buff bands and outside these a dark brownish bank along each flank with a blackish inner edge. Wings brown with pale tips and dark fore-edges. Dark patch on thigh. **Nestling period.** Tended by male alone. Young can run and dive soon after hatching. The adult broods them under his wings, against the flanks, and reports of transport of young under the wings may be due to inadvertent closing of wings by an alarmed bird.

OYSTERCATCHERS *Haematopodidae*

AMERICAN OYSTERCATCHER *Haematopus palliatus* **Pls. 11, 36**

Breeds on open sites, on coastal beaches; among rocks, on islands, in dunes, or on shingle beds, occasionally on saltmarsh.

Nest. A shallow hollow, unlined or with pieces of dead plants, small stones, or other debris. **Breeding season.** Begins mid-April in south, to June in north. Single-brooded but lost clutches replaced. **Eggs.** Usually 3, rarely 2–4. Subelliptical to oval. Smooth and glossy. Yellowish with stone, grayish or buffish tints, more rarely greenish or brownish; variably marked, but usually boldly spotted, blotched or irregularly streaked with brownish-black markings which vary considerably in size. 56 × 39 mm. **Incubation.** By both sexes, usually but not invariably beginning with the last egg. 24–27 days. **Nestling.** Precocial and downy. Down dark grayish-black above, finely tipped and tinted with grayish-white and buff; white on the underside. A blackish band across the breast at lower edge of dark breast shield, and a dark line on flanks separating blackish back and white underside. A narrow dark line from eye to nape, along centre of crown, two narrow longitudinal lines on back, and one across wing. Legs and feet light gray, irides brown. Bill dark with pinkish base. **Nestling period.** Young tended by both parents. They remain at the nest for 1–2 days. Some food is brought to them. Later they follow parents and pick up their own food, but may still be given some food. They can swim at an early age, and crouch motionless if alarmed. Independent in 34–37 days; but bill not fully developed for adult feeding until 8–9 weeks.

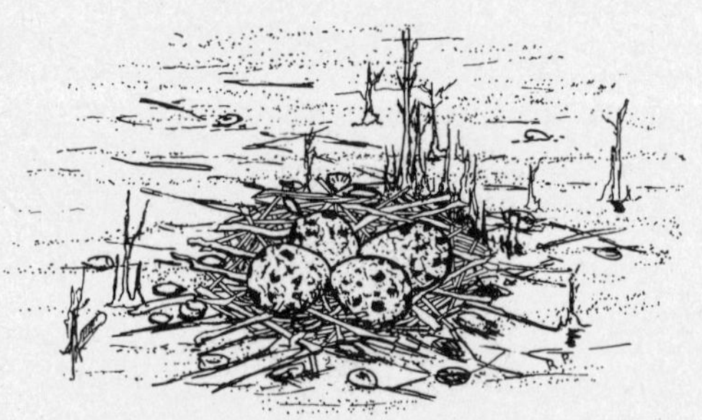

American Oystercatcher: *c.* 6-10in. across.

BLACK OYSTERCATCHER *Haematopus bachmani* **Pl. 36**

Breeds on coastal sites, preferring rocky shores, promontories and islands. Nest a hollow on the ground in shingle or turf, or on bare rock.

Nest. A shallow hollow, unlined or with a variable amount of small pebbles, fragments of shell, driftwood or other debris. Where dead plant material is present a gull-like nest is accumulated by sideways-building. Same site may be used in successive years. **Breeding season.** Begins late May to early June. Single-brooded, but lost clutches replaced. **Eggs.** Usually 2–3. Similar to those of American Oystercatcher in shape, color and size. **Incubation.** By both sexes. 26–27 days. **Nestling.** Precocial and downy. Down pattern like that of American Oystercatcher, but darker on face and back. **Nestling period.** Young tended by both adults. Begin to take insects at 5 days and some shellfish by 30 days. Young active but do not follow adults until 3–5 weeks. Fly at *c.* 5 weeks. Apparently continue to receive food from parents for a long period.

AVOCETS AND STILTS *Recurvirostridae*

Wading birds of shallow lagoons and muddy shores, nesting on sparse vegetation or dry mud near water. Nest-making, as in most other waders, by sideways-throwing and sideways-building. Young downy, with slender bills and legs, pale grayish or buffish with sparse dark marks.

BLACK-NECKED STILT *Himantopus himantopus* **Pls. 11, 39**

Breeds by water in shallow areas of lagoons, or edges of lakes or flood waters; where water is of little depth or muddy. Usually nests in colonies. Nest is on plant tuft or tussock in water, or built up in very shallow water, or on mud by the water's edge. Conditions may vary through change of water level during nesting.

Nest. A shallow hollow; with very variable amount of nest material which may be a few scraps in dry sites or a built-up accumulation of plant debris in wet sites. Material may be added during incubation if water level rises. **Breeding season.** Variable; beginning mid-April to early May. Single-brooded. **Eggs.** Usually 4, often 3, sometimes 5. Subelliptical to oval. Smooth but only slightly glossy. Pale brownish-buff, variable but usually marked with small black spots and blotches and sometimes grayish markings. Very similar to those of Avocet. 44 × 31 mm. **Incubation.** By both sexes. 25–26 days. **Nestling.** Precocial and downy. Down white below and finely freckled with pale gray and pale buff above, grayer on neck. Thin broken blackish line along mid-crown. Thin line through

Black-necked Stilt: *c.* 10in. across.

the eye and fine mottling on the head. Broader, very broken double blackish line down middle of upper back terminating in a dark spot on lower back; and broken blackish line along each flank. Thin black line on fore-edge of wings. **Nestling period.** Young tended by both parents, running and feeding soon after hatching. Independent at *c.* 4 weeks.

AMERICAN AVOCET *Recurvirostra americana* **Pls. 11, 39**

Breeds in open areas on the edges of salt or brackish lagoons, or on low islands, sands or mudflats, or meadows by salt or brackish waters. Usually nests colonially. Nest in the open on bare dry mud or sand near the water's edge, or in short sparse vegetation.

Nest. A shallow hollow, lining often absent or very sparse, usually a little dead plant material. **Breeding season.** Begins mid-April in south, to mid-May in north. Single-brooded. **Eggs.** Usually 4, sometimes 3–5, rarely less. Subelliptical to oval. Smooth, but non-glossy or with slight gloss. Pale brownish-buff, very variably marked but usually with scattered small spots and blotches of black, and rarely some gray spots. Very similar to those of Black-necked Stilt. 50 × 35 mm. **Incubation.** By both sexes. 22–24 days. **Nestling.** Precocial and downy. Down soft and silky; white on underside and pale buffish-gray on back. Pattern variable and very broken. Thin dark mark from bill through eye. Thin broken line or mottling along mid-crown. Sparse black blotches indicate relict paired lines in mid-back; single mid-line on lower back and line along each flank. Bill short, slender and almost straight at first. Bill blackish, legs and feet gray with orange edges to webs. **Nestling period.** Young tended by both parents, running and feeding themselves soon after hatching. Independent in *c.* 6 weeks.

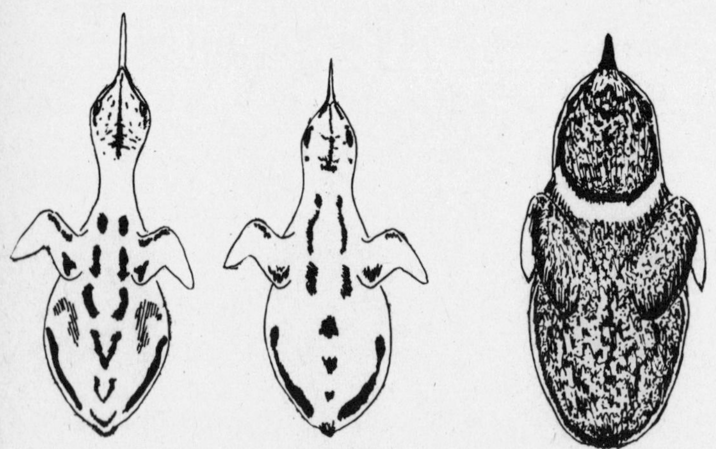

Dorsal pattern of downy chicks: *left,* Black-necked Stilt; *centre,* American Avocet. *right,* Semipalmated Plover.

PLOVERS *Charadriidae*

Short-billed waders, inhabiting drier terrain, and nesting on open ground with vegetation very short or absent. The nest is a shallow scrape, but often placed where it commands a view of surrounding country. Eggs tend to be more rounded and less pyriform than those of typical waders. Usually 3 or 4 eggs in a clutch. Young can run as soon as down is dry and may leave the nest quickly. Appear not to feed for first 24 hours. They crouch motionless when alarmed and may do so even when well-grown.

RINGED PLOVER *Charadrius hiaticula* **Pl. 36**

Usually breeds on open areas of shingle, sand, or mud, most often on the seashore; but also on bare or shingly areas at higher altitudes. Nest is on the ground.

Nest. A shallow scrape on the ground; usually exposed, but often near or sometimes sheltered by plant tuft. Lining varies with the availability of near-by material, and varies from tiny pebbles and debris to plant material. **Breeding season.** Begins mid-June. **Eggs.** Usually 4, rarely 3 or 5. Shorter pyriform or oval. Smooth and glossless or slightly glossy. Color and markings very variable. Pale bluish-gray, grayish-buff, stone-buff, yellowish or intermediate; usually marked with profuse blackish-brown and pale gray spots, sometimes with larger sparser black blotching or almost immaculate. 36 × 26 mm. **Incubation.** By both sexes, usually commencing before completion of clutch. 23–26 days. **Nestling.** Precocial and downy. Down pattern similar to that of Semipalmated Plover but ground color of back and head lighter. **Nestling period.** Young tended by both adults. Independent in *c.* 25 days.

SEMIPALMATED PLOVER *Charadrius semipalmatus* **Pls. 11, 36**

Breeds on coast or shoreline, on areas of sand, shingle, gravel or similar rubble; also away from water on gravel tundra or thin turf. Usually semi-colonial.

Nest. A hollow scrape; unlined or lined with a little debris, pebbles or shell fragments from near by. **Breeding season.** Begins early June in south to late June in north. Single-brooded, possibly double-brooded in south. **Eggs.** Usually 4, rarely 3–5. Shorter oval to pyriform. Smooth and slightly glossy. Buff, or pale creamy-buff or olive-buff. Heavily spotted and blotched with black, and with finer spots and specks of black and pale gray. Markings sometimes more concentrated towards larger end, large blotches sometimes black and brown. Eggs consistently more heavily marked than those of Ringed Plover. 33 × 23 mm. **Incubation.** By both sexes but mainly by male. 23 days. **Nestling.** Precocial and downy. Down white on underside to throat; white collar circling neck. Upperparts of body and crown dark grayish-buff, buffer on the mantle and wings, finely mottled overall with spots and short streaks of blackish-brown. Forehead white, a dark band bordering upper edge of collar round nape from eye to eye, and dark line from eye to bill. Sometimes a black broken line along mid-crown. Dark line to hind-edge of collar, and partial paired dark lines on mantle, dark band along flank bordering back. Short dark band across upper fore-edge of wing and dark band along hind-edge. **Nestling period.** Young tended by both parents. Active, leaving nest soon after hatching, and finding their own food. Guarded and brooded by adults. Young fly at 22–31 days.

PIPING PLOVER *Charadrius melodus* **Pl. 36**

Breeds on the higher parts of sandy shores, on the coast or larger inland lakes. Nest on the ground.

Nest. A shallow scrape. Unlined or lined with fragments of shells, driftwood or small pebbles. **Breeding season.** Begins late April on coast to late May inland. Single-brooded, but lost clutches replaced. **Eggs.** Usually 4, sometimes 3 in replacement clutches, exceptionally 5. Oval to pyriform. Smooth and non-glossy to slightly glossy. Creamy or ivory, to very pale creamy-buff; finely speckled and spotted with black and gray, the markings usually denser at the larger end, smaller and more sparse elsewhere. 32 × 24 mm. **Incubation.** By both sexes. 27 days. **Nestling.** Precocial and downy. Down white below, and white collar round hind-neck. Back, and upper parts of head, speckled buff and grayish and spotted with blackish-brown. Forehead buffish-white, and the dark speckling on crown may form a dark chevron at center. Dark spots on wings and thighs. **Nestling period.** Young tended by both parents. Fly at *c.* 30–35 days.

SNOWY PLOVER *Charadrius alexandrinus* **Pl. 36**

Breeds on open areas of shingle, sand or mud, most frequently on or near the sea but also on edges of saline lagoons or mud flats inland, and on areas of dry mud with scanty vegetation near brackish water. Nest is on the ground.

Nest. A hollow scrape; unlined or sparsely lined with fragments of plants and debris. Eggs are often partly buried. **Breeding season.** Begins from early April in south to early May in north. Probably double-brooded. **Eggs.** Usually 3, sometimes 2 or 4. Shorter oval to pyriform. Smooth but non-glossy. Buff, or sandy, sometimes tinted olive; with irregular lines and fine spots in black and pale gray. Markings at times concentrated towards the larger end. 33 × 23 mm. **Incubation.** By both sexes. 24 days. Eggs in sandy sites are often partially buried when found if adults are disturbed. **Nestling.** Precocial and downy. Down pattern like Semipalmated's but back and crown light creamy-buff with blackish mottling. Dark nape edge to crown absent; and dark streak from bill to eye faint or absent. **Nestling period.** As for Semipalmated Plover.

WILSON'S PLOVER *Charadrius wilsonia* **Pls. 11, 36**

Breeds on dunes, beaches or reefs. Nest on the ground in the open on sand and shingle; often by a piece of driftwood or some large object, or by grass tuft.

Nest. A shallow scrape, unlined or lined with fragments of shells and pebbles. **Breeding season.** Begins early April in south to early May in north. Single-brooded. **Eggs.** Usually 3, sometimes 2, rarely 4. Oval to short oval. Smooth and non-glossy to slightly glossy. Very pale creamy-buff to cream-colored. Heavily spotted and speckled and with more sparse small blotches and scrawls of black and pale gray. 36 × 26 mm. **Incubation.** By both sexes. 24–25 days. **Nestling.** Precocial and downy. Down grayish-white on underside and face. Broad white collar round hind-neck. Forehead buffish-white. Back and upper parts of head pale buffish very heavily speckled with black. Paired irregular lines on crown. Narrow paired black lines down mid-back, joining on the lower back. Black line along flank to tail, bordering pattern. Black line along wing. **Nestling period.** Young tended by both parents. Leave nest soon after hatching.

KILLDEER *Charadrius vociferus* **Pls. 11, 36**

Breeds in open spaces, usually on short turf or on bare sandy or gravelly areas. Often around lakes, ponds and rivers; also in meadows, on golf courses, airports and similar areas of open turf; and on bare cultivated land, or bare stony ground, gravel road, and railroads, and one record of a large gravelled roof being used.

Nest. A shallow scrape, unlined, or lined with near-by material – pebbles, woodchips, plant fragments and any small debris – sparsely lining the cavity. **Breeding season.** Begins mid-March in south to early April in north. Sometimes double-brooded. **Eggs.** Usually 4, rarely 3–5. Pyriform to oval. Smooth, non-glossy to slightly glossy. Very pale buff or creamy-buff; heavily marked with specks, spots and blotches or scrawls of black, blackish-brown and pale gray. Markings often overall, sometimes with a grouping of larger markings towards the larger end. 36 × 27 mm. **Incubation.** By both sexes. 24 days. **Nestling.** Precocial and downy. Down white on underside, with white on lower half of face continuing as collar round hind-neck, separated from underside by a black chest band. Forehead whitish with black band across forehead between eyes, from eye to base of bill, and around upper edge of white collar bordering nape. Crown of head and back mottled finely in buff and grayish-brown, with short broken black band along mid-back, and black edges to back pattern. Elongated tail tuft blackish, and barred at base. **Nestling period.** Young tended by both parents. Young leave nest soon after hatching and are often led to near-by water. They are brooded and guarded by adults, but feed themselves. First fly at *c.* 40 days.

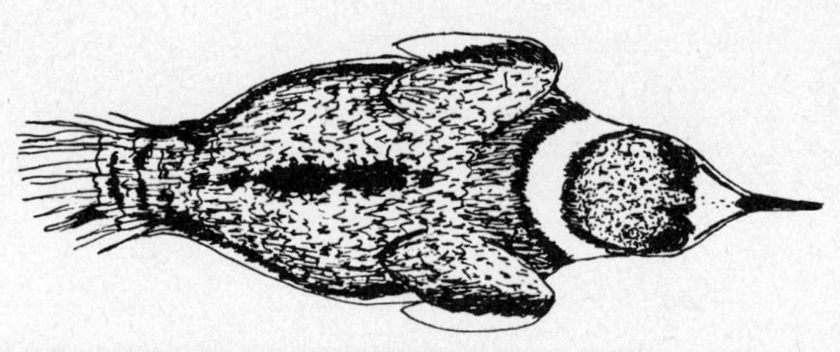

Killdeer: dorsal pattern of downy chick.

MOUNTAIN PLOVER *Charadrius montanus* **Pl. 36**

Breeds on shortgrass prairie or arid, high plains. Nest on the ground in an exposed site.

Nest. A shallow hollow, unlined, or lined with pieces of earth and plant material. **Breeding season.** Begins late April in south to late May in north. **Eggs.** Usually 3. Female may lay two clutches in two nests, one after the other with the same or a different mate. Oval. Smooth and slightly glossy. Drab light olive, or olive-buff, rarely pinkish-buff; finely speckled, spotted and scrawled with black and gray. 37 × 28 mm. **Incubation.** Eggs usually laid at 1–2-day intervals, exceptionally at longer intervals. By both sexes, or where more than one clutch laid, the first is incubated by male alone, the second by female. Period not recorded. **Nestling.** Precocial and downy. Down whitish below, pale yellowish-buff on flanks and more definite but pale yellowish-buff on back and head. Collar round hind-neck, and forehead, unmarked. Remainder of upper head and back and wings heavily spotted and mottled with black spots, those on the crown forming broken lines at times, and heaviest on hind-crown. Pale eye-stripe and thin dark line from eye to dark mark on ear-coverts. **Nestling period.** Young mostly tended by the single, incubating parent.

LESSER GOLDEN PLOVER *Pluvialis dominicus* Pls. 11, 36

Breeds on drier tundra areas, often on uplands; where ground herbage is scanty, often only mosses and lichens. Nests on the ground in an exposed site giving a wide view.

Nest. A shallow scrape, unlined, or lined with a variable amount of plant material. **Breeding season.** Begins late May in south of range to early or mid-June in north. Single-brooded. **Eggs.** Usually 4, sometimes 3–5, Pyriform. Smooth and slightly to moderately glossy. Buff, creamy-buff or ivory-yellow; heavily marked with spots and small blotches of black, and less frequently brown, and lighter shades of gray. Markings heaviest at or around the larger end. 48 × 33 mm. **Incubation.** By both sexes, but mainly by female. 27–28 days. **Nestling.** Precocial and downy. Down soft, with longer silky tips. Down grayish-white on underside. Back, head, thighs and wings are rich golden-yellow or greenish-yellow, finely mottled with black and with broken black patches of relic pattern. Crown thickly mottled black, but hind-neck and nape pale, unmarked or with a few dark marks down middle. Thin dark line through eye. Pale stripe above and below eye, with dark borders, form pale eye-patch. Forehead mainly yellow. **Nestling period.** Young tended by both parents. Adults may divide the brood between them but do not separate.

BLACK-BELLIED PLOVER *Pluvialis squatarola* Pl. 36

Breeds in arctic tundra regions, usually on a slightly raised area or ridge giving a wide view. Nest on the ground.

Nest. A shallow hollow sparsely lined with moss or lichen fragments. **Breeding season.** Begins late May in south-west of range to late June in north. **Eggs.** Usually 4, rarely 3. Oval to pyriform. Smooth but non-glossy or slightly glossy. Pale buff or grayish-stone, or sometimes tinged brownish, greenish, or reddish; variably spotted and blotched in black, and less frequently brown and pale gray. Marking tends to be concentrated towards the larger end, or in a zone around it. 52 × 36 mm. **Incubation.** By both sexes, but mainly by male. 27 days. **Nestling.** Precocial and downy. Down pattern like that of Lesser Golden Plover, but upper parts more grayish-buff and less golden. Markings larger and with more marbled effect. There is a bold white collar around nape. **Nestling period.** Young tended by both adults.

SANDPIPERS, SNIPE, PHALAROPES *Scolopacidae*

Small to medium, long-legged wading birds, occurring in a variety of habitats, but usually by water. Nest usually a hollow in the ground. Nest-lining added by sideways-throwing and sideways-building, and there may be considerable variation according to the nature of the site and the material available near by. Nests may be in bare, open sites or hidden in herbage. In the latter sites growing plants are usually pulled together over the nest, concealing it. The Solitary Sandpiper is an exception in habitually using an existing platform, usually the old nest of another bird, in a tree. Usually 4 eggs, pyriform or oval, cryptically colored and patterned. Young are downy and also cryptically colored and patterned. The patterns are rather like those of game-bird chicks. The dorsal pattern is basically a dark central stripe which may be split by a paler median band; and at either side one or two more dark stripes. The pattern becomes irregular, the central stripe varying in width along its length, and in the *Calidris* sandpipers and in the Snipe the dark bands are partly concealed by pale buff or white dots formed by specialised brush-tips to some down filaments, and the pattern is often not obvious.

The part played by the adults varies between species. In some cases both sexes incubate and care for young; but in the Pectoral Sandpiper the female does it all, while in the phalaropes sex roles are reversed and the male alone cares for eggs and young. In a number of instances the male plays a major role either in incubation or care of the young. It has been found that in some species the female may lay two clutches, one of which is incubated by the male; or may do so but involve two males, sharing incubation with the last male; or may initiate several such male-incubated clutches. The young are precocial and usually leave the nest as soon as the down is dry after hatching, being led away to better feeding by the adults. In most instances the young feed themselves, but are brooded and guarded by the parents. In such circumstances it is difficult to be sure of the point where independence is achieved.

SURFBIRD *Aphriza virgata*

Breeds on rocky areas of mountains, above the tree-line. Nests are in dry sites on rocky ridges with sparse vegetation, the nest in the open affording a wide view.

Nest. A shallow hollow with a thin lining of nearby plant material. **Breeding season.** Begins late May to early June. **Eggs.** Usually 4. Pyriform. Smooth. Buff to pale buff; marked with spots and small blotches of buffish-brown, reddish-brown or dark brown, and paler purplish-gray, the markings usually concentrated at or around the larger end. 43 × 31 mm. **Incubation.** By both sexes? Period unknown. **Nestling.** Precocial and downy. Down on underparts grayish-white, whiter on belly and throat; on upperparts finely mottled with buffish-white, warm buff, brown and brownish-black. The crown is more heavily marked with black, the sides of the head and the forehead are buffish-white spotted and mottled in black. The back and wings are browner, and there is some white spotting on head and back. **Nestling period.** Little information. Young tended by both parents, but mainly by male?

RUDDY TURNSTONE *Arenaria interpres* **Pls. 10, 37**

Breeds on open ground, usually on a small island near shore, or along river or delta; on bare stony area, but also among rocks or in rank herbage which shelters nest. Also on barren high ground, often near a source of water. Nest on the ground. Sometimes several near each other.

Nest. A shallow hollow; lining sometimes absent, or a variable lining of near-by vegetation, substantial at times. **Breeding season.** Begins in June. Single-brooded. **Eggs.** Usually 4, sometimes 3, rarely 5. Oval to short pyriform. Smooth, slightly glossy. Very pale green, bluish-green or light olive; usually irregularly blotched, spotted, and speckled with drab brown, olive-brown or blackish-brown, and paler gray markings. Most frequently marked with small blotches, tending to be densest at the larger end. Sometimes more heavily freckled with smaller markings. Marking often variably elongated into streaks slanting across shell. 40 × 29 mm. **Incubation.** By both sexes, at first mainly by female, with increasing help from male, beginning with third egg. 21–23 days. **Nestling.** Precocial and downy. Down white on underside, dark grayish-buff at sides of upper breast. Forehead and area round eyes buffish-white. Crown and sides of head around eye-patch mottled pale buff and blackish-gray; and black streak from bill to eye. Nape whitish, slightly mottled. Back yellowish-buff with blackish-gray mottling, at times in an indistinct triple-stripe pattern. Wing blackish with pale edge. **Nestling period.** Young tended by both adults, the male taking major share. Eggs hatch over 2 days. Young leave nest one day after completion of hatching and follow adults, but feed themselves. Fly at 24–26 days, when female usually leaves, but male may stay with brood a further two weeks.

BLACK TURNSTONE *Arenaria melanocephala*

Breeds on coastal tundra or offshore islands. Nest on wet tundra, near small open waters in grassy places. The nest is on the ground in an open site. A number of pairs may nest in close proximity.

Nest. A shallow hollow lined with grasses. **Breeding season.** Begins late May. Single-brooded. **Eggs.** Usually 4. Oval to short pyriform. Smooth, non-glossy to slightly glossy. Pale yellowish-olive to buffish-olive, or very pale greenish; marked with spots, small irregular blotches or scrawls, of buffish-olive, olive-brown and gray, sometimes poorly-defined. There are also markings of blackish-brown, the darker markings tending to be limited to the larger end, the others more overall in distribution. 41 × 29 mm. **Incubation.** By both sexes. 21 days. **Nestling.** Precocial and downy. Down pattern darker, finer and more uniform than that of Ruddy Turnstone. Down thick and soft. White on belly and chin. Remainder of head, body and wings finely and heavily spotted and speckled with black, pale gray and buffish-gray, to produce an overall effect of dark blackish-gray with a buffish tint in places. Upper breast dark gray. Blackish loral spot at base of bill. **Nestling period.** No information other than that young leave nest soon after hatching.

KNOT *Calidris canutus* **Pl. 38**

Breeds on barren ground at high or low altitudes, nesting on areas of bare stones and rock, scree or bare earth with some scanty vegetation. Nest sometimes made against a clump of vegetation.

Nest. A hollow lined thickly with lichens. **Breeding season.** Begins early to mid-June. Single-brooded. **Eggs.** Usually 4, rarely 3. Oval to pyriform. Smooth, slightly glossy. Very pale, green to greenish-olive; with small blotches, spots, specks and short streaks or scrawls, in medium to dark brown and sparse purplish-gray. Markings usually small and fairly evenly distributed. 43 × 30 mm. **Incubation.** Probably by both sexes, beginning with third or fourth egg. 20–25 days? **Nestling.** Precocial and downy. Down of underside white, throat sometimes buffish. Head cream-colored, whiter or buffer. Broken blackish and buff patch on crown, dark line from bill to crown, side of bill to eye, parallel low streak and dark irregular markings on ear-coverts. Nape whitish. Back mottled warm or grayish-buff and blackish-brown, finely dotted with creamy-white. **Nestling period.** Young tended mainly by male; leave nest soon after hatching and gradually move to more heavily vegetated area. Can fly at *c.* 18 days. Independent in *c.* 3 weeks?

SANDERLING *Calidris alba* **Pls. 10, 39**

Breeds on the tundra, usually near the coast, on drier sites with areas of stones or gravel scattered among clumps of low plants and herbage. Nest on the ground, usually against a clump of vegatation.

Nest. A neat deep cup well lined with dead willow leaves, or other plant material. **Breeding season.** Begins late June to July. Single-brooded, but possibly two clutches laid serially. **Eggs.** Normally 4, exceptionally 3. Pyriform to oval. Smooth and moderately glossy. Light olive or greenish; blotched, speckled, spotted or scrawled, with dull olive-brown, and purplish-gray. Markings tend to be concentrated towards the larger end, sparser towards the narrow end. 36 × 25 mm. **Incubation.** Eggs laid at 26–29-hour intervals. By both sexes, possibly mainly by female, beginning with completion of clutch. 23–24 days. In some instances female may possibly lay two clutches, one being incubated by her, the other by the male; incubation of the first clutch being delayed by 5–6 days. **Nestling.** Precocial and downy. Down on underside white, tinted light buff on throat. On upper parts buff, mottled with black and finely dotted with white. Black line from bill to crown, two from base of bill to eye; a few black marks on cheeks. Bill gray with black tip. Legs and feet black to bluish-black or greenish-gray. **Nestling period.** Young tended by both parents, but one appears to take major part. Possibly only one present if two clutches are produced. Leave nest soon after hatching. Fly at 17 days. Independent in 23–24 days.

SEMIPALMATED SANDPIPER *Calidris pusillus* **Pl. 39**

Breeds on grassy tundra, on areas of ridges and hummocks, usually near pools of water; or on dunes. Nest usually in herbage, often partly concealed by a tuft of vegetation.

Nest. A shallow hollow, lined with grasses, moss and dead leaves, *c.* 1½–2 in. diameter. **Breeding season.** Begins early to mid-June. Single-brooded. **Eggs.** Usually 4. Pyriform to oval. Smooth and glossy. Very pale olive, greenish or buff; very heavily spotted with reddish-brown, or more sparsely spotted, blotched or scrawled with dark brown or purplish-brown, and pale purple or gray. Speckling sometimes elongated into tiny streaks. 30 × 21 mm. **Incubation.** By both sexes. 17–19 days. **Nestling.** Precocial and downy. Down with long silky tips, but white-tipped (brush-tipped) down shorter. Underparts grayish-white, slightly buff on upper breast. Upper parts warm buff and blackish-brown in an ill-defined pattern, with areas of fine white tips along the dark parts. Buffish-white face with pair of small dark marks by bill, and some on ear-coverts. A brown stripe over eyes, broadening towards nape, and between these the dark crown is bordered by a pair of whitish lines converging at nape. Dark crown is golden-brown at nape, has narrow point at forehead, and short paired white marks on mid-crown. **Nestling period.** Young tended by both parents. Become independent early, before able to fly.

WESTERN SANDPIPER *Calidris mauri* **Pl. 39**

Breeds on raised and drier islands and ridges of heath tundra, surrounded by marsh areas and pools. Nest on the ground, usually under or partly hidden by a dwarf birch, heath or other plant tuft.

Nest. A shallow scrape formed by male, subsequently lined with lichen fragments and leaves, or other plant material. **Breeding season.** Begins late May. Single-brooded. **Eggs.** Usually 4, rarely 5. Pyriform to oval. Smooth and slightly glossy. Creamy-white to buffish or brownish; heavily speckled, spotted and blotched with light to dark reddish-brown and purplish-brown, and some faint grayish. The markings tend to be concentrated towards the larger end and often show spiral elongation. There may be a few blackish hair-lines or scrawls. 31 × 22 mm. **Incubation.** By both sexes, beginning with the next-to-last egg. 21 days. **Nestling.** Precocial and downy. Down whitish on belly and throat, and pale buff on breast. Cinnamon-buff on neck, sides of head and forehead. Blackish-brown crown patch, bordered by pale stripes from bill to hind-crown over eye. Paired pale marks on crown. Double dark marks at base of bill and dark markings on ear-coverts. Back, wings and thighs mottled heavily in black, brown and golden-brown, with an irregular pattern of pale buff tips on dark zones. Similar tips form the pale markings on the crown. **Nestling period.** Young tended by both parents. Leave nest soon after hatching, adults brooding and guarding the young. Young begin to fly and are independent at *c.* 17–18 days. Female may leave brood before this time.

RUFOUS-NECKED SANDPIPER *Calidris ruficollis*

Breeds on dry tundra or cottongrass bogs, or by water in high tundra. Nest on the ground in a tussock or hidden in growing herbage.

Nest. A small hollow lined with dry willow leaves and similar material. **Breeding season.** Begins mid-June. Single-brooded. **Eggs.** Usually 4. Pyriform to oval. Smooth and slightly glossy. Yellowish-buff; heavily speckled and spotted with reddish-brown or reddish-buff, with markings often concentrated in a zone around the larger end. 32 × 22 mm. **Incubation.** By female alone, or male may assist? Period not recorded. **Nestling.** Precocial and downy. Down whitish on underparts, but pale buff on breast. Neck, sides of head, forehead and eye-stripe bordering crown are warm buff. Crown blackish, variegated with brown, and with dark line down forehead. Broad dark mark from bill to eye. Upper parts are mottled in black, brown and warm buff (white or buff speckling is probably present, but lost on older young). **Nestling period.** Young tended by female only.

LEAST SANDPIPER *Calidris minutilla* **Pls. 10, 38**

Breeds in boggy places, with moss, grasses or sedges, usually close to water; sometimes on drier ridges or high ground. Nests in boggy sites usually on, or inside of a moss hummock or plant tuft. In drier sites usually by a heath-clump, shrub or small tree.

Nest. A small hollow, lined with dead leaves, grasses and stems. **Breeding season.** Early to mid-June. Single-brooded. **Eggs.** Usually 4. Pyriform to oval. Smooth and glossy. Creamy, tinted pale greenish, buff or reddish; with fine speckling and spotting, often dense, or sparser spotting and small blotches, in dark or medium brown or purplish-brown, and pale purple. Speckling often elongated into tiny streaks. 29 × 21 mm. **Incubation.** Apparently mostly by male. Period not recorded. **Nestling.** Precocial and downy. Down whitish on underside, tinted buffish on upper breast and sides of head and forehead. Black streak from bill to eye, and short malar streak. Dark marks on ear-coverts. Pale area around eye; blackish crown tapering to base of bill. Sides of crown, hind-crown and nape warm orange-buff with a little black mottling and four incomplete lines of whitish down tips. Back and wings mottled black and warm golden-brown, patterned with bands of whitish down tips, forming a diagonal cross on mid-back. **Nestling period.** Young tended by both adults.

WHITE-RUMPED SANDPIPER *Calidris fuscicollis* **Pl. 39**

Breeds on grassy or mossy tundra, from wet areas to dry eminences, but prefers wet, well-vegetated hummocks with persistent moisture. Nest on the ground, raised in a grass tussock, or moss hummock, in wet sites.

Nest. A shallow hollow, lined with dry grass, leaves and similar material. **Breeding season.** Begins early to mid-June. Single-brooded. **Eggs.** Usually 4 eggs. Pyriform to oval. Smooth and slightly glossy. Buff; spotted and blotched with medium to dark reddish-brown, mainly concentrated at larger end, and showing distinct spiral elongation; or pale green with similar markings in dark olive-brown and gray. 34 × 24 mm. **Incubation.** Eggs laid at intervals of *c.* 30 hours. Incubation by female only, beginning with completion of clutch. 22 days from laying to hatching of last egg. **Nestling.** Precocial and downy. Down on belly and throat whitish; on breast, sides of head, forehead and eye-stripe pale buff to buffish-white. The forecrown is warm brown, with a blackish stripe over forehead to bill, and sides of crown mottled blackish. Back and wings are variegated with dull tawny-brown and black; crown and back being patterned with zones of white down tips. **Nestling period.** Young tended by female only. Very active, leaving nest soon after hatching. Fly and are independent in *c.* 16–17 days.

BAIRD'S SANDPIPER *Calidris bairdii* **Pl. 38**

Breeds on tundra in dry areas with sparse grassy vegetation or low shrubby growth. Nest on the ground in fairly open site, or sheltered by a plant-tuft or rock.

Nest. A shallow hollow, sparsely lined with leaves and grasses, about 2½ in. across. **Breeding season.** Begins early June. Single-brooded. **Eggs.** Usually 4. Pyriform to oval. Smooth and glossy. Pale creamy-buff, or tinted pale buff, reddish or olive; with profuse speckling and spotting in reddish-brown and pale purple. Markings usually denser at the larger end and may be elongated. 33 × 24 mm. **Incubation.** By both sexes. 21 days. **Nestling.** Precocial and downy. Pale parts whiter than on other species. Underside, including breast, sides of face and forehead are white. Short dark malar streak and dark thin line through eye to blackish markings on ear-coverts. Blackish-brown crown

DUCKS (see also pl. 4). The downy young of these diving ducks are more boldly contrasting in color or more uniformly dark than those of dabbling ducks.

White-winged Scoter, *Melanitta fusca.* **page** 81

Black Scoter, *Melanitta nigra.* The Surf Scoter is similar but lacks the white spot over the eye and the down extends on to the upper bill as a wedge. 81

Common Eider, *Somateria mollissima.* The young of the King Eider is similar with more extensive paler buff on the face, and a dark eyestripe, and a pale underside. Steller's Eider has a more typical rounded head without the sloping forehead, and a light buff ring round the eye, with a streak back to the nape and a pale chin. The Spectacled Eider has a large buff spectacle mark around the eye, crossed by a dark streak, and down extending on to the bill base. 79

Harlequin Duck, *Histrionicus histrionicus.* 80

Oldsquaw, *Clangula hyemalis.* 80

Goldeneye, *Bucephala clangula.* Barrow's Goldeneye is similar. The Bufflehead is similar again but smaller and with some pale lateral spots on the back sometimes joining to form stripes. 82

Ruddy Duck, *Oxyura jamaicensis.* 83

Red-breasted Merganser, *Mergus serrator.* Common Merganser is paler and more rufous on side of head, with white streak from bill to below the eye, and small pale spot above it. The Hooded Merganser is less boldly marked; brown on back, head and upper breast, pale buffish-brown on cheeks and white on throat. 83

White-winged Scoter
Black Scoter
Common Eider
Harlequin Duck
Oldsquaw
Goldeneye
Ruddy Duck
Red-breasted Merganser

Bald Eagle
Golden Eagle
Osprey
Cooper's Hawk
Everglade Kite
Merlin
1st down
2nd down
Caracara
Turkey Vulture
Black Vulture

HAWKS and EAGLES. Young are downy, the down usually tinged white, buff or gray (see identification key, downy young). Hooked bill and sharp claws may help identify young, but young falcons and owls also share these characters, and some species of both use old nests of other raptors. Hawk and eagle young have two successive down coats, the first shorter and thinner, the second longer, coarser and usually darker. The various species are difficult to tell apart in early stages.

Bald Eagle, *Haliaeetus leucocephalus.* The White-tailed Sea Eagle has grayish-buff down. **page** 93

Golden Eagle, *Aquila chrysaetos.* 92

Osprey, *Pandion haliaetus.* 94

Cooper's Hawk, *Accipiter cooperii.* The second down is grayish on the Goshawk and purplish-buff to gray above on the Sharp-shinned Hawk. 87

Everglade Kite, *Rostrhamus sociabilis.* Down is buffish-white on Swallow-tailed Kite, upper parts tinged pinkish-buff on White-tailed Kite, buffish-brown on Mississippi Kite. 86

FALCONS. These also have two down coats like those of Hawks and Eagles. See also other comments under these species above.

Merlin (Pigeon Hawk), *Falco columbarius.* Shown here are both first and second down coats. Down is usually white on other falcon species, but second down buffish-gray on back on Peregrine. 97

Caracara, *Polyborus plancus.* 95

NEW WORLD VULTURES. Young downy, with two down coats on California Vulture, possibly on other? Down usually pale in color and absent altogether on head.

Turkey Vulture, *Cathartes aura.* 84

Black Vulture, *Coragyps atratus.* 84

has bordering white stripes converging on hind-crown and paired white marks on mid-crown. Back, wings and thighs mainly black with some lighter brown on flanks and wings; heavily spotted with white down tips. **Nestling period.** Young tended by both parents.

PECTORAL SANDPIPER *Calidris melanotos* **Pl. 38**

Breeds on grassy tundra of varying types, but at a dry site. Nest on the ground, usually concealed in grasses. Males possibly polygamous.
Nest. A shallow hollow, usually well-lined to form a definite nest of grass and leaves. 3–3½ in. diameter. **Breeding season.** Begins late May to early June. Single-brooded. **Eggs.** Usually 4. Pyriform to oval. Smooth and slightly glossy. Very pale olive or stone; heavily marked with small blotches and spots in dark brown or purplish-brown, and pale gray and purple; the markings often concentrated towards the larger end and showing some spiral elongation. 37 × 25 mm. **Incubation.** By female alone. 21–23 days. **Nestling.** Precocial and downy. Down of underside, head and forehead may be a warm orange-buff, or more whitish with warm buff on breast. Dark malar spot and thin black stripe through eye to hind-crown. Dark stripe down forehead from crown. Crown deep golden brown with blackish edges, and blackish median mark with paired white patches. Horseshoe-shaped pale buff stripe around hind and mid-crown, and broad brownish stripe from nape to above eye. Back mottled in warm golden-brown and black, with patterns of bands of whitish-buff down tips. **Nestling period.** Young tended by female alone.

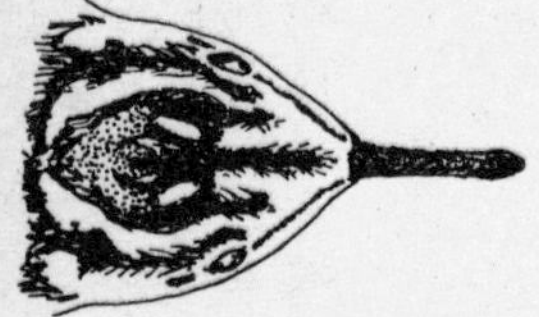

Pectoral Sandpiper: crown pattern of downy chick.

PURPLE SANDPIPER *Calidris maritima* **Pl. 38**

Breeds on the tundra, from sea-level to *c.* 1,500 ft., on barer, more open, peaty ground with some low shrubby cover and herbage, from ridge-tops and summits to hill-sides and tops of dry shingle ridges. Nest on the ground in the open.
Nest. Nest a fairly deep hollow lined with dead leaves. Nest hollow formed by male. **Breeding season.** Begins mid-May to early June. Single-brooded. **Eggs.** Usually 4, sometimes 3, subelliptical to oval and pyriform. Smooth and slightly glossy. Similar in appearance to Dunlin eggs but a little larger. Light to very pale olive, green or bluish-green; variably blotched, spotted, speckled or scrawled in drab, dark brown or olive-brown, and some pale purplish-gray. most typically blotched and with scattered smaller markings, tending to be sparser towards narrow end and largely concentrated towards larger end. Larger markings often show elongation and slant. 37 × 26 mm. **Incubation.** By both birds, but mainly by male. 21–22 days. **Nestling.** Precocial and downy. Down on underparts grayish-white with dark bases. On crown, ear-coverts and upperparts mottled yellowish-buff and blackish-brown with fine white dots. Forehead, forecrown, nape and sides of head otherwise light buff. Dark line from bill to crown, from side of bill above eye to nape, and short moustache streak. **Nestling period.** Young tended by male alone. Independent at *c.* 3–4 weeks.

ROCK SANDPIPER *Calidris ptilocnemis* **Pl. 38**

Breeds on tundra from sea-coast to hill-sides and mountain ridges, like Purple Sandpiper. Nest on the ground in the open.

Nest. A deep hollow lined with grasses and leaves; *c.* 3 in. across and *c.* 2 in. deep. **Breeding season.** Begins in early June. **Eggs.** Usually 4. Pyriform to oval. Smooth and slightly glossy. Pale green or olive; heavily spotted and blotched with medium to dark brown; usually concentrated at or around the larger end and sometimes showing spiral elongation. **Incubation.** Eggs usually laid at daily intervals. Incubation by both sexes. 20 days? **Nestling.** Precocial and downy. Down of underside, including breast, neck and throat, pure white. Head warm buff on upper parts, paler on sides. Converging loral and malar stripes. Crown mottled and striped black and buff, with tapering black stripe to bill. Nape dull and mottled. Back wings and thighs warm golden-brown and buff, mottled with black and patterned with narrow bands of bold buffish-white down tips. Hour-glass pattern of mid-back, typical of calidrine sandpipers, often well-defined. **Nestling period.** Young tended by both sexes, more specially by male. Young leave the nest soon after hatching.

CURLEW SANDPIPER *Calidris ferruginea*

Breeds on open tundra. Nest on the ground on slightly raised areas, in low grasses and sedges.

Nest. A shallow scrape among low herbage, with little or no lining. **Breeding season.** Begins mid-June. **Eggs.** Usually 4, sometimes 3. Long oval to pyriform. Smooth and glossy. Light olive-green; blotched, spotted and very sparsely speckled with dark olive-brown, blackish-olive, or reddish-brown. Markings tend to be more concentrated at larger end and to show some slanting elongation. 36 × 26 mm. **Incubation.** By female alone, male leaving after egg-laying. Period not recorded. **Nestling.** Precocial and downy. Pattern similar to that of Dunlin, but paler and yellower upperparts, more rufous on wings, ear-coverts and crown. Forehead, sides of breast and upper breast yellowish-buff, lower breast and belly white. Narrow black streak through eye, widening on nape. Pale patch around eye with dark, lower edge. Blackish square crown patch, bordered by pale buff stripes converging on nape, with small pale spots; lighter mottled area on mid-crown and narrow dark line to base of bill. Bill blackish. Legs and feet purplish-gray. **Nestling period.** Young tended by female only.

DUNLIN *Calidris alpina* **Pl. 39**

Breeds on tundra with pools and bogs, lowland grassy areas with similar water, or grassy coastal salt marshes. Nest on the ground, often on a slight eminence. Often a number of pairs nest in some proximity.

Nest. A cup-like hollow in a grass tussock, lined with grass or leaves. **Breeding season.** Begins late May to early June. Single-brooded. **Eggs.** Normally 4, occasionally 2–6. Oval to short pyriform. Smooth and slightly glossy. Pale to very pale olive or greenish, or blue-green; blotched, spotted, or speckled with dark brown, olive-brown and occasional pale purplish-gray. Markings very variable. Small specklings tend to be profuse, larger blotching more sparing. Markings often concentrated towards the larger end where they may form a cap. Larger markings often slanting and elongated. 36 × 28 mm. **Incubation.** By both sexes. 21–22 days. **Nestling.** Precocial and downy. Down of underparts white, breast tinted yellowish-buff. Head yellowish-buff, paler on cheeks, and back yellowish-tawny; both patterned with blackish-brown, the dark parts of the back being finely dotted with pale buff. Head has dark line from top of bill to crown, and crown mottled dark blackish and yellowish-tawny. Dark streak from side of bill to eye, and small moustache streak. Nape dark; back mottled dark and light. **Nestling period.** Female does most brooding for first few days. Both parents present at first, later only male may be apparent. Independent in *c.* 25 days; and flying at *c.* 28 days.

STILT SANDPIPER *Micropalama himantopus* **Pl. 39**

Breeds on open tundra, near marshy areas or shallow pools. Nest on the ground, among grasses, usually on slightly raised, drier sites. May be partly sheltered by a plant tuft.

Nest. A shallow hollow, unlined or sparsely lined with a few dead leaves and grasses. **Breeding season.** Begins mid- to late June. Single-brooded. **Eggs.** Usually 4. Oval to pyriform. Very pale creamy-olive or creamy-buff; blotched or spotted with reddish or purplish brown, and paler purple; often concentrated at or around the larger end and sometimes tending to show spiral elongation. 36 × 25 mm. **Incubation.** Eggs laid at an average 36-hour interval. Incubation by both sexes, usually male by day, female by night. 19–21 days. **Nestling.** Precocial and downy. Typical calidrine sandpiper pattern. Underside white and breast buffish; sides of head pale buff; forehead and throat drab white. Short black loral and malar streaks. Crown black, mottled brown, with black tapering stripe to bill. White band formed by down tips around crown, converging on hind-crown. Nape mottled. Back and wings mottled in black and warm golden-brown and patterned with narrow lines of bold white down tufts. **Nestling period.** Young leave nest soon after hatching. Tended by both parents at first, later by male only. Young left alone by 14 days. Can fly at 17–18 days.

BUFF-BREASTED SANDPIPER *Tryngites subruficollis* **Pl. 39**

Breeds on dry tundra, preferring grassy areas, with drier raised ridges where nests may occur. Nest in on the ground in an open site.

Nest. A shallow scrape, sparsely lined with dry grasses, dead leaves or moss. **Breeding season.** Begins in early June. Single-brooded. **Eggs.** Usually 4. Pyriform to oval. Smooth and slightly glossy. Very pale creamy, tinted greenish or olive; heavily blotched and spotted with medium to dark brown, the markings tending to be concentrated towards the larger end, and often showing slight spiral elongation. 37 × 26 mm. **Incubation.** Mainly by female. Period not recorded. **Nestling.** Precocial and downy. Down whitish below and brownish-gray above. The back mottled with blackish-brown in an irregular pattern, the dark areas more profusely spotted with zones of white down-tips. Dark eye-stripes to nape; and grayish-buff stripes above these bordering a dark crown patch with a poorly-defined short whitish chevron. **Nestling period.** No information.

COMMON SNIPE *Gallinago gallinago* **Pls. 10, 38**

Breeds in moist sites in a wide range of habitats at varying altitudes; in marshland, bogs and swamps, moorland, grassland, waterside vegetation, and sometimes in saltmarsh. Nest on the ground usually concealed in a clump of herbage partly pulled over to hide the nest. Exceptionally on bare sites.

Nest. A shallow hollow lined with grass. **Breeding season.** Begins mid-April to early June. Single-brooded. **Eggs.** Usually 4, sometimes 3. Oval to pyriform.

Smooth and slightly glossy. Very pale to pale green or olive, or deeper olive-buff to buff; exceptionally whitish-green. Marked with blotches, spots, specks and, more rarely, coarse scrawling, in dark brown, dark olive-brown, blackish-brown, reddish-brown and shades of gray or violet-gray. Markings often mainly small blotches, frequently rather sparing and often tending to be densest at the larger end. Sometimes with some blackish scrawling superimposed around the larger end. Blotches often irregular, or may show slanting elongation. 39 × 28 mm. **Incubation.** By female only, beginning with third or fourth egg. 18–20 days. **Nestling.** Precocial and downy. Down thick and soft. Dark chestnut-red and blackish-brown with fine white spots. Underparts pale tawny-buff with a pair of indistinct dark stripes down the front of the neck. Most of sides of head buffish-white, forming pale patch around eye, with warm buff patch on lower ear-coverts and streak from bill to over eye. Dark brown moustache streak, narrow dark streak from bill to eye. Dark patch on forehead separated from dark crown by pale transverse stripe. Rufous and blackish crown and nape patch bordered by pale stripe which constricts it over eyes. Pale streak across below eye. Mottling of body consists of median double dark streak with pale spots, and two pairs of lateral dark streaks with pale spots, but pattern is not obvious. Bill black, short and squat at first. **Nestling period.** Young tended by both parents. Leave nest as soon as down is dry. Apparently take food from parents' bills at first. Can fly at *c.* 19–20 days.

AMERICAN WOODCOCK *Scolopax minor* **Pls. 10, 38**

Breeds in drier woodland sites, in low shrubby cover, or tall herbage, bordering clearings, in thickets or under scrub oaks or pines, or in open woodland with dead leaf cover on ground. Usually near a moist area. Nest on the ground.
Nest. A hollow lined with dead leaves or other dry plant material from near by. **Breeding season.** Begins early January to February in south, to early April in north. **Eggs.** Usually 4, occasionally 3–5. Oval to short oval or subelliptical. Smooth and moderately glossy. Very pale creamy-buff, buff or creamy-olive; with spots, specks and blotches of light brown to reddish-brown and pale gray. Markings often rather sparse and sometimes concentrated around the larger end. 38 × 29 mm. **Incubation.** By female only. 20–21 days. **Nestling.** Precocial and downy. Underparts pinkish-cinnamon, upperparts light brownish-buff. Dark brown crown patch tapering forward to bill, narrowing on hind-crown and broadening on nape to extend along mid-back to tail and a dark band. Pale eye-stripes from the bill converge on the hind-crown as do the dark stripes through the eyes which join on the hind-edge of the ear-coverts with dark marks on the coverts. Dark bands along the sides from the shoulders meet the median band at the tail, and there is a dark band across the wing, and a thigh patch.

Downy chicks: *left*, Common Snipe, crown pattern; *right*, American Woodcock, dorsal pattern.

Bill is short at first. **Nestling period.** Young tended by female alone, led from nest soon after hatching, grow rapidly, can fly a little at 14–15 days. At 25 days well-grown and fly well.

SHORT-BILLED DOWITCHER *Limnodromus griseus* **Pls. 10, 39**
Breeds in muskegs, usually on mosses or sedges and at the base of a small tree or dead sapling.
Nest. A shallow hollow, a little above water level, lined with dry grasses, leaves and small twigs; *c.* 4 in. across. **Breeding season.** Begins late May to early June. Single-brooded. **Eggs.** Usually 4. Oval to pyriform. Smooth and slightly glossy. Pale greenish, olive or buff; speckled, spotted and blotched with dark brown and pale gray; the larger markings tending to wreath the larger end. 41 × 29 mm. **Incubation.** By both sexes? Period not recorded. **Nestling.** Precocial and downy. Sides of face, throat and breast are yellowish-buff, belly and chin whitish. Crown black with some brownish tips, tapering towards bill. Crown bordered by bold stripes over eyes, whitish by eyes and nape, otherwise buff. Black stripe from base of bill through eye to hind-edge of ear-coverts. Back and wings golden-brown with paired blackish-brown stripes down mid-back, and two short similar stripes along each side. Dark band and dark tips to wings. Bold white down tips border outer edge of paired dorsal stripes and occur along dark side stripes. **Nestling period.** Young tended by male alone?

LONG-BILLED DOWITCHER *Limnodromus scolopaceus* **Pl. 39**
Breeds in marshy areas and wet meadows near open water, on woodland edge or with scattered trees in more open areas. Nest on the ground among grasses or sedges.
Nest. A hollow, sparsely lined with grasses and small leaves. **Breeding season.** Begins late May to early June. Single-brooded. **Eggs.** Usually 4. Oval to pyriform. Smooth and slightly glossy. Pale greenish or olive. Speckled, spotted and blotched with medium to dark brown, and purplish-gray. Markings tending to wreath the larger end. 42 × 29 mm. **Incubation.** By both sexes at first, later by male alone. 20 days. **Nestling.** Precocial and downy. Down pattern like that of Short-billed Dowitcher, but ground color of back and wings a deeper brown. **Nestling period.** Young tended by male alone.

HUDSONIAN GODWIT *Limosa haemastica* **Pls. 10, 37**
Breeds on wet tundra near water at northern forest limits, and on bogs and marshes within the forest edge. Nest on the ground in a dry site on a grass tuft or a raised hummock.
Nest. A hollow sparsely lined with dry plant material. **Breeding season.** Begins mid-May in west to early June further east. Single-brooded. **Eggs.** Usually 4, sometimes 3. Pyriform to long oval. Smooth and moderately glossy. Pale to deep olive or greenish; with faint and indistinct spots, blotches and mottling in darker olive and gray; or with dark brownish spots or blotches concentrated at the larger end. 55 × 38 mm. **Incubation.** By both sexes. 22–23 days. **Nestling.** Precocial and downy. General down color very pale pinkish-buff, or pinkish-gray; becoming whiter on sides of face, throat and underside. Dark line from bill to eye. Forehead pale but squarish black patch on crown, with dark lateral spot at either corner on hind-crown, and narrow dark stripe down nape. Dark stripe continues down back, wider on shoulders; and on lower back widening to a lozenge shape with pale centre. Two dark patches on

wings, small one on foreflank, and dark band on hind-flank sometimes joining dorsal stripe at patch on rump. **Nestling period.** Young tended by both parents. Apparent tendency for adults to divide brood between them.

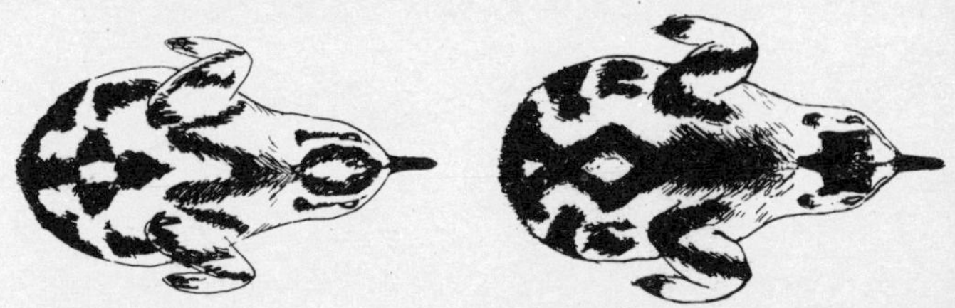

Dorsal patterns of downy chicks: *left,* Whimbrel; *right,* Hudsonian Godwit.

BAR-TAILED GODWIT *Limosa lapponica* **Pl. 37**

Breeds in swampy tundra, or marshes or heathland with pools bordering forest. Nest on the ground, on a dry site on raised ridge or mound.

Nest. A hollow lined with fragments of near-by plant material. **Breeding season.** Begins late May. Single-brooded. **Eggs.** Usually 4, sometimes 3 or 2. Subelliptical, oval or pyriform. Smooth and slightly glossy. Light to medium or olive brown, and paler gray. On shells with darker ground color markings are often indistinct, but on other markings are bold and may be evenly and fairly thickly distributed, or sparser and concentrated towards the larger end. 55 × 38 mm. **Incubation.** By both birds, mainly by male. 20–21 days. **Nestling.** Precocial and downy. Down pattern like that of other godwits but dark line from bill to crown, and lateral spot absent from hind-crown. Pale parts of back and head warmer buff, and underside drab, washed with buff. **Nestling period.** Young tended by both parents. Reports of single adults may refer to divided broods.

MARBLED GODWIT *Limosa fedoa* **Pl. 37**

Breeds on prairies and meadowland, on wetter areas near water. Nest on the ground. A number of pairs may nest in close proximity.

Nest. A shallow hollow, sparsely lined with dry grass. **Breeding season.** Begins mid- to late May. Single-brooded. **Eggs.** Usually 4, rarely 3, exceptionally 5. Oval, or pyriform. Smooth and moderately glossy. Pale buff or olive; sparsely spotted and with small blotches and scrawls of dark brown and pale purplish-gray. 57 × 40 mm. **Incubation.** By both sexes. Period not recorded. **Nestling.** Precocial and downy. Ground color pale buffish-brown. General appearance like that of Hudsonian Godwit, but face and belly whiter, dark head marking only begins on hind-crown with a separate lateral spot on each side, and the dark markings are browner. **Nestling period.** Young tended by both or one parent. Adults possibly divide brood between them.

ESKIMO CURLEW *Numenius borealis* **Pl. 37**

Very rare and almost extinct. Bred on barren grounds and tundra. Nest usually in an open site with a wide view.

Nest. A shallow hollow with a scanty lining of plant material. **Breeding season.** Began early June. **Eggs.** Usually 4, rarely 3. Oval. Smooth, non-glossy to slightly glossy. Pale olive to pale buff; speckled, spotted and with small blotches of varying shades of brownish-olive or dark brown and pale purplish-grey; the markings tending to be concentrated towards the larger end. 51 × 36 mm. **Incubation.** No information. **Nestling.** No information. **Nestling period.** No information.

WHIMBREL *Numenius phaeopus* **Pls. 11, 37**

Breeds on wet tundra in hummock areas with grasses, cottongrass and low heath scrub; on heathland and open areas in birch scrub. Nest on the ground in the open, often on a ridge or slight eminence.

Nest. A shallow hollow, sparsely lined with near-by plant material. **Breeding season.** Begins early June. Single-brooded. **Eggs.** Usually 4, occasionally 3, rarely 5. Oval to pyriform, or subelliptical. Smooth and slightly glossy. Pale green or olive to deeper olive-buff or buff; blotched, and more sparingly speckled and spotted, exceptionally coarsely scrawled with olive-brown, shades of medium to dark brown, and sometimes blackish-brown. Most frequently with irregular small blotches; occasionally well-distributed, sometimes more concentrated towards the larger end. 58 × 42 mm. **Incubation.** By both sexes. 27–28 days. **Nestling.** Precocial and downy. Down on upper parts pale buff, on underparts whitish-buff with warmer buff breast. Dark line from bill to crown and two dark brown bands over crown divided by a median buff streak. Dark line from eye to nape. Indistinct dark band down nape and four parallel dark stripes between wings. Large irregular dark patch around pale spot on lower back. Dark patch on flanks and dark hind-edge of flanks extending back to rump. Two small dark patches on wings. Bill short and straight at first. **Nestling period.** Young tended by both parents who divide brood between them. Young leave nest as soon as down is dry. Fly at 5–6 weeks.

LONG-BILLED CURLEW *Numenius americanus* **Pl. 37**

Breeds widely on open grassland, from wet meadows to dry prairie, often on uplands. Nest on the ground in growing herbage.

Nest. A shallow hollow, variably lined with near-by grasses and other plant material and debris, the rim sometimes raised. In damp sites a substantial layer of material may be accumulated. **Breeding season.** Begins late April to early May. Single-brooded. **Eggs.** Usually 4, rarely 5. Oval to pyriform. Smooth, non-glossy to slightly glossy. Pale greenish or olive; heavily speckled and spotted, and sometimes with small blotches or scrawls of medium to dark olive-brown and pale purplish-gray. 65 × 46 m. **Incubation.** By both sexes. 27–28 days. **Nestling.** Precocial and downy. Down creamy-buff on back, wings, underside and head, paler on throat; and warm buff on breast and flanks. The brownish-black pattern of head, back and wings is basically similar to that of the Whimbrel, but the markings are narrow and more broken, producing a more mottled appearance. Bill at first pink with black tip. **Nestling period.** Young tended by both adults. Adults may divide the brood between them since a number of broods of two young are recorded.

BRISTLE-THIGHED CURLEW *Numenius tahitiensis*

Breeds on drier rocky areas of upland tundra. Nest on the ground in open site.

Nest. A shallow hollow in moss, unlined or sparsely lined with plant material. **Breeding season.** Begins mid-May? **Eggs.** Usually 4. Similar to those of Whimbrel, but more buff and less greenish; with large, bold markings. 60 × 42 mm. **Incubation.** No information. **Nestling.** Precocial and downy. Down pinkish-buff, paler below; with blackish-brown pattern like that of Whimbrel. Crown has a pale centre, dark stripe from eye to nape is incomplete, and dark band on hind-flank does not meet tail mark. **Nestling period.** No information.

UPLAND SANDPIPER *Bartramia longicauda* **Pls. 11, 38**

Breeds on open grassland, prairies and meadows, usually by wet sites; and in clearings in spruce muskegs in north; but sometimes on dry areas. Nest in tall growing herbage.

Nest. A hollow, lined with grasses, leaves or small twigs, the surrounding grass pulled over, concealing the nest; *c.* 4–5 in. diameter, *c.* 2–3 in. deep. **Breeding season.** Begins late April to early May. Single-brooded. **Eggs.** Usually 4, sometimes 3. Oval to subelliptical. Smooth and glossy. Very pale buff, creamy-buff or pale stone; finely speckled and spotted, and occasionally with a few small blotches of reddish- or purplish-brown, and pale gray or lilac. Larger markings tend to be concentrated at the larger end, and the ground color predominates elsewhere. 45 × 33 mm. **Incubation.** By both sexes. 21 days. **Nestling.** Precocial and downy. Down of underparts and throat whitish; of breast, neck and sides of head buff. Back and wings mottled blackish-brown and buffish-brown, with overall buff and white tips, producing a spotted pattern with a few irregular black markings. Elongated black patch on ear-coverts and on nape. White stripe through eye to hind-crown, bordering a crown-patch which tapers to dark line on forehead and shows dark border and streaks converging completely or incompletely on hind-crown, the remainder mottled buff and white. **Nestling period.** Young tended by both parents. Full-grown in *c.* 30 days.

GREATER YELLOWLEGS *Tringa melanoleuca* **Pl. 38**

Breeds in muskeg country, along tundra/forest edge, and on high tundra. Nest on the ground in an open site, often on a slight ridge or hummock usually near a pool or open water. Nest often by a log or dead branch.

Nest. A shallow hollow in moss or dry peat, unlined or scantily lined with some grasses and dead leaves. **Breeding season.** Begins late May to early June. Single-brooded. **Eggs.** Usually 4. Pyriform to oval. Smooth and slightly glossy. Very pale creamy-buff or faintly olive, rarely pinkish-buff; speckled, spotted and blotched with dark brown or purplish-brown, and pale purple or gray. Larger markings often concentrated at the larger end, and sometimes spirally elongated. 50 × 33 mm. **Incubation.** Incubation by female alone. Period not

Greater Yellowlegs: dorsal pattern of downy chick.

recorded. **Nestling.** Precocial and downy. Down pattern shows variations. Paler parts of plumage grayish-white with slight buff tint on back and sides. Dark pattern blackish-brown. Narrow dark line from bill through eye. Dark crown patch with narrow line to bill, or smaller crown patch with dark line from above eye on either side converging on hind-crown. Dark spot at rear of ear-coverts. Dark patch on nape. Three dark bands down back, the middle one broad and sometimes divided on lower back to produce pale median streak. Dark lateral patches on flanks join outer dorsal bands. Two small dark wing patches. Bill black. Legs and feet yellowish-green. **Nestling period.** Young tended by both sexes.

LESSER YELLOWLEGS *Tringa flavipes* **Pl. 38**

Breeds in drier sites than Greater Yellowlegs, sometimes by a muskeg, but more often in clearings or burnt-off areas in forest, with or without secondary growth; on thinly wooded hillsides; on grassy marshland in clearings. Nest on the ground in the open; but by a branch or log, or sometimes sheltered by a shrub. **Nest.** A shallow depression lined with a few dry leaves and grasses. **Breeding season.** Begins mid-May in south, to early June in north. **Eggs.** Usually 4, sometimes 3. Pyriform to oval. Very pale creamy-buff, or faintly tinted olive or greenish; speckled, spotted and blotched, often profusely, with medium to purplish-brown, and pale purple or lilac. Larger markings sometimes concentrated at larger end. 42 × 29 mm. **Incubation.** By both sexes. Period not recorded. **Nestling.** Precocial and downy. Down pale grayish-white below and on neck and head; warm or pinkish-buff on back and wings. Pattern similar to that of Greater Yellowlegs; but crown-patch smaller, and dark lateral streaks over eyes more conspicuous. Broader black band across wings, and bolder band continuing along flanks to rump. **Nestling period.** Young tended by both sexes. Young leave nest soon after hatching, usually led by parents to nearest water.

SOLITARY SANDPIPER *Tringa solitaria* **Pl. 38**

Breeds in northern forests, tundra-forest edge, muskeg country, and in mountain forest. Usually near open water, lake or pool, in places where forest is open with scattered trees or broken cover. Nest is in the old nest of a robin or similar-sized bird, in a tree at any height.

Nest. The old nest of another bird species, no material other than that already present. **Breeding season.** Begins late May to early June. Single-brooded. **Eggs.** Usually 4, sometimes 3. Pyriform to oval. Smooth and slightly glossy. Creamy, tinted very pale green, olive or buff; speckled, spotted and with a few blotches of purplish or reddish-brown, and pale lilac or purple. Markings often sparse except at or around the larger end. 36 × 26 mm. **Incubation.** Role of sexes and period of incubation not recorded. **Nestling.** Precocial and downy. Down grayish on head and underside, buffish-brown on upperparts. Small dark spot on hind ear-coverts. Blackish patch with browner center on hind-crown; fore-crown mottled brown with dark median streak from hind-crown patch to bill, and lateral streaks from patch to just above eyes. Nape mottled. Back with three dark bands. Dark mark on thigh and dark stripe along hind-flank. Dark patches on wings. **Nestling period.** Young tended by both parents? Leave nest, probably dropping unaided, soon after hatching.

SPOTTED SANDPIPER *Tringa macularia* **Pls. 10, 38**

Breeds by freshwater – pools, lakes, streams, dams, rivers, marshes or flood-waters; in both open and wooded areas; and less frequently in open grassy areas away from water. At any altitude from tree-line to sea-level. Females often polyandrous.

Nest. Nest on the ground in growing herbage or low shrubby growth, or against plant-tuft, log or driftwood in an open site. **Breeding season.** Begins mid-May in south to mid-June in north of range. Single-brooded. **Eggs.** Usually 4, rarely 3 or 5. But female frequently lays more than one clutch, often two and sometimes more, with different males. Eggs pyriform to oval. Smooth and slightly glossy. Creamy or pale creamy-buff; usually with fine profuse speckling and sparser, more random spots or blotches in blackish-brown, purplish-brown or reddish-brown, and pale gray or purple. 33 × 24 mm. **Incubation.** Where several clutches are laid, earlier clutches incubated by males alone, last by both sexes. 20–24 days. **Nestling.** Precocial and downy. Some down with long fine tips. Underside, bill to vent, white. Sides of head and forehead pale buffish, with dark streak from bill through eye to hind ear-covert. Upperparts finely mottled in buffish-brown and blackish-brown; long down having black tips. Broad dark band over mid-crown tapering to forehead and nape. Dark stripe down mid-back. Down of rump elongated to form long wispy tuft. **Nestling period.** Young tended by male alone or by both parents. Young have teetering action of adults from the first. Leave nest as soon as down is dry. Fly in *c.* 16–18 days.

Spotted Sandpiper: dorsal pattern of downy chick.

WANDERING TATTLER *Heteroscelus incanus*

Breeds in mountain areas, by freshwater streams and pools. Nest in a level gravelly or rocky site by water.

Nest. A shallow scrape lined with a variable amount of rootlets and other plant material. **Breeding season.** Begins early June? **Eggs.** Usually 4. Pyriform to oval. Smooth and slightly glossy. Very pale greenish or olive, spotted and blotched with medium to dark brown, and paler brownish-gray. Markings mainly concentrated at larger end. 43 × 32 mm. **Incubation.** By both sexes. 23–25 days. **Nestling.** Precocial and downy. Down whitish below, becoming pale bluish-gray on sides, back and head. Dark line from bill through eye, but otherwise only a faint indication of a *Tringa*-sandpiper type pattern in darker brownish-gray on head and back. **Nestling period.** Young tended by both parents at first, but later usually only one present.

WILLET *Catoptrophorus semipalmatus* **Pls. 10, 38**

Breeds usually near, or in flying distance of, salt, brackish or fresh water. Nests in open places, coastal marshes, beaches or islands; and inland in wet grassland by lakes, or short grass or bare ground by water. Nest on the ground, in the open on bare ground or in short grass, or by a plant tuft, or well-concealed in grass-tufts or low bushes. Pairs often nest near each other.

Nest. A shallow scrape, lined to a varying degree with grasses or other vegetation, or shells, or other debris in barer sites. **Breeding season.** Begins mid-March in south to early June in north. Single-brooded. **Eggs.** Usually 4, rarely 5. Pyriform to oval. Smooth and moderately glossy. Very pale greenish, olive, buff, stone or slightly pinkish-buff; finely speckled, spotted and blotched with medium to dark brown, or purplish-brown, and pale gray or purple. Larger markings often concentrated at or around larger end. 55 × 39 mm. **Incubation.** By female, possibly male also? 22 days. **Nestling.** Precocial and downy. Down buffish-white on underside. Head pale buff, whiter on throat. Dark stripe through eye. Dark brown mottled patch on crown with dark streak to bill. Nape mottled. Back grayish to buffish-brown, patterned with blackish-brown. Three dark stripes down back, the middle one divided down the mid-back to enclose a long pale streak. Flanks and wings with dark patches. **Nestling period.** Young tended by both parents, but deserted at fairly early stage.

WILSON'S PHALAROPE *Phalaropus tricolor* **Pl. 39**

Breeds on the edges of shallow, inland waters, where wet meadows and grassy marshes with short vegetation are present, or on marshy islands. Nest on the ground, concealed by overarching grasses. Usually a number of pairs nest in close proximity. Sex roles reversed as in other phalaropes.

Nest. A hollow lined with dry grasses in variable amounts, *c.* 3–4 in. across; with grasses pulled over to hide nest. In wet sites nests may be larger accumulations of grasses, moss and twigs. **Breeding season.** Begins mid- to late May. Single-brooded. **Eggs.** Usually 4, sometimes 3. Pyriform to oval. Smooth and slightly glossy. Creamy to ivory or pale creamy-buff; usually heavily and profusely marked with speckling, spotting and blotching in blackish-brown or purplish-brown and sparse pale gray. 37 × 24 mm. **Incubation.** By male alone, with female nearby. 20–21 days. **Nestling.** Precocial and downy. Down buff on upperparts and across the breast, deepening to tawny-orange on crown, wings and back. Underside is white. Crown lacks the large dark patch present in other phalaropes, and is buff with a narrow median line from forehead to hind-crown where it terminates at a narrow transverse line joining two elongated lateral spots to produce an anchor-shaped mark. Bold dark stripe from nape to tail, two dark lateral stripes from wings to rump along flanks, and dark patches on wings and thighs. Pattern sometimes more broken. **Nestling period.** Little information. Young tended by male alone.

RED PHALAROPE *Phalaropus fulicarius* **Pl. 39**

Breeds on level areas with shallow pools and lagoons; or near coasts, or on offshore islands, where fresh-water pools are present. Nest on the ground, usually on slightly raised site, a grass tussock, ridge or shingle-bank, or small island in water. Usually a number of pairs nest in a small colony. Sex roles reversed, larger brighter female displays, male incubates and tends young. Female polyandrous.

Nest. A shallow hollow, material varying from sparse plant fragment in an open site to a substantial structure of grass and leaves in a grassy site. In the latter site grasses usually pulled over to hide the nest. Made by male. **Breeding**

season. Begins late June to early July, but may be late May in Alaska. Single-brooded. **Eggs.** Usually 4, rarely 3. Oval to pyriform. Smooth and slightly gloss. Light olive, or green, or deeper olive-buff; with irregular blotches, spots and specks of black and blackish-brown, and scarce paler purplish markings. Irregularly scattered large blotches combined with profuse finer markings very typical. Larger markings often concentrated towards the larger end. 30 × 22 mm. **Incubation.** By male only. 19 days. **Nestling.** Precocial and downy. Down on underside grayish-white. Yellowish-white or yellowish-buff on neck and throat; and warm buff marked with black on upperparts, forming a triple streak pattern on back. Forehead warm buff. Black crown with slight buff mottling, bordered by yellowish eye-stripe. Dark streak across lores to eye, and dark spot on cheek behind eye. Indistinct dark band down nape. Back has dark central stripe, bordered by two buff ones, these bordered in turn by irregular dark band along flanks and upper wings, and black patch on thigh. Dark spots on fore-edge and tip of wing. **Nestling period.** Young usually tended by male alone, although female may be present. Independent in 16–20 days.

Crown pattern of downy chicks: *left*, Red Phalarope; *right*, Wilson's Phalarope.

NORTHERN PHALAROPE *Phalaropus lobatus* **Pls. 10, 39**

Breeds on grassy or marshy ground by water or with some open pools, on marshy edges of lakes, low islands in rivers, or sometimes small offshore islands. Nest in a grass tussock near open water. As with Red Phalarope sex roles reversed. **Nest.** A hollow, built into a grass tussock with grass lining and grass pulled together over the nest. Built by both sexes. **Breeding season.** Begins late May to early June. Single-brooded. **Eggs.** Usually 4, sometimes 3. Oval to pyriform. Smooth and slightly glossy. Similar in color and pattern to those of Red Phalarope. 30 × 21 mm. **Incubation.** Eggs laid at 1–2-day interval. Incubation by male alone. 18–20 days. **Nestling.** Precocial and downy. Like that of Red Phalarope, but paler streaking on back is lighter and yellower; and dark streak from bill to eye absent but small spot may be present. **Nestling period.** Young tended by male alone; female sometimes present. Independent in 18–22 days.

JAEGERS, GULLS AND TERNS *Laridae*

JAEGERS *Stercorariinae*

Large to medium predators and scavengers. Nest on open ground, usually near the sea. Site often rather exposed. Nest a scrape with little or no lining although sideways-building may be used to accumulate some material. Usually 2 eggs, brownish with dark spots. Incubation begins with the first eggs, the young hatching at intervals and showing some difference in size. Young are downy, but not patterned. They may leave the nest after a few days, but remain in the parental territory.

PARASITIC JAEGER *Stercorarius parasiticus* **Pls. 13, 40**
Breeds on tundra near sea level, or on barer hills or cliffs, on low shingly areas, or on offshore islands. Nest on the ground, often in a swampy area or near water. Usually nests in large colonies, occasionally as scattered pairs.
Nest. A shallow depression, unlined or sparsely lined, in grass, heather or moss. **Breeding season.** Begins late May or early June. Single-brooded. **Eggs.** Usually 2, sometimes 1. Subelliptical. Smooth, and only slightly glossy. The ground color olive, greenish, dull buff or brown; with spots or blotches, of dark brown, light brown or gray. Markings are very variable, often sparse. Ground color rarely pale blue. 57 × 40 mm. **Incubation.** By both sexes, beginning with first egg. 24–28 days. **Nestling.** Semi-precocial and downy. Down thick and soft with fine silky tips. Down warm dark brown, or blackish-brown; lighter and gray-tinted around eyes, on chin, central underside and wing-tips. Down remains on tips of first feathers. **Nestling period.** Young are tended by both adults. They may leave the nest-site after a few days but remain in territory. They fly at 27–33 days, are independent at *c.* 7–8 weeks.

POMARINE JAEGER *Stercorarius pomarinus* **Pl. 40**
Breeds on swampy areas of level tundra. Less sociable in nesting than other skuas. Nest on the ground.
Nest. A shallow hollow in moss, unlined or scantily lined. **Breeding season.** Begins mid-June. Single-brooded. Lost clutch sometimes replaced. **Eggs.** Usually 2, rarely 3. Subelliptical. Smooth and very slightly glossy. Ground color buff, olive, or warm brown; with spots and flecks of dark blackish-brown. 64 × 44 mm. **Incubation.** By both sexes. 26–28 days. **Nestling.** Semi-precocial and downy. Down thick and soft, with fine silky tips. Pale brown on upperparts, paler grayish-brown on the underside. **Nestling period.** Young tended by both adults. Become independent after 30–35 weeks.

LONG-TAILED JAEGER *Stercorarius longicaudus* **Pl. 40**
Breeds on swamps and bogs bordering forests, bare stony flats and tundra. Often at some distance from the sea. Loose associations of scattered nests. Nest on the ground.
Nest. A shallow hollow, unlined or with a few fragments, in peat or moss. **Breeding season.** June. Single-brooded. **Eggs.** Usually 2, rarely 1–3. Subelliptical. Smooth and only slightly glossy. Olive-green to olive-brown, dull buff, or pale green; with spots, blotches, or scrawls, of dark brown or pale gray, mostly towards or around the larger end. 55 × 38 mm. **Incubation.** Eggs laid at 1½–2-day intervals. Incubation by both sexes, beginning with first egg. 23 days. **Nestling.** Semi-precocial and downy. Down thick and soft with fine silky tips. Dark brown but paler and grayer than that of Parasitic Jaeger. Sides of head and entire underside pale grayish-brown. Bill has upper mandible flesh-colored, lower bluish-pink, and tip black. Legs and toes pale blue, with webs pinkish. **Nestling period.** Young hatch over a period. Tended by both adults. They may leave the nest after 2 days. They fly at *c.* 3 weeks. Independent at *c.* 5 weeks.

GULLS *Larus, Rissa, Pagophila* species

Medium to large scavenging birds of coasts, marshes and inland waters. Nest on the ground near water, or on a ledge of cliff or rock outcrop. Usually nest in colonies. Nest material is carried to site, but sideways-building occurs at site. Amount of material is very variable and depends to some extent on the amount of excitement or discomfort at the site. Single-brooded, but lost clutches are usually replaced. Usually 2–3 eggs. Eggs cryptically colored, usually darker olive or buff in northern species, and much paler and more boldly marked in more southerly species. Young downy. Cryptically colored in variable, poorly-defined patterns. Well brooded for first few days but capable of leaving nest after first day. Parents swallow food and regurgitate it on the ground where small pieces may be given to the small young, but larger young pick up for themselves. Young peck at tip of parents' bills to encourage regurgitation. Young leave nest within a few days of hatching and when parents are not present may hide in near-by herbage. Right up to the point where they fly well they tend to crouch and remain motionless when alarmed. In colonies adults may kill and sometimes eat young of other pairs.

LAUGHING GULL *Larus atricilla* **Pl. 41**

Breeds on seacoasts; on saltmarshes, dunes, beaches, and shell and shingle ridges of coast and offshore islands. Nest on the ground in colonies, often large, with nests in close proximity. Nests in tall herbage, or weeds, or among bushes if present.

Nest. An accumulation of dry stems and plant material, thinner in drier sites and often substantial in wet sites, with a lining of thinner material. **Breeding season.** Begins early April in south to late May in north. Single-brooded. **Eggs.** Usually 3, sometimes 2–4. Subelliptical to oval. Smooth and slightly glossy. Pale to very pale olive-buff, olive, greenish or buff; spotted, speckled, blotched or scrawled with olive-brown to blackish-olive and paler gray or violet. Markings variable but usually small blotches or spots of fairly overall distribution. Occasionally larger markings concentrated at or around the larger end. 54 × 38 mm. **Incubation.** 21–23 days. **Nestling.** Semi-precocial and downy. Down long and soft. Down pale drab brown above tinted with cinnamon or warm brown. Underside a paler shade of the same with a warmer tint on the breast. Head, neck and throat are boldly spotted and streaked in blackish-brown to dark brown, and the back heavily mottled with the same. **Nestling period.** Young tended by both parents. Continuously brooded or shaded at first. After a few days leave nest to run and hide in herbage. Begin flying at 4–6 weeks?

FRANKLIN'S GULL *Larus pipixcan* **Pl. 41**

Breeds in marshy and reed-grown areas on the shores of inland lakes or on large marshes. Usually a large colony with nests close together. Nests built on floating vegetation held and anchored by growing stems of tall plants such as bulrushes (*Scirpus*).

Nest. A floating mass of dead plant material, built up 4–8 in. above water level and with a shallow nest cavity. **Breeding season.** Begins early May to early June. Single-brooded. **Eggs.** Usually 3, sometimes 2. Clutches of 4 possibly from two females. Subelliptical. Smooth and slightly to moderately glossy. Very pale to medium greenish, olive, olive-buff or buff; spotted, speckled, blotched or

Plate 7

GUANS. Downy young fairly large, with poorly-defined down pattern. More arboreal than most game birds.

Chachalaca, *Ortalis vetula.* **page** 98

GROUSE. Downy young boldly patterned when small, fairly stoutly-built like young of domestic hen. Usually with some down on the legs.

Sage Grouse, *Centrocercus urophasianus.* 98

Blue Grouse, *Dendragapus obscurus.* 99

Rock Ptarmigan, *Lagopus mutus.* 100

White-tailed Ptarmigan, *Lagopus leucurus.* 100

Willow Ptarmigan, *Lagopus lagopus.* 99

Greater Prairie Chicken, *Tympanuchus cupido.* Lesser Prairie Chicken similar but paler and less brown, without median stripe on head. 101

Sharp-tailed Grouse, *Tympanuchus phasianellus.* (head only). Similar to previous species but lacking warmer tints on back, and usually two dark spots behind eye. 102

Spruce Grouse, *Dendragapus canadensis.* 99

Ruffed Grouse, *Bonasa umbellus.* 101

Chachalaca

Sage Grouse

Blue Grouse

Rock Ptarmigan

White-tailed Ptarmigan

Greater Prairie Chicken

Willow Ptarmigan

Sharp-tailed Grouse

Spruce Grouse

Ruffed Grouse

8

Ring-necked
Pheasant
Turkey
Partridge
Chukar
Bobwhite Quail
Mountain
Quail
Scaled Quail
Montezuma Quail
Gambel's Quail
California Qua

TYPICAL GAMEBIRDS. Downy young usually boldly patterned, the pattern often differing between genera. Resembles the young of grouse but lack any down on legs. Quail chicks are usually small, and those with crests may show evidence of this at an early age.

Ring-necked Pheasant, *Phasianus colchicus.* **page** 107

Turkey, *Meleagris gallopavo.* 108

Partridge, *Perdix perdix.* 107

Chukar, *Alectoris chukar.* 108

Bobwhite Quail, *Colinus virginianus.* 106

Mountain Quail, *Oreortyx pictus.* 104

Scaled Quail, *Callipepla squamata.* 104

Montezuma Quail, *Cyrtonyx montezumae.* 106

Gambel's Quail, *Callipepla gambeli.* 105

California Quail, *Callipepla californica.* 105

scrawled with olive, brown, blackish-olive or black, and paler gray. Markings variable. Often a zone of heavier markings wreathing the larger end. 52 × 36 mm. **Incubation.** By both sexes. **Nestling.** Semi-precocial and downy. Down has two color phases. In brown phase down is pale brown becoming more buff posteriorly and paling to white below, while the throat and breast are yellowish-buff. Back heavily mottled with dark brown, densest along the mid-back, and the head also mottled. A black patch at the base of the bill and a few dark spots on throat. The gray phase has the buff and brown tints replaced by similar shades of gray. **Nestling period.** Young tended by both parents. Can swim at 3 days. Fly at 28–33 days.

LITTLE GULL *Larus minutus*

An uncommon visitor to the eastern seaboard where exceptionally it has bred. Breeds on marshes, lakes with marshy edges and shallow inland waters. Nests usually in colony, sometimes with other small gulls or tern species. Nests on tussocks of grass or rushes in water or marsh, or in shallow water among reeds and similar plants, or in open sites on low sandbanks or islands.

Nest. An accumulation of dead waterside plants, reeds, rushes and sedges. **Breeding season.** Single-brooded. **Eggs.** Usually 3, sometimes 2, rarely 4–5. Subelliptical. Smooth and slightly glossy. Light olive-green, olive or buff, sometimes very pale greenish or creamy. Buff eggs usually darkest. Finely and variably marked with specks, spots, and usually small blotches, of black, blackish-brown or olive, and with paler shades of gray. Markings sometimes overall, but often sparse with a thicker zone around larger end. Blotching sometimes large and concentrated towards larger end. 42 × 30 mm. **Incubation.** First 2 eggs laid at intervals of 1–2 days, later at less than 1-day intervals. Incubation by both sexes. 20–21 days. **Nestling.** Semi-precocial and downy. Down thick, soft and fairly long, with fine silky tips. Down has blackish-brown bases but appears buffish-gray on the underside; and on the upperparts is dark grayish-buff with irregular inconspicuous patches of blackish-brown with buff tips. **Nestling period.** Young tended by both parents. Young fly at *c.* 21–24 days.

SABINE'S GULL *Larus sabini* **Pls. 12, 42**

Breeds on swampy tundra on small islands and raised areas, or on tussocks; or on coastal islands. Breeds sociably, sometimes in company with Arctic Terns. Nest on the ground, in grass, or on drier sites on bare ground.

Nest. A shallow hollow, lined with plant stems and near-by plant debris. Coastal nests may have seaweed and feathers. **Breeding season.** Begins early June. Single-brooded. **Eggs.** Usually 3, sometimes 2. Subelliptical. Smooth, slightly glossy. Shades of deep olive to buffish-olive, darker than most gull's eggs. Indistinctly and variably marked with shades of olive-brown, sometimes widely distributed, sometimes mostly confined to a zone around the larger end. Some eggs paler greenish-olive with blackish-brown markings. 44 × 32 mm. **Incubation.** By both birds, probably beginning with first egg. 23–26 days. **Nestling.** Semi-precocial and downy. Down long and soft with silky tips. Underside buff, often white on mid-breast and belly. Upperparts deep brownish-buff mottled with black. Markings vary. Usually three lines of broken blotches over crown and broken line of spots under eye, and blotch on side of throat. Broken lines of black spots and blotches over back. **Nestling period.** No information.

BONAPARTE'S GULL *Larus philadelphia* **Pls. 12, 41**

Breeds in conifer forests near lakes and rivers. In scattered pairs in woodland areas, usually nesting on flatter branches of spruce trees, 4–20 ft. up, or more. **Nest.** A shallow cup of twigs, small sticks and a finer lining of grasses, mosses and lichens. Built by both sexes. **Breeding season.** Begins mid-June. Single-brooded. **Eggs.** Usually 3, sometimes 2, rarely 4. Subelliptical. Smooth and slightly glossy. Very pale to medium greenish, olive, olive-buff or buff; spotted, speckled, blotched or scrawled with shades of olive-brown, blackish-olive and dark brown, and paler gray or violet. Markings very variable, from fine overall speckling, to large blotching or scrawling mainly concentrated at or around larger end. 49 × 34 mm. **Incubation.** By both sexes, but chiefly by female? Period not recorded. **Nestling.** Semi-precocial and downy. Down yellowish-buff with blackish-brown mottling on upper parts and head. Breast pinkish-cinnamon. Flank and belly gray. Bill blue-black, dull flesh-color at base. Legs and feet buffish-pink with gray tint. **Nestling period.** Young begin to leave nest at end of 1 week.

RING-BILLED GULL *Larus delawarensis* **Pl. 41**

Breeds mainly at inland lakes, nesting on small islets or islands, isolated rocks, or islands formed by floating vegetation in marshy areas of lakesides. Nests on the ground, usually on the higher parts of islands, often in the open but sometimes in sites protected by rocks or shrubs. Nests in colonies with nests often close together, sometimes in company with other water birds.

Nest. A hollow lined with a variable amount of material, often sparse. Dead plant materials, green weeds, feathers and any available rubbish. On rock sites a pad of material a few inches thick. **Breeding season.** Begins early May in south to mid-June in north. Single-brooded. **Eggs.** Usually 3, sometimes 2, very rarely 4. Subelliptical. Smooth and slightly glossy. Very pale to medium olive, olive-buff or deeper buff; spotted, speckled, blotched or scrawled with olive-brown, brown or blackish. Markings very variable in size and number, but small markings tend to be overall, larger ones sparse and concentrated at larger end. 59 × 42 mm. **Incubation.** 21–23 days? **Nestling.** Semi-precocial and downy. Down has two color phases. Brown phase has pinkish or reddish-buff on upper parts, paler below and whiter on breast; spotted with dark brown on head and neck, and faintly mottled dark brown on the back. The gray phase has pale smoke-gray ground colour. **Nestling period.** Young tended by both parents. Fed until able to fly. Swim at an early age.

COMMON GULL *Larus canus* **Pl. 41**

Breeds on wet tundra, nesting on small islets or tussocks, or around lakes where low, scrubby conifers are present. Nest on the ground, or on a stump, or on the top of a spruce tree.

Nest. A shallow hollow with a variable accumulation of near-by plant material, varying according to site. Built mainly by female. In a tree a shapeless platform of plant material. **Breeding season.** Begins late May. Single-brooded. **Eggs.** Usually 3, sometimes 1–4. Subelliptical. Smooth and slightly glossy. Usually light olive, greenish, or buffish, but may vary from whitish-blue to deep brownish-buff. Very variably marked with spots, blotches, specks or short scrawls, in brown, blackish-brown, black and olive, with fainter gray markings. Markings may vary in distribution and intensity from unmarked shells to those with heavy overall pattern, but in general show an even distribution with a tendency, particularly on sparingly marked shells, for a heavier zone at the larger end. 57 × 41 mm. **Incubation.** By both birds, usually beginning with last egg. 22–27 days. **Nestling.** Semi-precocial and downy. Down long and soft, with silky tips. Upper parts pale buff to buffish-gray. Underparts buffish, yellowish or whitish, darker at the sides. Pattern on head, neck and back of spots or blotches of blackish-brown; spotted on head and forming broken irregular mottling elsewhere. Bill blue-gray with pink along cutting edge and at tip. **Nestling period.** Young leave nest in first day or two but remain near by. Tended by both parents. Begin flying at *c.* 4 weeks, fly well at 5 weeks.

HERRING GULL *Larus argentatus* **Pls. 12, 40**

Breeds on ledges of sea-cliffs, cliffs or edges of islands; or low in sand-dunes or on shingle, among rocks or on grass. On freshwater lakes inland. May nest on branches of conifers or roofs of buildings. Usually in colonies.

Nest. A usually large accumulation of grass, seaweed and other plant material; in hollow. Built by both birds. **Breeding season.** Begins early May in south to mid-June in north. Single-brooded. **Eggs.** Usually 2–3. Subelliptical. Smooth and non-glossy, or slightly glossy; and with finely granular surface. Very variable. Usually light olive, buffish or greenish, but may vary from pale whitish-blue to deep brownish-buff. Speckled, spotted and blotched, or rarely irregularly scrawled in black, blackish-brown or dark olive. Markings vary from profuse overall markings, to sparse speckling or blotches; rarely unmarked. Infrequently a zone of dark markings around larger end. Exceptionally creamy or pinkish with pink or reddish-brown markings. 70 × 48 mm. **Incubation.** Eggs laid at 2–3-day intervals. Incubation by both birds but mostly by female, beginning with first egg. 25–33 days. **Nestling.** Semi-precocial and downy. Down long and soft with fine silky tips. Upper parts and throat buffish-gray, lower throat buff, underside buffish-white. Head and throat marked with small numerous blackish-brown spots and small streaks forming a line of marks around eye, a series of blotches along mid-crown and nape, and streaks at sides of throat. Upperparts of body mottled with irregular patches of blackish-brown blotches. Bill black with pink tip. Legs and feet pinkish. **Nestling period.** Young tended by both parents. Brooded for first few days. Begin to fly at *c.* 6 weeks.

CALIFORNIA GULL *Larus californicus* **Pl. 41**

Breeds on prairie lakes, on islands. Nest on the ground, usually close to water, in the open or in short herbage. Usually nests in colonies, often in company with other water birds.

Nest. An accumulation of dead plant material, stems, feathers and rubbish; making a largish cup built up a few inches from the ground. **Breeding season.** Begins early May in south to early June in north. Single-brooded. **Eggs.** Usually 3, sometimes 2, rarely 4–5 and these possibly from two females. Subelliptical. Smooth or very slightly granular in texture. Very pale olive to olive-buff, greenish or deeper buff; spotted, speckled, blotched or scrawled in shades of olive-brown to blackish-olive, and paler gray or violet. Markings may be small and profuse, or very sparse and large, the latter often concentrated at the larger end. Rarely pale blue with or without pale violet markings. 68 × 46 mm. **Incubation.** By both sexes. 23–27 days. **Nestling.** Semi-precocial and downy. Down thick and soft. Pale buff, brighter on head and breast. Sparse dull black spotting on head. Back, wings and throat mottled or indistinctly blotched with light gray. The markings become obscured as the young grow. Bill black with creamy-pink tip which is gradually lost. Legs and feet black, becoming grayish-pink. **Nestling period.** Young tended by both parents. Leave the nest and run around and swim at a few days old.

WESTERN GULL *Larus occidentalis* **Pl. 40**

Breeds on islands and rocks offshore. Nests on the ground, at varying heights above the sea, sometimes in tideline debris, often in a sheltered hollow, niche or crevice in rocks, at the base of a cliff, or sometimes on grassy slopes and high exposed rocks.

Nest. Nest an often bulky cup of dead grasses, plant stems and other debris. Nests may be re-used in successive years. **Breeding season.** Begins early May in south to early June in north. Single-brooded, but lost clutches replaced. **Eggs.** Usually 3, often 2, sometimes 1, rarely 4. Replacement clutches usually 2. Subelliptical. Smooth or with slight granular texture. Non-glossy to slightly glossy. Very pale to medium olive or olive-buff; spotted, speckled, blotched or scrawled, often heavily, with olive-brown to blackish-olive, and pale gray or violet. 72 × 50 mm. **Incubation.** Eggs laid at 2–3-day intervals. Incubation by both sexes. 24–29 days. **Nestling.** Semi-precocial and downy. Down drab grayish to buff, with some variegation, becoming paler below. Head and throat spotted and irregularly streaked with black. The back and rump are heavily spotted with blackish-brown. Bill black with dull pink tip. Legs and feet pinkish-brown. **Nestling period.** Young tended by both parents. Leave the nest at 2–5 days and hide near by. Fly at 6–7 weeks.

GLAUCOUS-WINGED GULL *Larus glaucescens* **Pl. 40**

Breeds on steep coastal cliffs and on rocky islands offshore. Nests on rock ledges, and in hollows and niches, sometimes sheltered by shrubs, or on open sites on rock or turf on top of islands. In large colonies or scattered pairs. Sometimes with other gull species and seabirds.

Nest. Well-made bulky cup of grasses, seaweed, feathers, fish-bones and other debris. **Breeding season.** Begins late May to early June. Single-brooded. **Eggs.** Usually 3, often 2, rarely 4. Subelliptical. Smooth or very slightly granular texture. Non-glossy or slightly glossy. Very pale olive or stone, or slightly deeper buff; marked overall with spots, small blotches, some speckling or scrawling, in medium to dark olive-brown, and blackish-olive, and pale markings in gray or violet. 73×51 mm. **Incubation.** *c.* 26 days. **Nestling.** Semi-precocial and downy. Down pattern like that of Western Gull but the general ground color is grayer and the dark markings of the back are less bold. **Nestling period.** No information.

THAYER'S GULL *Larus thayeri*

Breeds on cliffs, on rock ledges.

Nest. A bulky, fairly deep cup of moss and plant material. **Breeding season.** Begins early to mid-June. **Eggs.** Usually 2–3. Subelliptical to oval, approaching pyriform. Smooth and slightly glossy. Very pale to pale olive, olive-buff, or buff; spotted, blotched or scrawled with olive-brown, brown or black, and pale gray or violet. 74 × 49 mm. **Incubation.** *c.* 26 days. **Nestling.** Semi-precocial and downy. Down very dark, blackish, in overall color. **Nestling period.**

Young tended by both parents. Chicks do not run from nest when alarmed, but become immobile like kittiwake young.

ICELAND GULL *Larus glaucoides* **Pl. 40**

Breeds on ledges of high cliffs and on low sandy shores.

Nest. A bulky cup of mosses and grasses. **Breeding season.** Begins late May. Single-brooded. **Eggs.** Usually 2–3. Subelliptical. Smooth or with fine granular texture. Pale to very pale olive, olive-buff or stone; spotted, blotched, speckled and sometimes scrawled with olive-brown to blackish-olive, and paler gray and violet. Size and density of markings varies but often a wreath of larger markings around the larger end. 69 × 48 mm. **Incubation.** Period not recorded. **Nestling.** Semi-precocial and downy. Down overall drab grayish-white, with brownish-gray spots on head and back, more distinct on the former. **Nestling period.** No information.

GLAUCOUS GULL *Larus hyperboreus* **Pl. 40**

Breeds usually in colonies, sometimes as single pairs. Nest on ledge of cliff, or on ground on small islands or at foot of cliff or rock outcrop.

Nest. An accumulation, frequently large, of moss and near-by plants, and seaweed. Sometimes the last alone. Usually built by both birds. **Breeding season.** Begins late May to early June. Single-brooded. **Eggs.** Usually 2–3, sometimes 1–4. Subelliptical. Smooth and non-glossy, with a fine granular texture. Light olive or creamy-olive to buff; exceptionally bluish-white. Very variably marked with spots, blotches, specks and occasionally thin scrawls, of black, blackish-brown, and olive-brown, and paler shades of gray. Markings are most frequently smallish and profuse, but sometimes a few large sparse blotches. Exceptionally pinkish varieties with reddish markings are known. 77 × 54 mm. **Incubation.** Eggs laid on alternate days. Incubation by both birds, beginning with first egg. 27–30 days. **Nestling.** Semi-precocial and downy. Similar in appearance to that of Greater Black-backed but dark markings on the back are paler and less well-defined. Bill, legs and feet dark brown. **Nestling period.** Young tended by both parents.

GREATER BLACK-BACKED GULL *Larus marinus* **Pl. 40**

Breeds in colonies or as single pairs. Nest on top of rock stack or island, or on ground on islands in lakes or estuaries.

Nest. A large accumulation of sticks, mosses, seaweed, grass and some feathers. Built by both birds. **Breeding season.** Begins mid-May. Single-brooded. **Eggs.** Usually 2–3, rarely 4? Smooth, non-glossy or slightly glossy; with a fine granular surface. Pale olive, olive-buff or greenish, exceptionally pale whitish-blue or buff; marked with specks, spots, small blotches or short scrawls of blackish-brown, olive or olive-brown, and fainter gray or blue-gray markings. Markings usually more consistently smaller and evenly distributed in comparison with other large northern gulls. Pinkish variety known. 77 × 54 mm. **Incubation.** Eggs laid on alternate days. Incubation by both sexes, beginning before completion of clutch. 26–30 days. **Nestling.** Semi-precocial and downy. Down long and soft with fine silky tips. Upperparts and throat gray, slightly buffish; lower throat buffish; underside whitish. Many small blackish-brown spots and blotches on head, chin and throat, and similar markings coalescing to form an irregular mottled pattern on back and rump. Bill dark blackish-purple. Legs and feet dull pink. **Nest-**

ling period. Young tended by both parents. Fed for *c.* 7 weeks at the end of which they begin to fly, and fly well within a week.

IVORY GULL *Pagophila eburnea* **Pls. 13, 42**

Breeds in colonies, on shores with shingle and boulders, or on ledges of cliffs; sometimes on similar sites inland.

Nest. A shallow hollow lined with moss, grass, and often some feathers, seaweed and driftwood splinters. **Breeding season.** Begins late June or early July. Single-brooded. **Eggs.** Usually 2, often 1, rarely 3. Subelliptical. Smooth, slightly glossy. Light olive to olive-buff, or buff; spotted and blotched, with blackish-brown, olive-brown and olive, and paler markings in varying shades of gray. 61 × 43 mm. **Incubation.** By both birds(?) beginning with first egg. Period unknown. **Nestling.** Semi-precocial and downy. Down long with fine, hair-like tips. Down gray with white tips. Unpatterned. **Nestling period.** Young tended by both parents. Period unknown.

BLACK-LEGGED KITTIWAKE *Rissa tridactyla* **Pls. 13, 42**

Breeds on ledges of cliffs at varying heights, and in sea-caves. Normally in colonies.

Black-legged Kittiwake: *c.* 1ft. across.

Nest. A solid drum of grass, mud, moss and seaweed, built up on some small projection or irregularity of rock face by continuous addition and firm trampling of material by both birds, the whole adhering to form a nest with a well-defined hollow. **Breeding season.** Begins mid-June. Single-brooded. **Eggs.** Usually 2, rarely 1–3. Subelliptical, smooth, non-glossy. Pale, creamy, or very pale greenish, yellowish, stone, buffish or olive; sometimes a warmer yellow or pinkish-buff. Very variably marked with specks, spots and blotches, of light brown, olive-brown, blackish-brown and paler gray or blue-gray. Frequently some fine speckling, occasionally some irregular scrawling. Markings often sparing, and where heavy blotching occurs it tends to be concentrated in a zone around the larger end. 56 × 41 mm. **Incubation.** Eggs laid on alternate days. Incubation by both birds. 25–30 days. **Nestling.** Semi-precocial and downy. Down long with fine, silky tips. Head and neck, tips of wings and edges creamy-white, glossy. Back dark grayish-brown mixed with some creamy-white. Underparts white. Down clings to tips of first feathers. **Nestling period.** Young tended by both adults. Usually leave at *c.* 43 days, but period may vary from *c.* 35–55 days.

SEA TERNS *Gelochelidon, Hydroprogne, Sterna* species

Small to medium-sized seabirds, catching fish by plunge-diving. Nests usually in colonies, with nests often only a bill-stab apart. More than one species may be present, and other birds may nest on the edges of such colonies to enjoy the protection afforded by the fact that terns may attack predators. The nest is a shallow scrape, often unlined. Material may be added by sideways-building, nest therefore dependent on near-by available material. One to three eggs, cryptically patterned but very varied. Incubation by both birds, usually beginning early in laying of clutch, and young may hatch at intervals of a day or two. Young are downy. Upperparts usually patterned in blackish-brown on buff or gray. Pattern often broken but may show paired dark dorsal streaks. In some species fine tips of down are joined in bunches to give down plumage a spiky appearance. Young fed by both parents on small fish brought in the bill. Young are vulnerable to bad weather conditions. They may leave nest after a few days. In some species they hide near nest while parents are away, but in others larger young gather in groups with a few adults present, usually near water's edge, where adults find and feed their own young. Observation is difficult after young fly but they may be wholly or partly dependent on adults for a month or two after leaving nest.

GULL-BILLED TERN *Gelochelidon nilotica* Pl. 42

Breeds on sandy beaches of coasts and offshore islands, on shores of saline lagoons or shallow lakes, on bare sand, soil or dry mud; in colonies with nests close together.

Nest. A shallow hollow in soft sand or soil, usually sparsely lined with grasses, seaweed or nearby vegetation, or with shells and other debris. **Breeding season.** Begins early May in south, early June in north. Single-brooded. **Eggs.** Usually 3, sometimes 2–5, larger number possible from two females. Subelliptical. Smooth and non-glossy, or very slightly glossy. Very pale creamy-buff to pale yellowish-buff; marked with spots, specks and blotches, usually small, of shades of dark brown, dark olive-brown, or blackish-brown, and paler shades of gray. Markings usually evenly distributed, often profuse, rarely with a concentration around larger end. 49 × 35 mm. **Incubation.** Eggs laid at daily intervals. Incubation by both birds, beginning with third egg. 22–23 days. **Nestling.** Semi-precocial and downy. Down soft and long with fine, hair-like tips. Upperparts buff to buffish-gray, patterned with blackish-brown. Forehead unmarked; three narrow irregular crown stripes, spots or short streaks on nape and behind eye. Pair of dark streaks along mid-back. Short streaks or spots at sides of mantle, along flanks and on upper wings. Rest of wings buff with whitish tip. Lores and lower face whitish, throat gray, and underside white. Down clings to tips of first feathers. **Nestling period.** Young tended by both parents. Fly a little at *c.* 4 weeks, well at *c.* 5 weeks.

CASPIAN TERN *Hydroprogne caspia* **Pls. 12, 44**

Breeds near coasts on sandy or stony beaches, on shores of large inland lakes, and on offshore islands. Nest on ground on bare sand, shell beach or shingle. Usually in colonies, occasionally as single pairs.

Nest. A shallow hollow, unlined, or with a sparse collection of near-by plant debris. **Breeding season.** Begins early April in south to late May in north. Single-brooded, but will replace lost clutch. **Eggs.** Usually 2–3, rarely 1. Subelliptical. Smooth, non-glossy or very slightly glossy; sometimes with a finely granular or textured surface. Pale creamy to creamy-buff; marked with specks, spots and rather small blotches of black, olive, brown, and pale gray. The markings are relatively small, usually finely and evenly distributed. Rarely odd large irregular blotches, sometimes at or around larger end. 64 × 45 mm. **Incubation.** By both birds, beginning with first egg. 20–22 days. **Nestling.** Semi-precocial and downy. Like that of Gull-billed Tern. Down soft and long with fine hair-like tips. Underparts white, sometimes buffish, and throat dusky. Upperparts dull buff or buffish-gray, with small blackish-brown markings, fewer than on Gull-billed Tern, on back and wings, but not on crown and nape. Bill red with dark patch near tip. **Nestling period.** Young tended by both parents. After a few days young leave nest and hide in nearby cover. Fly at 25–30 days.

ROYAL TERN *Sterna maxima* **Pl. 44**

Breeds on coastal beaches, sand-bars and islands. Nests in close-packed, often large, colonies; sometimes in company with other tern species. *Colony may desert if disturbed.*

Nest. A shallow scrape, usually unlined. **Breeding season.** Begins early April in south to mid-May in north. Single-brooded. **Eggs.** Usually 1, rarely 2, the latter possibly from two females. Subelliptical to oval. Smooth and non-glossy. Creamy-white to ivory-yellow, very pale buffish or greenish and rarely deeper buff or pinkish-buff; thickly marked overall with specks, spots and less frequently bold blotches and scrawls in black and gray, larger markings usually showing a blurred brown edge. 63 × 45 mm. **Incubation.** By both sexes. 28–35 days, usually 30–31 days. **Nestling.** Precocial and downy. Down stiff on head, long with fine tips on body. Color very varied. Ground color varies from pale pinkish-cinnamon or pinkish-buff, paler on the underside, deepening through shades of buff to a dusky form in which down tips are blackish and forehead and throat may be black. On palest forms markings may be absent except for a few on rump and head; on buff forms there is heavy spotting over back, wings, flanks, head and throat; and in dusky forms the markings are barely apparent. Bill, legs and feet vary from yellowish-flesh to gray or black. **Nestling period.** Young tended by both parents. Active at one day old and after 2–3 days leave nest and combine in a creche flock that roams about near colony. Young are recognised and fed by parents. Leave creche and can fly at 25–30 days. Adults recorded feeding young about 7 months old in wintering areas.

SANDWICH TERN *Sterna sandvicensis* **Pls. 12, 44**

Breeds on or near the coast, on sandy or shingle banks, sand dunes, offshore sandbanks and islands, and low rocky islands; or by lagoons near the sea. In colonies with nests near each other.

Nest. A shallow hollow, sometimes unlined, or sparsely lined with near-by material. **Breeding season.** Begins late April to early May. Single-brooded. **Eggs.** Usually 2, sometimes 1, rarely 3. Subelliptical. Smooth, slightly glossy. Pale yellow, yellowish-buff or creamy-white. Very variably marked with spots, blotches, specks and scrawls, of brown, blackish-brown, dark olive-brown, and paler gray. Great variation in size and distribution of markings. Large blotching frequently occurs, often concentrated towards larger end, occasional eggs show elongated, slanting markings, or blotches may show brownish blurring along one side. Smaller markings vary from profuse to very sparse. 51 × 36 mm. **Incubation.** Eggs laid at 2-day intervals. Incubation by both birds, beginning before second egg. 20–24 days. **Nestling.** Semi-precocial and downy. Down on head, neck, throat, back and wings long and soft with fine tips, but groups of tips joined in one sheath, giving down a spiky appearance. On flanks and underside down is normal. Spiky down light buff to gray, with blackish down-bases showing, and black spots and mottling on crown of head, and black line along wings. Downy sides buffish-white. Bill, legs and feet gray tinged with blue, pink or yellow. **Nestling period.** Young may hatch at intervals of up to 2–3 days. Tended by both parents. During second week young of colony tend to assemble, usually by water's edge, where they are fed by parents which recognise their own young. They fly at *c.* 35 days. Adults recorded still feeding young on migration in August.

ROSEATE TERN *Sterna dougallii* **Pl. 43**

Breeds on coastal sites; on sand, shingle banks, or low rocky shores or islands. Nests in colonies, often among other terns.

Nest. A shallow hollow, usually unlined, on rock or among shingle or shore plants. **Breeding season.** Begins early June. Single-brooded. **Eggs.** Usually 1–2, rarely 3. Subelliptical. Smooth, non-glossy. Light cream, or tinted yellowish, buffish or olive, or occasionally deeper olive or buff. Speckled, spotted or blotched, or occasionally with short lines or scrawls, of blackish-brown, black, dark brown or olive, and paler shades of gray. Markings very variable, often fine and rather profuse, sometimes more sparse. Occasionally a concentrated zone around the larger end. 43 × 30 mm. **Incubation.** Eggs laid at 2–3-day intervals. Incubation by both birds, mainly by female, beginning early in laying of clutch. 21–26 days. **Nestling.** Semi-prococial and downy. Down resembles that of Sandwich Tern in that, except on breast and belly, the filament tips are joined in groups, giving the down plumage a spiky appearance. Breast and belly white. Upper-parts gray tinted with pale to warm buff, and speckled with blackish down bases and dark markings. Bill bluish to pinkish-gray with darker reddish-brown tip. Legs and feet gray to pinkish-gray. **Nestling period.** Young tended by both parents.

COMMON TERN *Sterna hirundo* **Pls. 12, 42**

Breeds on shingle and sand banks, usually coastal or by large inland lakes, sometimes in rivers; sand dunes; sandy or rocky coastal islands; or salt marshes. Nest on the ground, occasionally on muskrat lodges or rafts of floating vegetation. Nests colonially.

Nest. A hollow, unlined, or variably lined with near-by plant material and odd feathers, built by female. **Breeding season.** Begins late May. Single-brooded.

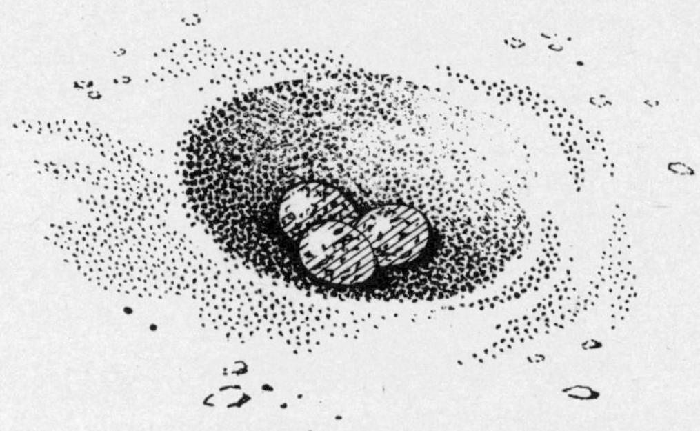

Common Tern: *above,* no nest material; *below,* with material near-by *c.* 8 in. across.

Eggs. Usually 2–3, rarely 4. Subelliptical. Smooth, non-glossy. Creamy, or tinted very pale yellowish, greenish or olive; or light to deep buff or olive; very variably marked with blotches, spots, specks and fine irregular lines of black, blackish-brown, dark to olive-brown, and paler shades of gray. Frequently irregular heavy blotching mixed with fine spots and specks; but markings may vary from sparse to profuse. Occasionally markings concentrated around larger end. Rarely pale bluish-white and very sparsely marked. 42 × 30 mm. **Incubation.** Eggs laid at 1–2-day intervals. Incubation by both birds, but mainly by female, beginning with first egg. 20–23 days. **Nestling.** Semi-precocial and downy. Down long and soft with fine, hair-like tips. Upperparts buff to gray; patterned with blackish-brown, usually as spots on head, but forehead usually uniform. Larger dark blotching on back and wings broken along flanks but tending to form paired dark streaks down mantle and back. Area round eyes buff with buff streak to bill, but chin white, upper lores and throat dusky blackish-brown, and rest of underside whitish. Legs and feet pink to yellowish-orange. Bill orange with dark brown or black tip. **Nestling period.** Young tended by both parents. May leave nest after 3 days but return for brooding. They can swim at an early age. Begin flying at *c.* 28 days.

ARCTIC TERN *Sterna paradisaea* **Pl. 42**

Breeds on small rocky islands, near or off shore, on sand or shingle banks, sand dunes, or grassy slopes. Usually on coast, sometimes inland. Usually in colony, sometimes with other terns or other sea-birds andsea-ducks.

Nest. A shallow hollow, often unlined or sparsely lined with near-by plant material and debris. Built by female. **Breeding season.** Begins mid-May to early June. Single-brooded. **Eggs.** Usually 2, sometimes 3 or 1. Subelliptical. Smooth, non-glossy. Often shades of buff or pale greenish or olive, but may vary from bluish-white or creamy through to deep brown; exceptionally pink. Marking variable. Blotching, sometimes extensive, spots, specks, and sometimes short scrawls, in blackish-brown, black, or dark olive. Sometimes a zone of heavy markings around larger end, or larger markings elongated and slanting in one direction. 40 × 29 mm. **Incubation.** By both birds. 20–22 days. **Nestling.** Semi-precocial and downy. Similar to that of Common Tern, but usually more heavily marked on the back, and the dusky blackish-brown of the throat usually extends to chin and forehead. **Nestling period.** Young tended by both parents. May leave nest soon after hatching but remain near by. Can swim at 2 days. Fly at 20–22 days, but are fed by adults for a longer period.

ALEUTIAN TERN *Sterna aleutica* **Pl. 43**

Breeds on offshore islands, on raised dry areas, in open places. Nest on the ground.

Nest. A hollow in moss, usually unlined. **Breeding season.** Begins late June. Single-brooded. **Eggs.** Usually 2, rarely 1–3. Smooth and non-glossy. Yellowish or olive to yellowish-buff or olive-buff. Heavily and boldly blotched, with more sparse spotting or speckling in medium to dark brown and pale gray. Markings often elongated and tending to be concentrated at the larger end. 42 × 29 mm. **Incubation.** 21 days? **Nestling.** Semi-precocial and downy. Down light buff to grayish-buff on upper parts, blotched with black. Black on chin and throat extending to upper breast, unlike Arctic Tern, and breast otherwise white, shading into very dark gray on belly and flanks. **Nestling period.** No information.

FORSTER'S TERN *Sterna forsteri* **Pl. 42**

Breeds on inland lakes and marshes, on floating masses of plant material held by growing stems of tall plants, tules, reeds or sedges; or on floating logs, old muskrat houses or occasionally old grebe nests; and on coastal or island sites on salt marsh, using drifted tideline debris or short herbage.

Nest. An accumulation of plant material, varying according to that available at site, from scantily lined hollow to a neat cup. **Breeding season.** Begins late May to early June. Single-brooded. **Eggs.** Usually 2–3. Subelliptical to oval. Smooth and non-glossy. Very pale olive or greenish to light buff or olive-buff; heavily speckled, spotted and blotched overall with dark brown, black and pale gray. 43 × 31 mm. **Incubation.** By both sexes. 23–25 days. **Nestling.** Semi-precocial and downy. Down varies in color from pale stone to cinnamon-buff or pinkish-buff, darkening to brown on the throat but not as dark as on the Common Tern. Underside similar but paler, almost white on belly. Upperparts spotted or streaked in blackish-brown, heavier on the back where it forms large irregular aggregations or longitudinal bands. **Nestling period.** Young tended by both parents. Remain in nest for a few days. Then run and swim actively.

SOOTY TERN *Sterna fuscata* **Pl. 43**

Breeds on open beach. In large colony with nests close together. Birds apparently visit and select sites by night.

Nest. A shallow scrape. Unlined, but some near-by stones or leaves may be pulled to edge of scrape. **Breeding season.** Begins early April to early May. Single-brooded, but lost clutch replaced. **Eggs.** Only one. Subelliptical. Smooth and non-glossy. White or tinted pink or more rarely buff. Usually profusely and finely spotted and speckled overall, or occasionally blotched, with deep reddish-brown and paler lilac. On some markings are sparse except for a concentration of bold dark blotches at or around larger end. Some larger markings show a blurred, paler edge. 50 × 35 mm. **Incubation.** By both sexes. Sitting periods variable but may be long at times, possibly several days. Change-over usually at night. 28–31 days. **Nestling.** Semi-precocial and downy. Down shortish and filaments may be grouped in sheaths as on Roseate Tern. Upper parts, head, throat and neck speckled with grayish-white and gray-black. Buff tips to down may also be present. Under parts white. **Nestling period.** Young tended by both parents. Brooded during first week. Usually leave nest and hide when alone. Feathered at *c.* 30 days. Fly at 55–60 days. Young probably remain with parents and are fed by them for some time after leaving nest and fledging.

LEAST TERN *Sterna albifrons* **Pls. 12, 43**

Breeds, usually in small colonies, on sand and shingle beaches on coast, or banks in estuaries and rivers.

Nest. A shallow hollow, usually unlined, or sparingly lined with near-by plant material or small pebbles or shell fragments. Made by female. **Breeding season.** Begins May. Single-brooded, but replaces lost clutches. **Eggs.** Usually 2–3. Subelliptical. Smooth, non-glossy. Very pale, tinted olive or buff, or cream-colored, sometimes slightly warmer buff. Spotted, blotched and speckled, in brown, blackish-brown, and shades of gray. Often finer dark markings are combined with larger pale gray ones. Markings variable but usually well-distributed, often profuse; with occasionally some concentration towards larger end. Exceptionally slanting elongated blotches or streaks towards larger end. 32 × 23 mm. **Incubation.** Eggs laid on consecutive days. Incubation by both birds, usually beginning with second egg. 19–22 days. **Nestling.** Semi-precocial and downy. Down shorter than that of other terns, with fine hair-like tips. Sandy-buff on head and upperparts, with mottling of darker brown, sometimes showing three parallel streaks on crown, and paired dark streaks on back, or so irregular that pattern is not obvious. Underparts white, or tinted light sandy-buff. Bill flesh-gray with dark brown tip. Legs and fleet flesh-colored. **Nestling period.** Young tended by both adults. Can leave nest after 1 day but remain nearby. Fly at 15–17 days.

MARSH TERNS *Chlidonias* species

Medium-sized terns feeding and nesting on still fresh and brackish waters with growing vegetation. Nests usually floating, with material more plentiful than with other terns. Material may occasionally be carried as well as being accumulated by sideways-building. Eggs heavily patterned, oval, and rarely pyriform. Young downy, warm buff mottled with black. Semi-precocial, but the aquatic nest-site limits wandering at first. Adults bring food in bill.

BLACK TERN *Chlidonias niger* **Pls. 12, 43**

Breeds on shallow, still waters, fresh or brackish, often with reedy vegetation; or sloughs and swampy marshes. Nest either as heap of floating vegetation in water, anchored by growing plants, or on mats of floating aquatic vegetation or heaps of fallen herbage; on old muskrat houses, old grebe or coot nests, or floating driftwood; or on firm ground among marshy herbage. Usually nests in colonies.

Nest. In water a heap of waterplants and reeds, formed by material pulled together, or rarely carried to the site, and lined with finer material. On firmer ground the nest is a scrape with a sparse lining of pieces of reeds and other plant matter. **Breeding season.** Begins mid- to late May. Single-brooded. **Eggs.** Usually 3, sometimes 2–4. Oval to subpyriform. Smooth and slightly glossy. Light buffish to brown, or pale yellowish or creamy; with irregular spotting or blotching, often large, in black and brown, frequently concentrated in a broad zone around the larger end. 34 × 25 mm. **Incubation.** By both sexes, beginning with last egg. 20–22 days. **Nestling.** Semi-precocial and downy. Down long and soft with fine silky tips. Upper parts warm buff mottled with black and extending to throat and chin. Mid-breast grayish-white, flanks and belly buffish-gray. Forehead, around base of bill, and patch around eyes white. Double row of small irregular blackish blotches over crown, dark streak down neck, double streak down mantle, broken line of blackish mottling along sides of back and dark median streak ending in a blotch; and dark mottling on the upper wings. **Nestling period.** Young tended by both adults. Young can move about but remain on nest for *c.* 2 weeks, start to fly at *c.* 3, are fully fledged at *c.* 4.

Black Tern: *c.* 8-10in. across.

NODDY TERNS *Anous* species

BROWN NODDY TERN *Anous stolidus* **Pls. 12, 43**

Breeds on keys and coastal islands, nesting on trees, shrubs, cacti, on rocks or on the ground. Nests mostly built on raised sites, in bush or low tree. Usually in colonies, with nests fairly close together.

Nest. A platform or shallow cup, of sticks, seaweed, and sometimes shells and coral fragments in the lining. Re-used in subsequent years and may become substantial. Built by both sexes. **Breeding season.** Begins early May. Single-brooded. **Eggs.** Only one. Subelliptical. Smooth and non-glossy. White or faintly tinted buff or pink, sparsely marked, mostly at the larger end, with specks, spots and blotches of reddish-brown, and paler shades of lilac and purple. 52 × 35 mm. **Incubation.** By both sexes. 35–36 days. **Nestling.** Semi-precocial and downy. Several color phases. May be uniform drab whitish, or overall dark brownish-black, or dark with white cap, or mainly white with grayish-brown on back and wings, or other intermediate states. **Nestling period.** Young tended by both parents. Normally remain in nest until fledged but will leave nests in low sites at a young age when alarmed; and climb back later or be fed on the ground by parents. Fly at 40–44 days.

SKIMMERS *Rychopidae*

BLACK SKIMMER *Rynchops nigra* **Pls. 12, 43**

Breeds on large beaches, or low sandy islands offshore or in estuaries; rarely on saltmarsh. Usually in an open site. Nest on the ground in a loose colony.

Nest. A bare shallow scrape, unlined. **Breeding season.** Begins early May in south to early June in north. Single-brooded. **Eggs.** 2–5. Subelliptical to oval. Smooth and non-glossy. White to creamy-white, or faintly tinted buff; irregularly and boldly blotched, and with some sparse spots and specks, of black, blackish-olive and shades of pale gray. Gray markings often numerous. 45 × 36 mm. **Incubation.** By female only, beginning with first egg. Period not recorded. **Nestling.** Semi-precocial and downy. Down thick and soft. Pale vinous-buff, lightly mottled with dusky brown on back and faint mottling on head. Underparts white. Mandibles of bill are of even length, adult bill only attained by fledging period. **Nestling period.** Young tended by both parents. Fed on regurgitated food at first, later on whole fish. Young have mandibles of even length and can pick up food and catch insects; when alarmed young may dig themselves into hollows in the sand, kicking up sand which partly hides them.

AUKS *Alcidae*

Medium-sized to small seabirds, living by diving for prey. Nest on shore at or near the sea, on rock ledges or in crevices or holes. Sideways-building is used but owing to sites nest material may be absent or very variable. Eggs are large for the size of the birds, and clutches of one or two. Young downy, and most are virtually altricial, remaining at the nest-site. They leave the nest and go straight to sea.

COMMON MURRE *Uria aalge* — Pls. 13, 46

Breeds on sea-coasts, on ledges of cliffs and on the level tops of isolated rock stacks, and on the slopes and tops of low rocky islands. Breeds colonially, with birds crowded very close together.

Nest. No nest, egg laid on bare rock. Individually variable egg patterns may assist adults to identify eggs. **Breeding season.** Begins mid-May in south to mid-June in north. Single-brooded. **Eggs.** Only 1. Large and pyriform. Surface finely granular and roughened, non-glossy. Color and markings extremely variable. Ground color from white through shades of buff, brown, reddish, cream, blue or green; immaculate or marked in shades of brown or black with variable combinations of dots, spots, blotches or intricate scribbling; at times uniformly dark in color or with pale or dark central zones. 81 × 50 mm. **Incubation.** By both sexes. Egg rests on the webs of the feet, covered by the belly feathers. 28–35 days. **Nestling.** Altricial and downy. Down thick, with fine tips; short on underside, longer and coarser on head and neck. Black on head and neck streaked with white sheaths enclosing several filaments. Body sooty-brown above with some grayish mottling, and buffish-white underneath. Feathers begin to show within a few days. Bill blue-gray. Mouth pale flesh. Iris brown. Legs and feet yellowish with blackish on back of legs and on webs. **Nestling period.** Young tended by both parents. Leave for sea at 18–25 days, only part-grown; accompanied, and possibly fed for a time, by an adult, probably not a parent? Cannot fly for *c.* 3 weeks after leaving.

THICK-BILLED MURRE *Uria lomvia* — Pl. 45

Breeds on sea-cliffs and rock stacks, in similar sites to the Common Murre, but further north; although sometimes in mixed colonies. Breeds in colonies, often large, with birds crowding very close together.

Nest. As for Common Murre. **Breeding season.** Begins early to mid-June. Single-brooded. **Eggs.** Only 1. Large and pyriform. Surface granular and roughened, non-glossy. Color and markings very variable. Ground color shades of white, cream, buff, reddish, greenish or blue; marked with buff, brown, purplish or black specks, spots, blotches, streaks or scribbling. 80 × 50 mm. **Incubation.** By both sexes. Eggs rest on the webs of the feet, covered by the belly feathers. 28–35 days. **Nestling.** Altricial and downy. Resembles that of Common Murre but shows more streaking, with white sheaths of head and neck more prominent and paler brown tips to down of back. Feathers begin to show after a few days. **Nestling period.** As for Common Murre.

RAZORBILL *Alca torda* **Pls. 13, 45**

Breeds on sea-coasts, on cliffs or on low rocky or boulder-strewn shores. Nest usually in a crevice or niche, more concealed than the exposed ledges used by murres, or holes between or under boulders.

Nest. Normally no nest material, occasionally a few loose fragments accumulated. **Breeding season.** Begins early to mid-June in north. Single-brooded. **Eggs.** Usually 1, rarely 2. Subelliptical to oval. Surface finely granular and roughened, non-glossy. Very variable in color. Ground color varies from white through yellowish, buff and shades of brown, or sometimes reddish or greenish; variably speckled, spotted, scribbled, blotched or banded with dark brown and/or black. The inner shell membrane is greenish. 73 × 47 mm. **Incubation.** By both sexes. 25–35 days. **Nestling.** Altricial and downy. Down short and thick, with fine silky tips. Lores, forehead and crown white; remainder of head, throat, back of neck blackish-brown with white tips. Upper parts and wings blackish-brown, tipped with pale buff above and on wings, white on mid-underside. Bill black, mouth pale yellow. Iris brown. Legs and feet black. **Nestling period.** Young tended by both parents. Leaves nest at 12–14 days for sea, accompanied by an adult.

BLACK GUILLEMOT *Cepphus grylle* **Pls. 13, 47**

Breeds on sea-coasts. Nest in a hole, under or among boulders, on low island, boulder beach, or base of a cliff; or in hole or crevice in cliffs. More rarely in hole in earth bank, or turf, or hole in building; or steep hillside near sea. Nests are in a loose colony of scattered pairs, due to dispersed nest-sites.

Nest. A hollow, normally unlined; sometimes with an accumulation of near-by debris. **Breeding season.** Begins early June in south to late June in north. Single-brooded. **Eggs.** Usually 2, often 1, sometimes 3. Shortish subelliptical. Smooth, non-glossy. White, sometimes lightly tinted with buff or bluish-green, marked with a mixture of various sized spots and blotches of black and pale gray, or reddish-brown at times. The inner shell membrane is green. 58 × 40 mm. **Incubation.** By both sexes, beginning with first egg, the male incubating by night, the female by day. 27–28 days?. **Nestling.** Altricial and downy. Down soft, thick and with silky tips. Blackish-brown, paler below. Bill black. Mouth pink. Legs and feet dark brown. The down remains on the tips of the first feathers. **Nestling period.** Young tended by both adults, leaving the nest at 34–40 days, fully fledged.

PIGEON GUILLEMOT *Cepphus columba* **Pl. 47**

Breeds on rocky coasts and offshore islands. Nests in cliffs, talus slopes, piles of

rocks and boulders on shores and caves. Nest in a cavity under a rock, in a crevice or a similar cavity site.
Nest. A natural hollow or slight concavity. Unlined, or tiny stones and other debris from immediately around site may be brought together to form a heap. **Breeding season.** Begins mid-May in south to mid-June in north. Single-brooded. **Eggs.** Usually 2 eggs. Similar to those of Black Guillemot in shape, color and markings. 61 × 41 mm. **Incubation.** By both sexes, beginning with first egg. Probably *c.* 28 days. **Nestling.** Semi-precocial and downy. Down soft and thick. Blackish-brown above, browner on underside. **Nestling period.** Young tended by both parents. After first few days young may leave nest itself and move around and hide, but do not leave nesting cavity until fledging. May come to entrance to take fish from adults. Probably fledge at *c.* 34–40 days.

MARBLED MURRELET *Brachyramphus marmoratum* **Pl. 47**
Only two nests known. These are in coastal coniferous forest, up to 5 miles from sea, 22-148 ft up a tree; near the trunk on a horizontal branch, sheltered but with direct access in flight. Probably re-used in successive years.
Nest. A thick pad of moss, consolidated with a ring of droppings around a hollow. **Breeding season.** Egg-laying begins early to mid-May, continuing to late June or early July. **Eggs.** Apparently only one. Long elliptical with bluntly rounded ends. Pale greenish-yellow or greenish-buff, with a thick spotting of dark brown, black and pale blue or gray. **Incubation.** Both sexes have brood patches. Period probably 30 days? **Nestling.** Altricial and downy. Down long, soft and thick, absent below eyes and around bill. Underside light buffish-gray, darker on flanks. Back and head yellowish-buff, the back mottled with black; head and neck with distinct black spots. Bill black. Legs and feet pinkish white to gray in front, black behind. Iris brown. **Nestling period.** Adults bring fish in bill. Young must fly to sea, appearing alone *c.* 20-22 days after probable hatching time.

KITTLITZ'S MURRELET *Brachyramphus brevirostre* **Pl. 13**
Breeds high on mountains, near tops, at some distance from sea. Nest on bare ground above tree-line, where snow may still be present.
Nest. Egg laid on bare ground in slight concavity. No material, or possibly a few small stones and fragments of moss pulled in. **Breeding season.** Begins late May to early June. **Eggs.** One only. Fairly long elliptical with bluntly rounded ends. Olive or olive-buff, with specks, spots and small blotches of light and dark brown, and black. 60 × 36 mm. **Incubation.** No information. **Nestling.** Semi-precocial? and downy. Down of body mainly medium gray, with blackish bases showing in places, and back suffused with buffish-yellow. Head and throat buffish-yellow with black spotting, becoming gray on breast and pale gray on belly. Bill black. Legs and feet pink at front, brownish-black at back. Nails black. Irides dark brown. **Nestling period.** Young still at nest at 13 days; downy, with wing quills showing.

XANTUS'S MURRELET *Endomychura hypoleuca* **Pls. 13, 47**
Breeds on rocky offshore islands in large colonies. Nest in a cavity, cliff crevice, cavity under rock, corner of a cave, or hollow under dense bush or agave foliage.
Nest. A bare natural hollow, or a scrape on soft earth; with no lining. **Breeding season.** Begins mid-March. Late eggs have been suggested as second broods, but might indicate extended breeding season as in Cassin's Auklet. **Eggs.**

Usually 1 or 2. Two eggs often differ in color. Long elliptical. Smooth and moderately glossy. Pale blue, greenish, olive, buff or brown, the last two sometimes darker. Speckled, spotted, blotched or scrawled with brown and paler purple. Smaller markings often fine and profuse, larger markings sparse and may be concentrated at the larger end. 53 × 36 mm. **Incubation.** By both sexes. Change-over at night. Period not recorded. **Nestling.** Precocial and downy. Down thick and fine, and very dense on underparts. Sooty-black on upper parts, including head down to lores and ear-coverts, with a small white mark above and below eye. Remainder of underside, from throat downwards, white. Color pattern similar to that of adult plumage. **Nestling period.** Young tended by both parents. Remain at nest for 2–4 days, then leave for sea at night, in down plumage, and swim away with parents. Can swim and dive easily at this age.

ANCIENT MURRELET *Synthliboramphus antiquus* **Pl. 47**
Breeds on offshore islands, nesting in very large colonies. Burrows into matted vegetation or soft soil, or uses old burrows of other species, cavities under rocks, crevices or similar sites.

Nest. A tunnel, sometimes 2–3 ft. long, with nest cavity at end, *c* 5 in. across and 2–3 in. deep; often but not always lined with dry grass brought in from outside. **Breeding season.** Appears to vary, beginning late April to early June. **Eggs.** Usually 2, sometimes 1. Long subelliptical. Smooth and slightly to moderately glossy. Very pale to medium creamy-buff or buff; evenly but not heavily marked with fine speckles and spots, and with some small blotches of light to medium brown and paler purplish-gray. The larger markings mainly of the last color. 61 × 39 mm. **Incubation.** No information. **Nestling.** Precocial and downy. Down of upperparts, including head to lores and lower edge of ear-coverts, black with a blue-gray tinge, and with a whitish patch on the hinder ear-covert. Underparts white, tinged yellow. **Nestling period.** Young tended by both parents, visited at night. At *c.* 4 days young leave burrow at night and go to sea in response to calls of parents. They can swim well and are led out to sea away from breeding ground.

DOVEKIE *Alle alle* **Pls. 13, 47**
Breeds on or near sea-coasts, on cliffs, or steep hillsides further inland, usually in very large colonies. Nest in holes or crevices in rocks or among piled boulders at the foot of slopes.

Nest. An unlined hollow. **Breeding season.** Begins mid-June. Single-brooded. **Eggs.** Usually 1, rarely 2. Subelliptical. Smooth, non-glossy. Pale blue, normally immaculate, rarely marked with spots or scribbles of buffish-brown at the larger end. 48 × 34 mm. **Incubation.** By both sexes. 24 days. **Nestling.** Altricial and downy. Down thick, soft and silky tipped. Blackish-brown, with paler brown on the underside (almost black when first hatched), and gray on mid-underside. **Nestling period.** Young tended by both parents. Later in period may come to entrance of hole and exercise wings while parents are present. Leaves nest at *c.* 3–4 weeks, usually going to sea accompanied by adults.

CASSIN'S AUKLET *Ptychoramphus aleuticus* **Pls. 13, 48**
Breeds on offshore islands, often in large colonies. Nests in burrows dug in sandy soil, in turf or under rocks, cavities under rocks, crevices in rocks, driftwood piles, or any similar site. From sea-level to *c.* 500 ft.

Nest. A burrow 2–6 ft. long, the nest cavity bare or with a nest of plant stems, twigs or any material that may be present near entrance to burrow. **Breeding season.** Information poor. Possibly begins about mid-May in north, but in south appears prolonged, with burrows being excavated in January, eggs from March to July, and young from May to July and possibly to October. **Eggs.** Only one. Subelliptical. Smooth and non-glossy. White, frequently nest-stained. 47 × 34 mm. **Incubation.** By both sexes. At least 37 days. **Nestling.** Semi-precocial and downy. Down varies from black to dark purplish-gray on back and from medium or pale gray to pale purplish-gray on underside. Absent from area around eye. Irides brown. Legs and feet pink with black claws at first; changing to blackish-gray by tenth day. **Nestling period.** Young tended by both parents. Brooded for first 3–4 days. Adults visit burrow at night. Birds defecate at burrow entrance. Young bird's feathers begin to appear at 12–16 days. Wing-exercise at entrance at 30–35 days. Young leave burrow at 41–50 days.

CRESTED AUKLET *Aethia cristatella* **Pl. 48**

Breeds on rocky shores and offshore islands. Nest in crevices or cavity among fallen boulders, on talus slopes, or similar sites.

Nest. Egg laid on a bare site, no nest. **Breeding season.** Begins mid- to late June. **Eggs.** Oval. Smooth or very slight granular texture, non-glossy. White. 54 × 38 mm. **Incubation.** By both sexes. Period not recorded. **Nestling.** Semi-precocial and downy. Down brown above and pale grayish-brown below. **Nestling period.** Young tended by both parents, food brought in throat pouch. Young leave nest at *c.* 4–5 weeks?

LEAST AUKLET *Aethia pusilla* **Pl. 47**

Breeds on rocky coasts and offshore islands. Nest in crevice in rocks, among fallen boulders, on talus slopes, or similar sites. Nests in large colonies.

Nest. Egg laid on a bare site, no nest. **Breeding season.** Begins mid- to late June. **Eggs.** Oval to subelliptical. Smooth and non-glossy. White. 39 × 29 mm. **Incubation.** By both sexes. Period not recorded. **Nestling.** Semi-precocial and downy. Down brown above and pale grayish-brown below. **Nestling period.** Young tended by both parents, fed on small crustaceans brought in throat pouch. Leave nest at *c.* 4–5 weeks.

PARAKEET AUKLET *Cyclorrhynchus psittacula*

Nests on offshore islands with cliffs and rocky slopes. Nest in turf-covered rock slopes where cavities and crevices occur, in crevices on cliff-face, among large boulders by shore, or under ledges. Breed in loose groups of pairs, with nests sometimes scattered.

Nest. Eggs laid on a bare site, rock or soil; or with near-by pebbles gathered together to line hollow. **Breeding season.** Begins mid- to late June. **Eggs.** One only. Subelliptical. Smooth with slight granular texture, non-glossy. Dull white, bluish-white, or rarely pale blue. 54 × 37 mm. **Incubation.** By both sexes. Period not recorded. **Nestling.** Semi-precocial and downy. Down blackish-brown on upperparts, back browner than head; underside paler and grayer. **Nestling period.** Young tended by both parents. Wing feathers developed rapidly. Young do not leave nest cavity until fully fledged.

RHINOCEROS AUKLET *Cerorhinca monocerata* **Pl. 48**

Breeds on offshore islands. Nest in a burrow dug by birds in steep slope or on more level ground. Nests in colonies.

Nest. A burrow 5–15 ft. long, or sometimes 4–25 ft.; sloping down at end to nest chamber *c.* 12 in. across and 6–8 in. high. Excavation by both sexes taking 1–2 weeks. **Breeding season.** Begins early May in south to early June in north. Single-brooded, but a lost egg may be replaced. **Eggs.** Only one. Subelliptical to oval. Smooth and non-glossy. Often nest-stained. White, unmarked, or marked sparsely with scrawls and spots of pale purplish-gray and light brown, often confined to a zone around the larger end. 68 × 46 mm. **Incubation.** By both sexes, changing over at night. 31–33 days. **Nestling.** Semi-precocial and downy. Down dark grayish-brown, paler below. **Nestling period.** Young tended by both adults. Little or no brooding occurs. Young can move around soon after hatching. Come to entrance to defecate. Fledge at 5–6 weeks, leaving for sea while still downy and only partly grown.

ATLANTIC PUFFIN *Fratercula arctica* **Pls. 13, 48**

Breeds on sea-coasts, on turf slopes on tops of cliffs. Cliffs with talus slopes, coastal hillsides, or the tops of islands down to sea-level. Nest in a burrow excavated by puffin; or in a hole among boulders or a natural crevice.

Nest. A shallow hollow, a few feet inside tunnel. Plant material and feathers are carried in, but not arranged systematically as a lining. **Breeding season.** Begins early June. Single-brooded. **Eggs.** Usually 1, rarely 2. Shortish subelliptical. Smooth, non-glossy. Usually white, but often with markings within the shell showing as faint brown or purplish blotches. Exceptionally shell buff or light brown with brown or purple blotches and spotting. 61 × 42 mm. **Incubation.** Usually by female alone, the male occasionally helping. 35–43 days? **Nestling.** Altricial and downy. Down long and soft with fine tips. Down buffish-brown to blackish-brown on upper parts. Down bases gray. Mid-underparts white. Bill black, lower mandible paler. Mouth pale flesh-color. Iris brown. Legs and feet black. **Nestling period.** Young tended by both adults. Leaves for sea alone at night after 47–51 days.

HORNED PUFFIN *Fratercula corniculata* **Pl. 48**

Breeds on rocky headlands and offshore islands. Nest a burrow in earth at varying heights from sea-level; may also use crevices or cavities in rocks occasionally. Often nests in large colonies.

Nest. Nest in a tunnel 2–10 ft. long. Shallow nest hollow bare, or sparsely lined with dry grasses or other near-by plant material. **Breeding season.** Begins early June. **Eggs.** Only one. Subelliptical to oval. Smooth and non-glossy. Dull white, often nest-stained; marked with faint spots or scrawls in pale gray or purplish-gray. 72–49 mm. **Incubation.** By both sexes. Period not recorded. **Nestling.** Semi-precocial and downy. Down long, soft and dense. Pale grayish-brown or darker brown above, paling to grayish-white or yellowish-white on belly. **Nestling period.** Young tended by both parents. Young leave nest when partly grown and feathered, unable to fly properly, and flutter down to sea, swimming away accompanied by parents.

TUFTED PUFFIN *Lunda cirrhata* **Pl. 48**
Breeds on rocky shores and offshore islands. Nest in a shallow burrow in the soil under turf, usually on the tops of islands, or in a rock crevice on a cliff or slope. Nests in colonies.
Nest. A shallow hollow, usually well lined with dry grasses, feather and other material brought in from near by; sometimes hollow unlined. **Breeding season.** Begins late April in south to early June in north. **Eggs.** Only one. Subelliptical to oval. Smooth and non-glossy. Dull white, often nest-stained; unmarked, or marked with sparse to profuse faint spots and scrawls in pale gray or purplish-gray and sometimes pale brown. 72 × 49 mm. **Incubation.** By both sexes. *c.* 30 days. **Nestling.** Semi-precocial and downy. Down long, soft and silky. Sooty-black above and sooty-gray below. **Nestling period.** Young tended by both parents. Young leave nest for sea when about half-fledged, accompanied by parents.

PIGEONS *Columbidae*

Medium-sized bird nesting in trees or shrubs, or on rocks. Nest thin, sketchy and platform-like. Material carried to the nest in the bill and added with small lateral quiverings of the bill as material is inserted. Male bringing material may land on back of female, and pass it to her over her shoulder. Clutch of 2, or sometimes 1, white egg. Eggs covered continually after first is laid. Male usually incubates by day, female by night, changing over in late afternoon. Young have sparse hairy down with bare skin showing through. The base of the bill is swollen and sensitive. They are fed by adults on a crop secretion for several days, then the amount of seed and plant material is increased. They take the food from inside the adult's bill. Young follow parents, or are visited and fed by them, after leaving the nest, but there is little information on this period and its duration.

ROCK DOVE *Columba livia* **Pl. 50**
Usually nest colonially. The wild form breeds in caves and crevices of sea-cliffs, gorges, or rock outcrops. Domesticated form breeds on ledges on or in man-made structures, sometimes at or below ground level. Nest on a ledge or in a hole, often well inside the various major sites, in almost dark situations.
Nest. A scanty layer, at times almost absent, at others more solid, of fine stems, roots, twigs, etc., or in towns sometimes pieces of wire of similar appearance. Both sexes build, but male usually brings material for female to incorporate. **Breeding season.** March or April to August or September. In urban situations may be longer. Double- or treble-brooded. **Eggs.** Normally 2, rarely 1. Subelliptical. Smooth and slightly glossy. White. 39 × 29 mm. **Incubation.** By both sexes, beginning with first egg. 17–19 days. **Nestling.** Altricial and downy. Down sparse and coarse, mainly yellowish with a slight reddish tint. Bill dull gray with pale, flesh-colored tip. Legs and feet grayish-pink. **Nestling period.** Young are brooded continually at first, and fed by both parents. Later left alone more. After flying they are still fed by parents for a time. Independent in 30–35 days.

WHITE-CROWNED PIGEON *Columba leucocephala* **Pl. 50**
Breeds in woodland, mangroves and low scrub. Nest in tree, or shrub, often low, or in cacti. Nest often in fairly open site. Usually nests in colonies.

Nest. A platform of twigs, roots and plant-stems. **Breeding season.** Begins late May. **Eggs.** Usually 2. Long elliptical to subelliptical. Smooth and fairly glossy. White. 37 × 27 mm. **Incubation.** No information. **Nestling.** Altricial and downy. Down sparse and pale buff with bare blackish skin showing. **Nestling period.** No information.

BAND-TAILED PIGEON *Columba fasciata* **Pl. 50**
Breeds in mountain and highland forest, particularly areas where oaks are plentiful. Nest in a tree or shrub, often standing above a small slope or precipice, and near a clearing. Often fairly low, 8–20 ft. up, occasionally much higher.
Nest. A typical shallow twig platform. **Breeding season.** Begins early March in south to early May in north. Prolonged. Probably several broods. **Eggs.** Only one. Long elliptical. Smooth and fairly glossy. White. 40 × 28 mm. **Incubation.** By both sexes. 18–20 days. **Nestling.** Altricial and downy. Down sparse, coarse and white, with yellow skin showing. **Nestling period.** No information.

RED-BILLED PIGEON *Columba flavirostris* **Pl. 50**
Breeds in woodland, or cultivated areas and open areas with patches of woodland or groves of trees; usually in semi-arid or arid areas but near water. Nest in a tree or shrub, 6–30 ft. up.
Nest. A shallow platform of twigs, sometimes with some finer stems, roots or grasses. *c.* 8 in. across by 2½ in. deep, and 1 in. depression. Built by both sexes. **Breeding season.** Begins early March. Prolonged. Several broods. **Eggs.** Only one. Long elliptical to subelliptical. Smooth and moderately glossy. White. 39 × 27 mm. **Incubation.** By both sexes. Period not recorded. **Nestling.** Altricial and downy. Down coarse and sparse; dark. Skin reddish-brown. **Nestling period.** Young tended by both parents. Adults appear to remove the droppings of unfeathered young.

WHITE-WINGED DOVE *Zenaida asiatica* **Pls. 14, 50**
Breeds in arid regions with scrub and thickets, woodland, and cultivated areas with trees. Nest in a tree or shrub. Often nests in loose colonies in mesquite thickets. Elsewhere nests singly or in loose groups. Nests may be 4–25 ft. up, but usually about 8–12 ft. up.
Nest. A shallow, thin platform of twigs, or occasionally weed-stems or grasses. **Breeding season.** Begins late March to early April. Prolonged. **Eggs.** Usually 2. Elliptical to long elliptical or subelliptical. Smooth and glossy. Buff to creamy or white. 31 × 23 mm. **Incubation.** By both sexes, or by female only? **Nestling.** Altricial and downy. Down long, straggling and sparse. Dull white tinged with buff. **Nestling period.** Young tended by both parents. Down mostly replaced by feathers in quill by end of first week.

MOURNING DOVE *Zenaida macroura* **Pl. 50**
Breeds in a wide variety of habitats. Open woodland, cultivated areas with trees or shrubs, semi-arid and arid areas within reach of water. Nest usually in a tree or shrub, often on the old nest of some other bird species; occasionally on a stump, exceptionally on a ledge of a building or on the ground.
Nest. A platform of twigs, sometimes with finer twigs as lining. **Breeding season.** Very prolonged. Begins December to February in south to late April in north. Double-brooded; possibly treble-brooded. **Eggs.** 2. Elliptical to long

Mourning Dove: *c.* 7-9in. across.

elliptical or subelliptical. Smooth and slightly glossy. White. 28 × 22 mm. **Incubation.** First egg laid in evening, second on early morning of next day but one. Incubation by both sexes, the male sitting most of the day, the female at night. 14–15½ days. **Nestling.** Altricial and downy. Down sparse and stringy, short and white; with yellowish skin showing through. **Nestling period.** Young tended by both parents, one usually present on nest most of the time. Young fledge at 13–15 days.

GROUND DOVE *Columbina passerina* **Pl. 50**

Breeds in open country with trees and shrubs, in cultivated areas and around human habitation. Nest in a tree or shrub, or occasionally on the ground in the shelter of a plant tuft or grasses.

Nest. A thin frail platform of fine twigs, grasses, stems, rootlets and occasionally feathers. *c.* 2½–3 in. across, 1–2 in. deep, with barely any central depression. **Breeding season.** Usually prolonged, February to November. Several broods; 2–3, possibly 4. **Eggs.** 2. Elliptical to long elliptical or subelliptical. Smooth and slightly glossy. White. 22 × 16 mm. **Incubation.** By both sexes. 13–14 days. **Nestling.** Altricial and downy. Down coarse and sparse, hair-like and dull gray. **Nestling period.** Young can fly at 11 days. They are brooded or shaded by an adult for much of the time until well feathered.

INCA DOVE *Scardafella inca* **Pl. 50**

Breeds in arid areas, and in cultivated places around human settlement, where trees and shrubs are present. Nest in a tree or bush, on a fork of flattened limb, or on the old nest of another bird species; on cacti, or occasionally on beams of open buildings. Usually 8–20 ft. up. Nests may be re-used for subsequent nestings with small addition to the linings.

Nest. A small, compact, flat platform of thin twigs, stems, grass-roots, etc., sometimes lined with finer material. 2–5 in. across, 1–1½ in. high with shallow center hollow. Built by both sexes, male carrying and female building. Usually takes *c.* 3 days. **Breeding season.** Often prolonged. Late February to October. Several broods, 2–3, sometimes 4–5. **Eggs.** 2. Long elliptical to long subelliptical. Smooth and glossy. White. 22 × 17 mm. **Incubation.** By both sexes. 13–14 days. **Nestling.** No information. **Nestling period.** Young tended by both parents. Brooded for 7–9 days. Young fledged at 14–16 days, becoming independent during a further week.

WHITE-FRONTED DOVE *Leptoptila verreauxi* **Pl. 50**

Breeds in drier open woodland, forest edge, scrub, and cultivated areas with trees and bushes. Nest in a tree or shrub, 3–15 ft. up, often low – about 3–6 ft. up or even to ground level.

Nest. A thick, slightly concave platform, variable in size and bulk but often substantial, more so than those of typical pigeons. Of twigs, or grasses and weed stems. **Breeding season.** Begins late March. **Eggs.** 2. Long elliptical to elliptical or long subelliptical. Smooth and slightly glossy. Dull white, to creamy or pale buff. 31 × 23 mm. **Incubation.** By both sexes. 14 days. **Nestling.** Altricial and downy. Down sparse and hair-like. Bill pinkish-brown, with black subterminal band and white tip. Eyes brown. **Nestling period.** Young tended by both parents. Nests are kept clean, presumably through removal of droppings by adults. Young are brooded even when well-feathered. Feathers out of quills at 9–10 days. Young leave nest at 15–16 days, and begin to feed themselves at *c.* 4 weeks.

BARBARY DOVE *Streptopelia roseogrisea* (‘*risoria*’) **Pl. 50**

Feral around Los Angeles and in parts of Florida, this species originates in arid areas with scrub or trees, but the present pale variant has for long been domesticated. In the wild, nests are in trees or bushes, often low.

Nest. A shallow platform of twigs and plant stems. **Breeding season.** No information. **Eggs.** 2. Elliptical to long elliptical or subelliptical. Smooth and glossy. White. 30 × 23 mm. **Incubation.** First egg usually laid in evening, second on morning of next day but one. 14 days. **Nestling.** Altricial and downy. Down sparse and stringy; yellowish. **Nestling period.** Young tended by both parents. Leave nest at 15–17 days.

SPOTTED DOVE *Streptopelia chinensis* **Pl. 50**
Feral in part of Los Angeles County, California. This species is a bird of open woodland and of cultivated areas and human settlement where trees or shrubs are present. Nest on a tree or shrub, or on the ledge of a building. Often quite low.
Nest. A small saucer-shaped structure of small twigs, grass-stems and roots. **Breeding season.** No information. **Eggs.** Usually 2. Elliptical to long elliptical or subelliptical. Smooth and glossy. White. 26 × 21 mm. **Incubation.** By both sexes. 14 days. **Nestling.** Altricial and downy. Down sparse and hair-like. **Nestling period.** No information.

CUCKOOS *Cuculidae*

Medium-sized, mainly insectivorous birds. Often partly terrestrial. Tend to nest low. Nests often loose and poorly-made twig structures. Eggs pale blue or greenish-blue, with white outer layer in some species. Some species may occasionally lay eggs in nests of other individuals of the same species, or of cuckoos of other species, or other birds, foreshadowing brood parasitism. In anis a number of pairs may nest communally. Nestling naked or with sparse coarse down. Feathers grow rapidly, remaining in sheath until most of plumage is present, and breaking out when young leave nest. Young leave nest early, some time before they are able to fly properly.

MANGROVE CUCKOO *Coccyzus minor* **Pl. 50**
Breeds in mangroves. Nest in mangrove tree, fairly low.
Nest. A shallow cup of dead twigs. **Breeding season.** Begins mid-May. Double-brooded? **Eggs.** Usually 2. Elliptical to subelliptical. Smooth and non-glossy. Pale blue, greenish-blue or pale green. 31 × 23 mm. **Incubation.** No information. **Nestling.** No information. **Nestling period.** Young tended by both adults.

YELLOW-BILLED CUCKOO *Coccyzus americanus* **Pl. 50**
Breeds in open woodland, scrub, parkland, orchards and gardens. Nest in a bush or tree, 2–20 ft. up, in a crotch or on a horizontal limb, usually concealed in foliage.
Nest. A very loosely built shallow twig platform, with rootlets, dry leaves, grass and other debris; loosely lined with grasses, pine-needles, flowering parts from trees and weeds, and mosses. Cup badly formed, the nest small for the size of the bird with many projecting twigs; and eggs may be lost. *c.* 5–8 in. diameter, by 1½ in. depth. **Breeding season.** Begins late March in south to late May in north. Single-brooded, or sometimes double-brooded in south. **Eggs.** Usually 3–4, sometimes 1–5. More may be from two females. Eggs occasionally laid in nests of other cuckoos or other bird species. Elliptical to subelliptical. Smooth and non-glossy. Light blue, greenish-blue or pale green. 30 × 23 mm. **Incubation.** By both sexes but mainly by female, beginning with first egg. *c.* 14 days. **Nestling.** Altricial. Almost naked with black skin, but some sparse, hair-like down also present. Feathers grow in sheath until young are covered with quills. **Nestling period.** Young tended by both parents. They hatch over a period; differ in size. Feather sheaths break to release feathers a day or two before young leave nest.

BLACK-BILLED CUCKOO *Coccyzus erythrophthalmus* **Pls. 14, 50**
Breeds in woodland. Nest in a tree or bush, on a fork or a horizontal branch, 2–15 ft. up, but usually low. At times almost on ground, partly concealed by tall herbage; exceptionally on a fallen log or in herbage on the ground.
Nest. A loosely-built cup, usually more substantial than that of Yellow-billed Cuckoo, rounded but with many projecting twig ends. Of twigs, grass, plant-stems, and seed-heads of weeds, lined with dried grass, leaves, flowering heads of trees and herbs and similar material. **Breeding season.** Begins early to mid-May. Single-brooded. **Eggs.** Usually 2–3, rarely 4–5. Larger clutches may be from two females. Eggs are sometimes laid in nests of other cuckoos or other bird species. Elliptical to subelliptical. Smooth and non-glossy. Light blue, bluish-green or light green. 27 × 21 mm. **Incubation.** Eggs are laid at irregular intervals. Incubation by both sexes, beginning with first egg. 14 days. **Nestling.** Altricial. Almost naked, skin black with sparse, coarse white hairs. These persist at tips of feather which follow. There is a complex pattern of white papillae inside the mouth. Tongue with black edges at tip. Feathers appear first as long quills, break later. **Nestling period.** Young tended by both parents. Hatch at intervals and differ in size. Adults bring insects carried in throat pouch and disgorge into mouth of nestling. Eyes open at 2–3 days. Young begin preening at 6 days, quill sheaths break at 7–9 days, and young leave nest and perch and climb on branches. Fly at *c.* 21–24 days.

ROADRUNNER *Geococcyx californianus* **Pls. 14, 51**
Breeds in arid desert areas. Nest usually in a low tree, shrubby thicket, or on cactus clump. 3–15 ft. up. Varies from well-concealed to exposed. Rarely nest on ground in cover.

Road Runner: *c.* 11-12in. across.

Nest. A compact cup of twigs or plant or grass stems, lined with leaves, grass, roots and feathers; and with debris such as snakeskins, flakes of cattle dung and seed-pods. **Breeding season.** May begin March, but more usually April. Single-brooded, possibly double-brooded at times. **Eggs.** Usually 3–6. Larger numbers may be from more than one female. Elliptical to subelliptical. Smooth and slightly glossy. White to creamy-white. 39 × 30 mm. **Incubation.** Eggs laid at irregular intervals. Incubation by female only? Beginning with first egg. 18 days? **Nestling.** Altricial. Almost naked. Shiny black skin with sparse, coarse whitish hairs followed by feathers in sheath. Gape flanges pink. Mouth bright red with white upper palate, white hind-edges to tongue and white lump on either side of throat. Legs and feet first dark, then blue-gray. Irides deep brown. **Nestling period.** Young tended by both parents. Hatch over long intervals, eggs and young in various stages may be present. Eyes open at 6–7 days. Feathers break sheaths at 10–14 days. Young probably leave nest at *c.* 11 days, before able to fly. Begin feeding themselves at *c.* 16 days.

SMOOTH-BILLED ANI *Crotophaga ani* — Pls. 14, 51

Breeds in brush, or trees around farmland. In social groups of 2–20 birds. Nest in a twig fork of tree or shrub, at times high.

Nest. Usually a loose mass of twigs, *c.* 12 in. across and 6 in. deep, with at times weed and vine stems and coarse roots; lined with green leaves which later wither. Fresh green leaves and sometimes twigs may be added during incubation change-overs. **Breeding season.** No information. In Central America has long breeding season and several broods. **Eggs.** Usually 4–7 from one female. With several birds nests may have up to 29. Elliptical to subelliptical. Light blue to greenish-blue, thinly covered with a smooth and fairly glossy white layer, the blue color showing through at times to varying degrees. Rarely the white layer absent. The layer tends to become scratched and stained during incubation. 35 × 26 mm. **Incubation.** Eggs laid at 2-day intervals. Incubation by both sexes and all members of group. 12–15 days for particular eggs, but with large numbers eggs may be in layers in nest and the lower ones may not hatch. **Nestling.** Altricial and naked. Skin black. Sheathed pin-feathers grow rapidly in first few days. **Nestling period.** Young tended by both sexes and all of group. Eyes open at 3 days. Pin-feathers begun by 3 days. Sheaths breaking by 5 days, and young may leave nest if disturbed. Young leave nest at 10–11 days. May remain with adults and help with later broods.

GROOVE-BILLED ANI *Crotophaga sulcirostris* — Pl. 51

Nest usually in a thick twiggy or tangled growth, often in thorny trees or shrubs, on the edge of an open area. Nest is in a fork or among twigs. 2–25 ft. up, but usually below 10 ft. Nesting may be by a single pair or by up to four breeding co-operatively.

Nest. A conspicuous bulky cup of loose coarse twigs, lined with green leaves. Both sexes may carry and build, but often the female, or females, build and males bring material. Green leaves and sometimes twigs are added during incubation. Where several females lay successively, earlier eggs may be covered with leaves. **Breeding season.** Begins mid-March. **Eggs.** Usually 4, sometimes 3–5, by one female, but up to 15 recorded from one nest with several females.

Eggs like those of Smooth-billed Ani. 31 × 24 mm. **Incubation.** Eggs laid at 2–3-day intervals, usually at midday. All birds of both sexes appear to incubate, male usually incubating at night. 13–14 days for individual eggs. **Nestling.** Altricial and naked. Black skin. Rapidly becomes covered with sheathed pin-feathers. **Nestling period.** Young tended by all birds of group. Brooded for first week. Sheathed feathers grow rapidly and burst from sheaths at *c.* 6 days. At 6 days young begin to leave nest and climb branches. Subsequently may roost out of nest. At 11 days can hop easily and make short flights. Young of earlier broods may help to feed later broods.

OWLS *Tytonidae and Strigidae*

Small to medium-sized raptors; usually nocturnal. No nest made, but female may make scrape by revolving on her breast on nest-site. A few species may collect material, but information is very unsatisfactory. Eggs white, and except in case of Barn Owl are usually rounded. Clutch may be large, and, in some species, regulated by food supply, being larger when food is plentiful. Incubation begins early in laying and young hatch at intervals, differing in size. Young covered in down, soon followed by first plumage of soft feathering, the first down persisting on the feather tips. If food becomes short smaller young die. Young of larger owls appear slow in achieving complete independence, possibly slower than our present information suggests.

BARN OWL *Tyto alba* — Pls. 14, 49

Generally distributed, breeding in cavities in trees, buildings of all types, crevices in rocks, outcrops, cliffs and quarries.

Nest. No nest material, but there may be a shallow hollow in existing debris, partly lined with owl pellets. **Breeding season.** May begin January in south to late February or March in north. Season prolonged. Often double-brooded. **Eggs.** Clutch variable, usually 4–7, occasionally 3–11. Long sub-elliptical to elliptical. Smooth but non-glossy. White. 42 × 33 mm. **Incubation.** Eggs laid at 2-day intervals, longer intervals at times. Female alone incubates, male bringing food. 32–34 days. **Nestling.** Altricial and downy. Unlike other owls has two down coats. First down white and short, sparse on the belly, covering legs to claws but absent on back of tarsus, also absent on sides of neck. Replaced in *c.* 12 days by a longer, thicker buffish-cream down, first down clinging to its tips. Down more sparse on lower legs and toes. Iris pale blue for first few weeks. **Nestling period.** Young vary in size. Tended and fed by both parents; feathering between third and seventh week; flying at *c.* 60 days; independent in *c.* 10 weeks.

FLAMMULATED OWL *Otus flammeolus*

Breeds in montane pine woods. Nest usually in a woodpecker hole, more rarely in a natural cavity.

Nest. An unlined cavity. **Breeding season.** Begins mid-May to early June. Single-brooded. **Eggs.** Usually 3–4. Elliptical to short subelliptical. Smooth and slightly glossy. White. 29 × 26 mm. **Incubation.** No information. **Nestling.** Altricial and downy. Down thick and white. Bill, legs and feet, flesh-colored. **Nestling period.** No information.

SCREECH OWL *Otus asio* **Pl. 49**

Breeds over a wide range, nesting in scattered trees around houses, parkland, cultivated areas with trees, orchards, and small groves and woodlots. Nest in a natural cavity or old woodpecker nest, including those in telegraph poles and cacti in some areas. Will also use a nest box.

Nest. A cavity unlined apart from any material already present. **Breeding season.** Begins early March in south to mid-April in north. **Eggs.** Usually 4–5, sometimes 3–7; but only 2–4 in some races. Elliptical, approaching spherical at times, to subelliptical. Smooth and slightly glossy. White. 36 × 30 mm. **Incubation.** Eggs laid at 2–3-day intervals. Incubation by female alone, beginning with first egg, male bringing food. *c.* 26 days. **Nestling.** Altricial and downy. Down thick and white, extending down toes to claws. **Nestling period.** Young brooded by female for first two weeks while male brings food. Young begin to feed themselves and cast pellets at *c.* 10 days, down replaced by downy feathering in second and third weeks. Young leave at *c.* 5 weeks.

WHISKERED OWL *Otus trichopsis*

Breeds in thick oak and oak-pine woods. Nest in a tree, in a natural cavity or woodpecker hole.

Nest. An unlined cavity. **Breeding season.** Begins early May. **Eggs.** Usually 3, sometimes 4. Elliptical to subelliptical. Smooth and slightly glossy. White. 33 × 28 mm. **Incubation.** No information. **Nestling.** No information. **Nestling period.** No information.

GREAT HORNED OWL *Bubo virginianus* **Pl. 49**

Breeds through a wide range of woodland habitat. Nest in a natural cavity in a tree, in a fork of a giant cactus, on a rock ledge, or in a rock or earth cave. Often in the old nest of a large bird in such sites. In some treeless regions on open ground.

Nest. An unlined cavity, or lined with any material already present. **Breeding season.** Begins late November or January in south to early April in north. Single-brooded, but lost clutch may be replaced. **Eggs.** Usually 2–3, sometimes 1–5. Subelliptical or short subelliptical to elliptical. Smooth and slightly glossy with slight granular texture. White. 56 × 47 mm. **Incubation.** By female only, beginning with first egg. 30–35 days? **Nestling.** Altricial and downy. Down white. **Nestling period.** Young hatch over a period of days. Tended by both parents. Brooded by female for first 3 weeks with male bringing all food. Eyes open at *c.* 10 days. Young leave the nest at 4½–5 weeks, but do not fly well until 9–10 weeks. Rely on adults for food for a long period afterwards.

SNOWY OWL *Nyctea scandiaca* **Pls. 14, 49**

Breeds in level, open country, on arctic tundra or bare stretches of higher fells and mountains, or on islands. Nest on the ground; usually sited on a slightly raised site with an extensive view around, often on a hummock, but at times on a large boulder or ledge of a crag.

Nest. A hollow scrape formed by the female, at times with some moss fragments and feathers. **Breeding season.** Begins late May to early June. Single-brooded; like other arctic breeders may not nest in some years. **Eggs.** Clutch varies with food supply, usually 4–10, sometimes up to 15. Short elliptical or subelliptical. Smooth and slightly glossy. White. 57 × 45 mm. **Incubation.** By female only, beginning with first egg, the male bringing food. 32–37 days. **Nestling.** Altricial and downy. Down white, soft, short and thick, extending down to the claws, but with bare patch on back of leg joint. Followed after 6–10 days by a first plumage of dark grayish-brown loose feathering which looks like down. **Nestling period.** Eggs hatch at 1–2-day intervals, a large clutch may hatch over 2 weeks. Female spends much time brooding, the male bringing food. When young are larger both adults hunt. Young leave the nest-site 3–4 weeks before they can fly. They fly well at *c.* 8–9 weeks but are still fed by adults.

HAWK OWL *Surnia ulula* **Pl. 49**

Breeds in conifers and birch forests. Nest in holes in trees, including old woodpecker holes; hollows at ends of broken tree-trunks; and old nests of large birds. **Nest.** An unlined hollow or cavity. **Breeding season.** Usually begins in April or early May. Single-brooded, possibly two in good food years. **Eggs.** Usually 3–10, rarely 13, depending on food supply. Short elliptical to short subelliptical. Smooth and glossy. White. 40 × 32 mm. **Incubation.** Mainly by female, beginning with first egg, but the male may take some part. 25–30 days. **Nestling.** Altricial and downy. Down white with a yellowish-buff tint. **Nestling period.** Young tended by both parents. Leave at *c.* 23–27 days.

PYGMY OWL *Glaucidium gnoma*

Breeds in forest, mainly in conifer forest. Nest in a natural hole or old woodpecker hole in a tree.

Nest. An unlined cavity. **Breeding season.** Begins late April to early May. Single-brooded. **Eggs.** Usually 4–6, sometimes 3–7. Short elliptical to short subelliptical. Smooth and slightly glossy. White. 29 × 24 mm. **Incubation.** Eggs laid at 3–4-day intervals. Incubation may not begin until clutch is almost complete. 28 days. **Nestling.** Altricial and downy. Down whitish. **Nestling period.** Female broods young and feeds them on food brought entirely by male. Young leave nest at 29–32 days.

ELF OWL *Micrathene whitneyi* **Pl. 49**

Breeds in desert regions. Nest usually in an old woodpecker nest in a giant cactus or tree. Rarely in a natural cavity.

Nest. An unlined cavity. **Breeding season.** Begins early May. **Eggs.** Usually 3, sometimes 2–5. Elliptical. Smooth and slightly glossy. White. 27 × 23 mm. **Incubation.** By both sexes, beginning with the first egg. 21 days. **Nestling.** Altricial and downy. Down sooty-white. **Nestling period.** Young tended by both parents. Leave nest at *c.* 33–34 days.

BURROWING OWL *Speotyto cunicularia* **Pl. 49**

Breeds on prairies and open grassy places. Usually occupies holes of ground squirrels, badgers or tortoises, but will enlarge or modify these if necessary and will excavate their own burrows if others are lacking.

Nest. Usually a burrow sloping down for 1½–3 ft. and then level and *c.* 5–10 ft. long, *c.* 5 in. diameter, and with a nest chamber of 12–18 in. Nest chamber lined with debris – cow dung, stalks, feathers, grasses, bones and any rubbish. This appears to be the only owl bringing material into a cavity. **Breeding season.** Begins late March in south to early May in north. Single-brooded. A lost clutch may be replaced by a smaller clutch. **Eggs.** Usually 5–6, sometimes 4–11.

Plate 9

CRANES and LIMPKIN. Young lack any distinctive pattern on the down. There is usually darker color on top of head and back. Downy plumage may be retained until the young have grown very large and appear rather incongruous.

Whooping Crane, *Grus americana.* **page** 109

Sandhill Crane, *Grus canadensis.* 109

Limpkin, *Aramus guarauna.* 110

RAILS. The young are active, with black down and unwebbed feet with long toes, but coots' toes have flange-like lobes along them. The young can move and swim actively at an early age, but may remain at the nest for a period.

American Coot, *Fulica americana.* The yellow and white sheaths and red tips are lost later; larger young are gray with white on throat, front of neck and underside 114

Purple Gallinule, *Porphyrula martinica.* 113

Common Gallinule, *Gallinula chloropus.* 114

Virginia Rail, *Rallus limicola.* King Rail has black down, Clapper Rail black with greenish sheen and usually a little white down just below and behind wings. 112

Sora Rail, *Porzana carolina.* 112

Black Rail, *Laterallus jamaicensis.* Yellow Rail is also very small with glossy black down and a pinkish bill. 113

Vhooping Crane
Sandhill Crane
Limpkin
American Coot
Purple Gallinule
Common Gallinule
Virginia Rail
Sora Rail
Black Rail

Spotted Sandpiper
Least Sandpiper
Sanderling
Northern Phalarope
Short-billed Dowitcher
Common Snipe
American Woodcock
Ruddy Turnstone
Hudsonian Godwit
Willet

SHOREBIRDS (see also pl. 11). These young are typically long-legged and slender-billed but the bills, although beginning to show the characters of the species, are usually shorter than those of adults. The basic down pattern of longitudinal stripes is similar on many species, but on some the darker stripes are masked by small white or buff spots formed by brush-tips to some down filaments, and on other patterns is so broken as to appear as dark mottling. The down pattern of the crown of the head may differ significantly between species.

Spotted Sandpiper, *Tringa macularia.* 139

Least Sandpiper, *Calidris minutilla.* Spots on the darker stripes are white on this and some other species, pale buff on Dunlin, Curlew Sandpiper, and Western Sandpiper, and buffish-white on Rock Sandpiper and Pectoral Sandpiper. 126

Sanderling, *Calidris alba.* 125

Northern Phalarope, *Phalaropus lobatus.* The Red Phalarope has a dark streak from bill to eye, and the pale dorsal streaks are darker. Wilson's Phalarope has a pale crown with a dark anchor-shaped mark on the hind-crown. 141

Short-billed Dowitcher, *Limnodromus griseus.* The Long-billed Dowitcher is similar but the ground color of back and wings is a deeper brown. 134

Common Snipe, *Gallinago gallinago.* 132

American Woodcock, *Scolopax minor.* 133

Ruddy Turnstone, *Arenaria interpres.* The Black Turnstone has an almost overall dark blackish-gray down with finely speckled pattern, and white on belly and chin. Wandering Tattler chick is also gray, with dark streak through eye. 124

Hudsonian Godwit, *Limosa haemastica.* Bar-tailed Godwit has dark line from bill to crown and lateral spots on hind-crown are absent. Marbled Godwit has dark markings only on hind-crown with separate lateral spots on each side. 134

Willet, *Catoptrophorus semipalmatus.* Three dark dorsal stripes are typical of *Tringa* sandpipers. Yellowlegs have dark crown patch, with bolder streaks over eyes of Lesser Yellowlegs. Solitary Sandpiper has dark crown patch with browner center and mottled forecrown. Wandering Tattler is pale gray with very faint pattern. 139

Elliptical, almost spherical at times, to short subelliptical. Smooth and glossy. White. 31 × 26 mm. **Incubation.** By both sexes? *c.* 21 days. **Nestling.** Altricial and downy. Down sparse and grayish-white, on feather tracts only, with bare areas showing. **Nestling period.** Young tended by both adults. As the young mature they spend increasing time at the mouth of the burrow, retreating into it when alarmed.

BARRED OWL *Strix varia* **Pl. 49**

Breeds in forest over a wide area. Nest in a natural cavity in a tree-trunk or stub, or in the nest of a large bird such as a hawk, or on an old squirrel nest. Very rarely on the ground.

Nest. An unlined cavity, or material already present on an old nest. **Breeding season.** Begins mid-January in south to mid-March in north. Single-brooded but lost clutches are replaced. **Eggs.** Usually 2–3, rarely 4. Elliptical, almost spherical at times; to short subelliptical. Smooth and slightly glossy. White. 49 × 42 mm. **Incubation.** By female only. *c.* 28 days? **Nestling.** Altricial and downy. Down thick and soft; white. **Nestling period.** Young tended by both parents. Brooded for the first 3 weeks. Eyes open at *c.* 7 days. Young may leave nest for adjacent branches at 4–5 weeks. Fly at *c.* 6 weeks.

SPOTTED OWL *Strix occidentalis*

Breeds in conifer forests and forested canyons. Nest in a natural cavity in a tree, more rarely in the nest of a large bird in a tree or cave, or on a bare site in cave or on rocky slope.

Nest. An unlined cavity. **Breeding season.** Begins early March. Single-brooded. **Eggs.** Usually 2, sometimes 3, rarely 4. Elliptical to short subelliptical. Smooth but with slight granular texture, non-glossy or slightly glossy. White. 50 × 41 mm. **Incubation.** No information. **Nestling.** No information. **Nestling period.** No information.

GREAT GRAY OWL *Strix nebulosa* **Pl. 49**

Breeds in conifer forests. Nests on the top of broken-off tree-trunks or on old nests of other large birds.

Nest. An unlined hollow, or old nest of another species. **Breeding season.** Begins late March. Single-brooded. Nesting may not occur in unfavorable years. **Eggs.** 3–5, sometimes fewer, but up to 9 in good years. Subelliptical, less rounded than those of most owls. Smooth and slightly glossy. White. 54 × 43 mm. **Incubation.** Eggs laid at variable intervals of 2–12 days. Incubation by female only, beginning with first egg. **Nestling.** Altricial and downy. Down pale gray on upperparts, white on underpart. Iris yellowish-gray; legs and feet pale yellow. **Nestling period.** Young hatch at different times and vary in size. The female guards the young and feeds them on food brought by the male. The young have eyes closed for first seven days; feather during 10–35 days; begin to leave the nest at 3–4 weeks but do not fly well until 5 weeks. They are still fed by adults and may remain together for months.

LONG-EARED OWL *Asio otus* **Pl. 49**

Breeds mainly in woodland, including riverine woodland belts; exceptionally in open areas of scrub and marsh. Nest frequently in a large old nest of another species, or a squirrel drey; more rarely on the ground sheltered by the base of a tree, or among low shrubby growth.

Nest. The nest of another bird, or an unlined hollow on the ground. **Breeding season.** Begins early March in south to mid-April in north. Usually single-brooded, occasional second broods in periods of good food. **Eggs.** Usually 4–5, rarely 3–8. Short elliptical. Smooth, moderately glossy and finely pitted. White. 41 × 33 mm. **Incubation.** Eggs laid on alternate days. Incubation normally by the female only, beginning with first egg. 25–30 days. **Nestling.** Altricial and downy. Down fairly thick, short and soft; white. Extending to the claws, with a bare patch on back of leg joint. **Nestling period.** Female feeds young with food brought by male. Often not all young are reared. Young leave nest at 23–24 days.

SHORT-EARED OWL *Asio flammeus* **Pl. 14, 49**

Breeds in open country, on plains, prairie, marshes or dunes. Nest on the ground sheltered by tall grass, reeds or bushes.

Nest. A shallow hollow, unlined. **Breeding season.** Usually begins late April, sometimes 2–3 weeks earlier. Usually single-brooded, but double-brooded when food is plentiful. **Eggs.** Usually 4–8, rarely 3; up to 14 when food is plentiful. Short elliptical. Smooth, non-glossy or slightly glossy. White. 40 × 31 mm. **Incubation.** Eggs laid at 2-day intervals, occasionally longer. Incubation by female alone, beginning with first egg. 24–28 days. **Nestling.** Altricial and downy. Down thick, short and soft, extending to the claws, with a bare patch on the back of leg joint. Creamy-buff to light warm buff on upperparts, with darker zone bordering mantle; white with a buff tinge on underside. **Nestling period.** Female broods and feeds young, the male bringing food. Young leave nest at 12–17 days, but do not fly until *c.* 10 days later.

BOREAL OWL *Aegolius funereus* **Pl. 49**

Breeds in woodland, usually in conifers. Nests in holes in trees, natural cavities and old holes of woodpeckers; sometimes in artificial nest-boxes.

Nest. An unlined cavity. **Breeding season.** Begins mid-April. Usually single-brooded, possibly double-brooded at times. **Eggs.** Usually 3–6, sometimes 10 when food is plentiful. Short elliptical. Smooth, moderately glossy and finely pitted. White. 32 × 27 mm. **Incubation.** Eggs laid at 2-day intervals. Incubation by female alone, beginning with first egg. 26–36 days. **Nestling.** Altricial and downy. Down sparse, short and soft; buffish-white on upper parts, white on underparts, extending down to claws. **Nestling period.** Young hatch at *c.* 1-day intervals and vary in size. The female broods the young for the first 3 weeks. Young leave nest at *c.* 30–36 days, occasionally longer.

SAW-WHET OWL *Aegolius acadicus* **Pl. 49**

Breeds in woodland, often in swampy areas. Nest usually in an old woodpecker hole, less often in a natural cavity.

Nest. An unlined cavity, or material from old nests of other birds or mammals already present. **Breeding season.** Begins mid-March to mid-April. **Eggs.** Usually 5–6, sometimes 4–7. Elliptical to short subelliptical. Smooth and non-glossy or slightly glossy. White. 30 × 25 mm. **Incubation.** Eggs laid at 2-day intervals. Incubation by female alone, beginning with first egg. 26–28 days. **Nestling.** Altricial and downy. Down sparse and white. When eyes open irides are brown. **Nestling period.** Young hatch at intervals, varying in size. Eyes open at 8–9 days. Down replaced by downy feathers during second to fourth week. Leave nest at 27–34 days.

NIGHTJARS *Caprimulgidae*

Medium-sized, nocturnal insect-eaters; highly modified with large mouths and weak feet. Ground-nesting, with no modified nest-site. The bird may roll the eggs under it when it settles. Clutches are of two eggs, with partially cryptic coloring, mainly concealed by the daytime brooding of the cryptically colored adults. Young are downy and protectively colored. Both eggs and young may be moved within the vicinity of the nest-site. The nestlings hatch with their eyes open. The young take food directly from the bills of the parents, seizing these in their own.

CHUCK-WILL'S-WIDOW *Caprimulgus carolinensis* **Pl. 51**
Breeds in woodland, particularly mixed oak and pine woods. No nest is built and eggs are laid on the leaves or pine-needles of open ground under the trees. **Nest.** No material is accumulated. Eggs or young may be gradually moved from site. **Breeding season.** Begins early March in south to mid-May in north. Single-brooded but lost clutches are replaced. **Eggs.** 2. Elliptical or subelliptical. Smooth and moderately glossy. White, cream or pinkish, mottled, blotched and spotted with large areas of pale gray or purple, often faint; and with, unusually, sparser markings in dark or pale brown. 36 × 26 mm. **Incubation.** Begins with first egg. 20 days. **Nestling.** Semi-precocial and downy. Down long and soft. Tawny-brown on the back and yellowish-tawny to yellowish-buff on the head and underside, becoming paler on throat and belly. **Nestling period.** Young have eyes open, but usually kept half-shut during day; and are active from first, moving in short hops if necessary.

WHIP-POOR-WILL *Caprimulgus vociferus* **Pls. 15, 51**
Breeds in drier, more open woodlands, or near woodland edge. No nest. Eggs are laid on the ground in an open site under trees or under a bush, usually on a bed of dead leaves.
Nest. No material is accumulated. The movements of the birds may produce a slight hollow. **Breeding season.** Begins early May. **Eggs.** 2. Long elliptical to subelliptical. Smooth and slightly glossy. White or creamy-white; with spots or small blotches of pale dull gray scattered overall, and occasional larger darker blotches and small spots and dots of warm brown. Rarely unmarked. 29 × 21 mm. **Incubation.** 17–20 days. **Nestling.** Semi-precocial and downy. Down long, soft and silky. Cinnamon-buff on the back, pinkish-cinnamon on the breast, and light pinkish-cinnamon on head and underside. **Nestling period.** Young tended mainly by female with the male bringing food at night. Young are active from an early stage and will leave nest and crouch if disturbed.

POOR-WILL *Phalaenoptilus nuttallii* **Pl. 51**
Breeds in open areas, on prairies, flats or hillsides, or in scrub or scattered brush of semi-arid regions. Nest-site a bare open area, rock, gravel or bare earth; usually shaded from strong sunlight by a bush or tuft of herbage.
Nest. No material accumulated, the site usually bare of herbage. **Breeding season.** Late March in south to late May in north. Single-brooded. **Eggs.** 2. Long elliptical to subelliptical. Smooth and slightly glossy. White or

creamy-white with faint pink tint, unmarked or with a few faint small markings. 26 × 20 mm. **Incubation.** No information. **Nestling.** Semi-precocial and downy. Down warm buff, paler on underside. **Nestling period.** No information.

PAURAQUE *Nyctidromus albicollis* **Pls. 15, 51**

Breeds in open brush on more level areas. Nest in the open on a bare site, usually at the foot of a low bush, sometimes partly hidden by it.

Nest. No material accumulated. Nest on bare ground. **Breeding season.** Begins early March. Single-brooded. **Eggs.** 2. Long elliptical to long sub-elliptical. Smooth, non-glossy or slightly glossy. Pale pinkish buff, variably but often heavily marked with specks, spots or small irregular blotches in pale lilac, light reddish-brown or light brown. 30 × 22 mm. **Incubation.** By both sexes. Period not recorded. **Nestling.** Semi-precocial and downy. Down long and soft. Forehead, crown and nape pinkish-buff; lores to ear-coverts brown. Back and rump brown with pinkish-buff band down middle. Chin and throat pale pinkish-cinnamon. Underparts pinkish-buff. **Nestling period.** Young tended by both adults. Adults feed young by inserting narrow tip of bill into the nestling gape and regurgitating insects from the parent's throat. Young can leave nest-site by hopping after parents at 2–3 days.

COMMON NIGHTHAWK *Chordeiles minor* **Pls. 15, 51**

Breeds in open areas, forest clearings, burnt-over areas, cultivation, barren rock, beaches. Nest on bare ground, infrequently on stumps. Also nests on flat, gravelled roofs of buildings.

Common Nighthawk: no nest; eggs laid on bare ground.

Nest. No material accumulated. Nest is on a bare site. **Breeding season.** Begins late March to early April in south, to late May or early June in north. Single-brooded. **Eggs.** Usually 2. Long subelliptical to almost elliptical. Smooth and moderately glossy. Pale creamy-white to creamy; very heavily speckled, spotted or freckled with pale gray or purplish-gray and dark olive-brown. Markings vary from mainly pale gray with sparse brown flecking to heavy overall brown mottling. 30 × 22 mm. **Incubation.** Eggs laid at 1-day intervals. Incubation by female alone with male near by. Beginning with first egg. 19 days. **Nestling.** Semi-precocial and downy. Down pale gray above, darker on chin, mid-throat and malar stripe. Upper parts and head mottled and marbled in pale and dark gray, with olive-buff tint on upper back and nape, and buff tint around base of bill. Bill pale gray at hatching, becoming darker gray. Legs and feet dull brown. **Nestling period.** Young tended by both parents; all brooding by female, and male bringing food. Feathers replace down during 10–20 days. Young begin making short flights at 23 days, begin feeding themselves at 25 days. Independent at *c.* 30 days.

LESSER NIGHTHAWK *Chordeiles acutipennis* Pl. 51

Breeds in open areas. Nest on a bare site.

Nest. No material accumulated. Nest on a bare open site. Eggs may be rolled a little distance, or young led to a new site, if frequently disturbed. **Breeding season.** Begins mid-April. Single-brooded. **Eggs.** 2. Long subelliptical to almost elliptical. White, creamy or faintly buff; very heavily marked with overall small speckling, spotting or freckling of pale gray and dull dark brown or olive-brown, or occasionally whitish with pale gray mottling. 27 × 20 mm. **Incubation.** By female only. 18–19 days. **Nestling.** Semi-precocial and downy. Upperparts and head mottled in buff and brown. Underside buff, paler on mid-breast and belly. **Nestling period.** Young tended by both parents. Hatch at 24-hour interval. Can walk towards parents from soon after hatching. Well feathered at 12 days. Food regurgitated into bills of young by pumping movements. Young fly at *c.* 3 weeks.

SWIFTS *Apodidae*

Small, insect-eating birds adapted for catching insects in the air. The bill is broad with a wide gape, and the legs are reduced since swifts rarely settle except at nest-sites. Nest material is difficult to collect and is scanty. It is frequently glued together and to the site with a copious saliva secretion which hardens. Eggs are white and elongated. Young are fed directly with insects brought back by the parents in a pouch below the tongue.

BLACK SWIFT *Cypseloides niger* Pl. 52

Breeds in areas with cliff faces, on coasts or inland in canyons. Nests are in sheltered crevices or ledges under overhangs, but usually in a moist situation near some source of seepage, or by or behind a waterfall; or on a cliff face over a river or deep pool. Pairs nest in close proximity in a colony where conditions allow.

Nest. A small rounded cup of moss, fern or other plant material, with some mud but apparently no saliva, sometimes built up on a small projection. 3–4 in. across, 3 in. deep. **Breeding season.** Begins mid-June. Single-brooded. **Eggs.** One only. Long subelliptical or long oval. Smooth and non-glossy. White. 29 × 19 mm. **Incubation.** No information. **Nestling.** Altricial. Naked when first hatched with bluish-black skin, eyes closed. Later covered with long soft blackish-brown down. **Nestling period.** Little information. Young fed at infrequent intervals, mainly at dawn and dusk. Young near fledging frequently exercise wings while clinging to nest.

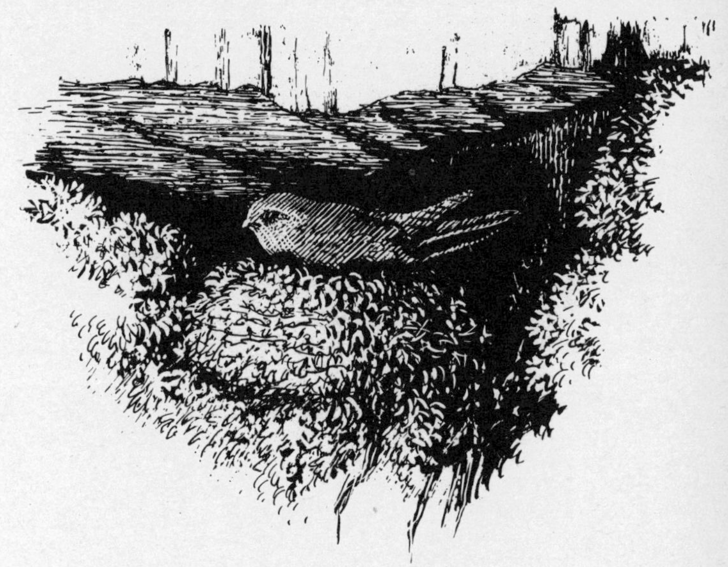

Black Swift: *c.* 3-4in. across.

CHIMNEY SWIFT *Chaetura pelagica* **Pls. 15, 52**

Breeds over a wide area where suitable sites are present. Nests are on the inside of hollow trees, large chimneys, open well shafts, open silos or exceptionally inside buildings. The nest is stuck to a vertical surface within a shaft, from just below the top aperture to 4–5 ft. above the bottom. One or two additional adults may help a nesting pair.

Nest. The nest is a shallow half-cup of short dead twigs broken off by the birds in flight and glued together and to the wall by saliva. There is no lining. **Breeding season.** Begins mid-May. Single-brooded. **Eggs.** Usually 4–5, sometimes 3–6. Long subelliptical to long elliptical, blunt-ended at times. Smooth and moderately glossy. White. 20 × 13 mm. **Incubation.** By both sexes and any helpers. 19 days. **Nestling.** Altricial. Naked at hatching, later covered with the spine-like quills of the first plumage. Mouth pink. No gape flanges. **Nestling period.** Young tended by both adults and any helpers. Adults bring insects in throat pouch and disgorge directly into mouths of young. Young can climb and move from hatching onwards, but eyes not open until 14 days. May leave nest and cling to, and climb on, walls at 19 days, fly at 24–26 days, leave nest at 28 days.

Chimney Swift: *c.* 5in. across at wall.

VAUX SWIFT *Chaetura vauxi*

Breeds where suitable sites are present. Nests on the insides of hollow trees, or tree-stumps, less frequently in chimneys, in woodpecker holes, or inside buildings. Nest placed relatively low, near the bottom of a shaft or cavity.

Nest. A small, narrow half-cup or hammock of dry twigs and conifer needles, glued together and lined with needles. **Breeding season.** Begins early May. **Eggs.** Usually 4–7, sometimes 3. Long oval to long subelliptical. Smooth and non-glossy. White or creamy-white. 18 × 12 mm. **Incubation.** By both sexes. 18–20 days. **Nestling.** Altricial. Naked at hatching, later covered with spine-like quills of first plumage. **Nestling period.** Young tended by both parents. Small young may starve in large broods. Young leave nest for wall that nest is built on at 20–21 days, but may not fly freely for a further 7 days.

WHITE-THROATED SWIFT *Aeronautes saxatilis*

Breeds on sea-coasts where steep cliffs are present, and on cliffs of mountain canyons. Nests are in rock cracks and crevices; and exceptionally in holes of Rough-winged Swallows, or crevices in buildings. Breeds in small colonies.

Nest. Rounded cup of feathers, plant-down, grass, bark or wool, or any material that can be snatched from the air; glued together and to site. Shape may be modified in confined spaces. **Breeding season.** Begins early May. **Eggs.** Usually 4–5, sometimes 3–6. Long oval, long subelliptical or long elliptical. Smooth and non-glossy. White to creamy-white. 21 × 14 mm. **Incubation.** No information. **Nestling.** No information. **Nestling period.** No information.

HUMMINGBIRDS *Trochilidae*

Tiny birds with hovering flight, taking nectar from flowers, and insects, on the wing. Nest a minute cup on a raised site, usually the upper surface of a plant-stem or twig. Made mainly of plant down and similar fine material, bound together and supported by spiders' webs. Web may be wound round structure by bird in flight. At times sites are re-used, several nests being built, one on the other, to produce an abnormally tall structure. Nest-building, incubation and care of young are by female alone. Laying and incubation may begin before nest-lining is complete. Eggs white, elongated and very large for the size of the bird. Incubation period long and variable. Young hatch with very little down. They have very short bills at first. Female inserts bill deep into mouth and throat of young and regurgitates food. Young may sit on nest edge and exercise wings 2–3 days before leaving nest.

Ruby-throated Hummingbird: *c.* 1½in. across.

RUBY-THROATED HUMMINGBIRD *Archilochus colubris* **Pls. 15, 51**
Breeds over a wide range. Nest on a tree or shrub, usually on a fork of a downward sloping twig. Usually in site near, and sometimes over, water. 5–50 ft. up; usually 10–20 ft.
Nest. A neat cup saddling the nest-site. Of small fragments of plant material with a thick lining of down; bound together smoothly and tightly with spiders' webs and covered on the outside with flakes of lichens. Built by female alone. **Breeding season.** Begins late March in south to early June in north of range. **Eggs.** Usually 2. Long subelliptical to long elliptical. Smooth and non-glossy. White. 13 × 8 mm. **Incubation.** By female only. 16 days. **Nestling.** Altricial. Nearly naked at first. Slate-blue skin, and line of yellowish down along back. Bill short and yellow. **Nestling period.** Young tended by female. Eyes open at *c.* 1 week; young leave nest at *c.* 19 days.

BLACK-CHINNED HUMMINGBIRD *Archilochus alexandri* **Pl. 51**
Breeds in drier mountain areas, in trees and shrubs along watercourses and canyons. Nest saddling a downward slanting small branch or twig; in shrubby growth 4–10 ft. up; occasionally in a creeper or on tall herbage plants; exceptionally in a tree at a greater height or on supports around buildings.
Nest. A deep rounded cup, the edge slightly incurved. Made almost entirely of plant down with occasional fragments of other material; firmly bound and felted together with spiders' webs. Colors usually shades of buff to whitish. Expands elastically as young grow. Built by female, taking several days. **Breeding season.** Begins early April. **Eggs.** Usually 2, rarely 1 or 3. Long elliptical to long subelliptical. Smooth and non-glossy. White 13 × 8 mm. **Incubation.** By female only. 13–16 days. **Nestling.** Altricial and almost naked. **Nestling period.** Young tended by female alone. Leave nest at 21 days.

COSTA'S HUMMINGBIRD *Calypte costae* **Pl. 51**
Breeds in desert areas. Nest in a variety of sites, usually near water and where shrubs and trees are present. Usually in fairly open site, on a dead yucca stalk, or on the stem or leaves of tall weeds, or in shrubs or trees, usually near the extremities of twigs. Usually 4–5 ft. up, occasionally 1–9 ft. up. A number of pairs may nest close together.
Nest. A small cup very variable in size and material. A mixture of pieces of down, fiber, tree-flowers, bud-scales, lichen fragments, leaves, feathers, etc., bound together with fine fibers and spiders' webs. Lined with plant down and sometimes small feathers. Outside dimensions $1\frac{1}{2}$–2 in. across, $1\frac{1}{4}$–$1\frac{1}{2}$ in. high. **Breeding season.** Begins mid-March. Single-brooded. **Eggs.** Usually 2. Long elliptical to long subelliptical. Smooth and non-glossy. White. 12 × 8 mm. **Incubation.** By female only. 15–18 days. **Nestling.** Altricial and with skin black above and brownish below; with a double line of yellow down filaments along mid-back. Down spreads within a few days over back, wings and top of head. Bill yellowish and triangular. **Nestling period.** Young tended by female only. Pin feathers appear at 6 days; well-feathered at 12 days. On last few days young perch on nest edge and exercise wings. Leave nest at 20–23 days.

ANNA'S HUMMINGBIRD *Calypte anna* **Pl. 51**
Widely distributed, usually in lower and less arid areas than previous species. Nest in a wide variety of sites, wherever a narrow support for a nest is present.

Nest. A fairly large and well-made cup, mainly of fine stems and plant down, bound with spiders' webs, lined with plant down and feathers, and often ornamented externally with lichen flakes. Egg-laying and incubation may begin before lining and outside are complete. **Breeding season.** Begins late December. **Eggs.** Usually 2. Long elliptical to long subelliptical. Smooth and non-glossy. White. 13 × 9 mm. **Incubation.** Eggs laid at *c.* 2-day interval. Incubation by female alone. 16–17 days. **Nestling.** Altricial. Skin black. Smoky-gray down along mid-back. Bill short and mouth yellowish. **Nestling period.** Young tended by female only. Eyes open at 5 days. Pin feathers well sprouted at 7 days. Not brooded after 12 days. Leave nest at 25–26 days.

Anna's Hummingbird: *c.* 1½in. across.

BROAD-TAILED HUMMINGBIRD *Selasphorus platycercus* **Pl. 51**

Breeds in mountain regions. Nest built on a low horizontal twig of a tree or shrub, often overhanging a stream. 3–30 ft. up, but often low.

Nest. A cup of variable plant material; fibers, rootlets, moss and plant down, lined with plant down and bound with spiders' webs and fine fibers, the outside decorated with flakes of lichen or more rarely shreds of bark or fibers. **Breeding season.** Begins early May in south to early June in north of range. **Eggs.** Usually 2. Long elliptical to long subelliptical. Smooth and non-glossy. White. 13 × 9 mm. **Incubation.** By female alone. **Nestling.** Altricial. **Nestling period.** No information.

RUFOUS HUMMINGBIRD *Selasphorus rufus* **Pl. 51**

Breeds over a wide range. Nest in a tree, frequently a conifer, or in shrub, bush or creeper, often low down. Tree nests are usually on lower branches. Nest is usually sited on a downward drooping twig or on a twig-fork or horizontal stem. A number of pairs may nest near each other.

Nest. A cup mainly made of soft cottony plant down, such as willow-seed, covered and built up outside with moss or similar material, bound with spiders' webs and covered on the outside with lichen flakes, or occasionally shreds of bark or fibers, helping to camouflage it. Diameter *c.* 2 in., *c.* $1\frac{1}{2}$ in. deep, inner cup *c.* 1 in. × $\frac{7}{8}$ in. deep. **Breeding season.** Begins late April to early May. **Eggs.** Usually 2. Long elliptical to long sub-elliptical. Smooth and non-glossy. White. 13 × 9 mm. **Incubation.** By female only. Period not recorded. **Nestling.** Altricial. Skin black. Mainly naked with a small double line of grayish down along mid-back. **Nestling period.** Young tended by female only. Eyes open at *c.* 6 days. Nestling down lengthens and pin feathers show at 6–7 days. Young leave at *c.* 20 days.

ALLEN'S HUMMINGBIRD *Selasphorus sasin*
Breeds in lightly wooded areas or thickets, often along streams. Nest on a tree, often low down, and saddling a twig or branch; on twigs or in twig forks of shrubs or bushes; occasionally on tall weed-stalks, in creepers, or on supports on buildings. At varied heights from 10 in. to 90 ft., but usually fairly low.
Nest. A cup, less deep than those of some other species; of moss, particularly in the bases of the walls, and of plant down, bound with spiders' webs and covered externally with lichen flakes or shreds of bark, pine needles or similar debris from near the site. *c.* $1\frac{3}{4}$–$1\frac{1}{4}$ in. external diameter, and *c.* 1 in. deep, with cavity *c.* $\frac{7}{8}$ in. across by $\frac{3}{4}$ in. deep. **Breeding season.** Begins early February. **Eggs.** Usually 2. Long elliptical to long subelliptical. Smooth and non-glossy. White. 13 × 9 mm. **Incubation.** Eggs usually laid on alternate days. Incubation by female alone, beginning with first egg. 16–22 days. **Nestling.** Altricial and downy. Sparse down along mid-back only. Skin dark. Mouth bright orange-yellow. Bill short, fleshy-yellow. **Nestling period.** Young tended by female alone. Leave nest at 22 days.

CALLIOPE HUMMINGBIRD *Stellula calliope*
Breeds on mountains and wooded hillsides. Nest usually on a horizontal or drooping twig or twig-fork of a conifer, near the end of a low branch and often partly hidden by a branch above. New nests may be built on old ones.
Nest. A cup of fine bark, fibers, mosses and pine-needles, mixed with plant down and bound with spiders' webs, the cavity thickly lined with down, and the outside covered with lichen flakes. *c.* $1\frac{1}{2}$–$1\frac{3}{4}$ in. diameter by $\frac{7}{8}$in. high, cup *c.* $1\frac{1}{8}$–$1\frac{7}{8}$ in. across and $\frac{7}{8}$ in. deep. **Breeding season.** Begins late May. **Eggs.** Usually 2. Long elliptical to long subelliptical. Smooth and non-glossy. White. 12 × 8 mm. **Incubation.** By female alone. 15 days. **Nestling.** Altricial. No description. **Nestling period.** Young tended by female only. Brooded and fed for 11–12 days, then only fed until young leave nest at 21–23 days.

RIVOLI'S HUMMINGBIRD *Eugenes fulgens*
Breeds in mountain regions, usually in trees along streams. Nest in a tree, often higher than those of other hummingbirds. 10–40 ft. up. Nest saddles a horizontal branch or twig, often overhanging a stream.
Nest. A cup, like a Ruby-throat nest, made of moss or plant fibers, bound together with spiders' webs, lined with plant down and covered outside with lichen flakes. *c.* $2\frac{1}{2}$ in. diameter by 2 in. deep, with cup $1\frac{1}{2}$ in. across and $1\frac{1}{4}$ in. deep. **Breeding season.** Begins early May. **Eggs.** Usually 2. Long elliptical to long subelliptical. Smooth and non-glossy. White. 15 × 10 mm. **Incubation.** No information. **Nestling.** Altricial. Not described. **Nestling period.** No information.

LUCIFER HUMMINGBIRD *Calothorax lucifer*
Breeds in mountain regions. Nest usually fairly low, in shrubs or agaves, 4–6 ft. up.
Nest. A cup of vegetable fibers, bud-scales, tree-blossoms and lichen, mixed with plant down, bound together with spiders' webs and fine fibers, lined with plant down, and sometimes a few feathers, and often decorated with whitish lichen flakes or small leaves on the outside. **Breeding season.** Begins in June. **Eggs.** Usually 2. Long elliptical to long subelliptical. Smooth and non-glossy. White. 13 × 10 mm. **Incubation.** No information. **Nestling.** Altricial and downy. Down very sparse, along mid-back only. **Nestling period.** Young tended by female only. Eyes open at 4–5 days. Feathered by *c.* 10 days. Leave nest at 21–23 days.

BLUE-THROATED HUMMINGBIRD *Lampornis clemenciae*
Breeds in mountain regions, frequently in rocky gorges. Nest in a twig fork, usually fairly low in a shrub, or on a weed stem, or fastened to a vine on a steep slope, often overhanging water.
Nest. A cup of fine moss, tree blossoms and small stems, firmly and smoothly bound together with down and spiders' webs. Inner cup small and deep. *c.* 2¾ in. across by 3 in. deep, inner cup 1¼ in. across by ¾ in. deep. **Breeding season.** Begins mid-May. **Eggs.** Usually 2. Long elliptical to long subelliptical. Smooth and non-glossy. White. 15 × 10 mm. **Incubation.** No information. **Nestling.** No information. **Nestling period.** No information.

VIOLET-CROWNED HUMMINGBIRD *Amazilia violiceps*
Breeds in mountain areas, in trees of canyons and streamsides. Nest on a high horizontal branch, near the extreme tip, and 30–40 ft. up.
Nest. No information. **Breeding season.** No information. **Eggs.** No information. **Incubation.** No information. **Nestling.** No information **Nestling period.** No information.

BUFF-BELLIED HUMMINGBIRD *Amazilia yucatanensis*
Breeds in lowland on woodland edge or in shrubby thickets. Nest in a small tree or shrub, usually by open space. The nest usually saddles a small horizontal or drooping twig, 3–8 ft. up.
Nest. A cup of plant and bark fibers, tiny leaves, and lichens, mixed with plant down, bound together with spiders' webs, lined with fine plant down; the outside decorated with shreds of bark, lichen flakes and dry tree-blossoms. **Breeding season.** Begins late March. **Eggs.** Usually 2. Long elliptical to long subelliptical. Smooth and non-glossy. White. 13 × 9 mm. **Incubation.** No information. **Nestling.** No information. **Nestling period.** No information.

BROAD-BILLED HUMMINGBIRD *Cynanthus latirostris*
Breeds usually in smaller trees and shrubs along streams. Nest built on to drooping or horizontal twig or stem, at times overhanging a stream. At heights of 4–12 ft.
Nest. A cup of stems, grasses, shreds of bark and parts of dry leaves, bound together with spiders' webs and lined with white down. Sometimes decorated on the outside with bark, small dead leaves or dry tree-blossoms, but not lichens. **Breeding season.** Begins mid-April. **Eggs.** Usually 2. Long elliptical

to long subelliptical. Smooth and non-glossy. White. 13 × 8 mm. **Incubation.** No information. **Nestling.** No information. **Nestling period.** No information.

WHITE-EARED HUMMINGBIRD *Hylocharis leucotis*

Breeds in mountain areas, in open woodland or clearings on mountainsides with shrubby growth. Nest built in fork of slender twigs of shrubs. At heights of 4–25 ft.

Nest. A deep rounded cup, usually built almost entirely of plant down, bound with spiders' webs and with the outside decorated with flakes of lichens and occasionally odd tree-blossoms or green mosses. *c.* $1\frac{3}{4}$–2 in. diameter and $1\frac{1}{2}$–$2\frac{3}{4}$ in. deep. Internal cup about 1 in. across and $1\frac{1}{8}$ in. deep. **Breeding season.** No information. **Eggs.** Usually 2. Long elliptical to long subelliptical. Smooth

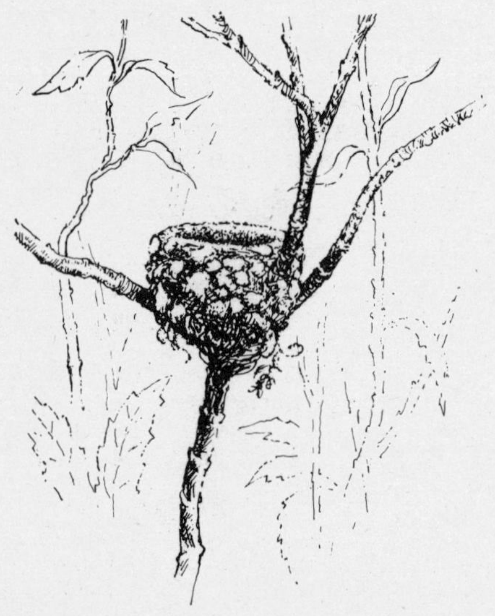

White-eared Hummingbird: *c.* $1\frac{1}{2}$-2in. across.

and non-glossy. White. 12 × 8 mm. **Incubation.** By female alone. Period not recorded. **Nestling.** Altricial. Naked skin black. Line of sparse, short down along mid-back. **Nestling period.** Young tended by female alone. Pin feathers sprout at 7–8 days. Eyes open at 9–10 days and feathers begin to break from sheath. Wing and tail feathers break out at 16 and 18 days. Young brooded until *c.* 18 days. Leave nest at 23–26 days. A young one seen fed by female at 40 days, although feeding itself by then.

TROGONS *Trogonidae*

COPPERY-TAILED TROGON *Trogon elegans* **Pls. 14, 52**
Occurs in dry woodland on mountain slopes. Nest in a natural cavity in a tree, or in an old woodpecker hole, 2–40 ft. up, rarely in hole in bank; but similar species are known to habitually dig, or bite, a cavity in rotten wood on a tree, using the bill.
Nest. A bare cavity, but later regurgitated seeds may be present. Cavities excavated by trogons are a little deeper than wide and have an upward-curved entrance tunnel. **Breeding season.** Begins late March. **Eggs.** Usually 3–4, sometimes 2. Short to very short subelliptical. Smooth and non-glossy. Dull white or bluish-white. 28 × 23 mm. **Incubation.** By both sexes. *c.* 19 days? **Nestling.** Altricial and naked. Pink skin. Eyes closed at first. Heel-joint of leg with pad of projecting papillae to protect it from abrasion. Two toes point backwards from the first. **Nestling period.** Young tended by both parents. No nest sanitation appears to occur. During first week all feathers grow as sheathed pin feathers. Eyes open at *c.* 1 week and feathers break from sheaths. Young leave at *c.* 15–17 days?

KINGFISHERS *Alcedinidae*

Small to medium, fast-flying predatory birds, diving for food or snatching it up. Bill well-developed, feet small and weak. Nest made by tunnelling with the bill; loose earth kicked out backwards with feet. Both sexes dig. No nest but debris from food castings may line cavity. Eggs white, nearly spherical. Young naked. Huddled together at first. No nest sanitation and although faeces are ejected for some distance by young the nest becomes foul before the young leave. All food brought to young is turned so that the creature is presented head first for ease in swallowing. After leaving the nest young remain together nearby and are fed by parents for some time afterwards.

GREEN KINGFISHER *Chloroceryle americana* **Pl. 52**
Breeds by freshwaters. Nest in a vertical bank alongside river or stream; usually 6–8 ft. up.
Nest. A burrow, *c.* 2–3 ft. long, 2 in. high by 2¼ in. wide. Small chamber at end and eggs laid on bare ground, later covered with cast-up fishbones and insect remains. **Breeding season.** Begins early April. **Eggs.** Usually 4–5, sometimes 3–6. Elliptical to short subelliptical. Smooth and glossy. White. 24 × 19 mm. **Incubation.** By both sexes. Period not recorded. **Nestling.** Altricial and naked. Skin pink. Small young have typical callosities on heels, and lower mandible longer than upper. **Nestling period.** Young tended by both parents. Can fly at *c.* 26 days. Independent of parents in further 4 weeks.

BELTED KINGFISHER *Megaceryle alcyon* **Pls. 15, 52**
Breeds by water – lakes, rivers, streams or sea-coast. Nest a burrow in a bank, usually near fresh water but occasionally at some distance when other sites are not available. Usually near the top of the bank or cliff. Exceptionally may nest in hole on shallow earth slope, or in natural cavity in a tree.

Plate 11

SHOREBIRDS (see also pl. 10). These young are typically long-legged and slender-billed, but the bills, although beginning to show the characters of the species, are usually shorter than those of adults. The basic down pattern is of longitudinal streaks, but mottled, with or without a white collar, in plovers.

Semipalmated Plover, *Charadrius semipalmatus.* Ringed Plover similar but paler. Other small species lack dark edge to collar. **page** 119

Wilson's Plover, *Charadrius wilsonia.* Piping and Snowy Plovers lack the dark lines on back and head and are paler. Mountain Plover is similar but yellowish. 120

Killdeer, *Charadrius vociferus.* 121

Lesser Golden Plover, *Pluvialis dominicus.* Black-bellied Plover has a grayer color, bolder markings and a bold white collar. 122

Black-necked Stilt, *Himantopus himantopus.* 116

American Avocet, *Recurvirostra americana.* 118

Jacana, *Jacana spinosa.* 115

Upland Sandpiper, *Bartramia longicauda.* 137

Whimbrel, *Numenius phaeopus.* Bristle-thighed Curlew is similar but stripe from eye to nape is incomplete and dark band on hind-flank does not meet tail mark. Long-billed Curlew has a broken, mottled dorsal pattern. 136

American Oystercatcher, *Haematopus palliatus.* Black Oystercatcher has similar pattern but face and back are darker. 115

Semipalmated Plover
Wilson's Plover
Killdeer
Lesser Golden Plover
lack-necked
tilt
American Avocet
Jacana
Upland Sandpiper
Whimbrel
American Oystercatcher

Noddy Tern
Black Tern
Least Tern
Sandwich Tern
Caspian Tern
Common Tern
Black Skimmer
Bonaparte's Gull
Herring Gull
Sabine's Gull

TERNS. In their earliest stages tern chicks may not be easy to tell apart from gull chicks, but they usually lack the very bold spotting or mottling on the head that most, but not all, gulls possess (note also that Black Tern chicks are heavily marked). They also tend to have shorter legs and more slender bills, and the adults are usually well in evidence. Young skimmers are tern-like and do not develop the characteristic bill until fledging.

Brown Noddy Tern, *Anous stolidus.* Three color forms are shown. The young may be white, brownish-black or in intermediate stages. **page** 159

Black Tern, *Chlidonias niger.* 158

Least Tern, *Sterna albifrons.* 157

Sandwich Tern, *Sterna sandvicensis.* Sooty and Roseate Terns also have the down sheathed in spiky tufts; grayer on Sooty Tern, more buff on back of Roseate Tern. 154

Caspian Tern, *Hydroprogne caspia.* Gull-billed and Royal Terns similar. The Gull-billed is more heavily marked in spots or streaks. The Royal Tern is very variable, some chicks being pale pinkish or buff with most markings absent and some dusky with blackish down tips. 153

Common Tern, *Sterna hirundo.* Forster's Tern has the throat brown, paler than the Common Tern's, and belly almost white; the Arctic Tern is usually more heavily marked with dark throat color extending to chin and forehead; the Aleutian Tern has the black extending from throat to upper breast. 155

SKIMMERS.

Black Skimmer, *Rynchops nigra.* 159

GULLS (see also pl. 13). In their earlier stages these are not easily told apart from young terns (see above) but as they grow the shorter, stouter bill becomes apparent. They usually have a bold, spotted or mottled down pattern.

Bonaparte's Gull, *Larus philadelphia.* The dorsal ground color of Common Gull is pale buff to buffish-gray, of Laughing Gull pale drab brown with warmer tints, of Franklin's Gull pale buffish-brown mottled dark brown, and of Ring-billed Gull pinkish or reddish buff. The last two species have a gray phase, pale with dark gray markings. 147

Herring Gull, *Larus argentatus.* Western Gull very similar. Greater Black-Backed Gull similar but with dark blackish-purple bill; Glaucous, Glaucous-winged and Iceland Gulls have ground color and markings paler, with dark brown legs and bill in the first. The California Gull is pale buff with indistinct gray markings on the back; and Thayer's Gull is very dark overall. 148

Sabine's Gull, *Larus sabini.* 146

Nest. Burrow usually slopes upwards from entrance. 3–6 ft. long, occasionally up to 15 ft. long, $3\frac{1}{2}$–4 in. wide, 3–$3\frac{1}{2}$ in. high. Egg chamber *c.* 10–12 in. diameter, 6–7 in. high. Excavated by both sexes in 3 days–3 weeks. Nest hollow usually bare when eggs are laid, but becomes lined with fishbones and insect remains. **Breeding season.** Begins early April to early May. Single-brooded but lost clutch may be replaced in new burrow. **Eggs.** Usually 6–8, sometimes 5–14. Elliptical to short subelliptical. Smooth and glossy. White. 34 × 27 mm. **Incubation.** By both sexes. *c.* 23–24 days. **Nestling.** Altricial and naked. Skin reddish. Feathers grow simultaneously in sheath, covering bird. Bill blackish. Mouth pink. No gape flanges. **Nestling period.** Young tended by both parents. Eyes open at *c.* 2 weeks. Feather quills begin to appear in first week. Sheaths break, freeing feathers, at 17–18 days. Young leave nest at 30–35 days.

RINGED KINGFISHER *Megaceryle torquata*

Breeds along deeper and smoother lowland streams, and shores of lakes, dams and lagoons, in more open sites. Nest a burrow in a steep earth or sand bank. Usually near the top of the bank face, overlooking the water or at a little distance from it.

Nest. A burrow 6–$8\frac{1}{2}$ ft. long, *c.* 4 in. high and 6 in. across, sloping upwards at the entrance, then more level. An enlarged brood chamber at the end is unlined. **Breeding season.** Begins early February. **Eggs.** Usually 4, sometimes 3–5. Elliptical to short subelliptical. Smooth and glossy. White. 44 × 34 mm. **Incubation.** By both sexes. Each incubating for 24 hours at a time. Period not recorded. **Nestling.** Altricial and naked. Skin pink and transparent. Lower mandible projects beyond blackish upper mandible. A callus pad on each leg joint is covered with small papillae. Skin rapidly covered by pin feathers in sheath. **Nestling period.** Young tended by both adults. Bill mandibles of equal length by 14 days and feather sheaths begin to break. Leaves nest at 33–38 days.

WOODPECKERS *Picidae*

Small to medium birds, gaining most of their food by climbing tree-trunks and branches. Nest bored in a hole in a tree, usually by both birds, and often in fairly firm wood. Similar holes may be made outside breeding season for roosting. A new hole is normally made each year. Eggs very smooth, white and rounded, but may become stained in damp nest cavities. Cavities are unlined and nestlings have a hard rough pad on the back of the leg joint, and rest and move on the whole tarsus when in the nest. On small young there is a sensitive swollen lump at the base of the lower mandible, on either side, and the adults touch this to induce the young to beg for food. The young are mainly fed on regurgitated food. They often keep up a harsh noise which may betray the nests.

COMMON FLICKER *Colaptes auratus* (Includes Yellow-shafted Flicker, *C. a. auratus*, Red-shafted Flicker, *C. a. cafer* and Gilded Flicker, *C. a. chrysoides*) **Pls. 15, 52**

Breeds in open or sparsely-wooded areas and cultivated areas with scattered trees. Nest-hole in a tree-trunk or stump; occasionally in telegraph pole, post, wooden building or in earth bank. Bird-boxes may be used. Holes usually at 8–25 ft., but may be 0–100 ft. up. Gilded Flicker, nesting in arid areas, often uses giant cacti.

Nest. Cavity sometimes in dead wood, more often in live wood. In cactus the pulp hardens around cavity after excavation. Entrance 2–4 in. diameter, depth of cavity usually 7–18 in., sometimes deeper, width varies, usually 7–8 in. Site apparently chosen by male, excavated by both sexes but mainly by male. Excavation takes 15–28 days. **Breeding season.** Begins mid-March in south to early June in north of range. Single-brooded but replaces lost clutches. **Eggs.** Usually 6–8, sometimes 3–14. Gilded Flicker clutches tend to be smaller, 3–5. Elliptical to subelliptical, long subelliptical, oval and long oval. Smooth and glossy. White. 28 × 21 mm. **Incubation.** Eggs laid daily. Incubation by both sexes, the male usually sitting at night. 11–12 days. **Nestling.** Altricial and naked. Skin warm brownish-orange, becoming reddish then blackish before feather quills appear. Swollen gape flanges whitish. **Nestling period.** Young tended by both parents, fed by regurgitation. Quills appear at 7 days, eyes open at 10 days. Young brooded by male for first 3 weeks. Begin climbing in nest cavity at 17–18 days, fed at entrance by 3 weeks. Leave at 25–28 days.

PILEATED WOODPECKER *Dryocopos pileatus* Pl. 52

Breeds in forest with large trees. Nest-hole bored in tree-trunk of conifer or deciduous tree, occasionally in telegraph pole. Usually chosen site is in close stand of living trees. 15–70 ft. up, but often at about 45 ft.
Nest. Cavity bored in dead wood. Entrance hole $3\frac{1}{4}$–$4\frac{1}{2}$ in. across, usually a little taller than wide. Cavity 10–24 in. deep, 6–8 in. across. **Breeding season.** Begins early March in south to mid-May in north of range. Single-brooded but replaces a lost clutch. **Eggs.** Usually 3–5. Subelliptical to elliptical. Smooth and glossy. White. 33 × 25 mm. **Incubation.** By both adults, male in cavity at night. *c.* 18 days? **Nestling.** Altricial and naked. **Nestling period.** Young tended by both parents. Fed by regurgitation. Eyes open at 9–10 days. Feathers break sheaths at 10–16 days. Young leave nest at 22–26 days.

RED-BELLIED WOODPECKER *Centurus carolinus* Pl. 52

Breeds in a variety of woodland habitats. Nest-hole in trunk of a variety of trees and stumps; sometimes in telegraph poles or fence posts. 5–40 ft. up, or occasionally up to 80 ft. Occasionally uses old nests of Red-cockaded Woodpecker.
Nest. Cavity bored in dead wood. Entrance hole slightly elliptical, $1\frac{3}{4}$–$2\frac{1}{4}$ in. diameter. Cavity 10–12 in. deep, 5–$5\frac{1}{2}$ in. across. **Breeding season.** Begins early to mid-April. Single-brooded, but lost clutch replaced. **Eggs.** Usually 4–5, sometimes 3–8. Subelliptical to long oval or elliptical. Smooth and slightly to moderately glossy. White. 25 × 19 mm. **Incubation.** By both sexes. 12–13 days. **Nestling.** Altricial and naked. **Nestling period.** Young tended by both parents. Closely brooded by either parent for first week. Leave nest at 26 days.

GOLDEN-FRONTED WOODPECKER *Centurus aurifrons* Pl. 52

Breeds in semi-arid areas, in mesquite in pure stands or mixed with larger trees. Nest-hole in trunk or branch of tree; occasionally in telegraph pole or nest-box. 6–25 ft. up, occasionally lower. Cavities may be re-used in subsequent years.
Nest. Cavity bored in live or dead wood. Cavity *c.* 15 in. deep. **Breeding season.** Begins late March. **Eggs.** Usually 4–5, sometimes up to 7. Subelliptical to oval or elliptical. Smooth and non-glossy or slightly glossy. White. 26 × 20 mm. **Incubation.** By both sexes, beginning with first egg. 12 days. **Nestling.** Altricial and naked. Skin pink. Callus on tarsal joint of leg with prominent

papillae for resting on wood. Upper mandible shorter but grows as long as lower by 8 days. **Nestling period.** Young tended by both parents. Eggs hatch over 2 days. Male broods at night while young are small. Eyes open at *c.* 9 days. Feathers grown but in sheath until 16–17 days, opening to full feathering in another 2 days. Young leave at 30 days. Remain with adults for some while after fledging.

GILA WOODPECKER *Centurus uropygialis* **Pl. 52**

Breeds in desert areas with cactus, and in river bottoms and canyons with mesquite or riverine woodland. Nest-hole in a cactus or tree such as cottonwood, willow or mesquite. 15–25 ft. up. Hole may be re-used in subsequent years. It has been suggested that cactus cavities are not suitable for use until the walls dry out.

Nest. Cavity bored in dead wood or live cactus. Entrance hole 2–2¼ in. diameter. Cavity 12–20 in. deep, *c.* 7–10 in. across. Made by both sexes. **Breeding season.** Begins in early April. Single- or double-brooded. **Eggs.** Usually 3–4, sometimes 5. Oval to long oval, and subelliptical. Smooth and moderately to very glossy. White. 25 × 19 mm. **Incubation.** By both sexes. 14 days? **Nestling.** Altricial and naked. **Nestling period.** No information.

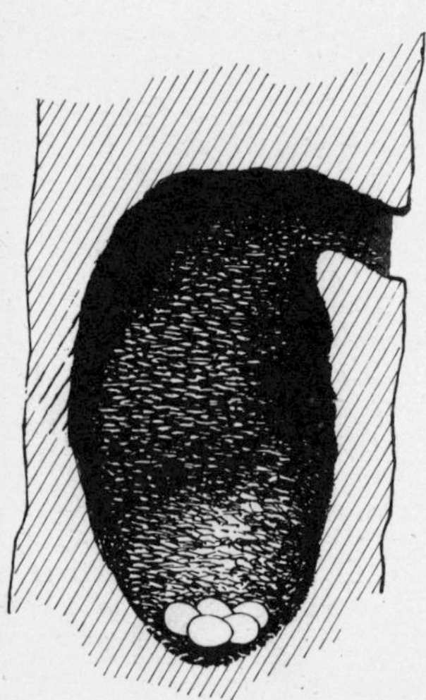

Nest cavity of Gila Woodpecker in cross-section.

RED-HEADED WOODPECKER *Melanerpes erythrocephalus* **Pl. 52**

Breeds in open and cultivated country with scattered trees. Nest-hole in a tree-trunk, large limb, or stump; occasionally in telegraph pole, fence post or roof of house. Cavity may be re-used for second brood. Nest from almost ground level to 80 ft. up.

Nest. Cavity usually bored in dead wood. Entrance hole 1¾ in. diameter. Cavity 8–14 in. deep, 3–4½ in. across. **Breeding season.** Begins late April in south to mid-May in north of range. Single- or double-brooded, and lost clutches are replaced. **Eggs.** Usually 5, sometimes 4–8. Subelliptical, oval or elliptical. Smooth and moderately glossy. White. 25 × 19 mm. **Incubation.** Eggs laid at daily intervals. Incubation by both adults, beginning before completion of clutch. *c.* 14 days? **Nestling.** Altricial and naked. **Nestling period.** Young tended by both parents. Hatch over a period, and differ in size. Leave at *c.* 27 days. Remain near nest-site but may be driven away if second brood is raised.

ACORN WOODPECKER *Melanerpes formicivorus* **Pl. 52**

Breeds in open woodland or partly wooded areas where oaks are present. Nest-hole in tree-trunk or larger limb, in large dead stubs, sometimes in telegraph poles, or power poles. 5–25 ft. up. Birds breed communally, in groups of 2–15 individuals, usually about 6, helping at a single nesting.

Nest. Cavity usually in dead wood. Entrance hole *c.* 1½ in. across. Cavity 8–24 in. deep. 4–5 in. diameter. **Breeding season.** Begins early April to early May. Sometimes 2 broods. **Eggs.** Usually 4–6, sometimes up to 10. Subelliptical to oval. Smooth and non-glossy or slightly glossy. White. 26 × 20 mm. **Incubation.** By both sexes and most individuals in group. *c.* 14 days? **Nestling.** Altricial and naked. **Nestling period.** Young tended by the whole group. Fed on insects brought in the bill.

LEWIS'S WOODPECKER *Asyndesmus lewis* **Pl. 52**

Breeds on forest edge, or in groves and scattered trees. Nest hole in a tree-trunk, in large dead stub, or in tree limb; in deciduous or coniferous tree. 6–100 ft. up. Sometimes several pairs have holes in one tree.

Nest. Cavity usually bored in dead wood. Entrance hole 2–2½ in. diameter, usually circular. Cavity up to 30 in. deep, *c.* 4 in. across. **Breeding season.** Begins mid-April in south to late May in north of range. **Eggs.** Usually 6–7, sometimes 5–9. Elliptical to subelliptical or oval. Variable in shape. Smooth and non-glossy. White. 26 × 20 mm. **Incubation.** By both sexes. *c.* 14 days? **Nestling.** Altricial and naked. **Nestling period.** Little information. Young tended by both parents. Leave nest at *c.* 21 days.

YELLOW-BELLIED SAPSUCKER *Sphyrapicus varius* **Pl. 52**

Breeds in forest, frequently in large dead trees. Nest-hole in tree-trunk. 5–60 ft. up.

Nest. Cavity may be bored in apparently live wood, but the heart-wood may be decaying inside an otherwise sound tree-trunk, hole usually neat and smooth-sided with some woodchips in bottom. Entrance hole 1¼–1½ in. diameter. Cavity 6–14 in. deep, 4–5 in. across. Bored by both sexes but mostly by male. Takes 15–28 days. **Breeding season.** Begins late April to May. Single-brooded but lost clutch replaced. **Eggs.** Usually 5–6, sometimes 4–7. Subelliptical to oval. Smooth, non-glossy or slightly glossy. White. 23 × 17 mm. **Incubation.** By both sexes. 12–13 days. **Nestling.** Altricial and naked. **Nestling period.** Young tended by both parents. Fed directly on insects brought in bill. Climb to upper nest for feeding by 18 days, to entrance by 20 days. Leave at 25–29 days. Dependent on parents for 1–2 weeks after leaving.

WILLIAMSON'S SAPSUCKER *Sphyrapicus thyroideus*

Breeds in mountain pine forests. Nest-hole in conifer tree-trunk. 5–60 ft. up. The same tree often used repeatedly over years, with new hole each time.

Nest. Cavity usually in dead wood. Entrance hole 1½ in. diameter. Cavity 8 in. deep, 5 in. across. **Breeding season.** Begins late May. Single-brooded. **Eggs.** Usually 5–6, sometimes 3–7. Smooth. Slightly glossy. White. 24 × 17 mm. **Incubation.** By both sexes. Period not recorded. **Nestling.** Altricial and naked. **Nestling period.** Little information. Young tended by both parents.

HAIRY WOODPECKER *Dendrocopos villosus* **Pl. 52**

Breeds in mature woodland, mainly deciduous, on woodland edge, in orchards, or parkland with scattered trees. Nest-hole in tree-trunk or large limb; occasionally in telegraph pole or bird-box. *c.* 3–55 ft. up, at average of *c.* 30 ft. up. **Nest.** Cavity more often in live wood. Entrance hole 2–2½ in. high by 1½–1¼ in. wide. Cavity 10–15 in. deep, *c.* 4½ in. across. Excavated by both sexes, taking 17–24 days. **Breeding season.** Begins late March in south to late May in north of range. Single-brooded, but lost clutches replaced, sometimes in same cavity. **Eggs.** Usually 4, sometimes 3–6. Subelliptical to almost elliptical or oval. Smooth and glossy. White. 25 × 19 mm. **Incubation.** By both sexes, male brooding at night. 11–12 days. **Nestling.** Altricial and naked. **Nestling period.** Young tended by both sexes. Regularly brooded for first half of period, decreasing later, mostly by female. Young fed directly on food carried in bill. Nest-sanitation mostly by male. Young climb to entrance for food at *c.* 17 days. Leave nest at 28–30 days. Rely on adults for *c.* 2 weeks after leaving. May return to roost in nest.

DOWNY WOODPECKER *Dendrocopos pubescens* **Pl. 52**

Breeds in open woodland, orchards, parkland and areas with scattered trees. Nest-hole in a branch or stub. *c.* 8–50 ft. up.

Nest. Cavity is in dead wood. Entrance hole 1¼ in. diameter. Cavity 8–12 in. deep. Excavated by both sexes in 13–20 days. **Breeding season.** Begins early April in south to late May in north of range. Single-brooded. **Eggs.** Usually 4–5, sometimes 3–6. Subelliptical to oval. Smooth and glossy. White. 19 × 15 mm. **Incubation.** By both sexes, male incubating at night. 12 days. **Nestling.** Altricial and naked. **Nestling period.** Young tended by both parents. Fed directly on food brought in bill. Climb to feed at top of cavity by 9 days, to entrance at 12 days. Leave nest at 20–22 days. Dependent on adults for up to 3 weeks after leaving nest.

LADDER-BACKED WOODPECKER *Dendrocopos scalaris* **Pl. 52**

Breeds in open woodland of arid areas, in scattered trees, trees along stream bottoms and creeks, and in mesquite. Nest-hole in trunk of a variety of trees, in a telegraph pole or fence post, cactus, or stem of agave or yucca. At *c.* 3–30 ft. up. Usually at 5–15 ft. up.

Nest. Cavity bored in dead wood. Entrance hole *c.* 1½ in. diameter. Cavity 7–10 in. deep. **Breeding season.** Begins mid-April. Single-brooded? **Eggs.** Usually 4–5, sometimes 2–7. Elliptical to subelliptical. Smooth and glossy. White. 20 × 16 mm. **Incubation.** No information. **Nestling.** Altricial and naked. **Nestling period.** No information.

NUTTALL'S WOODPECKER *Dendrocopos nuttallii* **Pl. 52**

Breeds in live oaks and mixed tree growth near watercourses. Nest-hole in a tree-trunk. 2–60 ft. up.

Nest. Cavity usually in dead wood. Usually *c.* 12 in. deep by 5 in. across. Excavated mostly by male. **Breeding season.** Begins late March. Single-brooded. **Eggs.** Usually 4–5, sometimes 3–6. Elliptical to subelliptical. Smooth and moderately glossy. White to creamy-white. 22 × 16 mm. **Incubation.** By both sexes. Period not recorded. **Nestling.** Altricial and naked. **Nestling period.** Young tended by both parents. Little information.

ARIZONA WOODPECKER *Dendrocopos arizonae*

Breeds in lower montane woodlands of pine-oaks areas. Nest-hole in tree-trunk, 8–50 ft. up, usually about 15–20 ft. up.

Nest. Cavity usually in dead wood. *c.* 12 in. deep. **Breeding season.** Begins late April. Single-brooded. **Eggs.** Usually 3–4. Subelliptical to oval. Smooth and glossy. White. 23 × 17 in. **Incubation.** No information. **Nestling.** Altricial and naked. **Nestling period.** No information.

RED-COCKADED WOODPECKER *Dendrocopos borealis*

Breeds in open long-leaf pine forest. Nest-hole in a tree-trunk or large limb. 18–100 ft. up. Some pairs may have one or more additional adult helpers.

Nest. Cavity bored in live wood. Small holes made around entrance produce resin flow which hardens around the hole. Cavity 8–12 in. deep. **Breeding season.** Begins in April. Single-brooded, but lost clutches replaced. **Eggs.** Usually 3–5. Subelliptical to oval. Smooth and glossy. White. 24 × 18 mm. **Incubation.** By both sexes. 10–11 days. **Nestling.** Altricial and naked. Skin pink. Legs and feet white. Swollen bill base white. **Nestling period.** Young tended by both parents and any helpers. Brooded for first 4 days. Young leave nest at 26–29 days. Fed by parents and possibly helpers for up to 5 months after fledging.

WHITE-HEADED WOODPECKER *Dendrocopos albolarvatus*

Breeds in mountain pine forest. Nest-hole in a tree-trunk. 3–50 ft. up.

Nest. Cavity usually in dead wood. Entrance $1\frac{1}{2}$–$1\frac{3}{4}$ in. diameter, usually circular. Cavity 10–15 in. deep. Width variable, wider towards base. **Breeding season.** Begins in late April. Single-brooded. **Eggs.** Usually 4–5, sometimes 3–7. Subelliptical to oval. Smooth and moderately glossy to very glossy. White. 24 × 18 mm. **Incubation.** By both sexes. 14 days? **Nestling.** Altricial and naked. **Nestling period.** Young tended by both parents.

ARCTIC WOODPECKER (Black-backed Three-toed Woodpecker)
Picoides arcticus **Pl. 52**

Breeds in northern woodland, in deciduous or conifer trees, usually near or in more open places. Nest-hole in a tree-trunk. Usually 2–15 ft. up. Rarely much higher.

Nest. Cavity usually in dead wood. Entrance hole 2 × $1\frac{1}{2}$ in., cavity 9–10 in. deep, width $4\frac{1}{2}$ in., narrower towards entrance. Excavated by both sexes but mainly by male. **Breeding season.** Begins mid- to late May. Single-brooded, but lost clutches may be replaced and cavity re-used if undamaged. **Eggs.** Usually 4, sometimes 2–6. Subelliptical to oval. Smooth, slightly glossy, and white. 21 × 19 mm. **Incubation.** By both sexes. 14 days? **Nestling.** Altricial and naked. **Nestling period.** Young tended by both parents. Food brought in bill and also regurgitated.

NORTHERN THREE-TOED WOODPECKER *Picoides tridactylus* **Pl. 52**

Breeds in conifer forests. Nest-hole in a tree-trunk. 5–40 ft. up.
Nest. Cavity usually in dead wood. Entrance hole *c.* 1 × 1½ in. Cavity *c.* 8–10 in. deep, *c.* 4–5 in. wide. **Breeding season.** Begins mid- to late May. Single-brooded. **Eggs.** Usually 4–5, sometimes 3–6. Subelliptical to oval. Smooth and moderately glossy. White. 23 × 18 mm. **Incubation.** By both sexes. 14 days? **Nestling.** Altricial and naked. **Nestling period.** Young tended by both parents. Fed directly on food brought in bill.

IVORY-BILLED WOODPECKER *Campephilus principalis*

Breeds, or bred, in forest with tall old trees. Nest-hole bored into large tree-trunk, 25–60 ft. up.
Nest. Cavity usually in dead wood. Entrance hole 5–6 × 4–4½ in. Entrance tunnel *c.* 5 in., and cavity 17–25 in. deep, and 6–10 in. across, elliptical, and 2–3 in. wider from side to side. Some loose sawdust and wood chips in cavity. Nest excavated by both sexes. **Breeding season.** Begins usually in March, sometimes February. Single-brooded. **Eggs.** Earlier clutches usually 1–2, later clutches 3–4. Long subelliptical to long oval. Smooth and glossy. White. 35 × 25 mm. **Incubation.** By both sexes, the male on the nest at night. *c.* 20 days? **Nestling.** Altricial and naked. **Nestling period.** Young tended by both adults. Brooded by the male at night, occasionally during day. Leave nest after *c.* 5 weeks. Fed by adults for further 2 months or more. Remain with parents until winter.

COTINGAS *Cotingidae*

ROSE-THROATED BECARD *Platypsaris aglaiae* **Pl. 53**

Breeds in trees near water. Nest a rounded pendant structure at the tip of a slender branch, 15–60 ft. up.
Nest. A pendant rounded or pear-shaped structure, *c.* 12–30 in. high by 9–12 in. wide, and with walls 1½–2½ in. thick, occasionally larger if made of coarser, loose material. The entrance at one side, near the bottom and directed downwards. Nest woven and suspended with bark strips, wiry vine stems, long pine needles, long branching lichen, weed stems, grasses and spiders' webs, and also using plant down, wool and moss. (Some mud in lining?) An inner cup lined with plant down and bark fiber. Building may continue during incubation. **Breeding season.** Begins early May. **Eggs.** 4–6. Subelliptical. Smooth and slightly glossy. White, creamy-white, or pale purplish or buffish, spotted and blotched with dull brown, olive-brown or purplish-red, and pale pinkish-cinnamon, buff or gray. Markings frequently elongated into poorly-defined short streaks. Markings often denser at, or around, the larger end. 23 × 17 mm. **Incubation.** By female alone. Period not recorded. **Nestling.** No information. **Nestling period.** Young tended by both parents.

TYRANT-FLYCATCHERS *Tyrannidae*

Small to medium-sized insectivorous birds. Nest usually a cup, domed in one species; in a tree or shrub fork, on a branch, in a cavity, on the ground or on a ledge under an overhang. Nest a miscellaneous array of debris, usually with a soft lining. Nest of phoebes stuck to site and largely built with mud; some other small species use spiders' webs for binding and attaching nests. Eggs usually white to creamy-yellow, with sparse bold spotting, or fine streaking in crested flycatchers. Incubation usually by female. Young hatch naked and grow down within several days. Fed on insects brought in bill by adults.

EASTERN KINGBIRD *Tyrannus tyrannus* **Pl. 53**

Breeds over a wide range, preferring farmland with scattered trees. Nest usually towards the end of a horizontal branch of a tree. Often over water. Where trees are absent, post or stump may be used, sometimes standing in water. Height very variable. 2–60 ft., but often fairly low.

Nest. A large, deep cup, with loose material at outside; of thin twigs, dry weed stems, straw, twine, plant-down and hair, sometimes with feathers, string and pieces of cloth or wool; lining of fine dry grass, rootlets and hair. **Breeding season.** Begins early May in south to late May or early June in north of range. **Eggs.** Usually 3–4, sometimes 5. Subelliptical, to long or short subelliptical. Smooth and slightly glossy. White, creamy-white or pinkish; speckled, spotted and blotched with purplish-brown, reddish-brown and blackish-purple, and paler brown, lilac and gray. Markings bold, often longitudinally elongated, with a concentration around the larger end. 24 × 18 mm. **Incubation.** By both sexes. 12–13 days. **Nestling.** Altricial and downy. Skin orange-yellow. Down white. Mouth orange-yellow. **Nestling period.** Young tended by both parents. Leave at 13–14 days? Parents continue to feed young for up to 35 days more.

GRAY KINGBIRD *Tyrannus dominicensis* **Pl. 53**

Breeds near the coast. Nest in a tree, mangroves in the swamps and scrub oak and palmetto elsewhere, or occasionally in shade trees. Often low, *c.* 3–12 ft. up.

Nest. A large, loose and flimsy cup of coarse twigs, vines and grasses; lined with fine grass and rootlets. **Breeding season.** Begins early April. **Eggs.** Usually 3–4, sometimes 2–5. Subelliptical to oval. Smooth and slightly glossy. Creamy-white, ivory-yellow or very pale pink; speckled, spotted and blotched with chestnut-red, purplish-brown and paler lilac and gray. Bolder markings usually in a zone at larger end with sparser and smaller markings elsewhere. Markings often longitudinally elongated. 21 × 18 mm. **Incubation.** No information. **Nestling.** Altricial and downy. Down buff to creamy-buff. **Nestling period.** No information.

TROPICAL KINGBIRD *Tyrannus melancholicus* **Pl. 53**

Breeds in chaparral regions. Nest usually in a tree near the end of a horizontal branch. 8–20 ft. up.

Nest. A cup of twigs, Spanish Moss, bark strips, and plant down; lined with fine rootlets and black, hair-like strands of moss. **Breeding season.** Begins early May. **Eggs.** Usually 3–4, sometimes 5. Subelliptical to long subelliptical. Creamy-white to ivory-yellow or very slightly tinted pink; speckled, spotted and blotched in deep chestnut-red, purplish-brown, reddish-brown and paler lilac and gray. Markings usually bold and fairly sparse except at larger end where they may form heavy wreath. Markings sometimes longitudinally elongated. 25 × 18 mm. **Incubation.** No information. **Nestling.** No information. **Nestling period.** No information.

WESTERN KINGBIRD *Tyrannus verticalis* **Pl. 53**
Breeds in open country in trees by water, or shade and orchard trees around settlement. Nest in a tree, well out on a horizontal limb or occasionally by the trunk, *c.* 15–30 ft. up, or sometimes 5–40 ft. up. Nests also on shrubs, telegraph poles, fence posts, buildings or similar sites.
Nest. A large untidy cup of weed stems, thin twigs, rootlets, plant fibers, coarse grasses, wool, hair, feathers, string, plant down, scraps of paper, snakeskin and catkins. Lined with similar but finer material felted together in a tight cup. **Breeding season.** Begins mid-April in south to late May or early June in north of range. **Eggs.** Usually 4, sometimes 3–5, exceptionally 6–7. Like those of Eastern Kingbird in shape, color and pattern, but slightly smaller on average. 23 × 17 mm. **Incubation.** 12–14 days. **Nestling.** No information. **Nestling period.** Young tended by both parents.

CASSIN'S KINGBIRD *Tyrannus vociferans* **Pl. 53**
Breeds in higher country with scrub, or open hillsides with scattered trees. Nests in trees along canyons, by streams, or in scattered oaks on hillsides. Nest in a tree, near the end of a horizontal branch, usually 20–40 ft. up, sometimes only 8–10 ft. up, and exceptionally on fence posts or gates.
Nest. A substantial cup of small twigs, weed stems, bark strips, rootlets and plant fibers, with dead leaves, string and rags; lined with finer grasses, rootlets and sometimes some feathers and thick cottonwood down. **Breeding season.** Begins late April to early May. Sometimes double-brooded? **Eggs.** Usually 3–4, sometimes 2–5. Subelliptical. Smooth and slightly glossy. White to creamy-white, or faintly buff; boldly blotched, speckled and spotted with reddish, purplish-brown or olive-brown, blackish-purple, and paler purple or gray. Markings rather sparse, usually concentrated at larger end, and often longitudinally elongated. 23 × 17 mm. **Incubation.** 12–14 days. **Nestling.** No information. **Nestling period.** *c.* 14 days.

SCISSOR-TAILED FLYCATCHER *Muscivora forficata* **Pl. 53**
Breeds in open country with scattered small trees and shrubs, open woodland edge, and shade trees around human settlement. Nest is typically on a horizontal branch or at a fork, 5–30 ft. up, in a tree or on the ledge of a man-made structure.
Nest. A loose cup of thin twigs, rootlets, weed stems, husk, twine, cotton, plant down, wool, paper, rags and other debris. Spanish Moss if available. Lined with rootlets, hair and cotton. Built by female alone. **Breeding season.** Begins early April in south to early June in north. **Eggs.** Usually 3–5, sometimes 6. Subelliptical. Smooth and slightly glossy. White, creamy-white or slightly pinkish; spotted, or blotched with dark brown, chestnut-brown, or purplish-brown, and paler gray, purple or brownish-gray. Markings sometimes very sparse or absent. 22 × 17 mm. **Eggs.** Eggs laid at daily intervals. **Incubation.** By female alone. 12–13 days. **Nestling.** No information. **Nestling period.** Young tended by both parents. *c.* 14 days.

KISKADEE FLYCATCHER *Pitangus sulphuratus* **Pl. 53**
Breeds in trees, usually by streams, rivers, lakes or swamps, in woodland, or in plantations and shade trees. Nest usually in a crotch of tree or similar site offering firm support, 10–30 ft. up.
Nest. A large domed structure, but the dome may not be completed until after

incubation has begun. A bulky mass of dry weed and vine stems, Spanish Moss, grasses, rags, plant-fibers, feathers, etc., the shallow cup lined with finer material such as wool, feathers and plant down. **Breeding season.** Begins late March. **Eggs.** Usually 4, sometimes 3–5. Smooth and slightly glossy. Pale creamy-white to ivory-yellow; very sparsely marked, often only at the larger end, with specks and spots of dark brown, blackish-brown and pale gray. 28 × 21 mm. **Incubation.** No information. **Nestling.** No information. **Nestling period.** No information.

SULPHUR-BELLIED FLYCATCHER *Myiodynastes luteiventris* Pl. 53

Breeds in larger trees of wooded canyons. Nest in a natural cavity in tree, or in an old woodpecker hole, 10–45 ft. up.

Nest. In a cavity which may be built up at base with twigs, bark and other debris; with a cup of leaf stems, fine weed stems, pine needles and an inner lining of finer stems. Built by female alone. **Breeding season.** Begins mid-June. **Eggs.** Usually 3–4. Subelliptical. Smooth and slightly glossy. White to rich creamy-buff; heavily spotted and blotched with deep chestnut-red, reddish-brown and purplish-brown, and paler purple and gray. Markings often profuse and distributed overall. 26 × 19 mm. **Incubation.** By female only. 15–16 days. **Nestling.** Altricial and downy. Skin pink at first, becoming dark gray. Down long and plentiful; dark gray. Mouth and gape flanges yellow. **Nestling period.** Young tended by both parents. Eyes open by 7 days. Young leave nest at 16–18 days.

GREAT CRESTED FLYCATCHER *Myiarchus crinitus* Pl. 53

Breeds in deciduous and mixed woodland, usually near clearings or woodland edge; in orchards, or scattered trees in cultivated regions. Nest in a cavity – whether natural or a woodpecker hole in a tree, or an artificial site, such as a pipe, nest-box or similar cavity. 10–70 ft. up.

Nest. A cavity built up at base with dead leaves, leaf stalks, twigs, and nest of stems, fibers, grass, pine-needles, feathers, rootlets, hair and various debris, including pieces of snakeskin or smooth paper; lined with hair, fur, feathers and fine material. **Breeding season.** Begins mid-March in south to mid-June in north of range. **Eggs.** Usually 4–5, rarely 6 or more. Subelliptical to short or long subelliptical or elliptical. Smooth and slightly glossy. Ivory-yellow to creamy-buff, or rarely creamy-white, pinkish or purplish-buff; heavily marked with irregular fine longitudinal streaks, sometimes thin hair lines, of purplish-red or purple, and paler gray and lavender. The lines may cross each other at times and sometimes show irregular scrawling. Usually a concentration of markings at larger end. 23 × 17 mm. **Incubation.** By female alone. 13–15 days. **Nestling.** Altricial and downy. Skin dark flesh-color. Young hatched naked, soon growing a scanty down, grayish in colour. Mouth orange-yellow. Gape flanges cream color. **Nestling period.** Young tended by both parents. Leave nest at 14–15 days.

WIED'S CRESTED FLYCATCHER *Myiarchus tyrannulus* Pl. 53

Breeds from open deciduous woodland to mesquite and dry plains with cactus. Nest in a natural cavity or woodpecker hole in tree or saguaro cactus.

Nest. A cup in a cavity. Of bark and fibers, hair, wool, feathers, and usually pieces of snakeskin. **Breeding season.** Begins late March to early April. **Eggs.** Usually 3–5. Subelliptical to short subelliptical. Smooth and slightly glossy. Creamy-white to creamy or ivory-yellow; with very fine small streaks, and more rarely heavier streaks or blotches at the larger end, of purple or purplish-red, and pale lavender or gray. Similar to those of Great Crested Flycatcher, but markings usually less profuse and ground color paler. 24 × 18 mm. **Incubation.** No information. **Nestling.** No information. **Nestling period.** No information.

ASH-THROATED FLYCATCHER *Myiarchus cinerascens* **Pl. 53**
Breeds in mesquite, oak scrub and dry plains with cactus, and in open deciduous woodland. Nest in a natural cavity in tree or stump, or in cactus, or a woodpecker hole, or behind loose bark, in dry inflorescent stems of yucca or agave, or in old nest of Cactus Wren. Also nests in man-made cavities; holes in posts, pipes, boxes or similar sites.
Nest. A cup of dry grasses, rootlets and weed stems; lined with finer grasses, hair and fur. Cavity base may be built up with dry cow or horse dung. **Breeding season.** Begins mid-April to early May. **Eggs.** Usually 4–5, sometimes 3–7. Subelliptical to elliptical. Smooth and slightly glossy. Creamy-white to ivory or pinkish-white. With fine longitudinal streaking, heavier streaking, or elongated blotches and spots, or more typical spots and blotches in purplish-red, reddish-brown, lilac or gray. Tending towards the pattern shown by Great Crested Flycatcher, but marking sparser, with more pale markings and more creamy ground color showing. **Incubation.** By female alone. **Nestling.** Altricial. Naked at hatching. **Nestling period.** Young tended by both parents.

OLIVACEOUS FLYCATCHER *Myiarchus tuberculifer* **Pl. 53**
Breeds in scrub oak thickets of lower mountain slopes, and dense growth along canyon streams. Nest in a natural cavity in a tree, or in a woodpecker hole, 4–40 ft. up.
Nest. A cup of fine grasses, weed stems, various plant fragments, bark strips, dead leaves, hair, fur or feathers; lined with finer grasses, hair and fur. **Breeding season.** Begins mid-May. **Eggs.** Usually 4–5. Subelliptical. Smooth and slightly glossy. Creamy-white or cream-coloured. Markings like those of Ash-throated Flycatcher. 20 × 15 mm. **Incubation.** No information. **Nestling.** No information. **Nestling period.** No information.

EASTERN PHOEBE *Sayornis phoebe* **Pl. 53**
Breeds usually around farms and other buildings. Exceptionally on a cliff niche or other natural site. More usually on a ledge, rafter or raised site with some overhanging protection, in or on a building, under a bridge, or in any niche of this kind.
Nest. A cup of mud pellets mixed with moss, dry grass, fibers of weeds and vine stems; lined with fine fibers, rootlets and hair. Built during 3–6 days. **Breeding season.** Begins mid-April in south to mid-May in north. Occasionally double-brooded. **Eggs.** Usually 5, sometimes 3–7, rarely 8. Subelliptical. Non-glossy or slightly glossy. White, usually unmarked, an occasional egg with a few small spots of light to dark brown. 19 × 15 mm. **Incubation.** By female alone. 14–16 days. **Nestling.** Altricial and downy. Down sparse and dark gray. Gape flanges yellow. Mouth orange-red. **Nestling period.** Young tended by both parents. Leave at 15–17 days. Fed by parents for a further 2–3 weeks.

Eastern Phoebe: *c.* 4-5in. across.

BLACK PHOEBE *Sayornis nigricans* **Pl. 53**
Breeds mainly around farms and human settlement. Nest on a ledge sheltered by some overhanging surface, on a beam or support in or on a building, under a bridge, in a niche in a wall, in a well or mine-shaft, or on a ledge of some other man-made structure.
Nest. A cup of mud pellets, dry grass, weed stems, plant and bark fibers and hair; lined with fine fibers, rootlets, grass-heads, hair, wool and sometimes feathers. **Breeding season.** Begins mid-March. Double-brooded. **Eggs.** Usually 4–5, sometimes 3–6. Subelliptical. Smooth and non-glossy or slightly glossy. White, usually unmarked, an occasional egg with a few specks and spots of reddish-brown. 19 × 14 mm. **Incubation.** By female alone. 15–18 days. **Nestling.** Altricial and downy. Down sparse; gray. **Nestling period.** Young tended by both parents. Leave nest at 21 days. Male may feed young after leaving while female re-nests.

SAY'S PHOEBE *Sayornis saya* **Pl. 53**
Breeds in open country where sites are available. Like other phoebes natural nest-site a sheltered ledge or crevice of cliff or cave, hole or crevice in steep bank,

or cavity in tree. Now nests on ledges with some sheltered overhang in or on buildings, and bridges, or down mine-shafts and wells, or in similar man-made sites.

Nest. A bulky, shallow cup of weed stems, dry grasses, plant fibers, moss, wool, hair and spiders' cocoons and webs; lined with hair. **Breeding season.** Begins early March in south to late May in north of range. Double-brooded. **Eggs.** Usually 4–5, sometimes 3–7. Subelliptical to short subelliptical. Smooth and non-glossy or slightly glossy. White, usually unmarked, rarely with a few brown or reddish spots. 20 × 15 mm. **Incubation.** By female alone. 12–14 days. **Nestling.** Altricial and downy. Skin deep yellow. Down very sparse and gray. **Nestling period.** Young tended by both parents. Eyes open at 6 days. Young leave at *c.* 14 days? The male feeds the first brood of fledged young while female re-nests.

YELLOW-BELLIED FLYCATCHER *Empidonax flaviventris* **Pl. 53**

Breeds in northern spruce forests in wet or swampy places. Nest on or near ground on moss hummock, mound, tree-roots, or among the raised roots of fallen tree. Nest sunk into a layer of moss, and usually hidden by moss or growing herbage, or under overhanging roots.

Nest. A cup of rootlets, weed stems, moss and grasses; lined with fine rootlets, black plant fibers and thin moss stems, occasionally fine grasses or pine-needles. **Breeding season.** Begins early June. **Eggs.** Usually 3–4, sometimes 5. Subelliptical to short subelliptical. Smooth and slightly glossy. White; sparsely speckled or with occasional blotches of brown, pinkish or buffish-cinnamon, and paler purple. 17 × 13 mm. **Incubation.** By female alone, beginning with last egg. 15 days. **Nestling.** Altricial and downy. Down brownish-olive. **Nestling period.** Young tended by both parents. Leave nest at 13 days.

ACADIAN FLYCATCHER *Empidonax virescens* **Pl. 53**

Breeds in swampy woodland, floodplain forest and cypress swamps, and in woodland along ravines and watercourses. Nest in a tree, suspended in a horizontal twig fork towards the end of a branch, often over water, 8–25 ft. up.

Nest. A cup partly suspended in a twig fork, with loose material hanging down from it. Caterpillar silk is used to bind the nest in place and plant fragments may hang from this. Cup of slender weed stems, twigs, vine tendrils, dead leaves, grasses, tree blossoms and bud scales; Spanish Moss used where available. **Breeding season.** Begins late April in south to early June in north of range. **Eggs.** Usually 3, sometimes 2–4. Subelliptical to elliptical. Smooth and non-glossy or slightly glossy. Creamy-white or buffish-white. Sparsely marked with minute specks and spots or blotches of dark brown and purplish-brown; mainly at larger end. 18 × 14 mm. **Incubation.** Eggs laid at daily intervals. Incubation by female alone. 13–14 days. **Nestling.** Altricial and downy. Skin pink or flesh-colored. Down sparse and white. **Nestling period.** Young tended by both parents. Brooded by female only. Eyes open by 4 days. Leave nest at 13 days. Fed by parents for *c.* 12 more days.

ALDER FLYCATCHER *Empidonax alnorum* **Pl. 53**

Breeds in alder swamps, low thickets along streams and lake edges in wooded areas, and open damp places with shrubs and bracken, usually near water. Nest low in a bush, shrub or small tree, or in the forks of tall bracken, 1–6 ft. up. Nest usually in an upright fork and built around supporting stems.

Nest. A neat cup of weed bark, soft dead grasses, plant fibers, bracken, moss and sometimes a few feathers; lined with finer grasses, hair and fruiting stems of moss. Material often hangs down in an untidy tail under the nest. **Breeding season.** Begins mid-May to early June. **Eggs.** Usually 3–4, sometimes 2. Subelliptical to short subelliptical. Smooth and non-glossy. White to creamy-white or tinted buff or pink. Unmarked or sparsely marked, mainly around the larger end, with fine specks, spots and small blotches of light red, reddish-brown and chestnut-red. 18 × 13 mm. **Incubation.** 13–15 days. **Nestling.** Altricial and downy. Down pale gray, brownish-gray on the head. Mouth yellow. Gape flanges deep yellow. **Nestling period.** Young tended by both parents. Eyes open at 6 days. Feathers break sheath at 5–8 days. Young leave nest at 12–15 days.

WILLOW FLYCATCHER *Empidonax traillii*

Breeds in dry scrub and dry overgrown upland pastures, or in low scrub by lakes and watercourses in open areas. Nest in a shrub or small tree, particularly rose and willow, usually in a vertical fork, built around supporting twigs, 5–20 ft. up.

Nest. A compact cup of weed bark, plant fibers, dry grasses and plant down such as willow down, often giving it a cottony appearance, like that of Yellow Warbler or Goldfinch; lined with finer grasses, plant down and hair. **Breeding season.** Begins mid-April. **Eggs.** Usually 3–4. Very similar to those of Willow Flycatcher. 18 × 13 mm. **Incubation.** *c.* 12 days. **Nestling.** Altricial and downy. Down pale olive-brown. **Nestling period.** *c.* 14 days.

LEAST FLYCATCHER *Empidonax minimus* **Pl. 53**

Breeds in open deciduous and mixed woodland, woodland edge, orchards, lake and stream edges, parkland, and shade trees around settlement. Nest in a tree, usually deciduous sometimes a conifer, often 5–20 ft. up, sometimes 2–60 ft. up. Nest on a horizontal branch, in a fork or against the trunk, or in a vertical crotch.

Nest. A small, deep and fairly compact cup; of bark fibers, shredded weed stems, fine grasses, and weed stems, dead weed and grass blossoms, plant down, cotton, and bound with spiders' webs and cocoons; lined with fine grasses, hair, plant down and feathers. **Breeding season.** Begins late May to early June. **Eggs.** Usually 4, sometimes 3–6. Subelliptical, short subelliptical or elliptical. Smooth and non-glossy. Creamy-white. Unmarked. 16 × 13 mm. **Incubation.** By female alone, beginning with third egg. 14–16 days. **Nestling.** Altricial and downy. Hatched naked, down appearing in 2–3 days. Down light gray. **Nestling period.** Young tended by both parents. Pin feathers appear at 8 days. Young leave at 13–16 days.

HAMMOND'S FLYCATCHER *Empidonax hammondii* **Pl. 53**

Breeds in mountain conifer or mixed woodland. Nest in a tree, often a conifer, from 6–60 ft. up, in a fork of a branch.

Nest. A loose cup of bark strips and fibers, rootlets, grass and weed stems, feathers, fibers, plant down, spider cocoons, lichen filaments; lined with grasses or feathers. **Breeding season.** Begins in early June. **Eggs.** Usually 3–4. Subelliptical. Smooth and slightly glossy. White to pale or deep creamy-white or yellow. Unmarked or with minute brown specks and larger purple spots. 17 × 13 mm. **Incubation.** By female alone, 15 days. **Nestling.** No information. **Nestling period.** Young tended by both parents. Brooded by female for first few days. Young leave nest at 17–18 days, fed by adults for *c.* 20 days more.

DUSKY FLYCATCHER *Empidonax oberholseri* **Pl. 53**
Breeds in mountain scrub, and scrub with scattered trees. Nest in a deciduous shrub or small pine, 4–7 ft. up, in a fork, along branch or resting in twigs.
Nest. A neat compact cup. Of bark fibers, fine grasses and dead weed stems, plant fibers, etc.; lined with similar but finer material with plant down and feathers. Bound with spiders' webs. The outside and base are more loosely built with odd ends hanging down. **Breeding season.** Begins late May to mid-June. **Eggs.** Usually 3–4, sometimes 2. Short subelliptical to subelliptical. Smooth and non-glossy. White or creamy-white. Unmarked. 17 × 13 mm. **Incubation.** By both sexes. 12–15 days. **Nestling.** No information. **Nestling period.** Young tended by both parents. Leave nest at 18 days.

GRAY FLYCATCHER *Empidonax wrightii* **Pl. 53**
Breeds in sagebrush, or semi-arid areas of juniper and scrub. Nest usually in a shrub in a fork or low on a main stem.
Nest. A bulky cup with untidy exterior; of bark strips, dead weed stems, plant down, grasses and hair. Lined with wool and small feathers. **Breeding season.** Begins late May to early June. Double-brooded. **Eggs.** Usually 3–4. Subelliptical to short subelliptical. Creamy-white. Unmarked. 18 × 13 mm. **Incubation.** By female alone. 14 days. **Nestling.** Altricial and downy. Down sparse: on head, wings and back. **Nestling period.** Young tended by both parents. Leave nest at 16 days, fed by adults for 14 days more.

WESTERN FLYCATCHER *Empidonax difficilis* **Pl. 53**
Breeds in deciduous woodland and mixed woodland on mountain slopes. Nest in a sapling or shrub, behind loose bark, in a cavity in a tree-trunk, a woodpecker hole, a crevice or cavity in a rock face, or on a ledge, on a stump or among tree roots by a stream, in or under low banks of streams, or on ledges or in crevices of buildings.
Nest. A cup of green moss, weed stems, dry grasses, plant fibers, bark strips, fine rootlets and dead leaves; lined with finer materials and hair. Sometimes only of moss with a lining. **Breeding season.** Begins mid-April in south to mid-June in north of range. Sometimes double-brooded. **Eggs.** Usually 4, sometimes 3, rarely 5. Subelliptical to short subelliptical, or elliptical. Smooth and non-glossy. White to creamy-white; speckled, spotted, and with small blotches usually concentrated at the larger end; of reddish-brown, cinnamon, buffish-pink or pale purple. 17 × 13 mm. **Incubation.** By female alone. 14–15 days. **Nestling.** No information. **Nestling period.** Young tended by both parents. Brooded by female. Young leave nest at 14–18 days, fed by parents for 10–11 days more.

BUFF-BREASTED FLYCATCHER *Empidonax fulvifrons*
Breeds on steep canyon slopes with pine-oak woodlands and shrub undergrowth. Nest in a tree, saddled on a near-horizontal branch or on a fork often high up and well out from the trunk, at from 4–45 ft. up.
Nest. A neat, compact and deep cup, bound together and to the branch with

spiders' webs. Of grasses, fine rootlets, plant fibers, leaf fragments, plant down and weed heads; lined with fine grasses, plant down, hair and some feathers. Decorated externally with lichen flakes or small grey leaves. **Breeding season.** Begins late May. **Eggs.** Usually 3–4, sometimes 2. Subelliptical. Smooth and non-glossy. Creamy-white. Unmarked. 15 × 12 mm. **Incubation.** No information. **Nestling.** No information. **Nestling period.** No information.

COUE'S FLYCATCHER *Contopus pertinax* **Pl. 54**

Breeds in pine-oak woodland on steep mountain slopes. Nest like that of a wood pewee, saddling a horizontal branch or in a horizontal fork, 10–40 ft. up. **Nest.** A deep cup, bound together and to the branch with spiders' webs. Of fine grass and weed stems, weed fibers, dead leaves and flower heads, and catkins, covered on the outside with lichen flakes; lined with fine grasses and grass heads. **Breeding season.** Begins mid-May. **Eggs.** Usually 3–4. Subelliptical. Smooth and non-glossy. White to creamy-white; sparsely marked, mostly at the larger end, with specks and spots of brown, blackish-brown, reddish-brown and paler gray. 21 × 16 mm. **Incubation.** No information. **Nestling.** No information. **Nestling period.** No information.

EASTERN WOOD PEWEE *Contopus virens* **Pl. 54**

Breeds in deciduous and mixed woodland, parkland, orchard, and in scattered plantings and shade trees. Nest usually saddling a small horizontal or sloping branch or in a level fork. Usually 8–20 ft. up, occasionally up to 45 ft., on a fairly open site.

Nest. A neat shallow cup, bound together and to the branch with spiders' webs and fine fibers. Of plant fibers, weed and grass stems, bark shreds, threads and wool; lined with plant down, finer grasses, wool and hair. The outside of the nest is decorated and camouflaged with lichen fibers. **Breeding season.** Begins mid- to late May. **Eggs.** Usually 3, sometimes 2, rarely 4. Creamy-white to very pale yellow; speckled, spotted or blotched in chestnut-red, reddish-brown and paler lilac and purple. Markings are mainly or entirely confined to a zone around the larger end, and paler markings often as numerous as dark ones. 18 × 14 mm. **Incubation.** 12–13 days. **Nestling.** Altricial and downy. Down whitish; on head and back. **Nestling period.** Young tended by both parents. Brooded by female for most of first four days. Feathered by *c.* 7 days. Leave nest at 15–18 days.

WESTERN WOOD PEWEE *Contopus sordidulus*

Breeds in coniferous and deciduous woodland, and in trees along watercourses Nest in a tree, like that of Eastern Wood Pewee, usually saddling a larger branch or in a near-horizontal fork, 15–30 ft. up, or rarely up to 75 ft.

Nest. A shallow but well-made cup, bound together and to the branch with spiders' webs and fine fibers. Of plant down, fine dry grasses, weed stems, bud scales and plant fibers; lined with fine grasses, hair and fibers and sometimes feathers. The outside is decorated with lichens or caterpillar cocoon. **Breeding season.** Begins early May in south to early June in north of range. **Eggs.** Usually 3, sometimes 2, rarely 4. Indistinguishable from those of Eastern Wood Pewee. 18 × 14 mm. **Incubation.** By female alone. *c.* 12 days? **Nestling.** No information. **Nestling period.** Young tended by both parents.

OLIVE-SIDED FLYCATCHER *Nuttallornis borealis* **Pl. 54**

Breeds in open conifer or mixed woodland in the north. Nest in a tree, frequently a conifer, sometimes deciduous. Usually on a horizontal branch, among twigs and foliage, at from 5–70 ft. up.

Nest. A cup with loose outer structure. Sometimes mainly of *Usnea* lichen or dead twigs, with dead grass stems, dead pine-needles and rootlets; lined with similar but finer material and hair. At times *Usnea* is lacking and twigs and moss form the main body. **Breeding season.** Begins late May to mid-June in north of range. **Eggs.** Usually 3, rarely 4. Short subelliptical. Smooth and non-glossy. Cream-colored or pinkish; spotted, and blotched with olive-brown, purplish-brown, and paler purple. Markings mostly confined to a broad wreath around larger end. 22 × 16 mm. **Incubation.** 16–17 days. **Nestling.** No information. **Nestling period.** Young leave at 15–19 days.

VERMILION FLYCATCHER *Pyrocephalus rubinus* **Pl. 54**

Breeds in trees along watercourses in arid areas. Nest in a tree, usually in a horizontal fork, 6–20 ft. up, sometimes up to 60 ft.

Nest. A flattish, well-made cup, sunk into a fork so that only the rim is obvious. Of short dead twigs, thinner twigs, weed stems, fine grasses, rootlets, dry leaves, bark strips, lichen, spiders' cocoons. Bound together and to the fork with spiders' webs, and decorated outside with lichen; lined with plant down, hair, fur and feathers. Built by female. **Breeding season.** Begins early to mid-March. **Eggs.** Usually 3, sometimes 2–4. Short subelliptical to short oval. Cream-colored to ivory-yellow or pale buff; spotted and blotched in light and dark olive-brown, black and pale gray. Usually a heavy zone of markings overlapping around the larger end, and a few specks or spots elsewhere. Pale markings often a prominent part of pattern. 17 × 13 mm. **Incubation.** Eggs laid at daily intervals. Incubation by female alone. 14–15 days. **Nestling.** Altricial and downy. Skin blackish with tufts of creamy-white down. Gape flanges yellow. **Nestling period.** Young tended by both parents. 14–16 days.

BEARDLESS FLYCATCHER *Camptostoma imberbe* **Pl. 54**

Breeds in trees, usually by water. Nest in a mistletoe clump, 25–50 ft. up (elsewhere have occurred lower in palmettos). Nest globular and among the mistletoe twigs.

Nest. A domed structure with an entrance on one side towards the top. Thick-walled, of grasses and fine weed stems, bark and fibers; the cup padded with plant down, fur and feathers. **Breeding season.** Begins mid-May. **Eggs.** Usually 1–3. Subelliptical. Smooth and non-glossy. White, very finely speckled, mainly at the larger end, with tiny specks and spots of brown, reddish-brown or gray. 16 × 12 mm. **Incubation.** No information. **Nestling.** No information. **Nestling period.** No information.

LARKS *Alaudidae*

Small birds, nesting on the ground, usually in open sites. The nest is often tucked into a natural, slightly-sheltered hollow. Small stones and similar objects often gathered around part of the nest, building up or paving one side of it. Eggs usually heavily speckled in buffish or olive-brown tints. Young have long down on the back which helps to camouflage them and sometimes scanty down on underside and usually show three small dark spots in the mouth. The young may leave the nest before they can fly properly, and crouch motionless to escape predators.

SKYLARK *Alauda arvensis* **Pl. 54**

Breeds on open, treeless areas, meadows, grasslands, stony or sandy tracts, dunes, marshes, or moorland, at varying altitudes. Nest in a slight depression in the ground; sometimes sheltered by a tuft of grass. Often exposed although grasses or crops may grow during the nesting period.

Nest. A shallow cup of grasses, with a lining of finer grasses and at times hair. Built by hen only? Occasionally small pebbles are placed around nests in more open sites. **Breeding season.** Begins in late April. Double- or treble-brooded. **Eggs.** Usually 3–4, sometimes 5, rarely 7. Subelliptical. Smooth and moderately glossy. Dull grayish-white or tinted buff or greenish, heavily spotted overall with medium brown or olive, tending to obscure ground color. 24 × 17 mm. **Incubation.** By female only. 11 days. **Nestling.** Altricial and downy. Down more scanty underneath but long and thick over upperside. Buffish-yellow. Mouth dull yellow. Three spots, one at tip of tongue, two at base. Bill flanges white. **Nestling period.** Young fed by both parents, leaving the nest at 9–10 days, but unable to fly. Hide by crouching motionless, fly well at *c.* 20 days.

HORNED LARK *Eremophila alpestris* **Pls. 16, 54**

Breeds in large areas of tundra or barren higher ground; usually bare, sandy and stony, but also in sparse grasses. Further south occurs in prairies, drier grasslands and larger treeless areas of cultivation. Nest on the ground in a small hollow, usually in the shelter of a plant-tuft or stone.

Nest. A cup of dry grass and plant stems, loosely put together, with a finer inner lining of plant down and hair. In a small hollow made by female. Small pieces of peat, dung or pebbles may be assembled around the nest or on one side of it. **Breeding season.** Late February in south to mid-June in north of range. Will replace lost clutch, and sometimes double-brooded. **Eggs.** Usually 4, sometimes 2–7. Subelliptical. Smooth and glossy. Pale greenish-white, heavily speckled with fine buffish-brown; often with a blackish hair-line, at times with sparse bolder spots or dark zones. 23 × 16 mm. **Incubation.** Eggs laid at daily intervals. Incubation by female alone. 10–14 days. **Nestling.** Altricial and downy. Skin brown. Down long and pale creamy-buff, covering much of upper surface of head and body. Mouth bright orange-yellow and gape flanges yellow; three dark spots on tongue. **Nestling period.** Young are tended and fed by both parents. Eyes open at 3–4 days. Leave nest at 9–12 days. Can fly 3–5 days later.

SWALLOWS AND MARTINS *Hirundinidae*

Small birds, taking their food on the wing. The nest is usually a mud structure, varying in shape with the species, fixed to rocks or walls, and sheltered by an overhang; or a more typical nest in a tree cavity or earth tunnel. The eggs are often elongated, white or finely spotted. Young are downy on head, back and sometimes thighs; with yellow, unspotted mouths.

VIOLET-GREEN SWALLOW *Tachycineta thalassina* **Pl. 54**

Breeds in mountains and around human settlement. Nest in a crevice or hole in cliff surface or rocky outcrop, or in old woodpecker hole, natural cavity in tree, old nest of Cliff Swallow or Bank Swallow, crevice or cavity in building, or in nest-box.

Nest. An accumulation of dry grasses with a cup lined with feathers and sometimes hair or fine fibers. Built by both sexes, but mainly by female. **Breeding season.** Begins early May in south to late May in north of range. Single-brooded. **Eggs.** Usually 4–5, sometimes 6. Subelliptical to oval. Smooth and non-glossy to slightly glossy. White and unmarked. 18 × 13 mm. **Incubation.** 13–15 days, beginning before completion of clutch. **Nestling.** Altricial and downy. Skin pale pink. Down cream-colored; on head, shoulders and back. Gape flanges whitish. **Nestling period.** Young tended by both parents and leave nest at 23–25 days. Eyes open at 10–11 days. Feathers break sheaths at 10–13 days. After leaving may be fed on the wing at times.

TREE SWALLOW *Iridoprocne bicolor* **Pl. 54**

Breeds over a wide range. Nest in a natural cavity or woodpecker hole in tree, often near water, also in cavity or crevice in building or wooden structure, and nest-box. Occasionally an additional adult assists the pair.

Nest. A collection of dry grasses, pine-needles, etc., with a cup lined with feathers. Built by female. **Breeding season.** Begins late April in south to mid-May in north of range. **Eggs.** Usually 4–6; larger clutches may be from two females. Subelliptical to oval. Smooth and non-glossy or slightly glossy. White and unmarked. 19 × 13 mm. **Incubation.** 13–16 days, usually beginning at completion of clutch. **Nestling.** Altricial and downy. Skin pale pink. Down whitish. Mouth pale yellow. Gape flanges creamy-white. **Nestling period.** Young leave nest at 16–24 days.

BANK SWALLOW *Riparia riparia* **Pl. 54**

Breeds in open country, usually near water. A colonial nester. Nest in a burrow in a vertical bank, natural or artificial, quarry or cliff; often high up but in extreme north of range where sites are scarce may nest almost at ground level. Existing artificial holes may be used.

Nest. A tunnel bored by both adults. The terminal chamber lined with plant stems, feathers and similar material. **Breeding season.** Begins late April in south to mid-June in north of range. Usually double-brooded. **Eggs.** Usually 4–5, sometimes 3–7. Subelliptical. Smooth and slightly to moderately glossy. White. 18 × 13 mm. **Incubation.** By both adults. 12–16 days. **Nestling.** Altricial and downy. Down, on head and back, short; pale gray. Skin pink. Mouth and gape flanges pale lemon-yellow. **Nestling period.** Young tended by both adults. Fed in nest cavity at first but later come to mouth of burrow. Leave nest at *c.* 19 days. Can already fly at 17–18 days.

ROUGH-WINGED SWALLOW *Stelgidopteryx ruficollis* **Pl. 54**

Breeds over a wide range, especially near water; nesting usually in solitary or scattered pairs. Nest a burrow dug in a steep-faced earth, sand or gravel bank. Banks may be from 2–50 ft. high. Burrows of variable length and old kingfisher burrows also used. Also crevices and holes in buildings and man-made structures, drainpipes, and, exceptionally, a hole in a tree.

Nest. Usually in burrow, 1–6 ft. long. Nest an accumulation of grasses, weeds and loose plant material; the cup lined with fine grasses and rootlets. Built by female. **Breeding season.** Begins mid-April in south to mid-June in north of range. Single-brooded. **Eggs.** Usually 6–7, sometimes 4–8. Subelliptical to oval. Smooth and glossy. White and unmarked. 18 × 13 mm. **Incubation.** By female only. 15–16 days. **Nestling.** Altricial and downy. Down very pale gray. Mouth yellow. Gape flanges yellow. Bill, legs and feet pink at first. **Nestling period.** Young tended by both parents. Female broods by day for first 5 days, by night for first 9. Eyes open at 7–8 days. Feathered at *c.* 12–13 days. Leave at 18–21 days.

BARN SWALLOW *Hirundo rustica* **Pl. 54**

Breeds in a variety of habitats, but more particularly near water and in open country. The nest is usually stuck against a vertical surface, but requires some support although often slight. The natural site probably a cave roof, but more often occurs on upper ledges such as rafters or girders in buildings of all kinds and under bridges or culverts. Exceptionally in sheltered sites on outside of building or on a tree.

Nest. An open shallow cup of mud pellets mixed with vegetable fibers and plant fragments; sparsely lined with feathers. Built by both adults. **Breeding season.** Begins early April in south to early June in north of range. Season prolonged. Double-brooded. **Eggs.** Usually 4–5, at times 3–8. Long subelliptical to long oval. Smooth and glossy. White, sparingly marked with variable spotting of

Barn Swallow: *c.* 4-5in. across.

reddish-brown, lilac or pale gray. 20 × 14 mm. **Incubation.** Only, or mainly, by female. 14–16 days. **Nestling.** Altricial and downy. Down on head and back, long and sparse; gray. Mouth lemon-yellow. Gape flanges whitish. **Nestling period.** Young tended by both adults. Food brought by parents in the throat. Nest left after 17–24 days. Young return to roost on nest at first. May be fed by adults in mid-air.

CLIFF SWALLOW *Petrochelidon pyrrhonota* Pl. 54

Breeds in places where rock outcrops or cliff faces or buildings provide sites. Nest a rounded mud structure fixed to a vertical surface and protected by an overhang. Most frequently on rock faces or under eaves of buildings; but nests have been recorded on very large tree-trunks, just below projecting limbs. Nests usually in crowded colonies, often large.

Nest. A rounded structure of mud pellets with some plant fiber or hair added; usually with a projecting and slightly downward-directed neck, 5–6 in. long. Cavity thinly lined with grasses and dry stems with an inner cup of feathers and finer fibres. **Breeding season.** Begins mid-April in south to late May in north of range. Double-brooded. **Eggs.** Usually 4–5, occasionally 3–6. Long subelliptical to long oval, or subelliptical. White, creamy-white or tinted pink; speckled, spotted or blotched in shades of light to dark brown, reddish-brown,

Cliff Swallow colony: nest *c.* 6-7in. across.

purplish-brown, and paler brownish-gray or gray. Markings often concentrated at or around the larger end and sparser elsewhere. 20 × 14 mm. **Incubation.** 16 days. Mainly or only by female. **Nestling.** Altricial and downy. Skin light pink. Down light gray. Mouth flesh-colored. Gape flanges pale flesh. **Nestling period.** Young tended by both parents. They fly first at 23 days but may return to the nest for 2–3 days.

CAVE SWALLOW *Petrochelidon fulva* Pl. 54

Breeds in the partially dark zones of large caves and caverns. Nest a half-cup attached to upper wall or irregularities of roof, or on a ledge. Usually more scattered than those of Cliff Swallows, but clustered where the site permits. **Nest.** A half-cup of mud pellets with some plant fiber or rock chips added; stuck to a steep surface under a partial overhang, and somewhat similar to that of a Barn Swallow in appearance. Lined with feathers, plant fragments and similar debris. Nests may be added to and re-used in subsequent years. **Breeding**

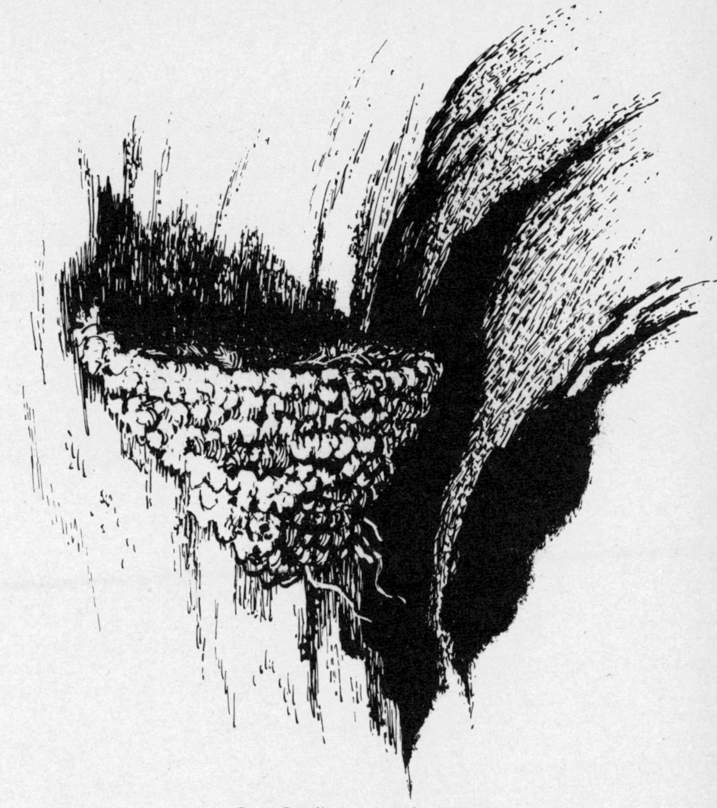

Cave Swallow: *c.* 4-5in. across.

season. Begins in April. Usually double-brooded. **Eggs.** Usually 4, and 3 in second brood. Oval. Smooth and moderately glossy. White, finely speckled and spotted in reddish-brown or purplish-brown. 20 × 14 mm. **Incubation.** No information. **Nestling.** No information. **Nestling period.** No information.

PURPLE MARTIN *Progne subis* **Pl. 54**
Breeds widely where human settlement occurs. Natural nest-site appears to be a cavity or crevice in rocks or tree, including old woodpecker holes. Now extensively uses artificial sites, nest-boxes or gourds put up by man. Usually nests in colonies varying in size according to site.
Nest. An accumulation of loose plant material, grass, leaves, stems, twigs, straws, feathers, rags and bark shreds. Built by both sexes. **Breeding season.** Begins late March in south to late May or early June in north of range. Single-brooded, possibly double-brooded at times. **Eggs.** Usually 4–5, sometimes 3–8. Oval to long oval. Smooth and non-glossy. White and unmarked. 24 × 17 mm. **Incubation.** Only by female. 15–18 days. **Nestling.** No information. **Nestling period.** Young tended by both parents. Leave nest at 24–28 days. Roost in nest after leaving.

CROWS, MAGPIES AND JAYS *Corvidae*

Medium to large perching birds, nesting in trees or bushes, or on rock ledges. In most species nests are made mainly of twigs and muddy earth is added to these, helping to bind the structure. There is a soft inner lining. The eggs are mostly blue or green with olive-green and blackish markings. In the true crows there are frequently one or two pale, atypical eggs in a clutch. Young are downy or naked, the mouth usually red or pink, and gape flanges pink or yellowish. Food is brought to the young pouched in the throat, and regurgitated.

GRAY JAY *Perisoreus canadensis* **Pl. 56**
Breeds mainly in conifer forests, sometimes in mixed woodland. Nest usually in a conifer, often hidden in the crown or out towards the end of a branch, sometimes exposed. Usually 5–12 ft. up, sometimes up to 30 ft.
Nest. Usually a thick-walled cup, of twigs, bark-strips, grass stems, moss, lichens and other soft materials, with spiders cocoons and nest on the outside; the inner lining thickly padded with fine dry grasses, moss, plant down, catkins, hair, feathers and fur. Built by both sexes. **Breeding season.** Begins late February to early March. **Eggs.** Usually 3–4, sometimes 2–5. Subelliptical to short subelliptical. Smooth and fairly glossy. Very pale greenish or gray-green; speckled, spotted and blotched fairly thickly with olive and paler gray. Markings tend to be concentrated at the larger end. 29 × 21 mm. **Incubation.** By female alone, beginning with first egg. 16–18 days. **Nestling.** No information. **Nestling period.** Young tended by both parents. For first few days female broods and male brings all food. Young leave at *c.* 15 days?

BLUE JAY *Cyanocitta cristata* **Pl. 56**
Breeds in woodland, particularly mixed woodland, cultivated areas with trees and parkland. Nest in tree, shrub or bush, at varying heights, usually 10–40 ft. up; rarely in or on buildings.

Nest. A cup of twigs, strips of bark, rootlets, grass and weed stems, paper, rags and feathers. Mud may be built into the structure. Thinner lining of fine rootlets or similar material. Built by both sexes. **Breeding season.** Begins mid-March in south to early May in north of range. Single-brooded in north of range, but lost clutches replaced. Occasionally double or treble-brooded in south. **Eggs.** Usually 4–5, sometimes 2–6. Subelliptical to short subelliptical. Smooth and fairly glossy. Very variable. Pale olive, buff, pinkish-buff, green, bluish-green, or rarely greenish-white; spotted, speckled or with small blotches of various shades of brown, olive and sometimes dark brown, with paler gray and purple. Markings tend to be small and generally distributed. 28 × 20 mm. **Incubation.** By female alone, fed by male. 16–18 days. **Nestling.** Altricial and naked. Mouth red. No distinct gape flanges. **Nestling period.** Young tended by both parents. Brooded by female only. Eyes open at *c.* 5 days, feathers break sheaths at 8–9 days. Young leave nest at 17–21 days, probably independent after *c.* 3 weeks more, but may be partly fed for further period.

STELLER'S JAY *Cyanocitta stelleri* **Pl. 56**

Breeds in woodland, coniferous or mixed, usually near an open space, or in open woodland, parkland, or cultivated areas with trees. Nest in a tree, usually a conifer, sometimes in shrub or bush, occasionally in a tree hollow or cavity, or in a building. Nest usually 8–16 ft. up, exceptionally from 2–100 ft. up.

Nest. A cup of twigs, usually with dead leaves in base, lined with mud, and with an inner lining of fine rootlets, and sometimes pine-needles, hair or grasses. Built by both sexes. **Breeding season.** Begins early to mid-April in south to early May in north of range. **Eggs.** Usually 4, sometimes 2–6. Subelliptical to short sub-elliptical. Smooth and fairly glossy. Similar to the bluish and greenish types of Blue Jay eggs. 31 × 22 mm. **Incubation.** By female only, fed by male. (Or by both sexes in north?) *c.* 16 days. **Nestling.** Altricial and naked. **Nestling period.** Young tended by both parents. Dependent on them for *c.* 1 month after leaving nest.

SCRUB JAY *Aphelocoma coerulescens* **Pl. 55**

Breeds in scrub woodland and low scrub, in arid and other areas; and open and broken woodland, shrubby forest edge, mangrove swamp, orchards and cultivated areas with many low trees. Nest in a tree, shrub, bush or vine tangle, usually fairly low, *c.* 3–10 ft. up.

Nest. A cup of twigs mixed with moss, weed stems and grasses; lined with fine roots, plant and bark fibers and occasionally hair. Built by both sexes. **Breeding season.** Begins mid-March. Single-brooded but lost clutches replaced. **Eggs.** Usually 2–3, sometimes up to 6. Clutches smaller in arid areas. Subelliptical to short subelliptical or oval. Smooth and fairly glossy. Blue, greenish-blue to pale olive-green, or blue with a pinkish wash; speckled, spotted and sometimes with blotches of light or dark drab or olive-brown, purplish-brown or reddish-brown, and paler gray and lilac. Rarely eggs are whitish, pale buff or light green with reddish markings. 28 × 20 mm. **Incubation.** By female alone, beginning before completion of clutch, fed by male. 15–17 days. **Nestling.** Altricial and naked. **Nestling period.** Young tended by both parents. Immature birds are often present as helpers, assisting in care of the young.

MEXICAN JAY *Aphelocoma ultramarina* **Pl. 55**

Breeds usually in oak or pine-oak woodlands of montane areas. Nest in a tree, usually in rock areas with steep slopes, or where the woodland canopy is broken by tall pines. Nest in a tree, usually a live oak, 6–50 ft. up, usually 15–25 ft. up. Breeds in small loose colonies or solitary pairs. Pairs in a breeding colony may assist members of other pairs in some breeding activities.

Nest. A cup of coarse twigs and sticks broken off trees, lined with smaller twigs, grass and weed stems and with an inner lining of vine tendrils, fine rootlets and hair. Built by both sexes. **Breeding season.** Begins late March to mid-April. **Eggs.** Usually 4, sometimes 3–7. Subelliptical to long subelliptical. Smooth and fairly glossy. Pale greenish-blue to yellowish-green, speckled, spotted and blotched with light to dark brown and paler gray; but usually unmarked in the Arizona subspecies. 30 × 22 mm. **Incubation** By female alone, fed by male or by other members of breeding flock. 18 days. **Nestling.** Altricial and naked. Skin purplish-pink or purplish-flesh color. Gape flanges pale yellow. Mouth pink. **Nestling period.** Young tended by both parents, and all other members of flock may help to feed young. Young brooded during most of first 2 weeks, feather between 10–20 days, leave nest at 24–26 days. Older young are fed by any adults.

GREEN JAY *Cyanocorax yncas* **Pl. 55**

Breeds in forest and thick scrub. Nest usually well-hidden in thicker shrubs and trees, often low, at 5–25 ft. up.

Nest. A cup, often of slight construction. Of twigs, sometimes thorny, with a shallowish inner cup of vine tendrils, fine rootlets, and sometimes dry grasses, moss or dead leaves. **Breeding season.** Begins early April. **Eggs.** Usually 4, occasionally 3–5. Subelliptical to short subelliptical. Smooth and slightly glossy. Creamy-white, or very pale greenish, or pale buff or olive; finely and profusely speckled and freckled, or more sparsely marked with small spots or blotches of olive, brown or buffish-brown, and pale gray or purple. 27 × 20 mm. **Incubation.** By female alone, fed by male. 15–17 days. **Nestling.** Altricial. Dark-skinned and naked at hatching. **Nestling period.** Young tended by both parents, at first brooded by female while male brings food. Begin feathering at *c.* 12 days. Leave nest at 19 days, but not able to fly properly. Independent in *c.* 2 weeks more.

BLACK-BILLED MAGPIE *Pica pica* **Pl. 55**

Breeds in canyons and valleys near water, wherever tall shrubby growth and scattered trees occur with open spaces. Nest usually in the top of a tall shrub, often thorny, or in trees where they are usually fairly low, up to 25 ft. Nest usually firmly set in a twig fork or among thick twigs. A number of pairs usually nest in the same locality.

Nest. A large, bulky cup of thick, often thorny twigs, with a heavy lining of mud or dung; and an inner lining of rootlets, thin weed or grass stems, and hair. The cup is covered with an openwork, sketchy-looking dome of twigs, with one or more openings. Nest built by both sexes, the male bringing material. **Breeding season.** Begins late March in south to late May in north of range. **Eggs.** Usually 5–9, rarely up to 12. Subelliptical, short subelliptical or oval. Pale greenish-blue, grayish-blue, blue, buff or olive; heavily spotted, and speckled or, more exceptionally, blotched, with olive-brown and gray. Markings sometimes heavier at one end. 33 × 23 mm. **Incubation.** By female only beginning with first egg. 17–18 days. **Nestling.** Altricial and naked. Skin pink at first, then yellowish and grayish. Mouth deep pink. Gape flanges pale pink. **Nestling period.** Young tended by both adults. 22–28 days in nest.

YELLOW-BILLED MAGPIE *Pica nuttalli* **Pl. 55**

Breeds in more open hilly country with scattered trees, cultivated areas with trees, or parkland. Nest usually in a tall or medium-sized tree, usually high up and well out on a branch. A number of pairs usually nest close together.

Nest. Similar to that of Black-billed Magpie. **Breeding season.** Begins early March. **Eggs.** Like those of Black-billed Magpie. 31 × 22 mm. **Incubation.** By female only, in part fed by male. **Nestling.** No information. **Nestling period.** Young tended by both parents. After leaving nest young remain near nest for further 5 days, and are fed to some extent for up to 7 weeks more.

WHITE-NECKED RAVEN *Corvus cryptoleucus* **Pl. 55**

Breeds in deserts, open plains and dry foothills, and around cultivation. Nest in a tree, shrub, or on old building. Low scrub trees often used.

Nest. A large cup of sticks and twigs, with a softer inner lining of hair, fur, wool and rags. **Breeding season.** Usually begins mid-May, exceptionally earlier. Single-brooded. **Eggs.** Usually 5–7, sometimes 3–8. Subelliptical to long oval. Smooth and slightly glossy. Pale to very pale blue, greenish-blue or grayish-blue; marked with black, dark olive-brown and shades of gray, the markings being usually fine and longitudinally elongated lines and scrawls forming a fine, rather poorly-defined lacy pattern, with paler markings predominating. 44 × 30 mm. **Incubation.** *c.* 21 days. **Nestling.** Altricial and downy? **Nestling period.** No information.

NORTHERN RAVEN *Corvus corax* **Pl. 55**

Breeds mostly in hilly and mountainous regions and on coasts, but also in forests. Nest on a sheltered rock ledge, or on a large fork of a tree.

Nest. A large mass of twigs, and larger sticks and coarser vegetable matter, bound with earth and moss, well-lined with grass tufts, leaves and moss; and inner lining of wool and hair. Built by both sexes. **Breeding season.** Begins February and early March in south to mid-April in north of range. Single-brooded. **Eggs.** Usually 4–6, rarely 3–7. Subelliptical. Smooth and glossy. Very variable in markings. Light blue, greenish-blue, or pale green; with specks, spots, irregular blotches, streaks or scribblings of light olive, olive-brown, or dark or blackish-brown, and light gray. Markings vary from sparse to very heavy, and sometimes show irregular patches of olive or greenish washes over more distinct markings. Often variations within a clutch, with one sparsely-marked blue egg. 50 × 33 mm. **Incubation.** Eggs laid at 1–2-day intervals. Incubation by female alone, fed by male, and beginning before clutch is complete. 20–21 days. **Nestling.** Altricial and downy. Down, on head, back and thighs, short and thick, dull brown. Mouth purplish-pink. Gape flanges yellowish-flesh. **Nestling period.** Young tended by both parents. They leave nest at 5–6 weeks.

AMERICAN CROW *Corvus brachyrhynchos* **Pls. 16, 55**

Occurs in a wide range of country where some trees or scrub are present; from open woodland and woodland edge to parkland and cultivation. Nest in a tree, shrub or bush; exceptionally on telegraph poles, or on the ground. Usually nests in single pairs, but sometimes several near each other.

Nest. A large cup of sticks and coarse stems, lined with bark strips and fibres and sometimes mud or earth, and with an inner lining of rootlets, grasses, fur, hair, moss, etc. **Breeding season.** Begins late January in south to early May in north of range. **Eggs.** Usually 4–5, sometimes 3–6. Subelliptical to oval and short to long. Smooth and slightly glossy. Greenish-blue to pale blue; very variably spotted, speckled and with small blotches of olive, olive-brown or blackish-olive, and a few paler gray or purplish markings. Markings vary from sparse to overall, usually small, and with markings often concentrated at the larger end. 41 × 29 mm. **Incubation.** *c.* 18 days. **Nestling.** Altricial and downy. Skin pink or flesh-colored, becoming brownish-gray. Down sparse and grayish-brown, on head and upperparts. **Nestling period.** Young tended by both parents. Feather between 20–30 days, leave nest at *c.* 35 days.

NORTH-WESTERN CROW *Corvus caurinus* **Pl. 55**

Breeds in coastal areas and on offshore islands. Nest in a tree, shrub or bush. Occasionally on ledge or recess of rocky outcrop or bank, or on the ground under an overhanging boulder.

Nest. A large cup of twigs and sticks, mixed with mud, and lined with bark fibers and strips, and grasses: with an inner lining of dead grasses, bark and plant fibers, hair, etc. **Breeding season.** Begins in May. **Eggs.** Usually 4–5. Very similar to those of Fish Crow and other crows. 40 × 28 mm. **Incubation.** No information. **Nestling.** No information. **Nestling period.** No information.

FISH CROW *Corvus ossifragus* **Pl. 55**

Breeds by marshes, rivers and lakes, coastal or inland. Nest in a tree, usually high, but sometimes as low as 6 ft. Usually in small colony of well-spaced pairs.

Nest. A large cup of sticks and twigs, lined with bark strips and fibers and sometimes with mud or dung; and with an inner lining of bark fibers, hair, grasses, pine-needles and similar material. **Breeding season.** Begins early April in south to early May in north of range. Single-brooded but lost clutches replaced. **Eggs.** Usually 4–5. Subelliptical to oval. Smooth and slightly glossy. Bluish-green, or pale green, rarely whitish or buffish-green; speckled, spotted, blotched or streaked with olive, olive-brown, blackish-olive or paler gray. Larger markings tend to be bolder and sparser than on eggs of American Crow, and often concentrated towards the larger end. 37 × 27 mm. **Incubation.** 16–18 days. **Nestling.** No information. **Nestling period.** No information.

PINYON JAY *Gymnorhinus cyanocephalus* **Pl. 55**

Breeds in hilly and mountain regions, where pinyon pines occur. Nest in a tree or shrub, usually pine, live oak or juniper. Nest usually in a fairly open site 3–80, but usually 5–30, ft. up. Nest in a loose scattered colony.

Nest. A large cup of twigs, weed stems and similar material, well-lined with rootlets, bark strips, vegetable fiber, grasses, hair and wool. **Breeding season.** Within a prolonged potential period, apparently dependent on pinyon seed supplies. Records from February to October. **Eggs.** Usually 3–4, sometimes 3–6. Elliptical to short elliptical. Smooth and slightly glossy. Pale bluish, greenish, or bluish-white; finely speckled and spotted with reddish-brown or, purplish-brown, and occasiona ,larger spots and blotches, usually concentrated about the larger end. 29 × 22 mm. **Incubation.** By female alone, fed by male.

15–17 days. **Nestlings.** Altricial, naked at first. Skin pink at first, later purplish-blue. **Nestling period.** Young tended by both parents. Leave nest at *c.* 3 weeks. Older nestlings sometimes fed by adults other than parents.

CLARK'S NUTCRACKER *Nucifraga columbiana* **Pl. 55**

Breeds in mountain conifer forest. Nest in a juniper or conifer, sheltered by foliage, often towards the end of a branch.

Nest. A large cup of twigs, sticks and sometimes bark strips, lined with bark fiber and wood pulp, and with an inner lining of dry grasses, and plant and bark fibers. There may be a layer of soil or mud in the base of the cup between the two linings. Built by both sexes, but mainly by female. **Breeding season.** Begins early March. **Eggs.** Usually 2–3, sometimes 4, rarely 5–6. Subelliptical to elliptical. Smooth and slightly glossy. Pale green, grayish-green or greenish-white; spotted and speckled with brown, olive and paler gray. Markings usually small and sparse. 32 × 23 mm. **Incubation.** By both sexes. 16–18 days. **Nestling.** Altricial. Naked at first, then with sparse white down. **Nestling period.** Young tended and brooded by both parents; leave nest at *c.* 22 days. Fed by adults for some time after leaving nest.

BUSHTITS *Aegithalidae*

BUSHTIT *Psaltriparus minimus* (Black-eared Bushtit included in this species) **Pl. 54**

Breeds in open woodland, scrub and areas with scattered trees and shrubs. Nest

Bushtit: *c.* 6-12in. across.

in a tree or shrub, 4–50 ft. up, suspended from a twig fork or two adjacent twigs. **Nest.** An elongated, pendant structure, with an entrance to one side of the top, the whole widening towards the base. 6–12 in. from top to bottom, and 3–4 in. wide at base. A ring of material between two twigs form the entrance and the structure is held together by spiders' webs. Material very variable, twigs, rootlets, lichens, moss, grass, blossoms of trees and shrubs, plant down, small dry leaves, spider cocoons, etc.; thickly lined with feathers, fur and down. **Breeding season.** Begins late February in California; early April elsewhere. **Eggs.** Usually 5–7, rarely up to 15, possibly from two females. Subelliptical. Smooth and non-glossy to slightly glossy. White, unmarked. 14 × 10 mm. **Incubation.** 12–13 days. **Nestling.** Altricial. Hatched virtually naked, then develops a scanty hair-like grayish-white down. **Nestling period.** Young tended by both parents. Eyes open at 8 days. Young leave at 14–15 days, independent *c.* 8 days later.

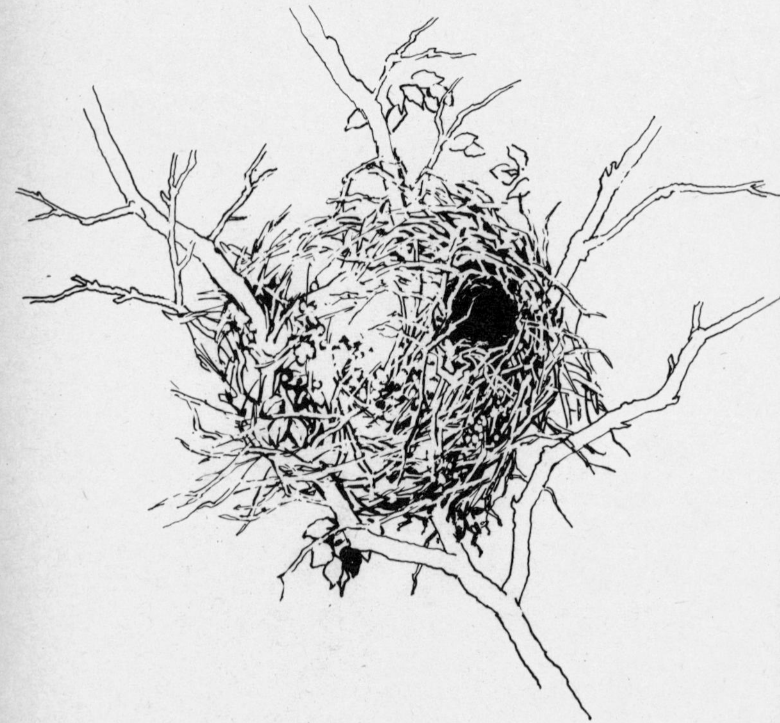

Verdin: *c*, 7-8in. across.

PENDULINE TITMICE *Remizidae*

VERDIN *Auriparus flaviceps* **Pl. 54**

Breeds in arid regions with sparse thorny scrub, bushy mesquite or dry chaparral. Nest in a shrub, low tree, or cactus; fixed into a twig fork, usually towards the end of a branch, 2–12 ft. up, but more often *c.* 5 ft. up. Nests are built and used for roosting also at most times of year.

Nest. A rounded prickly mass of small thorny twigs with many ends projecting; lined with spiders' webs, then fine grasses and dead leaves, and with a thick inner layer of feathers and plant down. Entrance at side. **Breeding season.** Begins late February. Possibly double-brooded. **Eggs.** Usually 4, sometimes 3–6. Subelliptical to short subelliptical. Smooth and moderately glossy. Very pale blue or greenish-blue; very finely speckled with reddish-brown, the markings often concentrated at or around the larger end. 15 × 11 mm. **Incubation.** By both sexes, or female alone. 14 days. **Nestling.** Altricial. Naked at hatching. **Nestling period.** Young fed by female at first, later by both parents. Leave at *c.* 3 weeks but roost in nest.

TITMICE *Paridae*

Small insectivorous birds, nesting in a variety of habitats but usually in association with trees. Nest in a hole in a tree, wall or bank, one or two species excavating their own in soft or rotten wood. Take readily to artificial bird-boxes. Nest a cup within the cavity, usually on a base of moss, leaves or earth, lined with hair and sometimes some feathers. Nest made by female, who may also excavate, or enlarge cavity. Eggs are white, variably patterned with small reddish markings. Incubation is by female, fed by male. Nestlings have grayish down, orange to yellow mouths, and pale yellow gape flanges. Broods are often large. Young fed by both adults on insects brought in the bill. After leaving nest the family party tend to remain together for some time after young become independent.

BLACK-CAPPED CHICKADEE *Parus atricapillus* **Pl. 54**

Breeds in northern forests, and in more open areas with scattered trees. Nest a cavity often excavated by the birds themselves in rotten wood. Often in a decayed birch or pine stump, but an existing cavity may also be enlarged, or an old woodpecker hole or bird-box used. At almost any height but often at only a few feet up.

Nest. A cavity made by both birds, 8–9 in. deep and 2–3 in. wide, with a moss base and cup of plant down, fibers, hair, wool, feathers and spiders' cocoon, in the bottom of it. **Breeding season.** Begins early April in south to mid-May in north of range. Single-brooded. **Eggs.** Usually 6–8, sometimes 5–13. Short subelliptical. Smooth and non-glossy. White to creamy-white; very finely speckled and spotted with reddish-brown or purplish-brown, sometimes with a heavier wealth of markings at the larger end. 15 × 12 mm. **Incubation.** Incomplete clutches are covered with nest lining. Incubation by female alone, beginning with completion of clutch. 12–14 days. **Nestling.** Altricial and downy. Down pale brownish-gray; sparse, on head, wings and back. Mouth pale yellow. Gape flanges white. **Nestling period.** Young tended by both parents. Leave nest at 16 days.

CAROLINA CHICKADEE *Parus carolinensis* **Pl. 54**

Breeds in woodland, mainly deciduous, and in scattered trees in cultivated areas, around buildings and elsewhere. Nest in a cavity in a tree or fence-post; and woodpecker holes and artificial cavities may also be used. Natural sites with decayed wood usually excavated by the birds themselves. At 1–22 ft. up, but usually 4–15 ft. up.

Nest. A cavity in decayed wood excavated by both sexes. About 5 in. deep and 2 in. wide at top, to 3 in. wide at base. Within a base of moss and a cup of plant down, feathers, hair and plant fibers. **Breeding season.** From mid-February in south to early April in north. **Eggs.** Usually 6, sometimes 5–8. Very like those of Black-capped Chickadee. 15 × 11 mm. **Incubation.** By female alone, beginning with last or next-to-last egg. 12–14 days. **Nestling.** Altricial and downy. Skin pale pinkish. Down dark gray. Mouth light yellow. Gape flanges white. **Nestling period.** Young tended by both parents. Leave nest at 17 days.

MEXICAN CHICKADEE *Parus sclateri* **Pl. 54**

Breeds in trees in mountain areas. Nest in a tree cavity excavated by the birds. **Nest.** A cavity in dead wood excavated by the birds, *c.* 8 in. deep. Contains a cup of wool, fur, hair and plant down. **Breeding season.** Begins early April. **Eggs.** Usually 6. Short subelliptical. Smooth and slightly glossy. White; profusely and finely speckled and spotted with reddish-brown and brown, and some paler purple. Often a concentration at larger end. 14 × 11 mm. **Incubation.** No information. **Nestling.** No information. **Nestling period.** No information.

MOUNTAIN CHICKADEE *Parus gambeli* **Pl. 54**

Breeds in mountain forest. Nest in a natural cavity in tree stump, tree-trunk or branch, woodpecker hole; or under rock in bank or hole in ground. Possibly does not excavate its own hole. Site usually low but at times up to 80 ft.

Nest. A cavity in dead wood or soil containing a cup of fur, hair, feathers and plant fibers. **Breeding season.** Variable, early April to mid-May. Possibly double-brooded. **Eggs.** Usually 6–12. Short subelliptical. Smooth and non-glossy to slightly glossy. White, usually unmarked, or with some very fine speckling of reddish-brown or light brown; or a ring of spots around the larger end which may be bolder reddish-brown or light red. 16 × 12 mm. **Incubation.** 14 days. **Nestling.** No information. **Nestling period.** Young tended by both parents. Leave nest at 20 days.

GRAY-HEADED CHICKADEE *Parus cinctus* **P. 54**

Breeds usually in conifer woods, occasionally in mixed woods. Nest a hole in a tree; a natural cavity or often an old woodpecker hole. In conifers, or in birch, alder or aspen. Nest often low, 2–15 ft. up.

Nest. Female will partly excavate hole in rotten wood. Nest of moss with a cup lined with hair. Built by female. **Breeding season.** Begins late May to early June. Single-brooded. **Eggs.** Usually 6–10. Subelliptical. Smooth and glossy. White; speckled, spotted or finely blotched with light red or reddish-brown; fairly evenly distributed but tending to form poorly-defined zone at larger end. 16 × 13 mm. **Incubation.** Eggs laid at daily intervals. Incubation by female alone, fed by male, beginning with last egg. 14–15 days. **Nestling.** No information. **Nestling period.** Young tended by both parents. Female broods for first few days while male brings food, insects carried in the bill. 19 days in nest.

BOREAL CHICKADEE *Parus hudsonicus* **Pl. 54**

Breeds in conifer forests, or mixed conifer and deciduous forest, often near bogs or muskegs. Nest in a natural cavity or woodpecker hole, in a tree or dead stump, from ground level to *c.* 10 ft. up.

Nest. A natural cavity in dead wood with a moss, lichens and bark base and a cup of hair and fur. **Breeding season.** Begins mid-May to early June. **Eggs.** Usually 4–9. Short subelliptical. Smooth and non-glossy. White; speckled or finely spotted with light reddish-brown, evenly distributed or concentrated in a ring around the larger end. 16 × 12 mm. **Incubation.** No information. **Nestling.** Altricial and downy. Down very sparse. **Nestling period.** Young tended by both parents.

CHESTNUT-BACKED CHICKADEE *Parus rufescens* **Pl. 54**

Breeds in conifer forests. Nest a cavity in the trunk of a tree or a dead stub, usually excavated by the birds in rotten wood, exceptionally in a woodpecker hole or artificial cavity. Usually low, up to 10 ft., but rarely very much higher in dead trees.

Nest. A cavity in dead wood excavated by the birds. Contains a base of thick moss and a cup of fur, hair, feathers and fibers. **Breeding season.** Begins mid-March to early April. **Eggs.** Usually 6–7, sometimes 5–9. Short subelliptical. Non-glossy and white. Speckled or finely spotted with light red, reddish-brown or brown. Markings evenly distributed or irregular, sometimes wreathing the larger end, sometimes absent altogether. 15 × 12 mm. **Incubation.** No information. **Nestling.** No information. **Nestling period.** Young tended by both parents.

TUFTED TITMOUSE *Parus bicolor* **Pl. 54**

Breeds in and around deciduous woodland. Nest in a natural cavity in a tree, or in old woodpecker hole or artificial cavity such as pipe, or bird–box. 3–90 ft. up.

Nest. A cavity in wood; containing a base of moss and dead leaves; and a cup of hair, fibers, fur, wool, cotton and similar material. Sometimes pieces of snakeskin. **Breeding season.** Begins late March in south to late April in north of range. **Eggs.** Usually 5–6, sometimes 4–8. Short subelliptical. Smooth and non-glossy or slightly glossy. White to creamy-white; finely speckled or spotted in chestnut-red, purplish-red or brown, and sometimes paler purple or lilac. Markings evenly distributed or with some concentration at larger end. 18 × 14 mm. **Incubation.** By female alone. 12–13 days. **Nestling.** Altricial and downy. Skin flesh-pink. Down scanty, dark bluish-gray; on head and back. **Nestling period.** Young tended by both parents. Brooded by female. Eyes open at 5–6 days. Well-feathered by 10 days. Leave nest at 15–16 days.

BLACK-CRESTED TITMOUSE *Parus atricristatus* **Pl. 54**

Breeds in deciduous woodland, scrub oaks and scattered trees. Nest in a natural cavity in a tree, stump or post, in old woodpecker hole or bird-box.

Nest. A cavity in dead wood, containing a base of moss, and a cup of fur, hair, wool, cotton, feathers, fibers, grass and occasionally snakeskin. **Breeding season.** Begins early March. **Eggs.** Usually 5–6, sometimes 4–7. Short subelliptical. Smooth and non-glossy. White; variably spotted or with tiny blotches of reddish-brown to buffish-brown. Often concentrated at the larger end.

17 × 15 mm. **Incubation.** No information. **Nestling.** Altricial and downy. Down very scanty, long and dark; on head and back. **Nestling period.** No information.

PLAIN TITMOUSE *Parus inornatus* **Pl. 54**
Breeds in woodland, oak or pinyon-juniper. Nest a natural cavity in tree-trunk or branch, an old woodpecker hole, or bird-box; exceptionally in an earth bank. **Nest.** A cavity containing a base of grasses or moss, and earth; and a cup of hair, fur and feather. Built mainly or entirely by female. **Breeding season.** Begins mid-March. **Eggs.** Usually 6–8. Short subelliptical to elliptical. Smooth and non-glossy or slightly glossy. Often white and unmarked. Sometimes with some minute speckling of very pale reddish-brown. 17 × 13 mm. **Incubation.** By female only. 14–16 days. **Nestling.** No information. **Nestling period.** Young tended by both parents. Leave nest at *c.* 3 weeks and remain with adults a further 3–4 weeks.

BRIDLED TITMOUSE *Parus wollweberi*
Breeds in oak and pinyon-juniper woodland. Nest in a natural cavity in a tree-trunk or stump. 3–30 ft. up.
Nest. A cavity in dead wood, containing a base of weed stems, leaves and grasses; and a lining of fur, plant down, cotton and spiders' cocoons. **Breeding season.** Begins mid-March to early April. **Eggs.** Usually 5–7. Subelliptical to short subelliptical. Smooth and non-glossy or slightly glossy. White and unmarked. 16 × 13 mm. **Incubation.** No information. **Nestling.** No information. **Nestling period.** No information.

NUTHATCHES *Sittidae*

Small birds, feeding over trunks and branches of trees. Nest in a cavity in dead wood, natural or excavated by birds themselves, or woodpecker hole. Hole sometimes surrounded by resin, smeared, or exuded by tree after pecking. Additional adults, usually single, may help pair in nest-making and rearing young. Nest usually a cup of hair or softer plant material in cavity. Eggs white with small reddish or brownish specks or spots. Incubation by female. Young have grayish down on head and back, mouth usually yellow and gape-flanges creamy-white. Young tended by both parents and any helpers. Fed on insects brought in bill.

WHITE-BREASTED NUTHATCH *Sitta carolinensis* **Pl. 56**
Breeds in deciduous woodland, and in conifer woodlands of mountain regions, also in orchards, and trees in cultivated areas and around houses. Nest in a natural cavity, deciduous or coniferous, or old woodpecker hole, often high but at times almost to ground level from as much as 50 ft. up. Bird-boxes are also used.
Nest. A cavity in dead wood. Cavity floored with bark flakes and strips and lumps of earth; with a cup of finer bark shreds, grasses and rootlets, but mainly lined with fur, wool, hair and feathers. **Breeding season.** Begins mid-March in south, to late April in north of range. Single-brooded. **Eggs.** Usually 5–9, sometimes 10. Subelliptical to short subelliptical. Smooth and slightly glossy.

White, sometimes tinted creamy or pink. Speckled and spotted with light red, reddish-brown, brown and purplish-red, and sometimes paler gray and purple. 19 × 14 mm. **Incubation.** By female alone, fed by male. 12 days? **Nestling.** Altricial and downy. Skin light pink. Mouth cream-colored. Gape flanges yellow. **Nestling period.** Young tended by both parents. Fed for two weeks after leaving nest.

RED-BREASTED NUTHATCH *Sitta canadensis* **Pl. 56**

Breeds in mixed or coniferous woodland. Nest in a natural cavity of deciduous or coniferous tree, or in old woodpecker hole, or bird may excavate its own. Will also use bird-box. Nest may be 5–40 ft. up, usually about 10–15 ft. up.

Nest. A cavity in dead wood, with cup of grasses, rootlets, hair and fur. Resin from pines, firs or balsams is smeared around the entrance hole of the nest. Building and resin-smearing by both sexes. **Breeding season.** Begins late April to early May. **Eggs.** Usually 5–6, sometimes 4–7. Subelliptical to short subelliptical. Smooth and slightly glossy. White, creamy-white or pinkish-white; usually speckled or spotted with reddish-brown, chestnut-red, purplish-red or brown. 15 × 12 mm. **Incubation.** 12 days? **Nestling.** Altricial and downy. Down dark gray. **Nestling period.** Young tended by both parents. Leave nest at 18–21 days.

BROWN-HEADED NUTHATCH *Sitta pusilla* **Pl. 56**

Breeds in open pinewoods, often in clearings or burnt-over areas with stumps remaining, and also in mixed woodland, and occasionally cypress swamp. Nest a cavity in dead wood, excavated by the birds, or a partial cavity enlarged, or an old one re-used. Usually less than 10 ft. up, and less deep and dark than those of Pygmy Nuthatch. May use bird-boxes. One or more additional birds may help pair.

Nest. A cavity in dead wood, entrance 2 × 1½ in, cavity *c.* 7 in. deep, 2–4 in. wide. Cup mainly of pine-seed wings, with cotton, feathers, wool, bark shreds and strips, pine-needles, weed stems and rootlets. Hole excavated by both sexes, may take 1–6 weeks, and additional adult may help. **Breeding season.** Begins early March in south to early April in north of range. **Eggs.** Usually 4–7, rarely 3–9. Short subelliptical to short oval. Smooth and moderately glossy. White, creamy-white or buffish; with bold profuse speckling, spotting and some blotching in purplish-red, chestnut-red and paler purple. Larger markings may be concentrated at large end with speckling elsewhere. 15 × 12 mm. **Incubation.** Eggs laid at daily intervals. Incubation by female alone, fed by male on or off nest. 13–15 days. **Nestling.** Altricial and downy. Skin brownish-pink. Down light brownish-gray; on head, back and shoulders. Mouth yellow. Gape creamy-white. Legs and feet light pink at first. Bill yellowish becoming gray. **Nestling period.** Young tended by both parents, and by any helper. Brooded by female only. Eyes open at 7 days. Feathers break sheaths at 7–10 days. Young leave nest at 18 days. Fed by parents and helper for 24–26 days more.

PYGMY NUTHATCH *Sitta pygmaea* **Pl. 56**

Breeds in mountain conifer woodland, often in open woodland with large trees. Nest a cavity in dead wood, excavated by the birds, or a partial cavity enlarged or an old one re-used. Usually more than 20 ft. up. An additional adult may aid pair during breeding season.

Nest. A cavity in dead wood. Entrance 1.8 × 1.5 in., cavity about 9 in. deep, and 2–4½ in. wide. Contains a cup, mainly of feathers, with bark shreds, plant fibers, moss, fur, hair, wool, plant down, leaves, and sometimes bits of snakeskin. Hole excavated by both sexes. May take 3–6 weeks. Additional bird may help. **Breeding season.** Begins mid-April to early May. **Eggs.** Usually 5–9, rarely 10. Short subelliptical to short oval. Little or no gloss. White; variably speckled or spotted with chestnut-red, reddish-brown, or purplish-brown, the heavier markings often concentrated at the larger end. 15 × 12 mm. **Incubation.** Eggs laid at daily intervals. Incubation by female alone, fed by male on or off nest. 15–16 days. **Nestling.** Altricial and downy. Skin brownish-pink. Down pale smoky-gray; on head, back and shoulders. Mouth yellow. Gape flanges creamy-white. Legs and feet light pink at first. Bill yellowish. **Nestling period.** Young tended by both parents and any helpers. Brooded by female only. Eyes open at 7–8 days. Feathers break sheaths at 7–10 days. Young leave nest at 20–21 days. Fed for 23–28 days after leaving nest.

TREECREEPERS *Certhiidae*

BROWN CREEPER *Certhia familiaris* Pls. 16, 56

Breeds in woodland, usually in coniferous woodland of northern or mountain regions, parkland or areas with scattered large trees. Nest is concealed in the

Brown Creeper; *c.* 3in. across.

narrow space behind loose bark on a tree, in a crevice in a tree, or where ivy or accumulated debris offers a similar site. Rarely in a crevice in a wall.
Nest. A loose cup of twigs, roots, moss and grass; lined with feathers, fine bark and wool. The base may be built up with twigs. Built by both sexes. **Breeding season.** Begins early April in south to late May in north. **Eggs.** Usually 6, occasionally 3–9. Subelliptical. Smooth and non-glossy. White, very finely speckled or spotted with pink or reddish-brown, the markings mostly or entirely confined to a cap at the larger end or a narrow zone around it. 15 × 12 mm. **Incubation.** By female alone, beginning with last egg. 14–15 days. **Nestling.** Altricial and downy. Down on head, thick and long; grayish-black. Mouth yellow. Gape flanges yellowish-white. **Nestling period.** Young tended by both parents. 14–16 days. On leaving nest young fly weakly but climb well.

BABBLERS *Timaliidae*

WRENTIT *Chamaea fasciata* Pl. 57

Breeds in low scrub and chaparral. Nest in a shrub or low tree, usually on the edge of a clearing or break in the thickets. Nest usually very low, 1–4 ft. up. Usually in a twig fork. Nest built around supporting stems, and well-concealed by foliage.
Nest. A compact cup. Spiders' webs form the base and bind material together. Of coarse bark fibers, fine bark strips, weed stems and grass blades; lined with finer fibers, grasses and hair. Small lichen fragments may ornament the outside. Built by both sexes. **Breeding season.** Begins late February to early March. **Eggs.** Usually 4, sometimes 3–5. Subelliptical. Smooth and non-glossy to slightly glossy. Uniform greenish-blue. 18 × 14 mm. **Incubation.** By both sexes, female incubating at night. Begins with next–to–last egg. 15–16 days. **Nestling.** Altricial and naked. **Nestling period.** Young tended by both parents. Leave nest at 15–16 days.

BULBULS *Pycnonotidae*

RED-WHISKERED BULBUL *Pycnonotus jocosus*

An introduced species breeding in one area of South-eastern Florida. In gardens, parkland and shrubberies. Nest in a shrub, small tree or creeper, usually in a twig fork, 2–8 ft. up.
Nest. A shallow cup of fine twigs and dead leaves, bound with spiders' webs and incorporating a variety of papery debris. Lined with fine rootlets and grass, sometimes with hair. **Breeding season.** Begins early February, but mainly from March onwards. Has two-three broods in India. **Eggs.** Usually 3, sometimes 2. Subelliptical to short subelliptical. Smooth and glossy. White, or tinted pink or purplish; speckled, spotted or blotched with purplish-red, chestnut-red or darker purple, and with paler lilac markings. Markings often profuse and fine; sometimes with a heavier zone around the larger end. 23 × 16 mm. **Incubation.** By both sexes. 12–14 days. **Nestling.** Altricial and naked. Skin mostly pink, gray on wings and head. **Nestling period.** Young tended by both parents. Eyes open at *c.* 3 days. Young leave nest at *c.* 13 days, independent in *c.* 12 days more.

DIPPERS *Cinclidae*

DIPPER *Cinclus mexicanus* **Pl. 56**

Breeds by mountain and hill streams. Nest built on a raised site overlooking and often overhanging water; on a bank, rock face, roots of waterside tree or fallen trunk, in a crevice or on a ledge under a bridge or culvert; sometimes behind a waterfall. Nest often tucked into a crevice or hole, or on a ledge or support, more rarely built on to top of a bank, or on a rock or stump in a stream. Some males polygamous, with two females.

Nest. A bulky domed structure of moss, with an internal cup of moss and grasses, lined with dead leaves. The canopy of the dome tends to overhang the edge of the cup to form a downward-pointing entrance, directed towards the water. Exceptionally a nest in a small cavity may lack the canopy. Built by both sexes. **Breeding season.** Begins late March in south to mid-April in north. **Eggs.** Usually 4–5, sometimes 3–6. Subelliptical to oval. Smooth and glossy. White and unmarked. 26 × 18 mm. **Incubation.** By female alone. 16 days. **Nestling.** Altricial and downy. Down long and thick, on head and back. Mouth and gape flanges yellow. **Nestling period.** Young tended by both parents. Leave nest at 18–25 days, and can dive and swim before they can fly. Fed by parents for *c.* 12 days more, and brood may be divided between parents.

WRENS *Troglodytidae*

Small birds, usually skulking in low cover, feeding on insects. Nest often a domed structure, in a tree and large and conspicuous with an entrance tunnel in the Cactus Wren; or small in a niche, crevice or cavity, in tree, shrub, bank, rocks, cliff, building or long grass of marshes, or bound to stems of tall waterside plants. Nests in cavities may lack a domed top. Males may be polygamous, and often build a number of rough nests, a female lining one for nesting. Eggs vary from white with reddish or brown specks or spots, or unmarked, to pinkish-buff or brown with indistinct dark zones. Females incubate. Young have scanty down, yellow or red mouths and yellow gape flanges, and are tended by both parents; the male feeding young of an earlier brood that have left the nest while the female re-nests.

HOUSE WREN *Troglodytes aedon* **Pl. 56**

Breeds over a wide range of country, from open woodland to cultivation and human settlement, wherever there is a low shrubby cover and thickets, with holes or niches for nesting. The typical nest-site is a natural cavity, hole or crevice in tree or rocks; but virtually any structure offering a cavity with restricted entrance, or a ledge or corner within a building, may be used. The male may build a number of rough nests and is probably often polygamous, different nests being taken and lined by different females.

Nest. A cavity filled with a mass of material to leave an entrance and cavity. Basically of plant material, twigs, stems, leaves and fibers, lined with softer material such as feathers, hair, wool, etc., but an incredible variety of debris has been recorded as nest material. **Breeding season.** Begins early April in south to late May in north of range. Double-brooded. **Eggs.** Usually 6–8, sometimes

5–12. Subelliptical to short subelliptical or oval. Smooth and glossy. White, or frequently tinted warm pink or buff, very finely and profusely speckled with purplish-red or purplish-brown, the markings so minute and numerous as to produce an overall mottling, or markings indistinct and tiny, producing an almost uniform tint. Often a band of denser markings around the larger end, and these may be duller, more purplish or grayish. Sometimes pinkish tints replaced by medium brown. 16 × 13 mm. **Incubation.** Eggs laid at daily intervals. Incubation by female only. 13–15 days. **Nestling.** Altricial and downy. Skin dark gray. Down dark gray and scanty; on head and back. Mouth pale yellow. Gape flanges whitish. **Nestling period.** Young tended by both parents. Leave nest at 12–18 days. Male may feed fledged young while female re-nests. Young begin feeding themselves at *c.* 13 days.

WINTER WREN *Troglodytes troglodytes* **Pl. 56**

Breeds usually in thick woodland, deciduous or coniferous, at varying altitudes, and mostly in moister places, but also on rocky islands and coasts of the north-west; in a wide range of sites which provide low cover. The nest is built into almost any type of hollow, cavity or hole available from ground level upwards, but most often on the side of a tree, wall or steep bank from about 0–10 ft. up. The male is often polygamous, building a number of nests within the territory and installing several females in succession in different nests.

Nest. A stout domed structure of leaves, moss, grass and other plant material; lined with feathers. The male builds the outer nest, the female selecting one of the several he builds and lining it. **Breeding season.** Begins late March in the south to mid-May at the north of its range. Single-brooded. **Eggs.** Usually 5–8, up to 16 have been recorded. Subelliptical. Smooth and glossy. White, at times immaculate, or with a limited area of minute speckling or tiny spots of black or reddish-brown at the larger end. 18 × 13 mm. **Incubation.** Eggs laid at

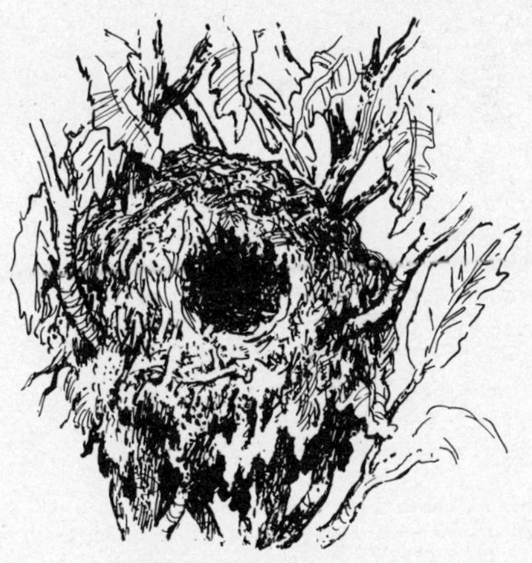

Winter Wren: *c.* 6-7in. across.

daily intervals. Incubation by female alone. 14–17 days. **Nestling.** Altricial and downy. Down, on head and back, short and sparse dark gray. Mouth bright yellow. Gape flanges very pale yellow. **Nestling period.** Fed by both parents. Polygamous males usually have broods which hatch at intervals, the male helping with first one, then another. 15–20 days in nest.

BEWICK'S WREN *Thryomanes bewickii* **Pl. 56**

Breeds in open woodlands and drier thickets, orchards, fencerows and gardens and shrubby growth round houses, replacing the House Wren in some areas. Nest a small natural cavity in tree or post, woodpecker hole, crevice in tree, wall or building, or between rocks or in brush pile, hole in a bank, or any kind of hollow object, including bird-boxes.

Nest. A bulky deep and irregular cup in a mass of varied material; plant material, bark and wood chips, rootlets and sticks; lined with feathers, moss, wool, hair, fur and similar material; and like the House Wren, liable to incorporate almost any material into the nest, including spiders' webs and caterpillar webs, and sometimes snakeskin. Both sexes take part in building. **Breeding season.** Begins late March to early April. Double- or possibly treble-brooded. **Eggs.** Usually 5–7, sometimes 4–9, exceptionally 11. Short subelliptical. Smooth and slightly glossy. White; very finely speckled, spotted and sometimes with a few small blotches in purplish-red, purplish-brown, reddish-brown and pale purple. The heavier markings mainly in a zone at or around the larger end. The finer spotting more widely distributed. 16 × 13 mm. **Incubation.** By female alone; fed wholly or partly by male. *c.* 14 days. **Nestling.** No information. **Nestling period.** Young tended by both parents. Leave nest at *c.* 14 days. Fed by parents *c.* 2 weeks more.

CAROLINA WREN *Thryothorus ludovicianus* **Pl. 56**

Breeds in woodland with low cover in the form of thickets, brushpiles or broken rocky areas, and along banks of streams or in overgrown swamps. Nest in a small niche or cavity in tree-trunk or stump, in a crotch, among roots, in a bank, or among low undergrowth. Usually up to 10 ft., exceptionally higher. Also in almost any cavity or niche around buildings and man-made structures.

Nest. A bulky and usually domed structure, but dome may be missing in cavity nests. Of plant material – grasses, weed stems, bark strips, leaves, moss and rootlets; lined with fine grasses and rootlets, hair and feathers. Fragments of a wide variety of other materials may also be incorporated. **Breeding season.** Begins mid-March to early April. Double- or possible treble-brooded. **Eggs.** Usually 4–6, sometimes 7–8. Short subelliptical to subelliptical or short elliptical. Smooth and moderately glossy. White; very finely speckled, spotted, or mottled in reddish-brown, purplish-brown and paler purple or gray. Heavier markings mainly in a zone capping or wreathing the larger end, with usually profuse speckling elsewhere. 19 × 15 mm. **Incubation.** By female only. 12–14 days. **Nestling.** Altricial and downy. Down slate-gray. Scanty. Mouth yellow. Gape flanges pale yellow. **Nestling period.** Young tended by both parents. Leave nest at *c.* 12–14 days.

CACTUS WREN *Campylorhynchus brunneicapillus* **Pls. 16, 56**

Breeds in arid regions with low scrub growth and cacti. Nest a bulky conspicuous mass on a cholla cactus, in low twiggy tree or shrub, often thorny, or on top of a yucca; occasionally in buildings. Usually well supported by twigs on site. Nest relined and used as winter roost, and additional nests built by male may be used by female for later broods.

Nest. A large domed structure, the cavity with a side entrance near top opening into an entrance tube, horizontal or sloping down into nest, and often curved to one side. Cavity *c.* 6 in. in diameter and entrance tube 5–6 in. long, the nest appearing horizontally elongated, the whole 12–18 in. long. Nest woven of dry grasses, fine twigs, dead leaves and rootlets, thick-walled but untidy on the outside. Cavity lined with feathers, plant down and fine grasses. **Breeding season.** Begins early to mid-March. Double or treble-brooded. **Eggs.** Usually 4–5, sometimes 3–7. Long to short subelliptical or oval. Smooth and slightly glossy. White, or pale pinkish or buffish; very finely speckled, spotted or mottled overall with purplish-red, buffish-brown, buffish-pink, pink and paler purple and lilac. Markings may be indistinct and sometimes tint or swamp ground colour. Usually a denser wreath or cap at larger end. 24 × 17 mm. **Incubation.** By female only. Partial incubation from first egg onwards. 15–18 days. **Nestling.** Altricial and downy. Down sparse and whitish. Mouth orange-red. Gape flanges yellow. **Nestling period.** Young tended by both parents. Eyes open at 6–8 days. Feathers begin to break sheaths at 8 days. Leave nest at *c.* 21 days.

Cactus Wren: *c.* 1ft. long with entrance tube.

Young return with parents to roost in nest for a period after leaving. Become independent *c.* 30 days after leaving nest. Young of earlier broods sometimes help tend young of later broods.

LONG-BILLED MARSH WREN *Telmatodytes palustris* **Pl. 56**

Breeds in tall rushes and marsh grasses along brackish estuaries, inlets and rivers, and in tall growth of cat-tails, bulrushes, sedges and rice of large inland freshwater marshes. Nest a domed structure raised on several stems of tall herbage over or by water. Height varies with growing herbage, 1–3 ft. for earlier nests, up to 6 ft. later. Exceptionally in mangroves 5–15 ft. up. Males build a series of unlined nests, nest is lined by female. Male occasionally polygamous. **Nest.** A rounded structure secured to two or more upright stems. Usually taller than wide with a rounded entrance on the side towards the upper end. Lower edge of entrance forms a thickened, inward-projecting sill, leaving the inner cavity retort-shaped with an upper entrance tube. Made of grass and sedge stems and long leaves woven around supports, filled in with leaves and small stems, plant fragments, rootlets, down and feathers; lined with fine plant fibres and feathers. **Breeding season.** Begins late March in south to late May in north of range. Double-brooded, sometimes treble-brooded. **Eggs.** Usually 4–5, sometimes 3–8, rarely to 10. Subelliptical or short subelliptical to oval. Smooth and moderately glossy. Very dark in color with a general dark brownish appearance. Dull buff, pinkish-buff or light brown ground color, very finely and heavily scribbled with minute freckling of dark purplish-brown or grayish-brown, the markings often indistinct and tinting the ground color but usually with a darker wreath or cap at larger end. 16 × 12 mm. **Incubation.** Eggs laid at daily interval. Incubation by female alone, beginning with third or fourth egg. 12–14 days. **Nestling.** Altricial and downy. Down whitish; on head and back only. Mouth deep yellow. Gape flanges yellow. **Nestling period.** Young tended by female alone, or by both parents, but male helps to feed older young. Young leave nest at 13–15 days. Male may feed them for further *c.* 7 days or so, while female re-nests.

SHORT-BILLED MARSH WREN *Cistothorus platensis* **Pl. 56**

Breeds in wet meadows or drier areas of marshes and bogs dominated by grasses and sedges. Nest is low in sedge grass or similar herbage, very near the ground, or over shallow water. Nest is globular and well-hidden in bases of growing vegetation, or rarely 1–2 ft. up. The male builds a number of nests.

Nest. A rounded ball with entrance at the side. Of dry grasses and sedges; lined with fine grass, hair, feathers and plant down. **Breeding season.** Begins late May to early June. Double-brooded. **Eggs.** Usually 6–7, sometimes 4–8. Short subelliptical to short oval. Smooth and moderately glossy. White and unmarked. 16 × 12 mm. **Incubation.** By female alone. 12–14 days. **Nestling.** No information. **Nestling period.** Young tended by both parents but mainly by female. Leave nest at 12–14 days.

CANYON WREN *Catherpes mexicanus* **Pl. 56**

Breeds on steep rocky walls of canyons, also around buildings and in cavities of man-made structures. Nest an open cup usually placed on a ledge or in a crevice, in a cave or recess in rocks, or in similar sites under, in or on buildings; the sites often similar to those used by Phoebes.

Nest. A cup with a base of twigs, and coarser material, of moss, dead leaves, lichens and a few weed stems, bark strips and similar material. Lined with plant down, wool, feathers or other soft material. At times a very considerable range of small debris may be incorporated. **Breeding season.** Begins early March in south to early May in north of range. **Eggs.** Usually 5–6, sometimes 4. Subelliptical. Smooth and moderately glossy. White; with very fine and minute dark speckling, mostly in an indistinct zone around the larger end. 18 × 13 mm. **Incubation.** No information. **Nestling.** No information. **Nestling period.** No information.

ROCK WREN *Salpinctes obsoletus* **Pl. 56**

Breeds on bare rocky slopes and hillsides, rock outcrops, quarries and erosion gullies, occasionally in crevices in stone or adobe walls. Also breeds on the rocky slopes of some offshore islands.

Nest. A cup in a cavity. The base of the nest and its surrounds are paved with small stones which may be built up in front of the nest, reducing the size of the entrance, or may form a paved approach to it. Nest of fine dry grasses, lined with hair or wool. Built by both sexes. **Breeding season.** Begins early February in south to early May in north of range. Double- or treble-brooded. **Eggs.** Usually 5–6, sometimes 4–8, rarely 9–10. Subelliptical to short subelliptical. Smooth and glossy. White; speckled, spotted and with a few small blotches of dark reddish-brown or lighter buffish-brown, and pale purple. Markings very sparse, mostly minute and mainly around or at the larger end. 19 × 15 mm. **Incubation.** By female fed by male. **Nestling.** No information. **Nestling period.** Young tended by both parents.

MOCKINGBIRDS AND THRASHERS *Mimidae*

Small to medium-sized songbirds; arboreal or partially terrestrial, feeding mainly on insects and fruit. Nest usually on bulky or loose cup set fairly low in thick cover. Both sexes build the nest, incubate eggs and rear the young. Eggs are blue or whitish-blue, sometimes unmarked, or often profusely marked in fine speckling or spots and blotches of reddish-brown. Young are downy, with yellow or orange-red mouth, gape flanges whitish. They are fed on insects brought in the bill.

MOCKINGBIRD *Mimus polyglottus* **Pl. 56**

Breeds in open woodland, scattered trees and bushes in more open country, and especially shade trees, shrubbery and plantings around buildings. Nest in a small tree, shrub, vine tangle, thicket, or large cactus; or exceptionally on a stump or fence post. Usually low, 3–10 ft. up, rarely up to 25 or 50 ft., or even higher.

Nest. A bulky cup of coarse dead twigs, sometimes thorny grasses, weed stems, decayed leaves, rags, string, cotton, etc.; lined with fine grasses, rootlets and sometimes hair or plant down. Built by both sexes. **Breeding season.** Begins mid-February in south-west to late April in north of range. Double- or treble-brooded. **Eggs.** Usually 3–5, very rarely 6. Subelliptical to elliptical. Smooth and glossy. Pale blue to greenish-blue, or with additional pinkish wash; speckled, spotted and blotched with light red, chestnut-red, or reddish-brown and paler lilac. Tends to have concentration of markings at larger end. Large blotches sometimes with indistinct edges. 25 × 18 mm. **Incubation.** Eggs laid at daily interval. Incubation by female alone. 11–14 days. **Nestling.** Altricial and downy. Down pale gray. Mouth yellow. Gape flanges yellow. Irides dark gray. **Nestling period.** Young tended by both parents. Brooded by female only. Eyes open at 3–5 days. Leave nest at 12–14 days.

GRAY CATBIRD *Dumatella carolinensis* **Pl. 56**

Breeds over a wide range in low thick vegetation. Often bordering woodland, marshes or watercourses; or in hedgerows, orchards or shrubberies. Nest usually low, 3–10 ft. up, in a small tree, shrub or bush; sometimes much higher, up to 60 ft. in trees, or rarely on the ground or in a tree cavity.

Nest. A bulky and thick cup of coarse sticks, weed stems, leaves and grasses; lined with fine rootlets, bark shreds, decayed leaves and pine needles, and sometimes hair. Other material, string, cotton or rags may be incorporated. Built by both sexes, but construction mainly by female. **Breeding season.** Begins early May. Sometimes double- or treble-brooded. **Eggs.** Usually 4, sometimes 3–5, exceptionally 6. Subelliptical. Smooth and glossy. Uniform deep blue or greenish-blue. Unmarked; or rarely with a few small reddish spots. 23 × 17 mm. **Incubation.** By female alone. 12–13 days. **Nestling.** Altricial and downy. Mouth orange-yellow. Gape flanges creamy-white. Some black on tip of tongue. Skin blackish gray on upper parts. Down dark blackish gray; on head, back, wings and thighs. **Nestling period.** Young tended by both parents. Closely-brooded by female for first few days. Leave nest at *c.* 10 days.

BROWN THRASHER *Toxostoma rufum* **Pl. 56**

Breeds over a wide range in low, thick cover, on woodland edge, in overgrown patches and secondary growth, hedgerows, dry scrub, shrubberies and garden growth in open areas. Nest very low in a shrub or bush, near the ground, or on the ground under a bush, shrub or small tree. Rarely more than 7 ft. up, usually under 3 ft.

Nest. A cup with a loose outer layer of twigs, then dead leaves, bark, small twigs and grass stems; lined with rootlets or fine grasses. **Breeding season.** Begins late March in south to mid-May in north of range. Sometimes double-brooded. **Eggs.** Usually 4–5, exceptionally 2–6. Subelliptical to long subelliptical or long oval. Smooth and glossy. White, or tinted pale blue or pale greenish-blue; minutely and very heavily speckled overall with tiny reddish-brown markings, often with a denser zone at or around the larger end. Markings occasionally larger and bolder. 26 × 19 mm. **Incubation.** By both sexes. 11–14 days. **Nestling.** Altricial and downy. Skin dark flesh-color. Down dark gray; on head, back, wings and thighs. Mouth creamy-yellow, orange towards throat. Gape flanges white. **Nestling period.** Young tended by both parents. Leave nest at 9–12 days.

LONG-BILLED THRASHER *Toxostoma longirostre* **Pl. 56**

Breeds in dense woodland along watercourses, in mesquite and in cactus chaparral. Nest in a low thick shrub or thicket. Resembles that of Curve-billed Thrasher. Usually 4–8 ft. up.

Nest. A compact layer of thorny twigs; lined with dry grasses. **Breeding season.** Begins early April. Sometimes double-brooded. **Eggs.** Usually 4, sometimes

2–5. Similar to those of Brown Thrasher. 27 × 20 mm. **Incubation.** No information. **Nestling.** No information. **Nestling period.** No information.

BENDIRE'S THRASHER *Toxostoma bendirei* **Pl. 56**

Breeds in dry scrub and cacti of desert areas in slightly more fertile areas than Le Conte's Thrasher occupies, with more vegetation; and around ranches. Nest in a low tree, shrub, or cactus clump; usually 2–4 ft. up, occasionally up to 12 ft.

Nest. A smallish cup of fine twigs, with an inner lining of grass, weeds, bark fibers, hair, rootlets, thread, wool and cotton; lined with softer material. **Breeding season.** Begins late February. **Eggs.** Usually 3, sometimes 4, rarely 5. Subelliptical to short subelliptical. Smooth and glossy. White or tinted very pale bluish, grayish and greenish; speckled, spotted and blotched with poorly-defined markings in light red, pale buff, and pale purple and gray. 26 × 19 mm. **Incubation.** No information. **Nestling.** No information. **Nestling period.** No information.

CURVE-BILLED THRASHER *Toxostoma curvirostre* **Pl. 57**

Breeds in arid places with sparse scrub growth and cacti, open areas in chaparral with prickly pears, and around settlements in arid areas. Nest frequently in cholla cactus, 3–5 ft. up, or in low trees where it may be up to 12 ft.

Nest. A cup of thorny twigs; lined with grasses and hair. **Breeding season.** Begins mid-March to early April. Double-brooded, and lost clutch replaced. **Eggs.** Usually 3, sometimes 2–4, rarely 1. Subelliptical to oval. Very pale blue to light blue; profusely and minutely speckled with reddish-brown, the markings so fine that color may not be obvious. Sometimes a dense cup or zone of markings at the larger end. 29 × 20 mm. **Incubation.** By both sexes. 13 days. **Nestling.** Altricial and downy. Dull grayish above, white on chin and below? Mouth yellow. Gape flanges yellow. **Nestling period.** Young tended by both parents. Eyes open at 6 days. Feathers break sheaths at 6–8 days. Young leave nest at 14–18 days, begin to feed themselves in 12 days more.

CALIFORNIA THRASHER *Toxostoma redivivum* **Pl. 57**

Breeds in scrub of lower mountain slopes and along watercourses. Nest in a low tree or shrub.

Nest. A cup of coarse twigs; lined with rootlets, fibers and grasses. **Breeding season.** Prolonged. Begins mid-December. Double-brooded. **Eggs.** Usually 3, sometimes 4, rarely 2. Subelliptical to long subelliptical. Smooth and glossy. Light to medium blue; very finely speckled, or more sparsely spotted or blotched with light to dark reddish-brown and paler lilac. Markings sometimes profuse minute speckling, occasionally indistinct, sometimes bolder sparser spots or few blotches with a tendency to concentration at larger end. 30 × 21 mm. **Incubation.** By both sexes. 14 days. **Nestling.** No information. **Nestling period.** Young tended by both parents. Young leave nest at 12–14 days. Male feed fledged young while female re-nests.

LE CONTE'S THRASHER *Toxostoma lecontei* **Pl. 57**

Breeds in desert with scattered shrubby growth and cacti; and in arid sagebrush. Nest in cholla cactus, sagebrush, or low tree or shrub, 2–8 ft. up.

Nest. A loose foundation of coarse twigs, with inner cup of slender twigs and grass stems; with inner lining of fibers, rootlets, small leaves, grasses and sometimes a few feathers. Built by both sexes. **Breeding season.** Prolonged. Begins late January to February. Double-brooded. **Eggs.** Usually 3, sometimes 2–4. Subelliptical. Smooth and glossy. Pale blue with a few specks, spots and small blotches of reddish-brown, mostly at the larger end. 28 × 20 mm. **Incubation.** By both sexes. **Nestling.** No information. **Nestling period.** Young tended by both parents.

CRISSAL THRASHER *Toxostoma dorsale* **Pl. 57**
Breeds on the edge of desert regions, in areas of low bushy scrub and small trees, along watercourses and valleys, and on hillsides. Nest in the fork of a low tree or shrub, often well-concealed and among close twiggy growth.
Nest. A cup with a rough, bristling outer layer of twigs, usually thorny, and within this a compact cup of dry grasses, plant stems, plant fibers, and bark shreds, with sometimes a few feathers. **Breeding season.** Begins early to mid-February. Double-brooded. **Eggs.** Usually 2–3, sometimes 4. Subelliptical. Smooth and glossy. Light blue or greenish-blue. Unmarked. 27 × 19 mm. **Incubation.** By both sexes. 14 days. **Nestling.** Altricial and downy. **Nestling period.** Young tended by both parents. Leave nest at 11–12 days.

SAGE THRASHER *Oreoscoptes montanus* **Pl. 57**
Breeds in semi-arid sagebrush regions, and in shrubby or open woodland growth on foothills. Nest usually very low in a fork of a shrub from ground level to 2–3 ft. up. Sometimes on the ground in brush.
Nest. A large cup, of coarse plant stems, twigs and bark shreds; lined with fine rootlets, hair and fur. **Breeding season.** Begins mid- to late April. Double-brooded. **Eggs.** Usually 4–5, sometimes 6, rarely 7. Subelliptical. Smooth and glossy. Medium to light blue; boldly speckled, spotted and blotched with chestnut-red, or reddish-brown, usually with a concentration at or around the larger end. 25 × 18 mm. **Incubation.** By both sexes. **Nestling.** Altricial and downy. Down blackish. **Nestling period.** No information.

THRUSHES *Turdidae*

Small to medium-sized insect and fruit-eating birds, feeding mainly on the ground. Breeds in various habitats from thick undergrowth of woodlands to scattered trees in open places. Nest in a fork or on a branch of a tree or shrub, on a ledge or in a cavity, or on the ground. Nest a stout cup in open sites, or a loose, shallow structure in a cavity. Many species incorporate a cup either of mud or of leaf-mould into the nest structure, strengthening it. Eggs blue, unmarked or variably marked with reddish-brown. Incubation usually by female. Young downy. They are fed by both adults on insects and invertebrates brought in the bill. The male may feed young which have left the nest if female re-nests.

AMERICAN ROBIN *Turdus migratorius* **Pl. 57**
Breeds over a wide range where nest-sites occur. Nest in a tree or shrub, in a fork or on a branch, on a ledge of a building, or occasionally on a post, or a cliff ledge, or on the ground. Usually 3–25 ft. up.
Nest. A bulky, untidy structure of twigs, coarse grass, weed and grass stems,

and sometimes string, rags and other debris; with a smooth inner cup of mud with a thin lining of fine dry grasses. **Breeding season.** Early April in south to mid-May in north of range. **Eggs.** Usually 4, sometimes 3–5, rarely 6–7. Subelliptical to oval. Smooth and glossy. Light blue. Unmarked. 28 × 20 mm. **Incubation.** By female alone. 11–14 days. A few records exist of apparent 8–9-day periods. **Nestling.** Altricial and downy. Skin pale flesh-color. Down whitish at first, becoming creamy, then gray? Down on head, back and wings. Present right along back. Mouth yellow, gape flanges yellow. **Nestling period.** Young tended by both parents. Leave nest at 14–16 days.

FELDFARE *Turdus pilaris* Pl. 57

Breeding in Greenland. In Europe breeds on woodland edge, or in woodland near clearings or marshes; in more open parkland or scrub; in gardens, orchards and other cultivated areas with trees; and in north in small areas of trees in open rough country, or in treeless moorland or tundra. Nest usually in a fairly open site, in a fork on a tree or among twigs, or on a post or stump, or on the ground. Nests are usually in colonies, often in a number of adjacent trees with several to a tree.

Nest. A bulky cup of grass, moss, twigs and roots, lined with a layer of mud forming a cup, lined in turn with fine grass. Built by female. **Breeding season.** Begins early or mid-June in north. Double-brooded at times in Europe. **Eggs.** Usually 5–6, sometimes 3–8. Subelliptical. Smooth and glossy. Light blue with reddish-brown markings. Markings often very small and profuse, covering much of the shell and partly obliterating ground color, sometimes markings sparse, or with heavier blotching, more sparingly distributed and at times capping the larger end. 29 × 21 mm. **Incubation.** By female alone. 11–14 days. **Nestling.** Altricial and downy. Down, on head and back, fairly long and sparse; pale buffish-gray. Mouth yellow. Gape flanges yellowish-white. **Nestling period.** Young tended by both parents. 12–16 days in nest.

VARIED THRUSH *Zoothera naevia* Pl. 57

Breeds in moist coniferous woodland. Nest in a tree, usually a small conifer, sometimes a deciduous tree. In a conifer usually against the trunk, hidden in foliage. 6–20 ft. up.

Nest. A bulky cup of dry twigs, dead leaves, bark shreds, weed and grass stems, with an inner layer of decayed leaves and mud, grasses and moss; lined with fine dry grasses. **Breeding season.** Begins mid-April in south to mid-May in north. **Eggs.** Usually 3, sometimes 2–5. Subelliptical. Smooth and glossy. Light blue. Unmarked. 30 × 21 mm. **Incubation.** By female only. **Nestling.** Altricial and downy. Down scanty and grayish. **Nestling period.** No information.

WOOD THRUSH *Hylocichla mustelina* Pl. 57

Breeds in moist woodland, usually near water. Nest in a sapling or shrub, or in a tree, *c.* 10 ft. up, but occasionally 6–50 ft. Nest in a fork or saddling a small branch.

Nest. A substantial cup of grass and weed stems, usually with a middle layer of mud and dead leaves; lined with dead leaves and fine rootlets. Paper or similar material may be present in base. Built by female. **Breeding season.** Begins late April to early or mid-May. Sometimes double-brooded. **Eggs.**

Plate 13

GULLS (see also pl. 12). In their earlier stages these are not easily told apart from young terns (see pl. 12) but as they grow the shorter, stouter bill becomes apparent. They often have a spotted or mottled down pattern.

Ivory Gull, *Pagophila eburnea.* **page** 151

Black-legged Kittiwake, *Rissa tridactyla* 151

JAEGERS. The chicks, are uniform dull brown but otherwise resemble gull chicks, web-footed and tending to have short stoutish bills. They leave the nest-hollow at an early stage, but remain nearby and adults may attack or mob intruders.

Parasitic Jaeger, *Stercorarius parasiticus.* Long-tailed Jaeger is also dark brown but a little paler and grayer, and the Pomarine Jaeger pale brown above and paler grayish-brown below. 142

AUKS. The chicks are downy, usually dark in color. The feathers appear quickly. The feet are webbed and the bird rests on the lower, tarsal part of the leg. Most remain in holes until ready for sea. Murres and Razorbill are on open cliff ledges and some murrelets on open, inland sites. The young usually leave for sea when only partly fledged.

Cassin's Auklet, *Ptychoramphus aleuticus.* Crested and Least Auklets are brown above, pale grayish-brown below; the Rhinoceros Auklet is grayish-brown, and the Parakeet Auklet blackish-brown above, paler below. 163

Kittlitz's Murrelet, *Brachyramphus brevirostre.* 162

Dovekie, *Alle alle.* 163

Xantus's Murrelet, *Endomychura hypoleuca.* The Ancient Murrelet is black, tinted blue-gray, with whitish patch on ear coverts, and belly white tinged yellow. 162

Black Guillemot, *Cepphus grylle.* The Pigeon Guillemot is similar. 161

Atlantic Puffin, *Fratercula arctica.* The Horned Puffin is similar or more grayish; the Tufted Puffin sooty-black above, sooty-gray below. 165

Common Murre, *Uria aalge.* The Thick-billed Murre has paler brown tips on back, and is more streaked on head and neck. 160

Razorbill, *Alca torda.* 161

Ivory Gull

Black-legged Kittiwake

Parasitic Jaeger

Cassin's Auklet

Kittlitz's Murrelet

Dovekie

Xantus's Murrelet

Black Guillemot

Atlantic Puffin

Common Murre

Razorbill

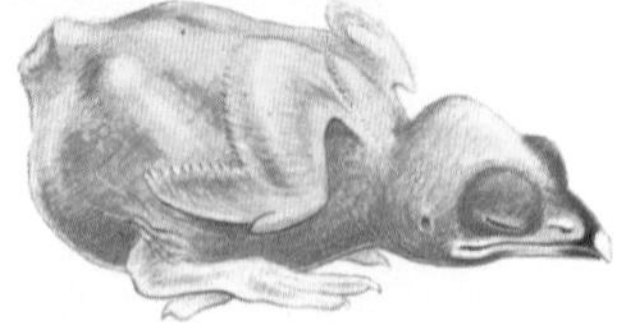
Coppery-tailed Trogon

White-winged Dove

Smooth-billed Ani

Roadrunner

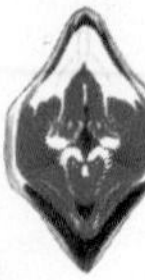

Black-billed Cuckoo

Snowy Owl

Short-eared Owl

Barn Owl

TROGONS. Young naked. Feathers grow in sheath and then break over a very short period.

Coppery-tailed Trogon, *Trogon elegans.* **page** 191

DOVES. Nestlings are covered with a coarse, sparse stringy down, the bare skin showing through. The base of the bill is swollen.

White-winged Dove, *Zenaida asiatica.* Band-tailed and Mourning Doves have white down, yellowish skin; White-crowned Dove has pale buff down, blackish skin; Rock and Barbary Doves have yellowish down, sometimes reddish in the former; Ground Doves have gray down, and the Red-billed Pigeon dark down and a reddish-brown skin. 167

CUCKOOS. Nestlings hatch naked or with sparse, coarse down; the feathers grow rapidly, remaining in sheath until well grown, then breaking out in a short time when young are about to fledge.

Smooth-billed Ani, *Crotophaga ani.* This is naked when hatched and the plate shows the later stage when the quills are growing. The Groove-billed Ani is similar. 172

Roadrunner, *Geococcyx californianus.* The mouth, which shows a pattern of white markings, is also shown. 171

Black-billed Cuckoo, *Coccyzus erythrophthalmus.* The mouth, which has a pattern of white papillae, is also shown. The Yellow-billed Cuckoo is similar. 171

OWLS. The nestlings have thick down extending down the legs to the claws in most species.

Snowy Owl, *Nyctea scandiaca.* The Long-eared, Flammulated, Screech, Pygmy, Barred and Saw-whet Owls also have white down. 174

Short-eared Owl, *Asio flammeus.* The down is buffish-white, white below' in the Boreal Owl, white with yellowish-buff tint in the Hawk Owl; sooty-white in Elf Owl, grayish-white in Burrowing Owl, pale gray above, white below in Great Gray Owl. 179

Barn Owl, *Tyto alba.* Unlike the other species, this has two down coats: the first short, white and sparse, the second a thicker, buffish-cream coat. 173

Usually 3–4. Subelliptical to oval. Smooth and glossy. Light blue and unmarked. 25 × 19 mm. **Incubation.** Eggs laid at daily intervals. Incubation by female alone, beginning with second or third egg. 12–14 days. **Nestling.** Altricial and downy. Down dark gray; on head, wings and rear half of back only. Mouth yellow. Gape flanges pale yellow color. **Nestling period.** Young tended by both parents. Eyes open at 5–7 days. Feathers break sheaths at 6–7 days. Young leave nest at 12–13 days. Adults divide brood between them. Young begin to feed themselves at *c.* 10 days.

HERMIT THRUSH *Hylocichla guttata* **Pl. 57**

Breeds in mixed or coniferous woodland. Nest on the ground, usually in a small depression under a conifer with low branches, or hidden by low plants. Occasionally nests a few feet up in conifer.

Nest. A compact but bulky cup. Of coarse grass, bark strips and fibers, ferns, moss and weeds, with a middle layer of mud, and a lining of fine grasses, rootlets, pine-needles or plant fibers. **Breeding season.** Begins early to mid-May. **Eggs.** Usually 3–4, sometimes 5–6. Subelliptical. Smooth and glossy. Light blue and unmarked. 22 × 17 mm. **Incubation.** By female only. 12–13 days. **Nestling.** Altricial and downy. Skin dark flesh-color. Down scanty and dark gray, on head, wings and lower half of back. Mouth orange-yellow. Gape flanges yellow. **Nestling period.** Young tended by both parents. Eyes open at 4 days. Young leave nest at 10 days.

SWAINSON'S THRUSH *Hylocichla ustulata* **Pl. 57**

Breeds in northern coniferous woodland, usually in moist and denser areas, or in thickets along watercourses. Nest in a small tree, close to trunk and well-hidden in foliage; usually low, 2–7 ft. up, exceptionally up to 30 ft. Often in a conifer, occasionally in deciduous tree or shrub.

Nest. A compact cup of fine twigs, mosses, lichens, weed stems, decayed leaves and mud, and bark shred, with inner lining of decayed leaves, rootlets, grasses, and other materials. **Breeding season.** Begins mid-April in south to early June in north of range. **Eggs.** Usually 3–4, sometimes 5. Subelliptical. Smooth and glossy. Light to medium blue; speckled, spotted and blotched with reddish-brown to purplish-brown, and paler lilac. Markings vary from profuse to very sparse, often with some concentration at larger end. 22 × 17 mm. **Incubation.** By female only. 10–13 days. **Nestling.** Altricial and downy. Down dark blackish-brown. **Nestling period.** Young tended by both parents. Brooded by female only for first few days. Eyes open at 2–3 days. Feathers break sheaths at 7–10 days, young leave nest at 10–12 days.

GRAY-CHEEKED THRUSH *Hylocichla minima* **Pl. 57**

Breeds in northern woodland and at woodland edge, in stunted spruce, and willow and alder thickets near water. Further south in similar stunted growth near tree line on mountains. Nest near the ground in the basal fork of a low shrub, or a few feet up in a small conifer; occasionally on the ground.

Nest. A compact cup of moss and thin twigs, consolidated with a middle layer of decayed leaves, leafmould and mud, and with an inner lining of rootlets and some grass or leaves. Sometimes moss is lacking and main structure may be of grasses, bark strips, weed stems and decayed leaves. **Breeding season.** Begins early June. **Eggs.** Usually 4, sometimes 3–5. Subelliptical. Smooth and glossy.

Light to medium blue; speckled, spotted, blotched or mottled, often indistinctly and sometimes sparsely with reddish-brown or purplish-brown. 23 × 17 mm. **Incubation.** By female alone. 13–14 days. **Nestling.** Altricial and downy. Down dark gray or blackish; on head, shoulders and back. **Nestling period.** Young tended by both parents. Brooded by female only for first few days. Feathers break sheaths at 7–10 days. Young leave nest at 11–13 days.

VEERY *Hylocichla fuscescens* **Pl. 57**

Breeds in deciduous woodland. Usually but not invariably in a moist or marshy area. Nest near or on the ground, in the base of a sapling or shrub, in shoots, fallen branches, briers, vines, on a stump or bank, or on the ground on a moss hummock or in a weed clump or grass-tussock.

Nest. A stout cup, often with a base of dead leaves. Of grass and weed stems, bark fibers, small twigs, moss and decayed leaves; lined with decayed leaves, rootlets, bark strips and pine needles. **Breeding season.** Begins early to late May. Possibly double-brooded. **Eggs.** Usually 4, sometimes 3–6. Subelliptical to short subelliptical. Smooth and glossy. Medium blue. Unmarked, or very rarely with some brown spots. 22 × 17 mm. **Incubation.** 10–12 days. **Nestling.** Altricial and downy. Down gray; on head and back only. **Nestling period.** Young tended by both parents. Leave nest at 10–12 days. Eyes open at 5–7 days.

EASTERN BLUEBIRD *Sialia sialis* **Pl. 57**

Breeds in open woodland, orchards, and in trees or man-made sites around farms and buildings. Nest in a natural cavity in a tree or post, old woodpecker hole in tree or post, old Cliff Swallow's nest, bird-box or similar site.

Nest. A loosely built cup in a cavity. Of dry grass and weed stems and fine twigs; lined with finer grasses, and sometimes hair or feathers. Built by both sexes. **Breeding season.** Begins mid-March to early April. Double- or sometimes treble-brooded. **Eggs.** Usually 4–5, sometimes 3–7. Subelliptical to short subelliptical. Smooth and glossy. Pale blue, unmarked. Rarely white. 21 × 16 mm. **Incubation.** By both sexes but mainly by female. 12 days. **Nestling.** Altricial and downy. Down dark gray; on head, wings and lower back. Mouth deep yellow, gape flanges pale yellow. **Nestling period.** Young tended by both parents. Eyes open at 4–6 days. Young leave nest at 15–18 days. Male tends fledged young while female re-nests.

WESTERN BLUEBIRD *Sialia mexicana* **Pl. 57**

Breeds in open mountain pinewoods. By clearings and open areas, particularly where dead trees are present. Nest in a natural cavity in a tree, or old woodpecker hole. Will use bird-boxes. 5–40 ft. up.

Nest. A slight cup in a cavity. Of dry grasses and a few feathers. Built by female. **Breeding season.** Begins early April to early May. Usually double-brooded. **Eggs.** Usually 4–6, sometimes 3–8. Subelliptical to short subelliptical. Like those of Eastern Bluebird. Blue and unmarked. 21 × 16 mm. **Incubation.** 13–14 days. **Nestling.** Altricial and downy. Down dark bluish-gray. **Nestling period.** Young tended by both parents. Male tends fledged young while female re-nests.

MOUNTAIN BLUEBIRD *Sialia currucoides* **Pl. 57**

Breeds in open woodland and scattered trees of higher altitudes. Nest in a natural cavity in tree, or old woodpecker hole. Sometimes hole in earth bank, or old mammal burrow, crevice or cavity in cliff or among rocks, or old swallow's nest. Will use bird box.

Nest. A loose cup in a cavity. Of weed and grass stems, rootlets and bark. **Breeding season.** Begins early April in south to late May in north of range. Double- or possibly treble-brooded in south. **Eggs.** Usually 5–6, sometimes 4–8. Subelliptical. Smooth and glossy. Pale blue to bluish-white; paler than those of other bluebirds. Unmarked. 22 × 17 mm. **Incubation.** By both sexes, but mainly by female, beginning with the last egg. 13–14 days. **Nestling.** Altricial and downy. Hatched naked, skin pinkish-gray. Thin down by second day on back and head, spreading gradually. **Nestling period.** Young tended by both parents. Eyes open at 5–6 days.

WHEATEAR *Oenanthe oenanthe* **Pl. 57**

Breeds on barer mountains and hillsides, in areas where broken rock occurs, and around settlements. Nest in a hole in rocks, walls, heaps of stones and other debris.

Nest. Large, loosely-constructed heap of grass, moss, plant stems, roots and leaves; with a shallow cup lined with grass, hair, wool and feathers. Built mainly by female but male may assist. **Breeding season.** Begins late May. **Eggs.** Usually 5–6, sometimes 3–8. Subelliptical. Smooth and non-glossy. Very pale blue. Unmarked; or rarely with a few fine dark specks at larger end. 21 × 16 mm. **Incubation.** By both sexes but mainly by female. 14 days. **Nestling.** Altricial and downy. Down, on head, shoulders and upper back, long and fairly plentiful; dark gray. Mouth pale orange. Gape flanges very pale yellow. **Nestling period.** Young tended by both parents. 15 days in nest.

BLUETHROAT *Luscinia svecica* **Pl. 57**

Breeds in irregular swampy ground with low shrubby growth and scrub, or tundra with little cover. Nest on the ground, usually hidden in a hollow on a slight bank, in a dense bush, or dead vegetation, or at base of a shrub.

Nest. A cup of plant stems, dead grass, roots and moss; lined with fine grass, hair, and rarely feathers. **Breeding season.** Begins early June. **Eggs.** Usually 5–7, sometimes 9. Subelliptical. Smooth and only slightly glossy. Pale green, bluish-green or blue, very finely speckled, mottled or tinted with light reddish-brown, the markings often poorly defined and giving a general rusty tint to some or all of shell. Occasionally more obviously marked. Markings sometimes concentrated at the larger end. 19 × 14 mm. **Incubation.** By female. 14–15 days. **Nestling.** Altricial and downy. Down, on head and back, fairly long and plentiful; dark gray. Mouth orange. Gape flanges whitish-yellow. **Nestling period.** Young tended by both parents. 14 days. Usually unable to fly when they leave.

TOWNSEND'S SOLITAIRE *Myadestes townsendi* **Pl. 57**

Breeds in mountain conifer woodland, more often in open woodland, on steep or rocky slopes. Nest low, in a cavity or crevice in rocks, in tree-stump or among tree-roots, at foot of tree on a steep slope, or in hollow or on ledge of steep earth bank.

Nest. A cup with a loose basal structure tailing off into material hanging down. Of weed stems, dry grasses, sticks and twigs, pine-needles and rootlets; with a finer lined cup of shredded grass stems and blades, moss and long pine needles. **Breeding season.** Begins late April in south to late May in north of range. **Eggs.** Usually 4, sometimes 3, rarely 5. Subelliptical, sometimes longer or shorter subelliptical, or oval. Smooth and slightly glossy. White, bluish-white or pale blue, or white tinted yellowish, greenish or pinkish. Heavily speckled, spotted or with small blotches or scrawls of varying shades of brown, reddish-brown or paler gray or purple. Markings sometimes concentrated at or around the larger end. 23 × 17 mm. **Incubation.** No information. **Nestling.** No information. **Nestling period.** No information.

OLD WORLD WARBLERS *Sylviidae*

ARCTIC WARBLER *Phylloscopus borealis* Pl. 57

Breeds in willow scrub. Nest on the ground at base of shrub or among herbage, moss, tree-roots or other cover. Usually built into dead vegetation so that only the entrance shows. Occasionally in shrubby growth. 2–3 ft. up.

Nest. A domed structure with side entrance. Of moss, dry grass and dead leaves; lined with fine grass, and rarely with hair. **Breeding season.** Begins late June. Single-brooded. **Eggs.** Usually 5–6, sometimes 3–7. Short subelliptical. Smooth and glossy. White; finely speckled and spotted with light reddish-brown or darker brown. Markings often rather sparse; finer specklings usually profuse but sometimes faint. 16 × 13 mm. **Incubation.** By female alone. Period unknown. **Nestling.** No information. **Nestling period.** Young tended by both parents. Period unknown.

GOLDEN-CROWNED KINGLET *Regulus satrapa* Pl. 57

Breeds in conifer woodland. Nest in a tree, suspended from stems or in a twig fork, under foliage near the end of an evergreen branch. 6–50 ft. up.

Nest. A deep, thick cup, bound together and to its supports with spiders' webs and hair, mainly of moss and *Usnea* lichen, with some plant fibers, dead grass and pine needles; lined with fine rootlets, fibers, hair and feathers. Built by female. **Breeding season.** Begins early April in south to early June in north of range. **Eggs.** Usually 8–9, sometimes 5–10. Short elliptical to short subelliptical. Smooth and non-glossy. Creamy-white to yellowish or buffish cream; speckled or spotted with drab brown and paler gray. Markings tend to form a wreath around larger end and may be indistinct and merge together. 13 × 10 mm. **Incubation.** By female alone? 14–17 days? **Nestling.** Altricial and downy. Down fine and gray. Mouth orange-red. **Nestling period.** Young tended by both parents.

RUBY-CROWNED KINGLET *Regulus calendula* Pl. 57

Breeds in northern conifer woodland. Nest in a coniferous tree, usually suspended in a similar site to that of Golden-crowned Kinglet, but occasionally nest saddles a branch. 4–100 ft. up.

Nest. A thick, deep cup of green moss and *Usnea* lichen, with plant fiber, grasses, plant down and bark shred, bound together and to supports with spiders' webs and hair; and thickly lined with feathers. **Breeding season.** Begins late May to early June. **Eggs.** Usually 7–8, sometimes 5–11. Short elliptical to short subelliptical. Smooth and non-glossy. White, to drab or buffish-white; spotted or speckled with dull brown or reddish-brown, often

Golden-crowned Kinglet: *c.* 3-4in. across.

poorly-defined and usually capping the larger end or forming a wreath around it. 14 × 11 mm. **Incubation.** By female alone. 14–15 days? **Nestling.** Altricial and downy. Mouth bright red. Gape flanges yellow. **Nestling period.** Young tended by both parents.

BLUE-GRAY GNATCATCHER *Polioptila caerulea* **Pl. 57**
Breeds widely where there are trees, from sparse scrub to heavy woodland, but more often near water, particularly in north of range. Nest in a tree, or shrub, saddling a branch or in a fork. From 3–80 ft. up.

Nest. A deep, rounded cup, neat and compact, narrowing slightly at the rim. Of plant down, bark and plant fibers, fine grasses, catkins, feathers and hair; bound together and to the support by spiders' webs; the outside covered with lichen flakes; and lined with plant down or feathers. Built by both sexes. **Breeding season.** Begins early to mid-April. **Eggs.** Usually 4–5. Short elliptical to short subelliptical. Very pale to pale blue. Speckled, spotted or blotched with chestnut-red, purplish-red, or reddish-brown and paler purple. Markings very variable, larger markings sometimes concentrated towards larger end. 14 × 11 mm. **Incubation.** By both sexes. 15 days. **Nestling.**

Altricial and naked. Mouth bright yellow, with two black spots on tongue. **Nestling period.** Young tended by both parents. Eyes begin opening at 5 days. Feathers break sheaths at 6–7 days. Leave nest at 12–13 days. Fed by adults for up to 19 more days.

Blue-gray Gnatcatcher: *c.* 2-2½in. across.

BLACK-TAILED GNATCATCHER *Polioptila melanura* **Pl. 57**

Breeds in arid regions. In mesquite, saltbush and pinyon-juniper woodland. Nest in a low tree or shrub, a few feet up.

Nest. A deep, compact cup, narrowing slightly at the rim; of plant fiber, bark and grasses, bound with spiders' webs; but lacking the external lichen covering. Lined with plant down, feathers and fur. **Breeding season.** Begins mid-March to early April. Double-brooded. **Eggs.** Usually 4, sometimes 3–5. Similar to those of Blue-gray Gnatcatcher. 14 × 11 mm. **Incubation.** Eggs laid at daily intervals. Incubation beginning with the first or second egg; by both sexes. 14 days. **Nestling.** Altricial and naked. Mouth yellow. Gape flanges yellow. **Nestling period.** Young tended by both parents. Leave nest at 9–15 days. Fed for further *c.* 3 weeks.

PIPITS AND WAGTAILS *Motacillidae*

Small insectivorous birds, mainly of open country. Ground-nesting, usually in a well-concealed cup nest. The eggs are usually cryptically colored, finely spotted in brown or gray. Young are downy, with yellow, orange or red mouths without spots. They are fed on insects carried by the adults in the bill.

WHITE WAGTAIL *Motacilla alba* **Pl. 58**

Breeds in a variety of habitats, usually with open stretches of level grass, often near water, frequently associated with human activity. Nest a cavity or hole in a great variety of sites – walls, buildings, pipes and drains, banks or old cup nests of other birds, from ground level upwards.

Nest. A cup of stems, twigs, leaves, roots and moss; lined with grasses, hair and feathers. Built by female alone. **Breeding season.** Begins late May to early June. **Eggs.** Usually 5–6, occasionally 3–7. Subelliptical. Smooth and glossy. Ground color gray or bluish-white; evenly and finely freckled with gray-brown and gray spots, occasionally with brown blotches, but predominantly of gray type. 21 × 15 mm. **Incubation.** Chiefly or entirely by female. 12–14 days. **Nestling.** Altricial and downy. Down dark gray; very scanty on underside. Mouth orange-yellow. Gape flanges very pale yellow. **Nestling period.** Young tended by both parents. Leave nest at 13–16 days.

YELLOW WAGTAIL *Motacilla flava* **Pl. 58**

Breeds on tundra and grassy areas near water. Nest on the ground in a hollow, or in thick herbage, or under a twig of a low-growing shrub.

Nest. A cup built into a hollow, of grasses, plant stems and roots; thickly lined with hair and occasionally fur or feathers. **Breeding season.** Begins early June. **Eggs.** Usually 5–6, rarely 7. Subelliptical. Smooth and glossy. Ground colour pale buff or grayish, heavily and finely speckled with yellowish-buff and appearing uniform, or mottled with buffish-brown. Often a dark hair streak present. 19 × 14 mm. **Incubation.** Chiefly by the female, beginning with last egg. 12–14 days. **Nestling.** Altricial and downy. Down fairly long and thick; on head and back. Sandy-buff or buffish-white. Mouth reddish-orange. Some populations may show two brown spots at base of tongue. Gape flanges pale yellow. **Nestling period.** Young tended by both parents. Leave nest at 10–13 days; fly at *c.* 17 days.

WATER PIPIT *Anthus spinoletta* **Pl. 58**

Breeds on alpine meadows and rocky slopes, or more level ground along water-courses at high altitudes, to cliffs and rocky coastlines, extending to level marshy coasts with occasional boulders or earth cliffs, and in extreme north on swamps and tundra near coast. Nest in a recess or shallow hole in bank or cliff, or on the ground concealed in a hole or under plants.

Nest. A cup built into a hollow, of plant stems and grasses and some moss; lined with finer grasses, fibers or hair. **Breeding season.** Begins early to mid-June. **Eggs.** Usually 4–6. Subelliptical. Smooth and glossy. Ground color whitish-gray, heavily spotted in brown and pale gray. Occasionally with a thin black hair streak, or with accumulated dark markings wreathing or capping the larger end. 21 × 15 mm. **Incubation.** By female alone. *c.* 14 days. **Nestling.** Altricial and downy. Down long and fairly thick. Brownish-gray; shorter and whiter on underside. Mouth reddish-orange. Gape flanges very pale yellow. **Nestling period.** Young tended by both adults. Eyes open at 4–5 days. Feathers break sheaths at 8–9 days. Young leave nest at 14–16 days. Become independent in *c.* 14 days more.

MEADOW PIPIT *Anthus pratensis* **Pl. 58**

Breeds in open country, in grassy areas. Nest on the ground, in herbage, usually well concealed from view, at times some distance under cover, occasionally just at edge of plant tuft.

Nest. A cup of dry grasses and plant material; lined with finer material, plant fiber and hair. **Breeding season.** Begins early June in north. **Eggs.** Usually 3–5, sometimes to 7; clutches larger in north. Subelliptical. Smooth and glossy. Variable in color, but with several distinct types – brownish, grayish or reddish. Ground color pale gray, buff, or pink; spotted or mottled with brown and pale gray, or so finely marked as to appear almost uniform dark gray or buff. Occasional blackish hair streaks. 20 × 15 mm. **Incubation.** By female only. 11–15 days. **Nestling.** Altricial and downy. Down long and thick, brownish-gray. Mouth red with whitish rear spurs on tongue. Gape flanges light yellow. **Nestling period.** Young tended by both adults. Eyes open at 4–5 days, feathers break sheaths at *c.* 12 days. Leave nest at 10–14 days, before they can fly well.

SPRAGUE'S PIPIT *Anthus spragueii* **Pl. 58**

Breeds on prairie grassland. Nest on the ground in growing herbage, usually set in a slight hollow and concealed by overhanging grasses.

Nest. A cup of fine grasses. **Breeding season.** Begins mid-May to early June. **Eggs.** Usually 4–5, rarely 3–6. Subelliptical to oval. Smooth and moderately glossy. Grayish-white to pale buff; finely speckled and spotted, or heavily mottled with buff, olive-brown, or purplish-brown and paler gray or purplish-gray. Markings usually fairly evenly distributed. Thin dark hair streaks sometimes present. 21 × 15 mm. **Incubation.** No information. **Nestling.** Altricial and downy. Down long and thick; light gray; on head and upperparts. **Nestling period.** No information.

RED-THROATED PIPIT *Anthus cervinus*

Has bred rarely in Alaska. Breeds in more open habitats, usually in damper sites, on higher ground in south to low levels in north. In moist grassy areas, usually with bushes and dwarf shrubs. Nest on the ground, usually tucked into the sides of grassy mounds or sheltered by plants.

Nest. A cup of drier grasses, lined with finer grasses and fibers, and hair. **Breeding season.** Begins mid-June. Single-brooded. **Eggs.** Usually 5–6, rarely 4–7. Subelliptical. Smooth and glossy. Variable in color, grayish, buffish, olive, or pinkish; finely speckled, spotted or indistinctly blotched with gray, buff, brown or reddish-brown. Lighter eggs may show fine black hair streaks. 19 × 14 mm. **Incubation.** By female alone; may be fed by male. **Nestling.** Altricial and downy. Down long and thick, dark grayish-brown. Mouth red. Gape flanges pale yellow. **Nestling period.** Young tended by both adults. Leave in 11–13 days.

WAXWINGS *Bombycillidae*

BOHEMIAN WAXWING *Bombycilla garrulus* **Pls. 16, 58**

Breeds in coniferous and birch forests. Nest in a tree, usually a conifer, 5–20 ft. up. Nest tree often on forest edge, or by lake or stream, or in a swamp.

Nest. A cup of conifer twigs, reindeer moss and grass; lined with hair and down.

Breeding season. Begins variably in late May to late June. Single-brooded. **Eggs.** Usually 5, sometimes 4–6. Subelliptical to oval. Smooth and glossy. Pale blue or grayish-blue, rarely slightly buffish; sparsely marked with spots of black and gray, spots occasionally showing blurred brownish edges. 25 × 17 mm. **Incubation.** By female alone, fed by male. 13–14 days. **Nestling.** Altricial and naked. Mouth bright red with violet-blue bands down either side, tongue purplish. **Nestling period.** Young tended by both parents. Fed on regurgitated insects and berries. Leave nest at 15–17 days.

CEDAR WAXWING *Bombycilla cedrorum* **Pl. 58**

Breeds irregularly over a wide range. Nest in a tree, usually fairly high, from 5 ft. upwards; frequently well out on a horizontal branch. Usually a number of pairs nest fairly near each other.
Nest. A bulky cup of twigs, dry grasses and weed stems, or *Usnea* lichen; lined with wool, pine-needles, rootlets, plant down or fine grasses. **Breeding season.** Begins early June, but variable and possibly dependent on food supply. **Eggs.** Usually 3–5, rarely 6. Subelliptical to oval. Smooth and moderately glossy. Very pale blue or grayish-blue; spotted and speckled with black and pale gray. Markings rather sparse, sometimes more numerous towards larger end, and sometimes with blurred brownish edges. 22 × 16 mm. **Incubation.** By female alone. 12–14 days. **Nestling.** Altricial and naked. Mouth bright red. Gape flanges creamy-yellow but not swollen. **Nestling period.** Young tended by both parents. Eyes open at 7–8 days. Feathers break sheaths at 8–14 days. Young leave nest at 16–18 days.

SILKY FLYCATCHERS *Ptilogonatidae*

PHAINOPEPLA *Phainopepla nitens* **Pl. 58**

Breeds in desert scrublands, dry oak woodland and trees bordering watercourses in arid areas. Nest in a tree usually well up in a stout fork or on a horizontal branch.
Nest. A shallow cup, compactly made of fine material. Small twigs, stem fragments, tiny leaves and oak blossoms, and plant down; bound together with spiders' webs and lined with hair, wool and plant down. Built by male at first but completed by female. **Breeding season.** Begins late February. Several broods? **Eggs.** Usually 2–3, rarely 4. Subelliptical to short subelliptical. Smooth and slightly glossy. Grayish-white or very faintly pinkish; finely and profusely speckled and spotted with black, and paler shades of lavender and gray. Markings becoming denser towards larger end. 22 × 16 mm. **Incubation.** By both sexes but possibly mainly by male. 14–15 days. **Nestling.** Altricial and downy. Skin purplish-black. Down white, in long tufts; on head, back wings and tail, but center of crown bare. Gape flanges yellow. Mouth flesh-colored. **Nestling period.** Young tended by both parents. Pin feathers appear at *c.* 7 days, crest begins to appear at 10–11 days. Young leave nest at 18–19 days.

SHRIKES *Laniidae*

Small predatory birds, mainly of open country with tree and shrubs. Nest a usually substantial, well-built cup of twigs and stems with a soft lining. Leafy fragments of fine-leaved aromatic plants are often used as nest material. Nests are in trees or tall shrubs, usually towards the outer end of a branch near the foliage canopy. Eggs of some species are very variable and show a series of distinct color types. Young are naked, or almost so, with yellow or pink mouths and yellow gape flanges. They are tended by both adults. The habit of impaling food items on thorns is an aspect of food abundance and not directly correlated with nesting.

NORTHERN SHRIKE *Lanius excubitor* **Pl. 58**

Breeds in open forest and forest clearings, open country with scattered trees, gardens, orchards and scrubland. Nest-sites vary from fairly low sites in thorn bushes and small trees, to sites high in taller trees.

Nest. A bulky cup of dry grass and moss on a foundation of twigs, greater use being made of twigs in more arid areas; lined with roots, wool, hair and feathers. **Breeding season.** Begins mid- to late May. Single-brooded. **Eggs.** 5–7, occasionally 8–9. Subelliptical. Smooth and glossy. White, tinged greenish or buffish, usually heavily marked with spots and small blotches of brown, light reddish-brown, olive, buff or pale purplish-gray; the markings present over most of the surface but also tending to concentrate in a wreath about the larger end. 26 × 19 mm. **Incubation.** Chiefly by female, fed by male. 15 days. **Nestling.** Altricial and naked. Flesh-colored, becoming darker after few days. Mouth pink. Gape flanges yellow. **Nestling period.** Young tended by both parents. Female broods for first day or two, male bringing food. Young leave nest *c.* 19–20 days, independent at *c.* 35 days.

LOGGERHEAD SHRIKE *Lanius ludovicianus* **Pl. 58**

Breeds in open country with scattered trees or shrubs, or open scrub or woodland. Nest in a thick shrub or low tree, usually 3–50 ft. up, occasionally higher in tall trees. Usually among twigs, sometimes well out in a fork of a branch, but concealed by foliage. Occasionally a number of pairs nest near each other.

Nest. A bulky cup of twigs, weed stems and rootlets; lined with plant down, bark, hair, rootlets and feathers. Built mostly or entirely by female. **Breeding season.** Begins mid-February in south to late April in north of range. Double-brooded, sometimes treble-brooded. **Eggs.** Usually 4–5, sometimes 6–7. Subelliptical. Smooth and moderately glossy. White, creamy-white or faintly tinted buff or gray; speckled, spotted and blotched in light to dark brown, or purplish-brown, and paler buff, purple or gray. Larger markings often concentrated at or around larger end; and paler markings may form a distinct band. 24 × 19 mm. **Incubation.** By female alone, beginning with next-to-last egg, and fed by male. 14–16 days. **Nestling.** Altricial and downy. Skin bright orange. Down very sparse, white; on body only. Bill buffish-yellow. Mouth yellow. Gape flanges yellow. **Nestling period.** Young tended by both parents. For several days female broods and male brings food. Young feathered by 15 days, leave at 20 days, become independent at 26–35 days.

STARLINGS *Sturnidae*

Small insect- and fruit-eating birds. Nests are untidy cups of plant material in holes and crevices. In areas where the Common Starling is resident the nest-hole may be used for roosting at other times of year. Eggs are glossy and light blue, with reddish spots in one species. The young are downy. Young are fed on insects and fruit brought in the bill. The young are noisy when in the nest, and when following the adults and begging for food after leaving it.

STARLING *Sturnus vulgaris* **Pl. 62**

Breeds in a range of habitats where nest-site holes occur with open areas of herbage. Nest in hole in tree, rocks, buildings, creepers on trees, or nest-box.
Nest. An untidy accumulation of stems, leaves and other plant material, with cup lined with feathers, wool and moss. Male begins nest before pairing, female completes nest. **Breeding season.** Begins mid-April, exceptionally at other times. Single- or double-brooded. **Eggs.** Usually 5–7, rarely 4–9. Subelliptical. Smooth and slightly glossy. Pale light blue, varying in tint. Very exceptionally a few brown spots. 30 × 21 mm. **Incubation.** By both sexes, beginning at completion of clutch. 12–15 days. **Nestling.** Altricial and downy. Down fairly long and plentiful; grayish-white. Mouth bright yellow. Gape flanges pale yellow. **Nestling period.** Young fed by both sexes. 20–22 days. Dependent on parents for food after leaving nest, following them and food-begging.

CRESTED MYNAH *Acridotheres cristatellus*

Breeds around cultivation and buildings, or open parkland, in natural cavities in trees, old woodpecker holes, or new ones taken over, crevices and holes in buildings, or any similar site.
Nest. Cavity lined with grasses and weeds, dead leaves, feathers, pieces of paper, rootlets and various debris and rubbish, to form a rough cup. **Breeding season.** Begins late April to early May. **Eggs.** Usually 4–5, sometimes 6–7. Subelliptical to oval. Smooth and glossy. Light blue or greenish-blue, normally unmarked, very rarely with a few dark spots. 31 × 22 mm. **Incubation.** By both sexes. *c.* 14 days. **Nestling.** No information. **Nestling period.** Young leave nest at *c.* 27 days; and are fed by parents for *c.* 1 week longer.

VIREOS *Vireonidae*

Small insectivorous and arboreal birds. Nest a pensile cup suspended in a thin twig fork. Nest bound together and the upper rim bound to the twigs with plant fibers, hairs and spiders' webs. Nest rounded, sometimes drawn in towards the mouth, and lined with fine grasses or fibers. Eggs usually 3–5, white and very sparsely speckled. Incubation and care of young usually by both sexes. Young altricial and downy. Fed on insects brought in the bill.

BLACK-CAPPED VIREO *Vireo atricapilla* **Pl. 58**

Breeds in scrub-oak woodland and shrubby growth in arid, hilly regions, often on steep hillsides near water. Nest in a twig fork of small tree or shrub, or in tangle of shrubby growth, usually *c.* 2–6 ft. up, rarely up to 15 ft.

Nest. A pensile cup, slung between twigs to which the rim is bound. Rather rounded and thick-walled; of leaves, coarse grasses, bark strips, catkins and spiders' cocoons, bound together and to supports with long plant fibers, spiders' webs and wool; and lined with finer grasses. **Breeding season.** Begins mid-April. **Eggs.** Usually 4, sometimes 3–5. Subelliptical to long subelliptical. Smooth and non-glossy. White and unmarked. 18 × 13 mm. **Incubation.** By both sexes, period not recorded. **Nestling.** No information. **Nestling period.** No information.

WHITE-EYED VIREO *Vireo griseus* **Pl. 58**

Breeds in lower shrub growth, thickets, woodland edge, hedgerows and scrub, usually in moist places. Nest usually suspended in a horizontal twig fork, 3–6 ft. up, or sometimes 2–25 ft. up.

Nest. A deep pensile cup, attached to twigs at the rim. The outer layer of coarse, looser material tapering away at the bottom. Outer layer dead or green leaves, wasp nest fragments, and bark flakes; cup of finer bark strips, fibers, spiders' cocoons, wool, plant down, lichen and moss, bound with spiders' webs; lined with fine grasses and hair. Built by both sexes. **Breeding season.** Begins late March in south to mid-May in north of range. **Eggs.** Usually 5, sometimes 3–4. Subelliptical to elliptical. White; very sparsely marked with minute speckling and spotting in black, sometimes with blurred edges to marks. 19 × 14 mm. **Incubation.** By both sexes. 12–15 days. **Nestling.** Altricial and downy. Mouth and gape flanges light yellow. **Nestling period.** No information.

HUTTON'S VIREO *Vireo huttoni* **Pl. 58**

Breeds in live oaks and other trees along mountain streams and canyons. Nest in a deciduous or coniferous tree, suspended from a twig fork, 5–35 ft. up.

Nest. A deep rounded cup, bound to twigs at the rim. *Usnea* lichen, Spanish Moss or plant down are extensively used where available, the structure bound with fine grasses, hair and spiders' webs, and incorporating small amounts of a wide range of other plant materials; lined with fine grasses or grass-heads, and sometimes a little hair. **Breeding season.** Begins late February to early May. **Eggs.** Usually 4, sometimes 3–5. Subelliptical to long subelliptical or oval. Smooth and moderately glossy. White; very sparsely marked with a few specks or spots of brown or reddish-brown at the larger end. Occasionally unmarked. 18 × 13 mm. **Incubation.** By both parents. 14–16 days. **Nestling.** No information. **Nestling period.** Young tended by both parents. Leave at *c.* 14 days.

BELL'S VIREO *Vireo belli* **Pl. 58**

Breeds in dense shrubby growth of thickets and woodland edge, scattered cover and hedgerows of cultivated areas, and in mesquite. Nest in a shrub or low tree, usually at *c.* 3 ft., or between 1–10 ft., and rarely up to 25 ft. Suspended usually in a horizontal twig fork.

Nest. A deep rounded cup, bound to twigs at the rim. Of bark strips, feathers, grass and leaf fragments, and plant down, bound with spiders' webs and cocoons; lined with fine grasses, or thin weed stems, and hair. Built by both sexes. **Breeding season.** Begins early April in south to late May in north of range. Double-brooded. **Eggs.** Usually 4, sometimes 3–5. Subelliptical. Smooth and non-glossy. White, with a few specks of dark brown or black, or spots of reddish-brown or brown. Sometimes unmarked. 17 × 13 mm. **Incubation.** By both sexes. 14 days. **Nestling.** Altricial and downy. Skin pinkish to reddish. Mouth yellow. Gape flanges yellow. **Nestling.** Young tended by both parents. Leave nest at 10–12 days. Remain with adults for 25–30 days more.

Bell's Vireo: *c.* 2½-3in. across.

GRAY VIREO *Vireo vicinior*

Breeds in chaparral scrub or pinyon-juniper woodland. Nest fairly low, 2–8 ft. up, in thorny or twiggy shrubs or trees, or in juniper. Nests often with several supporting twigs around, although basically pensile like those of other vireos.
Nest. A cup, bound to twigs at its rim. Of dry grasses, plant fibers, stems, shredded weed stems and spiders' cocoons. Bound together with spiders' webs and often decorated with sagebrush leaves externally. Lined with fine, hair-like fibers. **Breeding season.** Begins late April to May. **Eggs.** 3–4. Subelliptical. Smooth and moderately glossy. Pure white; with sparse minute specks at the larger end, of dark brown or black. 18–13 mm. **Incubation.** No information. **Nestling.** No information. **Nestling period.** No information.

YELLOW-THROATED VIREO *Vireo flavifrons* Pl. 58

Breeds in deciduous or mixed forest, by clearings or near water, and in scattered or shade trees elsewhere. Nest in a tree, usually deciduous, in a horizontal twig fork towards the end of a branch; usually more than 20 ft. up, sometimes 3–60 ft. up.
Nest. A deep rounded cup with thick walls and an incurved rim. Of plant fibers and very large amounts of spiders' webs, the outside and supports covered with flakes of lichen; the cup lined with fine grass-heads or thin pine-needles. **Breeding season.** Begins late April in south to late May in north of range. **Eggs.** Usually 4, sometimes 3–5. Subelliptical to oval. Smooth and slightly glossy. White, creamy-white or pale pinkish-white; spotted or with very small

blotches, mostly at the larger end, of black, brown, reddish-brown, and pale gray or purple. Larger spots may show blurred edges. 21 × 15 mm. **Incubation.** *c.* 14 days. **Nestling.** Altricial and downy. Down gray. **Nestling period.** No information.

SOLITARY VIREO *Vireo solitarius* **Pl. 58**

Breeds in mixed northern woodland. Nest in a tree or shrub, coniferous or deciduous, in a twig fork, 3–20 ft. up, exceptionally up to 40 ft.

Nest. A rounded cup, less deep than some other vireo nests, bound to twigs at its upper edges. Of bark strips, plant fibers, rootlets, threads, grasses, lichen, moss, fur, wool, plant down, cotton and feathers; bound together with spiders' webs and lined with finer grasses or moss stems, and some hair or fur. **Breeding season.** Variable, beginning mid-April to mid-May. **Eggs.** Usually 4, sometimes 3–5. Subelliptical to short oval. White or creamy-white; sparingly speckled or spotted in brown, chestnut-red or blackish. Markings mainly at the larger end. 20 × 14 mm. **Incubation.** 11 days? **Nestling.** No information. **Nestling period.** No information.

BLACK-WHISKERED VIREO *Vireo altiloquus* **Pl. 58**

Breeds in Florida in mangroves. Nest in mangrove tree on the edge of a group of trees, *c.* 7–10 ft. up, suspended in the fork of a horizontal twig, overhanging the water.

Nest. A pensile cup, bound to twigs at its rim; of grass-blades, plant down, dead leaves; bound with long plant fibers and spiders' webs; and lined with fine grasses. **Breeding season.** Begins late May. **Eggs.** Usually 2–3. Subelliptical to oval. Smooth and non-glossy. White with a few sparse specklings of black and purplish-brown; mostly at the larger end. 21 × 15 mm. **Incubation.** No information. **Nestling.** No information. **Nestling period.** No information.

RED-EYED VIREO *Vireo olivaceus* **Pls. 16, 58**

Breeds widely in deciduous woodland or scattered groups of trees in open or cultivated areas. Nest suspended in a horizontal fork, usually of a shrub or low tree branch, 5–10 ft. up, exceptionally 2–60 ft. up.

Nest. A pensile rounded cup, bound to twigs at its rim. Of vine-bark strips, thin grasses, rootlets and birchbark, bound with spiders' or caterpillar webs. Occasionally ornamented outside with lichen. **Breeding season.** Begins mid-May in south to mid-June in north of range. Occasionally double-brooded? **Eggs.** Usually 4, sometimes 3–5. Subelliptical to long subelliptical or oval. Smooth and non-glossy. White. Sparsely and finely speckled, spotted or rarely blotched with reddish-brown, brown or black. Rarely unmarked, or with larger light brown spots. Markings mostly at the larger end. Larger marks may show blurred edges. 20–14 mm. **Incubation.** By both sexes. 11–14 days. **Nestling.** Altricial and downy. Down pale gray. Skin yellowish flesh-color. Mouth pale yellow, gape flanges pale cream color. **Nestling period.** Young tended by both parents. Eyes open at 4–5 days. Young leave nest at 12 days.

PHILADELPHIA VIREO *Vireo philadelphicus* **Pl. 58**

Breeds on woodland edge, in deciduous scrub and open secondary growth, in trees along streams and rivers, and on lake islands. Nest in a horizontal twig fork 10–40 ft. up in a deciduous tree, usually near the upper canopy.

Plate 15

NIGHTJARS. The young remain at the rather exposed nest site, the mottled down aiding concealment. Mottling is mostly due to the difference in color between tips and bases of down filaments, but the Pauraque shows a more distinct pattern.

Whip-poor-will, *Caprimulgus vociferus.* Chuck-will's-widow is tawny-brown on the back, yellowish tawny to buff on head and underside, and the Poor-will is warm buff, paler on underside. **page** 180

Common Nighthawk, *Chordeiles minor.* The Lesser Nighthawk is mottled in buff and brown with buff on the underside. 181

Pauraque, *Nyctidromus albicollis.* 181

KINGFISHERS. The young are hatched naked, grow the feathers in quill and these break rapidly at a late stage.

4 (a-b). **Belted Kingfisher,** *Megaceryle alcyon.* The early naked stage and the later stage with feathers in quill are shown here. 191

SWIFTS. The young are hatched naked but later may grow down in some species. The feathers grow in quill and break rapidly at a late stage.

5 (a-b). **Chimney Swift,** *Chaetura pelagica.* As with the Kingfisher the early naked stage and later stage with feathers in quill are shown. Vaux Swift is similar, but the Black Swift is naked at first with bluish-black skin, later has long soft blackish-brown down. 183

WOODPECKERS. Young have large swollen and sensitive gape flanges projecting on either side of the head, and the lower mandible is longer than the upper at first. The young of different species are not easily told apart.

Common Flicker, *Colaptes auratus.* 194

HUMMINGBIRDS. Young usually nearly naked, with a narrow line of down along the middle of the back.

Ruby-throated Hummingbird, *Archilochus colubris.* Down yellowish on Costa's Hummingbird, gray on Anna's and Rufous Hummingbird. 186

Common Nighthawk
Whip-poor-will
Pauraque
Belted Kingfisher
Chimney Swift
Common Flicker
Ruby-throated
Hummingbird

16

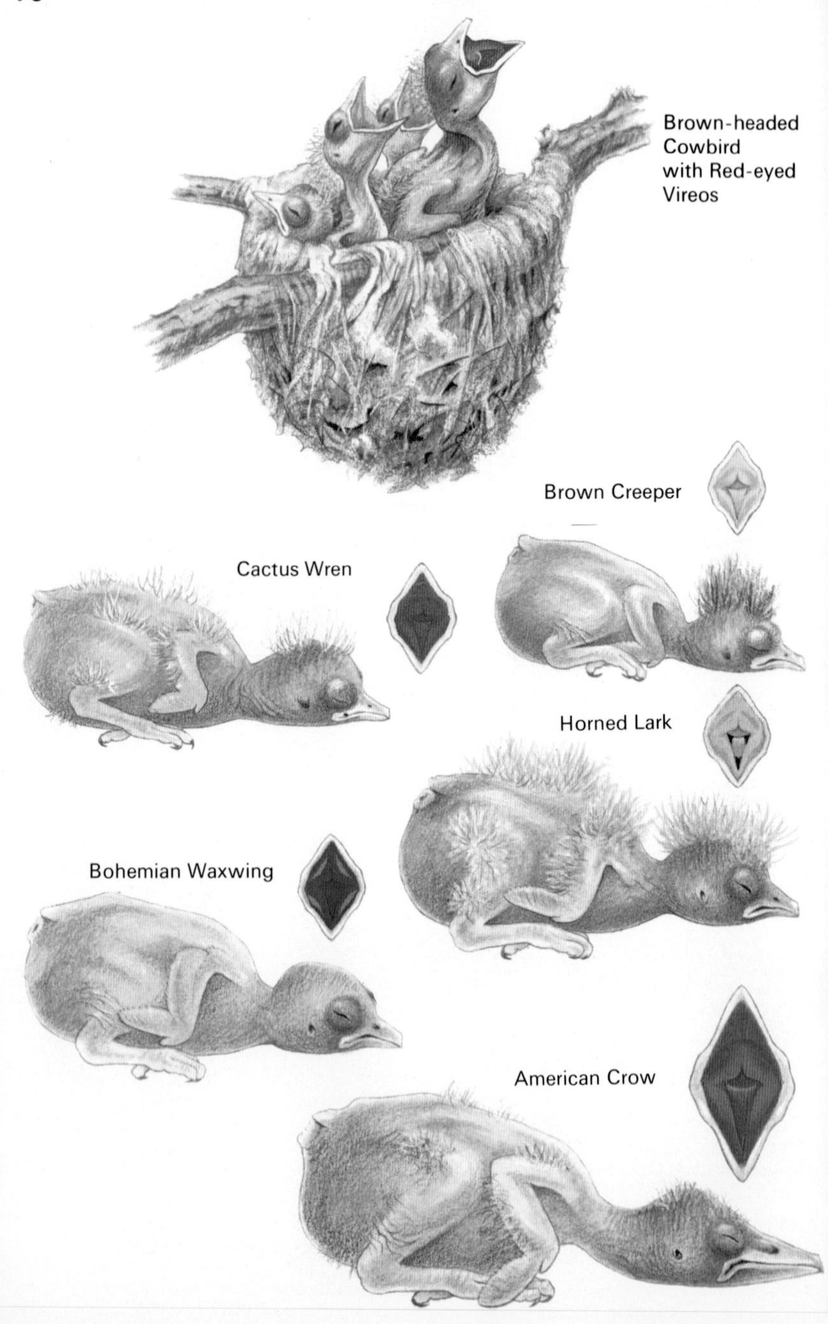
Brown-headed
Cowbird
with Red-eyed
Vireos
Brown Creeper
Cactus Wren
Horned Lark
Bohemian Waxwing
American Crow

SONGBIRDS. A selection of typical passerine nestlings is shown here. The colored pattern by each bird shows a simplified diagram of the colors of open mouth and gape flanges. A key to the mouth colors of songbird nestlings is given on p. 38. It should be noted that bills which are distinct in shape or length in adults are less obvious in the nestlings.

Brown-headed Cowbird, *Molothrus ater,* with young of the **Red-eyed Vireo,** *Vireo olivaceus.* The former is a brood-parasite of a family which has down varying from white through gray and brown, rarely buff, to blackish. The vireos have usually pale gray down. 282

Cactus Wren, *Campylorhynchus brunneicapillus.* Other wrens show dark to whitish-gray down. 232

Brown Creeper, *Certhia familiaris.* The down is confined to the head. On nuthatches it extends over the back. Titmice have down confined to the head and shoulders. 228

Horned Lark, *Eremophila alpestris.* The long down of back and head helps to conceal the huddled young in the nest, but usually sparse or absent on the underside. 211

Bohemian Waxwing, *Bombycilla garrulus.* 249

American Crow, *Corvus brachyrhynchos.* 219

Nest. A pensile rounded cup, narrowing at the rim where it is bound to twigs. Of bark fibres and strips, shreds of *Usnea*, grass-blades, twine and spiders' webs; lined with pine-needles, fine grass-stems and sometimes a few feathers. **Breeding season.** Begins early to mid-June. **Eggs.** Usually 4, sometimes 3–5. Long subelliptical. Smooth and non-glossy. White; sparsely speckled and spotted in black and brown. Larger spots sometimes with blurred edges. Markings often confined to the larger end. 19 × 14 mm. **Incubation.** 13–14 days. **Nestling.** Altricial and downy. Skin light orange-yellow. Down pale gray and short. Mouth yellow. **Nestling period.** Young tended by both parents. Leave nest at 13–14 days.

WARBLING VIREO *Vireo gilvus* **Pl. 58**

Breeds in large deciduous trees, roadside tree belts, orchards, scattered trees in cultivated areas, on hillsides, by lakes and streams and along canyons. Nest in a tree, usually high up in a horizontal twig fork, well out on a branch in the canopy. Usually 20–60 ft. up, occasionally lower and in the western race frequently lower, sometimes in shrubs down to 4 ft.

Nest. A rough, rounded pensile cup bound to twigs at its rim. Of hair, long grasses, threads and string, bark strips, plant down and lichen. Bound with spiders' webs and lined with fine shredded weed stems. Built by female. **Breeding season.** Begins mid-May. **Eggs.** Usually 4, sometimes 3–5. Long subelliptical or oval. Smooth and non-glossy. White; with a few specks and spots of black, brown or reddish-brown mostly at the larger end. 19 × 14 mm. **Incubation.** By both sexes. 12 days. **Nestling.** Altricial and downy. Skin dark yellow. Down pale brown. **Nestling period.** Young tended by both parents. Eyes open at 9 days. Young leave nest at 16 days?

AMERICAN WOOD WARBLERS *Parulidae*

Small insectivorous birds of trees, bushes and ground. Nest in a tree or shrub, on the ground or in a cavity. Usually a cup, sometimes domed. Nest usually built by female, male sometimes helping. Eggs plain or patterned. Incubation by female. Nestlings are downy; cared for by both parents, fed on insects brought in the bill. Usually only a single brood.

BLACK AND WHITE WARBLER *Mniotilta varia* **Pl. 59**

Breeds in deciduous woodland. Usually but not invariably in swampier places. Nest usually on the ground, in a hollow, against the foot of a tree or shrub, among roots, by a log, in a crevice or under an overhanging rock. Occasionally raised above ground in a cavity in a stump.

Nest. A stout cup of grasses, dead leaves, bark strips, rootlets and pine needles; lined with finer grasses, rootlets and hair. **Breeding season.** Begins mid-April to early May. **Eggs.** Usually 4–5. Short subelliptical to subelliptical. Smooth and slightly glossy. White or creamy-white; speckled, spotted or less frequently blotched; in light red, reddish-brown, purplish-brown, or dark brown, with paler lilac, purplish or olive spots. Markings often concentrated at or around the larger end, with a fine sprinkling elsewhere. 17 × 13 mm. **Incubation.** 11 days. **Nestling.** Altricial and downy. Skin pink. Down very dark gray; on head, lower back, wings and thighs. Mouth pink. Gape flanges pale yellow. **Nestling period.** Young tended by both parents. Leave nest at 8–12 days.

PROTHRONOTARY WARBLER *Protonotaria citrea* **Pl. 59**

Breeds along streams, and in flooded or swampy woodland areas of all kinds. Nest in a cavity, often near water, often low, sometimes up to 10 ft., occasionally to *c.* 35 ft. Nest in natural cavity in tree, woodpecker hole, hole or crevice in building or bridge, or post, or in any small artificial cavity.

Nest. A cup of small twigs, decayed leaves, moss, lichens, bark and plant down; lined with rootlets, fine grasses or sedge. **Breeding season.** Begins mid-April in south to mid-May in north of range. Double-brooded at times. **Eggs.** Usually 4–6, sometimes 3–8. Short elliptical to elliptical. Smooth and moderately glossy. Pale creamy, yellowish, white or tinted pale pink; spotted, or blotched with reddish-brown, purplish-red and dark brown, with paler lilac and purplish-grey. Markings are variable, often distributed overall, but sometimes a partial concentration at the larger end. 18 × 15 mm. **Incubation.** By female alone. 12–14 days. **Nestling.** Altricial and downy. Skin orange-red. Down brownish-grey; on head, back, wings and thighs. Mouth red. **Nestling period.** Young tended by both parents. Eyes open at *c.* 3 days. Feather sheaths break at 5 days. Young leave nest at 10–11 days.

SWAINSON'S WARBLER *Limnothlypis swainsonii* **Pl. 59**

Breeds typically in flood plain swamps, thickets and tangles, and in cane-brakes, in lowland regions; but also nests up to 3,000 ft. in mountains in areas of dense fern and evergreen shrubs. Nest in canes, shrubs, vine tangles and similar sites. 2–10 ft. up. Usually in a fork where dead leaves have lodged.

Nest. A bulky cup often based on lodged debris, of dead leaves of trees and bamboos, lined with pine needles or cypress leaves, moss fibers, rootlets, grass-stems and sometimes hair. Built by female. **Breeding season.** Begins early May. Possibly double-brooded. **Eggs.** Usually 3, rarely 4–5. Short subelliptical to subelliptical. Smooth and slightly glossy. White, sometimes faintly tinted bluish-greenish, pinkish or buffish. Unmarked or rarely with very sparse spotting. 19 × 15 mm. **Incubation.** By female alone, beginning with last eggs. 13–15 days. **Nestling.** No information. **Nestling period.** Young tended by both parents. Leave nest at 12 days, accompanying parents for 2–3 weeks more.

WORM-EATING WARBLER *Helmitheros vermivorus* **Pl. 59**

Breeds in deciduous woodland, usually in the leaf-litter on a bank or hillside. Nest on the ground, among and partly hidden by dead leaves, usually at the base of a shrub or sapling, among roots, or in a slight cavity.

Nest. A cup of skeletonised and decayed leaves; lined with fruiting stems of moss, fine grasses and hair. **Breeding season.** Begins mid- to late May. **Eggs.** Usually 4–5, sometimes 3–6. Short subelliptical to subelliptical. Smooth and slightly glossy. White, unmarked, or marked with fine speckling and spotting in reddish-brown. 17 × 14 mm. **Incubation.** By female alone. **Nestling.** Altricial and downy. Down brownish-gray; on head, back and wings. **Nestling period.** Young tended by both parents. Leave nest at 10 days.

GOLDEN-WINGED WARBLER *Vermivora chrysoptera* **Pl. 59**

Breeds in deciduous woodland, usually in areas of thick undergrowth in swampy areas; or on woodland edge with low cover, or in hillside scrub and overgrown pastures. Nest on or a little above the ground, in a grass-tuft, fern or weed clump, or concealed in herbage at the base of a shrub or tree.

Nest. A loosely built cup, often on a base of dead leaves, of grasses, vine tendrils and bark fibers; lined with finer material and hair. **Breeding season.** Begins mid- to late May. **Eggs.** Usually 4–5, sometimes 6–7. Short subelliptical to subelliptical. Smooth and slightly glossy. White or creamy-white; speckled, spotted or blotched with shades of brown or reddish-brown, and with paler gray or purple, and occasionally blackish spots or hairlines. Markings usually concentrated at larger end. 17 × 13 mm. **Incubation.** By female only. 10–11 days. **Nestling.** No information. **Nestling period.** Young tended by both parents. Leave nest at 10 days.

BLUE-WINGED WARBLER *Vermivora pinus* **Pl. 59**

Breeds in overgrown old pastures with secondary growth, woodland edge and clearings with low or shrubby cover, on hillsides or low, swampy areas. Nest on the ground or a little above ground concealed among ferns, in a grass tuft, or low plant growth.

Nest. A cup, usually narrow and deep, of coarse grass, dead leaves, and vine bark strips; lined with finer grass stems, fibers and hair. **Breeding season.** Begins mid- to late May. **Eggs.** Usually 5, sometimes 4–7. Short subelliptical to subelliptical. Smooth and slightly glossy. White; finely speckled or sparsely spotted with shades of brown, reddish-brown and paler gray. Markings often concentrated at larger end. Rarely unmarked. 16 × 12 mm. **Incubation.** Eggs laid daily. Incubation by female alone, beginning with last egg. 10–11 days. **Nestling.** Altricial and downy. Almost naked at hatching. Skin flesh-colored. Down grayish; on head and shoulders. Mouth pink. Gape flanges cream color. **Nestling period.** Eyes open at *c.* 5 days. Young leave nest at 8–10 days.

BACHMAN'S WARBLER *Vermivora bachmanii*

Breeds in thick swampy deciduous woodland. Nest in a fork, in vines or on palmetto leaf.

Nest. A cup of dead weed and grass stalks, decayed and skeletonised leaves, and sometimes Spanish Moss; lined with finer weed and grass stems, and black lichen fibers. **Breeding season.** Begins late March. **Eggs.** Usually 3–4, sometimes 5. Subelliptical. Smooth and glossy. White and unmarked. 16 × 12 mm. **Incubation.** No information. **Nestling.** No information. **Nestling period.** No information.

TENNESSEE WARBLER *Vermivora peregrina* **Pl. 59**

Breeds in northern conifer forests in a variety of sites. Nest on the ground, usually set in a hollow in moss and concealed by grasses and dead herbage.

Nest. A cup of thin grasses; lined with finer grasses and hair. **Breeding season.** Begins late May to early June. **Eggs.** Usually 4–6, sometimes 7. Subelliptical to short subelliptical. Smooth and slightly glossy. White to creamy-white; speckled and spotted with chestnut-red, reddish-brown or pale purple. Markings sometimes concentrated at the larger end. 16 × 12 mm. **Incubation.** No information. **Nestling.** No information. **Nestling period.** No information.

ORANGE-CROWNED WARBLER *Vermivora celata* **Pl. 59**

Breeds over a wide range. In shrubby growth along rivers and low, tangled growth at woodland edge, and overgrown clearings with shrubs and weeds, north to the tree-line; and in similar places on mountains at higher levels. Nest on the ground or in a bush, up to *c.* 2 ft.

Nest. A fairly bulky cup of coarse grasses, bark strips, plant down and finer grasses; lined with fur, hair and feathers. **Breeding season.** Begins early to mid-April. **Eggs.** Usually 5, sometimes 4–6. Short subelliptical. Smooth and moderately glossy. White; speckled, spotted or occasionally blotched, with light red to purplish-red, reddish-brown, brown and paler lilac, and gray, with occasionally blackish-brown scrawls. Markings often mainly or entirely around the larger end. 16 × 13 mm. **Incubation.** No information. **Nestling.** Altricial and downy. Mouth red. Gape flanges yellow. **Nestling period.** No information.

NASHVILLE WARBLER *Vermivora ruficapilla* **Pl. 59**

Breeds in saplings and thickets, on woodland edge, in shrubby areas of open woodland, and secondary growth in open spaces; and in the north on boggy forest edge. Nest on the ground, set in a hollow in moss, or against and concealed by shrubby growth, weeds or dead bracken.

Nest. A small, compact cup of rootlets and fibers; lined with hair. **Breeding season.** Begins early May in south to late May in north of range. **Eggs.** Usually 4–5. Subelliptical to short subelliptical. Smooth and slightly glossy. White to creamy-white; speckled, spotted and blotched or scrawled with chestnut-red to reddish-brown. Markings usually confined to a wreath at the larger end. Sometimes unmarked. 15 × 12 mm. **Incubation.** By female only. 11–12 days. **Nestling.** Altricial and downy. Down dark brown. **Nestling period.** Young tended by both parents. Leave nest at *c.* 11 days.

VIRGINIA'S WARBLER *Vermivora virginiae* **Pl. 59**

Breeds on steep slopes in mountain scrub-oak woodland. Nest on the ground, in dead leaves or earth, sunk into a small hollow, the rim at or near ground level, and concealed against an overhanging grass-tussock.

Nest. A shallow cup of shreds of weed and grass stems, bark strips, dry leaves, moss and lichen; lined with finer fibers. **Breeding season.** Begins mid-May to early June. **Eggs.** Usually 4, sometimes 3–5. Short subelliptical to subelliptical. Smooth and slightly glossy. White; finely speckled, and spotted with chestnut-red, reddish-brown and paler lilac. Markings vary from profuse to a concentration at the larger end. 16 × 12 mm. **Incubation.** No information. **Nestling.** No information. **Nestling period.** Young tended by both parents.

COLIMA'S WARBLER *Vermivora crissalis*

Breeds in northern deciduous woodlands, on slopes. Nest on the ground in dead leaves, concealed by low plants and shrubs.

Nest. A cup of grasses, dead leaves, moss and bark strips; lined with fine grasses, fur and hair. **Breeding season.** Begins mid-May. **Eggs.** Usually 4. Creamy-white; speckled or blotched, usually in a wreath at the larger end, in shades of dull brown and buff. 18 × 14 mm. **Incubation.** Eggs laid at daily intervals. Incubation by female only. **Nestling.** No information. **Nestling period.** No information.

LUCY'S WARBLER *Vermivora luciae* **Pl. 59**

Breeds in desert areas among mesquites, especially close to main watercourses. Nest in a natural cavity in a tree, behind loose bark, in a woodpecker hole, or in old verdin's nest; exceptionally in a bank. Up to 15 ft. up.

Nest. A small cup of bark, leaves and leaf-stems, and plant fibers; lined with hair, feathers and fur. **Breeding season.** Begins late April. **Eggs.** Usually 4–5, sometimes 3–7. Short subelliptical to subelliptical. Smooth and slightly glossy. White or creamy-white; finely speckled, with chestnut-red to reddish-brown, or light red and paler gray. Markings often concentrated at the larger end. 15 × 11 mm. **Incubation.** No information. **Nestling.** No information. **Nestling period.** No information.

NORTHERN PARULA *Parula americana* **Pl. 59**
Breeds mainly in woodland with pendant *Usnea* tree-lichen in north, and trailing Spanish Moss in the south. Nest built into hanging tufts of lichen or moss, but occasionally in more normal sites in conifers or deciduous trees.
Nest. A cup, built into pendant *Usnea* or Spanish Moss which may form the major part of it, elsewhere of thin grasses and bark shreds; lined with plant down and fine rootlets. **Breeding season.** Begins mid-April in south to mid- to late May in north of range. **Eggs.** Usually 4–5, sometimes 3–7. Subelliptical to short subelliptical. Smooth and slightly glossy. White to creamy-white; variably speckled and spotted with chestnut-red, purplish-red, reddish-brown, dull brown and paler gray and purple. Markings often mainly confined to larger end; paler markings may be prominent. 16 × 12 mm. **Incubation.** By female alone. 12–14 days. **Nestling.** Altricial and downy. Down smoke-gray, but may appear whiter at first. Skin yellowish-pink. **Nestling period.** Young tended by both parents.

TROPICAL PARULA *Parula pitiayumi* **Pl. 59**
Breeds in woodland in epiphytic growth on trees. Nest built into the pendant mass.
Nest. A cup built into pendant epiphytic growth. In Spanish Moss little material may be added. Growth is entered from one side, and may create a covered nest. Nest-cup of fine grasses, moss, rootlets, bark shreds and tree blossoms; lined with fine fibers, hair, plant down and some feathers. **Breeding season.** Begins late April. **Eggs.** Usually 3–4. Subelliptical to short subelliptical. Smooth and slightly glossy. White or creamy-white; speckled and spotted overall or in a wreath around the larger end with brown, cinnamon-brown and gray, and sometimes reddish-brown. 16 × 12 mm. **Incubation.** No information. **Nestling.** No information. **Nestling period.** No information.

OLIVE WARBLER *Peucedramus taeniatus* **Pl. 59**
Breeds in mountain conifer woodland. Nest often high up, 30–70 ft., usually out in the foliage and smaller twigs.
Nest. A neat compact cup of moss, lichens, bud and flower scales, fibers, rootlets and plant down; lined with fine rootlets and plant down. Built by female alone. **Breeding season.** Begins late May. **Eggs.** Usually 3–4. Subelliptical to short subelliptical. Smooth and slightly glossy. Very pale bluish or grayish, or pale blue; heavily speckled, spotted or blotched with shades of olive-brown to olive, olive-gray, gray and grayish-brown. The markings vary from bold to indistinct; often denser towards larger end. 17 × 13 mm. **Incubation.** No information. **Nestling.** Altricial and downy. Mouth red. **Nestling period.** No information.

YELLOW WARBLER *Dendroica petechia* **Pl. 59**

Breeds in shrubby growth bordering swamps or watercourses, in wet scrub and tree growth, also in gardens, shrubberies and berry patches. Nest in a twig fork of shrub or tree, usually low, 2–12 ft. up, and occasionally up to 40 ft.

Nest. A neat and compact cup of dry weed-stem fibers, fine grass stems, wool and plant down; lined with fine plant fibres, cotton, plant down and sometimes feathers. **Breeding season.** Begins mid-April in south to late May in north. **Eggs.** Usually 4–5, rarely 3–6. Subelliptical to short or long subelliptical. Smooth and slightly glossy. White, or tinted grayish or greenish; speckled, spotted or blotched in dull brown, olive-brown, or purplish-brown, and paler gray, purple or olive-buff. Markings mostly confined to a ring around larger end, often with bold spotting; and with paler markings prominent. 17 × 13 mm. **Incubation.** Eggs usually laid at daily intervals. Incubation by female only, beginning before completion of clutch. 11 days. **Nestling.** Altricial and downy. Down scanty and light cream colored; on head, wings, thighs and back. Mouth red. Gape flanges yellow. **Nestling period.** Young tended by both parents. Female broods for most of first few days. Eyes open at 4–5 days. Young leave nest at 9–12 days.

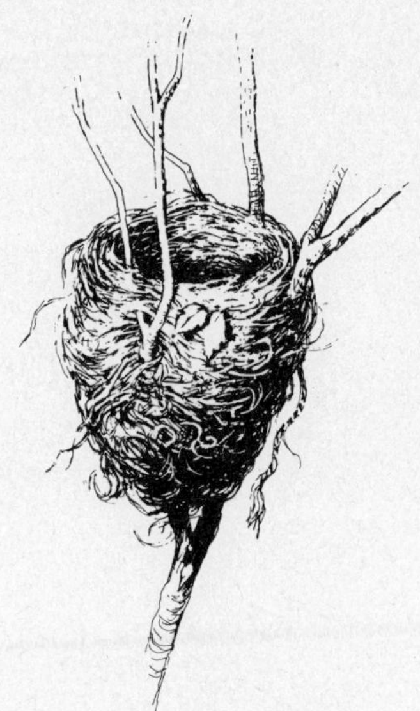

Yellow Warbler: *c.* 3in. across.

MAGNOLIA WARBLER *Dendroica magnolia* **Pl. 59**

Breeds in small conifers in bogs, and overgrown clearings and woodland edge, usually in lowlands. Rarely in drier oak-hickory-chestnut woodland. Nest on a branch out among twigs and foliage, or by trunk. Usually 1–15 ft. up, sometimes higher.

Nest. A loose cup of fine twigs, coarse grasses, moss stems, pine-needles and fine rootlets, sometimes bound with spiders' webs; lined with fine black rootlets and sometimes hair. **Breeding season.** Begins late May to early June. **Eggs.** Usually 4, sometimes 3–5. Subelliptical to short subelliptical. Smooth and slightly glossy. White, creamy-white or faintly tinted greenish; variably speckled, spotted and blotched or smudged in shades of brown, reddish-brown and olive-buff, with paler purple and gray. Markings may vary from dispersed speckling to a wreath or cap of overlapping brown and gray blotches at larger end. **Incubation.** Eggs laid at daily intervals. Incubation by female only, sometimes beginning with second egg. 11–13 days. **Nestling.** Altricial and downy. Down dark brown. **Nestling period.** Young tended by both parents. Brooded by female for first few days. Eyes open at 3–4 days. Feathers break sheaths at 6 days. Young leave nest at 8–10 days.

CAPE MAY WARBLER *Dendroica tigrina* Pl. 59

Breeds in conifer woodlands with mature spruces either in open woodland or scattered through canopy. Nest high in a spruce, 30–60 ft. up, near the trunk on short branches at the top of trees.

Nest. A bulky cup of twigs, stems, grass and moss; lined with hair, fur, feathers and some rootlets. **Breeding season.** Begins early June. **Eggs.** Usually 5–6, sometimes 4–9. Subelliptical to short subelliptical. Smooth and very slightly glossy. Creamy-white; spotted and blotched, mainly at larger end, with brown, reddish-brown, occasional blackish scrawls and paler buff, grayish-brown and gray. 17 × 13 mm. **Incubation.** No information. **Nestling.** No information. **Nestling period.** No information.

BLACK-THROATED BLUE WARBLER *Dendroica caerulescens*

Breeds in deciduous or mixed woodlands, preferring areas of saplings and secondary growth, or thick shrub layers for nesting. Nest in a small tree or sapling, or in a shrub, particularly evergreen. Nest low, *c.* 1–3 ft. up, in a twig fork.

Nest. A fairly bulky cup, with a base of bark and twigs. Of bark strips, moss, dead leaves and rotten wood fragments, partly bound together with spiders' webs; lined with hair, black hair-like rootlets and similar fibrous material. **Breeding season.** Begins late May to early June. **Eggs.** Usually 4, occasionally 3–5. Subelliptical to short subelliptical. Smooth and slightly glossy. White to creamy-white; speckled, spotted, blotched and clouded with shades of brown, cinnamon-brown, reddish-brown, brownish-gray, gray and pale purple. Markings very variable, sometimes indistinct and often concentrated at the larger end. 17 × 13 mm. **Incubation.** By female alone. 12 days. **Nestling.** Altricial and downy. Skin yellowish-flesh color. Down dark gray; on head, back, wings and thighs. Mouth pink. Gape flanges pale yellow. **Nestling period.** Young tended by both parents. Brooded by female only. 10 days.

YELLOW-RUMPED WARBLER *Dendroica coronata* Pl. 59

(Includes the Myrtle Warbler, *D. c. coronata*, and Audubon's Warbler, *D. c. auduboni*)

Breeds in conifer and deciduous woodland over an extensive area, often in more open areas or woodland edge, or in scattered conifers in open country. Nest on a branch at varying heights, 4–50 ft. up. Nest in twigs, on a fork, saddling a branch, or in foliage.

Nest. A cup of twigs, bark strips, moss, lichen, fibers, parts of weeds, grasses, rootlets and hair; lined with hair and feathers. **Breeding season.** Variable, beginning from mid-April to mid-June in various areas. **Eggs.** Usually 4–5. Subelliptical to short subelliptical. Smooth and slightly glossy. Speckled, spotted or blotched with shades of brown, chestnut-red, reddish-brown and pale gray or purplish-gray. The paler markings often prominent. Sometimes a few scrawls of blackish-brown present. Markings vary but often almost entirely concentrated in a wreath around, or a cap at, the larger end. 17 × 13 mm. **Incubation.** By female alone. 12–13 days. **Nestling.** Altricial and downy. Down dark brown. **Nestling period.** Young tended by both parents. Brooded by female only. Young leave at 12–14 days.

BLACK-THROATED GRAY WARBLER *Dendroica nigrescens* **Pl. 59**

Breeds mainly in mountain areas, in open woodlands, shrubby growth with scattered tall trees, or scrub, coniferous or deciduous. Nest in a tree or shrub, usually low, 3–10 ft. up, but occasionally up to 50 ft.

Nest. A cup of dry weed and grass stems, plant fibers and dead leaves; bound with spiders' webs, sometimes decorated with spiders' cocoons; lined with feathers, fur and hair. **Breeding season.** Begins early May in south to late May in north of range. **Eggs.** Usually 4, occasionally 3–5. Subelliptical to short subelliptical. Smooth and slightly glossy. White to creamy-white; speckled, spotted and occasionally blotched with chestnut-red, reddish-brown, brown and paler brownish-gray and purple. Markings usually a wreath at larger end, with paler markings prominent. 16 × 12 mm. **Incubation.** By female alone. **Nestling.** No information. **Nestling period.** Young tended by both parents.

TOWNSEND'S WARBLER *Dendroica townsendi* **Pl. 59**

Breeds in conifer woodland. Nest in a coniferous tree, from *c.* 8 ft. up to probably considerable heights and well out on a branch.

Nest. A compact, but rather large and shallow cup. Of plant fibers, slender twigs, bark strips, moss, lichens and plant down; lined with moss fruiting stems and hair. **Breeding season.** Begins late May to early June. **Eggs.** Usually 3–5. Subelliptical. Smooth and slightly glossy. White; speckled and spotted with chestnut-red, brown and brownish- or purplish-gray. Spotting may be denser at the larger end. 17 × 13 mm. **Incubation.** No information. **Nestling.** No information. **Nestling period.** No information.

BLACK-THROATED GREEN WARBLER *Dendroica virens* **Pl. 59**

Breeds in conifer woodland or mixed woodland where conifers predominate, over a wide range and at various altitudes. Nest often in conifers but also in deciduous trees, shrubs and vine tangles, from almost ground level up to *c.* 70 ft., but usually fairly low.

Nest. A compact deep cup, of twigs, bark strips, moss, grasses and plant fibers; lined with hair and feathers. **Breeding season.** Begins mid-May to early June. **Eggs.** Usually 4–5. Subelliptical to short subelliptical. Smooth and slightly glossy. Greyish-white to creamy-white. Speckled, spotted, blotched or with small scrawls of chestnut-red, reddish-brown, purplish-brown and paler brownish-gray or purple. Variably marked, usually with a heavy wreath at larger end. 17 × 13 mm. **Incubation.** By female alone. *c.* 12 days. **Nestling.** Altricial and downy. Skin dark orange. Down dark brown. **Nestling period.** Young tended by both parents. Eyes open at 3–4 days. Young leave nest at 8–10 days.

GOLDEN-CHEEKED WARBLER *Dendroica chrysoparia* **Pl. 59**

Breeds in shrubby hillside growth of juniper and oaks; nesting in thick shrubby juniper breaks or scattered clumps of junipers. Nest in juniper or deciduous tree, usually low, 4–20 ft. up, in a twig fork.

Nest. A compact but large cup of juniper bark strips, fine grasses, rootlets and fibers, bound with spiders' webs; lined with hair and feathers. **Breeding season.** Begins late March to early April. **Eggs.** Usually 4, sometimes 3–5. Subelliptical to short subelliptical. Smooth and slightly glossy. White to creamy-white; finely speckled and spotted in red, purplish-red or brown, and pale lilac and gray. Markings scattered or concentrated in dense mass at larger end. 18 × 13 mm. **Incubation.** No information. **Nestling.** No information. **Nestling period.** No information.

HERMIT WARBLER *Dendroica occidentalis* **Pl. 60**

Breeds in conifer woodland, preferably of a more open type with scattered large firs. Nest in a conifer, often high up, usually 20–40 ft., but sometimes 2–50 ft. up; often well out on a branch.

Nest. A cup of weed stalks, fine twigs, lichen, pine-needles and plant fibers; bound with spiders' webs; lined with fine grasses, plant fibers and hair. **Breeding season.** Begins mid-May in south to early June in north of range. **Eggs.** Usually 3–5. Subelliptical. Smooth and slightly glossy. Creamy-white or faintly pink; finely speckled or spotted, or sometimes heavily blotched in reddish-brown, brown and pale purple or brownish-gray. Markings usually concentrated at larger end. 17 × 13 mm. **Incubation.** No information. **Nestling.** Altricial and downy. Down dull brown. **Nestling period.** No information.

CERULEAN WARBLER *Dendroica cerulea* **Pl. 60**

Breeds in wooded swamps and moist bottomlands. Nest in a tall tree, deciduous or coniferous, often well out on a branch and high up, 15–100 ft., in a fork.

Nest. A neat cup of bark fibers and shreds, lichen, moss and fine grasses; bound with spiders' webs; lined with hair and fruiting moss stems. **Breeding season.** Begins mid-May to early June. Single-brooded. **Eggs.** Usually 4, occasionally 3–5. Subelliptical to short subelliptical. Smooth and slightly glossy. Creamy-white, grayish-white or very pale greenish-white; speckled, spotted and blotched with chestnut-red, reddish-brown, or purplish-brown and paler brownish-gray. Markings sometimes overall, often concentrated at larger end, varying from fine to heavy. 17 × 13 mm. **Incubation.** No information. **Nestling.** No information. **Nestling period.** No information.

BLACKBURNIAN WARBLER *Dendroica fusca* **Pl. 60**

Breeds mainly in conifer woodland, but also in hickory-oak woodland on mountains further south. Nest usually in a conifer, 5–85 ft. up, well-concealed in foliage or *Usnea* lichen.

Nest. A large compact cup of fine twigs, lichens, moss and rootlets; lined with plant down, hair, fine grasses and rootlets. **Breeding season.** Begins late May to early June. **Eggs.** Usually 4, sometimes 5. Subelliptical to short subelliptical. Smooth and slightly glossy. White or very pale greenish-white; spotted and blotched with chestnut-red, brown, occasionally blackish-brown scrawls, and pale brownish-gray and purple. Paler markings may predominate. Markings vary from even spotting to a heavy wreath around the larger end. 17 × 13 mm. **Incubation.** By female alone. Period not recorded. **Nestling.** Altricial and downy. Down dark brown. Gape flanges yellow. **Nestling period.** Young tended by both parents.

YELLOW-THROATED WARBLER *Dendroica dominica* **Pl. 60**

Breeds in areas of live oaks with Spanish Moss, in pine woodland and in deciduous woodland along watercourses. Where Spanish Moss occurs the nest is built into a moss clump, but elsewhere is built on to a horizontal branch. Nest from 3–120 ft. up; but usually 15–60 ft.

Nest. A cup of fine grasses, weed stems, bark shreds, plant fibers and down, hair or dead leaves, bound with caterpillar webs; lined with plant down and sometimes feathers, or with Spanish Moss strands and flowers. Built mostly or entirely by female. **Breeding season.** Begins early to mid-April. Sometimes double-brooded. **Eggs.** Usually 4, rarely 5. Subelliptical to short subelliptical. Smooth and slightly glossy. Pale greenish or grayish white; speckled, spotted and blotched in purplish-red, reddish-brown, blackish or grayish-purple, and paler purple and gray. Pale markings numerous. 17 × 13 mm. **Incubation.** No information. **Nestling.** No information. **Nestling period.** No information.

GRACE'S WARBLER *Dendroica graciae* **Pl. 60**

Breeds in mountain pine-oak woodland. Nest in a pine tree, usually high up, *c.* 20–60 ft., and well out on a branch, usually concealed in foliage.

Nest. A compact cup of hair, vegetable fibers, plant down, catkins and bud scales, wool and caterpillar webs; lined with feathers and hair. **Breeding season.** Begins early May. **Eggs.** Usually 3–4. Subelliptical. Smooth and slightly glossy. White or creamy-white; finely speckled and spotted, or sometimes blotched, with chestnut-red, reddish-brown, light olive, brown, grayish-brown and a few blackish-brown marks, with paler purple and gray. Markings often limited to a wreath at the larger end; sometimes speckled overall. 17 × 13 mm. **Incubation.** No information. **Nestling.** No information. **Nestling period.** No information.

CHESTNUT-SIDED WARBLER *Dendroica pensylvanica* **Pl. 60**

Breeds in deciduous secondary growth of open woodlands, clearings, woodland edge and cut-over areas, particularly on mountain slopes, and in overgrown pastures and roadsides. Nest low in a sapling, shrub, thicket or vine tangle; usually 1–3 ft. up.

Nest. A compact cup of fine grasses, bark fibers, shredded weed stems and plant down; lined with fine grasses and hair. **Breeding season.** Begins late May. **Eggs.** Usually 4, sometimes 3–5. Smooth and slightly glossy. Subelliptical to long subelliptical. White, creamy-white, or very pale greenish; speckled, spotted and blotched with light and dark reddish-brown, purplish-brown and dull brown, and paler gray and purple. Markings usually largely confined to a narrow ring around the larger end, but fine speckling may be more dispersed. 17 × 12 mm. **Incubation.** By female only. 12–13 days. **Nestling.** Altricial and downy.

Down fine and sparse, dark gray. Mouth red. Gape flanges yellow. **Nestling period.** Young tended by both parents. Eyes open at 3–4 days. Feathers break sheaths at 6–8 days. Young leave nest at 10–12 days.

BAY-BREASTED WARBLER *Dendroica castanea* **Pl. 60**

Breeds in northern conifer woodland, or mixed woodland. Nest in a tree, usually on a horizontal branch, 5–20 ft. up, sometimes up to 50 ft.; exceptionally on a shrub.

Nest. A bulky cup of fine twigs, dead grasses, bark strips and caterpillar webs; lined with fine black rootlets and hair. **Breeding season.** Begins early June. **Eggs.** Usually 4–5, sometimes 3–7. Subelliptical to long subelliptical. Smooth and slightly glossy. White, creamy-white or very pale bluish or greenish; boldly speckled, spotted and blotched with shades of reddish-brown or brown, and paler gray and lilac. Sometimes a few blackish scrawls. Markings variable, sometimes concentrated at the larger end. 18 × 13 mm. **Incubation.** By female alone. 12–13 days. **Nestling.** Altricial and downy. Down brown. **Nestling period.** 11 days.

BLACKPOLL WARBLER *Dendroica striata* **Pl. 60**

Breeds in northern spruce woodland, or in deciduous thickets beyond the tree limit. Nest in a small tree, 1–10 ft. up, usually well-hidden in foliage; rarely on the ground concealed in a grass-tuft.

Nest. A cup of small twigs, spruce shoots, bark fragments, dead grasses, weed stems, moss, wool and *Usnea* lichen; lined with plant fibers, fine rootlets, hair and feathers. **Breeding season.** Begins mid-June. **Eggs.** Usually 4–5, sometimes 3. Subelliptical. Smooth and slightly glossy. White, pale creamy-buff or very pale greenish; speckled, spotted and blotched with reddish-brown and brown, or paler purple and purplish-gray. Markings often concentrated at larger end. 18 × 13 mm. **Incubation.** By female alone, beginning with completion of clutch. 11 days. **Nestling.** Altricial and downy. Down gray; on head, back, wings and thighs. **Nestling period.** Young tended by both parents. Eyes open at 4–5 days. Feathers break sheaths at 5–8 days. Young leave nest at 10–11 days.

PINE WARBLER *Dendroica pinus* **Pl. 60**

Breeds in open pine woodland. Nest in a pine tree, on a horizontal branch or among the foliage at the branch tip, 15–80 ft. up.

Nest. A compact cup of weed stems, bark strips, pine twigs and needles, and plant fibers, bound with caterpillar or spiders' webs; lined with fern-down, pine-needles, hair and feathers. **Breeding season.** Begins early April in south to late May or June in north of range. **Eggs.** Usually 4, sometimes 3–5. Subelliptical to short subelliptical. Smooth and slightly glossy. White, grayish or greenish-white; speckled, spotted or blotched with shades of reddish-brown to brown, or paler brownish-gray or purplish-gray, and sometimes a few dark brown or blackish scrawls. Markings usually in a cap or wreath at the larger end. 18 × 13 mm. **Incubation.** By both sexes? **Nestling.** Altricial and downy. Down dark brown. **Nestling period.** Young tended by both parents.

KIRTLAND'S WARBLER *Dendroica kirtlandii* **Pl. 60**

Breeds only in thick stands of small pines in the Michigan Jack Pine plains. Nest on the ground very close to a pine-trunk and concealed under ground vegetation.

Nest. A compact cup of dry grasses and plant fibers; lined with finer grasses, fruiting stems of moss, and some hair. Built by female. **Breeding season.** Begins late May. Single-brooded or rarely double-brooded, but lost clutch replaced. **Eggs.** Usually 4–5. Subelliptical to short subelliptical. Smooth and slightly glossy. Creamy-white or faintly pink; speckled, spotted and blotched with buffish-brown or brown. Variably marked, often a concentration at larger end. 18 × 14 mm. **Incubation.** 14–15 days. **Nestling.** Altricial and downy. Down grayish-brown. Mouth red, gape flanges cream-colored. **Nestling period.** Young tended by both parents. Female broods for first few days while male brings food. Young leave nest at 12–13 days.

PRAIRIE WARBLER *Dendroica discolor* **Pl. 60**

Breeds in low scrub and secondary growth, in clearings, woodland edge, open woodland with low undergrowth, and roadside thickets. The southern subspecies nests in mangroves, bordering coastal marshes. Nest in a shrub, sapling, thicket or fern clump, usually 1–10 ft. up, occasionally up to 25 ft. in pines.

Nest. A compact cup of plant fibers, small dead leaves, fine grasses, bud scales, fern and seed down, bound with spiders' webs; lined with hair and feathers. Built by female. **Breeding season.** Begins late April in south to late May in north of range. **Eggs.** Usually 4, sometimes 3–5. Subelliptical to short subelliptical. Smooth and slightly glossy. White, creamy-white or with faint greenish tint; spotted and speckled with reddish-brown, chestnut-red and brown, with paler purple and gray. Spotting forms a denser band at larger end. 16 × 12 mm. **Incubation.** By female alone. 12 days. **Nestling.** Altricial and downy. Skin yellow-orange. Down dark gray. Mouth and gape flanges pale yellow. **Nestling period.** Young tended by both parents. Leave nest at 8–10 days.

PALM WARBLER *Dendroica palmarum* **Pl. 60**

Breeds in northern areas of scattered trees around wet or dry muskeg or similar areas. Nest on the ground, on a small hummock, in moss, concealed under a tuft of grass or other herbage or at the base of a spruce sapling. Occasionally up to 4 ft. up in spruce sapling.

Nest. A cup of plant fibers, bark shreds, dry grasses and shredded weed stems; lined with finer grasses and feathers. **Breeding season.** Begins mid- to late May. **Eggs.** Usually 4–5. Short to long subelliptical. Smooth and slightly glossy. White or creamy-white; speckled, spotted and blotched in chestnut-red, reddish-brown, or brown, with paler brownish-gray or gray. Sometimes a few blackish scrawls. Markings often in a wreath at larger end. 17 × 13 mm. **Incubation.** 12 days. **Nestling.** No information. **Nestling period.** Young tended by both parents. Leave nest at 12 days, cannot fly for several days and hide in herbage.

OVENBIRD *Seiurus aurocapillus* **Pl. 60**

Breeds in deciduous woodland with scanty secondary growth or thickets, where ground is covered in leaf-litter. Nest on the ground, in the open or partly hidden by plant growth; set in a small hollow and domed, covered with leaves and debris, with a side entrance invisible from above.

Nest. A rounded structure set in a small hollow made by the birds; of dead leaves, pine-needles, grass and weed stems, rootlets and moss; the inner cup lined with hair and fine rootlets. Built by female. **Breeding season.** Begins mid-May. **Eggs.** Usually 4–5, sometimes 3, rarely 6. Subelliptical to short subelliptical. Smooth and slightly glossy. White; speckled and spotted and with small blotches of reddish-brown, brown, and paler reddish-buff, lilac and gray. Markings usually in a wreath around the larger end, with a very fine speckling elsewhere. 20 × 15 mm. **Incubation.** By female alone, beginning with completion of clutch. 11–14 days. **Nestling.** Altricial and downy. Down medium gray; on head, back, wings and thighs. Mouth pink. Gape flanges pale yellow. **Nestling period.** Young tended by both parents. Leave nest at 8–10 days. Parents divide the brood once young leave the nest.

NORTHERN WATERTHRUSH *Seiurus novaboracensis* **Pl. 60**

Breeds in northern woodland in swamps or boggy areas, by streams or pond edges; particularly where fallen timber occurs. Nest in a cavity or hollow among roots of a fallen tree base, or in a bank, among tree-roots, or in the side of a decayed stump; the site normally raised and often over water.

Nest. A cup of moss, decayed leaves, bark strips, rootlets, small twigs and pine-needles; lined with fine grasses, hair or fruiting moss stems. **Breeding season.** Begins late May in south to early June in north of range. **Eggs.** Usually 4–5, sometimes 3–6. Subelliptical to short subelliptical. Smooth and slightly glossy or non-glossy. Creamy-white, buffish or yellowish-white; speckled, spotted or blotched with reddish-brown, brown or cinnamon-brown, and paler purplish-gray or brownish-gray. Occasionally clouded or scrawled with brown. Usually heavier markings concentrated at larger end with fine speckling elsewhere. 19 × 13 mm. **Incubation.** No information. **Nestling.** Altricial and downy. Down dark olive-brown. Mouth red. Gape flanges yellow. **Nestling period.** No information.

LOUISIANA WATERTHRUSH *Seiurus motacilla* **Pl. 60**

Breeds in swampy woodland and along wooded watercourses, but differs from the Northern Waterthrush in preferring running water. Nest-site, like that of previous species, in a crevice or raised site in tree-roots, banks of streams, and cliffs or ravines over water.

Nest. A cup of moss, decayed leaves, grasses and rootlets; lined with finer grasses, rootlets, hair and fruiting moss stems. Built by both sexes. **Breeding season.** Begins early April in south to early May in north of range. **Eggs.** Usually 4–6. Subelliptical to short subelliptical. Smooth and slightly glossy. White to creamy-white; speckled, spotted and blotched with reddish-brown to brown, and paler purple and purplish-gray. Variably marked and sometimes with heavy overall mottling. Paler markings sometimes prominent. 20 × 15 mm. **Incubation.** By female alone. Beginning with next-to-last egg. 12–14 days. **Nestling.** Altricial and downy. Down dark gray. Mouth red. Gape flanges yellow. **Nestling period.** Young tended by both parents. Leave nest at *c.* 10 days. Can fly at 6 days after leaving nest and begins feeding itself at *c.* 7 days.

KENTUCKY WARBLER *Oporornis formosus* **Pl. 60**

Breeds in moist, deciduous woodland with heavy undergrowth, thickets and ground vegetation. Nest on or just above the ground at the foot of a tree or shrub, or in a weed clump, or patch of weeds; usually hidden by overhanging vegetation or fallen branches.

Nest. A loose, bulky cup of dead leaves, with grass and weed stems, bark strips and rootlets; and a lining of rootlets and hair. **Breeding season.** Begins early to mid-May. **Eggs.** Usually 4–5, sometimes 3–6. Subelliptical to long or short subelliptical. Smooth and slightly glossy. White or creamy-white; speckled, spotted or blotched with chestnut-red, reddish-brown and pale gray. Fine speckling and spotting more typical, often denser at the larger end. 19 × 14 mm. **Incubation.** By female alone. 12–13 days. **Nestling.** No information. **Nestling period.** Young tended by both parents. Brooded by female only. Eyes open at 5 days, young leave at 8–10 days, before they can fly. Fed by adults for up to 17 days more.

CONNECTICUT WARBLER *Oporornis agilis* **Pl. 60**

Breeds in woodland, often in moist or boggy areas, with low shrubby growth, thick undergrowth, or sapling thickets. Nest on the ground, in a small hollow, on a moss mound, or in grasses or weeds, or at the base of a shrub. Usually concealed by overhanging herbage or shrubby growth.

Nest. A deep compact cup of fine dry grasses and rootlets; lined with fine rootlets and hair. **Breeding season.** Begins mid-June. **Eggs.** Usually 4–5. Subelliptical. Smooth and slightly glossy. Creamy-white; speckled, spotted and blotched with reddish-brown, chestnut-red and paler purple, gray and brownish-gray. Occasionally streaked with brown. Markings usually concentrated at the larger end but do not form a distinct wreath. 19 × 14 mm. **Incubation.** No information. **Nestling.** No information. **Nestling period.** No information.

MOURNING WARBLER *Oporornis philadelphia* **Pl. 60**

Breeds in northern woodland where heavy undergrowth occurs, on edges of swamps, on steep slopes, and in bushy thickets. Nest on or near the ground in thickets, thorny briers or similar growth, in fern or weed clumps, grass-tussocks, or sometimes up to 3 ft. in thickets.

Nest. A bulky but compact cup of dead leaves, vine stems, and with inner cup of grasses, weed stems and leaves; lined with fine grasses and hair. **Breeding season.** Begins late May to early June. **Eggs.** Usually 4, sometimes 3–5. Subelliptical to short subelliptical. Smooth and slightly glossy. White to creamy-white; speckled, spotted and blotched with chestnut-red, reddish-brown, and paler purple, brownish-gray and gray. Sometimes a few spots or specks of black. 18 × 14 mm. **Incubation.** By female alone. 12–13 days. **Nestling.** Altricial and downy. Down dark gray. Mouth red. Gape flanges yellow. **Nestling period.** Young tended by both parents. Leave nest at 7–9 days, unable to fly. Begin to fly in second week out of nest. Remain with adults for *c.* 3 weeks.

MACGILLIVRAY'S WARBLER *Oporornis tolmiei* **Pl. 60**

Breeds in low moist thickets in or around woodland, often on hill slopes, and in secondary growth or cut-over areas, and moist hillside scrub. Nest low in a thick shrub, conifer sapling, weed clump or fern clump; 1–5 ft. up.

Nest. A small compact cup of fine blades and stems, dead grasses, weed stems and bark shreds; lined with fine grasses, rootlets and hair. **Breeding season.** Begins early May in south to late May in north of range. **Eggs.** Usually 4, sometimes 3–5, rarely 6. Subelliptical. Smooth and slightly glossy. White or creamy-white; speckled, spotted and blotched with chestnut-red, reddish-brown and paler brownish-gray, gray or purple. Occasionally clouded with brown or with small blackish spots or scrawls. 18 × 14 mm. **Incubation.** Eggs laid at daily intervals. Incubation by female only, beginning with last or next-to-last egg. 13 days. **Nestling.** Altricial and downy. Scanty down on head, back and wings. **Nestling period.** Young tended by both parents. Eyes open at 4–5 days. Feathers break sheaths at 7–8 days. Young leave nest at 8–9 days.

COMMON YELLOWTHROAT *Geothlypis trichas* **Pl. 60**
Breeds in low undergrowth by water, in sloughs, on islands, and by creek and swamp edges. In tangled thickets of shrubs, weeds and vines, along hedgerows, woodland edge and similar sites. Nest just above the ground, or over water, in weeds, reeds, cat-tails, tule, grass-tussocks, brier bushes or similar situations; often at base of shrub or sapling, sometimes higher in weeds or shrubs up to 3 ft.
Nest. A bulky cup of dead grasses and leaves, ferns, weed stems, bark strips, grass-blades and moss; lined with fine grasses, vine tendrils, bark fibers and often hair. Loose material is occasionally built up above the rim of the cup, forming a partial hood. **Breeding season.** Begins late April in south to early June in north of range. Double-brooded. **Eggs.** Usually 4, sometimes 3–6. Subelliptical. Smooth and slightly glossy. White or creamy-white; speckled, spotted or blotched, and with occasional dark scrawls, of reddish-brown, brown, black, and paler reddish-buff, lilac and gray. Markings often form a wreath about the larger end. Pale markings may predominate. 17 × 13 mm. **Incubation.** By female only. 12 days. **Nestling.** Altricial and downy. Skin light orange. Down dark gray; on head, lower back and wings. Mouth red. Gape flanges yellow. **Nestling period.** Young tended by both parents. Eyes open at 4–5 days. Feathers break sheaths at 6–7 days. Young leave nest at 9–10 days.

GRAY-CROWNED YELLOWTHROAT *Geothlypis poliocephala* **Pl. 59**
Breeds in areas of grassland with scattered thickets and low trees, or dry hill-sides with scattered shrubs. Nest on a grass-tussock.
Nest. A stout cup of dry grasses and dead leaves; lined with finer grasses and hair. **Breeding season.** Begins late April? **Eggs.** Usually 4. Subelliptical. Smooth and slightly glossy. Creamy-white; speckled, spotted and blotched with chestnut-red, reddish-brown, brown and paler brownish-gray or buffish-gray. Sometimes a few small scrawls of blackish-brown. 17 × 14 mm. **Incubation.** No information. **Nestling.** No information. **Nestling period.** No information.

YELLOW-BREASTED CHAT *Icteria virens* **Pl. 60**
Breeds in thick tangled shrubby growth on woodland edge, old pastures; stream, pond and swamp edges, hedgerows and scrub country. Nest in a dense shrub or tangle, from about ground level to *c.* 5, sometimes 8 ft. up.
Nest. A cup of coarse grasses, dead leaves, weed and grass stems and bark strips; lined with finer grasses and weed stems. **Breeding season.** Begins early April in south to mid-May in north of range. **Eggs.** Usually 3–5, sometimes 6. Subelliptical. Smooth and slightly glossy. White or creamy-white; speckled, spotted and occasionally blotched boldly with chestnut-red, reddish-brown, brown, and paler gray and purple. 22 × 17 mm. **Incubation.** 11–15 days?

Nestling. Altricial and naked. Skin dull yellow. Mouth red. Gape flanges creamy-white. **Nestling period.** Young tended by both parents. Leave nest at 8–11 days?

RED-FACED WARBLER *Cardellina rubrifrons* **Pl. 59**
Breeds in northern woodland, coniferous or deciduous. Nest on the ground, on a bank or slope, against and concealed by a shrub, sapling, log, rock or herbage. **Nest.** A cup sunk in a small hollow made by bird. Of dead leaves and grasses, pine-needles, and cedar bark strips; lined with fine grasses and hair. **Breeding season.** Begins early May. **Eggs.** Usually 3–4. Long to short subelliptical. Smooth and slightly glossy. White; finely speckled, rarely spotted or with small blotches, of brown and pale gray. Often speckled overall with a slight concentration at larger end. 16 × 13 mm. **Incubation.** No information. **Nestling.** Mouth deep orange-yellow. **Nestling period.** No information.

HOODED WARBLER *Wilsonia citrina* **Pl. 60**
Breeds in moist deciduous woodland, where shrubby growth or thick undergrowth is present. Nests low in sapling, shrub, palmetto, cane clump or vine tangle. Often about 2 ft. up, sometimes 1–6 ft. up. Usually in a twig fork, often resembling lodged dead leaves.

Nest. A compact cup with a loose outer layer of dead leaves; a main cup of vine-bark strips, plant fibers, weed stems, down and dry catkins; lined with plant fibers, fine rootlets and moss fibers. **Breeding season.** Begins late April in south to late May in north of range. Double-brooded, and lost clutches replaced. **Eggs.** Usually 3–4, rarely 5. Subelliptical, sometimes short or long subelliptical. Smooth and slightly glossy. Creamy-white; speckled, spotted or blotched with reddish-brown, brown, and paler purplish-brown or brownish-gray. Markings often concentrated at the larger end, forming a wreath. 18 × 14 mm. **Incubation.** 12 days. **Nestling.** Altricial and downy. Down gray or brown? **Nestling period.** Young tended by both parents. 8–9 days

WILSON'S WARBLER *Wilsonia pusilla* **Pl. 60**
Breeds in open areas of northern forest, in willow and alder thickets, bogs with scattered small trees, and wet clearings with secondary growth. Nest on the ground, in moss or soil, at the base of a shrub or sapling, or hidden in herbage, in a grass-tussock, hidden in dry grass under low willow branches, or in a hollow in a bank with overhanging plants.

Nest. A bulky cup of dead leaves, bark shreds and strips, thin dead weed stems, grass blades and stems; lined with fine dry grasses, rootlets and hair. **Breeding season.** Begins late April in south to early June in north of range. **Eggs.** Usually 5, sometimes 4–6. Subelliptical to short subelliptical. Smooth and slightly glossy. White or creamy-white. Finely speckled, and spotted with chestnut-red, reddish-brown and paler brownish-gray. Often a wreath of speckling at the larger end. 16 × 12 mm. **Incubation.** By female alone, beginning with last egg 11–13 days. **Nestling.** No information. **Nestling period.** Young tended by both parents. Eyes open at 5–6 days, feathers break sheaths at 6–8 days. Young leave nest at 10–11 days.

CANADA WARBLER *Wilsonia canadensis* **Pl. 60**

Breeds in moist mixed woodland, usually where the canopy is broken by streams, bogs or gullies. Nest on or near the ground, in the roots of a fallen tree, in a cavity of a bank, or on the side of rocks, on a ledge, on a hummock, stump or fallen log, or on the ground under a shrub. Often concealed by overhanging plants.

Nest. A bulky cup of dry or decayed leaves, bark shreds, dead grass and weed stems, fern leaves, pine-needles and plant fibers; lined with plant fibers, fine rootlets and hair. **Breeding season.** Begins late May. **Eggs.** Usually 4, sometimes 3–5. Subelliptical to short subelliptical. Smooth and slightly glossy. White to creamy-white. Speckled, spotted and blotched with chestnut-red, reddish-brown and paler purple or gray. Sometimes marked in duller brown and black. Markings tend to form a wreath round larger end. 17 × 13 mm. **Incubation.** No information. **Nestling.** Altricial and downy. Down dark brown. **Nestling period.** Young tended by both parents.

AMERICAN REDSTART *Setophaga ruticilla* **Pl. 60**

Breeds in open deciduous woodland, or mixed woodland, orchards, secondary growth, trees in clearings, cultivated areas and bordering water, shade trees and shrubberies. Nest usually in a vertical fork of a sapling, shrub or tree; occasionally in vine tangle, or in old nest of a vireo. Nest usually 5–10 ft. up, sometimes 2–20 ft. up, or exceptionally much higher in big trees.

Nest. A firm, compact cup of grasses, bark fibers and strips, small rootlets, and vine tendrils; bound with spiders' webs and ornamented externally with lichen flakes, birch bark, seed heads and plant down; lined with fine grasses, plant and bark fibers and often hair. Built by female. **Breeding season.** Begins late May to early June. Single-brooded. **Eggs.** Usually 4, sometimes 3–5. Subelliptical to short subelliptical. Smooth and slightly glossy. White to creamy-white, or tinted grayish or greenish; speckled, spotted and blotched with shades of brown and reddish-brown, and with paler brownish-gray, gray and purple. Heavier markings often concentrated at larger end forming wreath, with finer speckling elsewhere. 16 × 12 mm. **Incubation.** By female alone. *c.* 12 days. **Nestling.** Altricial and downy. Down brown; on head and upper parts. Mouth red. Gape flanges yellow. **Nestling period.** Young tended by both parents. Eyes open at 4 days. Feathers break sheaths at 6–8 days. Young leave nest at 9 days.

PAINTED REDSTART *Setophaga picta* **Pl. 59**

Breeds in canyon oakwoods. Nest on the ground, on a slope or rocky face, under a tree or shrub root, or under a projecting rock, against an overhanging grass-tuft, or among grasses, ferns or vines which hide it.

Nest. A bulky, rather shallow cup of bark strips, weed-stem fibers, dead grasses and leaves; lined with finer grasses and hair. **Breeding season.** Begins late April. **Eggs.** Usually 4, sometimes 3–5. Subelliptical. Smooth and slightly glossy. Creamy-white; finely speckled with chestnut-red or reddish-brown, and paler brownish-gray or buffish-gray. Markings concentrated towards larger end. 16 × 13 mm. **Incubation.** No information. **Nestling.** Mouth deep orange-yellow. **Nestling period.** No information.

BLACKBIRDS AND ORIOLES *Icteridae*

Medium-sized insect- and fruit-eating birds. Arboreal or feeding on the ground. Nest a pensile cup, or long pensile bag suspended from a twig fork or loop of material at a twig tip; or a bulky cup in tree or shrub, or tall herbage, or a deep cup bound to stems of waterside plants, or a cup or domed nest on the ground in grasses. Two species are brood parasites, laying eggs in the nests of other birds which hatch them and rear the young. Eggs blue, pinkish or purplish, boldly marked, often with heavy scrawling or scribbling. Male's role varies from help with nest-building and feeding of young to none at all. Young with down, often long and scanty, brown to buff, gray or white. Mouth usually red and gape flanges yellow. Young fed on insects brought in bill. Male may take over care of young after they leave nest while female re-nests.

BOBOLINK *Dolichonyx oryzivorus* **Pl. 61**

Breeds in open grassland, preferring moist, lusher areas, meadows, and cultivated clovers and grain. Also in grassy marshland. Nest on the ground, in a small hollow.

Nest. A shallow hollow, sometimes made by the bird, containing a thin, shallow cup of dead grass and weed stems; lined with finer grasses. **Breeding season.** Begins mid- to late May. **Eggs.** Usually 5–6, sometimes 4–7. Subelliptical to oval. Smooth and glossy. Very pale blue or greenish, sometimes tinted by a brownish or purplish wash; boldly but sometimes sparsely blotched, mottled and scrawled, and sometimes with finer speckling and spotting of medium to deep brown, purplish-brown, or blackish-brown. 22 × 16 mm. **Incubation.** 11–13 days. **Nestling.** Altricial and downy. Down buffish. **Nestling period.** Young tended by both parents. Leave nest at 10–14 days. Cannot fly for some days.

EASTERN MEADOWLARK *Sturnella magna* **Pl. 61**

Breeds in open grassland, meadows and pastures, and in similar low herbage such as clover, alfalfa or young corn. Will also use areas such as orchards, with scattered trees. Nest on the ground in growing herbage, concealed by a domed top and overhanging grasses.

Nest. A large domed structure, nests usually having a roof of grasses woven into the growing herbage around the nest, leaving a fairly large side entrance. Of dry grasses, the cup lined with finer grasses and sometimes hair. Nest set into a small hollow which may be made by bird. Built by female only. **Breeding season.** Begins early April in south to early May in north of range. Double-brooded, and lost clutches may be replaced. **Eggs.** Usually 3–5, sometimes 2–7. Short subelliptical to short oval. Smooth and glossy. White; speckled, spotted or with small blotches of reddish-brown, purplish-brown, chestnut-red, light red, light brown and pale lilac and purple. The markings tend to be sparse and largely concentrated at larger end with fine speckling elsewhere. 28 × 20 mm. **Incubation.** By female only. 13–15 days. **Nestling.** Altricial and downy. Skin orange-red. Down abundant, pale gray; on head, back, wings and thighs. **Nestling period.** Young tended by both parents, but mainly by female. Eyes open at 5 days. Young leave nest at 11–12 days. Male may take over feeding of young out of nest while female re-nests.

WESTERN MEADOWLARK *Sturnella neglecta* **Pl. 61**

Breeds on open grassland of prairies and river valleys, in mountain areas of open and broken woodland, in more open sagebrush, in pastures, and in cultivated areas with clover, alfalfa and grain or similar crops.

Nest. A domed structure like that of Eastern Meadowlark. In both species the birds' visits to the nest entrance through tall grass may result in a small tunnel being formed. **Breeding season.** Begins mid-February in south to mid-June in north of range. Double-brooded and lost clutches may be replaced. **Eggs.** Usually 5, sometimes 3–7. Similar to those of Eastern Meadowlark. 28 × 21 mm. **Incubation.** Eggs laid at daily intervals. Incubation by female only. 13–15 days. **Nestling.** Like that of Eastern Meadowlark. **Nestling period.** Young tended by both parents. Leave nest at *c.* 12 days, before being able to fly. Fed by parents for *c.* 2 weeks more.

YELLOW-HEADED BLACKBIRD *Xanthocephalus xanthocephalus* **Pl. 61**

Breeds in tall herbage growing in water on the edge of lakes and open waters, and on deeper marshes or sloughs. Nest in a thick growth of tall vegetation – tule, reeds, bulrushes or cat-tails – over water of reasonable depth. The nest is bound to several stems, usually 2–3 ft. up, occasionally ½–6 ft. up. Pairs nest in colonies, often very large, with nests fairly close together.

Nest. A deep cup of long stems and blades of wet, partly decayed grasses, woven around supporting stems to form a tight cup, lined with dead leaves of plants, coarse grasses, roots and decayed plant material, firmly packed and with an inner lining of narrow leaves, leaf strips or fine grasses. Occasionally fine material

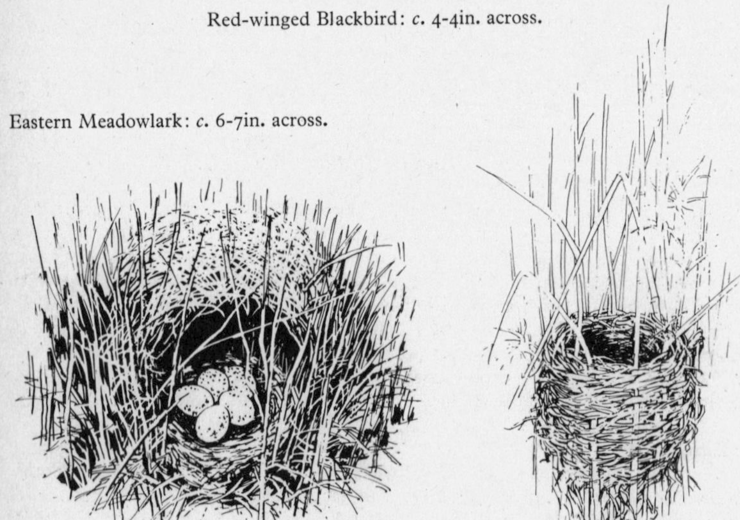

Red-winged Blackbird: *c.* 4-4in. across.

Eastern Meadowlark: *c.* 6-7in. across.

built above rim to form a partial canopy. **Breeding season.** Begins late April in south to early June in north. **Eggs.** Usually 4, occasionally 3, rarely 5. Long subelliptical to long oval. Smooth and glossy. Very pale bluish-white; profusely and finely speckled and mottled with brown, purplish-brown or reddish-brown, usually with denser markings at the lower end. Markings occasionally coalescing to form heavier but poorly-defined overall spotting or blotching. 26 × 18 mm. **Incubation.** By female alone. 10–13 days. **Nestling.** Altricial and downy. Down sparse, buff; on head and back. **Nestling period.** By female alone or by both parents. Young feather by 8–9 days, leave nest unable to fly at 9–12 days, and can make short flights by *c.* 20 days.

RED-WINGED BLACKBIRD *Agelaius phoeniceus* Pl. 61

Breeds usually by or over water in marshes, swamps or wet meadows, or in tall herbage bordering open water or slower streams; in cat-tails, rushes, sedges, large grass tussocks, waterside shrubs or low trees. Occasionally in shrubs, bushes, and tall herbage some distance from water. Exceptionally in trees.

Nest. A deep cup of long leaves and stems woven tightly around the upright supports, with a layer of broken plant material and fibers, roots, decayed leaves, and some mud, firmly shaped; and lined with fine dry grasses or thin rushes. **Breeding season.** Begins late March in south to late May in north of range. Possibly double- or treble-brooded. **Eggs.** Usually 4, sometimes 3–5. Subelliptical to long subelliptical. Smooth and glossy. Very pale blue, sometimes tinted pinkish or purplish; sparingly scribbled, scrawled or with a few blotches or spots of black, blackish-brown or blackish-purple, and paler purple and gray. Larger markings sometimes superimposed on pale brown or purple marks. Sometimes indistinct blotching or clouding of brown or purple. Markings tend to be concentrated towards the larger end. 25 × 18 mm. **Incubation.** By female alone. 10–12 days. **Nestling.** Altricial and downy. Skin scarlet. Down whitish, scanty; on head, lower back, wings and thighs. Mouth red. Gape flanges yellow. **Nestling period.** Young tended by both parents. Feather sheaths break at 6–8 days. Young leave at 10–11 days. Present around nest area for *c.* 10 days longer.

TRI-COLORED BLACKBIRD *Agelaius tricolor* Pl. 61

Breeds in sloughs, swamps, marshes where tall growth of water plants – cat-tails, tule and the like – is present. Or in similar growth bordering open water. Nesting usually occurs in dense and sometimes enormous colonies. Nests may be very close together and colonies may extend into shrubs and trees in the area, or into grain or similar crops nearby, or tall herbaceous growth on dry ground. Nest may be almost at ground level or several feet up.

Nest. A deep cup, bound to upright stems of growing plants, the outer layer of long leaves and stems woven tightly around supports, and long coiled leaves inside. There is a middle layer of broken and decayed leaves, roots and muddy plant material, compacted together; and an inner lining of fine grasses. **Breeding season.** Begins late March to early April; but in south-west may occasionally breed in fall, October to November. **Eggs.** Usually 4, rarely 5–6. Similar to those of the Red-winged Blackbird. 28 × 20 mm. **Incubation.** 11 days. **Nestling.** Altricial and downy. **Nestling period.** Young tended by female alone or by both parents. Young leave at *c.* 13 days, but may leave much earlier if disturbed.

ORCHARD ORIOLE *Icterus spurius* **Pl. 61**

Breeds in tree belts and riverine woodland along watercourses, in orchards, in shade trees around farms and settlements, or in scattered trees in cultivated areas. Nest in a tree, less frequently in a shrub, 4–50 ft. up. Has also been found nesting in *Phragmites* reeds down to 2–3 ft. Nest usually suspended in a twig fork at the tip of a branch, but may be built into a vertical fork, or a hanging tuft of Spanish Moss.

Nest. A pensile or semi-pensile rounded cup, attached to supports at the rim and sometimes at the sides. Of long fine stems and fibers woven around to form a thick cup, lined with some plant down. **Breeding season.** Begins late April in south to early June in north of range. **Eggs.** Usually 4–5, sometimes 3–7. Long subelliptical to long oval. Smooth and glossy. Very pale blue; with scrawls, small blotches, spots and specks of black, blackish-brown, blackish-purple, and paler gray and purple. Markings often sparse and mainly around or at the large end. 20 × 15 mm. **Incubation.** By female alone. 12–15 days. **Nestling.** Altricial and downy. Down sparse; on head and back. **Nestling period.** Young tended by both parents. Leave nest at 11–14 days.

BLACK-HEADED ORIOLE *Icterus graduacauda*

Breeds in dense thickets with scattered taller trees along watercourses. Nest usually in a tree or shrub, 5–15 ft. up, suspended in an upright fork of a terminal branch. Attached at both rim and sides to twigs, like that of Orchard Oriole.

Nest. A semi-pensile structure. A smallish, rounded cup of fine long grasses woven, often while green, around the supports and twigs to form a firm cup lined with finer grasses or grass-heads. **Breeding season.** Begins late April. **Eggs.** Usually 3–5. Long subelliptical to subelliptical. Smooth and slightly glossy. Very pale bluish or grayish white, sometimes with a purple wash. Scribbled, scrawled, blotched or sometimes spotted or speckled with brown, purplish-brown, blackish-purple, purplish-red or paler purple or gray. Sometimes with only a few spots or fine scribbles at the larger end; sometimes clouded or blotched with lighter reddish-brown and with darker speckling of the same. 26 × 19 mm. **Incubation.** No information. **Nestling.** No information. **Nestling period.** No information.

SPOTTED-BREASTED ORIOLE *Icterus pectoralis*

Breeds in tall trees, up to 60 ft. Nest an elongated pensile bag suspended from a twig fork or tip, at the end of a branch.

Nest. An elongated pear-shaped bag, 18 in. long by 6 in. wide at the bottom end. Suspended from forked twigs which form part of the rim of the entrance. Shallower, cup-shaped nests have been built by introduced Florida birds. Nest of long plant fibers and fine aerial roots of epiphytic plants woven together. Some of the material ends may hang down below the bottom of the nest. Nest cavity with a thick lining of fine plant fibers. Built by female alone in 6–7 days. **Breeding season.** No information. **Eggs.** Usually 3–4. Long subelliptical. Smooth and slightly glossy. Pale bluish-white, scribbled and scrawled with black and pale lilac. **Incubation.** No information. **Nestling.** No information. **Nestling period.** No information.

HOODED ORIOLE *Icterus cucullatus* Pl. 61

Breeds in woodland along watercourses and in shade trees and shrubs around houses. Nest a cup in a tree or shrub, 10–45 ft. up, suspended between twigs, or in a fork and attached at sides as well as rim, or sewn by fibers to the underside of a palm or palmetto leaf, the bird entering between nest-rim and the leaf above. At earlier periods nest recorded in, and of, Spanish Moss.

Nest. A cup a little deeper than wide. Woven of fine grasses and long plant fibers to form a strong, firm, fibrous cup; lined with some plant down, or occasionally a little wool, feathers or hair. **Breeding season.** Begins early April to early May. Two or sometimes three broods. **Eggs.** Usually 4, sometimes 3–5. Long subelliptical to long oval. Smooth and glossy. Very pale blue, sometimes with a slight pink or purple wash. Finely scribbled and scrawled or with a few elongated blotches or specks of black, usually with the markings concentrated at the larger end. Sometimes almost unmarked. 22 × 15 mm. **Incubation.** Eggs laid at daily intervals. Incubation by female alone. 13 days. **Nestling.** Altricial and downy. Down sparse; on head and back. **Nestling period.** Young tended by both parents. Leave nest at *c.* 14 days.

LICHTENSTEIN'S ORIOLE *Icterus gularis*

Breeds in low trees of semi-desert areas. Nest suspended from a twig near the tip of a branch in a tree, usually 15–30 ft. up, sometimes 7–50 ft. up, in an exposed position.

Nest. A very elongated, pear-shaped bag, 1–2 ft. long and *c.* 6 in. wide at the basal nest cavity. Woven mainly or entirely of aerial roots of epiphytic plants and long plant fibers. Loose ends of material may hang down around and below the nest. Suspended from a twig fork or a loop of material bound to a twig and forming an entrance at the top. The entrance may be widened and the side torn open during the nestling period. Nest cavity lined with plant fibers and plant down. **Breeding season.** Begins late April. Possibly double-brooded. **Eggs.** Usually 3–4. Long subelliptical to long elliptical. Smooth and glossy. Pale bluish-white; scribbled, scrawled and with irregular spots and small blotches of black and paler lilac. 29 × 19 mm. **Incubation.** No information. **Nestling.** No information. **Nestling period.** Young tended by both parents. Male feeds young of fledged first brood while female re-nests.

SCOTT'S ORIOLE *Icterus parisorum* Pl. 61

Breeds by semi-arid and desert areas, on the edges of dry plains and in open pinyon-juniper woodland on foothills and mountains. Nests are frequently in yuccas where these are present but elsewhere in trees 4–20 ft. up. A typical site is in dead leaves under a yucca crown. Nest a semi-pensile cup attached to the edges of yucca leaves or bound to supporting twigs in trees.

Nest. A semi-pensile or pensile cup, strongly woven of fine grasses and plant fibers and attached to supports at its rim and sometimes at its sides. Lined with fine grasses and down. **Breeding season.** Begins late April to mid-May. Double-brooded. **Eggs.** Usually 3, sometimes 2–4. Long subelliptical to subelliptical. Smooth and slightly glossy. Very pale blue; blotched, streaked and spotted with black, purplish-brown, chestnut-red, and paler brownish-gray, gray or purple. 24 × 17 mm. **Incubation.** By female alone. 14 days. **Nestling.** No information. **Nestling period.** No information.

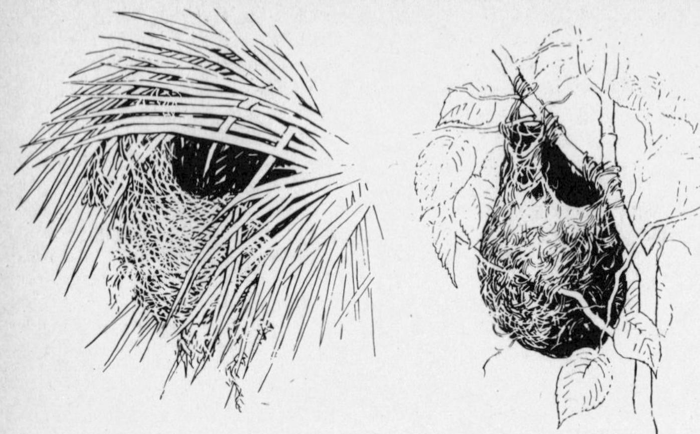

Scott's Oriole: *c.* 4-5in. across. Northern Oriole: *c.* 3-4in. across.

NORTHERN ORIOLE *Icterus galbula* (Includes Baltimore Oriole, *I. g. galbula*, and Bullock's Oriole, *I. g. bullocki*) **Pl. 61**

Breeds in scattered trees in more open areas, in shade trees, orchards and similar sites. Nest suspended in a twig fork, usually at the end of a branch, mostly about 20–30 ft. up, sometimes 6–60 ft. up. Bullock's Oriole nests often fastened to supporting twigs at sides as well as at top; in a tree or shrub, 6–15 ft. up, exceptionally up to 50 ft., set among twigs, sometimes in a mistletoe bunch.

Nest. A deep pensile pouch, bound to forked twigs at its rim and with twigs sometimes extending down and bound to the sides. Of long plant fibers, vine bark, hair, string when available, and similar long material, woven into a deep cup; lined with hair, plant down, wool and fine grasses and moss. Built by both sexes. **Breeding season.** Begins late April in south to late May in north of range. **Eggs.** Usually 4–5, sometimes 3–6. Long oval to long subelliptical, sometimes biconical. Smooth and glossy. Very pale bluish, sometimes with faint purplish tint. Scribbled and scrawled with black or blackish-purple and paler purple or gray. Markings often fine and may form a wreath of scribbling around larger end, often sparse elsewhere. There may be limited purple suffusion around heavier markings. 24 × 16 mm. **Incubation.** By female alone. *c.* 14 days. **Nestling.** Altricial and downy. Skin pink. Down long and scanty, white; on head and back. Mouth reddish. Gape flanges yellow. **Nestling period.** Young tended by both parents.

RUSTY BLACKBIRD *Euphagus carolinus* **Pl. 61**

Breeds usually by open waters with swampy shores, in woodland areas, where trees mix with swamp. Nest in a tree or shrub usually growing in or by water, frequently in conifers. 2–20 ft. up.

Nest. A stout bulky cup of twigs, lichens, including *Usnea*, and sometimes long grasses. A middle layer is a firmly moulded bowl of decaying plant material smoothed and lined with dry grasses, fibers and sometimes thin twigs. **Breeding season.** Begins early to mid-May. **Eggs.** Usually 4–5, sometimes 6. Eggs similar to those of Brewer's Blackbird. 26 × 19 mm. **Incubation.** By female alone, beginning with first egg. 14 days. **Nestling.** Altricial and downy. Down long and thin, dark brown. **Nestling period.** Young tended by both parents. Eyes open at 5–6 days. Young leave nest at *c.* 13 days.

BREWER'S BLACKBIRD *Euphagus cyanocephalus* **Pl. 61**

Breeds in a variety of habitats and sites, but more particularly in trees or shrubs adjoining open water or marshy areas or along watercourses. Also in shade trees and shrubs of cultivated or urban areas. Usually in small colonies or groups or pairs. Males sometimes polygamous. Nests in a variety of sites, in trees or shrubs, in a fork or on a branch, often in conifers, from 150 ft. downwards, to bushes, tall sedges in wet marshes, or on the ground in plant tufts on the top of a steep bank or growing in water. Nest sometimes in cavity or broken tree.

Nest. A stout cup of fine twigs and grasses with a middle layer of grasses, pine-needles and fibres mixed with mud and dung and forming a firm cup, with an inner lining of rootlets and hair. **Breeding season.** Begins late March in south to late May in north of range. Double-brooded. **Eggs.** Usually 5–6, sometimes 3–7. Subelliptical to short subelliptical or oval. Smooth and glossy. Very pale blue or greenish-blue, sometimes suffused by a pink, brown or purple wash; speckled, spotted, blotched or mottled in purplish-brown, brown or purple, and paler purple and purplish-brown or buff. Markings are frequently poorly-defined and additional spots or scrawls of blackish-brown may be present. Occasionally markings are sparse and largely confined to the larger end. 25 × 19 mm. **Incubation.** By female alone. 12–13 days. **Nestling.** Altricial and downy. Down blackish. **Nestling period.** Young tended by both parents. Leave nest at 13 days and fed for further 12–13 days.

BOAT-TAILED GRACKLE *Cassidex major* **Pl. 61**

Nest usually in vegetation by or over water, in sawgrass, bulrushes, flags, shrubs and trees. Nest usually low, 3–12 ft. up, but sometimes up to 50 ft. in trees. Usually breeds in colonies. Male takes no part in nesting other than defence against predators.

Nest. A bulky and compact cup of rushes, flags, coarser grasses and stalks, with an inner lining of bark strips and fibres, grass stems and decayed waterplant material bound with rotted plant material and mud to form a firm cup, lined with fine rootlets and dry grasses. Built by female alone. **Breeding season.** Begins early March in south to late April in north of range. Breeding in November–December has occurred in Florida. Double- or sometimes treble-brooded. **Eggs.** Usually 3–4, sometimes 5. Long subelliptical to subelliptical or long oval. Smooth and glossy. Pale blue or tinted to varying degrees with pink or purple. Boldly scribbled or scrawled and with occasional blotches or spots of black, and paler purple or gray. Dark markings may have blurred purplish edges or pale purple suffusion around them. Markings often sparse. 32 × 22 mm. **Incubation.** By female alone. 13–14 days. **Nestling.** Altricial and downy. Down long and sparse, gray; on head, back, wings and thighs. Mouth bright red. **Nestling period.** Young tended by female alone. Eyes open at 3–5 days. Young feathered at *c.* 14 days. Leave nest at 20–23 days.

GREAT-TAILED GRACKLE *Cassidex mexicanus* **Pl. 61**

Nests most frequently in vegetation by or over water, in rushes, reeds and canebrakes, shrubs and trees; in trees or thickets along watercourses in drier regions; in chaparral and mesquite; in coastal cactus, yuccas and grasses; and shade trees around houses. On Texas coast nests in large numbers in heron colonies, with some nests in herons' stick nests. Usually breeds in colonies, often very large with nests close together. Male takes no part in nesting other than defence against predators.

Nest. A bulky cup of weed stems, coarse grasses, strips of bark, plant fibers, or sometimes Spanish Moss, lined with mud or cowdung to form a firm structure with an inner lining of fine grasses and rootlets, feathers and other soft material. Built by female alone. **Breeding season.** Begins early April. Sometimes double-brooded. **Eggs.** Usually 3–4, sometimes 5. Long subelliptical to subelliptical or long oval. Smooth and glossy. Pale blue or tinted to varying degrees with pink, purple or brownish. Boldly scribbled or scrawled and with occasional blotches or spots of black, and pale purple or gray. Dark markings may have blurred purplish edges or pale purple suffusions around them, less widely dispersed than in the Boat-tailed Grackle and more apparent at the larger end. Markings often sparse. 33 × 22 mm. **Incubation.** Eggs usually laid at daily interval. Incubation by female alone. 13–14 days. **Nestling.** Altricial and downy. Skin salmon-colored. Down long and sparse; gray; on head, back, wings and thighs. Mouth bright red. **Nestling period.** Young tended by female alone. Eyes open at 3–5 days. Young feathered at *c.* 14 days. Leave nest at 20–23 days.

COMMON GRACKLE *Quiscalus quiscula* **Pl. 61**

Breeds through open and cultivated country, especially in wetter areas. Nests in trees, particularly conifers, in low shrubs and bushes, on dry land and in marshes and in tall swamp vegetation. Also in shade trees around houses, and in niches and ledges on or in buildings. Sometimes in holes in large dead trees and stumps, or in stick nests of large birds. Nests from ground level to *c.* 45 ft. up, but often low. Nests usually in colonies, and at times close together.

Nest. A bulky, externally loose cup, of twigs, weed stems, coarse grasses, *Usnea* lichen, Spanish Moss or seaweed in some areas, pine-needles and inner cup of mud or dung; lined with fine dry grasses and rootlets, a few feathers, or hair, and sometimes paper, string or rags. **Breeding season.** Begins late March in south to mid-May in north of range. Sometimes double-brooded. **Eggs.** Usually 4–5, sometimes 6, rarely 7. Long to short subelliptical. Smooth and glossy. Pale blue, sometimes tinted pinkish; with bold scrawls or scribbles, spots or blotches, and a little fine speckling or spotting in black, blackish-purple or blackish-brown. Markings often show blurred purple or brown edges; and paler parts of shell may show variable clouding or suffusion with brown or purplish-brown. 28 × 21 mm. **Incubation.** By female alone, beginning with next-to-last egg. 12–14 days. **Nestling.** Altricial and downy. Down pale brown. Irides brown. **Nestling period.** Young tended by both parents. Brooded by female only. Leave nest at 10–17 days; usually at *c.* 12 days, and only remain in vicinity of nest for 2–3 days.

BROWN-HEADED COWBIRD *Molothrus ater* **Pls. 16, 61**

Breeds over a wide range on and around farmland. Promiscuous and a brood parasite, eggs being laid in the nests of other bird species and the young reared by these hosts, sometimes at the expense of the host's young. The principal hosts are various species of finches, vireos, warblers and flycatchers; but eggs appear to be laid at times in almost any available nest of birds of moderate size, some of which might rear young, but some wholly unsuitable. Usually only one egg is laid in a nest, but several eggs may be laid by different cowbird females. Occasionally eggs are ejected or built over by the host. **Breeding season.** Begins early April in south to mid-May in north of range. **Eggs.** Up to *c.* 30 laid by a female in one season. Short subelliptical to elliptical, or subelliptical. Smooth and glossy. White or faintly bluish or greenish; profusely and finely speckled or mottled with brown, purplish-brown, or reddish-brown, and paler gray or purple. Markings sometimes show longitudinal elongation. Usually finely marked overall but sometimes greater concentration at larger end. 21 × 16 mm. **Incubation.** 11–12 days. Often hatching a little sooner than eggs of host. **Nestling.** Altricial and downy. Skin flesh-color. Mouth deep pink. Gape flanges cream color. **Nestling period.** Young develop very rapidly. The young of the host often survive with the cowbird but sometimes fail to compete successfully for food. Cowbird leaves nest at 10 days. Host continues to feed it for a further *c.* 2 weeks.

BRONZED COWBIRD *Tangavius aeneus* **Pl. 61**

Breeds in open areas and farmland. Like the Brown-headed Cowbird a brood parasite. The typical hosts for this species are the various orioles (*Icterus* species) but occasionally eggs are laid apparently at random in almost any nest of birds of moderate size, some of which might rear young, but some wholly unsuitable. Includes grosbeaks, sparrows, thrashers, wrens, warblers, flycatchers and even ground doves. Normally only one egg laid in a nest, but several females may lay in the same nest. **Breeding season.** Begins early April. **Eggs.** Number normally produced by a single female not known. Subelliptical or tending to biconical. Smooth and glossy. Very pale blue or greenish-blue. Sometimes with a few scattered pale specks of brown. 23 × 18 mm. **Incubation.** Period not recorded. **Nestling.** Altricial and downy. Skin pinkish-orange becoming brownish. Down gray; on head, back, wings and thighs. Mouth reddish. Gape flanges white. Bill, legs and feet yellowish. **Nestling period.** Young develop very rapidly. Young of host sometimes survive with young cowbird, but are sometimes unable to compete. Eyes open at 5 days. Feathers break sheaths at 6–7 days. Young cowbird leaves at *c.* 11 days. Fed by hosts for a further *c.* 2 weeks.

OLD WORLD SPARROWS *Ploceidae*

Small, seed-eating birds. Usually sociable, nesting near each other. Build domed nests in trees or bushes; in holes make domed nests or cups. Eggs very variably patterned, without apparent need for pattern. Young naked; with yellowish-pink to red mouth and yellow to pale yellow gape flanges; fed mainly on insects.

EURASIAN TREE SPARROW *Passer montanus* **Pl. 58**

Breeds in sites offering nest-holes in regions of cultivation or wasteland. Nest a hole in a tree, cliff, quarry, wall or thatched roof, haystack, thick creepers on walls or rocks, pipe or mammal hole.

Nest. A domed structure or untidy cup of plant stalks and twigs; lined with down and feathers. Built by both sexes. **Breeding season.** Begins April. Double- or treble-brooded. **Eggs.** Usually 4–6, rarely 2–9. Subelliptical. Smooth and slightly glossy. Variable, but less so than those of the House Sparrow, being darker, browner and smaller. Ground color white to very pale gray; heavily marked with spots, small blotches or speckling, usually in dark brown, sometimes purplish or grayish. Markings often heavy enough to obscure ground color. At times very fine speckling makes eggs appear uniform in color but usually darkening towards the larger end. Markings tend to concentrate towards the larger end. Many clutches show one or two pale, sparsely-marked eggs. 19 × 14 mm. **Incubation.** By both sexes. 11–14 days. **Nestling.** Altricial and naked. Mouth pink, sometimes with dark spot at tongue tip. Gape flanges pale yellow. **Nestling period.** Young tended by both parents. 12–14 days in nest.

HOUSE SPARROW *Passer domesticus* **Pl. 58**

Breeds around or near human habitation, usually in association with cultivation. Nest in a hole or crevice of any kind in or near a building. In creepers growing on buildings, or occasionally among twigs in trees.

Nest. In trees a neat rounded domed structure with side entrance, in creepers or crevices an untidy domed structure, or in holes may be a cup. Of straw, plant stems and any rubbish such as paper, string or cloth; lined with feathers, hair and wool. Built by both sexes, but mainly by the male. **Breeding season.** Usually begins about May, but variable, and exceptional nests have been recorded in most months. Double- or triple-brooded. **Eggs.** Usually 3–5, rarely up to 8. Subelliptical. Smooth and only slightly glossy. White, or faintly tinted greenish or grayish; very variably marked with spots, speckling or small blotches of gray, blue-gray, greenish-gray, purplish-gray, black, brown or purplish-brown. Eggs may vary within a clutch, usually one being much more sparsely marked and appearing whiter. Rarely unmarked. 23 × 16 mm. **Incubation.** Chiefly by the female, beginning with the completion of the clutch. 11–14 days. **Nestling.** Altricial and naked. Mouth pinkish-yellow. Gape flanges pale yellow. **Nestling period.** Young fed by both parents, mainly on insects brought in the bill. 15 days in nest.

FINCHES *Fringillidae*

Small, seed-eating birds. Nests in trees, shrubs or terrestrial herbage. Nest a cup, usually substantial and well-made; varying from the neat downy cup of the Goldfinch to the looser stick nest of the Evening Grosbeak. Nest usually built by female. Eggs usually very pale blue, variably but often sparsely marked in purplish or red, the markings largely confined to the larger end. Often several broods. Sometimes a number of pairs nest near each other in a social group. The female incubates alone and may be fed by the male. Young are downy, with red mouths and yellowish or white gape flanges. Both adults tend them, but if successive broods overlap the male may care for fledged young while the female begins re-nesting. Young are usually fed on regurgitated seeds and plant material. Young rely on parents for food for a while after leaving the nest and may follow them, noisily begging for food.

EVENING GROSBEAK *Hesperiphona vespertina* **Pl. 62**

Breeds in northern spruce forest, and in montane conifer forest elsewhere. Nest usually high in a tree, coniferous or deciduous, in a crotch, or close to the trunk, or well out towards the end of a conifer branch, where foliage offers concealment.

Nest. A loosely constructed cup of sticks, untidily put together and elliptical in shape, with some moss, lichens and rootlets woven into it, and an inner cup of finer material; rootlets and some hair and fibers. **Breeding season.** Begins mid-May in south to late June in north of range. **Eggs.** Usually 3–4, sometimes 2–5. Subelliptical. Smooth and glossy. Light blue or greenish-blue, speckled, spotted and with blotches and large scrawls of dull purplish-brown, olive-brown or purplish-gray; the markings very sparse and bold and mainly concentrated at the larger end. Resembles egg of Red-winged Blackbird in color and pattern. 24 × 17 mm. **Incubation.** Eggs laid at daily intervals. Incubation by female only, fed by male. 12–14 days. **Nestling.** Altricial and downy. Skin dark. White down on head, wings, back and thighs. Bill yellow, gape flanges white. Mouth violet and red. **Nestling period.** Young tended by both parents. Fed on regurgitated insects. Eyes open at 4–6 days. Young leave nest at 13–14 days.

PURPLE FINCH *Carpodacus purpureus* **Pl. 62**

Breeds in open woodland, parkland, cultivation with trees, and areas of scattered trees and shrubby growth; favoring conifers in the east part of the range. Nest in a tree, in conifers usually high up and well-hidden in foliage, elsewhere in deciduous trees and in lower sites.

Nest. A cup of fine twigs, grasses and rootlets; lined with moss, hair or wool. **Breeding season.** Begins early to mid-May. Usually single-brooded, but may be double-brooded in the south-west. **Eggs.** Usually 4–5, sometimes 3–6. Subelliptical to oval. Smooth and slightly glossy. Pale light blue, finely speckled, spotted and with, occasionally, scrawls in black and paler purple; the markings small and sparse, often concentrated at the larger end, the purple markings often larger and more numerous. 20 × 15 mm. **Incubation.** By female only, fed by male. 13 days. **Nestling.** No information. **Nestling period.** Young tended by both parents. Leave nest at *c.* 14 days.

CASSIN'S FINCH *Carpodacus cassinii* **Pl. 62**

Breeds in mountain conifer forests. Nest usually in a conifer, high up and usually well out on a branch. Also occurs at lower levels and in deciduous trees.

Nest. A loose cup of thin twigs, weed stems, rootlets and lichen; with a finer lining of rootlets, hair, wool and bark fiber. **Breeding season.** Usually begins mid-May. Probably double-brooded at times. **Eggs.** Usually 4–5, sometimes 3–6. Subelliptical to long subelliptical. Smooth and slightly glossy. Light blue, finely speckled and spotted in black and pale purple, the markings sparse and often concentrated at the larger end. Purple spots tend to be larger and more numerous. Eggs sometimes unmarked. 20 × 15 mm. **Incubation.** By female only. 12–14 days. **Nestling.** No information. **Nestling period.** Young tended by both parents. Fed by regurgitation.

HOUSE FINCH *Carpodacus mexicanus* **Pl. 62**

Breeds in cultivated areas and around buildings. More rarely in trees, near water, in montane country. Nests in a variety of sites, where a raised ledge or cavity is available. On branches of trees or shrubs, on cacti, in cavities of trees or walls, old nests of other birds, from grosbeaks to cliff swallows, very exceptionally on the ground. Built by female. Nests may be re-used for second broods and in subsequent years.

Nest. Cup of fine weed and grass stems, leaves, rootlets, thin twigs, string, wool and feathers, with similar but finer material as lining. **Breeding season.** Begins late February in south to mid- or late April in north of range. Often double-brooded, sometimes treble-brooded. **Eggs.** Usually 4–5, sometimes 2–6. Subelliptical to long subelliptical. Smooth and slightly glossy. Very pale blue, with or without some very fine but scanty black and pale purple speckling, usually confined to the larger end; or a wreath of very fine scrawls around the larger end. 19 × 14 mm. **Incubation.** Eggs laid at daily intervals. Incubation by female alone, fed by male. 12–14 days. **Nestling.** Altricial and downy. Down long and greyish-white. **Nestling period.** Young tended by both parents. Brooded mainly by female. Fed by regurgitation. Droppings are not removed after first 3 days and nest-edge becomes soiled. Eyes open at 4 days. Main feather growth at 3–6 days. Young leave nest at 14–16 days.

PINE GROSBEAK *Pinicola enucleator* **Pl. 62**

Breeds in coniferous or mixed forest. Nest in birch, conifer or juniper, fairly low, about 2–10 ft. up.

Nest. A loose structure of twigs; with an inner cup of fine roots, grass and moss. Built by female. **Breeding season.** Begins late May to early June. Single-brooded. **Eggs.** Usually 4, sometimes 2–5. Subelliptical. Smooth and moderately glossy. Deep light blue; sparsely spotted and blotched with bold black and purplish-brown spots or small blotches, and more profusely marked with pale lilac or purplish speckling or spotting. Often most heavily marked at the larger end. 26 × 18 mm. **Incubation.** By female only, fed by male. 13–14 days. **Nestling.** No information. **Nestling period.** Young fed by both parents. Food regurgitated. *c.* 14 days.

ROSY FINCH *Leucosticte tephrocotis* (All three forms are included here) **Pl. 62**

Breeds on mountains at high altitudes where bare rocky slopes are present. Nest on a sheltered rock ledge, or in a crevice, hole or cave.

Nest. A cup of Sphagnum moss or dry grasses, with coarser stems, grasses and rootlets towards the inside, and lined with soft material; feathers, fur, hair, fine grasses and similar material. Built by female. **Breeding season.** Mid-May to mid-June. Single-brooded, but lost clutches may be replaced. **Eggs.** Usually 4–5, sometimes 2–6. Subelliptical to oval. Smooth and slightly glossy. Pure white and unmarked. 23 × 16 mm. **Incubation.** By female alone. 12–14 days. **Nestling.** Altricial and downy. Down sparse, long and white, on head and back. Gape flanges yellow. Mouth bright red. **Nestling period.** Young tended by both parents. Fed by regurgitation. Eyes open at 4 days, feathers break sheaths at 7–11 days. Young leave nest at 18–20 days, fed by adults for 2 weeks more and remaining with them until Fall.

COMMON REDPOLL *Acanthis flammea* **Pl. 62**

Breeds in mixed conifer and birch woodland, cultivation with plantations and shrubberies, birch scrub, dwarf trees of semi-barrens and tundra. Nest in a tree, shrub, or bush, often high in trees, but at times down to ground level. Pairs often nest near each other in loose associations.

Nest. A small, untidy cup of fine twigs, grass and plant stems; lined with plant down, feathers and hair. In arctic areas old nests may be relined and re-used in subsequent years. **Breeding season.** Begins late April in west to June in east. Single- or double-brooded. **Eggs.** Usually 4–5, sometimes 3–7. Subelliptical. Smooth and slightly glossy or non-glossy. Pale blue, marked with fine specks, spots, small blotches and scrawls; many of them in pale pink or lilac, and sparser reddish-brown and purple marks. Markings mostly concentrated at larger end. 17 × 13 mm. **Incubation.** By female alone. 10–13 days. **Nestling.** Altricial and downy. Down fairly long and thick; dark gray. Mouth red with two pale spots on palate. Gape flanges yellow. **Nestling period.** Young tended by both parents. Eyes open at 5 days. No removal of dropping by adults during most of period. Young leave at 11–14 days.

HOARY REDPOLL *Acanthis hornemanni* **Pl. 62**

Breeds in northern scrub and tundra. Nest in a low tree or shrub, or on the ground sheltered by a rock.

Nest. A cup of grasses and twigs, sometimes rootlets; lined with feathers, hair and plant down. Old nests may be relined and re-used in subsequent years. **Breeding season.** Begins late May to late June. Single-brooded. **Eggs.** Usually 4–5, rarely 3–6. Similar to those of Common Redpoll but larger and a little paler in ground color. 18 × 13 mm. **Incubation.** By female alone, beginning with second or third egg, 14–15 days in all. **Nestling.** No information; probably similar to Common Redpoll. **Nestling period.** Young tended by both parents. Brooded by female only for *c.* 10 days. Young leave nest at 10–14 days.

PINE SISKIN *Spinus pinus* **Pl. 62**

Breeds in forests, usually conifers. Nest in a tree or shrub, usually at medium height but sometimes 3–50 ft. up. Frequently in a conifer out on a branch, well-hidden in foliage; usually resting in or on a twig fork.

Nest. A fairly large cup of twigs, rootlets and grass; with a finer lining of feathers, hair, fur, fine rootlets and fibers. **Breeding season.** Begins late March to early April. Possibly double-brooded. **Eggs.** Usually 3–5, sometimes 2–6. Subelliptical to short subelliptical. Very pale blue or greenish-blue; speckled, spotted, blotched or scrawled with purplish-black and pale lilac. The markings usually sparse and confined to a wreath around the larger end. 17 × 12 mm. **Incubation.** Eggs laid at daily intervals. Incubation by female alone, fed by male. 13 days. **Nestling.** Altricial and downy. **Nestling period.** Young tended by both parents. Fed by regurgitation. Brooded for first *c.* 9 days by female with male bringing food. No droppings removed after *c.* 9 days. Young become active at *c.* 11 days. Leave nest at 14–15 days.

AMERICAN GOLDFINCH *Spinus tristis* **Pl. 62**

Breeds over a wide range where trees and shrubs are present. Nest in a tree or shrub, usually 3–10 ft. up, occasionally 1–33 ft. or higher in trees; sometimes

Plate 17 Approx. ¾ life-size

LOONS. The eggs are large, rather elongated and blunt-ended. They have a slightly granular or rough texture. They are usually olive-brown but may vary to more buff or greener tints, and the markings, although usually small, may sometimes be large or rarely absent. The usual clutch is two eggs, laid in a hollow scrape or on a pile of near-by material pulled together, by the water's edge

1. **Red-throated Loon,** *Gavia stellata.* Eggs smaller and often more buff than others. **page** 43
2. **Arctic Loon,** *Gavia arctica.* 42
3. **Common Loon,** *Gavia immer.* The markings are often sparse and eggs at times unmarked. 41

(**Yellow-billed Loon,** *Gavia adamsii,* not shown, has eggs similar to those of common Loon, but often lighter in color and more buff than brown.)

GANNETS. The egg has an uneven white surface, thin enough in places to show the bluish shell underneath, and liable to scratch or flake away during incubation. The nest is a pile of seaweed and debris and the outer shell may be stained buff or brown by rotting nest material. Nests are in colonies, a bill-stab apart.

4. **Gannet,** *Morus bassanus.* 52

SHEARWATERS. The eggs are usually blunt-ended but may show a more distinct taper in larger species. The eggs are usually white, smooth and non-glossy, and only a single one is laid, usually in a burrow or crevice by the sea, the Fulmar being exceptional in nesting on an open cliff ledge. Nest material usually sparse or absent, but burrow-nesters may gradually accumulate near-by material.

5. **Northern Fulmar,** *Fulmarus glacialis.* 50

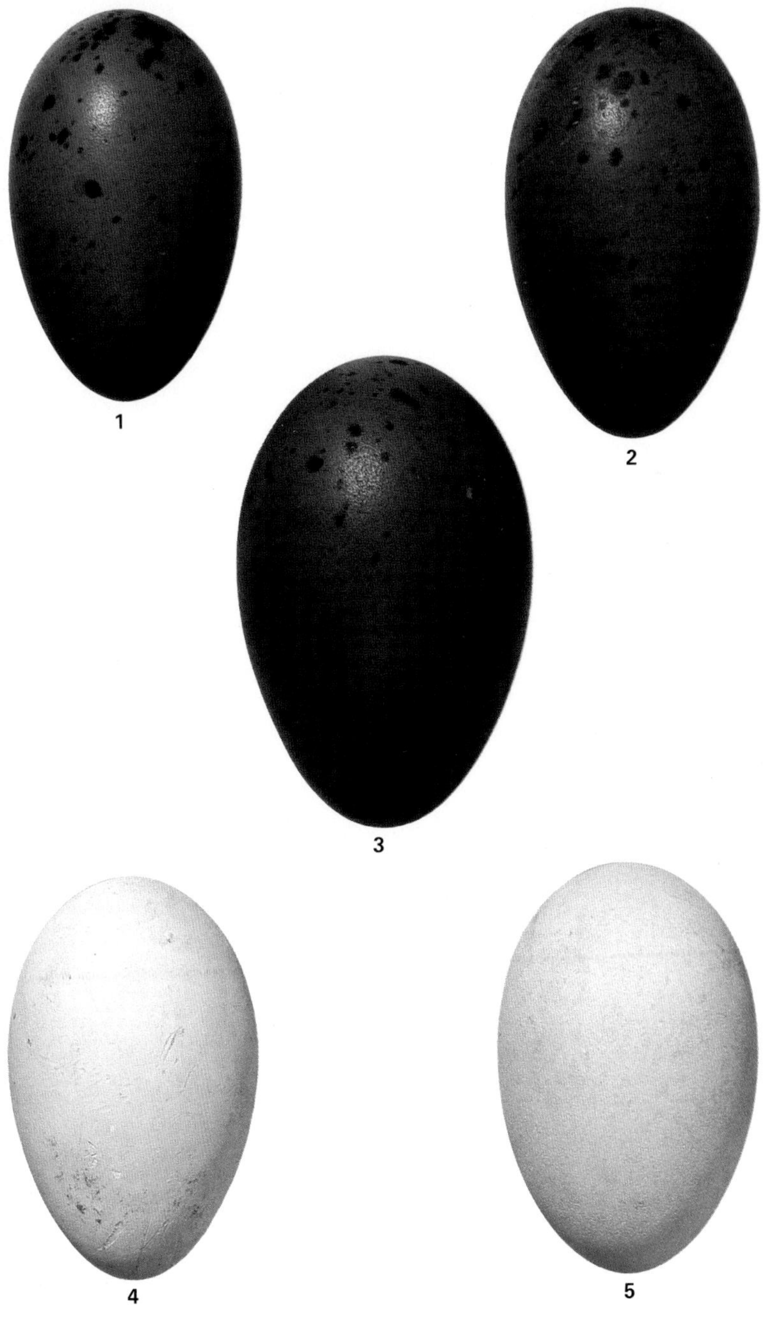
1
2
3
4
5

Plate 18 Approx. ¾ life-size

PETRELS. The eggs are usually blunt-ended and may be almost elliptical in smaller species. They are white and may show tiny reddish or violet specks at the larger end. They are smooth and non-glossy and only a single egg is laid, usually in a burrow or crevice by the sea. Nest material is often sparse or absent, but burrow-nesters may gradually accumulate near-by material over a period.

1. **Leach's Petrel,** *Oceanodroma leucorhoa.* **page** 51

(**Fork-tailed** and **Ashy Petrels,** not shown, have very similar eggs, all usually having a zone of fine reddish specks around the larger end.)

GREBES. The eggs tend to be biconical, wider towards the middle and tapering to both ends. They are smooth but not glossy and almost white when new-laid. Usually a clutch of 3–6 eggs on a nest of waterweed, often floating. The birds cover the eggs with weed when they leave the nest, and eggs soon become stained buff or brown.

2. **Least Grebe,** *Podiceps dominicus.* 46

3. **Horned Grebe,** *Podiceps auritus.* 44

4. **Red-necked Grebe,** *Podiceps griseigena.* 44

5. **Eared Grebe,** *Podiceps nigricollis.* 49

6 (a-b). **Pied-billed Grebe,** *Podilymbus podiceps.* One example is included to show how nest-stained a grebe egg may become. 50

7. **Western Grebe,** *Aechmophorus occidentalis.* 46

CORMORANTS and ANHINGA. Eggs are rather elongated and blunt-ended. The pale blue or greenish-blue shell has an outer surface layer of irregular thickness, the under shell often showing through. A clutch of *c.* 3–6 eggs is laid in a cup of twigs in a tree or pile of seaweed and debris on rocks. Eggs may become stained.

8. **Great Cormorant,** *Phalacrocorax carbo.* 54

9. **Double-crested Cormorant,** *Phalacrocorax auritus.* 54

10. **Neotropical Cormorant,** *Phalacrocorax olivaceus.* 56

11. **Brandt's Cormorant,** *Phalacrocorax penicillatus.* 56

12. **Pelagic Cormorant,** *Phalacrocorax pelagicus.* 56

(Eggs of **Red-faced Cormorant,** not shown, are similar in appearance and size to those of Brandt's Cormorant.)

13. **Anhinga,** *Anhinga anhinga.* 57

3
2
1
5
6a
4
6b
7
9
8
10
11
12
13

Plate 19 Approx. $\frac{3}{5}$ life-size

PELICANS. The eggs are large and blunt-ended. They have a rough, uneven chalk-like layer which may become scratched and stained during nesting. The shell beneath is white. The nest is a hollow on the ground with a variable amount of material, or a stick platform in a bush or low tree.

1. **Brown Pelican,** *Pelecanus occidentalis.* **page** 53

2. **White Pelican,** *Pelecanus erythrorhynchus.* 53

STORKS. The eggs are smooth with a finely granular texture. Usually a clutch of 3–4 laid in a large stick nest with a finer lining, in a tree.

3. **Wood Stork,** *Mycteria americana.* 63

IBISES and SPOONBILLS. The eggs are subelliptical to elliptical. Smooth and non-glossy or, in the Glossy Ibis, slightly glossy. Usually a clutch of 2–4 in a rough nest of sticks, usually with leaves in lining, in a tree, shrub or on the ground. Nests usually in colonies.

4. **Glossy Ibis,** *Plegadis falcinellus.* 66

5. **Roseate Spoonbill,** *Ajaia ajaja.* Markings vary from reddish-brown to light buffish-brown. 66

6 (a-b). **White Ibis,** *Eudocimus albus.* Two examples show the range of variation. Ground color may be buffish, bluish or greenish, and the variable markings light to dark brown. 67

HERONS. Eggs always greenish-blue. Smooth but non-glosssy and rather blunt-ended, Usually a clutch of 3–7, in a twig nest in a tree or shrub, or on the ground or on rock ledge.

7. **Great Blue Heron,** *Ardea herodias.* 57

1
2
4
3
5
6a
7
6b

Plate 20 Approx. $\frac{9}{10}$ life-size

HERONS and BITTERNS. The eggs are elliptica to subelliptical, smooth and non-glossy, greenish-blue except in the American Bittern. Usually a clutch of 3–5 eggs in a stick nest in tree or shrub, plants by or in water, or on the ground. Normally a shallow structure in smaller species, sometimes massive in larger ones. Often nests in colonies.

1. **Reddish Egret,** *Dichromanassa rufescens.* **page** 60
2. **Great Egret,** *Egretta alba.* 60
3. **Little Blue Heron,** *Florida caerulea.* 58
4. **Yellow-crowned Night Heron,** *Nycticorax violaceus.* 62
5. **Snowy Egret,** *Egretta thula.* 61
6. **Black-crowned Night Heron,** *Nycticorax nycticorax.* 61
7. **Least Bittern,** *Ixobrychus exilis.* 62
8. **Green Heron,** *Butorides virescens.* 58
9. **Cattle Egret,** *Bubulcus ibis.* 59
10. **American Bittern,** *Botaurus lentiginosus.* 62
11. **Tricolored Heron,** *Hydranassa tricolor.* 61

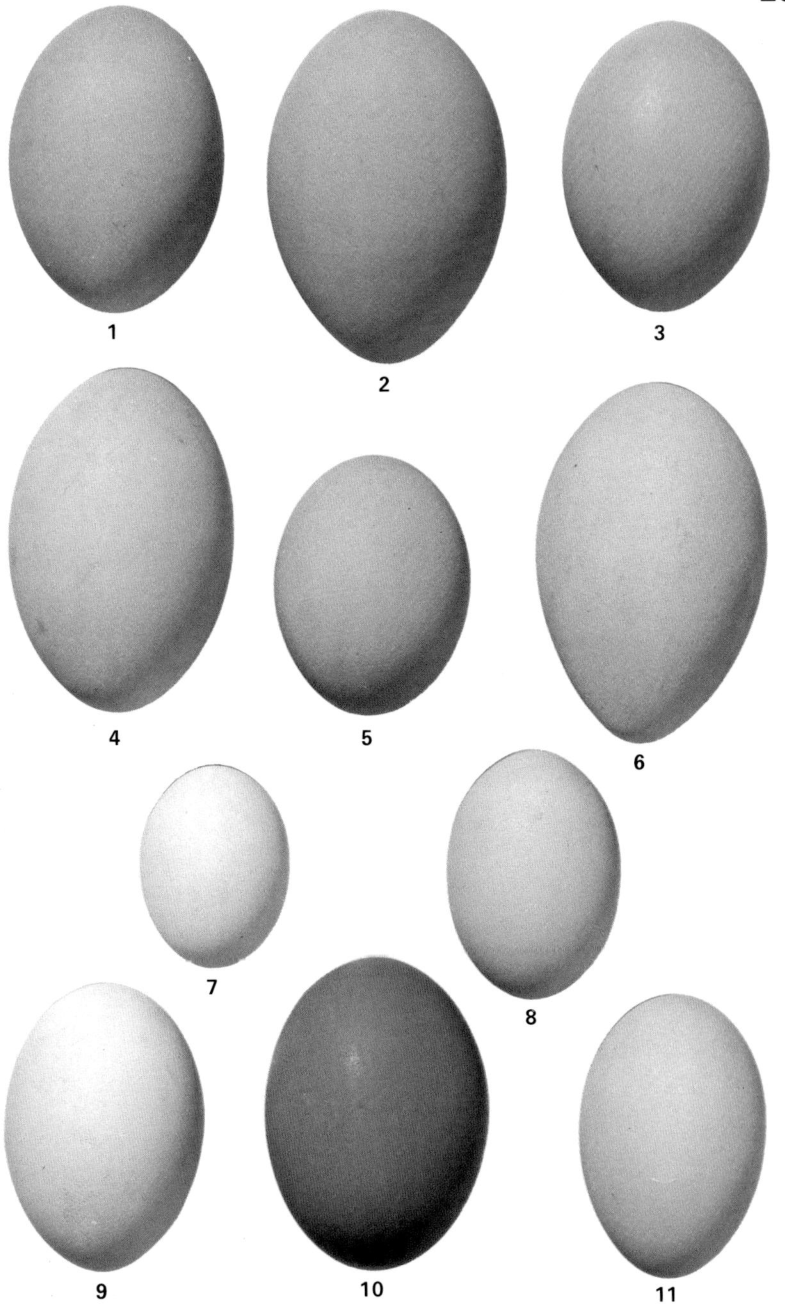
1
2
3
4
5
6
7
8
9
10
11

Plate 21 Approx. $\frac{3}{4}$ life-size

SWANS. The eggs are large, smooth and slightly glossy, usually with a fine granular surface texture. The clutch usually of about 5 eggs is laid in a nest formed of a large heap of plant material just in or by water; with a shallow central hollow usually containing a small amount of white down.

1. **Mute Swan,** *Cygnus olor*. The egg color may vary from almost white to blue-gray or blue-green. **page** 68
2. **Whistling Swan,** *Cygnus columbianus*. 69
3. **Trumpeter Swan,** *Cygnus buccinator*. 69

1
2
3

Plate 22 Approx. ¾ life-size

BRANTA GEESE and GRAY GEESE. The eggs are smooth with a fine granular texture, and non-glossy to slightly glossy. Usually a clutch of 3–6 eggs laid in a large nest which may be a shallow scrape or low mound of material, lined with plant fragments, down and some feathers. Down tufts are grayish-brown with white centers and pale tips in Canada Goose, brownish-gray with whitish centers in Brant, and dark gray with whitish centers in Barnacle Goose.

1 (a-b). **Canada Goose,** *Branta canadensis.* Some races differ considerably in size, and eggs of two different races are shown. **page** 72

2. **Emperor Goose,** *Anser canagicus.* 71

3. **Brant,** *Branta bernicla.* 72

4. **Barnacle Goose,** *Branta leucopsis.* 72

1a

2

1b

3

4

Plate 23 Approx. ¾ life-size

GRAY GEESE. The eggs are smooth with a fine granular texture, and non-glossy to slightly glossy. Usually a clutch of 4–6 eggs is laid in a shallow scrape or low mound of plant material, lined with plant fragments, down and a few feathers. Down tufts pale gray in White-fronted Goose, and Snow Goose, gray with pale tips in Pink-footed Goose, and white in Ross's Goose.

1. **White-fronted Goose,** *Anser albifrons.* **page** 70

2. **Snow Goose,** *Anser caerulescens.* 71

(**Ross's Goose,** not shown, has similar but smaller eggs.)

3. **Pink-footed Goose,** *Anser fabalis.* 69

TREE and DABBLING DUCKS (see also pls. 24-26). Eggs are smooth and vary from non-glossy to fairly glossy or with a waxy surface, and subelliptical to elliptical or oval. A clutch usually of 8–12 eggs is laid in a tree cavity or hollow among vegetation on the ground, and lined with down; except in the Tree-ducks which use no down lining. Down tufts white in Wood Duck, brown with paler centers and tips in Mallard, similar but with less conspicuous pale centers in Black Duck, and dark with small pale center and distinct pale tips in Gadwall.

4. **Wood Duck,** *Aix sponsa.* 77

5. **Black-bellied Tree-duck,** *Dendrocygna autumnalis.* 73

6. **Fulvous Tree-duck,** *Dendrocygna bicolor.* 73

7. **Mallard,** *Anas platyrhynchos.* Egg color varies to pale green, bluish-green, pale blue, buffish-green, or creamy with a greenish tint. 74

8. **Black Duck,** *Anas rubripes.* Egg color varies from green and greenish-buff to yellowish-buff or creamy tinged green. 74

9. **Gadwall,** *Anas strepera.* Egg color varies from creamy to very pale green. 74

1
4
2
5
6
3
7
8
9

Plate 24 Approx. $\frac{9}{10}$ life-size

DABBLING and DIVING DUCKS (see also pls. 23, 25 and 26). The eggs are smooth with a waxy rather than a glossy surface. A clutch usually of 7–12 eggs is laid in a hollow on the ground in vegetation usually near water. The hollow is lined with down. Down tufts are small and very dark with white centers in the Green-winged Teal, dark brown with large whitish centers in Blue-winged and Cinnamon Teals, dark sooty-brown with indistinct pale centers in the Greater Scaup, dark with indistinct pale centers and pale tips in the American Wigeon, warm medium brown with white centers in the Ring-necked Duck, brown with light centers in the Shoveler, light brown and longish with pale centers in the Pintail, and very pale grayish-white in the Redhead.

1. **Green-winged Teal,** *Anas crecca.* Egg color varies from pale cream to pale olive-buff. **page** 75
2. **Shoveler,** *Anas clypeata.* Egg color varies from creamy-buff to olive. 76
3. **Cinnamon Teal,** *Anas cyanoptera.* Egg color varies from white to creamy or warm buff. 76
4. **American Wigeon,** *Anas americana.* 76
5. **Redhead,** *Aythya americana.* Egg color varies from greenish to pale olive or olive-gray. 77
6. **Pintail,** *Anas acuta.* Egg color varies from yellowish-cream to greenish or bluish tints. 75
7. **Ring-necked Duck,** *Aythya collaris.* Egg color varies from pale or grayish olive to greenish tints. 77
8. **Blue-winged Teal,** *Anas discors.* Egg color varies from white to pale olive. 75
9. **Greater Scaup,** *Aythya marila.* 78

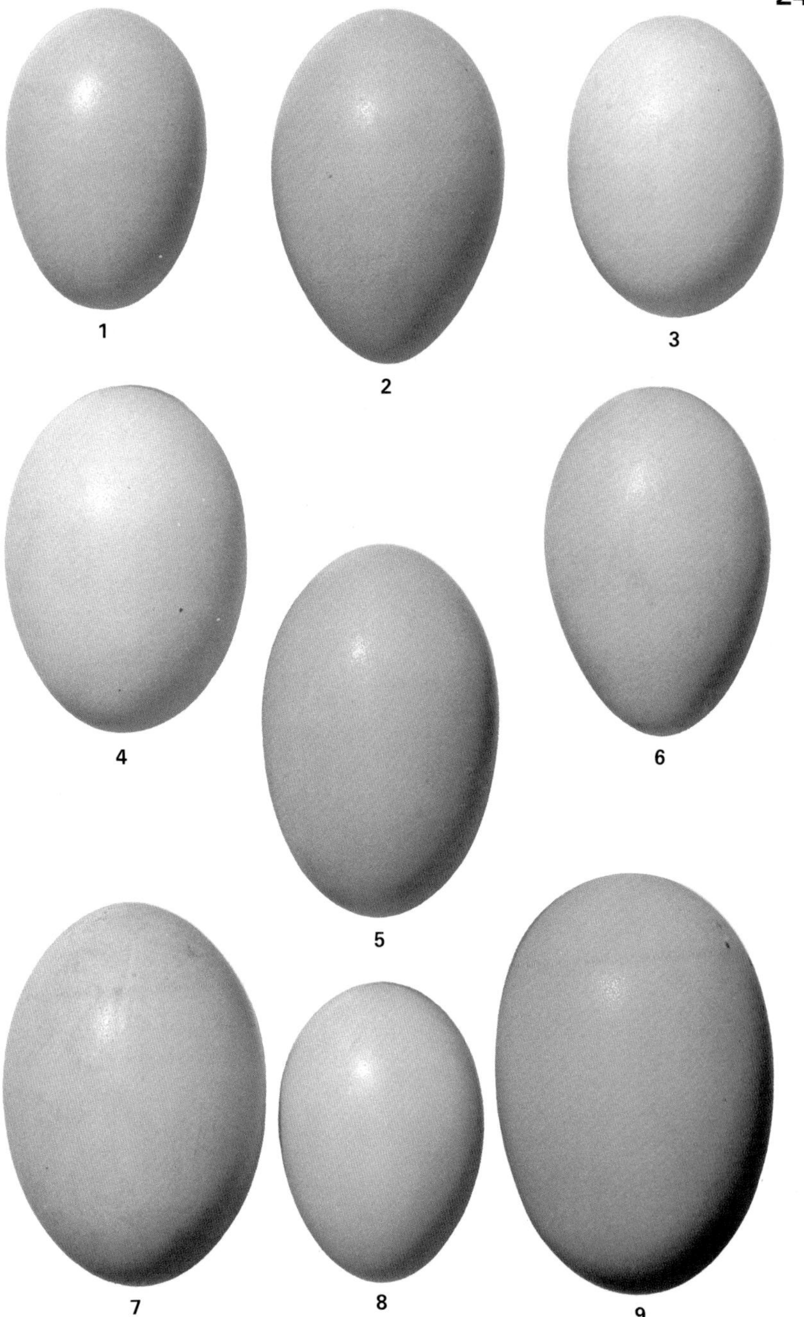
1
2
3
4
5
6
7
8
9

Plate 25 Approx. ¾ life-size

DIVING and SEA DUCKS (see also pls. 23, 24, and 26). Eggs smooth and non-glossy to slightly glossy. Elliptical to subelliptical or oval. A clutch usually of 5–12 eggs is laid in a tree cavity or hollow among vegetation on the ground near salt or fresh water. The nest is lined with down. Down tufts are dark brown with indistinct pale centers in Lesser Scaup, Black and White-winged Scoters, dark brown with whitish centers and tips in the Surf Scoter, dark grayish-brown with paler centers in Oldsquaw, light gray-brown with indistinct paler centers in Canvasback, pale gray tinted brown with indistinct pale centers in Bufflehead, grayish-white in Goldeneye, and white in Barrow's Goldeneye.

1. **Canvasback,** *Aythya valisineria.* Egg color varies from grayish-olive through pale, bluish or olive green. **page** 78
2. **Lesser Scaup,** *Aythya affinis.* Egg color varies from olive to greenish-buff. 78
3. **Oldsquaw,** *Clangula hyemalis.* Egg color varies from yellowish to faintly olive or greenish. 80
4. **Barrow's Goldeneye,** *Bucephala islandica.* 82
5. **Bufflehead,** *Bucephala albeola.* Egg color varies from creamy-white to olive-buff. 81
6. **Goldeneye,** *Bucephala clangula.* 82
7. **White-winged Scoter,** *Melanitta fusca.* Egg color varies from creamy to buff. 81
8. **Surf Scoter,** *Melanitta perspicillata.* Egg color varies from creamy-white to pinkish-buff. 81
9. **Black Scoter,** *Melanitta nigra.* Egg color varies from creamy to creamy-buff. 81

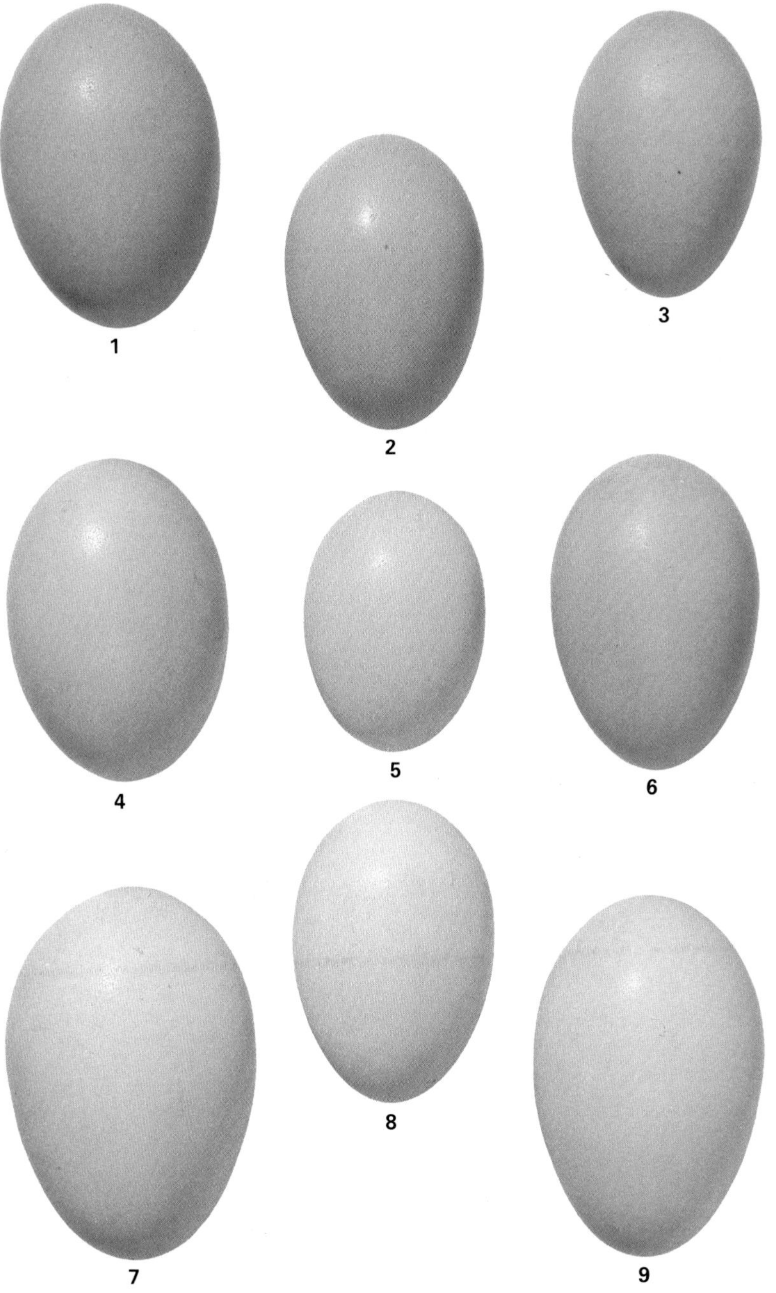
1
2
3
4
5
6
7
8
9

Plate 26 Approx. ¾ life-size

SEA DUCKS, STIFFTAIL and SAWBILLS (see also pls. 23–25). The eggs are smooth and slightly glossy, subelliptical to elliptical. A clutch of 5–8 eggs in sea ducks, 5–12 in sawbills, in a hollow on the ground in vegetation by salt or fresh water, and in tree cavities, hollows in banks, among stones or under bushes in sawbills. Nests lined with down except in the Ruddy Duck. Down tufts are very dark brown with occasional white tufts in Steller's Eider, sooty-brown with indistinct pale centers and occasional white tufts in the King Eider, medium brown with indistinct pale centers in the Spectacled Eider, light brown with pale centers in the Harlequin Duck, light grayish-brown with indistinct pale centers and palish tips in the Common Eider, large and pale gray in the Common Merganser, darker gray tinged brown with pale centers and palish tips in the Red-breasted Merganser, and very pale gray with slightly paler centers in the Hooded Merganser.

1. **Steller's Eider,** *Polysticta stelleri.* Egg color varies from yellowish-olive to greenish or olive-buff. **page** 80
2. **Harlequin Duck,** *Histrionicus histrionicus.* Egg color varies from pale creamy to buff. 80
3. **Spectacled Eider,** *Somateria fischeri.* Egg color varies from green to bluish-green or olive-buff. 79
4. **King Eider,** *Somateria spectabilis.* 79
5. **Ruddy Duck,** *Oxyura jamaicensis.* 83
6. **Common Eider,** *Somateria mollissima.* Egg color varies from pale green to olive, grayish, bluish or rarely buffish. 79
7. **Common Merganser,** *Mergus merganser.* 83
8. **Hooded Merganser,** *Mergus cucullatus.* 82
9. **Red-breasted Merganser,** *Mergus serrator.* 83

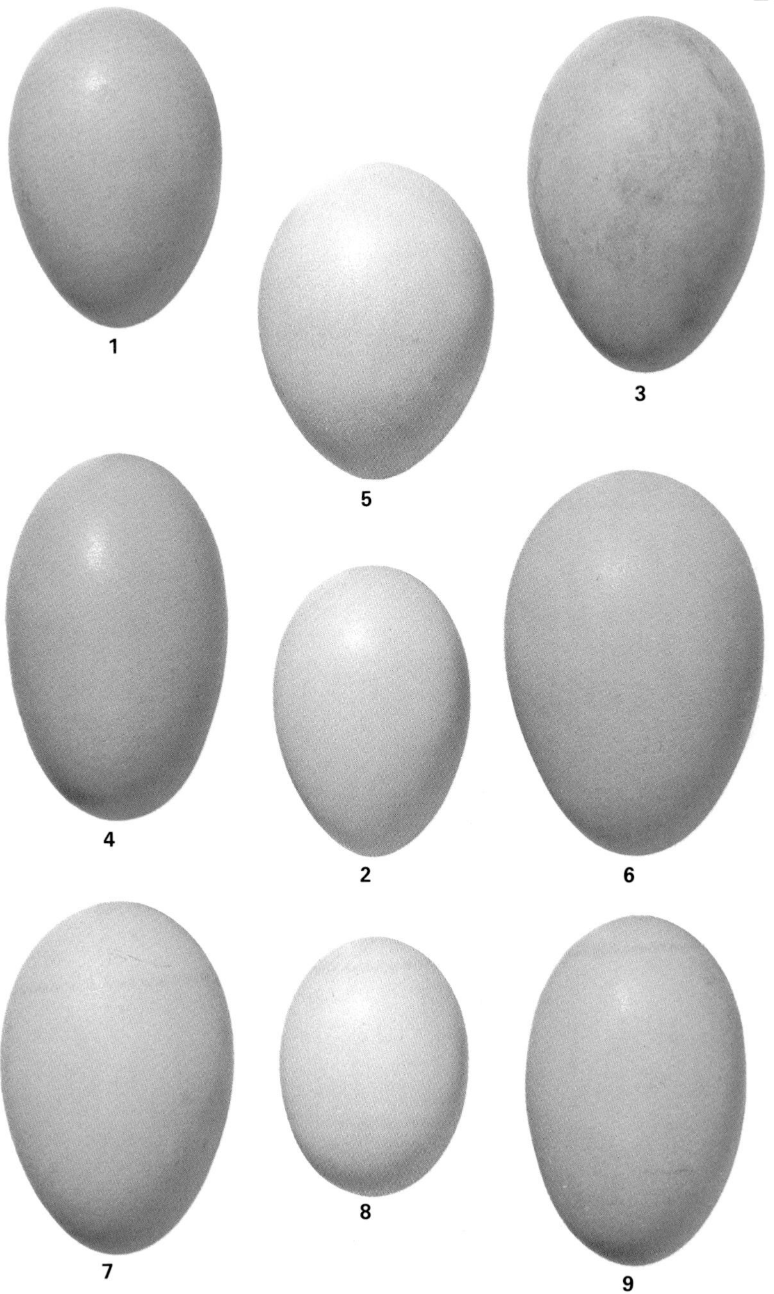
1
5
3
4
2
6
7
8
9

Plate 27 Approx. $\frac{9}{10}$ life-size

NEW WORLD VULTURES. Eggs smooth and slightly glossy, and that of California Condor finely pitted. Long subelliptical to subelliptical and blunt oval. Clutch of one or two eggs laid in a bare cavity or sheltered site with no nest.

1. **California Condor,** *Gymnogyps californianus.* **page** 85
2. **Turkey Vulture,** *Cathartes aura.* Markings very variable, usually a combination of fine small markings and larger irregular markings, but rarely large blotches. 84
3. **Black Vulture,** *Coragyps atratus.* Color varies from pale gray-green to creamy-white or buff. Markings variable. 84

27

Plate 28 Approx. $\frac{9}{10}$ life-size

KITES and HAWKS (see also pls. 29-31.). The eggs are smooth and non-glossy, sometimes slightly glossy in the kites. Short subelliptical to elliptical, generally rather rounded. Clutch of 2–4 eggs laid in a stick nest, usually in a tree, sometimes on the ground in swampy areas in the Everglade Kite.

1. **White-tailed Kite,** *Elanus leucurus.* **page** 85
2. **Swallow-tailed Kite,** *Elanoides forficatus.* 86
3. **Mississippi Kite,** *Ictinia mississippiensis.* 86
4. **Everglade Kite,** *Rostrhamus sociabilis.* Markings vary from speckling, spotting and irregular blotching to extensive pale blotching. 86
5. **Goshawk,** *Accipiter gentilis.* 87
6. **Sharp-shinned Hawk,** *Accipiter striatus,* Markings very variable. 87
7. **Red-tailed Hawk,** *Buteo jamaicensis.* Markings vary from heavy to indistinct blotching, sometimes combined with fine speckling. 88
8. **Cooper's Hawk,** *Accipiter cooperii.* Eggs normally unmarked but rarely may show a few brown specks or tiny blotches. 87
9. **Red-shouldered Hawk,** *Buteo lineatus.* Markings vary in size and intensity. 88

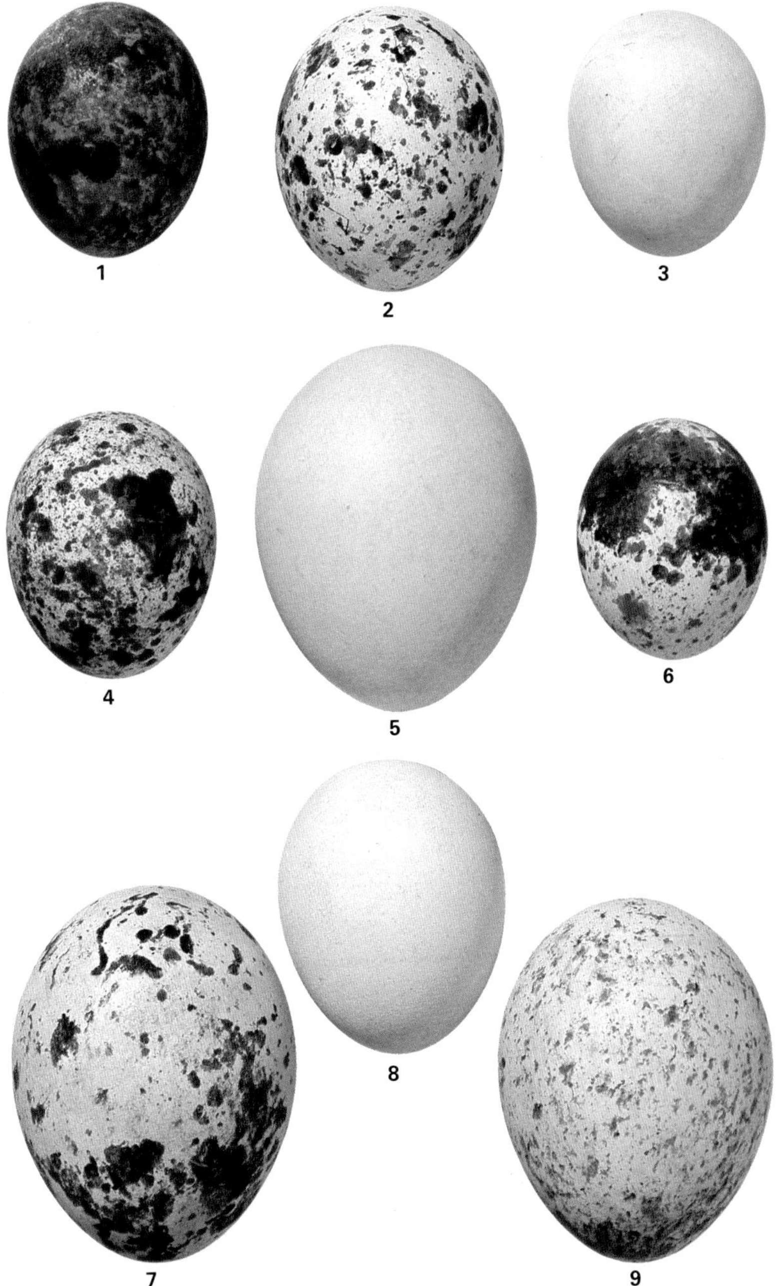
1
2
3
4
5
6
7
8
9

Plate 29 Approx. life-size

HAWKS (see also pls. 28, 30 and 31). The eggs are smooth and non-glossy, usually rather rounded. A clutch usually of 2–4 eggs, is laid in a stick nest, usually with green leaves in lining. Nest in a tree, shrub, cactus, or on rock ledge, exceptionally on ground.

1. **Broad-winged Hawk,** *Buteo platypterus.* Markings vary in color from buff and brown to reddish or purplish brown. **page** 89

2. **Swainson's Hawk,** *Buteo swainsoni.* 89

(**Zone-tailed Hawk,** not shown, has white or bluish-white eggs, usually unmarked, exceptionally with a few fine brown spots, of similar size to those of Rough-legged Hawk.)

3 (a-b). **Rough-legged Hawk,** *Buteo lagopus.* The markings are very variable and two examples are shown here. 91

4. **White-tailed Hawk,** *Buteo albicaudatus.* Markings may be absent or if present are fairly faint and sparse. 90

(**Short-tailed Hawk,** not shown, has eggs bluish-white, dull white or buffish; unmarked or variably marked with speckling, scrawls or sparse to heavy blotching in light to dark brown. Similar in size to previous species.)

5. **Ferruginous Hawk,** *Buteo regalis.* Markings vary from almost absent to sparse specks, spots and blotches, in various brownish tints. 90

1
2
3a
3b
4
5

Plate 30 Approx. $\frac{3}{4}$ life-size

EAGLES (see also pls. 28, 29 and 31). The eggs are non-glossy with a finely granular texture, and rounded in shape. A clutch usually of 2 eggs is laid in a large nest of sticks and other debris with softer lining and leafy twigs regularly added. Nest in a large tree, on a rock ledge or outcrop, or sometimes on the ground.

1 (a-c). **Golden Eagle,** *Aquila chrysaetos*. The eggs vary from unmarked to spotted and blotched patterns in brown chestnut-red or purplish-red. The three examples shown indicate common varieties, and typical clutches of two eggs may show distinct differences in markings, one egg sometimes being unmarked. **page** 92

2. **White-tailed Sea Eagle,** *Haliaeetus albicilla*. 92

3. **Bald Eagle,** *Haliaeetus leucocephalus*. 93

1a
1b
1c
2
3

Plate 31 Approx. life-size

OSPREY and HAWKS (see also pls. 28-30). The eggs are smooth or slightly granular in texture, non-glossy or slightly glossy. A clutch of 2–4 eggs is laid in a stick nest in a tree, or shrub, or in the case of the Osprey sometimes on a low rock outcrop, or on the ground, in the Marsh Hawk always on the ground.

1 (a-b). **Osprey,** *Pandion haliaetus.* The eggs are usually heavily but variably marked and two examples are shown here. **page** 94

2. **Marsh Hawk,** *Circus cyaneus.* Eggs usually unmarked, infrequently blotched with light brown. 93

3. **Gray Hawk,** *Buteo nitidus.* The eggs are usually unmarked, rarely with a few tiny pale brown marks. 91

4. **Black Hawk,** *Buteogallus anthracinus.* Markings vary from small specks to indistinct smudging. 92

5. **Harris's Hawk,** *Parabuteo unicinctus.* Often unmarked. Sometimes with small markings of pale brown or lavender-gray. 91

1a
1b
2
3
4
5

Plate 32 Approx. life-size

FALCONS. The eggs are rather rounded, non-glossy and often heavily freckled overall with reddish or red-brown. No nest is made but a clutch of 2–4 eggs is laid on a rock ledge, in a cavity in cliff or broken tree, on the ground or in large nests of other birds.

1. **Caracara,** *Polyborus plancus.* Color very variable, white, pinkish-white, buff, orange-buff to purplish; marked often heavily with brown or reddish-brown, which may obscure the ground color. **page** 95
2. **Gyrfalcon,** *Falco rusticolus.* 95
3. **Merlin (Pigeon Hawk),** *Falco columbarius.* 97
4. **Peregrine Falcon,** *Falco peregrinus.* 96
5. **Prairie Falcon,** *Falco mexicanus.* 96

(**Aplomado Falcon,** not shown, has eggs similar in color and markings to those of Prairie Falcon, but smaller.)

6. **American Kestrel (Sparrowhawk),** *Falco sparverius.* Color and markings variable; white, creamy, pink or pale buff, with variable but usually fine markings. 97

INTRODUCED GAMEBIRDS (see also pls. 33 and 34). The eggs are smooth and glossy, and usually subelliptical. A clutch, usually of 5–15 eggs, is laid in a hollow in the ground, usually concealed in herbage and sparsely lined with near-by vegetation.

7. **Partridge,** *Perdix perdix.* The egg color may vary through buff, brown and olive. 107
8. **Chukar,** *Alectoris chukar.* 108

1
2
3
4
5
8
7
6

Plate 33 Approx. life-size

GAMEBIRDS (see also pls. 32 and 34).

GUAN. Eggs smooth but with finely granular surface, non-glossy or slightly glossy, and often nest-stained. A clutch usually of 3 eggs in a nest of twigs in a tree.

1. **Chachalaca,** *Ortalis vetula.* **page** 98

TURKEY and GROUSE. The eggs are smooth, subelliptical to oval, and slightly glossy to moderately glossy. A clutch of 4–12 eggs, usually a smaller clutch in ptarmigans, in a scrape nest on the ground, often concealed in vegetation, lined with a little plant material.

2. **Turkey,** *Meleagris gallopavo.* The egg color is white, yellowish or buff; marked with brown, purplish-brown or buff. 108
3. **Blue Grouse,** *Dendragapus obscurus.* 99
4. **Spruce Grouse,** *Dendragapus canadensis.* 99
5. **White-tailed Ptarmigan,** *Lagopus leucurus.* 100
6. **Willow Ptarmigan,** *Lagopus lagopus.* The egg ground color may vary from yellow to reddish; and markings are variable and deep brown to reddish-brown. 99
7. **Ruffed Grouse,** *Bonasa umbellus.* The egg color varies from pale creamy to pale or pinkish buff; often unmarked, sometimes with fine brown speckling. 101
8. **Rock Ptarmigan,** *Lagopus mutus.* 100

1
2
4
3
5
7
6
8

Plate 34 Approx. life-size

GROUSE and TYPICAL GAMEBIRDS (see also pls. 32 and 33). The eggs are smooth and glossy, usually subelliptical to oval. A clutch of 7–14 eggs is laid in a shallow scrape, usually on the ground and concealed in herbage, lined with some plant material.

1. **Greater Prairie Chicken,** *Tympanuchus cupido.* The egg color varies through shades of buff; sometimes eggs are unmarked. **page** 101

2. **Lesser Prairie Chicken,** *Tympanuchus pallidicinctus.* Eggs may be with or without fine markings. 102

3. **Sharp-tailed Grouse,** *Tympanuchus phasianellus.* The egg color is in varying shades of buff, unmarked or with fine speckling or a few larger spots. 102

4. **Scaled Quail,** *Callipepla squamata.* The markings may vary from pale buff to reddish-brown. 104

5. **Sage Grouse,** *Centrocercus urophasianus.* 98

6. **California Quail,** *Callipepla californica.* The egg color varies from creamy-white to yellowish or buffish; marked with golden-brown, buff or dull brown. 105

7. **Bobwhite Quail,** *Colinus virginianus.* 106

8. **Gambel's Quail,** *Callipepla gambeli.* 105

9. **Mountain Quail,** *Oreortyx pictus.* The egg color varies from pale cream to deep pinkish-buff. 104

10. **Ring-necked Pheasant,** *Phasianus colchicus.* The egg color may vary through brown, olive or blue-gray. 107

11. **Montezuma Quail,** *Cyrtonyx montezumae.* 106

1
2
3
4
5
6
7
8
9
10
11

Plate 35 Approx. ¾ life-size

CRANES and LIMPKIN. The eggs are large, smooth and slightly glossy or non-glossy. A clutch, usually of 2 eggs, is laid in a nest on the ground in an open site, sometimes in very shallow water; a large heap of vegetation with a shallow central hollow.

1. **Whooping Crane,** *Grus americana.* The egg color varies from creamy to olive buff or greenish, marked with light to reddish brown. **page** 109

2. **Sandhill Crane,** *Grus canadensis.* The egg color varies from pale to olive buff, marked with light to reddish brown. 109

3. **Limpkin,** *Aramus guarauna.* The egg color varies from creamy to olive buff, and medium to dark brown. 110

JACANAS. The eggs are smooth and highly glossy. A clutch of 3 – 4 eggs is laid in a scanty nest lying on floating plants.

4 (a-b). **Jacana,** *Jacana spinosa.* 115

RAILS. The eggs are smooth and moderately glossy. A clutch, usually of 6 – 12 eggs, is laid in a nest which is usually a substantial mound or cup of plant material hidden in marsh or waterside vegetation.

5. **Black Rail,** *Laterallus jamaicensis.* Yellow Rail has similarly small eggs of warm buff sparsely and finely marked in reddish-brown and lilac, usually mostly at large end. 113

6. **Purple Gallinule,** *Porphyrula martinica.* 113

7. **Common Gallinule,** *Gallinula chloropus.* 114

8. **King Rail,** *Rallus elegans.* 111

9. **Sora Rail,** *Porzana carolina.* 112

10. **Virginia Rail,** *Rallus limicola.* 112

11. **Clapper Rail,** *Rallus longirostris.* 111

1
2
3
4a
5
6
4b
7
8
9
10
11

Plate 36 Approx. $\frac{9}{10}$ life-size

RAILS (continued from pl. 35).

1. American Coot, *Fulica americana.* **page** 114

OYSTERCATCHERS. The eggs are smooth and glossy, less pyriform than those of most shorebirds. Usually a clutch of 3 in a bare hollow in a variety of open sites, unlined or lined with various debris.

2. American Oystercatcher, *Haematopus palliatus.* The egg color varies through various tints on a mainly yellowish ground. 115

3. Black Oystercatcher, *Haematopus bachmani.* 116

PLOVERS. The eggs are smooth and non-glossy or slightly glossy, varying from oval to pyriform, but less pyriform than those of most other shorebirds. The clutch, usually of 3–4 eggs, is laid in a shallow hollow on open ground, sparsely lined or unlined.

4. Ringed Plover, *Charadrius hiaticula.* Egg color variable, from yellowish to bluish. 119

5. Semipalmated Plover, *Charadrius semipalmatus.* 119

6. Piping Plover, *Charadrius melodus.* 120

7. Snowy Plover, *Charadrius alexandrinus.* 120

8 (a-b). **Killdeer,** *Charadrius vociferus.* 121

9. Wilson's Plover, *Charadrius wilsonia.* 120

10. Lesser Golden Plover, *Pluvialis dominicus.* Egg color varies from ivory-yellow to buff. 122

11. Mountain Plover, *Charadrius montanus.* 121

12. Black-bellied Plover, *Pluvialis squatarola.* 122

1
2
3
5
6
4
7
8a
8b
9
10
11
12

Plate 37 Approx. ¾ life-size

SHOREBIRDS (see also pls. 38 and 39). The eggs are smooth and glossy, usually pyriform and cryptically patterned. A clutch, usually of 4 eggs, is laid in a shallow hollow lined with vegetation, in a variety of sites, exposed or set against a stone, log or plant tuft, or concealed in vegetation sometimes pulled together over the nest.

1. **Whimbrel,** *Numenius phaeopus.* The egg color varies from pale green through olive and buff, and is variably marked. **page** 136

(**Bristle-thighed Curlew,** not shown, has eggs like those of Whimbrel but more buff, less greenish.)

2. **Eskimo Curlew,** *Numenius borealis.* 135

3. **Long-billed Curlew,** *Numenius americanus.* 136

4 (a-b). **Bar-tailed Godwit,** *Limosa lapponica.* The egg color varies from light to medium green and olive. Markings may be bold or indistinct. Two examples are shown here. 135

5. **Ruddy Turnstone,** *Arenaria interpres.* The egg color varies from very pale green to light olive, variably marked with shades of brown to blackish-brown. 124

(**Black Turnstone,** not shown, has eggs pale yellowish to buffish olive, with small markings or scrawls of buffish-olive or olive-brown.)

(**Surfbird,** not shown, has eggs buff to pale buff, with spots and small blotches of buffish, reddish or dark brown.)

6. **Hudsonian Godwit,** *Limosa haemastica.* The egg color varies from pale to deep olive or green, and with markings bold or indistinct. 134

7. **Marbled Godwit,** *Limosa fedoa.* Egg color varies from pale buff to olive with dark markings. 135

1
2
3
4a
4b
5
6
7

Plate 38 Approx. life-size

SHOREBIRDS (see also pls. 37 and 39). The eggs are smooth and glossy, usually pyriform and cryptically patterned. A clutch, usually of 4 eggs, is laid in a shallow hollow lined with vegetation, in a variety of sites, exposed or set against a stone, log or plant tuft, or concealed in vegetation which may be pulled together over the nest. The Solitary Sandpiper nests on a raised site, an old bird nest in a tree.

1. **Upland Sandpiper,** *Bartramia longicauda.* **page** 137
2. **Lesser Yellowlegs,** *Tringa flavipes.* 138
3. **Greater Yellowlegs,** *Tringa melanoleuca.* The egg color varies from pale creamy-buff or faint olive to pinkish-buff, marked with dark or purplish brown. 137
4. **American Woodcock,** *Scolopax minor.* The egg color varies from pale creamy-buff to creamy-olive, marked with light to reddish-brown. 133
5. **Willet,** *Catoptrophorus semipalmatus.* The egg color varies from very pale greenish to olive buff and pinkish-buff, marked with medium to dark or purplish brown. 139

(**Wandering Tatler,** not shown, has eggs very pale greenish or olive, marked with medium to dark brown.)

6. **Common Snipe,** *Gallinago gallinago.* The egg color varies from pale green or olive to buff, marked in varying shades of brown. 132
7. **Solitary Sandpiper,** *Tringa solitaria.* 138
8. **Spotted Sandpiper,** *Tringa macularia.* 139
9. **Baird's Sandpiper,** *Calidris bairdii.* 127
10. **Least Sandpiper,** *Calidris minutilla.* 126
11. **Knot,** *Calidris canutus.* 124
12. **Purple Sandpiper,** *Calidris maritima.* 130
13. **Rock Sandpiper,** *Calidris ptilocnemis.* 131
14. **Pectoral Sandpiper,** *Calidris melanotos.* 130

1
2
3
4
5
6
7
8
9
10
11
12
13
14

Plate 39 Approx. life-size

SHOREBIRDS (see also pls. 37 and 38). The eggs are smooth and glossy, usually pyriform and cryptically patterned. A clutch, usually of 4 eggs, is laid in a shallow hollow lined with vegetation in a variety of sites, exposed, or set against a stone, log or plant tuft, or concealed in vegetation sometimes pulled together over the nest.

1. **White-rumped Sandpiper,** *Calidris fuscicollis.* **page** 127

2. **Dunlin,** *Calidris alpina.* The egg color varies from pale olive to green or blue-green, marked with dark or olive brown. 131

(**Curlew Sandpiper,** not shown, has eggs light olive-green, marked in olive-brown, blackish-olive or reddish-brown.)

3. **Short-billed Dowitcher,** *Limnodromus griseus.* The egg color varies from pale greenish to buff. 134

4. **Long-billed Dowitcher,** *Limnodromus scolopaceus.* 134

5. **Stilt Sandpiper,** *Micropalama himantopus.* 132

6. **Semipalmated Sandpiper,** *Calidris pusillus.* The egg color varies from very pale olive to buff, marked with reddish, dark or purple brown. 125

7. **Western Sandpiper,** *Calidris mauri.* The egg color varies from creamy-white to buff or brownish. 126

(**Rufous-necked Sandpiper,** not shown, has eggs yellowish-buff, heavily speckled and spotted with reddish-brown or reddish-buff.)

8. **Buff-breasted Sandpiper,** *Tryngites subruficollis.* 132

9. **Sanderling,** *Calidris alba.* 125

10. **Red Phalarope,** *Phalaropus fulicarius.* The egg color varies from greenish to buff. 140

11. **Northern Phalarope,** *Phalaropus lobatus.* Egg color varies as in Red Phalarope. 141

12. **Wilson's Phalarope,** *Phalaropus tricolor.* 140

13. **American Avocet,** *Recurvirostra americana.* 118

14 (a-b). **Black-necked Stilt,** *Himantopus himantopus.* Two varieties are shown here. 116

1
2
3
4
5
6
7
8
9
10
11
12
13
14a
14b

Plate 40 Approx. ¾ life-size

GULLS and JAEGERS (see also pls. 41 and 42). The eggs are smooth and non-glossy or only slightly glossy, with a slightly granular surface evident on the larger eggs. A clutch, usually of 2-3 eggs, is laid in a nest formed from accumulated plant material, seaweed and debris, large at times, but usually sparse in warmer climates. Nest site on a rock ledge, stack or small island, on coastal sand or shingle, or on marshland, grassland or tundra by water.

1. **Pomarine Jaeger,** *Stercorarius pomarinus.* The egg color varies from buff to warm brown. **page** 142
2. **Parasitic Jaeger,** *Stercorarius parasiticus.* The egg color varies from olive to deeper buff or brown. 142
3. **Long-tailed Jaeger,** *Stercorarius longicaudus.* 142
4. **Glaucous Gull,** *Larus hyperboreus* The egg color varies from light or creamy olive to buff, exceptionally bluish-white; with very variable markings. 150
5. **Iceland Gull,** *Larus glaucoides.* 150
6. **Glaucous-winged Gull,** *Larus glaucescens.* The egg color varies from very pale olive to buff. 149
7. **Western Gull,** *Larus occidentalis.* The egg color varies from very pale olive to olive-buff. 149
8. **Greater Black-backed Gull,** *Larus marinus.* The egg color varies from pale greenish to olive-buff, exceptionally whitish-blue or deeper buff. 150

(**Thayer's Gull,** not shown, has eggs pale olive to buff, marked with olive-brown, brown or black.)

9. **Herring Gull,** *Larus argentatus.* The egg color varies through pale olive, greenish and buff, exceptionally pale whitish-blue or deep buff. 148

4
2
6
8
1
3
7
5
9

Plate 41 Approx. ¾ life-size

GULLS (see also pls. 40 and 42). The eggs are smooth and non-glossy or only slightly glossy, with a slight granular surface evident on larger eggs. A clutch, usually of 2–3 eggs, is laid in a nest formed from accumulated plant material, seaweed or debris, large at times but usually sparser in warmer climates. Nest site on a rock ledge, stack or small island, on coastal sand or shingle, or in or by water in marshland, grassland or tundra. Bonaparte's Gull nests in spruce trees.

1 (a-d). **California Gull,** *Larus californicus.* Although most gulls' eggs are rather similar there is a wide range of possible varieties within a species. In most instances only a single typical egg has been shown but 4 eggs are used here to show the problem of variation. **page** 148

2. **Ring-billed Gull,** *Larus delawarensis.* The egg color varies from pale olive to deeper buff. 147

3. **Common Gull,** *Larus canus.* The egg color varies from greenish to buff, exceptionally whitish-blue to deep brownish-buff. 147

4. **Franklin's Gull,** *Larus pipixcan.* The egg color varies from greenish to buff. 143

5. **Laughing Gull,** *Larus atricilla.* The egg color varies from greenish to buff. 143

6. **Bonaparte's Gull,** *Larus philadelphia.* The egg color varies from greenish to buff. 147

1a
1b
1c
2
1d
3
4
5
6

Plate 42 Approx. life-size

GULLS (see also pls. 40 and 41). The eggs are smooth and non-glossy or only slightly glossy. A clutch, usually of 2 – 3 eggs, is laid in a nest formed from accumulated plant material, seaweed or debris, large at times. Nest site on a rock ledge, stack or small island, coastal sand or shingle, or in or by water on tundra, marsh or tall grasses.

1. **Ivory Gull,** *Pagophila eburnea.* The egg color varies from light olive to buff. **page** 151

2. **Black-legged Kittiwake,** *Rissa tridactyla.* The egg color varies from cream to pale greenish, yellowish, stone, buff or olive, exceptionally yellow or pinkish-buff. The markings are very variable. 151

3. **Sabine's Gull,** *Larus sabini.* 146

TERNS (see also pls. 43 and 44). The eggs are smooth and non-glossy. A clutch, usually of 2–3 eggs, is laid in a shallow hollow, sparsely lined or unlined, on an open site usually on sand or shingle by water. The nests are usually close together in colonies, sometimes of several species nesting together.

4. **Gull-billed Tern,** *Gelochelidon nilotica.* The egg color varies from pale yellowish to creamy buff. 152

5. **Forster's Tern,** *Sterna forsteri.* The egg color varies from very pale olive or greenish to light or olive buff, marked with dark brown and black. 157

6. **Common Tern,** *Sterna hirundo.* The egg color varies from creamy and pale yellowish through greenish tints to deep buff or olive; very variably marked with shades of black and brown. 155

7 (a-c). **Arctic Tern,** *Sterna paradisaea.* The egg color varies through shades of pale greenish, olive or buff, exceptionally from bluish-white or creamy to deep brown. The markings are variable. Three examples are shown here. 156

4
2
1
5
6
3
7a
7c
7b

Plate 43 Approx. life-size

TERNS and SKIMMER (see also pls. 42 and 44). The eggs are smooth, non-glossy, and cryptically patterned. The clutch usually of 2–3 eggs, or one in species of warmer climates, is laid in a shallow hollow on an open site with little or no nest material, usually on sand, shingle or dry mud; or a nest of plant material floating on water plants for the Black Tern; and a more substantial nest in a shrub or on a ledge for the Noddy Tern. Nests are usually close together in a colony.

1 (a-b). **Roseate Tern,** *Sterna dougallii.* The egg color may vary to yellowish, buffish or olive, occasionally of deeper tint, and with markings very variable, but often fine and profuse. Two examples are shown here. **page** 154

2 (a-c). **Sooty Tern,** *Sterna fuscata.* The egg color may vary from white to pale pinkish or buff, markings are variable and often small and profuse. Three examples are shown here. 157

3. Aleutian Tern, *Sterna aleutica.* The egg color varies from yellowish or olive to yellowish or olive buff. 156

4 (a-b). **Least Tern,** *Sterna albifrons.* The egg color varies through pale olive, buff and cream. Markings are variable. Two examples are shown here. 157

5. Black Tern, *Chlidonias niger.* The egg color varies from light buff to brown, pale yellowish or cream, with irregular heavy marking. 158

6. Brown Noddy Tern, *Anous stolidus.* The color is usually white, but may be tinted buff or pink. 159

7. Black Skimmer, *Rynchops nigra.* 159

1a
2b
3
2a
1b
2c
4a
4b
5
6
7

Plate 44 Approx. $\frac{9}{10}$ life-size

TERNS (see also pls. 42 and 43). The eggs are smooth and non-glossy, and cryptically patterned. The clutch, usually of 2–3, sometimes one only, is laid in a shallow hollow, usually on shingle, sand or dry mud. The nests are usually close together in colonies, sometimes of several species.

1. Royal Tern, *Sterna maxima.* The egg color varies from creamy-white to ivory-yellow, pale buffish or greenish, or buff and pinkish-buff. Markings are variable. **page** 153

2. Caspian Tern, *Hydroprogne caspia.* 153

3 (a-f). **Sandwich Tern,** *Sterna sandvicensis.* Some tern species show considerable variation in egg color. This might be of value in helping birds to recognise eggs where nests are scantily lined and very close together, but the amount of variation differs from one species to another. The 6 eggs shown here illustrate the amount of variation occurring in one species. 154

3a

3b

1

3c

3d

2

3e

3f

Plate 45 Approx. ¾ life-size

THICK-BILLED MURRE and RAZORBILL. The eggs of these two larger auks are large, usually long and pyriform, although those of the Razorbill are a little shorter and rounder. The surface is finely granular and roughened, lacking gloss. Apart from this there is little consistency, the eggs showing a great individual variation in color and markings, some examples being shown here. It is thought that the variations may enable birds to recognise their own eggs in sites where no nest is made, where one egg is laid, and where a number of birds may be crowded close together.

1 (a-c). **Thick-billed Murre,** *Uria lomvia.* The egg color may vary through shades of whitish, cream, buff, reddish, greenish or blue; and markings may be buff, brown, purplish or black. **page** 160

2 (a-c). **Razorbill,** *Alca torda.* The egg color may vary from white, through yellow, buff, brown, reddish or greenish tint; variably marked with dark brown or black, the markings including scribbling and banding. 161

1a
1b
1c
2a
2b
2c

Plate 46 Approx. $\frac{3}{4}$ life-size

COMMON MURRE. The eggs of this larger auk are large, usually long and pyriform, occasionally more oval. The surface is finely granular and roughened, lacking gloss. Apart from this there is little consistency, since the eggs show great individual variation in color and markings. The group shown here indicate the range of variation with some types of color and markings. It is thought that these variations enable birds to recognise their own eggs, and since this species makes no nest and single eggs are laid on bare rocky ledges or the flatter tops of rock stacks closely crowded with birds, there would be an exceptional need for this.

Common Murre, *Uria aalge.* The egg color may vary from white through shades of brown, buff, reddish, cream, blue or green. Markings may be brown or black, and some larger markings show a mixture of both colors. Markings are sometimes in the form of continuous zones of pigment, or sometimes absent altogether. **page** 160

Plate 47 Approx. $\frac{9}{10}$ life-size

AUKS (see also pls. 45, 46 and 48). The eggs are smooth and non-glossy to moderately glossy, subelliptical to long elliptical, sometimes with bluntly rounded ends. The eggs of most species are concealed in crevices or burrows near the sea, but Kittlitz's Murrelet breeds on bare places in mountains some miles inland and the Marbled Murrelet apparently uses a platform of debris in a forest tree near the shore.

1 (a-b). **Black Guillemot,** *Cepphus grylle.* The egg color may be tinted with buff or bluish-green; and markings are variable and reddish-brown at times. **page** 161

2 (a-b). **Pigeon Guillemot,** *Cepphus columba.* The eggs are similar to those of the Black Guillemot in color and range of variation. 161

3. Dovekie, *Alle alle.* 163

4. Least Auklet, *Aethia pusilla.* 164

5. Xantus's Murrelet, *Endomychura hypoleuca.* The egg color may vary from pale blue to greenish, olive, buff or brown. 162

6. Ancient Murrelet, *Synthliboramphus antiquus.* 163

7. Marbled Murrelet, *Brachyramphus marmoratum.* The egg color may vary to pale greenish-yellow or greenish-buff. 162

(**Kittlitz's Murrelet,** not shown, has a similar long elliptical, egg with an olive or olive-buff tint and brown and black markings.)

1a
6
1b
2a
3
2b
4
5
7

Plate 48 Approx. ¾ life-size

AUKLETS and PUFFINS (see also pls. 45-47.) The eggs are smooth and non-glossy, sometimes with a finely granular surface texture; and sub-elliptical to oval. The nests are burrows or rock crevices or cavities, on the coast or offshore islands.

1. **Cassin's Auklet,** *Ptychoramphus aleutica.* **page** 163

2 (a-d). **Atlantic Puffin,** *Fratercula arctica.* The eggs may be unmarked, or may show faint brown or purplish blotches, or exceptionally be more heavily marked and tinted pale to deep buff. 165

3. **Crested Auklet,** *Aethia cristatella.* 164

(The **Parakeet Auklet,** not shown, has eggs of white, bluish-white or pale blue, of similar size to those of the Crested Auklet.)

4. **Rhinoceros Auklet,** *Cerorhinca monocerata.* The eggs are white and unmarked or sparsely marked with scrawls and spots of gray or light brown. 165

5. **Horned Puffin,** *Fratercula corniculata.* 165

6. **Tufted Puffin,** *Lunda cirrhata.* The egg markings vary from pale gray to pale brown. 166

1
2a
3
2b
2c
2d
4
5
6

Plate 49 Approx. $\frac{9}{10}$ life-size

OWLS. The eggs are rounded or blunt-ended, but those of the Barn Owl are more elongated. They are smooth, but occasionally show small, pimple-like excrescences; and are non-glossy or slightly glossy. They may become slightly stained in the nest. The clutch is usually of 2–6 eggs, but in some species may be larger, of 10–15 eggs in seasons when food is plentiful. Usually no nest is built, the clutch being laid in a hollow tree or large cactus, hollow on the ground in herbage or in the open, on a ledge or the old nest of another bird, or in a burrow.

1. **Great Gray Owl,** *Strix nebulosa.* **page** 178

2. **Barn Owl,** *Tyto alba.* 173

3. **Barred Owl,** *Strix varia.* 178

(The **Spotted Owl,** not shown, has eggs similar in shape and size to those of the Barred Owl.)

4. **Snowy Owl,** *Nyctea scandiaca.* 174

5. **Elf Owl,** *Micrathene whitneyi.* 175

(The **Pygmy Owl** and **Flammulated Owl,** not shown, have small eggs similar to and slightly larger than those of the Elf Owl.)

6. **Great Horned Owl,** *Bubo virginianus.* 174

7. **Short-eared Owl,** *Asio flammeus.* 179

8. **Hawk Owl,** *Surnia ulula.* 175

9. **Long-eared Owl,** *Asio otus.* 178

10. **Screech Owl,** *Otus asio.* 174

11. **Boreal Owl,** *Aegolius funereus.* 179

(The **Whiskered Owl,** not shown, has eggs of similar shape and size to those of the Boreal Owl.)

12. **Saw-whet Owl,** *Aegolius acadicus.* 179

13. **Burrowing Owl,** *Speotyto cunicularia.* The eggs are glossier than those of most owls. 175

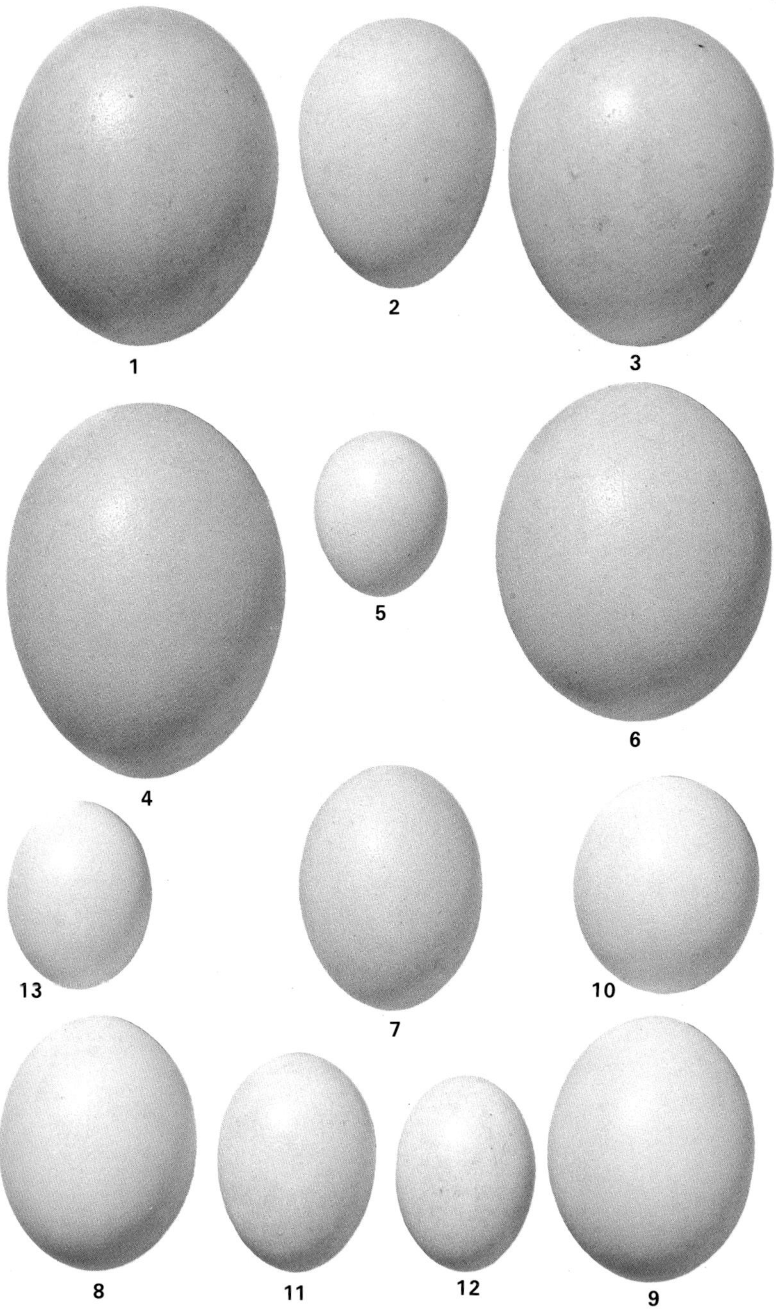
1
2
3
4
5
6
13
7
10
8
11
12
9

Plate 50 Approx. life-size

PIGEONS. The eggs are smooth and slightly to moderately glossy, and when freshly laid may have a faint pink tint that soon fades. The clutch is usually of two eggs, but only one in some larger species. The nest is a thin platform of twigs in a tree or shrub, or on a ledge, rarely on the ground.

1. **Band-tailed Pigeon,** *Columba fasciata.* **page** 167
2. **Red-billed Pigeon,** *Columba flavirostris.* 167
3. **Rock Dove,** *Columba livia.* 166
4. **White-crowned Pigeon,** *Columba leucocephala.* 166
5. **White-winged Dove,** *Zenaida asiatica.* 167
6. **Mourning Dove,** *Zenaida macroura.* 167
7. **Ground Dove,** *Columbina passerina.* 168
8. **Barbary Dove,** *Streptopelia roseogrisea.* 169
9. **Spotted Dove,** *Streptopelia chinensis.* 170
10. **Inca Dove,** *Scardafella inca.* 169
11. **White-fronted Dove,** *Leptoptila verreauxi.* 169

CUCKOOS (see also pl. 51.) The eggs are smooth and non-glossy, elliptical to subelliptical. The clutch, usually of 2 – 4 eggs, is laid in a loose and poorly-made nest of twigs in a tree or shrub.

12. **Mangrove Cuckoo,** *Coccyzus minor.* 170
13. **Yellow-billed Cuckoo,** *Coccyzus americanus.* 170
14. **Black-billed Cuckoo,** *Coccyzus erythropthalmus.* 171

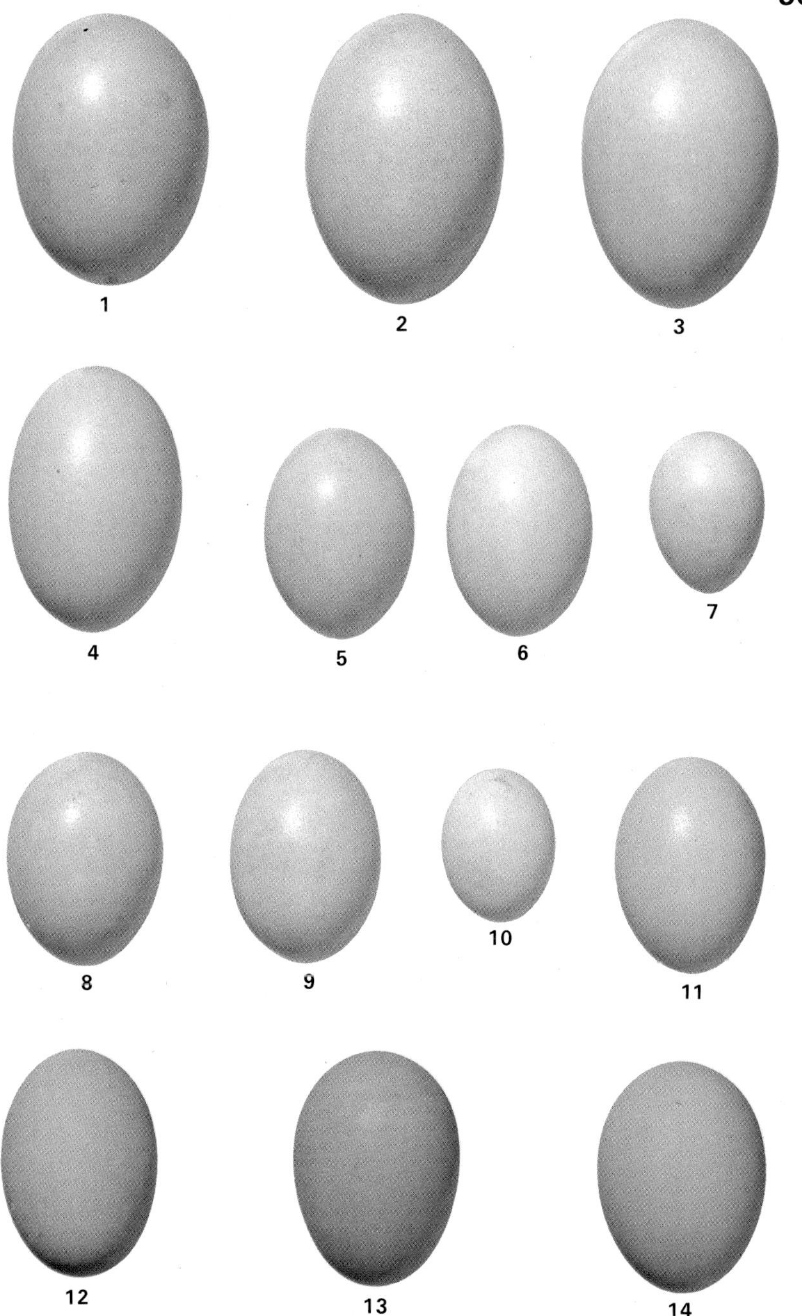
1
2
3
4
5
6
7
8
9
10
11
12
13
14

Plate 51 Approx. life-size

CUCKOOS (see also pl. 50). The eggs are smooth and slightly or fairly glossy. Ani eggs are blue with a white outer layer of varying thickness with the underlying color showing through at times. The Roadrunner has a clutch of 3–6 eggs in a well-made cup of plant material in a tree or shrub. Anis build loose cups of twigs, lined with fresh leaves, and a number of females lay eggs in one nest.

1 (a-c). **Smooth-billed Ani,** *Crotophaga ani.* The three examples show variation from the typical white covering to absence of the layer. **page** 172

2. **Roadrunner,** *Geococcyx californianus.* 171

3. **Groove-billed Ani,** *Crotophaga sulcirostris.* 172

NIGHTJARS. The eggs are elongated, biconical and blunt-ended, showing little evidence of a taper towards the narrow end. They are smooth and moderately glossy, and cryptically patterned. Usually 2 in a clutch, laid on a bare, open site with no nest.

4. **Chuck-will's-widow,** *Caprimulgus carolinensis.* The eggs may be tinted cream or pinkish. 180

5. **Whip-poor-will,** *Caprimulgus vociferus.* 180

6. **Poor-will,** *Phalænoptilus nuttallii.* 180

7 (a-b). **Pauraque,** *Nyctidromus albicollis.* 181

8 (a-b). **Common Nighthawk,** *Chordeiles minor.* The markings vary from mainly pale gray to heavy brown, and two examples are shown here. 181

9 (a-b). **Lesser Nighthawk,** *Chordeiles acutipennis.* The markings vary from heavy brown to pale gray, and two examples are shown here. 182

HUMMINGBIRDS. The eggs are smooth and non-glossy, long elliptical to long subelliptical, blunt-ended. A clutch, normally of 2, is laid in a small tight neat cup with a deep cavity, fixed on a twig or branch of a tree, shrub or more rarely a ledge or support on a building. All eggs are very similar and only a selection is shown here.

10. **Ruby-throated Hummingbird,** *Archilochus colubris.* 186

11. **Black-chinned Hummingbird,** *Archilochus alexandri.* 186

12. **Costa's Hummingbird,** *Calypte costae.* 186

13. **Anna's Hummingbird,** *Calypte anna.* 186

14. **Broad-tailed Hummingbird,** *Selasphorus platycercus.* 187

15. **Rufous Hummingbird,** *Selasphorus rufus.* 187

1a
1b
1c
2
3
4
5
6
7a
7b
8a
8b
9a
9b
10
11
12
13
14
15

Plate 52 Approx. life-size

SWIFTS. The eggs are elongated, smooth and non-glossy. A clutch, usually of 4–5 eggs, but only one in the Black Swift, is laid in a nest of plant debris or small twigs, glued together with saliva; on a ledge or crevice of cliffs or rocks, or glued to an upright surface in a hollow tree or chimney.

1. **Chimney Swift,** *Chaetura pelagica.* **page** 183

(**Vaux** and **White-throated Swift,** not shown, have similar eggs to those of the Chimney Swift.)

2. **Black Swift,** *Cypseloides niger.* 182

KINGFISHERS. The eggs are smooth, very glossy, and sometimes almost spherical. A clutch, usually of 4–7 eggs, is laid in an unlined tunnel in a bank or natural cavity, but may gradually become surrounded by food castings such as fish bones.

3. **Belted Kingfisher,** *Megaceryle alcyon.* 191

(**Ringed Kingfisher,** not shown, has similar but larger eggs.)

4. **Green Kingfisher,** *Chloroceryle americana.* 191

TROGONS. The eggs are smooth and non-glossy. A clutch, usually of 3–4 eggs, is laid in a natural cavity, old woodpecker hole, or possibly hole excavated by the bird itself on rotten wood.

5. **Coppery-tailed Trogon,** *Trogon elegans.* 191

WOODPECKERS. The eggs are smooth, rounded and glossy. A clutch, usually of 3–7 eggs, is laid in an unlined cavity in a tree, pole or cactus.

6. **Pileated Woodpecker,** *Dryocopos pileatus.* 195
7. **Common Flicker,** *Colaptes auratus.* 194
8. **Lewis's Woodpecker,** *Asyndesmus lewis.* 197
9. **Red-bellied Woodpecker,** *Centurus carolinus.* 195
10. **Golden-fronted Woodpecker,** *Centurus aurifrons.* 195
11. **Gila Woodpecker,** *Centurus uropygialis.* 196
12. **Red-headed Woodpecker,** *Melanerpes erythrocephalus.* 196
13. **Acorn Woodpecker,** *Melanerpes formicivorus.* 197
14. **Yellow-bellied Sapsucker,** *Sphyrapicus varius.* 197
15. **Nuttall's Woodpecker,** *Dendrocopos nuttalli.* 198
16. **Hairy Woodpecker,** *Dendrocopos villosus.* 198
17. **Downy Woodpecker,** *Dendrocopos pubescens.* 198
18. **Ladder-backed Woodpecker,** *Dendrocopos scalaris.* 198
19. **Arctic Woodpecker,** *Picoides arcticus.* 199
20. **Northern Three-toed Woodpecker,** *Picoides tridactylus.* 200

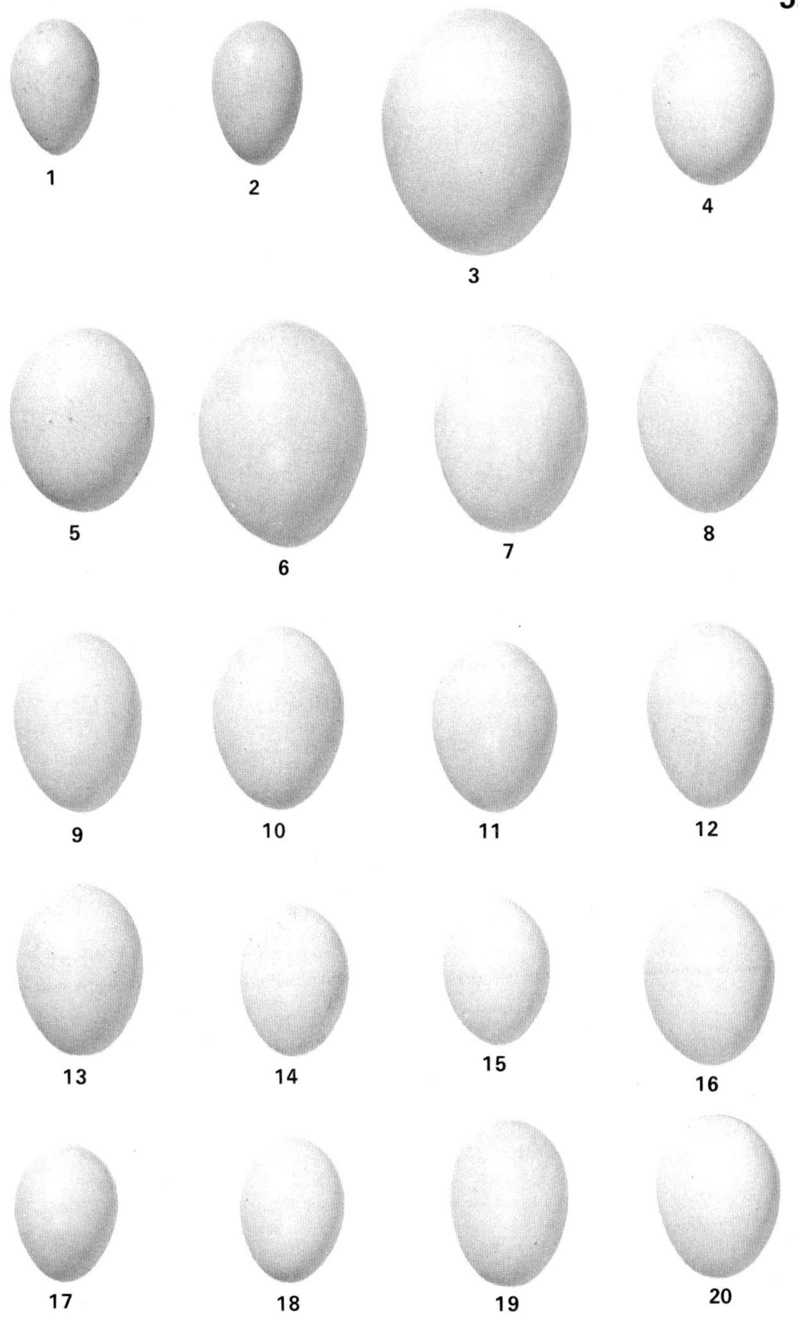
1
2
3
4
5
6
7
8
9
10
11
12
13
14
15
16
17
18
19
20

Plate 53 Approx. life-size

BECARDS. The eggs are smooth and slightly glossy. A clutch of 4–6 is laid in a rounded pendent nest of plant material hung from a twig of a tree.

1. **Rose-throated Becard,** *Platypsaris aglaiae.* **page** 200

TYRANT-FLYCATCHERS (see also pl. 54). The eggs are smooth, and slightly glossy. A clutch, usually of 3–6 eggs, is laid in a nest, usually a cup, domed in a few species, on a tree or shrub, in a cavity, on the ground or on a ledge.

2. **Eastern Kingbird,** *Tyrannus tyrannus.* 201
3. **Gray Kingbird,** *Tyrannus dominicensis.* 201
4. **Tropical Kingbird,** *Tyrannus melancholicus.* 201
5. **Western Kingbird,** *Tyrannus verticalis.* 202
6. **Cassin's Kingbird,** *Tyrannus vociferans.* 202

7 (a-b). **Scissor-tailed Flycatcher,** *Muscivora forficata.* 202

8. **Kiskadee Flycatcher,** *Pitangus suphuratus.* 202
9. **Sulphur-bellied Flycatcher,** *Myiodynastes luteiventris.* 203
10. **Great Crested Flycatcher,** *Myiarchus crinitus.* 203
11. **Wied's Crested Flycatcher,** *Myiarchus tyrannulus.* 203
12. **Ash-throated Flycatcher,** *Myiarchus cinerascens.* 204
13. **Olivaceous Flycatcher,** *Myiarchus tuberculifer.* 204
14. **Eastern Phoebe,** *Sayornis phoebe.* 204
15. **Black Phoebe,** *Sayornis nigricans.* 205
16. **Say's Phoebe,** *Sayornis saya.* 205
17. **Yellow-bellied Flycatcher,** *Empidonax flaviventris.* 206
18. **Acadian Flycatcher,** *Empidonax virescens.* 206
19. **Willow Flycatcher,** *Empidonax trailli.* Alder Flycatcher eggs are similar. 206
20. **Least Flycatcher,** *Empidonax minimus.* 207
21. **Hammond's Flycatcher,** *Empidonax hammondi.* 207
22. **Dusky Flycatcher,** *Empidonax oberholseri.* 208
23. **Gray Flycatcher,** *Empidonax wrightii.* 208
24. **Western Flycatcher,** *Empidonax difficilis.* 208

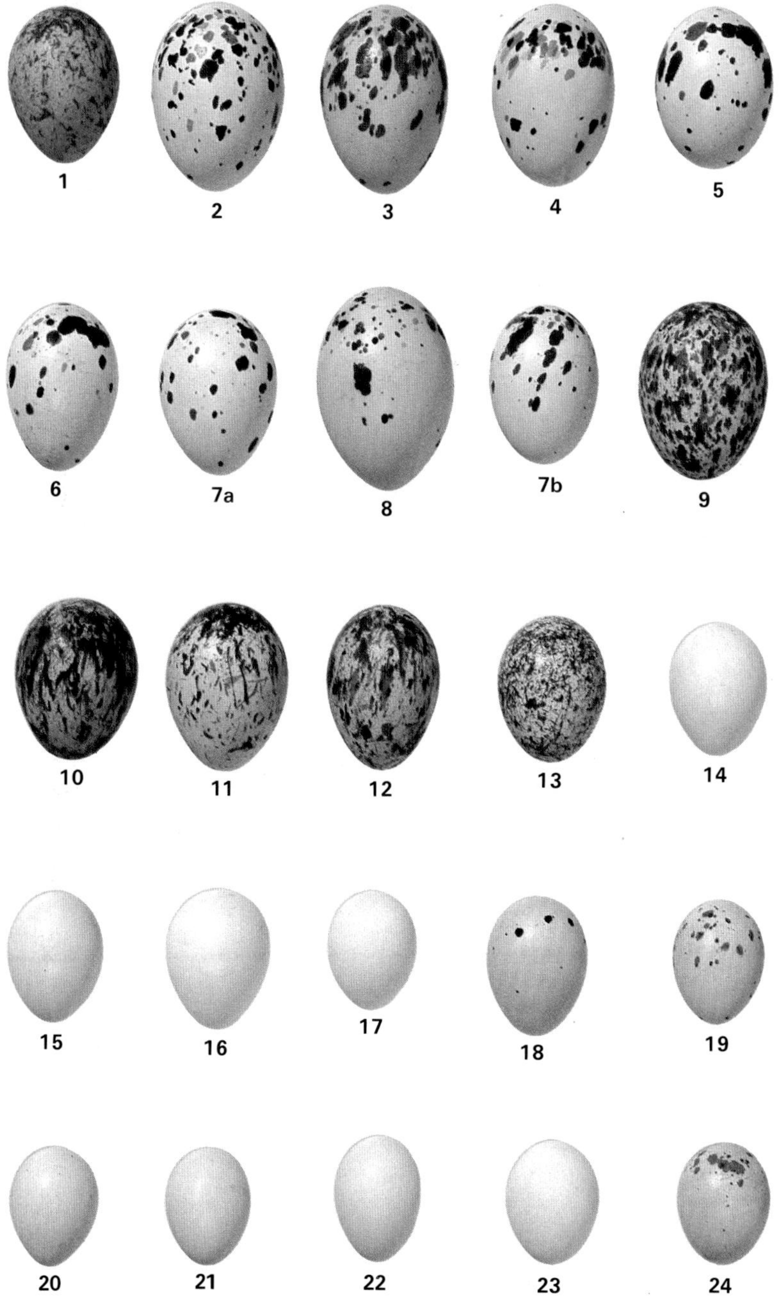
1
2
3
4
5
6
7a
8
7b
9
10
11
12
13
14
15
16
17
18
19
20
21
22
23
24

Plate 54 Approx. life-size

TYRANT-FLYCATCHERS (see also pl. 53). The eggs are smooth and slightly glossy. A clutch, usually of 3–6 eggs, is laid in a nest, usually a cup, domed in a few species, on a tree or shrub.

1. **Coue's Flycatchers,** *Contopus pertinax.* **page** 209

(**Buff-breasted Flycatcher,** not shown, has unmarked creamy-white eggs.)

2. **Eastern Wood Pewee,** *Contopus virens.* Western Wood Pewee has similar eggs. 209
3. **Olive-sided Flycatcher,** *Nuttallornis borealis.* 210
4. **Vermilion Flycatcher,** *Pyrocephalus rubinus.* 210
5. **Beardless Flycatcher,** *Comptostoma imberbe.* 210

LARKS. The eggs are smooth and glossy and cryptically patterned. A clutch, usually of 3–5 eggs, is laid in a cup nest on the ground.

6. **Skylark,** *Alauda arvensis.* 211
7. **Horned Lark,** *Eremophila alpestris.* 211

SWALLOWS and MARTINS. The eggs are smooth and non-glossy or slightly glossy, and often elongated. A clutch, usually of 2–5 eggs, is laid in a cup nest in a tree cavity or earth tunnel, or in a mud nest fixed to rocks or walls.

8. **Violet-green Swallow,** *Tachycineta thalassina.* 212
9. **Tree Swallow,** *Iridoprocne bicolor.* 212
10. **Bank Swallow,** *Riparia riparia.* 212
11. **Rough-winged Swallow,** *Stelgidopteryx ruficollis.* 212
12. **Barn Swallow,** *Hirundo rustica.* 213
13. **Cliff Swallow,** *Petrochelidon pyrrhonota.* 214
14. **Cave Swallow,** *Petrochelidon fulva.* 215
15. **Purple Martin,** *Progne subis.* 216

BUSHTIT, VERDIN and TITMICE. Eggs smooth and often rather rounded. Non-glossy or slightly glossy. A clutch, usually of 5–8 eggs, is laid in a pendent domed nest in the Bushtit, rounded domed nest in the Verdin and in a natural or excavated tree cavity in other species.

16. **Bushtit,** *Psaltriparus minimus.* 221
17. **Verdin,** *Auriparus flaviceps.* 223
18. **Black-capped Chickadee,** *Parus atricapillus.* 223
19. **Carolina Chickadee,** *Parus carolinensis.* 224
20. **Mexican Chickadee,** *Parus sclateri.* 224
21. **Mountain Chickadee,** *Parus gambeli.* 224
22. **Gray-headed Chickadee,** *Parus cinctus.* 224
23. **Boreal Chickadee,** *Parus hudsonicus.* 225
24. **Chestnut-backed Chickadee,** *Parus rufescens.* 225
25. **Tufted Titmouse,** *Parus bicolor.* 225
26. **Black-crested Titmouse,** *Parus atricristatus.* 225
27. **Plain Titmouse,** *Parus inornatus.* 226

(**Bridled Titmouse,** not shown, has unmarked eggs similar to those of the Plain Titmouse.)

1
2
3
4
5
6
7
8
9
10
11
12
13
14
15
16
17
18
19
20
21
22
23
24
25
26
27

Plate 55 Approx. life-size

JAYS, MAGPIES and CROWS (see also pl. 56). The eggs ar smooth and glossy. A clutch, usually of 3–4 eggs, is laid in a largish stick nest with soft lining in a tree or shrub, or on a ledge.

1. **Scrub Jay,** *Aphelocoma coerulescens.* The egg color varies from blue to pale olive green, sometimes washed with pink, rarely whitish, pale buff or light green; marked in olive-brown or reddish. **page** 217
2. **Mexican Jay,** *Aphelocoma ultramarina.* The egg color varies from greenish-blue to yellowish-green. Sometimes unmarked. 218
3. **Green Jay,** *Cyanocorax yncas.* The egg color varies from creamy-white to pale greenish, buff or olive. 218
4. **Pinyon Jay,** *Gymnorhinus cyanocephalus.* The egg color is bluish, greenish or bluish-white. 220
5. **Black-billed Magpie,** *Pica pica.* The egg color varies from greenish-blue to grayish, blue, buff and olive. 218
6. **Yellow-billed Magpie,** *Pica nuttalli.* The eggs are similar to those of the Black-billed Magpie. 219
7. **Clark's Nutcracker,** *Nucifraga columbiana.* 221

8 (a-b). **American Crow,** *Corvus brachyrhynchos.* The egg color varies from greenish-blue to pale blue, with variable markings. Two examples are shown here. 219

9. **Northern Raven,** *Corvus corax.* The egg color varies from light blue to pale green. 219
10. **White-necked Raven,** *Corvus cryptoleucus.* 219
11. **North-western Crow,** *Corvus caurinus.* The egg color varies from blue to green with variable markings. 220
12. **Fish Crow,** *Corvus ossifragus.* The egg color varies like those of other crows. 220

1
2
3
4
5
6
7
8a
9
8b
10
11
12

Plate 56 Approx. life-size

JAYS (see also pl. 55). The eggs are smooth and glossy. A clutch, usually of 3–4 eggs, is laid in a stick nest in a tree or shrub.

1. **Gray Jay,** *Perisoreus canadensis.* **page** 216
2. (a-b). **Blue Jay,** *Cyanocitta cristata.* The egg color varies from pale olive to green, bluish-green, buff, pinkish-buff or whitish. Two examples are shown here. 216
3. **Steller's Jay,** *Cyanocitta stelleri.* 217

NUTHATCHES and BROWN CREEPER. Eggs are smooth and slightly glossy, non-glossy in the creeper, and rather rounded. A clutch, usually of 4–9 eggs, is laid in a cup nest in a cavity in a tree, or in a crevice in the case of the creeper.

4. **White-breasted Nuthatch,** *Sitta carolinensis.* 226
5. **Red-breasted Nuthatch,** *Sitta canadensis.* 227
6. **Brown-headed Nuthatch,** *Sitta pusilla.* The egg color varies from white to buff. 227
7. **Pygmy Nuthatch,** *Sitta pygmaea.* 227
8. **Brown Creeper,** *Certhia familiaris.* 228

WRENS and DIPPER. The eggs are smooth and glossy. A clutch, usually of 4–8 eggs, is laid in a domed nest – in the dipper sited by and overlooking water, in wrens in a tree, shrub, grasses, cavity or crevice.

9. (a-c). **House Wren,** *Troglodytes aedon.* Egg color may vary from white to pinkish or brown. Three examples are shown. 230
10. **Winter Wren,** *Troglodytes troglodytes.* 231
11. **Bewick's Wren,** *Thryomanes bewickii.* 232
12. **Carolina Wren,** *Thryothorus ludovicianus.* 232
13. **Dipper,** *Cinclus mexicanus.* 230
14. **Long-billed Marsh Wren,** *Telmatodytes palustris.* 234
15. **Short-billed Marsh Wren,** *Cistothorus platensis.* 234
16. **Canyon Wren,** *Catherpes mexicanus.* 234
17. **Rock Wren,** *Salpinctes obsoletus.* 235
18. **Cactus Wren,** *Campylorhynchus brunneicapillus.* 232

MOCKINGBIRDS and THRASHERS (see also pl. 57). The eggs are smooth and glossy. A clutch, usually of 3–5 eggs, is laid in a cup nest in a tree, shrub or cactus.

19. **Mockingbird,** *Mimus polyglottus.* The egg color varies from pale to greenish blue. 235
20. **Gray Catbird,** *Dumatella carolinensis.* 236
21. **Brown Thrasher,** *Toxostoma rufum.* 236
22. **Long-billed Thrasher,** *Toxostoma longirostre.* 236
23. **Bendire's Thrasher,** *Toxostoma bendirei.* 237

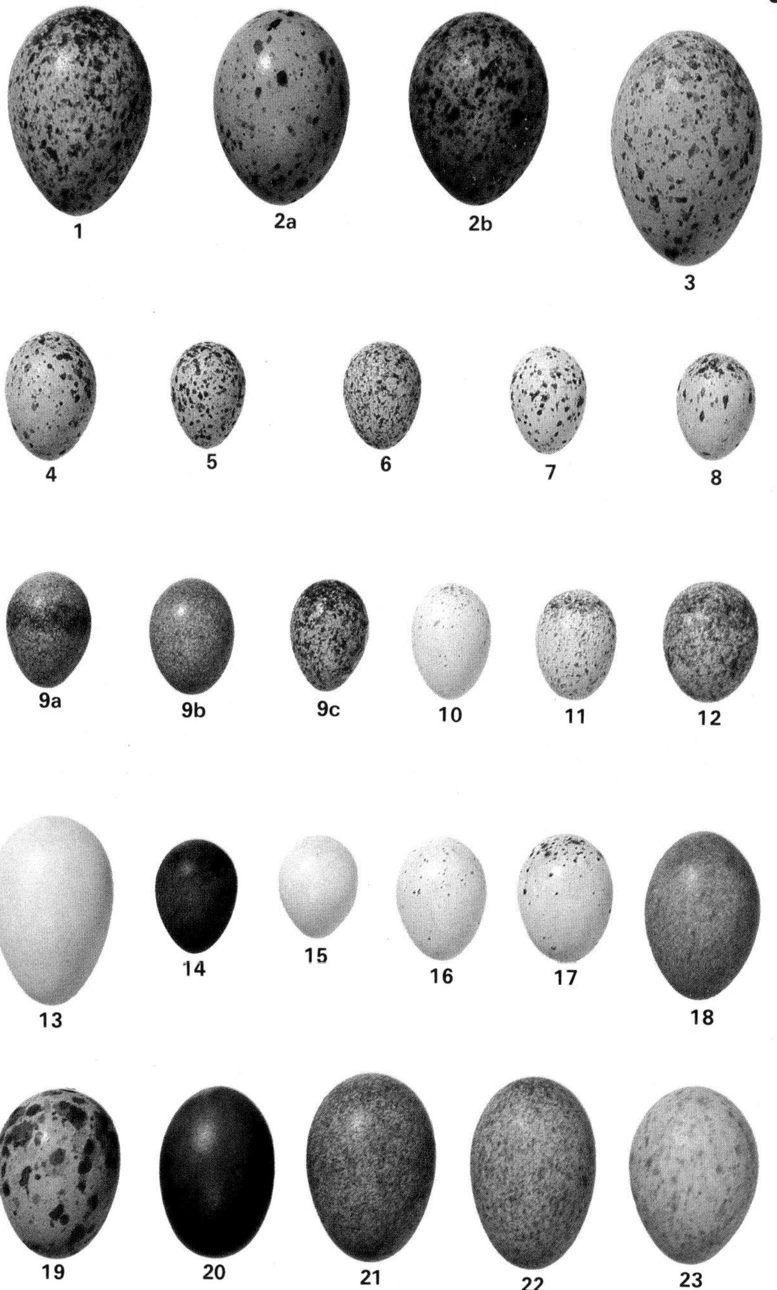
1
2a
2b
3
4
5
6
7
8
9a
9b
9c
10
11
12
13
14
15
16
17
18
19
20
21
22
23

Plate 57 Approx. life-size

THRASHERS (see also pl. 56). The eggs are smooth and glossy. A clutch, usually of 3–5 eggs, is laid in a cup nest in a tree, shrub or cactus.

1. **Curve-billed Thrasher,** *Toxostoma curvirostre.* **page** 237
2. **California Thrasher,** *Toxostoma redivivum.* 237
3. **Le Conte's Thrasher,** *Toxostoma lecontei.* 237
4. **Crissal Thrasher,** *Toxostoma dorsale.* 238
5. **Sage Thrasher,** *Oreoscoptes montanus.* 238

THRUSHES and BLUEBIRDS. The eggs are smooth and glossy. A clutch, usually of 3–6 eggs, is laid in a cup nest, in a tree or shrub, on a ledge or on the ground. Bluebirds build skimpy nests in natural cavities.

6. **American Robin,** *Turdus migratorius.* 238
7. **Fieldfare,** *Turdus pilaris.* The pinkish wash and reddish markings may obliterate the blue ground color. 239
8. **Varied Thrush,** *Zoothera naevia.* 239
9. **Wood Thrush,** *Hyocichla mustelina.* 239
10. **Hermit Thrush,** *Hyocichla guttata.* 242
11. **Swainson's Thrush,** *Hylocichla ustulata.* 242
12. **Gray-cheeked Thrush,** *Hylocichla minima.* 242
13. **Veery,** *Hylocichla fuscescens.* 243
14. **Wheatear,** *Oenanthe oenanthe.* 244
15. **Bluethroat,** *Luscinia svecica.* 244
16. **Eastern Bluebird,** *Sialia sialis.* 243
17. **Western Bluebird,** *Sialia mexicana.* 243
18. **Mountain Bluebird,** *Sialia currucoides.* 243
19. **Townsend's Solitaire,** *Myadestes townsendi.* 244

BABBLER. The eggs are smooth and non-glossy to slightly glossy. A clutch, usually of 4 eggs, is laid in a cup nest in a tree or shrub.

20. **Wrentit,** *Chamaea fasciata.* 229

NEW WORLD WARBLERS, KINGLETS and GNATCATCHERS. The eggs are smooth and glossy to non-glossy. A clutch usually of 4–6, or 7–9 in the kinglets, is laid in a nest, domed and on the ground, or a cup supported or suspended in a tree or shrub.

21. **Arctic Warbler,** *Phylloscopus borealis.* 245
22. **Blue-gray Gnatcatcher,** *Polioptila caerulea.* 246
23. **Black-tailed Gnatcatcher,** *Polioptila melanura.* 247
24. **Golden-crowned Kinglet,** *Regulus satrapa.* 245
25. **Ruby-crowned Kinglet,** *Regulus calendula.* 245

1
2
3
4
5
6
7
8
9
10
11
12
13
14
15
16
17
18
19
20
21
22
23
24
25

Plate 58 Approx. life-size

WAGTAILS and PIPITS. Eggs glossy. 4–6 eggs laid in a cup nest on the ground among herbage or in a cavity or crevice.

1. **White Wagtail,** *Motacilla alba.* **page** 248
2. **Yellow Wagtail,** *Motacilla flava.* 248
3. **Water Pipit,** *Anthus spinoletta.* 248
4. **Meadow Pipit,** *Anthus pratensis.* 249
5. **Sprague's Pipit,** *Anthus spragueii.* The egg color varies from grayish-white to pale buff. 249

SHRIKES. The eggs are smooth and glossy. A clutch, usually of 4–7, is laid in a bulky cup nest in a tree or shrub.

6. **Northern Shrike,** *Lanius excubitor.* The egg color varies from white to greenish or buff, with markings of variable color. 251
7. **Loggerhead Shrike,** *Lanius ludovicianus.* 251

SILKY FLYCATCHER and WAXWINGS. Eggs slightly to moderately glossy. 2–5 eggs, laid in a cup nest in a tree or shrub.

8. **Phainopepla,** *Phainopepla nitens.* 250
9. **Bohemian Waxwing,** *Bombycilla garrulus.* 249
10. **Cedar Waxwing,** *Bombycilla cedrorum.* 250

VIREOS. Eggs smooth and non-glossy to moderately glossy. 3–4 eggs laid in a pensile cup nest suspended between horizontal twigs.

11. **Black-capped Vireo,** *Vireo atricapillus.* 252
12. **White-eyed Vireo,** *Vireo griseus.* 253
13. **Hutton's Vireo,** *Vireo huttoni.* 253
14. **Bell's Vireo,** *Vireo belli.* 253

(**Gray Vireo,** not shown, has eggs similar to those of Bell's Vireo.)

15. **Yellow-throated Vireo,** *Vireo flavifrons.* 254
16. **Solitary Vireo,** *Vireo solitarius.* 255
17. **Black-whiskered Vireo,** *Vireo altiloquus.* 255
18. **Red-eyed Vireo,** *Vireo olivaceus.* 255
19. **Philadelphia Vireo,** *Vireo philadelphicus.* 255
20. **Warbling Vireo,** *Vireo gilvus.* 258

OLD WORLD SPARROWS. Eggs slightly glossy. 3–6 laid in a domed nest or untidy cup, usually in a hole or crevice, rarely in a more open site.

21 (a–c). **House Sparrow,** *Passer domesticus.* Markings highly variable. A clutch may contain one or two very pale eggs. 284

22 (a–b). **Eurasian Tree Sparrow,** *Passer montanus.* The eggs are variable but less so than those of the House Sparrow. 284

1 2 3 4 5

6 7 8 9 10

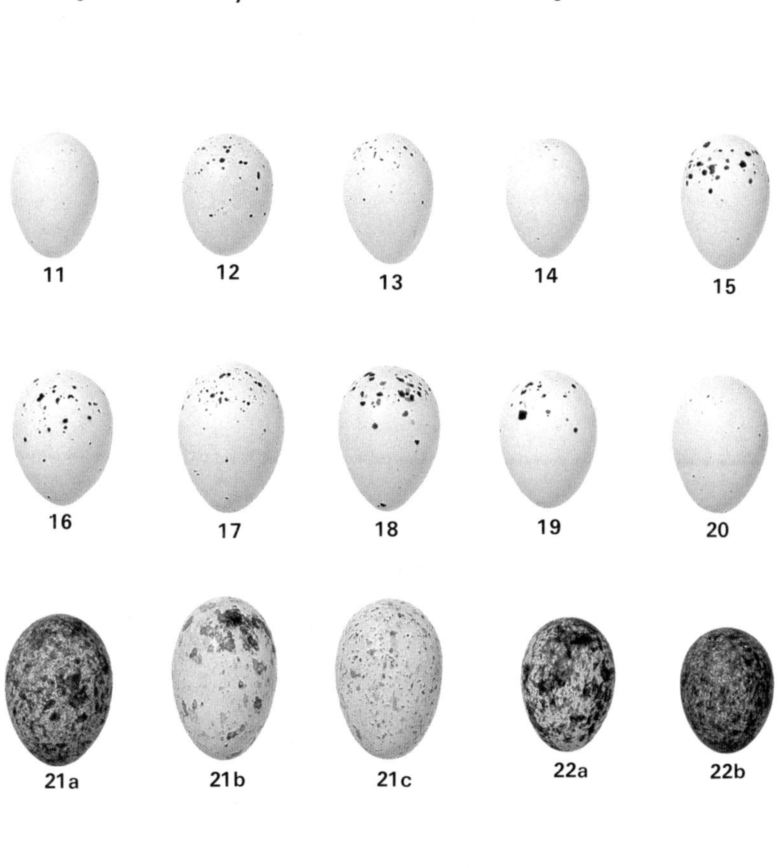

Plate 59 Approx. life-size, but nos. 5, 8, 18, 22, 23 and 24 are approx. ¾ life-size.

AMERICAN WOOD WARBLERS (see also pl. 60). The eggs are smooth and slightly glossy; sometimes rather rounded. 3–5 eggs laid in a cup or sometimes a domed nest, in a tree or shrub, on the ground or in a cavity.

1. **Black and White Warbler,** *Mniotilta varia.* **page** 258
2. **Prothronotary Warbler,** *Protonotaria citrea.* The egg color varies from yellowish to white or pale pink. 259
3. **Swainson's Warbler,** *Limnothlypis swainsonii.* 259
4. **Worm-eating Warbler,** *Helmitheros vermivorus.* The eggs are unmarked or finely spotted. 259
5. **Golden-winged Warbler,** *Vermivora chrysoptera.* 259
6. **Blue-winged Warbler,** *Vermivora pinus.* 260

(**Bachman's Warbler,** not shown, has unmarked, white eggs.)

7. **Tennessee Warbler,** *Vermivora peregrina.* 260
8. **Gray-crowned Yellowthroat,** *Geothlypis poliocephala.* 272
9. **Orange-crowned Warbler,** *Vermivora celata.* 260
10. **Nashville Warbler,** *Vermivora ruficapilla.* 261
11. **Virginia's Warbler,** *Vermivora virginiae.* 261
12. **Lucy's Warbler,** *Vermivora luciae.* 261

(**Colima Warbler,** not shown, has creamy white eggs, speckled or blotched in dull brown and buff, often wreathing larger end.)

13. **Northern Parula,** *Parula americana.* 262
14. **Tropical Parula,** *Parula pitiayumi.* 262
15. **Olive Warbler,** *Peucedramus taeniatus.* 262
16. **Yellow Warbler,** *Dendroica petechia.* 263
17. **Magnolia Warbler,** *Dendroica magnolia.* 263
18. **Cape May Warbler,** *Dendroica tigrina.* 264
19. **Painted Redstart,** *Setophaga picta* 274
20. **Yellow-rumped Warbler,** *Dendroica coronata.* 264

(**Black-throated Blue Warbler,** not shown, has eggs white to greenish-white variably marked in brown, reddish and gray.)

21. **Red-faced Warbler,** *Cardellina rubrifrons.* 273
22. **Black-throated Gray Warbler,** *Dendroica nigrescens.* 265
23. **Townsend's Warbler,** *Dendroica townsendi.* 265
24. **Black-throated Green Warbler,** *Dendroica virens.* 265
25. **Golden-cheeked Warbler,** *Dendroica chrysoparia.* 265

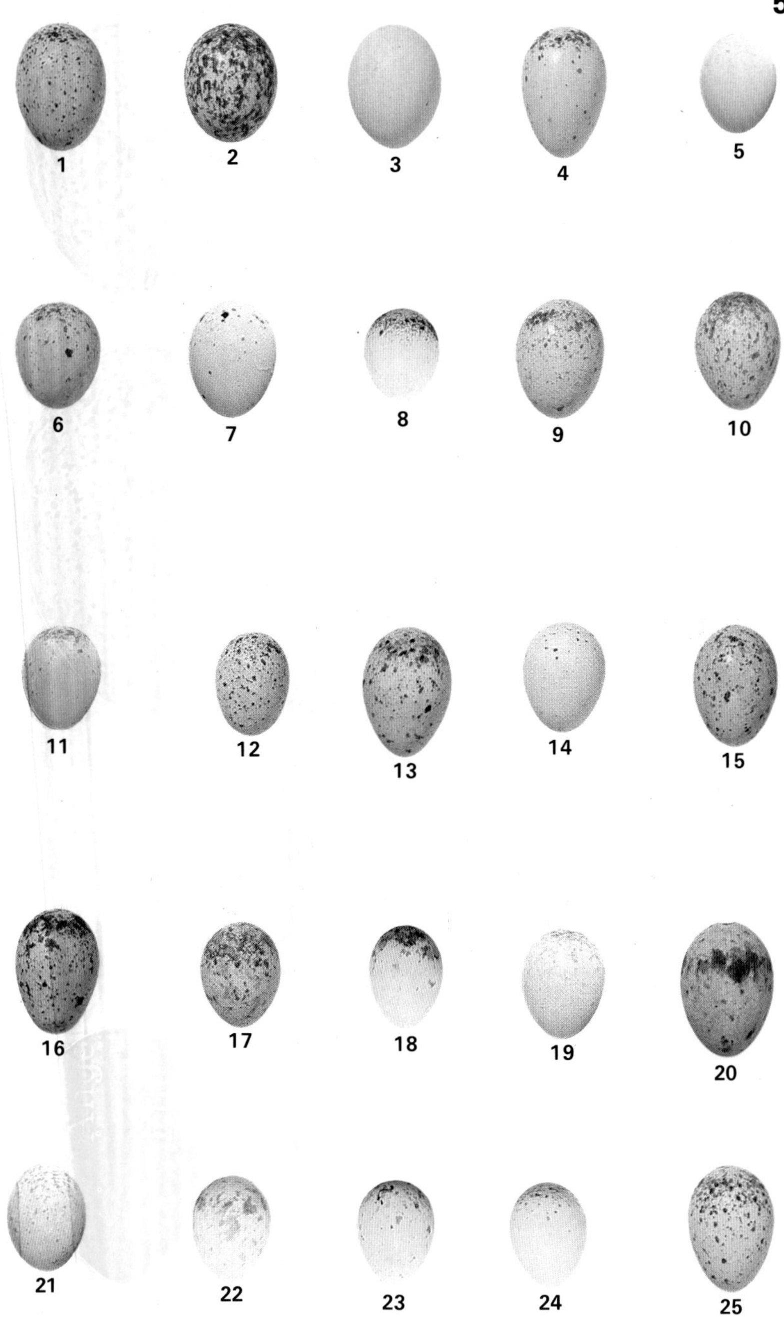
1
2
3
4
5
6
7
8
9
10
11
12
13
14
15
16
17
18
19
20
21
22
23
24
25

Plate 60 Approx. life-size, but nos. 5, 17 and 18 are approx. ¾ life-size.

AMERICAN WOOD WARBLERS (see also pl. 59). The eggs are smooth and slightly glossy; sometimes rather rounded. A clutch, usually of 3–5 eggs, is laid in a cup or sometimes a domed nest, in a tree or shrub, on the ground, or in a cavity.

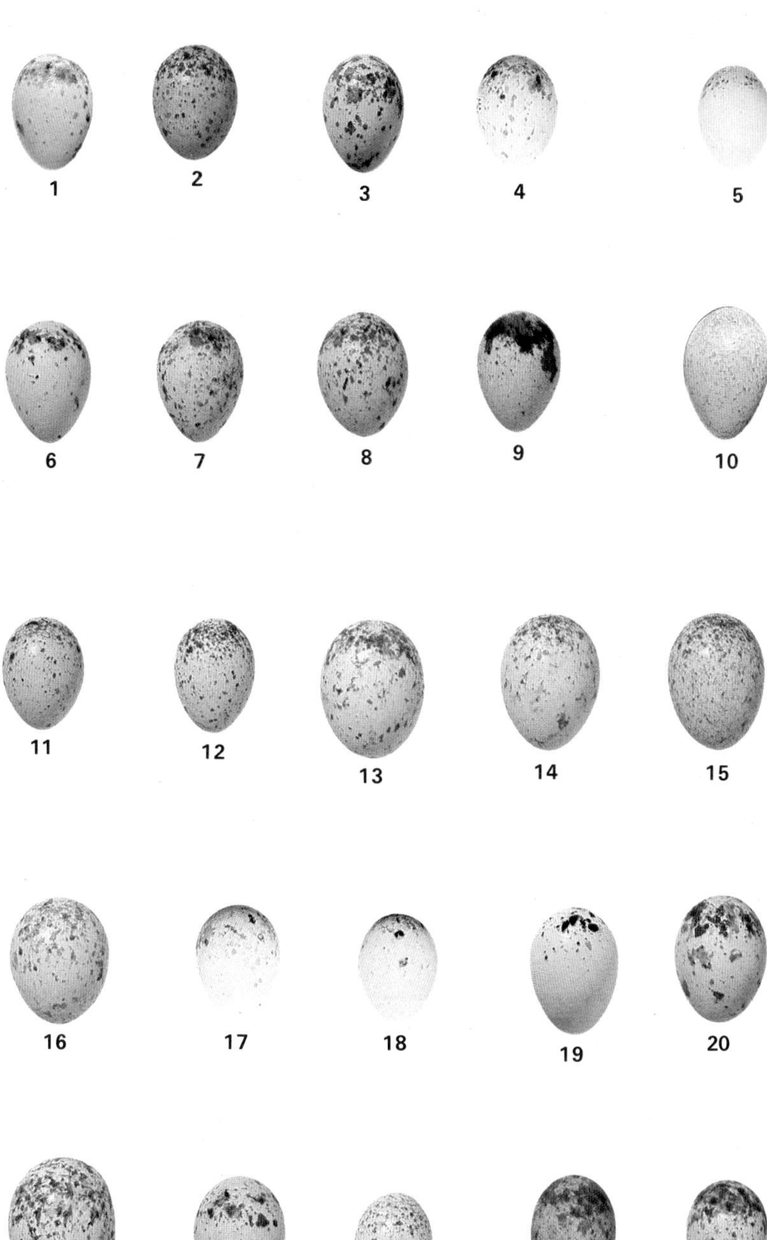
1
2
3
4
5
6
7
8
9
10
11
12
13
14
15
16
17
18
19
20
21
22
23
24
25

Plate 61 Approx. life-size

BLACKBIRDS and ORIOLES. The eggs are smooth and glossy, varying in different species from elongated to rather round. A clutch, usually of 3–5 eggs, is laid in a bulky cup in a tree, shrub or herbage, in a deep cup among waterside plants, a domed nest on the ground in grasses, or a pensile cup or long pensile bag suspended from a twig. Cowbirds are brood parasites, laying single eggs in other birds' nests.

1 (a–b). **Eastern Meadowlark,** *Sturnella magna.* There is some variation in markings and two examples are shown here. **page** 275

2 (a–b). **Western Meadowlark,** *Sturnella neglecta.* Two examples are shown. 276

3. **Tri-colored Blackbird,** *Agelaius tricolor.* 277

4 (a–c). **Red-winged Blackbird,** *Agelaius phoeniceus.* The egg color varies from blue to purple with variable markings. Three examples are shown here. 277

5. **Yellow-headed Blackbird,** *Xanthocephalus xanthocephalus.* 276

6. **Orchard Oriole,** *Icterus spurius.* 278

7. **Bobolink,** *Dolichonyx oryzivorus.* 275

8. **Scott's Oriole,** *Icterus parisomum.* 279

9. **Hooded Oriole,** *Icterus cucullatus.* 279

10 (a–b). **Northern Oriole,** *Icterus galbula.* Two examples are shown. 280

(**Black-headed Oriole, Lichtenstein's Oriole** and **Spotted-breasted Oriole,** not shown, have similar eggs to those of the Northern Oriole.)

11. **Common Grackle,** *Quiscalis quiscala.* 282

12. **Rusty Blackbird,** *Euphagus carolinus.* 280

13. **Brewer's Blackbird,** *Euphagus cyanocephalus.* 281

14. **Great-tailed Grackle,** *Cassidex mexicanus.* 282

15. **Boat-tailed Grackle,** *Cassidex major.* 281

16. **Brown Cowbird,** *Molothrus ater.* 282

17. **Bronzed Cowbird,** *Tangavius aeneus.* 283

1a
1b
2a
2b
3
4a
4b
4c
5
6
7
8
9
10a
10b
11
12
13
14
15
16
17

Plate 62 Approx. life-size

STARLINGS. The eggs are smooth and glossy. A clutch, usually of 4–7 eggs, is laid in a cup nest in a cavity.

1. **Starling,** *Sturnus vulgaris.* **page** 252

(**Crested Mynah,** not shown, has eggs like those of the Starling.)

FINCHES. The eggs are smooth and non-glossy to moderately glossy. A clutch, usually of 3–5 eggs, is laid in a cup nest in a tree, shrub or ground herbage.

2. **Evening Grosbeak,** *Hesperiphona vespertina.* 285
3. **Purple Finch,** *Carpodacus purpureus.* 285
4. **Cassin's Finch,** *Carpodacus cassinii.* 285
5. **House Finch,** *Carpodacus mexicanus.* Markings are sometimes absent. 286
6. **Pine Grosbeak,** *Pinicola enucleator.* 286
7. **Rosy Finch,** *Leucosticte tephrocotis.* 286
8. **Hoary Redpoll,** *Acanthis hornemanni.* 287
9. **Common Redpoll,** *Acanthis flammea.* 287
10. **Pine Siskin,** *Spinus pinus.* 287
11. **American Goldfinch,** *Spinus tristis.* 287
12. **Lesser Goldfinch,** *Spinus psaltria.* 385
13. **Lawrence's Goldfinch,** *Spinus lawrencei.* 386
14. **Red Crossbill,** *Loxia curvirostra.* 386
15. **White-winged Crossbill,** *Loxia leucoptera.* 386

BUNTINGS. The eggs are smooth and slightly to moderately glossy. A clutch, usually of 3–5 eggs, is laid in a cup nest, or rarely a domed structure, on the ground among herbage, or in a shrub or low tree.

16. **Olive Sparrow,** *Arremonops rufivirgatus.* 391
17. **Green-tailed Towhee,** *Chlorura chlorura.* 391
18. **Rufous-sided Towhee,** *Pipilo erythrophthalmus.* 391
19. **Brown Towhee,** *Pipilo fuscus.* 392
20. **Abert's Towhee,** *Pipilo aberti.* 392
21. **Lark Bunting,** *Calamospiza melanocorys.* 392
22. **Savannah Sparrow,** *Passerculus sandwichensis.* 392
23. **Grasshopper Sparrow,** *Ammodramus savannarum.* 393
24. **Baird's Sparrow,** *Ammodramus bairdii.* 393
25. **Le Conte's Sparrow,** *Ammospiza leconteii.* 394

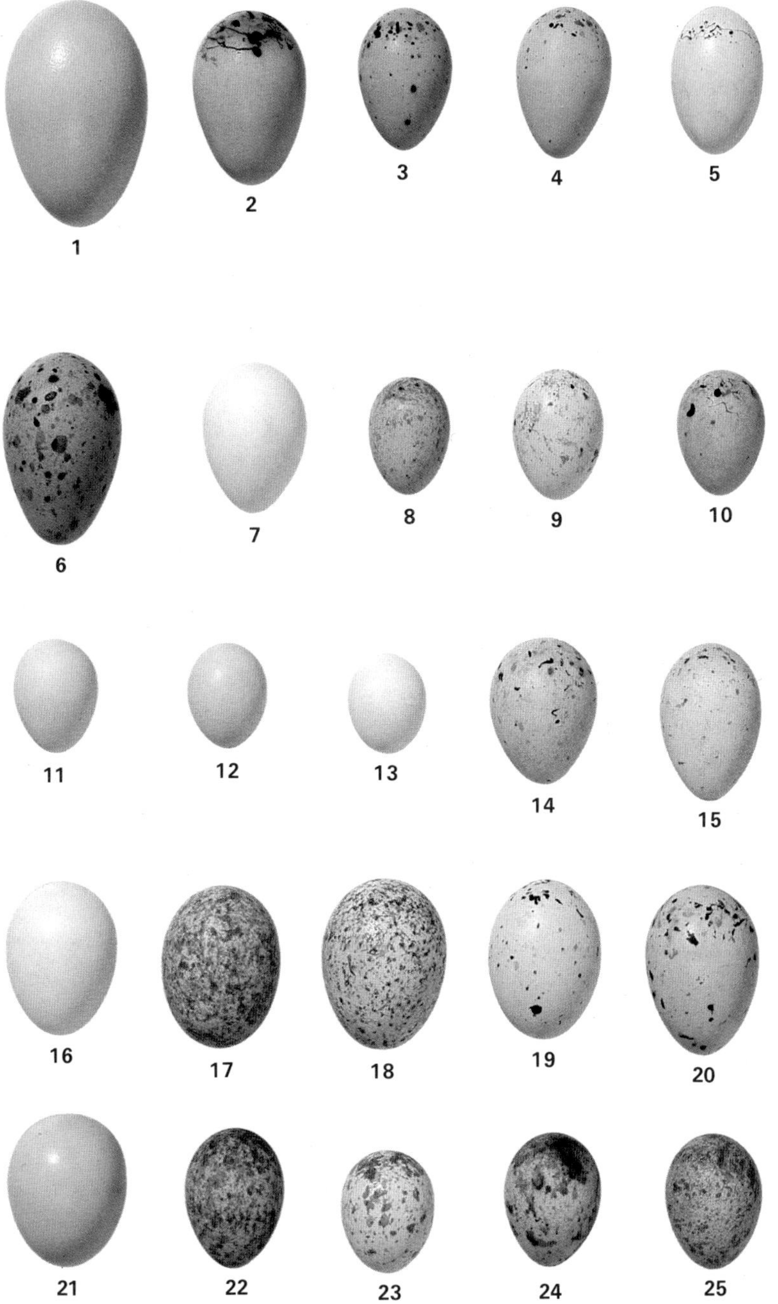

Plate 63 Approx. life-size

BUNTINGS. The eggs are smooth and slightly to moderately glossy. A clutch, usually of 3–5 eggs, is laid in a cup nest on the ground among herbage, or in a shrub or low tree.

(**Harris's Sparrow,** not shown, has white to pale greenish-white eggs marked with brown to reddish-brown.)

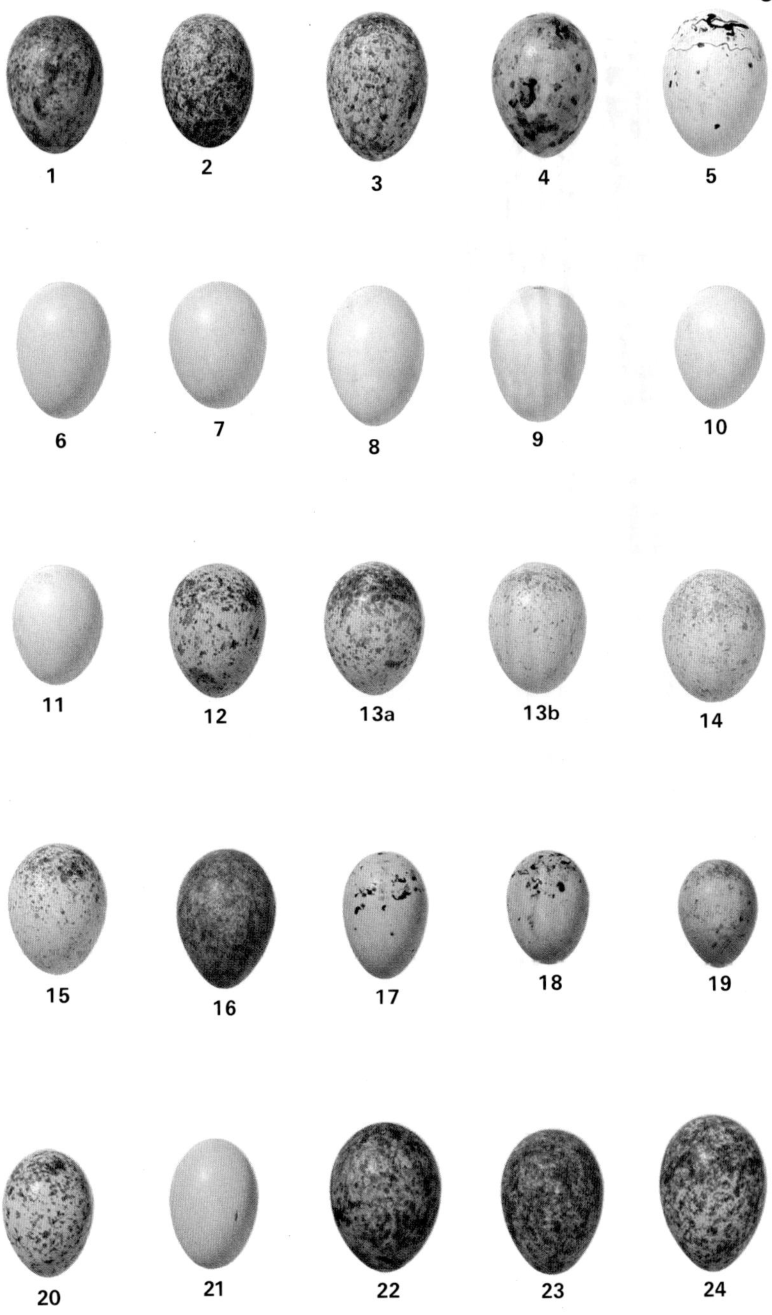
1
2
3
4
5
6
7
8
9
10
11
12
13a
13b
14
15
16
17
18
19
20
21
22
23
24

Plate 64 Approx. life-size

BUNTINGS, GROSBEAKS and TANAGERS. The eggs are smooth and slightly to moderately glossy. A clutch, usually of 3–5 eggs, is laid in a cup nest, on the ground among herbage, or in a shrub or low tree.

1. **Fox Sparrow,** *Passerella iliaca.* The egg color varies from blue to greenish-blue. **page** 401
2. **Lincoln's Sparrow,** *Melospiza lincolnii.* 402
3. **Swamp Sparrow,** *Melospiza georgiana.* 402
4. **Song Sparrow,** *Melospiza melodia.* 402
5. **White-collared Seedeater,** *Sporophila torqueola.* 388
6. **McCown's Longspur,** *Calcarius mccownii.* 403
7. **Lapland Longspur,** *Calcarius lapponicus.* 403
8. **Smith's Longspur,** *Calcarius pictus.* 404
9. **Chestnut-collared Longspur,** *Calcarius ornatus.* 404
10. **Snow Bunting,** *Plectrophenax nivalis.* 404
11. **Cardinal,** *Cardinalis cardinalis.* 388
12. **Pyrrhuloxia,** *Pyrrhuloxia sinuata.* 388
13. **Rose-breasted Grosbeak,** *Pheuticus ludovicianus.* 389
14. **Black-headed Grosbeak,** *Pheucticus melanocephalus.* 389
15. **Blue Grosbeak,** *Guiraca caerulea.* 389
16. **Indigo Bunting,** *Passerina cyanea.* 389
17. **Lazuli Bunting,** *Passerina amoena.* 390
18. **Varied Bunting,** *Passerina versicolor.* 390
19. **Painted Bunting,** *Passerina ciris.* 390
20. **Dickcissel,** *Spiza americana.* 390
21. **Western Tanager,** *Piranga ludoviciana.* 387
22. **Scarlet Tanager,** *Piranga olivacea.* 387
23. **Hepatic Tanager,** *Piranga flava.* 387
24. **Summer Tanager,** *Piranga rubra.* 387

1
2
3
4
5
6
7
8
9
10
11
12
13
14
15
16
17
18
19
20
21
22
23
24

low on tall weeds. Nest often near water or in swampy area. Nest placed on twigs or in fork or between uprights with nest material bound around supports. **Nest.** A neat compact cup of plant fibers and strips of bark, with catkins, plant down, cotton and wool; lined with plant down. Nest edges and probably elsewhere bound with spiders' and caterpillar webs and strengthened with long fibers. **Breeding season.** Begins April or May in south-west to mid-June or early July in east. **Eggs.** Usually 5, sometimes 4–6. Smooth and slightly glossy. Subelliptical to oval. Very pale blue or greenish-blue, unmarked. 16 × 12 mm. **Incubation.** By female alone, fed by male. 12–14 days. **Nestling.** Altricial and downy. Pale grayish down on head and body. Mouth pinkish-red. Gape flanges pale creamy-yellow. **Nestling period.** Young tended by both parents. Brooded by female during first week and all food brought by male. No droppings removed after *c.* 1 week. Young leave nest at 11–17 days.

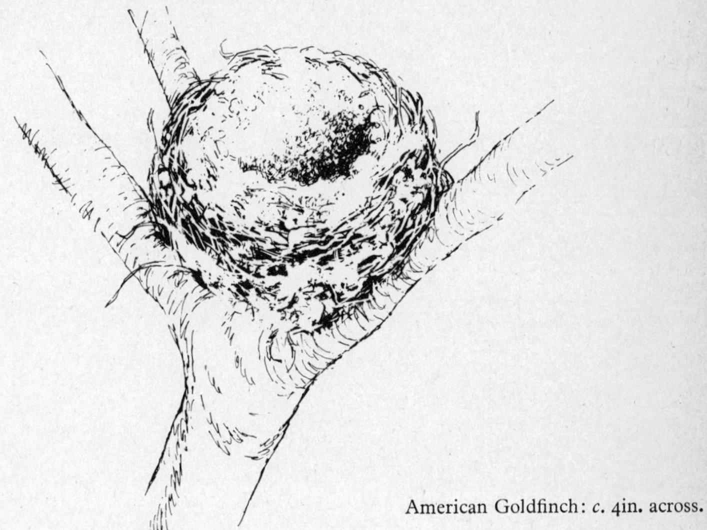

American Goldfinch: *c.* 4in. across.

LESSER GOLDFINCH *Spinus psaltria* **Pl. 62**

Breeds in more arid open country, in trees and shrubs close to water. Nest in a twig fork, usually well-hidden in foliage, and in larger trees may be well out in canopy. 2–30 ft. up, more usually 5–10 ft. up. Usually nest in solitary pairs. **Nest.** Fairly compact cup of fine grass stems, plant and bark fiber, and moss or wool; lined with very fine fibrous material or plant down. Built mostly or entirely by female. **Breeding season.** Begins late March in south to early May in north of range. **Eggs.** Usually 4–5, sometimes 3–6. Subelliptical to oval. Smooth and slightly glossy. Very pale blue or greenish-blue. Unmarked. 15 × 12 mm. **Incubation.** By female alone, fed by male. 12 days. **Nestling.** Altricial and downy. **Nestling period.** Young tended by both parents. Fed by regurgitation. Nest sanitation ceases about halfway through period.

LAWRENCE'S GOLDFINCH *Spinus lawrencei* **Pl. 62**

Breeds in drier regions with scattered trees or open woodland. Nest often, but not always, in conifers from 3–40 ft. up, but usually 15–20 ft. up; in a twig fork. Pairs nest singly or with a number nesting near each other.

Nest. A small cup, usually of coarser material; stems, grasses and lichen towards the outside, but including grass and flower heads, wool, hair and feathers. Built by female. **Breeding season.** Begins late March to early April. **Eggs.** Usually 4–5, sometimes 3–6. Subelliptical to oval. Smooth and slightly glossy. White and unmarked. 15 × 12 mm. **Incubation.** By female alone, fed by male. **Nestling.** Altricial and downy. **Nestling period.** Young tended by both parents. Leave at *c.* 11 days.

RED CROSSBILL *Loxia curvirostra* **Pl. 62**

Breeds in conifers on edges of woodland, or in scattered groups of trees. Nest at varying heights, 6–60 ft. up, usually high and well out on a branch, among twigs and foliage.

Nest. A basal cup of pine twigs, built up with grasses, moss, lichen and wool; and with a finer inner cup of fine grass, moss, hair, fur and feathers. **Breeding season.** Very variably, usually beginning in January or February, but at times earlier, and extending sometimes to July. Single-brooded. **Eggs.** Usually 3–4, sometimes 2–5. Subelliptical. Smooth and glossy. Very pale blue or bluish-white, variable and sparsely marked with specks, spots and short scrawls of purple or purplish-black, and fainter pale pink and lilac, mostly limited to the larger end. 22 × 16 mm. **Incubation.** Eggs laid at daily intervals. Incubation by female only, beginning with first egg. 13–16 days. **Nestling.** Altricial and downy. Down dark grey. Mouth yellow and purplish-pink? Gape flanges pale yellow. **Nestling period.** For about a week the female broods the young while the male brings food, later both parents bring food. Young leave nest at 17–22 days, but depend on adults for 3–4 weeks afterwards.

WHITE-WINGED CROSSBILL *Loxia leucoptera* **Pl. 62**

Breeds in conifer forests. Nest in a tree, usually a conifer, built on branches, at varying heights and well-hidden in foliage.

Nest. A cup built on a foundation of twigs, of grass, lichens, moss and leaves; with inner lining of roots, lichen, moss, wool, hair and feathers. **Breeding season.** Begins early February. Usually single-brooded. **Eggs.** Usually 3–4, rarely 5. Subelliptical. Smooth and glossy. Like the eggs of Red Crossbill. Pale bluish or greenish-white, spotted or variably marked in dark purple and sometimes pale lilac at the larger end. 21 × 15 mm. **Incubation.** No information. **Nestling.** Altricial and downy. Mouth bright purplish-red. Mandibles not crossed. **Nestling period.** No information.

TANAGERS, GROSBEAKS AND BUNTINGS *Emberizidae*

Small seed-eating birds, chiefly nesting in more open habitats. Cup nests, or rarely domed structures, usually built by the female, often on or near the ground and well concealed in vegetation. Eggs with pale ground color, sometimes spotted and blotched but more often marked with intricate scrawling and scribbling. Incubation is usually by female alone. Nestlings downy. Down sparse or sometimes absent on the underside. Mouths usually pink or red, and gape flanges yellow or creamy-yellow. Young fed mainly on insects brought in the bill. With ground-nesting species young may leave the nest fairly early on, while still unable to fly.

WESTERN TANAGER *Piranga ludoviciana* **Pl. 64**

Breeds in mountain conifer forests. Nest in a tree, usually a conifer, rarely deciduous; at varying heights, 6–50 ft. up, usually well out on a branch, often at the fork of a horizontal limb.

Nest. A stout cup of twigs, rootlets and moss; lined with finer rootlets and hair. **Breeding season.** Begins early May in south to early June in north of range. **Eggs.** Usually 3–5, clutches smaller in south. Subelliptical to short subelliptical. Smooth and moderately glossy. Light blue or greenish-blue; finely speckled and spotted with brown, dark brown and paler gray. 23 × 17 mm. **Incubation.** By female alone. 13 days. **Nestling.** Altricial and downy. Down pale gray, on head, back and wings. Mouth orange-red. Gape flanges yellow. **Nestling period.** Young tended by both parents.

SCARLET TANAGER *Piranga olivacea* **Pl. 64**

Breeds in deciduous and pine-oak woodland, and orchards. Nest in a tree, usually well out on a branch at a twig fork. 15–45 ft. up.

Nest. A rather shallow and loose cup of twigs, grass, weed stems and rootlets; lined with finer grasses, weed stems and rootlets. **Breeding season.** Begins late May. **Eggs.** Usually 4, sometimes 3–5. Subelliptical to short subelliptical. Smooth and moderately glossy. Light blue or greenish-blue; finely speckled and spotted, and sometimes with small blotches of chestnut-red or purplish-red and paler lilac. Markings often finer than those of Summer Tanager. 23 × 16 mm. **Incubation.** By female alone. 13–14 days. **Nestling.** Altricial and downy. Down plentiful, light gray; on head, back and wings. Mouth orange-red. Gape flanges yellow. **Nestling period.** Young tended by both parents. Leave nest at 15 days.

HEPATIC TANAGER *Piranga flava* **Pl. 64**

Breeds in trees of mountain canyons. Nest on a conifer or deciduous tree, usually high up and well out on a branch at a fork. 18–30 ft. up.

Nest. A rather shallow cup of grass, weed stems and flower stalks; lined with finer grasses. **Breeding season.** Begins mid- to late May. **Eggs.** Usually 4, sometimes 3–5. Subelliptical to short subelliptical. Light blue or greenish-blue; speckled and spotted with chestnut-red, reddish-brown and brown, and paler lilac. Markings usually fine and profuse, but often with a concentration at or about the larger end. 24 × 18 mm. **Incubation.** No information. **Nestling.** No information. **Nestling period.** No information.

SUMMER TANAGER *Piranga rubra* **Pl. 64**

Breeds in open oak-pine woodland. Nest in a tree, usually well out on a horizontal lower branch. 10–35 ft. up.

Nest. A flimsy-looking shallow cup of grasses and weed stems, and sometimes Spanish Moss; lined with finer grasses. **Breeding season.** Begins late March in south to mid-May in north of range. **Eggs.** Usually 4, sometimes 3–5. Subelliptical to short subelliptical. Light blue or greenish-blue; speckled, spotted and blotched with chestnut-red or purplish-red, and paler lilac. Markings often sparse with a concentration at the larger end. 23 × 17 mm. **Incubation.** No information. **Nestling.** No information. **Nestling period.** Young tended by both parents.

WHITE-COLLARED SEEDEATER *Sporophila torqueola* **Pl. 64**
Breeds in open grassy areas with some shrubs or tall herbage. Nest 3–5 ft. up in a low bush or tall weed. Nest in a fork.
Nest. A thin, delicate cup of fine stems or rootlets; lined with a little very fine dry grass and hair. **Breeding season.** Begins mid-March. **Eggs.** Usually 3–4. Subelliptical. Smooth and moderately glossy. Very pale blue to greenish-blue; speckled, spotted and blotched in shades of brown and sometimes paler purple. Markings bold, often profuse, sometimes concentrated at the larger end. 16 × 12 mm. **Incubation.** By female alone. 13 days. **Nestling.** No information. **Nestling period.** Young tended by both parents. Leave nest at 10–11 days.

CARDINAL *Cardinalis cardinalis* **Pl. 64**
Breeds in a wide variety of sites but usually in a shrubby thicket or vine tangle, overgrown clearing, woodland edge or other secondary growth, open woodland with undergrowth and cane thickets, and in mesquite and thickets along streams in drier regions. Nest usually in a shrub or vine tangle, 1–12 ft. up, usually 4–5 ft. up.
Nest. A cup of thin twigs, weed stems, grasses, bark fibers, vines and rootlets, mixed with large dead leaves, rags, paper and other debris; lined with rootlets, fine grasses and sometimes hair or Spanish Moss. Usually built by female alone. **Breeding season.** Begins late March to early April. 3–4 broods at times. **Eggs.** Usually 3–4, sometimes 2–5. Subelliptical to short subelliptical. Smooth and slightly glossy. White or very slightly greenish; speckled, spotted and with small blotches of medium to dark brown, rarely reddish-brown, and paler purple or gray. Markings often profuse and usually present overall but with some concentration at larger end. 25 × 18 mm. **Incubation.** Usually by female alone, beginning with third egg. 11–13 days. **Nestling.** Altricial and downy. Skin orange. Down blackish-gray. Mouth red. Gape flanges cream colored. **Nestling period.** Young tended by both parents. Young leave nest at 9–11 days, fly well at 19 days, become independent at 38–45 days.

PYRRHULOXIA *Pyrrhuloxia sinuata* **Pl. 64**
Breeds in more arid regions, on mesquite edge and in more open sites in shrub growth than the Cardinal uses. Nest in a shrub, 5–7 ft. up, in a twig fork or against the trunk.
Nest. A small and fairly compact cup, but with loose outer layer; of twigs, weed stems, coarse grass and bark fibers and spiders' webs; lined with fine grasses, fibers, rootlets and hair. Built by female. **Breeding season.** Begins mid-March to early April. Prolonged, but birds probably single-brooded. **Eggs.** Usually 2–3. Short subelliptical to subelliptical. Smooth and slightly glossy. White or very pale greenish; speckled, spotted and blotched with brown and pale purple and gray. Very like those of Cardinal but markings often a little finer. 24 × 18 mm. **Incubation.** By female alone, fed by male. 14 days. **Nestling.** No information. **Nestling period.** Young tended by both parents. Leave nest at *c.* 10 days.

ROSE-BREASTED GROSBEAK *Pheucticus ludovicianus* **Pl. 64**
Breeds in scrub woodland and shrubby growth by streams and woodland edge, and in parkland shrubbery. Nest in a shrub or small tree. Usually in a twig fork, 4–20 ft. up, occasionally much higher in trees.
Nest. A loose cup of small twigs, coarse grasses, weed stems and decayed leaves; lined with fine twigs, rootlets and hair. Built by female. **Breeding season.** Begins mid- to late May. Double-brooded. **Eggs.** Usually 4, sometimes 3–5. Subelliptical to short subelliptical. Smooth and slightly glossy. Light blue to greenish-blue; blotched, spotted and speckled with reddish-brown or purplish-red, the markings being sparse at the narrow end, increasing in density towards the larger end. 25 × 18 mm. **Incubation.** By both sexes. 12–14 days. **Nestling.** Altricial and downy. Skin orange. Down white but grayish on head. Mouth reddish-orange. Gape flanges yellow. **Nestling period.** Young tended by both parents. Leave nest at 9–12 days. Male may feed fledged young while female re-nests. Young dependent on adults for *c.* 3 weeks more.

BLACK-HEADED GROSBEAK *Pheucticus melanocephalus* **Pl. 64**
Breeds in thickets and in trees along streams and in swampy places; or in open woodlands, orchards or parkland. Nest in a tree or shrub usually 6–12 ft. up, in a twig fork.
Nest. A loose, bulky cup, of thin twigs, weed stems and rootlets; lined with finer grasses, stems and rootlets. Built by female in 3–4 days. **Breeding season.** Begins late April in south to early June in north. **Eggs.** Usually 3–4. Short subelliptical to subelliptical or oval. Smooth or slightly glossy. Pale blue; speckled, spotted or blotched with light to medium brown, and scarcer pale gray. Markings tend to be more concentrated at larger end. 28 × 18 mm. **Incubation.** By both sexes, beginning with next-to-last egg. 12–13 days. **Nestling.** Altricial and downy. Down grayish-white, sparse. Mouth red. Gape flanges yellow. **Nestling period.** Young tended by both parents. 12 days.

BLUE GROSBEAK *Guiraca caerulea* **Pl. 64**
Breeds in shrubby growth, thickets, tall herbage, vines and low trees. Nest from *c.* 6 in. to 15 ft. up. Nest in a twig fork or among stems.
Nest. A cup of stems, thin twigs, bark strips, rootlets, dead leaves, corn-husks and occasionally cotton, paper or cast snakeskins; lined with fine rootlets, tendrils, hair and fine grasses. **Breeding season.** Begins mid-April in south to mid-May and early June in north of range. Double-brooded in south of range. **Eggs.** Usually 4, sometimes 2–3, rarely 5. Subelliptical to short subelliptical. Smooth and slightly glossy. Very pale blue. Unmarked. 22 × 17 mm. **Incubation.** Eggs laid on successive days. Incubation by female alone. 11 days. **Nestling.** No information. **Nestling period.** Young tended by both parents. Leave nest at 9–13 days. Male feeds fledged young while female re-nests.

INDIGO BUNTING *Passerina cyanea* **Pl. 64**
Breeds in scrub, on forest edges and clearings, and in hedgerows and orchards. Nest in a shrub, low bush, tree sapling, vine tangle or on tall weeds; usually in a twig fork *c.* 5–15 ft. up, sometimes lower.
Nest. A well-made cup of dry grass and weed stems, dead leaves, Spanish Moss, etc.; lined with fine grasses, rootlets, hair, wool, cotton, feathers and occasionally pieces of snakeskin. **Breeding season.** Begins mid-May to early June. Sometimes double-brooded. **Eggs.** Usually 3–4, sometimes 2. Sub-

elliptical to oval. Smooth and slightly glossy. Very pale bluish to greenish-white. Unmarked. 19 × 14 mm. **Incubation.** By female alone? 12–13 days. **Nestling.** Altricial and downy. Skin pinkish-orange. Down sparse and gray. Mouth red. Gape flanges yellow. **Nestling period.** Young tended by female only? Eyes open at 4–5 days, feathers break sheaths at 5–6 days. Young leave nest at 9–13 days. Male may feed fledged young, possibly while female re-nests.

LAZULI BUNTING *Passerina amoena* **Pl. 64**

Breeds in trees and shrubby growth along streams, or on near-by hillsides. Nest in low thick shrubby growth, vine tangles, sapling or small tree, 1–10 ft. up, but usually low. In twig fork or similar site.

Nest. A cup of coarse dry stems and leaves of grass, bark strips and rootlets; lined with hair and fine grasses. Nest is bound to supporting stems. **Breeding season.** Begins late March in south to early June in north of range. Sometimes two or more broods? **Eggs.** Usually 4, sometimes 3–5. Subelliptical to oval. Smooth and slightly glossy. Very pale bluish or greenish white, or very pale blue. Unmarked. 19 × 14 mm. **Incubation.** By female alone? 12 days. **Nestling.** Altricial and downy. Down gray; on head and back. **Nestling period.** Young tended by both parents or female alone. Leave nest at 10–15 days. Male feeds fledged young, possibly while female re-nests.

VARIED BUNTING *Passerina versicolor* **Pl. 64**

Breeds in arid and semi-arid scrub and brushes. Nest in a low tree, shrub or vine tangle, 1–12 ft. up.

Nest. An untidy cup of dry grasses, small weed stems, plant fibers, plant down and other debris; lined with rootlets, fine grasses and hair. **Breeding season.** Begins early April. **Eggs.** Usually 3–4. Very similar to those of Indigo Bunting. 18 × 14 mm. **Incubation.** No information. **Nestling.** No information. **Nestling period.** Young tended by both parents?

PAINTED BUNTING *Passerina ciris* **Pl. 64**

Breeds in low shrubby growth, hedgerows and rank herbage. Nest in a bush or vine tangle, usually 3–6 ft. up. Sometimes in a tree in thick Spanish Moss at much greater height.

Nest. A neat, deep cup, partly woven around its supports. Of grasses, finer weed stems and leaves; lined with hair and fine grasses. Built by female. **Breeding season.** Begins late March in south-west, to early to mid-May elsewhere. Usually double-brooded, sometimes up to four. **Eggs.** Usually 3–4, sometimes 5. Subelliptical to short subelliptical. Smooth and slightly glossy. White; very finely speckled with chestnut-red and purple, often with a wreath or cap of heavier spotting at the larger end. 19 × 14 mm. **Incubation.** By female alone. 11–12 days. **Nestling.** No information. **Nestling period.** Young tended by female alone? Leave nest at 8–9 days. Male may feed fledged young, possibly while female re-nests.

DICKCISSEL *Spiza americana* **Pl. 64**

Breeds on prairies and meadow grassland, with or without scattered shrubs. Nest on the ground in grass or rank herbage, or raised a little above ground, in grass tufts or tall weeds, or in low shrubs or trees, up to about 6 ft., but usually low. Males often polygamous.

Nest. A loose cup of coarse grass and weed stems, plant fibers and leaves; lined with finer grasses, rootlets and hair. Nest built by female alone. **Breeding season.** Begins late April in south to mid-May in north of range. **Eggs.** Usually 4, sometimes 3–5. Light blue, unmarked. 21 × 16 mm. **Incubation.** By female alone. 11–13 days. **Nestling.** Altricial and downy. Down white; on head, wings and body, but absent from underside. **Nestling period.** Young tended by female alone. Brooded for most of first 6 days. Feathers break sheaths at *c.* 6 days. Young leave nest at 7–10 days, unable to fly until *c.* 11–12 days.

OLIVE SPARROW *Arremonops rufivirgatus* Pl. 62

Breeds in shrubby thickets, chaparral, cacti and undergrowth at forest edge. Nest low in a bush, 2–5 ft. up.

Nest. A domed structure with a large entrance; of fine twigs, grass and weed stems, pieces of bark and leaves; the cup lined with finer grasses and hair. **Breeding season.** Begins mid-March. **Eggs.** Usually 4–5, sometimes 3. Subelliptical. Smooth and glossy. White and unmarked. 22 × 16 mm. **Incubation.** No information. **Nestling.** Altricial and downy. Bare skin flesh-colored. Down dark gray. Mouth red. Gape flanges yellow. **Nestling period.** No information.

GREEN-TAILED TOWHEE *Chlorura chlorura* Pl. 62

Breeds in scrub and brush of montane areas. Nest on or near the ground in the base of a bush, up to *c.* 2 ft., usually well-concealed.

Nest. A large, deep and thick-walled cup. Of twigs, grasses, weed stems and bark. Lined with fine stems, rootlets and hair. **Breeding season.** Begins mid- to late May. **Eggs.** Usually 4, sometimes 2–5. Subelliptical to short subelliptical. Smooth and moderately glossy. White, finely speckled and spotted, and occasionally blotched in reddish-brown to dull brown, with paler gray or purple markings. Larger markings often concentrated at the larger end. 22 × 16 mm. **Incubation.** No information. **Nestling.** Altricial and downy. Down gray. Mouth bright red. Gape flanges yellow. **Nestling period.** Young tended by both parents.

RUFOUS-SIDED TOWHEE *Pipilo erythrophthalmus* Pl. 62

Breeds in low shrubby growth or undergrowth. Nest on the ground hidden in or under undergrowth or tangled brush; or occasionally sheltered by a large plant tuft. Some nests built a little above ground in brushwood piles, dense bushes or vine tangles. Usually 1–5 ft. up. Rarely in sites up to 18 ft.

Nest. A stout cup of grasses, bark shreds, rootlets and dead leaves; lined with finer dry grasses and hair. Set in a small hollow made by bird, the rim at ground level. Built by female alone. **Breeding season.** Begins late April to early May. Double-brooded in southern part of range? **Eggs.** Usually 3–4, sometimes 2–6. Subelliptical to short subelliptical. Smooth and moderately glossy. White or slightly greenish or grayish; finely speckled, spotted and sometimes with a few blotches, of chestnut-red, purplish-red, reddish-brown or brown, and paler purple or gray. Markings usually fine and profuse with a concentration at the larger end. 23 × 17 mm. **Incubation.** By female only. 12–13 days. **Nestling.** Altricial and downy. Skin flesh-colored. Sparse gray down on head, wings, back and thighs. Gape flanges pale yellow, mouth red. **Nestling period.** Young tended by both parents. Brooded by female only. Fed by regurgitation at first. Young leave nest at 8–10 days.

BROWN TOWHEE *Pipilo fuscus* **Pl. 62**

Breeds in areas of shrubby thickets, edges of dry scrub, in shrubby growth and low trees of arid slopes, canyons and gullies, and in cover around buildings. Nest in a small tree or shrub, often against the trunk or in a strong twig fork, well-hidden by foliage; or in vines, low bushes, cacti and tall herbage. 2–25 ft. up, sometimes higher in large trees.

Nest. A bulky, poorly-made cup of thin twigs, weed stems with leaves and flower-heads, and grasses; lined with fine thin stems, grasses and hair. **Breeding season.** Begins early March to early May. Sometimes treble-brooded. **Eggs.** Usually 3–4, sometimes 2–5, rarely 6. Smooth and slightly glossy. Subelliptical. Pale blue, occasionally with a pinkish wash; very sparsely marked, mostly in a zone at or around the larger end, with some specks, spots, small blotches and scrawls of black, purplish-black or purplish-brown, and pale gray or lilac. Larger markings sometimes have blurred reddish edges. 24 × 18 mm. **Incubation.** By female only. 11 days. **Nestling.** Altricial and downy. Down brown. **Nestling period.** Young tended by both parents. Fed on insects. Leave at *c.* 8 days. First brood driven away when next brood hatch, but may otherwise remain for 4–6 weeks.

ABERT'S TOWHEE *Pipilo aberti* **Pl. 62**

Breeds in trees and shrubs along creeks and watercourses, and in mesquite and occasionally orange groves. Nest usually in a low bush or tree.

Nest. A bulky cup of weed stems, bark strips, vines and green leaves; lined with finer bark strips, dry grasses and hair. **Breeding season.** Begins late February. **Eggs.** Usually 2–4. Subelliptical. Smooth and slightly glossy. Very similar to those of Brown Towhee. 24 × 18 mm. **Incubation.** No information. **Nestling.** No information. **Nestling period.** No information.

LARK BUNTING *Calamospiza melanocorys* **Pl. 62**

Nest on the ground in growing grass, sometimes against a grass tuft or weed clump, or under a low shrub or cacti. In a slight hollow with the rim a little above or level with the ground. Rarely in a raised site.

Nest. A cup in a small hollow made by the bird. Of dry grass stems and blades; with an inner lining of fine grasses, rootlets and hair. **Breeding season.** Begins mid- to late May. Probably double-brooded at times. **Eggs.** Usually 4–5, sometimes 3–6, rarely 7. Short subelliptical to subelliptical. Smooth and slightly glossy. Light blue and unmarked. 22 × 17 mm. **Incubation.** By female alone, or with male assisting? 12 days. **Nestling.** Altricial and downy. Down dark blue-gray. **Nestling period.** Young tended by both parents.

SAVANNAH SPARROW *Passerculus sandwichensis* (Includes the Ipswich Sparrow, *P. s. princeps*) **Pl. 62**

Breeds in open areas with grass or short vegetation, including meadows, dunes, tundra sedge bogs, prairie, salt marsh and grass islands. Nest on the ground, sunk in a small hollow and usually concealed by a tuft of vegetation overhanging it.

Nest. A hollow scratched out by the bird in soft soil; nest rim level with the ground. Lined with a cup of coarser grasses, sedges or salicornia and similar material, depending on habitat; lined with fine grasses, rootlets and hair. Does not use feathers. **Breeding season.** Begins mid-March in south-west to late

May or early June in north of range. Double-brooded. **Eggs.** Usually 4–5, sometimes 3–6. Second clutches usually smaller. Subelliptical. Smooth and slightly glossy. Very pale greenish or bluish, or dull white; speckled, spotted and blotched with brown, purplish-brown or chestnut-red, and paler lilac or gray. Markings often heavy, often concentrated at the larger end. Markings sometimes indistinct on eggs with general reddish or brownish wash. 19 × 15 mm. **Incubation.** By both sexes. 12 days. **Nestling.** Altricial and downy. Down grayish-brown to dull brown. **Nestling period.** No information.

GRASSHOPPER SPARROW *Ammodramus savannarum* **Pl. 62**

Breeds on grasslands, prairie, cultivated clovers and large grassy forest clearings; in Florida in stunted and sparse saw palmetto and burnt-off places. Nest on the ground, sunk in a small hollow at the base of a tuft of overhanging grass or weeds. A number of pairs may nest within a limited area.

Nest. A hollow made by the bird, with a cup of stems and blades of grass, the rim level with or slightly above the ground; the inner lining of fine grasses, rootlets and hair. **Breeding season.** Begins early April in south to late May or early June in north of range. Double- or treble-brooded. **Eggs.** Usually 4–5, sometimes 3–6. Short subelliptical to subelliptical. Smooth and moderately glossy. White. Speckled, spotted or blotched with brown to reddish-brown. Markings usually concentrated at larger end, sparse elsewhere. 19 × 14 mm. **Incubation.** By female alone. 11–12 days. **Nestling.** Altricial and downy. Down grayish-brown; on head, wings and body. **Nestling period.** Young tended by female alone, but male reacts to predators near nest. Young begin feathering at 4 days, leave nest at 9 days, unable to fly, run through grass if disturbed.

BAIRD'S SPARROW *Ammodramus bairdii* **Pl. 62**

Breeds in open grassland, preferring taller grasses. Nest on the ground, concealed under a grass tuft or a small shrub, among a tangle of grasses, or occasionally in grass but exposed from above. Nest sunk in a small hollow.

Nest. A poorly-made and short-lived cup. Nests in tangled grasses may be deep thin cups of dead grasses with raised entrances. Where nest is sunk in a hollow made by the bird it may be a thicker cup. The lining is of finer grasses, or rarely with hair. **Breeding season.** Begins early June. Single-brooded. **Eggs.** Usually 3–5, rarely 6. Subelliptical. Smooth and slightly glossy. White, speckled, spotted and blotched with chestnut-red or brown, and with pale gray, and exceptionally black spots. Markings in general similar to those of Savannah Sparrow. 19 × 15 mm. **Incubation.** By female alone. 11–12 days. **Nestling.** Altricial and downy. Skin reddish-flesh. Down pale smoky-gray. Longest and thickest on head, present on back, wings and thighs. Irides brown. Bill pale to pinkish-gray, brown along culmen. Legs and feet pink. **Nestling period.** Young tended by female alone for first few days. Later male helps. Young fed on insects. Daytime brooding stops at *c.* 5 days, eyes open at 3–4 days, young leave nest at 8–10 days and hide in grass, begin to fly at 13 days and wander at 19 days.

HENSLOW'S SPARROW *Ammodramus henslowii* **Pl. 63**

Breeds on rough meadows and grassland with taller weeds or scattered small shrubs; often in damp, low-lying areas. Nest well-hidden in grass, either at the base of a tuft under overhanging grass, or raised in the stems of growing herbage up to 20 in. above ground. A number of pairs usually nest within a limited area. **Nest.** Usually a deep cup, of coarse grasses and dead leaves; lined with finer grasses and occasionally hair. Built mainly or entirely by female in 4–6 days. **Breeding season.** Begins mid- to late May. Possibly double-brooded. **Eggs.** Usually 3–5. Subelliptical. Very pale greenish or creamy-white; speckled, spotted and with some blotching in chestnut-red, reddish-brown and brown, and paler purple and gray. Markings like those of Grasshopper Sparrow, tending to be very sparse except at larger end. 18 × 14 mm. **Incubation.** By female alone. 11 days. **Nestling.** Altricial and downy. Down smoky-gray to brownish-gray; on head, back, wings and thighs. **Nestling period.** Young tended by both parents. Leave nest at 9–10 days.

LE CONTE'S SPARROW *Ammospiza leconteii* **Pl. 62**

Breeds in herbage of drier edges of marshes. Nest on or a little above the ground, concealed in a thick and tangled growth of rushes, sedges or tall grasses. Varies from a sunken cup to a site about 9 in. above ground.

Nest. A compact cup of grasses, the outermost layer of grasses and rushes woven around supporting stems; inner lining of finer grasses. **Breeding season.** Begins late May to early June. **Eggs.** Usually 4, sometimes 3–5. Subelliptical. Smooth and moderately glossy. White, faintly bluish, greenish or grayish; very heavily speckled, spotted or blotched with reddish-brown or brown. Markings usually concentrated at larger end. 18–14 mm. **Incubation.** By female alone. 11–13 days. **Nestling.** Altricial and downy. Down sparse and dull brown. **Nestling period.** Young tended by female alone at first, male helps later?

SHARP-TAILED SPARROW *Ammospiza caudacuta* **Pl. 63**

Breeds on coastal salt-marsh, but with one race on swampy edges of freshwater prairie lakes. Nest is in the taller, drier grasses and sedges bordering creeks and pools; built among the stems and raised a few inches from the ground, usually concealed by overhanging vegetation. At freshwater sites nests in tule.

Nest. A loosely-woven cup of dry grasses and other plant material, built up around supporting stems, often high-sided and almost as deep as wide with the opening slightly to one side as though tending towards a domed structure. The inner lining of finer grasses is at the bottom of the cavity. **Breeding season.** Begins early May in south to mid-June in north of range. **Eggs.** Usually 3–5, sometimes 6, rarely 7. Subelliptical to short subelliptical. Smooth and slightly glossy. Very pale greenish-white; speckled, spotted, blotched or finely mottled with shades of brown or reddish-brown, the markings often fine and profuse. 19 × 15 mm. **Incubation.** By female alone. 11 days. **Nestling.** Altricial and downy. Down grayish-brown. Mouth pinkish. Gape flanges yellow. **Nestling period.** Young tended by female alone. Eyes open at 3 days, feathers break sheaths at 7 days, leave at 10 days. Young dependent on female for *c.* 20 days after leaving nest.

SEASIDE SPARROW *Ammospiza maritima* (Includes Dusky Seaside Sparrow, *A. m. nigrescens*, and Cape Sable Sparrow, *A. m. mirabilis*) **Pl. 63**

Breeds on salt marshes. Nest in wetter parts in tufts of rushes, cord-grass and similar growth, 7 in. to 3 ft. above ground level; or in salicornia, marsh shrubs or low mangrove, in twig forks up to 5 ft., or at times to 14 ft. above ground level.

Nest. Simple open cup of rush stems, or grass stems and blades; lined with finer grasses; apparently built up at the sides to an almost semi-domed structure in some instances. **Breeding season.** Begins mid-April to early May, sometimes with second brood late June to early July. Cape Sable Sparrow may begin mid-March or a little earlier. **Eggs.** Usually 4–5, sometimes 3–6. Subelliptical to short subelliptical. Smooth and slightly glossy. Very pale greenish-white, grayish-white or white; speckled, spotted and blotched with purplish-brown, reddish-brown or dull brown, and some paler purple or gray. Markings very variable, often bold, and with some concentration at larger end. 21 × 16 mm. **Incubation.** By female alone. 11–12 days. **Nestling.** Altricial and downy. Skin pink, darkening to blue-gray. Down smoky-gray on head, back, wings and thighs; whiter on legs and flanks. Mouth red. Gape flanges yellow. **Nestling period.** Young tended by both parents. Eyes open at 3–6 days, feathers break sheaths at *c.* 7 days, young leave nest at 9 days. Can run well but cannot fly at first. Dependent on parents for a further 3 weeks.

VESPER SPARROW *Pooecetes gramineus* **Pl. 63**

Breeds in drier grassland on upland or well-drained soils; and in open or burnt-over forest clearings where vegetation is scanty in places. Nest on the ground, often near patches of scanty or absent herbage. In a small hollow against the base of a weed or grass tuft, concealed or exposed.

Nest. A cup in small depression made by bird. A loose structure of grass and weed stems and rootlets; lined with finer grasses, rootlets and hair. Sometimes with pine needles. **Breeding season.** Begins late April in south to late May in north of range. Double-brooded at times. **Eggs.** Usually 3–5, sometimes 6. Subelliptical to oval. Smooth and slightly glossy. White, with fine speckling or indistinct mottling of paler purplish or pinkish-buff; and very sparse bold markings, chiefly towards the larger end, of reddish-brown, brown or blackish-purple in irregular blotches or scrawls. 21 × 15 mm. **Incubation.** By female alone? 11–13 days. **Nestling.** Altricial and downy. Skin flesh-colored. Down gray. Mouth deep pink. Gape flanges pale yellow. **Nestling period.** Young tended by both parents. Brooded and shaded by female. Leave nest at 9–13 days, unable to fly. Dependent on adults for 20–22 days more. Male feeds fledged young while female re-nests.

LARK SPARROW *Chondestes grammacus* **Pl. 63**

Breeds on open grassland, weed-grown or old pastures, and in areas of low scrub or scattered trees. Nest usually low in a shrub or tree, usually up to 7 ft., rarely up to 25 ft., sometimes on the ground, often sheltered by a weed or grass tuft, exceptionally in a low rock crevice.

Nest. On the ground, a hollow made by the bird containing a thin cup of grasses; above ground, a stouter cup with a base of small twigs and walls of thicker grass and weed stems, lined with finer grasses and rootlets and rarely hair. **Breeding season.** Begins early April in south to early June in north of range. Probably single-brooded but period prolonged. **Eggs.** Usually 4–5, sometimes 3–6. Short subelliptical to subelliptical. Smooth and glossy. White; sparsely marked with specks, spots, scrawls or scribbles of black or purplish-black and paler gray and lilac. Markings irregular, often very sparse and sometimes with a scribbled wreath around the larger end. Paler markings often conspicuous. 20 × 16 mm. **Incubation.** By female alone. 11–13 days. **Nestling.** Altricial and downy. Down sparse, brownish-gray. **Nestling period.** Young tended by both parents. Eyes open at 4 days, feathers grow at 3–4 days, break sheaths at 6–7 days. Young leave nest at 9–10 days, only able to fly short distances. If disturbed will leave nest at 6 days.

RUFOUS-WINGED SPARROW *Aimophila carpalis* **Pl. 63**

Breeds in drier areas with grass and shrubby growth, usually in low-lying areas or by watercourses. Nest in a low thick bush or cactus, 1–6 ft. up. Nest in a twig fork.

Nest. A deep stout cup of dead weed stems, coarse grasses, bark strips, or fine twigs; lined with finer grasses and hair. **Breeding season.** Begins mid-April. Variable, depending on rainfall. **Eggs.** Usually 4, rarely 2–5. Subelliptical. Smooth and slightly glossy. Very pale bluish-white and unmarked. 19–14 mm. **Incubation.** By female alone. Period not recorded. **Nestling.** Altricial and downy. Down sparse and brown. **Nestling period.** Young tended by both parents. Leave nest at 9–10 days.

RUFOUS-CROWNED SPARROW *Aimophila ruficeps* **Pl. 63**

Breeds on montane areas of open woodland with sparse undergrowth, low shrubs and grasses, or widely-spaced shrubs. Nests on the ground, usually at the base of a grass-clump or sapling.

Nest. A loosely-constructed, thick-walled nest of coarse dry grasses, grass-roots, twigs, fibers; and lined with hair or fine dry grasses. Sunk in a small hollow made by the bird, the rim level with the ground. **Breeding season.** Begins mid- to late March. **Eggs.** Usually 3–4, rarely 2–5. Subelliptical. Smooth and slightly glossy. Very pale bluish-white and unmarked. **Incubation.** By female only, beginning with last egg. Period not recorded. **Nestling.** Altricial and downy. Skin orange. Down blackish. **Nestling period.** Young tended by both parents.

BACHMAN'S SPARROW *Aimophila aestivalis* **Pl. 63**

Breeds in open pinewoods with shrubby secondary growth, or in open grassland overgrown with tall weeds. Nest on the ground, partly concealed, against a grass-tuft or under a low shrub.

Nest. A cup of weed stems and grasses; lined with finer grasses and hair. In some instances the nest sides are built up high, with the opening deflected to one side, producing a virtually domed nest. **Breeding season.** Begins mid-April to early May. Possibly double-brooded in south. **Eggs.** Usually 3–5. Subelliptical. Smooth and slightly glossy. White and unmarked. 19 × 15 mm. **Incubation.** By female only, beginning with third egg. 13–14 days. **Nestling.** No information. **Nestling period.** Young tended by both parents. Leave nest at 10 days, unable to fly properly.

BOTTERI'S SPARROW *Aimophila botterii* **Pl. 63**

Breeds in drier grassland with scattered shrubs and small trees, or small bushes or cacti. Nest on the ground?

Nest. No information. **Breeding season.** Begins in May. **Eggs.** Usually 4, sometimes 2–5. Subelliptical. Smooth and glossy. White and unmarked.

20 × 15 mm. **Incubation.** No information. **Nestling.** Altricial and downy. Down buffish-gray on crown and nape; whitish on back, wings and sides of rump. Irides dark brown. Bill yellowish-pink to yellowish-flesh. Feet flesh to yellowish-flesh colored. **Nestling period.** No information.

CASSIN'S SPARROW *Aimophila cassinii* **Pl. 63**
Breeds in short grass plains with scattered shrubs, cacti or yuccas, or scrub areas broken by open grassy spaces. Nest usually on the ground in cover, either against or under a shrub or low bush, or grass-tuft; or in tall grasses. Sometimes raised in a low bush or cactus.
Nest. A deep cup of dead grasses, weed stems, bark and plant fibers and sometimes grass flowers; lined with finer grasses and grass flowers, rootlets and sometimes hair. **Breeding season.** Begins early April. **Eggs.** Usually 4, sometimes 3–5. Subelliptical. Smooth and slightly glossy. White and unmarked. 19 × 15 mm. **Incubation.** No information. **Nestling.** Altricial and downy. Down sparse and very dark. **Nestling period.** Young tended by both parents.

BLACK-THROATED SPARROW *Amphispiza bilineata* **Pl. 63**
Breeds on arid or desert hillsides with sparse cover of shrubs or cactus. Nest low in small bush or cactus, about 6–18 in. up, in a fork; occasionally higher.
Nest. A cup of fibers, blades and stems of grasses, weed stems, small twigs; lined with fur, hair, wool, fine grasses and plant down. The lining is usually pale in color. **Breeding season.** Begins mid-April to early May. **Eggs.** Usually 3–4, larger in the north. Subelliptical. Smooth and slightly glossy. Bluish-white to white and unmarked. 17 × 14 mm. **Incubation.** No information. **Nestling.** Altricial and downy. Down buffish-white with slight gray tint. **Nestling period.** No information.

SAGE SPARROW *Amphispiza belli* **Pl. 63**
Breeds in sagebrush and other low arid scrub. Nest low in a thick bush, 3–4 in. up; sometimes on the ground in a small hollow.
Nest. A cup of dry twigs, sticks and weed stems; lined with shreds of bark and grass stems; and with inner lining of finer bark fiber, grasses, with fur, hair, wool tufts and sometimes feathers. **Breeding season.** Begins late March in south to late May in north of range. **Eggs.** Usually 3–4, rarely 5. Subelliptical. Smooth and moderately glossy. White or faintly greenish or bluish; speckled, spotted and with a few small blotches of reddish, purplish-brown or brown, and paler purple. Markings mostly fine, with heavier markings confined to larger end. Occasionally brown or blackish scrawls or spots present. Paler markings may be conspicuous. 19 × 15 mm. **Incubation.** 13 days. **Nestling.** Altricial and downy. Down pale. **Nestling period.** No information.

DARK-EYED JUNCO *Junco hyemalis* (Includes Slate-colored Junco, *J. h. hyemalis*, and Oregon Junco, *J. h. oreganus*) **Pl. 63**
Breeds in open woodland, woodland clearings and forest edge. Nest on the ground among tree-roots, or partly hidden by brushwood, stump or rock, often in ferns or herbage on a bank or rocky slope, or in more open site against a plant tuft. Exceptionally in low shrubs or on conifer branches, in tree cavities or on raised sites on ledges and niches of buildings.
Nest. In a small hollow made by bird where site is soft. A cup, often substantial,

of thin twigs, fine stems, dry grasses, bark strips, rootlets and moss; lined with finer stems, grasses and hair. Built by female. **Breeding season.** Begins mid-March in south to mid-May in north of region. Double- or treble-brooded in some areas. **Eggs.** Usually 3–5, rarely 6. Short subelliptical to subelliptical. Smooth and slightly glossy. White or slightly greenish or grayish; speckled, spotted and blotched in reddish-brown, chestnut-red and purplish-brown. Markings usually very sparse except as a cap or wreath at larger end. 19 × 14 mm. **Incubation.** Eggs laid at daily intervals. Incubation by female alone, beginning with next-to-last egg. 12–11 days. **Nestling.** Altricial and downy. Skin dark reddish-orange. Down dark gray. Mouth deep pink. Gape flanges pale yellow. **Nestling period.** Young tended by both parents. Eyes open at *c.* 5 days, feathers showing at 7 days. Young fed on insects, regurgitated at first, fed directly later. Young leave nest at 10–13 days, partly dependent for *c.* 3 weeks more.

GRAY-HEADED JUNCO *Junco caniceps* **Pl. 63**
Breeds in dry or wet mountain forest. Nest on the ground, usually hidden by a rock, shrub or grass-tuft, tree-root or log; or in a small hollow in a bank. Rarely low in a tree, or on a building.
Nest. Usually in a small hollow made by bird, the rim level with the ground. A cup of coarse grass, pine needles, dead leaves and bark fibers; lined with finer grasses, hair, fur and sometimes feathers. **Breeding season.** Begins early May to June. Possibly double- or treble-brooded at times. **Eggs.** Usually 3–5. Like those of other juncos, but markings tend to be browner or more buff, and sometimes diffuse and indistinct. 20 × 15 mm. **Incubation.** By female alone. **Nestling.** Altricial and downy. Skin pink. Down sparse and gray, on head and upperparts. Mouth bright red. Gape flanges yellow. **Nestling period.** Young tended by both parents. Eyes open at 4–6 days. Young may leave nest hollow to meet parents with food at 7–10 days, leave nest for good at 10–13 days, unable to fly for several days more. Partly dependent for 18–20 days more.

YELLOW-EYED JUNCO *Junco phaeonotus* **Pl. 63**
Breeds in mountain conifer forest. Nest on the ground hidden under plant tuft or grass-tuft, log, fallen branch, or rock. Exceptionally in conifer tree to 9 ft. up.
Nest. Nest in small hollow made by bird in soft site. A cup of coarse grasses and moss; lined with finer grasses, hair and fur. Built by female. **Breeding season.** Begins mid-April. **Eggs.** Usually 3–4, sometimes 5. Subelliptical. Smooth and slightly glossy. Similar to those of Gray-headed Junco. 20 × 15 mm. **Incubation.** By female alone. 15 days? **Nestling.** Altricial and downy. Down sparse and gray; on head and body. Irides dark brown. **Nestling period.** Young tended by both parents. Eyes open at 4–5 days, feathers break sheaths at 6–8 days, young leave nest at 10 days.

TREE SPARROW *Spizella arborea* **Pl. 63**
Breeds in low shrubby growth along northern tree limit, tundra edge and river flats of north. Nest on the ground, at the base of a small tree, shrub, grass-tuft or dead branch which hides it; or in a grass tussock, or occasionally in dwarf willow at height of up to 4 ft.
Nest. A cup of coarse grass and weed stems, bark shreds, rootlets, moss and lichen; lined with fine dry grasses and moss and with an inner lining of feathers, hair and fur. **Breeding season.** Begins early June. **Eggs.** Usually 3–5, occa-

sionally 6. Subelliptical to short subelliptical. Smooth and slightly glossy. Very pale blue or greenish, sometimes with dull buffish or pinkish wash; speckled, spotted, blotched or indistinctly mottled with chestnut-red, purplish, or reddish-brown, and pale lilac. Marking often more concentrated at larger end. 19 × 14 mm. **Incubation.** Eggs laid at daily interval. Incubation by female alone, beginning with last egg. 12–13 days. **Nestling.** Altricial and downy. Skin pinkish-yellow. Down dark grayish-brown. Mouth pinkish-orange. **Nestling period.** Young tended by both parents. Eyes open at 4–5 days, feathers break sheaths at 6–8 days, young leave nest at 9–10 days, unable to fly for 5–6 days, fed by parents for *c.* 2 weeks more.

CHIPPING SPARROW *Spizella passerina* **Pl. 63**

Breeds in open woodland, on woodland edge and in clearings, in parkland, cultivation with trees and gardens. Nest in a tree, usually a conifer, a shrub, or a vine, occasionally in other sites. From 3–60 ft. up, but mostly between 3 and 20 ft. up. Nest in a twig fork or among foliage.

Nest. A cup of dead grasses, weed stems and rootlets; lined with finer grasses and hair. Built by female. **Breeding season.** Begins mid-March in south to late May or early June in north of range. **Eggs.** Usually 4, sometimes 3–5. Subelliptical to short subelliptical. Smooth and moderately glossy. Light blue; very sparsely marked, mostly at larger end, with irregular spots, small blotches and specks in black, blackish-brown and paler purple and lilac. 18 × 13 mm. **Incubation.** Eggs laid at daily intervals. Incubation by female alone, beginning with next-to-last egg. 11–14 days. **Nestling.** Altricial and downy. Skin dark red. Down fairly thick, dark gray. Mouth pinkish-red. Gape flanges pale yellow. **Nestling period.** Young tended by both parents. Female broods young for most of first 4–5 days. Young leave nest at 9–12 days, can fly at 14 days.

CLAY-COLORED SPARROW *Spizella pallida* **Pl. 63**

Breeds on prairies and upland plains where some shrubby cover is present, and on scrubland by cultivated areas, on hillsides or bordering swamps and woodland. Nest a little above ground level in the base of a shrub, weed clump or grass-tuft, or in the lower branches of a shrub. From almost ground level to *c.* 5 ft. up. Usually well-hidden. Nests tend to be higher up in taller herbage.

Nest. A cup of thin twigs, weed stems, grasses and rootlets; lined with finer grasses and rootlets, and hair. **Breeding season.** Begins late May to early June. Probably double-brooded at times. **Eggs.** Usually 3–4, occasionally 5. Short subelliptical to subelliptical. Smooth and moderately glossy. Eggs very similar to those of Chipping Sparrow. 17 × 13 mm. **Incubation.** By both sexes, beginning with third egg. 10–11 days. **Nestling.** Altricial and downy. Skin flesh-colored. Down very sparse and dark gray, on head and back only. Gape flanges white becoming yellow. Mouth bright orange-red. **Nestling period.** Young tended by both parents. Both sexes brood. Young leave at 7–9 days. Adults continue feeding for at least 8 days more.

BREWER'S SPARROW *Spizella breweri* **Pl. 63**

Breeds in sagebrush, with a northern subspecies in exposed scrub of mountain tree-lines. Nest low in a small shrub, in a twig fork, a few inches to *c.* 4 ft. up, but usually very low.

Nest. A cup of dry grass stems, dead weeds and rootlets; lined with dried grasses, rootlets and hair. **Breeding season.** Begins mid-April in south to late

May or early June in north of range. **Eggs.** Usually 3–4, occasionally 5. Subelliptical. Smooth and moderately glossy. Similar to those of Chipping Sparrow. 17 × 13 mm. **Incubation.** No information. **Nestling.** Altricial and downy. Down light to dark gray. **Nestling period.** No information.

FIELD SPARROW *Spizella pusilla* **Pl. 63**

Breeds in old pastures and clearings overgrown with low scrub and bushes. Early nests are on or near the ground in weed clumps or grass tufts, later ones may be higher in small thick shrubs as leaves grow. Nests a few inches to *c.* 1 foot up.

Nest. A cup of coarse grasses and leaves; lined with finer grasses, rootlets and hair. Built by female in *c.* 5–7 days. **Breeding season.** Begins mid-April in south to early May in north of range. Probably treble-brooded, and in addition lost clutches are replaced. **Eggs.** Usually 3–5, rarely 6. Subelliptical. Smooth and slightly glossy. White or tinted very pale bluish or greenish; finely speckled, spotted or with small blotches of medium brown, reddish-brown, or purplish-brown, and paler purple or gray. Markings usually minute or very sparse except at the larger end where they form a cap or wreath. 18 × 13 mm. **Incubation.** Eggs laid at daily intervals. Incubation by female alone. Usually 10–11 days, exceptionally up to 17 days in cold weather. **Nestling.** Altricial and downy. Skin pinkish to orange. Down light to dark gray. Mouth bright red. Gape flanges yellow. **Nestling period.** Young tended by both parents. Brooded by female for most of first few days. Young leave at 7–8 days, can fly only short way 5 days later. Independent 18–26 days later.

BLACK-CHINNED SPARROW *Spizella atrogularis* **Pl. 63**

Breeds in sagebrush and chaparral. Nest in a shrub, 1–3 ft. up, in a twig fork.

Nest. A cup, often of loose construction, of dry grasses and weed stems; lined with finer grasses, plant fibers, hair or feathers. **Breeding season.** Begins late April. **Eggs.** Usually 2–4, occasionally 5. Subelliptical. Smooth and moderately glossy. Light blue, unmarked or with a few scattered specks or spots of black or dark brown. 18 × 13 mm. **Incubation.** No information. **Nestling.** No information. **Nestling period.** Young tended by both parents.

HARRIS'S SPARROW *Zonotrichia querula*

Breeds in stunted trees of forest along the northern treeline, and along woodland edge, by clearings or in burnt-over areas. Nest on the ground on a hummock among trees, usually sheltered by a low shrub or small tree.

Nest. A bulky cup in a hollow made by the birds; of coarse rootlets, dead grass stems, and sometimes mosses; lined with finer grasses. **Breeding season.** Begins early June. Single-brooded, but a lost clutch may be replaced. **Eggs.** Usually 4, sometimes 3–5. Subelliptical. Smooth and slightly glossy. White to pale greenish-white; speckled, spotted, blotched and scrawled with brown or reddish-brown. Markings usually heavy and sometimes with a concentration at the larger end. 22 × 17 mm. **Incubation.** 13–14 days. **Nestling.** No information. **Nestling period.** No information.

WHITE-CROWNED SPARROW *Zonotrichia leucophrys* **Pl. 63**

Breeds in open, stunted woodland and scrub in the north, similar habitat on western mountains and in cleared, cultivated or burnt-over areas in forest. Nest on the ground, partly concealed in moss and low shrubby growth, or in or under a grass-tuft or fern, or at the base of a shrub. Or a few feet above the ground in a bush, or low tree branch, exceptionally much higher in trees.

Nest. A cup of grass stems, dead leaves, thin twigs, pine-needles, bark shreds, and some moss; lined with fine rootlets, hair and feathers. Built by female. **Breeding season.** Varies in different populations. May begin early March to April in west to early June in north. Lost clutches usually replaced. **Eggs.** Usually 2–5, rarely 6. Subelliptical. Smooth and slightly to moderately glossy. Very pale blue or greenish-blue; spotted, speckled or mottled in light red, reddish-brown or purplish-red. The markings usually fine and profuse. 21 × 16 mm. **Incubation.** By female alone, beginning at or just before completion of clutch. 9–15 days. **Nestling.** Altricial and downy. Down brownish-gray; on head, back, wings and thighs. Mouth bright red. Gape flanges yellow. **Nestling period.** Female broods for first 2 days fed by male. Young tended by both parents. Eyes open at 4 days. Leave nest at 9–11 days. Young still fed to some extent for 25–30 days more. Male may feed fledged young, possibly for a shorter period, if female re-nests.

GOLDEN-CROWNED SPARROW *Zonotrichia atricapilla* Pl. 63

Breeds in willow and alder scrub and herbage along the tree-line of northern mountains; and in similar types of growth near sea-level. Nest on the ground at the base of a small shrub or in a bank under overhanging plants. Rarely on a low branch of a shrub within thick cover.

Nest. A thick cup of small twigs, bark flakes, fern leaves and stems, dry grasses and dead leaves; lined with fine grasses, and hair and feathers. **Breeding season.** Begins late May to early June. **Eggs.** Usually 3–5. Subelliptical to long subelliptical. Smooth and slightly glossy. Very similar in color and markings to those of White-crowned Sparrows. 23 × 16 mm. **Incubation.** No information. **Nestling.** No information. **Nestling period.** No information.

WHITE-THROATED SPARROW *Zonotrichia albicollis* Pl. 63

Breeds on forest edge, in partly open areas, clearing with scrub, shrubby growth on bog edge, and open woodland on mountain slopes. Nest on the ground at the edge of clearing, usually by or under low shrubs, tree branches, grass-tufts, weed clumps and ferns. Exceptionally above ground in thick bushes or low in trees.

Nest. A cup of coarse grasses, wood chips, twigs, pine-needles and rootlets; lined with fine grasses, rootlets and hair. Built by female. **Breeding season.** Begins mid- to late May. Usually single-brooded. Lost clutches are usually replaced. **Eggs.** Usually 4–6. Subelliptical or long subelliptical. Smooth and slightly glossy. Very pale blue or greenish-blue; speckled, spotted or blotched in purplish-red, or chestnut-red, and paler lilac. Markings variable, sometimes fine and profuse, sometimes concentrated about the larger end. 21 × 15 mm. **Incubation.** Eggs laid at daily intervals. Incubation by female alone. 11–14 days. **Nestling.** Altricial and downy. Almost naked at hatching. Down sparse and brown. **Nestling period.** Young tended by both parents. Usually brooded by female. Eyes open at 3–4 days. Young leave nest at 7–12 days, usually 8–9. Can fly 2–3 days later.

FOX SPARROW *Passerella iliaca* Pl. 64

Breeds over a wide range in a variety of habitats where thick shrubby growth is present, ranging from the stunted northern trees of conifer tree-line to south-

western arid chaparral; and including smaller areas in cultivated and cleared regions. Nest frequently on the ground in thickets, or above ground in shrubs or low branches of trees up to *c.* 7 ft.
Nest. A bulky and deep cup of twigs, bark shreds, grass and weed stems, wood chips or moss; lined with fine rootlets, fur and sometimes feathers. **Breeding season.** Begins early to mid-May. Double-brooded at times? **Eggs.** Usually 3–5. Subelliptical. Smooth and slightly glossy. Pale blue or greenish-blue; heavily speckled, spotted or mottled with chestnut-red or purplish-brown. Markings sometimes evenly distributed or with concentration at or around larger end. 23 × 16 mm. **Incubation.** Mostly by female? Beginning with first egg? 12–14 days? **Nestling.** No information. **Nestling period.** Young tended by both parents.

LINCOLN'S SPARROW *Melospiza lincolnii* **Pl. 64**
Breeds in shrubby growth on forest edge, clearings, borders of bogs and water-courses in forest and secondary growth; often on the edge of wet areas. Nest on the ground hidden by plant growth or shrubs, or in wet places usually on drier raised mounds.
Nest. A cup of dry stems and blades of grass, and dead leaves; lined with finer grasses and a little hair. **Breeding season.** Begins late May in south to mid-June in north. Probably double-brooded at times. **Eggs.** Usually 4–5, sometimes 3–6. Very similar to those of Song Sparrow, but markings often browner. 19 × 14 mm. **Incubation.** Eggs laid at daily intervals. Incubation by female only. 13–14 days. **Nestling.** Altricial and downy. Skin dark reddish-buff. Down dark blackish-gray; on head, back, wings and thighs. Mouth bright red. Gape flanges creamy-white at hatching, becoming yellow. **Nestling period.** Young tended by both parents. Eyes open at 5–6 days. Young leave nest at *c.* 10–12 days.

SWAMP SPARROW *Melospiza georgiana* **Pl. 64**
Breeds in marsh vegetation of freshwater swamps, marshes and bogs, marshy edges of lakes and streams, and wet meadows, freshwater or brackish. Nest in large grass or sedge tussock, or suspended in tall plants such as cat-tails growing in water, or in shrub growing in water; but usually with foliage concealing the nest from above. Male polygamous at times.
Nest. A cup, often with bulky foundations of coarse stalks and leaves, supporting a neater cup of coarser grasses; lined with fine grass stems. **Breeding season.** Begins early or mid-May. **Eggs.** Usually 4–5, sometimes 3–6. Subelliptical. Smooth and slightly glossy. Very pale blue or greenish-blue; speckled, spotted or blotched in purplish-red, purplish-brown or reddish-brown, and paler lilac or purple. Markings often concentrated at or about the larger end. Occasionally with very sparse, bold spots or blotches. 19 × 15 mm. **Incubation.** By female alone. 12–13 days. **Nestling.** Altricial and downy. Skin pink. Down blackish-brown, with some white on undersides. Mouth reddish-orange. Gape flanges yellow. **Nestling period.** Little information. Young leave nest at 9–10 days.

SONG SPARROW *Melospiza melodia* **Pl. 64**
Breeds in low shrubby growth and thickets in a variety of habitats, but most often in moist or swampy places. Earlier nests mostly on the ground under a tuft

of grass or weed clumps. Later nests often in shrubs or trees, usually up to *c.* 4 ft., exceptionally in trees up to 30 ft., usually in a twig fork. Rarely in a cavity.

Nest. A cup, with a rough outer layer, of dead grasses and weed stems, with some rootlets and bark shreds; lined with finer grasses and sometimes hair. **Breeding season.** Begins in April. Normally by female alone. Often treble-brooded and lost clutches replaced. **Eggs.** Usually 3–5, rarely 2–6. Subelliptical to short subelliptical, or oval. Smooth and slightly glossy. Very pale blue or greenish-blue, rarely pale buff; finely speckled, spotted or mottled, or with some blotching in purplish-red or purplish-brown, reddish-brown or dark brown, and some pale lilac. Markings often more concentrated towards larger end. 22 × 17 mm. **Incubation.** By female alone. 12–14 days. **Nestling.** Altricial and downy. Skin yellowish. Down is dark gray; on head, back, wings and thighs. Mouth red. Gape flanges bright yellow. **Nestling period.** Young tended by both parents. Brooded by female for most of first 5–6 days. Eyes open at 3–4 days. Young leave nest at *c.* 10 days, can fly well at 17 days, and independent in 18–20 days more. Young may be fed by male while female re-nests.

McCOWN'S LONGSPUR *Calcarius mccownii* **Pl. 64**

Breeds on more arid prairie grasslands. Nest on the ground, often at the base of a grass tuft, weed clump or small shrubby growth.

Nest. A cup in a small hollow made by the bird, its rim at or near ground level. Of coarser stems and blades of grass; lined with finer grasses and sometimes plant-down, fur, hair and wool. **Breeding season.** Begins early to mid-May. **Eggs.** Usually 3–4, occasionally 5. Very pale buffish or olive, grayish-white or pinkish, or with a wash of buff or purplish; blotches and scrawled with olive-brown, brown, blackish or paler lilac; the markings sometimes sparse and faint. 20 × 15 mm. **Incubation.** Eggs usually laid at daily intervals. Incubation by female only. 12–13 days. **Nestling.** Altricial and downy. Skin pale reddish. Down long and pale buff; on head and back. Mouth deep pink. **Nestling period.** Young tended by both parents. Female broods for first 3 days. Eyes open at 4–5 days, feathers break sheaths at 6–7 days, young leave nest at 10 days, can fly short distances at 12 days.

LAPLAND LONGSPUR *Calcarius lapponicus* **Pl. 64**

Breeds on open tundra or on similar habitat on northern mountain tops, often in moist places. Nest on the ground in a depression; may be in the side of a bank or hummock, usually well hidden by surrounding vegetation.

Nest. A cup of grasses, moss and roots; lined with finer grass, hair and feathers. Built by female. **Breeding season.** Begins end of May to June. Single-brooded. **Eggs.** Usually 5–6, sometimes 2–7. Clutches may be small in cold seasons. Subelliptical. Smooth and glossy. Pale greenish, buffish or grayish; usually largely obscured by indistinct mottling of dull reddish-brown or purplish-brown, and with some sparse dark spots or scrawls of black or purplish-black, the darker markings sometimes absent. 21 × 15 mm. **Incubation.** Eggs laid at daily intervals. Incubation by female, beginning with completion of clutch. 10–14 days. **Nestling.** Altricial and downy. Down light brown. Mouth red. Gape flanges yellow. **Nestling period.** Young brooded and fed by both parents, leave nest at 8–10 days. They leave 3–5 days before they are able to fly.

SMITH'S LONGSPUR *Calcarius pictus* **Pl. 64**

Breeds on moister, grassy tundra. Nest on the ground, on slightly raised hummock or grass tussock, often sunk into small hollow probably made by bird.

Nest. A cup of dry grasses; lined with finer grasses, hair, down and feathers. **Breeding season.** Begins early June. **Eggs.** Usually 3–4. Subelliptical to short subelliptical. Smooth, non-glossy or slightly glossy. Very pale olive, bluish or greenish, sometimes with a purplish wash; spotted, blotched or mottled in pale dull purplish-brown, or lilac; and with sparse dark scrawls and specks in dark brown, purplish-black or black. 21 × 15 mm. **Incubation.** By female only, beginning before completion of clutch. 11–14 days. **Nestling.** Altricial and downy. Down buff with dark gray tips; on head, back, wings and thighs. Skin pale orange. Mouth bright pink, becoming red. **Nestling period.** Young tended by both parents. Eyes open at 3–4 days. Feathers break sheaths at 4–6 days. Young leave nest at 7–9 days. Fed by one parent (parents may divide brood?). Fed for *c.* 3 weeks after leaving nest.

CHESTNUT-COLLARED LONGSPUR *Calcarius ornatus* **Pl. 64**

Breeds on prairie grassland where grass is short and sparse. Nest on the ground in shorter grass.

Nest. Nest built in a small hollow made by the bird, the rim level with the ground. A cup of dry grass blades and stems, with a lining of finer grasses and some feathers and hair. Built by female. **Breeding season.** Begins May. **Eggs.** Usually 3–5, sometimes 6. Short subelliptical to elliptical. Smooth and slightly glossy. Creamy-white, or usually tinted faintly blue or gray, with very minute speckling in purplish or blackish, and sparse irregular spots and blotches of reddish-brown, purplish-brown or black, and pale purple or lilac. 19 × 14 mm. **Incubation.** Eggs laid at daily intervals. Incubation by female alone, beginning at completion of clutch. 11–13 days. **Nestling.** Altricial and downy. Down buffish-gray; mainly on head and back. Legs and feet pale flesh color. Bill flesh-colored with dark tip. **Nestling period.** Young tended by both parents. Brooded by female for first *c.* 5 days. Eyes open at 5–6 days, leave nest at 9–11 days.

SNOW BUNTING *Plectrophenax nivalis* **Pl. 64**

Breeds on bare rocky areas and screes, from sea-level to mountain. Nest on the ground, concealed in a crevice among rocks and boulders, or hole in a wall or old building. Male sometimes polygamous.

Nest. A cup of dry grass, moss and lichens; lined with finer grass, hair, wool and feathers. Built by female. Old nests may be re-used. **Breeding season.** Begins late May to mid-June. Varying with locality and altitude. Double-brooded. **Eggs.** Usually 4–6, rarely 3–9. Subelliptical. Smooth and glossy. Very pale blue or greenish-blue, very variably blotched, spotted or speckled with light reddish-brown, dark brown, purplish-brown, light purplish-gray and occasionally purplish-black. Markings may be sparse and concentrated at the larger end, or heavier and more widely distributed. 23 × 16 mm. **Incubation.** By female alone. 10–15 days. **Nestling.** Altricial and downy. Down fairly long and plentiful but absent from underside; dark gray. Gape flanges yellow. Mouth deep red. **Nestling period.** Young brooded by female for *c.* 5 days while male brings food. Later both parents bring food. 10–14 days. Young are active at 8 days and may come out of nest and return.

INDEX OF COMMON NAMES

Numbers in **bold** type refer to plates

INDEX OF SCIENTIFIC NAMES

Numbers in **bold** type refer to plates